Praise for *Prisoners of the Japanese*

"Brilliant and unflinchingly honest"
—San Francisco *Chronicle*

"Sears the reader's memory with unforgettable images"
—*The Japan Times Weekly,* international edition

"Heartbreaking reading ... Japanese prison camps killed more than ten thousand Americans, and this book, so far, is their only memorial."
—*American Heritage*

"Seldom is history written with such intensity *and* restraint, and with such narrative power"
—Manchester *Journal Enquirer*

"A moving saga of human endurance in the face of slavery, torture, murder, starvation and disease."
—*The Washington Post Book World*

"This remarkable book will move, startle, and possibly engulf you."
—Honolulu *Weekly*

"Explicit, truthful, and impeccably researched"
—*Retired Officers* magazine

"A masterwork"
—Gerrit Bras, POW

"A scorching indictment. Gavan Daws has performed a service equal to those who will not let the Holocaust be forgotten or excused. Destined to be read and referred to for generations to come."
—Richard Selzer, author of *Raising the Dead*

"Daws has done for the POW saga what *Schindler's List* and *The Diary of Anne Frank* did for the Holocaust."
—*The Asian Wall Street Journal*

"A rigorously authenticated masterwork ... Daws gives his chronicle a thoroughly considered historical and psychological context ... The ultimate effect is strangely, unexpectedly uplifting."
—*Cleveland Plain Dealer*

"Vividly brings to light the random killing of prisoners during the infamous Bataan Death March and the use of POW slave labor in the construction of the Burma-Siam railroad."
—*The New York Times Book Review*

"It is a disgrace, really, that because of political priorities this story has never been systematically recorded or documented, and hence has never been fully told to the public."
—*The Wall Street Journal*

"A powerful, disturbing, and necessary book"
—*Parameters,* U.S. Army War College quarterly

"My story is told in this book. Every word is true."
—Houston Tom Wright, POW

"All of us recognize how well you have captured the truth. Thanks for telling the world."
—Guy Kelnhofer, POW

PRISONERS
OF THE
JAPANESE

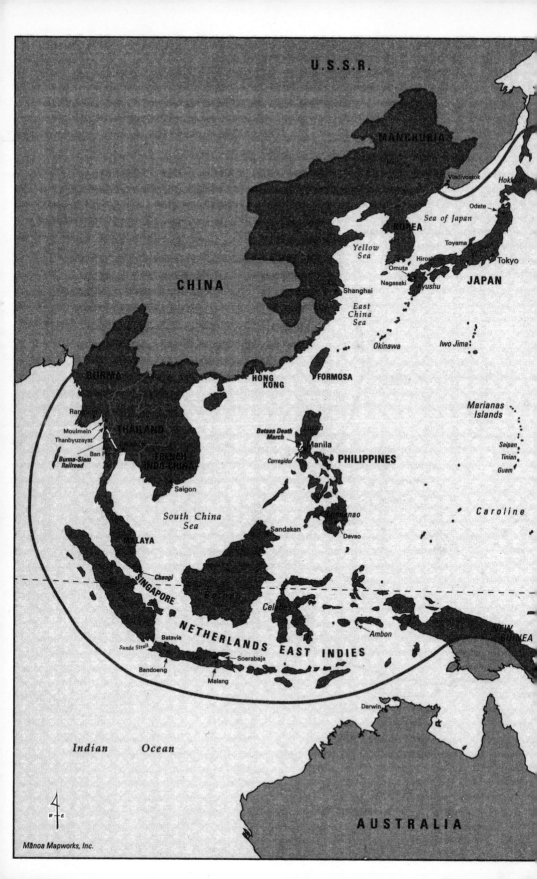

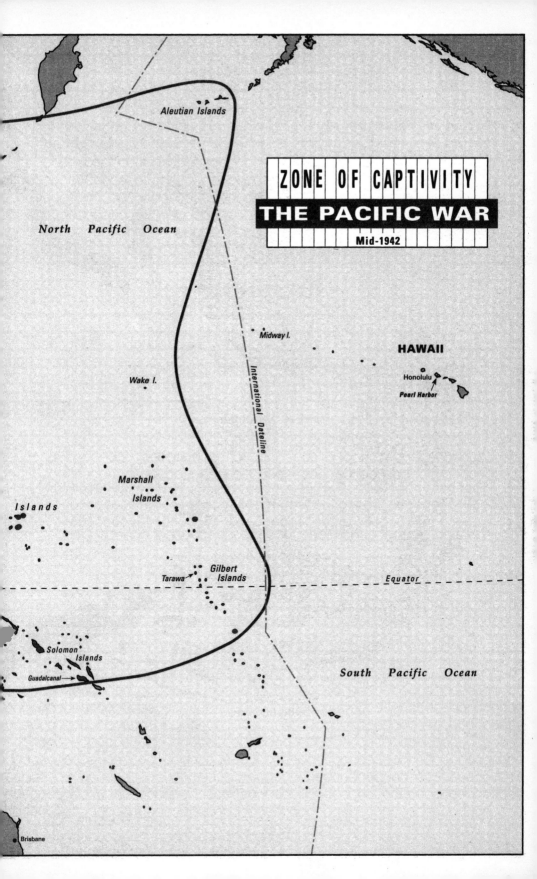

ALSO BY GAVAN DAWS

Books

A Dream of Islands

Holy Man

Night of the Dolphins

Shoal of Time

Land and Power in Hawaii (with George Cooper)

The Hawaiians

Hawaii: The Islands of Life

Hawaii 1959–1989

Documentary Films

Angels of War

Man Without Pigs

Plays

Dolphin Play

PRISONERS
OF THE
JAPANESE

GAVAN DAWS

SIMON &
SCHUSTER

London · New York · Sydney · Toronto

A VIACOM COMPANY

First published in Great Britain by Simon & Schuster UK Ltd, 2006
A Viacom company

1 3 5 7 9 10 8 6 4 2

Simon & Schuster UK Ltd
Africa House
64–78 Kingsway
London WC2B 6AH

www.simonsays.co.uk

Simon & Schuster Australia
Sydney

A CIP catalogue record for this book is available from the British Library.

Hardback ISBN 0-7432-8528-X
EAN 9780743285285
Trade paperback ISBN 0-7432-8547-6
EAN 9780743285476

Printed and bound in Great Britain by
The Bath Press, Bath

Cover image: an Australian prisoner of war (who we believe to be Private Lloyd
Sibraa), captured by soldiers of the Imperial Japanese Army at Kavieng in
Papua New Guinea in January 1942. The Publishers would welcome
correspondence from any reader who can confirm the prisoner's identity and
the circumstances of his capture.

Sometimes, when crimes have been committed it is

necessary to go back and mark the spot.

—Bill Young, POW

ACKNOWLEDGMENTS

First and foremost, my grateful thanks to the many ex-POWs who have taken so much time and trouble with me. Their names appear in their rightful place, at the head of the list of indispensable sources for this book, beginning on page 397.

I thank especially Slug Wright, Forrest Knox, Harry Jeffries, and Oklahoma Atkinson. They put up with my questions for years—for longer than they were POWs. Forrest, Harry, and Oklahoma are gone now. Slug is still around, and he still hears from me.

Otto Schwarz of the USS *Houston* Survivors Association has been outstandingly generous with help from day one; likewise, Roger White of the Lost Battalion Association. My thanks also to representatives of other ex-POW and related groups: Alex Dandie of J Force; Ralph Levenberg and Joe Vater of American Defenders of Bataan and Corregidor; Franklin Gross of Wake Defenders; Genevieve Donoho of Survivors of Wake, Guam, Cavite; Sjoerd Lapré of Stichting Japanese Ereschulden; Mrs. J. H. van Kempen of Stichting Nederlandse Schlachtoffers Japanse Vrouwenkampen; Marjoke Schepel of Werkcollectief Kongsis; Hank Neumann of Pakan Baroe Spoorwegcomite; Graham McMillan of the New Zealand Ex-Prisoners of War Association; John Stroud of the Hong Kong Veterans Association of Canada; and Harold Payne of the National Federation of Far Eastern Prisoners of War Clubs and Associations of Great Britain.

Special thanks to four ex-POW doctors, Gerrit Bras, Henri Hekking, Tom Hewlett, and Ian Duncan—two Dutchmen, one

American, and one Australian—for invaluable insight into the humane practice of medicine in inhuman conditions. Other individual ex-POWs have gone well beyond the call, in particular John Olson and John McInerney.

Next, my thanks to people who have thought hard and written well about POWs of the Japanese. At the top of my list is Hank Nelson, with whom I worked for many years. Hank has written the best book on Australians in Japanese hands: *POW: Prisoners of War—Australians Under Nippon*. Watching him put together his book—and the fine sixteen-part radio documentary he and Tim Bowden produced for the Australian Broadcasting Commission—first made me aware of the voices of POWs and the stories they had to tell. Hank has been a friend and a guide to me, and no one could ask for a better pathfinder.

The late Donald Knox, whose book *Death March* is an excellent oral history of the Bataan campaign and the years of captivity that followed, took a friendly interest in my work and introduced me to Forrest Knox—no relation, but a teller of true stories.

Ronald Marcello led me to Slug Wright. Marcello's hundreds of hours of interviews with Texans captured by the Japanese are a rich basic source, the best possible introduction to the Lost Battalion and the *Houston* survivors.

I have been helped greatly by others with specialized knowledge: Louis Allen, Joan Beaumont, Dorothy Cave, Charlotte Carr-Gregg, P. N. Davies, Edward Drea, Richard Glenister, E. Bartlett Kerr, Arnold Krammer, Bill Powell, David Sissons, Gregory Urwin, George Von Peterffy, Ian Watt, and Walter Wynne Mason. Special thanks to Charles Roland, a medical historian whose research into POW medicine in both the Asian and European theaters of World War II makes him an exceptionally knowledgeable professional consultant.

My thanks to those who helped me to understand the situation of the Dutch in the Netherlands East Indies who became POWs or civilian internees: Willi Banens, John Bange, Len de Bruijn, Henri de Monchy, J. J. Duizend, Frans Dumoulin, Ruurdje Laarhoven, Lucas Lindeboom, N. G. W. Luitsz, Derk Nooij, Rita Powning, Anthony Reid, Frank Samethini, Teunis Stahlie, C. J. Stolk, Eve ten Brummelaar, Cornelius van Heekeren, Regy van Iterson, and Leonie Voorhoeve.

For help with Philippines material, thanks to: Stephanie Castillo, Dan Doeppers, Lewis Gleeck, Rico Jose, and Glenn May. Special thanks to Al McCoy, and to Morton and Petra Netzorg of Cellar Book Shop.

I have benefited greatly from conversation and correspondence with students of the history, politics, and culture of Japan: Harold Bolitho, Ian Buruma, Hilary Conroy, Haruko Taya Cook and Theodore Cook, Alvin Coox, John Dower, John Fincher, Theodore Friend, Mikiso Hane, Meirion Harries and Susie Harries, Akira Iriye, Marius Jansen, Donald Keene, Margaret Lock, John McBride, Gavan McCormack, Richard Minear, Richard Mitchell, Emiko Ohnuki-Tierney, Roger Pineau, John Pritchard, Donald Richie, Edward Seidensticker, Peter Suzuki, David Titus, John Toland, Paul Varley, and William Wetherall. Special thanks to John Stephan, for answers to innumerable ignorant questions.

My thanks also to the many citizens of Japan whose help I sought. I know that what I asked of them often caused them great personal and professional strain and difficulty. To name them here might well cause more. Forty and fifty years on from World War II, Japan is still a country where a warning shot can be fired at an ex-prime minister for suggesting that Japan would do well to apologize for waging a war of aggression, where the mayor of Nagasaki can be shot for suggesting that Emperor Hirohito had some responsibility for war crimes, and where Japanese scholars can be threatened with death for researching what their country did to subject peoples in occupied territory in Asia. So—to all the men and women in Japan whom I contacted, my sincere thanks, and the assurance of anonymity.

I thank librarians and archivists at the following institutions. In Japan: the National Diet Library, Tokyo. In Australia: the Australian Archives and the Australian War Memorial, Canberra; and the Medical Army Museum, School of Army Health, Healesville. In New Zealand: the Alexander Turnbull Library, Wellington. In Singapore: the National Archives. In the Netherlands, at The Hague: Algemeen Rijksarchief; Statische Archief; Centraal Archievendepot, Ministerie van Defensie; Sectie Militaire Geschiedenis, Koninklijke Landmacht; Afdeling Maritieme Historie van de Marinestaf; and in Amsterdam, Rijksinstituut voor Oorlogsdocumentatie. In Great Britain: the Imperial War Museum, London, and the Public Record Office, Kew. In the United States, in the Washington, D.C., area: the Library of Congress; the Center of Military History; the Naval Historical Center; the United States Marines History and Museum Division; the Modern Military History Branch of the National Archives; and the National Area Records Center, Suitland. In New York State: the United States Military Academy Library, West Point, and the Franklin D. Roosevelt Library, Hyde Park. In Pennsylvania: the United States Military History Institute, Carlisle Barracks. In Oregon: the Douglas County Museum, Roseburg. In Texas: the United States Army Academy of Health Sciences, Fort Sam Houston; and the Oral History Program, University of North Texas, Denton. In Kentucky: the United States Army Armor School Library, Fort Knox. In Alabama: the United States Air Force Historical Research Center, Maxwell Air Force Base. Special thanks to Edward Boone of the Douglas MacArthur Memorial Archives and Library, Norfolk, Virginia; and to Chieko Tachihata of Hamilton Library, University of Hawaii, Honolulu.

For help with document and picture searching, I thank: Leimomi Apoliona-Brown, Charles Balaza, Tim Bowden, Jack Chalker, Patricia Edwards, Frank Fujita, Neal Hatayama, Eugene Jacobs, Patricia Keen, Terence Kirk, Al McGrew, Luther Prunty, Lester Rasbury, and Jess Stanbrough. Every effort has been made to credit pictures correctly. If errors or omissions remain, I would appreciate being informed so that correct attributions can be made in any future edition.

For access to unpublished materials, I thank: Leon Beck, Lee Bendell, John Blinko, Roy Bodine, Lindy Bradley, Alex Dandie, Tom Douglas, Ewart Escritt, Frank Fujita, Jose Holguin, Hans Lüning, Woodrow Kessler, John McBride, Diane McIntosh, James McMurria, Refugio Medina, Robert Mitchell, Ian Sayer, J. C. Sharp, Ash Tisdelle, JoAnn Pryor Wychopen, and Roy Whitecross. Special thanks to Adaline Knox, Kathleen Rucker, and Geoffrey Pharaoh Adams.

The endmaps were drawn by Jane Eckelman of Mānoa Mapworks.

For help with logistics at the level of national governments and affiliated institutions, my thanks to: Henry Ryan of the United States embassy in Canberra; Sue Gerson and Barbara Vasko of the USIA Office for International Visitors, Washington, D.C.; Herman Meijer of the Royal Netherlands embassy in Canberra; John Wilton and Jim Wollraven of the Ministry of Foreign Affairs at The Hague.

For various services, much appreciated, I thank: Peter Allen, De Soto Brown, James Dooley, Sally Drake, Tom Farber, Laura Figueira, Evangeline Funk, Bill Gammage and Jan Gammage, Julie Gordon, Gerald Green, Karen Haines, Jerry Hopkins, Ken Inglis and Amirah Inglis, Ron Jacobs, Marilyn Kim, David Krogh, Constance Larmour and Graeme Larmour, Don McDonald, Dorothy McIntosh, Paula and William Merwin, David Rick, Robin Rowland, Shiro Saito, Jenny Stewart and Ron Stewart, Paul Theroux, John Turpin, Eric Weyenberg, and the late Irwin Shaw. Special thanks to Norah Forster, for many years of knowledgeable and capable assistance.

Grateful thanks to my energetic, resourceful and thoughtful agent, Gordon Kato of ICM, and to Andy Dutter and Gail Kinn at William Morrow.

Thanks above all, and always, to my wife, Carolyn. Words have never been enough.

To all the good people in the long list above I am heavily indebted. That having been said, it is my name that is on the title page of the book; responsibility and accountability for everything in it is mine alone.

—**G.D.**

CONTENTS

AUTHOR'S NOTE

This book is about Allied prisoners of war taken by the Japanese in World War II. With those POWs, the cliché that every human life has a book in it takes on the force of a real truth: the life of any one of them is worth a book. My book is necessarily a single volume about all of them—who they were, how they came to be taken prisoner, what happened to them in prison camp, and what being a POW did to them for the rest of their lives.

There were more than 140,000 of them. A roster of just their last names and first initials would come close to filling a book this size. Complete names would fill a book the size of *Gone with the Wind*. Name, rank, serial number, and a single sentence about what happened to each of them, those who survived and all those who did not, would fill a book the size of *War and Peace* four times over. The POWs who died at the hands of the Japanese have no single monument. Their names carved in stone would cover a mass of granite that could stand beside the Vietnam Veterans Memorial and not be overshadowed.

The war in Asia and the Pacific was a clash of armies, a clash of cultures, and—most brutally—a clash of races. Race war was the way the conflict was understood on both sides, that was the way it was fought, and the POWs suffered for it.

They were white men,★ and yellow men had life-and-death power over them. The Japanese had a formal warrior code, *bushidō,* that taught soldierly correctness and right attitudes to duty in the warrior's life and the warrior's death. But anything touching upon respect for the enemy, or mercy, or restraint, did not carry over into the POW camps of World War II. In the eyes of the Japanese, white men who allowed themselves to be captured in war were despicable. They deserved to die.

The Japanese were not directly genocidal in their POW camps. They did not herd their white prisoners into gas chambers and burn their corpses in ovens. But they drove them toward mass death just the same. They beat them until they fell, then beat them for falling, beat them until they bled, then beat them for bleeding. They denied them medical treatment. They starved them. When the International Red Cross sent food and medicine, the Japanese looted the shipments. They sacrificed prisoners in medical experiments. They watched them die by the tens of thousands from diseases of malnutrition like beriberi, pellagra, and scurvy, and from epidemic tropical diseases: malaria, dysentery, tropical ulcers, cholera. Those who survived could only look ahead to being worked to death. If the war had lasted another year, there would not have been a POW left alive.

Almost all of them had been captured in the first months of the war, a disastrous time for the Allies. By three weeks after Pearl Harbor—Christmas, 1941—Guam, Wake Island, and Hong Kong had fallen; Malaya fell in January, 1942; Singapore in February, the greatest British military disaster ever in Asia; the Netherlands East Indies and Burma in March. In April–May the Japanese took the Philippines, capturing the entire army of Douglas MacArthur— the greatest overseas military disaster in the history of the United States up to that point. This brought on the Bataan death march, the worst single atrocity committed against American POWs. In Southeast Asia, POWs from all the major Allied armies—American, Australian, British and Dutch—were set to slave labor, building the Burma–Siam railroad, the biggest sustained POW atrocity

---

★The Japanese also captured large numbers of Asian troops fighting with Allied forces: Filipinos with the Americans, Indians and Chinese with the British, Indonesians with the Dutch, a total of something like 180,000. Thousands of these Asians died in their first weeks as prisoners; of those surviving, the great majority were released within months. This book is about the POWs who were held for the duration of the war: whites, plus Eurasian Dutch from the Netherlands East Indies who were treated as whites.

of the Pacific war. From the beginning, and increasingly as the war turned against Japan, POWs were shipped to the Japanese home islands for slave labor, on transports that were objectively—measured by numbers of bodies crammed into airless holds fulminating with disease—as bad as slave ships from Africa in the eighteenth century. These transports came to be known as *hellships,* and it is the right name. Thousands of prisoners died at sea, sick, starved, suffocating—or killed when the transports, sailing unmarked by decision of the Japanese, were bombed or torpedoed by the Allies. In Japan, the killing went on to the last moments of the war; downed airmen by the hundreds were tortured and beheaded, and POWs were killed as well when the Americans dropped A-bombs on Hiroshima and Nagasaki.

In a Japanese prison camp, under guards holding life-or-death power, what was it going to take to stay alive, stay sane, stay human? When the body is savagely beaten, what happens to the mind and to the spirit? Among starving men, can common human decency survive? What is the calorie count on friendship, on personal loyalty, on moral agreements, on altruism? In prison camp, what would it mean to say that a man is his brother's keeper?

Every POW saw men like himself die horribly. Every POW saw men like himself offer themselves up to death so that others might live. Those who survived had to struggle to keep themselves alive in the camps, and then struggle to live with themselves afterward, back in the world. They were branded by the experience. They have borne the tribal scars of the POW ever since.

This is what my book is about. What got me firmly pointed in the direction of writing it was overhearing an ex-POW talking in a bar. I talked with him. We went on to talk again. He gave me the name of another POW, who introduced me to yet another. Soon more and more names were coming my way, in the end hundreds. Many times an opening conversation turned into the first of a series. And each time I thought I had arrived at an answer to one question of fact or meaning, a dozen more questions came to my mind. There are a good number of men I have been talking with for more than ten years now.

To borrow a phrase from another book about World War II, I did not interview the dead. But I have listened to all kinds of survivors. Some ex-POWs find it next to impossible to talk. Some find it next to impossible to stop talking. For all of them, the POW years are alive—still, fifty years on. *Time does not heal all wounds; it buries them in very shallow graves.* That is an American POW's way of putting it. An Australian says it this way: *Every last detail comes crystal clear, out of all those years, like a photo developing.* Sometimes the developing takes days, and sometimes the developing fluid is alcohol; but suddenly it happens—the POW and the men who were with him in prison camp are alive again as they were half a century ago, half the world away. Officers good, bad, and worthless. Doctors and medical orderlies. Cooks. Genius scroungers. Black marketeers. Men with no idea that they harbored a latent talent for cat burglary. Gamblers who dealt the cards for rice and stayed alive by winning, and losers who in betting their rations forfeited life. Traders in food who got rich, and men who wound up on the wrong side of this trade, bankrupt of food and thus bankrupt of life. Men who traded their rice for tobacco and smoked themselves to death. Men who could not stand slave labor anymore and had themselves mutilated for surcease—and men who did the mutilating for money. Men who stopped wanting to live and let themselves die. Men who were sure God would save them, and men who wound up just as certain there was no God, only fate and blind luck. Unassuming saints. Genial villains. And one ordinary prisoner who had to kill another ordinary prisoner to save other ordinary prisoners from being killed.

And above all, POWs who, against terrible odds, kept the faith and kept each other alive. These little brotherhoods have stayed close ever since, closer than with any other human beings. Fifty years on, they would still do anything for each other, unquestioningly, to the death. Their closeness as POWs has been the meaning of their whole lives.

I have been amazed at the fullness of memory among the survivors, the detail and the emotional power of their recall. Sometimes, all these years later, they will get a date wrong, or forget a man's first name, or remember something as happening on one side of the river when in fact it was the other. But always they are telling the human truth about what it was like for them to be POWs. That truth is burned into them, body and brain.

As for verification, the other side of work on this book has been with the documentary record, in archives in the United States, Australia, Great Britain, the Netherlands, and Singapore. On the subject of POWs of the Japanese there is no shortage of surviving paper—thousands and thousands of archive boxes. (To take just one class of documents, testimony from the war crimes trials fills a linear mile of file drawers.) Time and again along the road I have heard a story from a seventy-year-old, and then, months or years later, in an archive thousands of miles away, I have come across that story as he set it down in his twenty-year-old handwriting, in his secret diary, or in his statement written at liberation, lodged in a file that no one has looked at in forty or fifty years.

I was not a POW, but I have tried as best I can to write about their experiences from their point of view, putting on the page their life in captivity the way they saw it, in language they would recognize. Whenever I quote them, I quote them exactly. When they recall a conversation, I reproduce it as they gave it to me: no invented or reconstructed dialog of my own making. When I paraphrase, when I have to compress scores of prisoners' utterances on a given subject into a few lines, it is always the POWs' view of the POWs' life that I am trying to convey: not only what they thought of what happened to them, but their way of expressing it.

As often as possible I use their vocabulary. Take one universally recurring example. The Japanese prison camps were filthy with dysentery. The prisoners did not think of themselves as living in *feces* or *excrement;* what they were condemned to live in was their own shit. That is the word I use.

POWs were and are not greatly given to using Latin-based expressions in long sentences with qualifying clauses; their kind of truth was and is spoken in plain Anglo-Saxon. To say that the Japanese *executed* prisoners, *decapitated* them, has an abstract, sanitary sound, almost a legally validated ring to it. What ex-POWs say—and they were the ones who were repeatedly forced to watch it happening—is that the Japanese chopped heads off, far more often than not without trial, often enough just for Japanese-warrior sport, and as often as not incompetently, needing more than one hacking blow to finish the bloody work. In this and in other such instances I follow the prisoners' use of language.

A different kind of example. Psychological concepts such as post-traumatic stress disorder and survivor guilt were never in the heads of POWs in the camps, and were not available to them in their postwar lives. The way they saw things—the way they still see things—is this: As POWs they did what they had to do, and afterward they had to try to live with it or it would destroy them.

Political correctness was not in their thinking either. At the time they were taken prisoner, the armed forces of the United States were still segregated; African-Americans were not even Blacks yet, they were coloreds, niggers. For the British, in their own famous phrase, Wogs (meaning lesser breeds with a touch of the tar brush) began at Calais. Australia was White Australia, by official national policy. American, British, and Australian POWs—Anglos all—instantly perceived and labeled Eurasian prisoners from the Netherlands East Indies as Black Dutch.

As for the enemy, the Japanese were *fucking Japs, Nips, yellow-bellied bastards, rattlesnakes, vipers, vermin, human cockroaches, mad dogs, crazed gorillas, jaundiced baboons, monkey men.* That was the language of the racial world the POWs lived in. What was racially true for the POWs in the years of their growing up and the years of their captivity is set down here in their words, in their tone of voice.

If anyone reading this book at an emotional remove of fifty years from World War II is minded to think that the way I phrase racial utterances about the Japanese is gratuitous Japan-bashing, the product of some nasty prejudice of my own, I recommend, by way of a reality check, John Dower's exhaustively researched, meticulously documented, and alarmingly illustrated *War Without Mercy: Race and Power in the Pacific War.* And, even closer to the mind-set of the war years, the many surveys on race attitudes reported in Samuel Stouffer's large-scale study, *The American Soldier.* For my own part, I have not set out to bash the Japanese with words. I record what POWs say it was like to be in Japanese prison camp, with the Japanese physically bashing their prisoners, to the death.

Race was a vicious thing in prison camp. Between prisoners, there was also nastiness and hostility about nationality. To most Americans, the British remained forever and without distinction Limeys. To most of the British, all Americans—southerners equally with northerners—were Yanks. Of the various nationalities whose men became POWs, the British and the Australians, by the facts of imperial-colonial history, knew most about each other already; but in prison camp, just as in the world outside, their knowledgeable understandings were not necessarily cordial, in fact often—most often—the reverse. As another corollary of imperial-colonial history, Australians and Americans were likely to make common cause out of being strongly anti-British. And, in general, the British, Australians, and Americans—all English speakers, however differently they used the language, and whatever they thought of each other—were strongly anti-Dutch.

I began in great ignorance, imagining that if human beings were worked and starved and beaten to the point of death, they would be reduced to barely functioning skeletons, scraps of biology, with

all the so-called veneer of civilization flayed away, all national culture and character trampled out of them. Not so. The juices
crushed out of the POWs were of course human in the most fundamental sense. But at the same time, all the way down to starvation rations, a thousand calories a day and less, to a hundred
pounds of body weight and less, to the extremities of degradation—all the way to death—the prisoners of the Japanese remained
inextinguishably American, Australian, British, Dutch.

Some of these manifestations are so clear as to register on the
written page, fifty years later, as nothing but clichés. The Americans were the great individualists of the camps, the capitalists, the
cowboys, the gangsters. The British hung on to their class structure
like bulldogs, for grim death. The Australians kept trying to con-
struct little male-bonded welfare states. None of the Anglos had
much useful experience of the tropics; the colonial Dutch did,
centuries of it. These national-cultural differences were obvious
everywhere in the camps, in matters crucial to survival, from discipline to food gathering to medical-surgical doctrine on amputation. What emerges is that much of the life-or-death behavior
of POWs was based on national origin, the sum of what men
carried with them from the place of their birth and upbringing into
prison camp. I would go so far as to say that it was nationality
above all that determined, for good or ill, the way POWs lived
and died, often *whether* they lived or died.

In fact, the most surprising and unexpected impression left on
me is the force and inextinguishability of these national-cultural-
ethnic differences and divisions, and all the behaviors that went
with them, including the most extreme behaviors imaginable. For
example, it came as a surprise to me—indeed a shock—to find
that of all nationalities who were POWs of the Japanese, only
Americans killed each other in captivity.

I started coming across national differences in behavior from
the very first days of my research, and the evidence kept piling up.
When I tried to think of simple expressions to describe what I was
finding, just filenames, the words that came immediately to mind
were *tribes* and *tribalism*. That was ten years ago, and since then I
have been interested—more and more so every year—to note how
often those words have come to be used about the way ethnic and
cultural groups around the globe continue to behave in the world
we live in now: tribalism in society, tribalism in war, tribalism to
the death. Tribalism has always had enormous power; it still does.
And certainly it did in the POW camps.

There were small subtribes, intimate little groups of men help-ing each other to stay alive, that could rightly be called moral communities. But the big ethnic-cultural-national tribes simply were what they were, for good and ill—for good and evil.

As for the ruling tribe of the camps, the Japanese, almost none of the POWs had the slightest idea what a Japanese was. Not one in a thousand prisoners would have so much as seen a live Japanese before the war (the possible exception here would be some West Coast Americans). Going into prison camp, not one out of five thousand men would have spoken fluent Japanese. From the first, the Japanese appeared to their prisoners as the ultimate alien tribe, grotesque, brutal, incomprehensible, barely human, in fact non-human. This was how the POWs saw them going in; it was how they saw them coming out. And, start to finish, the Japanese saw their white prisoners the same way.

The undeniable, incontrovertibly documented record of bru-tality, disease, and death in the POW camps, plus what happened in the civilian internment camps for white men, women, and chil-dren, and the massacres and atrocities perpetrated on native Asian peoples in occupied territory—all this shows the national tribe of Japan at its worst as a power in the world. That worst was humanly dreadful, a terrible chapter in the world's twentieth-century book of the dead.

What the Japanese did, the human pain they inflicted, the hu-man ruin they left behind, was on a huge scale. The pain remains unassuaged. The more so as the world sees Japan dominating Asia again, with the underlying economic and grand-strategic impera-tives of the region looking much the same as they did in the 1930s: Japan a formidable global power, Japanese nationalism on the rise, even signs and omens that Japan might be on the cusp of rearming.

What the Japanese people of the postwar decades—all the way to the fiftieth anniversary years of the war—were told about World War II in their own language was very little indeed. Typically, Japanese school and college textbooks gave only half a dozen or so pages to the war in its entirety, phrased in sanitized language officially enforced by the Ministry of Education. In the orthodox teaching of the Japanese national tribe, Japan was the victim of white aggression, and the atrocities of the war began and ended with the atom-bombing of Hiroshima and Nagasaki. World-scale atrocities like the Rape of Nanking were reduced to *incidents,* and POW camps were cleansed out of existence altogether.

That has been "history" for the general Japanese population. Neither do POWs figure at all in the one hundred-plus volumes of the official Japanese military history of World War II, *Senshi Sōsho*. Perhaps that is not surprising. What did strike me as truly surprising was to find that on the other side of the ledger, in the Allied official histories written soon after the war, the POWs did not do markedly better overall. Oddly, New Zealand POWs of the Japanese, very few in number, were allowed the most official pages—a volume shared with POWs of the European war. The British gave their POWs not so much as a ceremonial bow. The Australians gave theirs better than that, but still not fair measure. The Dutch took more than forty years to focus detailed official-historical attention upon what happened to their people in the Indies. As for the Americans, the Navy and the Air Force, with few POWs, gave them only peripheral mention. The Marine history isolated their POWs in a kind of appendix. And the Army volume on the campaign in the Philippines—where the entire army of Douglas MacArthur was captured—made a deliberate point, overtly stated, of excluding POWs.

Why should this have been so? The answer to that question is above my pay grade.

My own book, which was not researched and written under official auspices, turns out to be the reverse side of official history. Not that I am anti-official history on principle or by prejudice, any more than I am a principled or prejudiced Japan-basher. Rather, this book is my best effort to tell a story conspicuously absent from the official histories of both sides, missing in action, so to speak: the truth of life according to the POW.

The official military histories are multivolume. In starting to lay out my single volume, I had to concede from the beginning that I would not have space to tell the story of the war itself in any detail. I focus on the POWs and only on them. Everything else is seen only peripherally, which is the way the POWs saw things. The world of the POWs was not the vast Asia-Pacific theater of war, it was the prison camp. Life was the sum of what happened in the huts and at the work sites where they labored as slaves. What went on among prisoners, and between prisoners and guards—that was the sum of existence. The war itself was something else, somewhere else.

The course of military events became known in the camps by way of clandestine news—especially through the work of men who built and operated secret radios at the risk of their lives. I have had the good fortune to be able to talk to a number of these extraordinary men, and it is through them that the story of the war comes into the book. I have chosen secret radio stories from different times and places and situations: Java in 1942, the Burma–Siam railroad in 1943, Davao in the southern Philippines in 1944; and for 1945 a very different kind of radio story, about an American POW forced to work at a Japanese propaganda radio station in Tokyo, only eight blocks from the emperor's palace.

Another major choice I had to make was whether to try to give equal coverage to all groups of POWs in all camps. When I was in the army (post–World War II, an eighteen-year-old dumb private who never had to fire a shot in anger, and with not the slightest idea that anything such as a POW camp might ever have existed), I was forever being told that *time spent in reconnaissance is very rarely wasted.* In the very first of my research reconnaissances I learned that there were hundreds of POW camps. In book terms, equal time for every camp would amount to only a few hundred words on each—not enough, in my opinion, to say anything humanly useful. So, for me, the better working choice was to select carefully from this known universe a few groups of POWs, and then within those groups to follow a few men through the years of their captivity and the years that followed—do close-ups of them against the panorama of the whole experience, in the responsibly reconnoitered knowledge that, by having chosen well, in a single book this would convey human truth better than any other method.*

I chose Americans to follow in detail for the simple reason that Americans covered the whole range of experience, across the broadest geographical sweep of territory. They were the only white Allied troops captured in the Philippines, and elsewhere they found themselves with POWs of all the other nations: on Java and other islands in the Indies, on the Burma–Siam railroad, in China, on Formosa, in Korea, in Manchuria, on hellships to Japan, and in the Japan camps. They were everywhere; it is through their eyes that we see the other national POW tribes.

In close-up I follow, first, Harry Jeffries and Oklahoma Atkin-

---

*The downside of this approach is that some groups of prisoners get short shift, some virtually no mention at all. However, these groups are small in number, and as it happens there are good books already dealing with their experiences: New Zealanders, Canadians, and one quite different and separate category of POW—female army nurses.

son, technically civilian construction workers on Wake Island, who took up arms, fought as soldiers, and were captured early and imprisoned as POWs along with United States marines, transported by ship to Shanghai, then later by ship to Japan, where in the last days of the war they tried to escape.

Next, Slug Wright, captured with his battalion of Texans on Java, shipped through the enormous multinational POW camp at Changi in Singapore to labor on the Burma–Siam railroad, where he became (with no previous training) a medical orderly for a Dutch doctor who taught him wisdom about the larger human tribe. And then Forrest Knox, captured in the Philippines, survivor of the Bataan death march, survivor of the appalling months that followed at Camp O'Donnell, and finally survivor of a hellship voyage to Japan during which he had to kill to keep himself and others alive.

Many things were done among POWs that might seem dreadful or shameful to people who were not there, meaning privileged and protected people, of whom I am one. It does not behoove someone like me to sit in lofty judgment. My own judgment of myself is that as a POW I would have lasted about three and a half days. They had to try to last three and a half years. I do my best to describe what they did and explain why they did it; judgment on their actions I leave to others.

But how to handle such matters on the printed page? I have changed the names of three men and altered a few small personal details. In no way do these changes diminish or distort essential truth. Anyone who was in the camps with those three will recognize them immediately; and anyone else who has a genuine need to know their real identities and is prepared to do some digging can find out.

For the same sort of reason, I have not named POWs who suffered atrocious death at the hands of the Japanese. Even after all these years, it is still possible that family and friends do not know how they died, and the worst way to find out would be to come across it unexpectedly in a book written by a stranger.

These are judgment calls. I can only hope that my calls have been sensible and humane.

On the other side of the balance, the judgment on the Japanese that is recorded in these pages is the judgment of the prisoners themselves—moral truth according to the POW.

I do have opinions of my own to offer on some large and consequential issues. For one: the appallingly high percentage of

POWs killed by Allied friendly fire, and the reasons for it. For another: the reputation of Douglas MacArthur among the tens of thousands of men he left to be captured by the Japanese in the Philippines. Another matter involving MacArthur: the deal he made at the end of the war not to try Japanese military scientists for the war crime of killing prisoners in lethal medical experiments—immunity from prosecution in return for information useful to the United States about biological and chemical warfare. On another level of consideration of responsibility: the important human question of what kind of justice was arrived at in the Allied war crimes trials. Among POWs themselves: the overall performance or nonperformance of POW officers in the camps; and the tragically blinkering effect of national tribalism in matters crucial to survival, such as POW medical practice. In the postwar years: the record of veterans administrations around the world. And so on.

I have matured these opinions by the simple method of listening as closely as possible for as long as possible to what the POWs told me, and reading official documents with that in mind.

Finally, some nuts-and-bolts items. All times given are local: for example, Sunday, December 7, 1941, at Pearl Harbor was Monday, December 8, on Wake Island and in the Philippines. Concerning place names, I use designations and spellings from the period: for example, Formosa, not Taiwan; Batavia, not Jakarta; Burma, not Myanmar. Siam officially changed its name to Thailand in 1939; during the war both names were used. Regarding place names for prison camps along the Burma–Siam railroad, it has been next to impossible to find one universally accepted standard spelling from the period (Tamarkan or Tha Makhan? Nonpladuk or Nong Pladuk?). For Japanese personal names in the text, I follow Japanese usage—family name first, then individual name: for example, Tōjō Hideki, Yamashita Tomoyuki, Homma Masaharu.

One last item needs to be flagged. After working my way through all kinds of arithmetical calculations concerning POWs, I count myself among those who know from experience that there are lies, damned lies, and statistics. Figures on combat and captivity are often shaky. Between Japanese and Allied figures there are serious discrepancies at almost every turn: how many men fought on either side in the Malaya campaign, how many prisoners survived the Bataan death march, how many were worked to death on the Burma–Siam railroad, and so on. Often, in writing about large numbers, the best I can do is indicate orders of magnitude. At the level of single camps and small groups of POWs, just as often the arithmetic in the surviving documentary record does not add up. So it goes, POWs gone missing forever, reduced to gaps in columns of figures that do not tally, blank spots in human history.

At the end of it all, I think of what Michelangelo said about sculpture and about life. The statue is there in the marble; endless labor is required to discover and uncover its true human form; and the hope all the way through the work must be that within the rough stone a shape good and strong can be found, just as the hope must be that within human beings, under the crude coarse encrusted skin, there is something essentially of value. Michelangelo carved a group of statues called *The Captives*. He shows prisoners struggling out of the imprisoning stone, the marks of their struggle forever upon them. That suggests a way to think of the life and death of POWs. And a way to think of a book about POWs—as a piece of work that tries hard to give an awful subject human shape and human scale, an effort to comprehend and convey the human meaning of struggle and suffering.

SITTING DUCKS

HARRY JEFFRIES WAS CRUISING, COUNTING THE DAYS TILL HIS divorce papers came through and he could make his getaway from San Fancisco. He was an ironworker, his trade was bucking hot rivets, and his place of employment was the Golden Gate Bridge, the south tower, hundreds of feet above the waters of the bay. In his last week on the job—his last days as a married man—the world below appeared to him like a map laid out to show his life and times, past and future. Turn one way and there was the city, the cold-water hotel where he had been living out of a suitcase, separated from his wife and little daughter, the bars where he drank when he was not working, the blind alleys in the Tenderloin where he gambled when he was not drinking. Turn the other way and there was the blue Pacific, stretching off to the west—and

31

the instant he was single again, that was where he was headed, over the horizon and out. On the stroke of noon, August 21, 1941, his big moment came up, and all the married men who worked on his level of the tower cheered and beat on the steel girders with their sledges and wrenches, wedding bells in reverse, as he climbed down off the bridge, free at last.

He and his friend Oklahoma Atkinson had their ship's passage booked for that same afternoon, and before the day shift on the tower downed tools they were sailing in style out through the Golden Gate.

They were going to be gone for nine months—which would make it June of 1942 when they came cruising back, flush with money, set for life. They had it all worked out.

They had met at the building trades labor temple. Harry was hanging around waiting for a poker game to materialize when Oklahoma came walking in with his little tin suitcase, looking all wide-eyed and countrified. They got to talking, and they clicked right off. They were a pair, a couple of healthy young physical specimens, the same age, twenty-six, the same height and weight, six feet one, one hundred ninety-five pounds, full of beans, purpose-built for bridge building. They organized things so that they could work the same shift in the same gang.

And they started running around together after hours, nightclubbing along North Beach, picking up women. Harry was the date maker. On the bridge he was known as Hollywood—a snappy dresser with slick hair and a movie-star moustache—and in the clubs no one was speedier with a silver Ronson when some good-looking blonde sitting at the bar crossed her legs and tapped her cigarette. Oklahoma with his average man's Zippo was forever a step behind, meaning he was the one who always drew the good-looking girl's less good-looking friend.

Not that he was complaining. Before San Francisco he had not seen a great deal of the world, not much beyond the flatlands for a day's drive or so around his tiny little hometown, and a military base or two from his hitch in the peacetime army of the United States, one lowly private soldier among thousands, grateful just to be fed and clothed and in out of the cold in the worst years of the Great Depression. Now here he was in the big city, with Hollywood Harry ordering up the high life.

Harry had started out a poor boy too, and that pointed him toward the service the same way as Oklahoma. Not the Army, though, the Marines. An elite corps—Harry liked the sound of those words. So he signed up with the reserves. But he never did make it to the real Corps. In the dark days of the 1930s recruiting lines in the big cities were as long as soup kitchen lines, and because the Marines were elite, for every one keeper they came across they could afford to throw back dozens. Harry was well set up, big and strong, but he was bowlegged; when the recruiters stood him at attention, daylight showed between his knees, and that was enough to wipe him out. It was a blow to his pride. He had to settle for the Navy.

His big cruise, aboard the battleship U.S.S. *Colorado,* took him from Bremerton in Washington State down the West Coast, through the Panama Canal, and up the East Coast to New York. It was the time of the World's Fair, and Harry was detailed to march with his shipmates in a big parade along Fifth Avenue. Passing the Empire State Building, the tallest skyscraper on earth, some of the young sailor boys got carried away and tilted their heads back to gawk; they lost their step and bumped into each other and fell down in a heap and took Harry with them.

Harry did not need the embarrassment. He was doing the parade the hard way already. In Havana, on liberty, his first ever night of catting around in a foreign port, he had picked up his first ever dose of the clap. All the way north to New York he had to suffer the Navy's fearsome gonorrhea treatment, standing at a trough, a nozzle stuck up his urethra to drench his inflamed plumbing with purple potassium permanganate, let that drain out, then take a syringe of Argyrol straight up. He made the Fifth Avenue march feeling sorry for himself, his greatest item of value and distinction tied with a butterfly bandage, and for extra protection a leather Bull Durham sack, so that the gonorrhea drip would not weep all over the crotch of his Navy whites.

By the time his ship got back to the West Coast the drip had dried up. But in Seattle he found a more serious sort of woman trouble to get himself into, a shotgun marriage, and that turned into a curse worse than the clap.

If he could not be a Marine he was looking to be career Navy, but now here he was, condemned to be a family man as well, and he could not carry the weight of both. He felt as if his life was all bent out of shape. He did so many things wrong that finally the Navy threw him out on a bad conduct discharge.

He bummed his way down the West Coast and got lucky in San Francisco, seventy-five cents an hour as a starting ironworker on the new suspension bridge over the Golden Gate. He stuck with the job, rising to twelve dollars a day on a union ticket, very respectable money. He tried to stick with his wife and daughter as well, but he could not, and the marriage went from bad to divorce court.

Where Harry did far and away the best for himself was not on the job or at home but at the gambling table. He had found out how good he was as early as his middle teens, when he was running loose in the deep south of California, around Mexicali and Calexico. In the Hoovervilles, the Depression shantytowns along the border, there was all kinds of action. It was only penny ante stuff, down-and-outers hustling each other for small change, but that was all Harry could afford anyway. He watched for a while and then threw in for a quarter. He knew he would come up a winner, and he was right. He was a natural. From the beginning he could count the cards at blackjack, remember the fall of a whole deck. Not many players along the border could do that, in fact not many in the world, and if it was done right, meaning inconspicuously, it was the next thing to a guaranteed income. At poker, Harry was as good as any grown man he ever came across—from game one he knew better than to draw to an inside straight, the mathematics of it coming to him as clear as day. On top of which, he could instinctively read the tells, the different little bodily giveaways of the players around the table. And once he caught on to the fact that there were ways and ways of working a deck, he practiced forcing and second-carding and dealing off the bottom, and quickly became perfect. He was put on earth to be a card sharp.

Oklahoma knew a thing or two himself. He might have looked and sounded like a yokel, but he had a calculating brain, all the way to the fine point of figuring that, in a big-city game, looking like a bumpkin could tilt the percentages his way. And he suffered no real disability with the cards by losing the first joint of his left index finger in an accident on the bridge. In fact, he came out ahead, because he learned to use the sensitive stump to do things to a deck, undetectable except by the sharpest of sharpies.

Of all the sharpies in San Francisco, Harry had to be one of the sharpest. Oklahoma watched him operate and judged him to be the best he had ever seen—he could take a deck of cards and make them dance.

So when those two sat down across a poker table, it took no more than a couple of hands for them to see possibilities. They worked up some secret signals, and then all it required was getting into games with strangers, arriving separately, leaving separately,

meeting later in a quiet little bar across town to count their winnings. After Harry split up with his wife they were in a game every
night, making a lot more money than they ever did on the bridge.

The trouble was, the more they made the more they spent,
and all they had to show for their talents was a somewhat better
grade of blonde on a barstool. Then it came to them: If they truly
wanted to move up in class, meaning money unlimited and
women laid end to end, they would need to move up to being
the house.

They put out feelers around the Tenderloin, and a vision began
to form in their brains: a club, a place with a bit of style, the right
class of blonde on a barstool downstairs, the right class of game
upstairs. It would be illegal, but that was nothing. Back home,
Oklahoma used to have a deal going, bootlegging liquor into
counties that stayed dry after the end of Prohibition, selling fifths
to thirsty men off the back of a truck. As for Harry, never for a
moment did he doubt that he was naturally wiser than the law.

Getting their dream club up and running was going to take a
sizable bankroll. But that was not the hard part; all they had to do
was keep winning at poker. The real problem would be hanging
on to their winnings. What kept cleaning them out was women.
So it came down to this: They were going to have to put a lock
on sex, for however long it took, even if that meant months. They
gave a big sigh and set about looking for some place on earth with
a deal that offered big money and no women at all.

Contractors Pacific Naval Air Bases fit their specifications to a tee.
CPNAB was the umbrella name for a group of heavy construction
companies building bases for the United States Navy on strategic
islands in the Pacific. By mid-1941 the wisdom in Washington was
that Japan was secretly getting ready to attack the United States.
The Japanese empire had bases on Formosa and in three scattered
island groups in Micronesia: the Carolines, the Marianas, and the
Marshalls. The United States urgently needed a defensive screen
to shield the Navy's Pacific Fleet, home-ported at Pearl Harbor in
Hawaii. So CPNAB was constructing island bases, to be manned
by marines, with submarines patrolling and Wildcat fighter-
bombers combing the skies.

CPNAB paid top dollar. If a man could sit on his wallet for a
full nine-month tour, he would come home thousands to the
good, more money than most American working men in the 1930s
would ever see at one time.

The CPNAB projects were run by the Navy book, meaning

no liquor and no women on base. Gambling was banned, too. But every military installation and every construction project on the face of the earth had games going perpetually; it was a truth of life. And especially on remote island bases—men only, by the hundreds, and no way to blow off steam—of course there was going to be intense gambling.

CPNAB bases were custom-built for Harry and Oklahoma, machines for converting pay packets into poker winnings. They flipped a coin for an island, and up came Wake.

They did not plan to cut the cards immediately they got there. They had a long-term strategy worked out: Stay strictly away from the cards for the first six months, then come on fast and be gone with their winnings.

An excellent scheme, and it lasted all of three hours, the time it took for their ship to clear the Golden Gate and make the open ocean.

The first leg of their journey was to Honolulu. They were traveling courtesy of Morrison-Knudsen, the lead contractor for Wake, first class on the famous South Seas luxury liner S.S. *Matsonia*. In international waters it was legal to play the ship's slot machines, or wager money on the races held in the lounge with wooden horses advanced by the throw of dice. This was beneath their gambling dignity. But when Harry saw all those CPNAB roughnecks milling around bored and restless, he had a rush of blood to the brain. After dinner the first evening, he and Oklahoma got a game going, and by breakfast time they had cleaned every last player out of cash and were piling up IOUs against a draw on wages to be paid in Honolulu.

Hawaii was only a four-day sail. Ten days there, then the time lock on sex was going to snap shut for nine months. So, Hollywood Harry and his magic Ronson went to work—their second night out, he came up with two nice young California girls from Salinas, traveling first-class on daddy's money. He took the better-looking one and dealt her friend to Oklahoma. Working the other side of the blanket, he negotiated an exclusive private arrangement with a hooker. She was shipping out for her third tour at one of the high-volume short-time houses on Hotel Street in Honolulu that serviced the military—soldiers from Schofield Barracks, airmen from Hickam Field, sailors from Pearl Harbor. She did business under the name of Raceboat Sally, and she had a first-timer with her, a snappy little redhead. Class acts, both of them, happy to accommodate men of distinction like Harry and Oklahoma. And so the blue Pacific days and nights went sailing by, all the way to Hawaii.

Honolulu to Wake was a big step down, ten days on a rust-bucket merchant ship, with stacked bunks in the hold and no air-conditioning, and nothing but beans and corn bread for meals.

Wake was about twenty-three hundred miles south and a long way west into the empty Pacific. On the map it was only a bug speck, an atoll, actually three tiny linked coral islets: Wake, Peale, and Wilkes, total land area less than three square miles. The highest point was about twenty feet. There was no drinkable ground water. It was a tropical island without palm trees, in fact there was almost nothing green above knee-height except thick ugly scrub. And the place was teeming with rats, different from American rats, beady-eyed, with short front legs that gave them a nasty hunch-backed look, rats everywhere, even at the Pan Am Inn where the passengers on the China Clipper stayed overnight. Pan Am had a rack of air rifles, complimentary to any passenger who felt like killing rats, and that was the most excitement to be had on Wake.

Morrison-Knudsen laid on all comforts for their contractors: a mess serving three meals a day and a fourth at midnight for the graveyard shift, excellent food with unlimited seconds, plus a canteen that featured homemade ice cream and cookies; a rec hall; a free outdoor movie show; a library that checked out more than a hundred books a day; tennis courts; and a protected swimming pool on the reef.

Females were the most serious deficiency. At Pan Am there were a couple of women, management wives, and twice a week there was the long shot of a glimpse at the Clipper's cabin crew. Six nights a week at the movies there were good-looking blondes on the silver screen, cleavage in close-up, and a man could think whatever he was moved to think. But day by day in the real world, CPNAB-Navy doctrine was no females on base.

Yet against all expectations and regulations there was one. She was the wife of Morrison-Knudsen's head man, the contractors' overall boss on Wake, Dan Teters. Her name was Florence. Dan had brought her out on the principle of morale boosting. Florence was an all-American blonde, and the sight of her strolling about in shorts in the hot Wake sun was certainly a boost. The word was that when Dan and Florence went to bed at night in their private quarters, Dan slept only lightly and with a gun under his pillow.

Wake was a strange place, in fact a kind of prison. Some men could not handle it—they came down with rock fever. Under the CPNAB agreement, if a contractor quit in less than three months he had to pay his own fare back to civilization. That was no deterrent. The instant an incoming supply ship hove over the horizon, a knot of defecting contractors would form at the water's edge, champing to get away to Hawaii and then the West Coast. Once they cleared Honolulu, the joy of being back on a shiny white Matson cruise liner headed for San Francisco at a rate of knots moved many of them to strip off their last change of Wake work clothes and race around first-class wearing nothing at all.

For every one contractor who bailed out, though, fifty stayed. The money kept them hanging on. Some of the pioneer party from January even re-upped in October. But they considered themselves to be paying a heavy price for the paycheck, and they made a public show of it. Harry and Oklahoma used to watch the performance. Away would go the latest bunch of happy defectors, in would come the latest batch of hopefuls, and over at the entrance to Camp 2 the long-timers would be standing, like lifers in some maximum-security prison, razzing the new intake: *Sucker, sucker, sucker.*

Any contractor who wanted to could take weapons instruction with the marines. A couple of hundred signed up, but the better part of a thousand did not. The average contractor on Wake did not see war as a great worry, and that included Harry and Oklahoma. If the Japanese took on the United States, it would only prove they were slant-eyed fools; they would get their whipping, six weeks maximum, more likely two.

Then, early in November, Dan Teters sent Florence home on the Clipper. The Pan Am managers sent their wives, too. This was on the advice of the marine officers, who were not the least bit hazy about the situation of Wake. Only six hundred miles away, in the Marshall Islands, the Japanese were massing forces: fighting ships by the dozen, airplanes by the score, combat troops by the thousand.

Major J.P.S. Devereux had arrived in mid-October to take over the marine battalion. His orders were to have things complete and one hundred percent operational by March 1942. His opening declaration of intent was to crank up the workday of his marines from twelve hours, already severe, to sixteen. The enlisted men named him Just Plain Shit.

In late November, Wake was named a naval air base, and with that new designation it came under a new senior officer, a navy commander, Winfield Scott Cunningham. As of the day Cunningham took over, there still had been no chance to see if the island's whole defense system would work properly together, indeed if it would work at all. By November–December the physical fortifications were only about two thirds complete, and the island was still radically undermanned; there were only about 520 men in any kind of United States uniform, fewer than 400 marines, the others navy and miscellaneous. The rest of the men, approximately 1,200, were civilians: contractors, and 50 or so Pan Am employees.

On the morning of Saturday, December 6, Devereux called a mock alert. It was the first day ever for many of the gun crews to work together as a team. The drill went well enough to please Devereux, which was something, he being a career marine officer impossible to please. He told his men they could have the afternoon off, and the next day too, Sunday, unheard of from Just Plain Shit.

Wake was west across the international date line from Hawaii. The morning of Sunday, December 7, at Pearl Harbor was the morning of Monday, December 8, on Wake. Coming up to 0700 hours, the marines were still easing themselves into the idea of yet another work week when a radio message came beaming in from Hawaii, uncoded: *SOS. ISLAND OF OAHU ATTACKED BY JAPANESE DIVE BOMBERS. THIS IS THE REAL THING.*

Devereux was caught in the middle of shaving. He waited for a coded confirmation, then yelled for his bugler, the marine field music, who in his agitation blew pay call, church call, and fire call before he hit upon the call to arms.

The marines could not credit what they were hearing. When they finally fell out, some had weapons and helmets, some had sand buckets for fire drill, some were still chewing on their breakfast bacon, and very few were moving at speed.

The contractors took even longer getting the word. The morning shift was on the job already, spread out everywhere, hard to contact in a hurry. As the shore battery marines were being trucked out, they went bouncing by a new barracks building, and there was a sight—contractors up ladders with brushes and buckets, painting the place spic-and-span white to impress an admiral scheduled to visit in a couple of weeks.

They were still painting when, just before noon, big planes

broke by the dozen from the cover of a rain squall, red circles at the wingtips, bomb bays open, sticks of bombs loose and tumbling.

The Japanese caught eight Wildcats still sitting on the ground, knocked out seven, killing more than half the men of the squadron, and blew up a twenty-five-thousand-gallon aviation gas tank. They strafed the marine barracks at Camp 1, the contractor barracks at Camp 2, flattened everything at Pan Am including the Inn—and then they were gone, less than twelve minutes start to finish.

The marines did not lose any dead, but a crowd of contractors got caught on their lunch break at Camp 2, and about fifty were killed. Contractors were civilians, and for hundreds of them that was enough war. They grabbed food and took off for the scrub, as far away as they could get from anything built up, dug themselves holes, and crawled in.

The next day, Tuesday, the bombers came back, and again on Wednesday, and that was when the war turned personal for Harry and Oklahoma. They were caught out in the open, a stick of bombs walking its way straight at them, *crump, crump, crump,* and they had nowhere to go to ground, the closest even remotely safe place a big steel dragline bucket a hundred yards away. They felt as if they made it to the bucket in ten strides, yet every stride felt like it took ten minutes. They piled in a split second ahead of an explosion that would have pulverized them. The concussion was a colossal thump, like being beaten inside the biggest bass drum in the world, and when they flopped out onto the ground they were oozing blood from the ears.

Their great card game of March 1942 was off without ever being on. Bombing raids three days in a row meant the Japanese were softening Wake up, getting ready to invade. On the subject of CPNAB lifting the civilians out, as per contract in the event of war, there was deafening silence.

The marines were handing out spare Springfield rifles. Now they had more civilian volunteers than weapons. Some of the contractors went across to the wrecked Pan Am Inn and came back with complimentary rat-shooting air rifles. The rest were going to have to make do with pick handles and iron bars, or settle for working unarmed as ammunition passers on the heavy machine guns or sandbaggers and searchlight crews on the shore batteries.

Harry and Oklahoma both had put in time in the service, they could claim weapons proficiency, and they talked their way into a Browning Automatic Rifle each.

Harry had always wanted to be a Marine. But J.P.S. Devereux would not let him. Not Harry, and not any other civilian. Not even with a Japanese invasion force steaming toward Wake. It would contaminate the holy purity of the Corps. To the willing contractors that was craziness, Devereux saving his Marine officer face while his Marine officer ass was on fire. Harry was insulted, but not enough to turn in his BAR.

The invasion of Wake was announced just before 0300 hours on Thursday, December 11, when the shore lookouts spotted the Japanese coming up from the south in the moonlight—three cruiser-class vessels, six destroyers, and troop transports. By 0530 the big ships had closed to where they could bombard, and for forty minutes they fired their heavy guns unopposed, driving in to where the landing craft could disembark troops. By 0610 they had come well within range of the shore batteries. The marine gunners opened fire and did phenomenal execution. They sank one destroyer almost immediately, disabled another, and scored repeated hits on the lead cruiser. In less than an hour the Japanese ships were scattered and in retreat. The four remaining flyable Wildcats went out after them, scored damaging hits, and sank a destroyer. It was a great morning's work.

But on Friday the twelfth the bombers came back, and from then on they pounded away day after day. Keeping the base in working order was nonstop labor, brutal on the body. And being under the bombs was hard on the nerves. The air raids drove the Wake rats crazy; they came leaping into the dugouts, frantic, scratching and biting—Harry hated that. The concussion of the bomb blasts killed birds in flight by the hundred. They screamed and fell dead out of the sky and lay on the ground in heaps, rotting in the heat and drawing flies. Men in foxholes with nowhere to go for a latrine had to go on the spot. The flies flocked to the smell, and diarrhea and dysentery flared up all across the island.

Everybody was on the raw edge, fatigued and stinking and starving. Then on the afternoon of Saturday the twentieth, a single flying boat appeared, a PBY sent from Hawaii, bringing good news. A task force was on its way, with marine reinforcements, millions of rounds of ammunition, plus an aircraft carrier with planes to stop the disastrous hole the Japanese had blown open in Wake's air cover. Every wounded marine was going to be carried out. Most of the contractors would be able to get away, too. All this was definitely going to happen on the twenty-fourth.

The Navy wanted 350 contractors to stay. Harry and Oklahoma did not wait to be fingered; that would have been beneath their dignity. They held on to their BARs and threw in as volunteers. Yet J.P.S. Devereux still refused to let them be marines, and they resolved that if ever they ran across him up close, they were going to call him by his true name, to his face.

At about 0100 on Tuesday, December 23, the day before the relief force was due, the lookouts sighted flashes to the northeast, repeated flickerings, like heat lightning on a hot Indiana night. It could have been the Japanese signaling back and forth among themselves. Or it could have been them firing at what they thought was Wake, but from a long way off, and missing by miles, because no sound of gunfire or exploding shells was heard. It could even have been—and it should have been—the task force out of Pearl Harbor. But whatever it was, it was not that. Cunningham and Devereux heard not a word about friendly forces in the area.

Relief was nowhere in sight, and now in the darkness the Japanese were everywhere. The shore lookouts could feel them. They strained their senses. Lights started showing on the water, little flare-ups. Messages ricocheted around the communications net: *I see boats!* and from somewhere else: *I don't see any boats!* and instantly from somewhere else again: *I see boats!* At about 0245 a machine gun fired a burst from the shore, a question in tracers, lighting up the blackness enough to show something solid looming. A searchlight flicked on and caught a landing craft. And there, frozen in the beam, were the Japanese, a hallucinatory first sighting that branded itself into the brain—squat, yellow-skinned men, in drab uniforms, with strange webbed helmets and bizarre animal-looking split-toed boots, rifles with long fixed bayonets that stuck up straighter and taller than the little bandy-legged soldiers themselves, some of them even with swords, charging into war against Americans in the middle of the twentieth century with a weapon out of some alien Asiatic past. Then the searchlight shorted and hissed into blackness, the after-image on the eyes burned down to nothing, everyone was unsighted, and in the pitch dark the Japanese came on again.

They put 750 men ashore, and the battle was on in the night. Mortar and machine-gun fire, and then the marines and the volunteer contractors were fighting by muzzle flare and grenade flash, making contact, losing contact, falling back, moving out, colliding and flailing and shooting and thrusting, knots of bodies, voices without faces; and in the blackness it was impossible to know what was happening anywhere beyond bayonet point.

Devereux and Cunningham in their separate underground command posts did not know much more. The Japanese were cutting the communications wires, and the radio net was next to worthless. Long before dawn the phones from Wilkes islet went silent. Much of Wake islet was dead, too. For all the command posts knew, there were only dead men at the other end of the line. Or men marked for death. A voice kept whispering, *There are Japanese in the bushes,* never saying where, never saying anything else, until inhuman sounds came down the wire and the voice was gone.

At 0500, Cunningham radioed Pearl Harbor: *ENEMY ON ISLAND. ISSUE IN DOUBT.* By then the issue was not really in doubt. The Japanese had landed a thousand men, and they had hundreds more in reserve aboard ship. The rising sun showed twenty-seven Japanese ships steaming in a beleaguering circle. The Japanese owned the seas, by United States Navy forfeit. They owned the skies, too; they could bomb and strafe at will—the Wildcat squadron was down to zero planes, and only one antiaircraft battery could still fire.

Devereux's assessment was that there was no way forward, no way out. The only options were to fight to the death or stop fighting. He did not want to be the first marine officer of his lifetime to have to say the word *surrender.* It came down to Cunningham, the navy commander, as senior officer. Cunningham left the decision as long as he could bear to. Finally, at 0752, with the Japanese moving to land more troops, he radioed a last message to Pearl Harbor, put on a clean blue uniform, and set out to find a Japanese to surrender to.

The marines and contractors fighting at the dead end of cut phone lines did not know that they had been surrendered. All through the morning little separate wars kept grinding on, bodies piling up on both sides, until Devereux or Cunningham appeared, one or the other, surrounded by Japanese, under a grubby white rag knotted to a mop handle.

Harry and Oklahoma were holding their own. Better than that, they were actually taking back some ground. Harry was firing his BAR in bursts; he was excited, he could see himself winning the war out of the barrel of his own gun. A marine runner showed up, shouting, *Stay under cover, hold your fire!* but just then five Japanese came at Harry and he flipped to full automatic and riddled them. Even when the runner blurted out the last part of his message—*The island has surrendered!*—Harry and Oklahoma did not get it, or rather they got it wrong. They saw the white flag coming, but they thought it must be the Japanese giving up. They could not understand why there were Americans with their arms in the air. Then the dirty white flag came closer, and they saw that the man directly under it was Devereux. Everyone around was letting their weapons fall. They looked at each other and cursed and slipped the firing bolts out of their BARs and tossed them.

As a major in the United States Marine Corps, J.P.S. Devereux would never willingly have lowered himself to talk to a yellow man on equal terms. Now he had to learn to speak lower than low, in the voice of unconditional surrender. Of course he did not know a word of Japanese. Scarcely an officer in the United States military did. So Devereux was forced to ask a Japanese officer junior to him, *Do you speak English?* The Japanese replied, in perfect English, *No, I do not speak English. Do you speak Japanese?* Then this yellow man who spoke both languages said not a word more in either, just walked along behind Devereux, swinging his sword as though he had an appetite to use it.

It would not be the last time, not by a thousand times in the next months and years, that a white prisoner would find himself under the absolute control of a Japanese who had had experience with white men and come away seething with blood hate, blood contempt. The yellow man knew what the white man thought of him; on that subject the white world had taught him bitter lessons in the twentieth century, and the yellow man returned the white man's hate and contempt. In the Pacific war, with race hate coursing through both sides like an electric current, white men and yellow men behaved like magnetic poles identically charged—the closer to each other, the more violent the repulsion.

By midafternoon the Japanese had all their prisoners, more than sixteen hundred, herded onto the runway at the airfield. They stripped them and laid them out in rows like trussed pigs, wrists tied with ropes and lengths of cut phone wire and a loop around the neck so that if a man moved his arms he would noose himself tighter, struggle and he would strangle.

There was no talking to the guards, nobody knew how to in

Japanese, and if a man so much as opened his mouth to speak English all he would get back was an alien growl or an animal grunt, if he did not get a rifle butt in the teeth. The only understandable message was in Japanese gestures, with grins, about how they were all going to be dead by sundown.

A captured American truck came grinding into view, with a Japanese driving. A Japanese naval officer stepped out. He was in immaculate whites, with a chestful of ribbons and a ceremonial sword. It was Rear Admiral Kajioka Sadamichi, commander of the invasion fleet. He spoke to the army officer who had led the landing force, and the talk turned into a fifteen-minute shouting match. To Harry and Oklahoma and the rest of the prisoners it was Japanese jabber, but it was about them, their life or their death. The army officer was more than ready to kill them all. The admiral was not. He had the rank, and he prevailed. He climbed back into the truck and drove off. The army officer gave some reluctant-sounding orders; the soldiers uncocked their machine guns; and an interpreter shouted out a proclamation in stiff and clumsy English, to the effect that the peace-loving imperial forces would not inflict harm upon those of the enemy who did not hold hostility, but that any who violated the Japanese spirit or were disobedient would be punished by martial law. *The Emperor,* he wound up, *has gracefully presented you with your lives.* And out of the hog-tied mass of naked bodies on the runway came the graceful American response: *Well, thank the son of a bitch.*

The Japanese ringed the airfield with barbed wire. The prisoners were untied, then left on the blinding white coral of the runway, to burn and blister in the afternoon heat of the tropical sun, with no shade, no hats for their heads, no shirts for their backs, no boots for their feet, no food, no water, nowhere to go with their diarrhea and their dysentery.

Once the sun went down, the wind blowing in off the ocean turned cold, robbing body heat. Everyone froze, Harry and Oklahoma too, shivering and shaking uncontrollably; they had to huddle for warmth.

The next morning nothing happened, just the day heating up again to unbearableness; tongues grew dry, and lips blistered, parched with thirst. About noon the Japanese trucked in some water in fifty-five-gallon drums. They rolled the barrels under the barbed wire, and the prisoners stampeded for them like crazed cattle.

There were sixteen hundred Americans, one in five of them

highly trained marines, and in only twenty-four hours as prisoners they had degenerated into animals. Not all of them, of course, but it did not take a majority to make a mob. As a matter of urgency the marine officers and the contractor foremen set about getting servicemen back in their squads and civilians in their gangs, answering to American authority. When the trucks came with food, discipline held; the prisoners lined up and waited to be fed like civilized human beings.

Harry and Oklahoma got on line like everyone else for a slice of old moldy bread with a smear of jelly from the remains of the Camp 2 kitchen. They ate naked behind barbed wire, with the Japanese sighting at them over the barrels of machine guns, and that was Christmas dinner.

When the Japanese announced that the prisoners were going to be moved back to the contractors' barracks at Camp 2, Harry and Oklahoma volunteered to go with an advance group to get things ready.

All the time Wake was being raided from the air it had been next to impossible to bury the dead, and at Camp 2 the corpses were stacked in the kitchen reefer, the refrigerated storeroom. The power was out, and the bodies were rotting along with the last of the prime steaks. So Harry and Oklahoma had no trouble getting on the cleanup detail.

When they got there they waited for the right moment, Harry gave the high sign, and Oklahoma slipped away to reconnoiter their old room in the barracks. The guards did not see him make his move. They did not fancy the reefer detail, either; they were staying outside, upwind of the stink. Lucky for Oklahoma and Harry, their room was still standing; and luckier still, the Japanese who looted the place had been hasty and sloppy; they missed certain small items.

By the time Harry and Oklahoma finished with the dead bodies, they smelled like corpses themselves, so dreadful that the guards did not shake them down. They even scored a bonus point. The barracks still had running water, and soap, and they talked their way into a shower, not using words, just standing up close to the guards and smelling hideous.

When they were through they put on a fresh change of clothes from their room, topped off with a selection from the other rooms, boots and everything, the best available; and as they buttoned up and laced up, they stowed their salvaged small items about their persons, unobserved.

*   *   *

On January 11, out of the blue, on one hour's notice, all but three hundred or so of the prisoners were ordered to get themselves down to the beach, to be moved off Wake. The word was that they were going to be taken to Japan.

Harry and Oklahoma had no wish to go. Japan was thousands of miles farther from home. It was not that they had any doubt about the United States winning the war, even if it took months; but the Japanese islands were bound to be the last place to fall, meaning that prisoners in Japan would be the last to be liberated. And who could tell what being a prisoner would be like there, a handful of Americans among millions of Japanese?

Their best guess about Wake was that they could make it there. It was the poorest imitation of life, disgusting. Still, they had their own room at the barracks. And they had a hole card: out in the brush they had located a little cache of canned food, and of course they were keeping it to themselves. But the Japanese were dealing, Harry and Oklahoma had to play the hand they were dealt, and they were forced to fold.

Before they were lightered out to a ship standing offshore, the guards shook them down one last time, late looting, slim pickings. The seas were heavy. To get themselves aboard, they had to sling their bags up, then time a jump between the surges of big waves and the kicks and curses of the Japanese, and cling and claw their way up the side on a rope ladder. They never saw their bags again. On deck a new squad of guards body-searched them and kicked and cursed them for being bare of loot. Then they were run through a gauntlet, beaten with four-foot clubs of heavy bamboo, booted and shoved, all twelve hundred of them, into the forward cargo holds, and when they were jammed in solid the hatches were dogged down on top of them.

The ship was the *Nitta Maru,* a luxury liner made in Japan, still new, and fast, in fact the holder of a transpacific speed record. But down among the prisoners, it was a *Matsonia* cruise turned upside down and inside out. They were packed to suffocating, bodies on bodies on bodies. They were ordered to lie still—anyone the Japanese caught moving got a beating. The air was foul, the heat fierce. The Japanese refused them drinking water, and men went so crazy for moisture they were down to licking like dogs at the condensation of sweat and breath vapor on the steel bulkheads. Twice every twenty-four hours, buckets of a miserable thin rice gruel came down on ropes, one time out of two with a few slivers of some sort of smelly pickled radish. And tiny fish, head, eyes, guts and all, rotting. The dysentery that had been so bad on Wake got worse, with men not even able to make it to the slop buckets in the corners of the hold.

In the first days at sea the men at the outside edge of the stinking mass of humanity felt the hull of the ship with their hands and told the others the steel was warm, which meant the water outside must still be warm, and that they must still be in the tropics—perhaps they were not being taken to Japan at all but to a tropical island. But after a few more days the hull cooled to the touch, then turned cold, then iron cold. They were heading toward Japan, into the high latitudes of the Northern Hemisphere, into freezing midwinter.

They were in remnants of warm-weather clothing, with one flimsy Japanese cotton blanket for covering. More blankets were thrown down, but even two Japanese blankets were not enough. The guards beat them for shivering and shaking, and for huddling together for body warmth. *You are war prisoners and should be cold, if you are sick you should die.*

Time passed, perhaps a week—it was impossible in the hold to say how long—until one freezing day they felt the motion of the ship slowing to a halt, the vibration of the engines winding down to stillness. The *Nitta Maru* had reached Japan, the island of Honshu, the port of Yokohama, just miles from the city of Tokyo and the palace of the emperor. The guards, in the joy of their homecoming, pulled back the hatches and pelted the prisoners with snowballs.

After just one day, the hatches were dogged down again without warning, and the *Nitta Maru* cast off and headed to sea again.

A few days out, the guards pulled five men from the hold, and they did not come back. That was unusual. Between Wake and Yokohama some men had been taken topside for interrogation, and others had been singled out so that the guards could do *judo* moves on them up on deck, throwing them down, kicking them up onto their feet again, throwing them down some more. With white prisoners, the Japanese had the pleasure of choosing men bigger than themselves to throw. That was part of the sport. One marine had it done to him over and over again because he had red hair—the Japanese, for whatever reason, hated red hair. But every time when they had thrown him down enough, they threw him back into the hold. The same with the other big men, and the men taken for interrogation. But not these five men after Yokohama. Two marines and three navy men, two of the five of them redheads—their friends could not imagine what had become of them.

What happened was this: When they were taken on deck there were Japanese everywhere, a crowd of well over a hundred. They were made to line up in front of the commander of the prisoner escort, a navy lieutenant named Saitō Toshio, and a squad of his petty officers with swords. Saitō got up on a box and read to them from a paper, in Japanese. They had no idea what he was saying. It was this: *You have killed many Japanese soldiers in battle. For what you have done you are now going to be killed—for revenge. You are here as representatives of your American soldiers and will be killed. You can now pray to be happy in the next world—in heaven.*

The five were blindfolded, and one after the other they had their heads chopped off. For each one a different guard stepped up, forced the prisoner to his knees, and swung his long sword. The blade swished through the air. When it bit into the neck, it made a noise like a wet towel being cracked. The Japanese applauded, even if the blow was botched and the head was not chopped off properly and the swordsman had to make a second chop or even a third. When all five heads were finally chopped off, other men took the swords for the sport of trying to cut the corpses in two with a single stroke, like warriors of the old *samurai* times in Japan. But none of them were samurai; they were just hackers, slashing away in a welter of blood. When they had had enough, Saitō had the bodies propped against a *sake* barrel so that his guards could stick them for bayonet practice. When the bayoneters had had enough, the carcasses and the chopped-off heads were thrown overboard. That night, Saitō invited some guests to celebrate the satisfactions of the occasion.

The next day, January 23, four days out of Yokohama, twelve days out of Wake, the *Nitta Maru* made the coast of China and put in at the port of Shanghai, where the Yangtze River came to the sea. The Japanese controlled the city and big stretches of territory inland. Their intention was to offload the prisoners and herd them through the streets, fifteen miles to prison camp at Woosung. Along the way they would be exhibited to the Chinese in all their filthy surrendered weakness, as a demonstration of what the Japanese empire could do to white men. But that particular midwinter day was especially cold and wet. A satisfactory turnout of Chinese watchers could not be guaranteed. So, to avoid loss of face, the

Japanese canceled the procession and the *Nitta Maru* went on up the Whangpoo River to Woosung.

Harry and Oklahoma were in terrible shape. Oklahoma had drawn a bad blanket, infested with vermin, and he caught the crabs. His dysentery kept him miserable nonstop. Harry's bowels had gone the other way, seizing up altogether. Twelve days breathing foul air, starving, no soap and water, no shave, stubble growing out into dirty beard—when the Japanese kicked them up out of the hold into the light of day at Woosung, for a moment they did not recognize each other.

They were marched, under armed guard, stiff-legged and staggering, five miles through the freezing late afternoon, to the Shanghai War Prisoners Camp. They thought about those undeserving contractors who had shipped with them to Wake and then bailed out right away for the States: weak characters, with no plan, ruled by thirst for whiskey, driven by their gonads. Those men were back on the West Coast, on the right side of the Pacific, the right side of the war, the right side of the bar, the right side of the blanket. And here were Harry and Oklahoma, smart guys with a plan, and look where it had got them.

In the first minute on the *Nitta Maru* they had lost their bags. All their smoking stuff was gone. For clothes, they had only what they stood up in. Oklahoma's good leather belt with the cowboy buckle had been ripped off him before he made it to the hold; he was keeping his pants up with string. Still, he had pants, Harry did too, and they had shirts. Boots too, good ones, and they were likely to keep them, because they were big men with big feet; their boots were too big to be objects of attraction for the average looting Japanese. They were luckier than some other big men; they had not been singled out for beatings and judo throws, not yet, anyway. And—most important—even if their Wake moneymaking plan was shot to bits, they never stopped working on their edge. They had been shaken down any number of times, but they had quick hands and quick minds; and as they went through the barbed wire entrance to the camp and passed inside the electric fence, they still had, safely concealed about their persons, those certain small items from Wake—a deck of cards and a wad of banknotes.

::

IN SEPTEMBER of 1941, when Harry and Oklahoma were on their way to Wake, Houston Tom Wright, known as Slug, was in Louisiana, playing war games with the 2nd Battalion of the 131st Field Artillery. On December 7–8, when the Japanese were bombing Wake, Slug and the 131st were on a troopship in the middle of the Pacific, headed for the Philippines. They never got there, because on that first day of the war the Japanese bombed the Philippines, too. Their convoy was diverted to Australia. They got there the day before Wake surrendered. By the time Harry and Oklahoma were being shoved down into the hold of the *Nitta Maru,* Slug and the 131st were on their way to the Netherlands East Indies, to Java. Harry and Oklahoma were behind barbed wire at Woosung before the ground war hit the Indies. When it did hit, Java lasted less than two weeks. By the middle of March 1942, Slug and all the rest of the 2nd Battalion were prisoners of the Japanese.

The 131st Field Artillery was a Texas National Guard outfit, and Slug himself was essence of Texas. His great-great-grandfather was one of the first captains of the Texas Rangers, and he and his brothers fought in the Battle of San Jacinto. From then on down the generations, there were always Wrights in the Rangers. Slug's own father, Will, was a Ranger captain. Slug was raised in Ranger camp, and he was named for Sam Houston, meaning he was baptized by total immersion in the glories of Texas.

Slug had a family history with the 131st Field Artillery as well. In World War I his older brothers, Charlie and Maurice, were with D Battery of the 2nd Battalion in Europe. So when the 131st was federalized in 1940 along with the rest of the National Guard, nothing was more natural for Slug than to want to get himself placed in a Texas outfit that was also the Wright family outfit. He reported to the 131st at Camp Bowie at Brownwood with an album full of stories and pictures of his family's history as fighting Texans, from his father's pistol duel on the border with an outlaw Mexican general all the way back to his great-great-grandfather, the original Ranger captain.

He wanted his brothers' old battery, D. But there was no vacancy, so he wound up in F. F Battery came out of Jack County, farm country north and west of Dallas, south and east of Wichita Falls, no spot within its boundaries more than fifty miles at the most from another, county seat Jacksboro, population less than three thousand. At Camp Bowie everyone knew F Battery as the Jacksboro boys.

They were a natural tribe, and Slug came in among them as an outsider. He was in his mid-twenties, whereas most of the Jacks-boro boys were barely out of their teens. For them Jack County was the world, but Slug had traveled to distant parts of Texas, even out of state, as far as California. He had worked in big business, for Standard Oil. He had a trained job where he wore eyeglasses and sat at a desk and used his mind. To the Jack County farm boys and the Jacksboro day laborers and auto mechanics Slug appeared to be some kind of bank clerk. What it amounted to was that he was different, and for that the Jacksboro boys gave it to him. They apple-pied his bed. They put snuff in his gas mask bag to make him sneeze during drills (in Jack County in those days there were snuff dippers even among the young). Once when Slug had guard duty they stole his issue Smith and Wesson .44. And any time they felt so moved they dog-piled him, jumped on him, five or six big, healthy Jacksboro boys at a time all over Slug, who was smaller than average, and they stayed piled on until he hollered uncle.

Slug had the chance to get out from under, because he was a Wright. The adjutant general of Texas, the man in charge of both the Guard and the Rangers, was a Wright family friend, and he told Slug he could fix it for him to apply to officer school for radio training. But Slug said no. Dog-piling and all, he wanted to stay with the 131st, for Wright family tradition. Also, the Louisiana Maneuvers were coming up, and he did not want to miss out on a great experience like that.

The Louisiana Maneuvers of August–September 1941 were the biggest war games in the history of the United States to that time, and the last before the real war. A Red Army of 180,000 had to defend against an invading Blue Army of 240,000, a greater number than General Ulysses S. Grant had under his command in the last real invasion of the South. The 131st were with the Blues.

No sooner had F Battery set up camp in the Kisatchie National Forest, part piney woods, part swamp, than a hurricane blew in out of the Gulf of Mexico, the drenching rain running off hat brims into mess kits, turning everything underfoot muddy and wallow-ish. After the storm died down, the nights were filled with the croaking of thousands of bullfrogs—a sound never heard in Jack County, where the world was drier. One of the untraveled Jacks-boro boys asked what kind of animal it might be making that strange noise. The other boys told him crocodiles. He wrote his parents that he was in *crocodeel country,* and forever after he was known as Croc.

The 131st's artillery pieces were World War I vintage, and the gun crews were not going to be firing real shells, but they were all keen to play the game of war. The 131st liked to win. They were great competitors against other outfits, and among themselves, battery versus battery. Jack County boys were taught that F Battery from Jacksboro was the best artillery battery in the army. Every other 131st battery was taught the same thing. And the way they heard it, all of them were right. The Blues won the war games, and the 131st's unit firing record was judged to be the best of all, so outstanding that they were going to be specially outfitted to go to the Texas State Fair as a showpiece. Or, so good that they were going to be sent to Fort Sill for artillery officer training.

What happened was this: The 2nd Battalion—D, E, and F batteries, plus headquarters battery, service battery, and a medical detachment—were singled out to go overseas.

There was a war story about the way the 2nd Battalion came by this distinction. Late in the maneuvers, on a Sunday, a Blue motorcycle dispatch rider saw some Red trucks coming at him. He hightailed it to the nearest Blues, F Battery's forward observers, and by the time he got there his agitated mind had turned those few Red trucks into the whole Red Army. The sergeant at the observation post called for fire from F Battery. But the private who actually spoke the phone message was conscious of its being Sunday, the day of rest, and he decided that if F Battery was going to have to exert itself on the Sabbath, the whole battalion should have to. So he called for maximum fire. Which for no more than a few Red trucks would have been ridiculous. But, by the ironic maneuverings of the gods of war games, in fact there *was* a huge Red force coming. So calling down maximum fire turned out to look like a master stroke. The war game umpires ranked this action as the single most decisive factor in the Blue victory. Meaning F Battery won the maneuvers.

Less than six months on from that Sunday morning phone call in Louisiana, the 2nd Battalion of the 131st Field Artillery were prisoners of the Japanese.

National Guard units like the 131st had a nickname, *brother-in-law outfits.* Everyone knew everyone else, and many were related. In F Battery alone, among about a hundred who went overseas, there were seven sets of brothers, all Jacksboro boys. And among some late transfers from C Battery of the 1st Battalion were the Barnes twins, Dan and Don.

Nearly all the family names on the battalion roster were Anglo-

Saxon. There were no blacks, and not simply because the 131st was from Texas—all the armed forces of the United States were segregated. There was a sprinkling of Spanish-sounding names, Mexican-Americans; E Battery had a number, F Battery three. And there were two other non-whites of a kind unusual for Texas. In fact, either of them would have been rare anywhere in the army.

Eddie Fung was Chinese, born and brought up in Chinatown in San Francisco. In his teens he ran away to be a cowboy. He was caught and dragged back, but he ran away again, and finally he was allowed to do what he wanted where he wanted, which was rope cattle in Texas. He was not the only Texas cowboy to join the 131st, but he would have been among the slightest in build, and certainly he was the only Chinese-looking one. He wound up with the Jacksboro boys, a private first class in F Battery.

Frank Fujita was even more unusual, in fact unique. He was American by birth, but by blood he was half Japanese. His mother was American; his father had come to the United States from a place called Nagasaki. After Pearl Harbor, the United States interned Japanese living on the American mainland, approximately 110,000 men, women, and children. Military-age Japanese males born in the United States—thus not aliens but American citizens by birth—were formed into special segregated units and sent to fight in Europe, on the far side of the globe: The Army did not want them in the Pacific, looking like the enemy in American uniform. Frank Fujita turned out to be one of a kind. He had joined the 131st at Abilene in 1938, still in school, under-age by six months, under-weight by thirty pounds. Under-height too—at drill, when it came to *dress right* at arm's length, with the fingers of the left hand supposed to be touching the right shoulder of the man to the left, Fujita always had tall Texas-boy fingers in his mouth. He used to bite at them for fun, and for this he was called (also in fun) Mad Dog. He rose by 1941 to be a sergeant. He went overseas with E Battery of the 2nd Battalion and became a prisoner of the Japanese with them. In all the Pacific-Asian war he was the only POW with a Japanese last name and a Texas accent.

When the 2nd Battalion were told they were being sent overseas, they were not told where, for security reasons. But the code name they were given to stencil on their kits was *PLUM,* and anyone could break that down to *Philippines-LUzon-Manila.*

At 11:00 a.m. on November 11, 1941, they left for the West Coast. For most of them it was their first time crossing the Texas border heading west, and their first long train trip. Corky Woodall of Headquarters Battery was a natural country-boy comedian, and he figured out how to imitate the noise of a train going through a tunnel—very amusing, except that he kept doing it all the way.

The troops were on the train ten days. They had one day on the loose in San Francisco, before heading to Angel Island to board their navy transport, and on November 22 they were sailing out through the Golden Gate. The *Republic* was nothing like a Matson liner. It was slow, it pitched and rolled and wallowed, and from the first meal, fish and cabbage, it stank. The enlisted men were packed belowdecks in stacked bunks, queasy territory. The smart money said to get in the middle of the ship, but no one could seem to find the middle, and a lot of men spent a lot of time on deck with the heaves. Slug Wright had intelligently bought himself some seasick pills. The package said *KEEP IN A DRY PLACE,* so he did. He did not open it till he was seasick already, and then the directions said, *TAKE TWO PILLS BEFORE EMBARKA-TION.* Too late.

The *Republic* made a stopover at Honolulu, time enough for a four-hour leave. Slug fell in with some other F Battery boys heading for Hotel Street to get laid. Slug had no money. All he could do was sit in the parlor while the others were enjoying their short time. One of the girls went by with a john in tow, and lo and behold Slug knew her; they had belonged to the same church back in Corpus Christi. Between tricks she told Slug her story, how she had fallen in love with a sailor in Corpus and followed him to Hawaii. He had dumped her, and she was grinding it out for her fare home. She bought Slug two flower *leis* and made him swear he would not tell about her, and he did not. But of course when he got back to the ship wearing the leis, the others fired up a story to the effect that she had been his girlfriend, and so on and so forth.

At sunrise on December 2 the *Republic* left Honolulu to join a convoy headed for *PLUM.* To stay clear of the Japanese-held islands in Micronesia, they made a big swing to the south. Four days out they crossed the equator into the Southern Hemisphere. The next day came the news that the Japanese had bombed Pearl Harbor. *PLUM* was out. The new destination was Australia. On December 22 they docked at the port of the city of Brisbane in the northernmost state, Queensland.

They were among the first Americans in uniform ever in Australia, and the Brisbane people could not do enough for them. It was all the rage to bring American soldiers home for Christmas dinner: enormous slabs of roast beef and giant dobs of plum pudding with custard sauce, served piping hot in the steam heat of the Brisbane summer. In the pubs no American fighting man was allowed to pay for a drink; the Australians force-fed them unlimited local beer—powerful, ice-cold—for free. Cash offers were made for American uniforms, right on the street, pants and all. And at night in the dance halls Australian girls lined up by the dozen for the sophisticated experience of fox-trotting with an American.

One day between Christmas and New Year, Slug was doing temporary MP duty at a pub. There was a church opposite with a wedding going on. The bridal party insisted on Slug joining the procession. All the bridesmaids hugged him and kissed him, he loved it, and he went on loving Australians forever.

At the turn of the year the 131st were shipped out. They still did not know where they were headed, but it had to be the combat zone. When they were finally told where they were headed—Java, in the Netherlands East Indies—they had to look it up on the map.

They landed at Soerabaja. Some British and Australian troops were on the island, and of course many Dutch, but the 131st were just about the only Americans, and Java was nothing like Texas. They were camped at an airfield at Singosari, near the town of Malang, in a valley between two green mountains, rice paddy country. It was the most manicured land on earth; it looked as though even the weeds were planted where they were supposed to be. And they had never seen so many human beings per square inch: peasant men hoisting heavy loads on yokes over their shoulders, looking like little moving haystacks; brown-skinned children riding on the backs of water buffaloes; and women, bare-breasted in sarongs, bathing in the streams.

On the streets of Malang there were Dutch girls who could speak English, and Eurasian girls, Javanese-Dutch, who knew how to jitterbug—they had been to the movies, and they would hang around the Hunque House for the thrill of jitterbugging with a handsome American from Hollywood, U.S.A. And prostitutes. The 131st had never seen so many whores per square yard, not even on Hotel Street. *Macmac OK! Macmac very cheap!* And it was— converting from Dutch guilders, about ten cents.

From the air-raid watch at Camp Singosari to the macmac girls, then back to base to sleep on the floor on a straw mattress, war and peace were washing over each other, with war gaining in surges every day. Singapore was gone; the Indies were threatened. By the middle of February the Japanese were raiding Java every day from the air. The bombing was making everybody jumpy. Corky Woodall, the comedian who made train noises all the way from Texas to California, learned how to do a siren, and when he did it in the mess he cleared the place, all two hundred men; in fact he was so convincing that he bailed out himself.

At the beginning of March the Japanese made lightning landings on Java, in force. At Singosari a couple of dozen of the 131st had been working on B-17s in from the Philippines, and they were flown out to safety ahead of the invasion. Slug could see Java was a sinking ship. He had the chance to go, and if he had been a rat he would have. But he was a Wright of the Texas Ranger Wrights, and a Wright of the 131st, so of course he stayed.

F Battery was trucked westward, to fight in the area around Bandoeng. The move-out was so sudden that Slug did not even have time to pick up his family album. He never saw it again.

Slug was out forward of a four-gun detail near Buitenzorg with his phone and a Springfield rifle, when he came under sniper fire. He spotted two Japanese soldiers and shot at them. Then the thought struck him that where there were two Japanese there were bound to be more, and he was gladder than he could begin to say when the gun trucks came by, changing locations in a hurry.

The new setup was near a Dutch farmer's house, a lovely-looking spot. They were firing across rice paddies and dumping the brass shell casings down a well so that the Japanese spotter planes would not catch the shine. But this place got too hot, and the guns were moved into a rubber plantation, for natural camouflage. Slug was told to stick by his phone; the others would come for him when the Japanese got tired of searching. But they never did come, the phone went dead, and suddenly the war was right on top of Slug, shot-up Australians staggering by in retreat, bleeding, whole platoons of Javanese Dutch on bicycles, pedaling like crazy.

Slug took off to look for his gun crew. It turned dark and started raining. He fell in a ditch and almost drowned. He came out filthy and bedraggled, his helmet and rifle gone, his eyeglasses smeared and the cigarettes in his ditty bag all soaked. He was a long, long way from home, and he had no trouble admitting to himself that he was scared.

In the first Javanese *kampong* he stumbled into, a little village, the people would not feed him. He came upon an abandoned half-track and found a machete and a Bren gun, and at the next kampong this weaponry was all that got him some food; he had to threaten the Javanese with killing before they would let him have a hand of bananas and some rice on a green leaf.

He was hungry again when he ran into some Englishmen. They had food and tea, but they told him flat out, *Not for you, Yank,* and turned him away empty.

Whenever he heard engine noises along the road, he faded into the underbrush. Finally he peeked and saw a big white passenger car with flags on the fenders. It was a brigade officer and his driver. Slug stepped out and hailed them. *Soldier,* said the officer, *are you a deserter? No,* said Slug, *my group deserted me.* So the officer carried him to the Japanese, and they surrendered themselves.

Capitulation—the 131st had never heard the word. They had only lost three dead: one of the Barnes twins, Don, helping out in a B-17 over Singosari before the land invasion; Jack Bingham the same way; and Bruce Rhodes, killed near Bandoeng when he propped his rifle against a tree and it fell over and went off. If the Texans had ever been asked about surrender, and they never were, they would have said it would have to be in a situation where they were out of ammunition and physically overwhelmed by superior numbers. And even then it would have to be their own officers making the decision. But here it was some Dutch general who did not even speak American ordering them to lay down their arms while they were still capable of fighting. E Battery went through the astounding experience of having not the Japanese but the Dutch turn machine guns on them and threaten to shoot them if they did not capitulate.

They set about disabling their artillery pieces, nicking the sights crooked, pouring salt brine in the recoils. They shot out the tires of their trucks, drained the sumps and the radiators, and ran them off the mountain roads at full throttle and listened while the engines cooked; and in a detached way they were interested to note that the Chevy engine lasted longer than the Plymouth, the Studebaker command car longer than either.

Altogether more than 530 of the 131st were taken. Slug and his bunch were moved to Tanjong Priok in the port district of Batavia, the capital city of the Netherlands East Indies. They were herded in with other prisoners, Australians and British, plus some

Sikhs, Indians who had been fighting under the colors of the British empire. Then on May 14 they were put on a train through Batavia, and when they were offloaded they were marched to a barracks built before the war for the 10th Battalion of the Dutch colonial army, KNIL, Koninklijk Nederlands-Indisch Leger. The 10th was a bicycle unit. The prisoners called the place Bicycle Camp.

When the 131st came dragging in, other prisoners were in the barracks already—Australian, British, and Dutch.

And yet others, in a building to the right of the main gate, with barbed wire strung across the porch. Men were peering out, starved bodies, terrible-looking scarecrows in shorts made of sacking, green straw hats, sarongs, bits of native blanket, anything and nothing, bodies starved and unwashed, worse than unwashed, coated in fuel oil.

They turned out to be Americans. They were all that was left of the crew of the heavy cruiser U.S.S. *Houston,* caught and sunk in Sunda Strait during the Japanese invasion of Java. About 700 of them did not make it away from the sinking. The rest, some 350, washed up on Java. The Japanese herded most of them to the town of Serang, into a commandeered movie house, along with some Australians off H.M.A.S. *Perth,* sunk with the *Houston,* other Australian troops surrendered on Java, more Australians and British from the stampede out of Singapore, and Dutch civilians with their children—about 1,500 white bodies in a movie house that would have been full at 500 Javanese. The guards made everyone sit at attention for hours while they tried over and over to count them and failed. An officer with the face of a malignant frog was strutting around with his hand on his sword, serving the emperor by kicking the wounded. They got no medical treatment. At night they had to lie on top of each other in the stink of festering wounds. The latrine was an open pit outside, with flies rising off it in huge clouds, making a blaring noise like a brass band.

They were fed one ounce of rice each once a day, plus a tiny loaf of bread, two by two by four inches. One of the marine privates, only a boy, said, *This is not the way my mother made bread.* He was the first off the *Houston* to die.

The Japanese took the senior officers away. The others were herded from the movie house to the town jail. They were packed into the cells, lying stacked like fish in a shop window, starved, parched for water. The *kempeitai,* the Japanese military police, had their interrogators at work; they had a Dutchman tied to a chair, a metal band around his head; they were screwing it tight and he was screaming.

The Japanese kept them at Serang through March, and then in April, badly down in weight, they were trucked off to Batavia, to Bicycle Camp. They had been only there a few days when the 131st turned up, Americans in full uniform, and for about a tenth of a second it was possible for the *Houston* men to imagine a liberating force had arrived. But of course not, it was only more prisoners. The *Houston* men had no idea who they might be. Then they heard guitar music and singing from a barracks just down the way. It was the Brimhall brothers, Clifford and Onis, F Battery of the 131st, and the song was "Deep in the Heart of Texas."

::

BY THE time Slug Wright and the 131st were on their way from Australia to Java instead of to Philippines-LUzon-Manila, Douglas MacArthur's combined American and Filipino forces were in serious trouble. The Japanese had invaded Luzon in strength in the last days of December. In the first days of January, Manila fell. By March, when Slug and his gun crew were in combat on Java, MacArthur's army was in even worse trouble. The last holdout on Luzon, the peninsula of Bataan, was under siege; and MacArthur himself was gone, lifted out to safety in Australia. By the time the 131st were behind the fence at Bicycle Camp in May, the Philippines had fallen. It was the biggest American disaster of the ground war in the Pacific.

The Japanese attacked the Philippines from the air on the afternoon of December 8, 1941, local time. The raid came nine hours after MacArthur was told about Pearl Harbor. Nine hours—longer than a standard peacetime working day for MacArthur's troops. Yet most of the planes of the Army's Far East Air Force were still on the ground at Clark Field, sitting ducks. In a matter of minutes the Japanese destroyed half the bombers and two thirds of the fighters. In those minutes, after those nine hours, on that first day of war in the Pacific, MacArthur lost control of the air.

On December 22 the Japanese landed in force on north Luzon, at Lingayen Gulf. MacArthur's strategy called for a grand-gesture defense at the water's edge. Straightaway it turned into a second disaster. MacArthur's Filipino battalions did not stand with the

Americans and fight; they broke and ran. They did not collapse just because they were Filipinos. In among the panicked mass were units of the Philippine Scouts, professional soldiers, and at Lingayen they fought as well as any well-trained white Americans. But the Scouts were only a small minority of the Filipinos in uniform, thousands only among scores of thousands. The great majority were draftees, green, not properly trained and disciplined, and never properly equipped. They had no steel helmets, not even boots; and many of them had not so much as fired their rifles before they had to face the Japanese. When the Japanese attacked they fell to bits, and so did the world according to MacArthur.

After his beach strategy at Lingayen blew up in his face, it took MacArthur forty hours to respond to the fact that he had been disastrously wrong a second time. Not until December 24, when the Japanese made another landing, at Lamon in south Luzon, putting Manila Bay under the sudden threat of a pincer movement, did MacArthur finally give the order to bring into effect War Plan Orange-3, the old-established strategy against a Japanese invasion.

On the map of Luzon he drew lines of defense, D1, D2, D3, D4, D5—hold and fall back, hold and fall back, through the end of December. When Manila fell at the turn of the year, MacArthur had to move his headquarters offshore to Corregidor. Everything was down now to the peninsula of Bataan.

From the moment the first bomb fell at Clark Field on the afternoon of December 8, till dawn on January 7 at the entrance to Bataan, the 192nd Tank Battalion had been in the thick of MacArthur's war.

The 192nd was a National Guard unit like the 13th Field Artillery. But not from a single state. One company was from Maywood, Illinois; one from Port Clinton, Ohio; one from Harrodsburg, Kentucky; and one, Company A, from Janesville, Wisconsin.

Janesville was famous for being the home of the Parker Pen Company. For an American businessman of his day, George S. Parker was a world thinker. By the 1930s he was selling more pens in Asia than anywhere else; Parker was a famous name in Japan and China. But no one from Company A had ever seen an Asian up close. Not one of them had ever been out of the country. Next to none had so much as seen the Pacific. Forrest Knox had been in Mr. Parker's house once, and he saw a room that was papered in gold-leaf tea wrappers, but that was as close as he had come to anything Asiatic.

When the National Guard was federalized, Company A was assigned with the rest of the 192nd to the armored school at Fort Knox in Kentucky. From there they went to the 1941 Louisiana Maneuvers. Lousy Anna, they called the place, but they did well enough to catch the eye of Major General George S. Patton, Jr., who knew about tanks. He picked the 192nd to go overseas—destination *PLUM,* like the Texans of the 131st, the difference being that the 192nd actually made it to the Philippines. They docked at Manila on November 20. A train took them up-country, and they unloaded at Fort Stotsenburg and Clark Field just in time for Thanksgiving.

Once they set themselves up in their tent city, they could start getting into the swing of things in the bars at Barrio Sapangbato, known to all as Sloppy Bottom. The best fun they had there was with Bernard Shea, known to all as One-Horse. One-Horse was not bright. Forrest Knox, a sergeant, and smarter than most in Company A, never thought One-Horse should have made the final cut to the Philippines. Bernard was a good Christian boy and he tried hard, but he just did not have it. He would practice his close-order drill for hours, and as long as he could shout out the commands himself he was fine, but in an actual drill he was nowhere. At Stotsenburg he wore all his issue at all times—pistol belt, canteen, steel helmet, gas mask in holder—and he kept every one of his pockets buttoned, but underneath he was still One-Horse.

The boys paid a Sloppy Bottom bar girl to eat a *balut* in front of him. Balut was a Filipino delicacy, a duck egg taken when it was ready to hatch and matured for months in brine. When One-Horse saw the tiny claws and the beginning feathers and the reproachful little eyes peering out at him he went straight under the table. The next plan was to smuggle a balut into his mess kit at breakfast back on base instead of a hard-boiled egg, so the whole company could watch. But that very morning turned out to be December 8, and nobody had breakfast. And the other project—to decoy One-Horse into a Sloppy Bottom cathouse and turn the girls loose on him, the way they had done to him before with some Kentucky whores—that one never came off, either.

The war overwhelmed One-Horse. He convinced himself he was going to die. He would walk from one tank crew to another without much to say, and no one had much to say to him. One day Company A was in reserve and One-Horse was hanging around Forrest Knox's crew when a dive-bomber came over. Forrest and the others piled into the hole they dug under their M–3 whenever they were out of the lines. One-Horse beat them to it. When the dive-bomber went away, Forrest and the others climbed out and dealt the cards again. Half an hour went by; then One-Horse poked his head out and cracked the one joke Company A ever heard from him: *What do you think of the situation as a hole?*

The farther south the Japanese penetrated on Luzon, the more chaotic things got. The main lifeline of retreat to the Bataan peninsula, Route 7 to Layac, turned into one big blocked artery, clogged with tens of thousands of men swarming to the rear on foot, bowed down under their loads of supplies and equipment, remnants of units that were broken up and scattered; command cars, trucks, horses, Filipinos clinging to the outside of *pambasco* buses; and in among all this the tanks grinding along, chewing up the roadbed, throwing tracks on turns, sitting stalled like big metal blood clots.

The final crossing into Bataan was at the Culo bridge. The tanks were the last to make it, at about 0200 hours on January 7, and Forrest's tank was the last of all. In ten days he had managed five hours of rest. He found himself a stretcher someone had left behind. It was covered with blood, but he lay down on it anyway and slept.

The Bataan peninsula was only a few hundred square miles, and packed into it now were the better part of eighty thousand men in uniform, about six thousand Filipino civilian army workers, and about twenty thousand refugees. The sea was on three sides of them, the enemy on the fourth. One of the Japanese generals said it was like watching a cat go into a sack.

The weather was seething hot, 90 degrees and up. The tankers of Company A were fighting the war in overworked high-revving superheated steel sweatboxes. Forrest Knox was not much impressed with the M-3 in combat. The machine guns spewed shell cases, burning hot, that showered all over the crew, down the neck of the shirt, down the waistband of the trousers. The way to tell a tanker was by his burns and blisters. Forrest worked out a defense; he cut the pockets off his coveralls and wrapped a towel around his neck.

He was not getting nearly enough to eat. Nobody was. Their mess truck driver never seemed to be able to find them on the front line; he wanted to spend his day holed up out of sight under the trees. When the tankers were not in combat, they had to do their own reconnaissance, on foot. Forrest and his crew were out in the heat one day, it was all steep hills and all uphill, and it got to be too much for one of the bunch. He sat down on a rock and said, *This is as far as I go. I am going to sit right here till Jesus Christ comes by on a bicycle.* The only force powerful enough to get him up on his feet was the certainty that if he was late back for chow, nobody would be holding a serving for him.

It was true for the 192nd, and true all over Bataan; there was not enough food anywhere on the peninsula. That was a consequence of the disaster of MacArthur's beach defense plan, and it was bound to come back and bite every one of his men in the empty belly. Luzon had food all over the place, in big dumps, but MacArthur never got nearly enough of it to where it was supposed to be under War Plan Orange-3. The Japanese were too quick, and he was too slow.

At Fort Stotsenburg food was stored by the hundreds of tons. But Stotsenburg was abandoned—many would have said well before it needed to be—and the food was left behind. Cabanatuan had a rice dump, containing millions of pounds; but not American military rice, Philippine civilian rice. The Philippine government had some crazed regulation about not moving rice from one province to another, and MacArthur never overrode it. Along the railroads the Filipino workers were deserting, there were no crews left to run the trains, and the government would not let American troops take over—and so trainloads of food never got moved into Bataan. At Tarlac there were businesses owned by Japanese civilians, stores full of canned fish and corned beef—yet permission to confiscate was never issued. In fact, when a colonel was about to do the obvious logical useful thing and take the lot, MacArthur's headquarters threatened to have him court-martialed. So it went, all over Luzon. Before Manila fell in the first week of January, food was being moved out of the city to Corregidor and Bataan by barge and tugboat and motor launch, but not nearly enough. When the Japanese occupied Manila, the bleachers at Rizal Stadium were still piled high with quartermaster stores.

On Bataan, WPO-3 called for 180 days' worth of food for forty-three thousand men. But crammed into the peninsula were more than a hundred thousand—seventy-eight thousand troops and twenty-six thousand civilians. This worked out to only thirty days' worth of full rations. MacArthur had to order everyone onto half rations, two thousand calories a day, against the thirty-five hundred to four thousand that an active soldier needed. Those figures were for American troops, big white men, calculated ideally in meat and potatoes and bread. Filipino soldiers, being smaller, were to be fed proportionately less, calculated ideally in Filipino native chow: fish and rice.

Forrest Knox and some of the other Company A sergeants were hungry enough to go out with tommy guns to hijack a food truck. They picked their spot, a curve in the road with a high bank, and sat there all night, hoping they would not have to go up against shotgunner MPs. Not a single truck came along, and at dawn they hiked back emptier than when they started. Forrest was a skinny type going in; now he had run out of holes in his belt at the skinny end.

He was fighting the war again, yet another day in the steel sweatbox on half rations, when his company commander got on the radio and said the mess sergeant had a big pan of baked beans and bacon waiting for them, plus all the hot coffee they could drink. The whole radio net heard. Straightaway officers came flocking from the rear area. They helped themselves, taking seconds and thirds and fourths, and they were not even from Janesville. When the Company A tankers came wheeling in in their banged-up M-3s, nothing was left but a few beans burned onto the side of the pan. The Janesville tribe took one look and walked away. Flies on a turd, that was the way it hit Forrest, and he marked that day as the time he lost respect for officers.

The last ones to be looked after for food were the frontline troops. If anyone needed and deserved full rations, they did. But they were down on paper the same as everyone else, for only two half-meals a day, one around dawn, the other around dusk. And nothing like even that puny amount was showing up in their mess kits. Forrest could see everything coming to be calculated in calories—combat efficiency, obedience to orders, esprit de corps, morale, morality, common humanity, altruism, being your brother's keeper, the brother in arms who was fighting in front of you or alongside you—all the way to life or death.

Douglas MacArthur was seldom seen in the combat zone. After he moved his headquarters to Corregidor, he made only one foray to Bataan, early on, January 10, a day tour in a Ford staff car. But according to the radio news—shortwave from KGEI, San Francisco, featuring the famous voice of William Winter—MacArthur was everywhere. In the three months from the beginning of the war at Clark Field, up through Lingayen and the retreat south, on into early March on Bataan, when the Japanese sack was drawing down tight, MacArthur issued 142 communiqués—more than one a day, all vividly written and making wonderful reading—and in 109 the only man in uniform identified by name was MacArthur. Practically never did MacArthur name even big units. It was always MacArthur's men, MacArthur's left flank, MacArthur. On Bataan they choked on the sound of the name. One man at Cabcaben Field used to do an impression: *Ladies and gents, KGEI now brings you fifteen minutes of the latest war news from the Pacific. MacArthur, MacArthur, MacArthur, etc. And now to repeat the headline news— MacArthur, MacArthur, MacArthur. . .*

The Japanese were dropping propaganda leaflets. The Americans were targeted with the standard item about war profiteers back home putting the make on their girlfriends. The Filipinos were shown in pictures how sweet it would be after they surrendered—wonderful food to eat, served by a loving wife, child in arms—*Don't wait to die . . . before the terror comes, let me walk beside you in garden deep in petalled sleep . . . rest your warm hand on my breast . . .* , et cetera, et cetera. And for the friendliest of friendly persuasion, pictures of a beautiful blonde stripper, private parts and all: *You too can enjoy this if you will surrender.*

The propaganda bombers came droning over every day. It was like having the morning paper delivered. Some of the troops started trading the leaflets like baseball cards. The top-value item was addressed from commander to commander, Lieutenant General Homma Masaharu telling General Douglas MacArthur he was doomed: *You have already cut rations by half . . . Your prestige and honor have been upheld. However, in order to avoid needless bloodshed and save your . . . troops you are advised to surrender . . . failing that our offensive will be continued with inexorable force.* This drop of Homma's came in empty beer cans with streamers of red and white, the colors of the Japanese flag, and the streamers commanded top dollar. For all ranks below MacArthur there was a Ticket to Armistice: *Use this ticket, save your life, you will be kindly treated . . . Come towards our lines waving a white flag . . . Any number of you may surrender with this one ticket,* et cetera, et cetera. That item was plentiful; the Americans used it to wipe their behinds.

From his headquarters underground in Malinta Tunnel on Corregidor, MacArthur was forever telling the troops on Bataan that help was on the way: thousands of reinforcements with millions of rounds of ammunition, hundreds of planes with tons of bombs, shiploads of food. But nothing materialized. The only re-liable report about reinforcements was that one of the army nurses was pregnant.

A poem turned up on the front line. It was written by Frank Hewlett, a war correspondent with United Press International who spent a lot of time at the front with the men in their foxholes. The poem traveled faster than news, faster even than scuttlebutt, it reached farther than food, and it spread like a contagion. The troops made up verses of their own, but there was one verse that everyone recited, as the truth:

> *We're the battling bastards of Bataan;*
> *No mama, no papa, no Uncle Sam;*
> *No aunts, no uncles, no nephews, no nieces;*
> *No pills, no planes, no artillery pieces;*
> *And nobody gives a damn.*

Then orders came for MacArthur from Washington: to get out of the Philippines while he still could, make for Australia, and run the war against Japan from there. Whereupon a song turned up on Bataan, sung to the tune of "The Battle Hymn of the Repub-lic":

> *Dugout Doug MacArthur lies ashaking on the Rock*
> *Safe from all the bombers and from any sudden shock*
> *Dugout Doug is eating of the best food on Bataan*
> *And his troops go starving on.*
>
> *Dugout Doug's not timid, he's just cautious, not afraid*
> *He's protecting carefully the stars that Franklin made*
> *Four-star generals are rare as good food on Bataan*
> *And his troops go starving on.*
>
> *Dugout Doug is ready in his Kris Craft for the flee*
> *Over bounding billows and the wildly raging sea*
> *For the Japs are pounding on the gates of Old Bataan*
> *And his troops go starving on. . . .*

So MacArthur disappeared from the Philippines, gone to Australia to eat steak and eggs, and the United States government decorated him with a Medal of Honor for his accomplishments on the island of Luzon and the peninsula of Bataan. For MacArthur's seventy-eight thousand troops there was no way out. There were not enough ships in the ocean, and even if there had been, MacArthur sent orders from Australia that his forces must stay and fight to the death.

He announced, in the MacArthur imperial first-person singular, *I shall return*. On Bataan, the way they said it was, *I am going to the latrine, but I shall return.*

The longer Bataan hung on, the shorter food got. The calorie count, even the official one on paper, dropped from two thousand to fifteen hundred and looked to be headed for one thousand, down from one-half rations to three-eights, on the way to one-fourth.

Real American beef was disappearing. Filipino beef was *carabao*, water buffalo, the skinny overworked peasant beast of burden. MacArthur had forbidden his troops to shoot at carabao as targets of opportunity. They were supposed to eat only official carabao, quartermaster issue, livers inspected for disease. But close to the front it was amazing how many fierce wild Filipino carabao attacked Americans and had to be killed in self-defense.

Next came *calesa* pony. Company A of the 192nd had one cowboy. He always swore he would never eat horse. He was eating calesa and trying to convince himself it was real beef, or at worst carabao, when Forrest Knox said, for the fun of it, *Shucks, I got proof, I just bit a saddle gall.* The cowboy threw his meal away and washed out his mess kit. But on two meals a day, less than twelve hundred calories, he was the only one who did that.

Next came the mules and horses of the 26th Cavalry. The horses were in the last American cavalry charge in history, at Morong on January 26, but there was no forage left for them on Bataan, or for the mules. They had eaten all the stacks of rice straw, they were down to the last of the oats, they were starving. But so were the troops.

An officer ranked mule as succulent and tender; calesa pony better-flavored than carabao, if a little tougher; iguana fair. Most men would not balk at wild boar, or even python meat and python eggs. Rat was excellent with *mongo* beans. The big worry was monkey. Not so much the taste, more that when a man peeked into the pot and saw the little bleached hands and the little scrunched-up face, like a boiled baby's, it tended to take away his appetite.

Down by the coast the fashion was blast fishing. Forrest Knox scrounged some dynamite and a Filipino showed him how: You folded the stick over and made a fat little bomb with a short fuse, only about an inch and a half, and then, when you spotted a ripple on the water, you lit the fuse and timed the throw so the bomb went off right at the surface—under water the explosion churned up the coral and you could not find the fish. That was the sophisticated way. The unsophisticated way was to pack a milk can with blasting powder, or lob a grenade, then wade in and grab the concussed fish before the blood brought sharks.

Sugar was a craving. A can of Eagle Brand sweetened condensed milk would bring $20, and any later than February no one could find one. In March a Milky Way bar was $37.50 bid, no seller. Sugarcane was free; sucking on a cut length for the juice would send a jolt through the body like a sweet electric shock. In the sugar mills there might still be blackstrap molasses in the refining tanks; men would carry five-gallon gas cans of it back to camp, and everyone would fall on it and eat it straight, like candy. Another sugar item came in big patties, dark congealed stuff, very crude. The Filipinos used to feed it to their calesa ponies. It was dirty and contaminated, it brought on disastrous runs, but it was a sugar fix.

For as long as the rice straw stacks lasted in no-man's-land, there might be grain to be gleaned. At Pilar some men went out to a rice mill to bring back a set of grindstones, but the stones were gone; the Japanese had been there ahead of them. In an abandoned Japanese camp there might be food leavings among the split-toe shoe tracks. And after a firefight there were Japanese rations to be had. All a man had to do was get used to rolling corpses.

Hospital No. 1 was in the South Mariveles Mountains, No. 2 was at Cabcaben, both in southern Bataan. They were big campaign hospitals, intended to handle a thousand patients each. After a month or two they had three thousand each. By the end of March, twenty-four thousand men on Bataan were sick, being treated where they lay, or not getting treatment at all. At the front there were men too weak to climb out of their foxholes at chow time, and other men who fainted before they reached the food. There was no guarantee of a full stomach for casualties, either—in more than one place with the official title of a medical station, the sick and wounded were fighting the wild dogs for food.

The Filipino draftees did not have training in battlefield hygiene. They did not boil their drinking water, sterilize their mess kits, or bury their garbage; they dropped empty cans that stank of rotting fish. They did not build good latrines, just straddle trenches dug next to the kitchens. There was so much filth that diarrhea and dysentery ran wild. And so little food that deficiency diseases were turning up: scurvy, pellagra, beriberi. Food was going, strength was gone: bloated belly, swollen legs, mind in a fog, vertigo, lassitude. If a man tried to move quickly his heart thumped like a tractor bogged in a swamp.

Bataan, especially the southern part of the peninsula, was malaria country. There was no such thing as a working mosquito control plan; no one had the energy. Malaria was awful, chills and shakes, racking fevers and splitting headaches, hallucinations and terrible debilitating depression. Prophylaxis was five grains of quinine a day, meaning three million tablets a month were needed on Bataan. Through part of February there was enough, but not beyond then, and by the start of March only men already suffering were getting their dose. Some of the doctors had a certain amount of pure quinine sulfate, a flaky powder. One teaspoon per day equaled the prophylactic dose. Get the dose slightly wrong, which was easy with powder, and the ears rang. On top of that, quinine was as bitter-tasting as anything on earth. The powder, even taken stirred in water, was horrible going down. It left the mouth and tongue numb for twenty-four hours—meaning, with a daily dose, perpetually. By March, with the Japanese sack drawing down more and more tightly, the disease was turning epidemic. By the end of the month, 75 to 80 percent of frontline troops had malaria, and quinine was down to a week's supply.

By March, the Japanese propaganda leaflets were featuring less of the private parts of blondes, more the dinner menus of fine Manila hotels. When General Homma sent down another message, by dive-bomber in beer cans, it was about food as ranking with honor and military inevitability. Homma said he was speaking in accordance with the humanitarian principles of *bushidō,* the way of the Japanese warrior. He could either attack and rout the defenders of Bataan at will or just wait until they starved in the narrow confines of the peninsula. Homma said that Hong Kong, Singapore, and the Netherlands East Indies had accepted what he called *honorable defeat;* the Americans and Filipinos should, too. The Imperial Japanese Forces would adhere strictly to international law, and the surrendering forces would be treated accordingly. They had until March 22 to reply by special messenger. After that, Homma said, he would consider himself at liberty to take any action whatsoever.

By Homma's deadline of March 22, MacArthur was ten days gone, and Jonathan Wainwright was running the Bataan campaign from Corregidor. Wainwright did not respond to the Japanese offer of honorable surrender. On April 3, Homma opened his offensive.

For the last stand, Wainwright put his Bataan troops on double rations, with extra food sent across from Corregidor. That did not make a double full ration, just double what they had been getting, rice up from 8.5 to 17.0 ounces a day, flour from 1.22 to 2.44, and more fish for the Filipinos. It was the best Wainwright could do, but it was not enough. He said so to Washington—it would not put sufficient food in the belly to nourish a dog.

On the morning of April 6, unit commanders were supposed to report their percentage of effectives, an *effective* being defined as a man who could walk a hundred yards, carrying his weapon, without stopping to rest, and still shoot. Some commanders had no units left to report on; their troops had scattered and vanished. Among groups that could still be described, however loosely, as units, effectives were estimated at 15 percent. They were bone weary, exhausted; one man said even his *hair* was tired.

All they could do, in their tens of thousands, was drag themselves away from the Japanese, on foot. They drained the oil from the cars and trucks in the motor pools and set the engines running, that terrible wail of American humiliation. They lit their last cigarettes with their last fifty-dollar bills. They buried their family letters and photos and fled, and the last wild pigs of Bataan, the ones too cunning to be caught and eaten, came snouting among their memories. The Japanese kept bombing and shelling: shrapnel and phosphorus, the smell of burned human flesh in the air, bits of bodies stuck in the scrub and pasted on trees. Bombs fell on the hospitals; Alvin Poweleit, the surgeon of the 192nd, was operating among arms and legs and heads flying everywhere. On the jungle trails the litter bearers were carrying wounded men, but the wounded were too many, they had to be left behind, by the hundred. At night the Japanese pushed closer and closer, and the noise of butchery was frightful in the dark; they were bayoneting the dying, hacking at the corpses with their swords. It was fixed in the minds of the Americans, the Filipinos too, that the Japanese did not take prisoners. Anyone who had been out on patrol on Bataan had seen men strung up by the thumbs, their guts trailing, and bodies lying on the ground, their mouths stuffed with their own penises.

By April 8 the shambles was total. Orders came to the 192nd

to destroy their tanks. Company A drove into the jungle and drew up their M-3s in a fan shape. They shot each other's engines dead with their 37-millimeter cannons. They broke off the gas valves in the crew compartments to flood the insides, stripped the machine guns and threw the parts in, lit matches, and watched the Armored Force burning down into scrap iron. Forrest Knox had to turn away, he could not stand to look.

Ammunition dumps were going up all over the place. The whole southern end of Bataan was like a volcano erupting, with white-hot metal fountaining from exploding bombs and shells, colored flares rocketing everywhere, snaking through the air like crazed disintegrating rainbows. Between Bataan and Corregidor the falling debris was lashing the water; and under the hail, small craft of all kinds were making for The Rock, yachts, motor launches, barges, canoes, knocked-together rafts, flat bits of board hand-paddled with smaller bits of board, logs kick-powered with legs shrinking from the sharks.

Jonathan Wainwright was still under MacArthur's orders to fight to the death. If the troops on Bataan were to be wiped out, MacArthur told Washington from Australia, let it be on the actual field of battle, taking full toll of the enemy. If the food gives out, MacArthur told Wainwright, counterattack.

On Corregidor, Wainwright issued the counterattack order. On Bataan the command sounded crazy. Major General Edward P. King, Jr., was in charge of the remnants of Luzon Force, human rags and tatters only. King could see the Japanese pushing to the south end of the peninsula. For the life of him he could not imagine that anything Luzon Force could do would delay them a minute. So King made the dreadful decision—and made it alone—to surrender Bataan.

In the early hours of April 9, the darkest hour before the darkest dawn in the history of the United States Army, King sent two officers to make contact with the enemy. For their white flag they had a dirty bed sheet. It came from Company A of the 192nd. Phil Parrish, the supply sergeant, found it for them.

The Japanese general who took King's surrender spoke no English. Through an interpreter, King's sword was demanded of him. He had no saber; he had left his in Manila when the war began. A general with no sword—the Japanese could not conceive of such a barbarism. King offered his pistol, it was laid on the table, and all of MacArthur's Luzon Force, Americans and Filipinos, were unconditional prisoners of the Japanese.

*   *   *

Homma Masaharu was under heavy pressure. Of all the commanding generals in Japan's Greater Asian War, he was the only one behind schedule. He made up time in his final offensive; in fact, Bataan fell to him sooner than he expected. But still Imperial Army headquarters in Tokyo was coming down on him severely. They even sent some specially picked senior officers to lean on him.

Now Homma had Corregidor in front of him, vital to Japanese control of the Pacific. But underfoot he had prisoners, scores of thousands of them.

In March, thinking ahead, Homma had had some of his staff officers draw up a plan for the disposition of captives. It was issued as an order by Homma along with his orders for the final Bataan offensive: Move all prisoners out of the peninsula, north into central Luzon, and herd them into Camp O'Donnell. It was a hundred miles at the most—not all that far by Imperial Japanese Army standards. A Japanese infantryman with full pack could be marched, routinely, as much as twenty-five miles a day, another twenty-five the next, and the next, at an average pace of two and a half miles an hour, speeding up to four on command, all on a few rice balls and sticks of dried fish and slivers of pickled vegetable and a shot of sugar. So, by Japanese thinking, it was only a few days and a few food stops: Balanga, Orani, Lubao, San Fernando Pampangas, Capas, O'Donnell.

The problem with this simple plan and neat itinerary was that it was never going to work. A few months earlier, MacArthur had had a paper plan to go by, but in the shambles of retreat under fire he made a mess of moving food and medicine into Bataan, and his men paid the price in sickness and starvation. Now, under the Japanese paper plan for moving prisoners, the same scores of thousands of men—less the dead, but with the living even closer to total exhaustion after months more of fighting and losing—were going to be rounded up and marched for days, at speed, in tropical heat, by a Japanese army in the flush and arrogance of victory.

When Edward King surrendered Luzon Force, he made a point of telling the Japanese that he had many more men than their intelligence had estimated, most of them sick and hungry. He said he would assemble them, organize them, and move them wherever the Japanese directed him to, using American trucks and ambulances.

The Japanese turned up their noses at King's proposal. To them King was a worthless white general who had surrendered his

worthless troops. The Japanese senior officer who took King's surrender would not lower himself so much as to look at him. The
surrender was unconditional; now the Japanese could do—or not
do—anything they wanted.

They wanted the prisoners swept out of their way. And the
greater the number of prisoners, the rougher the sweep was going
to be.

So it began. The Japanese herded their captives north out of Bataan
on foot, like driven cattle. The East Road was jammed, and the
Japanese truck convoys bringing troops south for the Corregidor
offensive had to bull their way through.

General King was permitted to ride to O'Donnell in a car, total
driving time less than a day. For a white general surrendering to
the Japanese without a sword, that was getting off light. Another
general was hauled out of his car and beaten by a Japanese officer.
He was allowed to get back in, but later a different bunch of Japanese hauled him out again, trussed him up, and left him lying on
the ground overnight. Other generals had to walk from the start,
the first generals in the military history of the United States reduced
to trailing into captivity on foot, on the far side of the world. The
Japanese put captured colonels on show to humiliate them, fingered their insignia of rank, poked at them like monkeys, strung
them up and beat them. They ransacked officers' bags and took
eyeglasses and cigarette cases and Parker pens. They came swag-
gering through collecting officers' wristwatches in five-gallon cans,
and they said that anyone who held back would have his throat
cut. They chopped the fingers off officers to get at their gold West
Point rings. One captain had some Japanese money, and for that
they chopped his head off. Another officer was holding his men's
money, white money; the Japanese took it and shot him. A lieutenant bent to help a captain who had fallen; the Japanese shot the
captain and ran a bayonet up the lieutenant from behind.

All this was before Balanga—meaning that even before the first
big staging point on the way to O'Donnell, the Japanese were
randomly killing surrendered American officer prisoners of every
rank below general.

As for Filipino prisoners, after the surrender some Japanese
were halting men from the 91st Division at a roadblock, shaking
them down group after group, sending the privates on their way,
holding the noncoms and officers. On the third day, the Japanese
tied them at the wrists with phone wire, then tied them man to

man, and herded them to a ravine near the Pantingan River. There they got a speech, through an interpreter: *Dear friends, pardon us. If you surrendered early, we will not kill you. But we suffered heavy casualties. So just pardon us. If you have any last wish before we kill you, just tell us.* The Japanese officers and noncoms started at one end of the line with their swords, the Japanese enlisted men at the other end with their bayonets. They killed from behind. The butchering took two hours. Between three and four hundred bound men were killed. There was blood and screaming until nightfall. And by the best-informed guess, the Japanese senior officer who turned up in person at the ravine to give the killing order was Nara Akira, a general, a brigade commander. Nara graduated before the war from the United States Army's infantry school at Fort Benning, Georgia, and before Benning he had been a student at Amherst College; but with him the white American liberal arts education did not take.

It is conventional wisdom in war to say that a captive is in the greatest danger of being killed right after he is taken. His captors may not have eaten or slept for days themselves. They may be close to the edge of craziness. They have the smell of death in their nostrils; they are still wound up tight to kill. They have seen their comrades-in-arms killed; their blood runs hot for revenge. Not long into the march, before Balanga, between Cabcaben and Lamao, the surgeon of the 192nd, Alvin Poweleit, was seeing a dead American every couple of hundred yards, and more dead Filipinos than he could count. Poweleit was only one pair of eyes on one short stretch of road, less than five miles. The slow limping march of the prisoners out of Bataan went on for days more, lengthening to weeks, and all that time the killings went on, from the battle front to the rear, south to north, start to finish. Beyond Balanga, meaning days into the march, one American started counting bodies with their heads chopped off. At twenty-seven he stopped because he could not bear to count any more, it was driving him out of his mind, and he was still far short of Lubao—meaning more than one head chopped off per mile while he was keeping count, probably closer to two. Not deaths of all kinds, just heads chopped off, and only the heads this one man saw.

These were killings not only by combat soldiers, but rear-echelon troops too, Japanese who had never used their guns and bayonets and swords in battle, slaughtering prisoners days and weeks after surrender.

The Japanese did not have to answer to Western reason in their killing; they were Japanese in victory, and that was enough. They would see a man desperate for water, catch him throwing himself down at some filthy pond and chop his head off. They would kill a man even if they did not catch him drinking, bayonet him for having water stains on his trousers. They would bayonet a man squatting with dysentery, leave him bleeding to death, fouled, with his pants down around his ankles. They killed men for going too slow, exhausted men dropping back through the column, Japanese buzzard squads coming along behind to finish them off. The Japanese might order prisoners to dig graves and dump corpses in, one on top of the other. Some were thrown in alive, and the Japanese made other prisoners bash them down with shovels, or be bashed themselves and buried, alive or dead.

All along the way Filipinos were watching, and if they tried to help the prisoners they put themselves in danger. They tried anyway, amazing numbers of them, and they suffered for it. Before Balanga, three of them were trying to hand some prisoners rice wrapped in banana leaves. The Japanese tied them up and chopped off their heads. At Limay a farmer and his wife tried to give the marchers rice. The Japanese staked them and burned them alive. The prisoners could hear them screaming, and the groups that passed by the spot later saw the bodies still hanging there, blackened and charred.

At Hospital No. 2, the Filipino sick and wounded got it into their heads that the Japanese were letting them go home. They took off, thousands of them, crutches and all, branches of trees if they had no crutches. The Japanese went after the slowest, the halt and the blind, the compound fractures, amputees and gut-shots, and left the ditches clogged with bodies.

There were terrible things to see, things that the brain could not block out: the print of a bloody foot in the dirt, just one foot, not two, step after step for a mile, and then it disappeared. No one who saw that ever forgot it.

From the start, there was next to no cohesion among the prisoners. And not enough leadership: Officers were tearing off their insignia because the Japanese were zeroing in on officers for beating. The marchers started out in groups large or small, with many guards or only a few, sometimes no guards for miles at a time. After Balanga the organization was supposed to be separate groups of a hundred, Filipino soldiers, Filipino civilians, or American soldiers. A man might be with his outfit, or the remnants of it, or with anyone, or with no one, alone under the sun, struggling among strangers.

By blind luck a few men got to ride in Japanese trucks going north empty after they had unloaded in the south. It was better by far to be riding than on foot, because the Japanese heading south in the truck convoys made a game of throwing rocks at the prisoners, or else they would whack at them with rifle butts, bayonets, lengths of bamboo, looted golf clubs, anything—they appeared to be keeping score, points for knocking off a hat or a helmet, higher points for raising a welt on a skull.

If the guards were on bicycles, they might make the marchers keep up with bicycle speed. If the march was halted because the road was blocked, the guards might keep the prisoners out in the sun with no water, hours at a time, even if there was shade, even if there was water.

This was called the sun treatment. Forrest Knox's group got theirs in an open rice paddy. An interpreter came through, a Frisco Nip, meaning a Japanese who had spent time on the West Coast before the war—there were a lot of those in the emperor's army. This one dumped out an officer's musette bag—it was full of money. He kicked at the bills and scattered them, and said in his Frisco Nip American accent: *Where the hell do you think you're going, to whorehouse?* and laughed and walked away. Men were passing out in the heat. The Japanese took this as a signal that the prisoners were ripe to be force-marched some more. They herded them back onto the road and double-timed them. They kept changing guards so the fresh ones could keep the pace up, and after a couple of miles Forrest heard the shooting start again at the back, the buzzard squads.

How to stay alive—Forrest learned his lessons along with everyone else. One: Never fall back. From the first day, men were hanging on to each other's belts to keep going; the strong were towing the weak, joshing them, razzing them, anything to keep them on their feet and pointed forward. Two: Never get on the outside of the column; you could get whacked or worse. Three: Never lose your hat; the sun will kill you.

April was the hottest month in the Philippines, and the driest before the monsoon. The marchers started out in shadeless heat, temperatures in the 90s, stumbling across smoking battlefields, then north along roads churned into choking dry dust. There was some water, lying stagnant in carabao wallows, many times with dead animals or dead men floating. Sometimes for sport the Japanese would let the prisoners drink this foul stuff. Sometimes for sport they would not. There was clean water too, artesian, bubbling up out of the ground, but the chances of the Japanese letting a man get to it were next to zero. That was the worst torture of all, to see clean water and know that to run for it was as much as life was worth.

By Orani, only a few days into the march, so many men had already fetched up there that the groups following after could smell the place coming, a sickening gas in the air, straddle latrines pullulating with maggots, dead bodies in the pits, men falling in. After Orani, Lubao. The prisoners of each day were herded in with the dead of the night before, in a sheet-iron warehouse—thousands of bodies, crammed up against each other, men fighting to keep standing because if they fell underfoot they might never be able to get up again. A prisoner with the rank of general asked the Japanese to allow the dead to be taken out, but of course he was refused, so the corpses lay among the living.

San Fernando Pampanga was next, and Forrest almost did not make it. He was with one other Company A man, Herb Durner. They hooked up at the start of the march and managed to stay together. Along the road they were shaken down any number of times. Janesville men offered exceptional pickings for the Japanese—all those Parker pens. Forrest and Herb were different; they both happened to prefer Sheaffers, with the little white dot signifying the lifetime guarantee. They got heavy whacks on the head for this, and the Japanese took their Sheaffers anyway. Whenever they could, they scooped water out of the ditches. Herb had a bottle of iodine; he put it in the filthy water drop by drop. Approaching San Fernando, they were on a stretch of asphalt road, black tarmac chewed up and melting in the sun; it was like walking on sticky hot coals, burning and blistering, enough to rip the skin off the soles of the feet. The Japanese double-timed them, and the last mile they ran them through a gauntlet. Forrest was on the verge of heat stroke, he had no water left in his canteen and none in his body, he could not even sweat anymore. Herb took the chance; he scooted over to a ditch and came back with water, just his canteen cup full—one quick scoop was all he could get away with. Forrest had a neck towel, the one he wore in the tank to stop the hot machine-gun shell casings getting in his clothes. He hung it over the back of his neck like the flap of a French Foreign Legion cap. Herb poured water on it a bit at a time to keep him cool, and that was all that got Forrest to San Fernando, a little thing the size of his life.

The Japanese had the San Fernando cockfighting pit jammed

to bursting with prisoners, the elementary school too, an old factory, a pottery shed, and the Blue Moon dance hall. Forrest and Herb drew the school. Food came to the gate, watery rice, one five-gallon can per hundred men and the can not even filled, meaning on average five ounces of slop per man, more for the lucky few, less for most, none for men too weak to struggle to the gate and fight for their share. Through the night the guards played a game, running in and poking with their bayonets at sick and wounded men lying on the ground, and if a man had strength enough to jump up and try to defend himself he got bayoneted.

From San Fernando to Capas it was twenty-five miles by rail, on narrow-gauge tracks, in boxcars built to carry freight. The cars came in two shapes and sizes. One was wood, small, so low in the roof that a tall white man had to crouch. Into this sort of car the Japanese packed fifty prisoners. The other kind was bigger, about the size of the World War I Forty and Eight, meant for forty men or eight horses. Into those the Japanese forced a hundred bodies. These cars were fierce sweatboxes, steel-sided, so hot they burned the skin. Most of the time the doors were locked. When they were open, the strongest men forced their way to the fresh air; the weakest breathed only foulness and got weaker. Good luck was a strong man to lead, officer or not; the only leadership that counted was being able to get everyone to rotate past the open door. Better luck was a door open when the train stopped, so that the prisoners could get food from the Filipinos by the track. Freely given or sold at extortionate prices, it did not matter—to a prisoner any price was a good price. Bad luck was if a man took his change in Japanese occupation money. This was a little thing that could get him killed later on.

Starting, stopping, jerking along—average time for the twenty-five miles was four hours. Men died standing up, with no room to fall, and the others cursed them for not dying at a stop so that they could be thrown out to make more room.

At Capas it was down off the train, for the final few miles on foot. This part of central Luzon was not blasted to bits; there was some blessed greenness to it, even if it was only miles of *cogon* grass. The Filipinos were coming up with food, the Japanese seemed to be easing off, and the road was flat all the rest of the way to O'Donnell.

In January, MacArthur had about seventy-eight thousand men in uniform on Bataan. By Japanese numbers, something like sixty-three thousand made it to O'Donnell. By American numbers the

O'Donnell figure was much less, something like fifty-four thousand.

No one knows exactly how many men, American or Filipino, were killed in combat. Or how many died of wounds and disease, or how many dropped dead along the road. Or how many were outright murdered by the Japanese. No one knows how many Filipino soldiers disappeared from the military head count in the course of the fighting. Filipino civilians were forced to make the march, and no one knows how many survived it. Or how many Filipino soldiers managed to fade out of the march, strip off their uniforms, and turn themselves back into civilians—probably some thousands. Or how many Filipinos slipped away into the mountains to fight on as guerrillas—certainly hundreds. Some Americans escaped from the march and turned themselves into guerrillas too—not many, some few dozen.

Even approximately, then, how many dead bodies were left lying along the hundred miles of road and railroad track between southern Bataan and O'Donnell? American bodies: hundreds, probably between five hundred and a thousand, meaning between five and ten dead white bodies per mile. Filipino bodies: thousands, possibly as many as ten thousand, meaning a hundred per mile. Total: a body every ten or fifteen paces, and every death a Japanese atrocity.

In Homma Masaharu's orders for the prisoners of Bataan, he said they were to be well treated. If Homma meant what he said, he failed to make himself heard, understood, and obeyed among his own officers and men. He did not even manage to raise his own head and see for himself what was happening before his eyes, every day for weeks. After the surrender on Bataan, Homma had his headquarters at Balanga and his forward command post at Lamao, south of Balanga on the East Road, nearer the start of the march. At either place, he was within hundreds of yards of thousands of prisoners passing by every day. Riding in his staff car between the two places, or anywhere along the East Road, he would not have been able to make any kind of speed through the milling herds of marchers; he would have had hundreds of prisoners at a time jammed up against his eyes, ears, and nose. Yet Homma said he never saw anything he would have described as *extraordinary*—that was the word he used—and he also said none of his officers ever reported any atrocities to him.

After the long march, Homma sent his chief of staff to a memorial service at O'Donnell for dead prisoners. But never while Homma was in the Philippines did he have a single soldier of his army, officer or enlisted man, punished for mistreating a prisoner in any way.

Of course, Homma had a war to fight. Corregidor was ahead of him, and on his list of priorities the prisoners of Bataan would have been last. It was also true that the prisoners were sprung upon him in greater numbers than he anticipated, and sooner than he was ready for. And it was true that Homma did not have food or medicine to spare; he had thousands of sick and hungry Japanese soldiers to provide for.

Homma said he only learned much later how sick and hungry the prisoners really were, and it came as a surprise to him. But if he had thought about it at the time—and it ought not to have taken much thought—all those Americans and Filipinos had been in the malaria country of Bataan longer than his own troops. And they had collapsed in such a hurry that it surprised him—in other words, they were much weaker as fighting men than he had thought. So it should not have been difficult to conclude that they were as badly off physically as his own troops, or even worse. Particularly since they were white Americans and brown Filipinos. It was a well-known fact among Japanese that troops of other races were inferior to the emperor's warriors in every way: physique, stamina, character, and will.

Then again, if Homma really did not think of the Americans and Filipinos as being sick and hungry, he must not have believed his own propaganda—the broadcasts over Manila radio after the city fell, the scores of thousands of air-dropped leaflets. In particular Homma must have forgotten the message he signed and dropped on MacArthur early in January, the one about knowing that the defenders of Bataan were on half rations already. And the other message he dropped on Wainwright in March, after two more months of appallingly short rations, this one about being able to starve the Americans and Filipinos out without difficulty.

There were Japanese eyewitnesses to the march who later on were ready to say under oath that they saw nothing unusual. Some were even willing to say nothing happened on the march that did not happen as a matter of course in basic training in the Japanese Army. True, Japanese enlisted men had a more rigorous time of things physically than Americans or Filipinos: routinely long marches, short rations, and rough discipline, including corporal punishment. In the Japanese armed services, a senior officer could slap a junior officer, a lieutenant could hit a sergeant, a sergeant could beat a three-star private, a three-star a two-star, a two-star a one-star. And the lowest of the low had to take it. But basic training in the Imperial Japanese Army did not routinely include hundred-mile marches with Japanese privates bayoneting and shooting their own officers and burying men alive. The forced march out of Bataan to O'Donnell was many things, but never was it merely the continuation of Japanese basic training by other means.

Some Japanese described what happened on the march as a failure of discipline. Not a policy, not an intention, merely an aberration, possibly conceded to be a regrettable aberration, but still no more than that. It was true that the Japanese Army at the senior officer level was a mix of fanaticism and indiscipline, full of faction fighting taken all the way to assassination. And it was true that by the time of the Nanking massacre in China in 1937, tradition-minded officers were worried about indiscipline in the lower ranks. Yet for all that, the Imperial Japanese Army was still a rigid structure, with a fetish for total obedience and instant physical punishment for the most minor of transgressions by inferiors. So it is asking a lot to accept what happened in China for years, what began to happen wherever the Japanese invaded in the first months of the Pacific war, and specifically what happened on Bataan, as nothing more than a failure of discipline.

It was true on the march out of Bataan that every so often along the road a good-hearted Japanese enlisted man, or an honorable sergeant, or even an officer, a warrior of bushidō, might behave kindly to a prisoner, or at least not unkindly—offer a ride on a truck, return loot, show consideration about the pace of the march, come up with a cigarette or a swig of water. But this kind of thing was so unusual that the prisoners took indelible note of it. Receiving a kindness from a Japanese was as rare as winning a prize in a lottery.

At Homma's headquarters at Balanga there were those senior officers sent to stiffen him for his final offensive. They were professional Japanese military hardheads, most of them from what was known as the China gang. They wanted all prisoners killed, and they put it about that death to prisoners was the policy of the emperor.

The officer who spread this word most insistently was Lieutenant Colonel Tsuji Masanobu. Wherever Tsuji went in the war he trailed atrocities. He was one of the masterminds of the Malayan campaign, and after the surrender of Singapore he organized mass murders. He came to Bataan fresh from that. Out on the march, along the East Road, an officer who looked like Tsuji was seen behaving like Tsuji, a Japanese lieutenant colonel killing a surrendered prisoner with his own hands. Some of Homma's staff did not like that sort of thing, and they said so. But then other senior officers were riding up and down the East Road in their staff cars, and they said and did nothing about what they saw, except that one of them drove over a prisoner.

Some Japanese officers demanded the killing of prisoners. Some encouraged it. Some tolerated it. A few opposed it; but even they endured it. No doubt any number of Japanese, officers and enlisted men, were just following orders, doing their job, whatever that might have meant to them in the service of their emperor. But nothing and nobody stopped the Japanese from doing whatever they felt like to their surrendered prisoners. Bushidō, the way of the warrior, meant whatever officers wanted it to mean. Discipline likewise meant whatever they wanted it to. The result was mass atrocity.

::

ANYWHERE from two days to three weeks after the surrender, the survivors of the Bataan death march came stumbling into Camp O'Donnell, group by group, hundreds early on, rising to thousands of Americans and tens of thousands of Filipinos.

Inside the barbed wire, they were made to stand yet again for shakedown. This time they were frisked all the way to nail files, pen knives, notebooks, pipe tobacco and matches. By O'Donnell there were not many Rolex watches and Parker pens left to be looted, but some men still had Japanese things on them, souvenirs of battle, Japanese *yen* in bills, coins, small change. Inconsequential things, forgotten in pockets in the daze of the march. But by Japanese thinking, anything Japanese found on a prisoner must have come off a dead Japanese on the battlefield, and that was death to the prisoner.

The quick scuffed a hole in the dirt, or just stood on whatever they needed to hide, hoping the Japanese would not slug them for nothing and knock them off it. One man with some Japanese paper yen managed to chew the bills and swallow them without gagging. A captain had a Japanese fan, given to him by a guard to fan a sick man, one of those rare small Japanese acts of kindness on the march; at O'Donnell it got the captain killed.

In the first few days about twenty Americans were killed for small Japanese things; and over on the other side of camp the Japanese were marking Filipinos with a big red X on their chests, condemning them to death for the same reason, in job lots.

Every incoming group got a speech from the camp commandant. Captain Tsuneyoshi Yoshio's harangue was famous in the annals of O'Donnell. Tsuneyoshi gave his speech in Japanese, through an interpreter, a set oration with daily variations. One of the first groups got their version at sunrise. They had to stand and watch Tsuneyoshi eat his breakfast, stringing out his meal for half an hour. He was about five feet three, with a shaven head, a little Hitler mustache, and riding boots (he always wore his riding boots, even when he was walking around in his underwear the way the Japanese did, even the officers). When he was ready, he got up on a box to deliver his speech. In the world according to Tsuneyoshi, the domination of the white man in Asia was over, but the prisoners were still the eternal enemies of Japan. They were an inferior race, in fact worthless. They owed their lives to the benevolence of the emperor. Tsuneyoshi himself would just as soon see them dead; he regretted he could not destroy them all, but unfortunately the spirit of bushidō forbade it. All prisoners, regardless of rank, were to salute all Japanese; even a prisoner general must salute a Japanese private. That was an order. At O'Donnell there were going to be orders about everything, Tsuneyoshi's orders, and if prisoners violated his orders they would instantly be executed.

O'Donnell was flat, bleak, treeless, with virtually nothing but cogon grass outside the barbed wire. Before the war the area was used as a firing range. Then in 1941 construction was started on a barracks for some Philippine infantry, bamboo-framed huts with *nipa* grass roofs, and Filipino-size double-tier bunks of split bamboo with no mattresses. The construction was never finished; the war cut it short. The camp was supposed to be for eight thousand men, and it was small even for that number. It was disastrously short of water—one miserable stream, a couple of small storage tanks, narrow pipes, and on the American side of the camp a maximum of three taps.

Now upwards of fifty thousand bodies were jammed inside the barbed wire, in less than a square mile. The place stank, and every day the stink got worse. Forrest Knox thought the smell was him, but of course that was taking far too much on himself. The word was that Tsuneyoshi had put out an order against bathing, as a waste of water. Forrest was not the only one who thought Tsuneyoshi was crazy enough for this to be believable. He organized himself his first O'Donnell wash, with a scrounged canteen cup of water and a sliver of soap that he had kept hidden through the shakedowns. After that, all the way to the start of the rainy season, his water for bathing was captured morning dew, for armpits and crotch.

What water there was came into camp through half-inch pipes. The line at the spigot was endless. Twenty-four hours a day the noise of clanking canteens filled the air like mournful cattle bells at a dried-up carabao wallow. Some marines had managed to keep their money; they could afford to buy their way out of the line, ten to twenty dollars for a full canteen. Everybody else had to wait. Group by group they learned the lesson and made up their own duty rosters, doing shifts, taking over from each other with their friends' canteens strung on a bamboo pole. Men went to sleep waiting and had to be shaken awake to get them up and shuffling forward. Some of them did not get up when they were shaken, they had died waiting.

Water came out of the spigot in surges and spurts and gurgles, but mostly dribbles, and sometimes nothing at all. It was weeks before the prisoners were able to get a generator and pumps up and running properly, and until then the only way to bring in water in quantity was by water details, half a mile to the stream and half a mile back with five-gallon cans. The dry season stretched on. The stream ran shallow and sluggish, lethal with disease, not fit to be drunk without boiling. And still the Americans had to post guards at the stream to stop men crazy with thirst from throwing themselves in and gulping down the filth.

The morning meal was a watery rice gruel that went by the Filipino name of *lugao.* For the other meals it might be nothing but rice. Sometimes there was *camote,* the Filipino sweet potato, or little bits of squash. One day for nine hundred forty American officers it was three fourths of a sack of camotes and four squash. Another day, for the whole American camp, eight thousand-plus appetites, it was rice with one small carabao forequarter. Other days, it was lugao with salt, or with rice-flour gravy and a thin squash soup, or a smidgeon of pork gravy on rice.

The Japanese were farming ducks. Not that the Americans ever saw duck meat or duck eggs—the Japanese took the lot. The only prisoners who scored were the few men on the duck detail. They got into the duck feed ahead of the ducks, and on short rations the ducks came down with vitamin deficiency diseases, just like prisoners.

Anything that ran, swam, flew, jumped, or crawled slower than a prisoner was hunted for eating. Monkey would have been fine, if there had been any monkeys in the cogon grass, but there were none. There were dogs, wild ones howling at night around the camp burial ground, chewing on the corpses, dragging the bones about. Five months into war and one month into O'Donnell, the howling noise raised a fine point of taste: *Would you eat the dog that ate the dead?*

Tsuneyoshi used to say the only thing that interested him about the prisoners was the number of them dead. The prisoner doctors kept after him to bring in supplies for the sick. He said all his requests were refused from above. Perhaps so, perhaps not, perhaps he never even bothered to put in requisitions. When the prisoners were out on work details, they saw all kinds of American food in stacks at Tarlac, but none of it ever got to their kitchens at O'Donnell. Two of the American doctors went to Tsuneyoshi early on and asked for the Philippine Red Cross to be allowed into O'Donnell. Tsuneyoshi blew up and told them never to raise that subject again, on pain of severe punishment. The Red Cross sent volunteers anyway, with trucks of supplies from Manila. Tsuneyoshi refused to let them unload. He said it was against regulations. When they tried to talk him around, his interpreter said, *You talk too much,* and knocked one of them down.

Day by day the prisoner head count went up and up, to more than 50,000, mostly Filipinos. The highest count of Americans came on May 2, just over three weeks after the start of the long march—8,675 Bataan survivors, plus a scattering of troops rounded up from other parts of Luzon, plus something like eighty white civilians trapped in the Japanese sack along with the military.

The dead count went up with the head count. By mid-May, on the American side, as many as thirty were dying every day, sometimes more, one every forty-five minutes.

The doctors and their medical corpsmen had next to nothing to work with, and they were likely to be in bad shape themselves. One day Forrest Knox was at the latrine trench, contributing to the dysentery overflow, and it turned out that the man squatting next to him had the reverse problem, he could not go at all. Forrest watched him straining, pulling at the cheeks of his ass, and asked him if he was constipated. *No,* said the man, *I got bleeding hemorrhoids and I haven't shit in ten days and it has growed shut.* Forrest said, *Why not go to the medics?* And the man said: *I am a medic.*

The dysentery ward was filthy. It could not be anything but. There was next to no water, no soap, and no disinfectant. Cleaning was a matter of moving the sick from one side of the hut to the other, coming through with long scrapers and pushing the mess out of the way, like a cow barn, then sprinkling sand on the floor, or slaked lime if there was any, moving the sick back to lie with their bedsores and ulcers in the lime, and crossing over to scrape the other side the same way.

The dead of each day were brought to the morgue underneath St. Peter's Ward, where the dying lay waiting for death, skin and bones, open ulcers, and in their last hours maggots and blowflies. Bodies waiting for burial had their dog tags stuffed in their mouths. If a corpse did not have tags but someone knew who it was, the name was written on a piece of paper and put in its hand to hold. It was a half-mile carry to where the day's gravediggers were working nonstop. Forrest learned the ins and outs of burying like everyone else. Try to be at the head of the litter detail so that you could drop your corpse straight down the near side of the grave and not have to burn up energy swinging it out into the middle. Leave that extra labor for the ones coming after you. Working down in the hole, lay the bodies head to foot, so as not to have to dig any more than the minimum depth.

Mass graves were dug in rice-paddy land, and once the rainy season came the soil was soaked. The bodies would come floating up, and they would have to be held down with a rake or piled with rocks while the shovelers covered them again. A man could go mad working down in the hole, straightening bodies with more bodies forever falling on top of him. It was eerie to take hold of an arm, feel the skin strip off like a glove, and see a tattoo of propeller and wings, the insignia of the 17th Pursuit Squadron. Or turn a body over and see the face of a friend.

Inside six weeks, one of every six Americans who survived the march out of Bataan was dead. Forrest did his sums. He was like everyone else at O'Donnell; he knew at least six men, and at least six men knew him.

Bernard Shea, One-Horse, made it to O'Donnell, a fact that Forrest found remarkable. But after One-Horse got there he lasted only a few weeks. Company A had been doing better than most at surviving, at least up to O'Donnell. Two men wounded and evacuated. Only one man killed in actual combat, one other killed fusing a land mine, both of them officers, as it happened. On the march, only two dead: one officer, one sergeant. And George McCarthy managed to escape and find guerrillas. All the rest of Company A, ninety-plus of the original hundred-plus, wound up at O'Donnell. Twelve died there: one diphtheria, one beriberi, all the rest dysenteries or malarias or both. One of the twelve was One-Horse.

He was close to the last from Janesville to make it into camp, and the first to die, on May 19. On the American death list he was number 556, cause DU, meaning dysentery, type undetermined. That was the official cause, but something else worked on One-Horse to kill him. Forrest knew what it was, because One-Horse told him. On the march out of Bataan, some Japanese commandeered One-Horse. They made him drive a captured American truck for them because they did not know how. So far so good; he did not have to walk. Then they turned him into their *tōban,* their orderly. Not so bad either—One-Horse had been a dog robber at Stotsenburg, he knew how to do that. Then they started killing prisoners, and they made him bury the bodies. One day he had to dig a hole for a Filipino corpse. He threw the body in, and to his horror it was not dead, it was a living human being, and the Japanese made him bash this human being to death with his shovel. One-Horse was a Christian. He could not get over his guilt. Forrest was an atheist; he tried to talk One-Horse out of his despair. No good. One-Horse walked around with his head down, weeping. Forrest could tell he was going to die, and he did. He still had his dog tags, so at least he was on the death list under his right name. The list had a space for Nearest Relative, but for One-Horse that part was blank; he had told Forrest before he died that he did not want his parents to know what he had done.

Ted Lewin was a survivor. He was a civilian, and by rights he should not have been at O'Donnell in the first place; he should have been interned with the other American civilians. If that. He was what was called *connected;* he used to run gambling ships off the California coast, out of Catalina, and when he came to Manila before the war he built up connections there. He should have stayed in Manila at his night club, the Alcazar, or his whorehouse, the Golden Gate. Have the Japanese come to him, buy them a drink, let them feel the merchandise, see what sort of a deal he could cut. But he made the wrong move at the wrong time and ended up at O'Donnell.

Lewin kept his Manila connections. A lot of food and medicine floated miraculously into O'Donnell through the barbed wire and landed at Lewin's feet, to be dealt out to others, at his price. He never had to work. He could always arrange that for himself, and for others too, for a price. He had ways of shuttling from the American camp to the Filipino camp and back. The millionaires' row on the Filipino side was his kind of place. The chief of the Manila police department was there, and a big Filipino firearms dealer, and a mogul of Filipino show business. Lewin was a gambler; at night he would shoot craps with the Filipino corpsmen behind their hospital barracks, by the light of a salmon-can oil lamp. One night, most of the money was in front of the Filipinos. Lewin knew how to arrange such hopeful signs. But late in the game, with all the pesos magically sliding over to Lewin, the Filipinos blew out the light, grabbed everything and took off. In the morning Lewin complained to their officer, but he could not finger the guilty; all Filipinos looked alike, especially in the dark. Win some, lose some—Lewin was the house, and he was going to survive.

Forrest was not a Lewin, any more than he was a One-Horse. He figured the odds his own way. He saw the medics at St. Peter's Ward stacking bodies, the lines to the graves getting longer every day, and he decided that if he was going to live he had to get out of O'Donnell.

He had another reason for wanting out. The Japanese had him working on a regular detail, and one of the guards was forever kicking him in the knees. Forrest was forever cursing him, and it was the longest time before he realized he was bringing it upon himself. The guard understood English. He knew Forrest was cursing him, so he kept on kicking him.

The Japanese were drafting work details, back into Bataan to do salvage work, back to anywhere the war had been on Luzon, to rebuild roads and bridges and airfields—Bagac, Balanga, Calumpit, Capas, Gapan, Lubao, Lubang, Salcot, Tayabas, and up into the mountain provinces. By the time the last of the Bataan prisoners were rounded up and marched to O'Donnell, three thousand or so were out again on details.

Not that getting away from O'Donnell was any guarantee of survival. The Balden twins from Janesville, Fay and Ray, went on a detail back to Bataan, and Ray died there, of dysentery and dengue fever, the first of the brothers in Company A to die.

Janesville doctrine was for brothers to stick with each other. The Luther twins, John and Henry, were determined to do that, all the rest too. Forrest and his brother Henry decided differently. They had been separated in combat and on the march anyway. Now Henry was too sick to leave O'Donnell. So the question was whether Forrest should stay with him. They had a heart-to-heart talk and decided to split up, trusting to the odds that one or the other would make it home. They did not see each other again until after the war was over, back in Janesville late in 1945, and when they did their head count they found out they were the only pair of Company A brothers left alive.

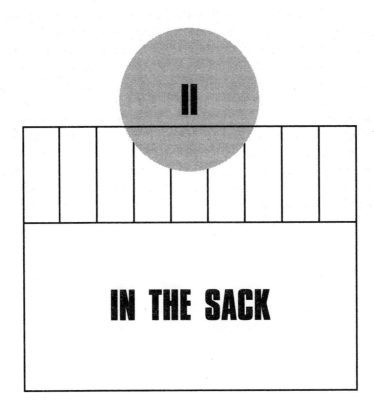

IN THE SACK

JUST BEFORE THE WAR HIT JAVA, SOME OF THE TEXANS FROM the 131st Field Artillery managed to make time for a last peaceable beer at a high-class Dutch hotel in Malang. They were sitting minding their own business when out of a table of Hollanders drinking in the corner one man rose up in his jungle uniform, green-colored like a parrot, and started waving his Dutch dress sword. He was well into the Heineken, and he wanted the room to know he could do many things with the saber. Everyone was giving him respectful attention, except for the 131st—which, of course, impelled him to dance toward them. In among them was a sergeant wearing an absentminded shirt and an Australian slouch hat he had scrounged from somewhere; in other words he did not look anything at all military. So of course he was the one the

Dutchman had to single out for special treatment, swinging in expertly with his saber, closer and closer. But the Dutchman, being a Dutchman, did not know about Texans and how they drew lines in the sand. All unbeknownst, he waltzed himself and his saber across the line. Whereupon the sergeant, without making a big flourish, in fact scarcely troubling to look up from his beer, drew his .45 and shot the chandelier stone dead. Of all the parrot-green Dutch in the room, not one so much as came up out of his chair. Out on the Texas front the saber expert was left lonely, being rained on by cut glass, and without a word he put away his saber and about-faced and retreated to the corner he came from and sat down facing the wall.

Less than three weeks from that night, the 131st were prisoners of the Japanese. Looking back, they came to believe that in the hotel at Malang they had seen a true preview of their short and sorry war. They set it down forever in their book of life that the Dutch threw the fight.

Of course the Dutch had their own need to add up the score-card so that they did not appear too terrible to themselves in defeat. Everybody on the losing side did that. It was a round-robin.

The Dutch pointed the finger at the British as the ones who rolled over first and most disgracefully, in the Malaya campaign. Everyone in the world, and especially white men in Asia, was brought up on the article of faith that Singapore, the British empire's great island fortress, was impregnable—that was the virtuous word the British loved to use. But the British left the back door of Malaya open, the Japanese kicked their way in and raped Singapore; and after that, the chances of the Netherlands East Indies being able to stand were zero.

To the Dutch this was a terrible shock. Yet, to be betrayed by the British was not a real surprise, because the British had been spitting on them for centuries. In the English dictionaries every word under D for Dutch was full of contempt and abuse, for example *Dutch courage,* meaning bravery only when a man was drunk, and *Dutch defense,* meaning a garrison delivered up to the enemy by treachery. The Americans had their own insults to pile on: to *do a Dutch,* meaning to desert or run away, and to *be in Dutch,* meaning to be in disgrace. The Australians who were surrendered in the Indies along with the Americans called the Dutch terrible names too: *Huns with their guts ripped out, Huns who would not fight,* and *papayas, green on the outside, yellow on the inside.*

When it came to the British, though, the Australians were with the Dutch. By the time Singapore fell and Australia itself looked to be going under the Japanese gun, for every trained Australian soldier still free on Australian soil there were two who were prisoners of the Japanese in Southeast Asia. In the Australian book of life, the British were the ones who dropped them into the stinking pit of captivity.

There were Canadians captured at Hong Kong who felt the same way about the British—Winnipeg Grenadiers and Royal Rifles, a battalion of each, thrown into battle without enough training, too few too late, in a hopeless campaign.

On Bataan there were Americans convinced that their high command had left them in the lurch. Some of them cursed Douglas MacArthur for bailing out to Australia. Some cursed Jonathan Wainwright. The commander of the tank force, Forrest Knox's senior officer, was one who had nothing but curses for Wainwright as an obsolete horse soldier with scarcely a notion of what a tank was, much less how to use it in war; and so, beginning the first day of his captivity, he started setting down his own bitter version of what happened on Bataan.

Prisoners everywhere were putting themselves through that kind of exercise, or exorcism. They went over and over their own campaigns, trying to figure out how their superior officers could have gotten things so wrong, and after that they tried to get the whole picture of the Pacific war straight—which was no consolation, since all it amounted to was piling others' disasters on top of their own.

The terrible truth—and every prisoner was seared and scarred by it—was that less than six months after Pearl Harbor the Japanese were all over China, Southeast Asia, the Philippines, and the western Pacific, millions of square miles of the globe, trampling on the lives of hundreds of millions of people.

The standard prewar wisdom of empire was that it took only a handful of white men to run the lives of millions of yellow or brown subjects. In the Philippines, fifteen thousand white Americans to sixteen million Filipinos. In the Indies, a quarter of a million white Dutch to nearly sixty million Indonesians. In Hong Kong, less than twenty thousand white British to more than a million Chinese. In Malaya and Singapore, less than twenty thousand white British to about five and a quarter million Malays, Chinese, Tamils, and Sikhs. On the island of Singapore itself, whites (including women and children) were less than .2 percent of the population, and yet Britain ruled.

The arithmetic of war was bound to be a bit more demanding, but everyone knew that one white fighting man was worth ten yellow men. Yet in actual combat the Japanese, with nothing like a ten-to-one advantage, were winning everywhere.

On Wake, and on Guam, the Japanese did have the numbers on their side. At Hong Kong they were on the high side too; there were 20,000 to 30,000 Japanese attackers to 14,000 or 15,000 defenders. In the Philippines, the Japanese started out on Luzon with the numbers against them—something like 74,000 to 105,000—but by the time of Bataan, what with Japanese reinforcements and Allied losses, the figures were tilted the Japanese way. In the rest of Southeast Asia, though, the arithmetic was a terrible embarrassment for the Allies. In the Indies, it took no more than 1,000 Dutch soldiers killed to convince tens of thousands to about-face and go sit in the corner. In Malaya, the British had 130,000 soldiers of the empire, more than two to one over the Japanese, possibly closer to three to one. Yet the Japanese general, Yamashita Tomoyuki, who had less than three full divisions, turned down the suggestion of reinforcements and went straight ahead and took Singapore far ahead of schedule and on the cheap—less than 10,000 Japanese casualties, only 3,000 of them dead. Yamashita was the yellow Tiger of Malaya; he made the British and Australian generals and their troops look like white goats.

There never was an even remotely reliable count of how many men fought in the first months of the war, on either side. Probably the Allies overstated the strength of the Japanese; probably the Japanese understated their own numbers. But in approximate figures, the Japanese, in those five months of fighting, took something like 320,000 Allied troops out of the war, killed, wounded, and captured, for a loss of about 15,000 of their own killed and wounded. In other words, the overall ratio in favor of the Japanese was more than twenty to one.

This was factoring in all colors of men on the Allied side, all the soldiers of subject Asian peoples fighting in the armies of white empires. Of the 320,000 taken out of the war, 140,000-plus were white. As against 15,000 Japanese casualties. So, in head-to-head race war, Japanese versus whites, the score was indeed close to ten to one, but it was the Japanese who won.

What all this added up to was a disastrous white man's miscalculation about the Japanese, a world-scale mistake. The sorry truth was that for years, white men—including professional soldiers and politicians who should have known better—had been looking at the Japanese without ever registering what was before their eyes. They saw only what they wanted to see.

In 1940 Air Marshal Sir Robert Brooke-Popham, commander-in-chief of the combined forces of the British empire in the Far East, was visiting Hong Kong, and while he was there he looked across the border at the Japanese army in China. He saw nothing better than what he called *sub-human specimens* in dirty gray uniforms, and he could not believe they would form an intelligent fighting force.

The Japanese could not even beat the Chinese, so how could they defeat the white man? And what did they imagine they would be using for weapons? For one thing, a fighter plane, made in Japan by Mitsubishi, the Type O, known to white military men as the Zero. Long before the start of the war in the Pacific, the Allies had had the chance to look at the Zero in action over China. Zeroes flew hundreds of missions and shot down scores of Chinese planes. Objectively, meaning by measurable performance, the Zero was the best aircraft of its kind in the world. But among white men it continued to be a well-known fact that Japanese planes were made out of bamboo and rice paper and rags, with rigid landing gear and mouse-powered engines. How could they maneuver? The little yellow Japanese pilots were all nearsighted, their eyes were ruined from eating fish heads and rice, they had to wear thick corrective lenses. They were racially incapable of closing just one eye, so they could not aim a gun accurately. And on top of everything, the way they were physically and nervously constituted they could not perform violent aerobatics, because as babies they were strapped to their mothers' backs and bounced around, which caused them to grow up pigeontoed and with no sense of balance.

The Japanese navy's big fighting ships had no sense of balance either, they had top-heavy superstructures that looked like Oriental pagodas, they would roll over and sink.

In fact everything about the Japanese was strange and laughable. They had a weird way of rowing a boat, a weird way of bathing. They had handsaws that cut on the pull instead of on the push. They ate one-handed, with little wooden sticks, chasing grains of rice, a pitiful starch that was no competition for white potatoes. They wrote back to front and upside down and in any case indecipherably. They named themselves back to front too, family name first, given name last. They bowed uncontrollably, a nervous tic. They had funny buckteeth and funny slanty eyes. And every white man knew the joke about Oriental women being built on the cross.

Out of these cross-built women came little yellow boy babies who turned into little bandy-legged Japanese soldiers. The Japanese soldier was so short that his Arisaka rifle and bayonet stood taller than he did, and an Arisaka was only a popgun, 6.5mm, it could only make miniature holes in white muscle—a white man could squeeze the bullet out like a blackhead. The Australian army's training pamphlets actually did say the Japanese knew how to fight in the jungle, but the British wisdom, which carried the real weight, gave that idea no points at all. The Japanese were not real soldiers with real fighting weapons. Their tanks were Tinkertoys. Their support services were so puny that their troops had to be ordered to live off the land, a shambles of a system that could not possibly work for any length of time. They did not even have enough trucks to bring their fighting men forward; their infantry had to ride bicycles through the jungle.

Yellow monkeys just down out of the trees, doing circus tricks on bicycles. And yet the white empires of Asia fell to them. Whites were on the bottom now, Japanese on top.

::

SOMETHING like 320,000 prisoners taken in less than six months, whole armies of captives—the Japanese had never had anything like it on their hands. They decided to turn native prisoners loose, a sensible move in logistical terms and good propaganda for them as racial liberators in Asia. That left 140,000-plus white military prisoners. How were they going to be treated?

The Japanese had regulations about prisoners of war dating from when they first fought against white men, in the Russo-Japanese War, 1904–1905. The Japanese won that war. They were concerned at the time to be seen as a people of elevated morality in the modern world, fitted to make twentieth-century war in a civilized way, up to Western standards. Prisoners of war of the emperor, the Japanese regulations said, were to be treated with a spirit of goodwill, never subjected to cruelty or humiliation, et cetera. And that is how the Russians were treated.

In 1907 the Japanese took part in an international conference at The Hague, where they agreed to the terms of a white man's convention about the proper treatment of POWs.

In 1914 the Japanese came into World War I against Germany. They did not fight in the European theater out of devotion to the cause of the British and the French, only in Asia and the Pacific, for the purpose of staking out imperial territory of their own. They took some small Pacific islands that the Germans had occupied since the late nineteenth century, also the German empire's holdings in China. They treated their German prisoners according to The Hague convention: like men, not like animals.

After the end of World War I, when the Western powers were trying to put down the Bolshevik revolution in Russia, the Japanese went with them on an expedition into Siberia. A white man from the International Red Cross gave two nations top marks for scrupulous treatment of prisoners—the United States and Japan.

In 1929 some improved ideas for the humane treatment of prisoners of war were put forward by the Red Cross at a conference held in the world capital of white civilized internationalism, Geneva. Japan, along with more than forty other nations, signed agreements at the conference table. But at home the Japanese government never did ratify the Geneva convention on POWs. Going into the 1930s, the Japanese were cranking up their military machine. They were on their way into aggressive war against China, and on their way out of the white version of an international community with Western rules of war. By the mid-thirties, the Japanese were saying that whenever and however the white man's way of doing things conflicted with the Japanese way, Japan would go ahead and do things its way. The way the Japanese read the 1929 Geneva convention, an enemy prisoner of war in their hands would be entitled to a softer time than a Japanese fighting man in the field with the emperor's army, and to them that was absurd. As for a Japanese taken prisoner, there was not going to be any such thing. No Japanese fighting man was ever going to be taken alive: *Do not survive to suffer the dishonor of capture.* So why should the Japanese bother about the Geneva convention? There was nothing in it for them.

That was how they operated in China, especially from 1937 on. By 1941 they were ready to take on the white world in war, and they truly did not care anymore what the white man thought of them. They had torn the Geneva convention to pieces. White men could go to hell, and the Japanese would be the ones to send them there.

Once the Pacific war began, the Japanese foreign minister told the rest of the world that even though the Japanese had not ratified the Geneva convention, they would have no objection to acting in accordance with its terms, giving consideration to national and racial customs about food and clothing, et cetera. Except—and this was the crucial part—where such things conflicted with existing Japanese policies.

Between December 1941 and March 1942, offices were set up in Tokyo, within the Military Affairs Bureau of the Ministry of War, for a small prisoner-of-war information bureau and a small administrative section, which were to oversee the handling of prisoners both in Japan itself and in the captured territories of China, Korea, Manchuria, Formosa, the Philippines, and what was called the Southern Region, the *Nan'yō*. The Japanese Navy was going to be administering some island groups in the south: Celebes, part of Borneo, the Moluccas, Timor, the Lesser Sundas, New Guinea, Rabaul, the Bismarck Archipelago, Guam, and Wake. The rest of the south was to be the army's, including Malaya and Singapore, Burma and Siam, some parts of the New Guinea islands, and the big islands of the Netherlands East Indies.

In all this, the man whose voice counted for most was the army minister, General Tōjō Hideki, who was also the prime minister. His orders to officers in charge of prison camps were strict: They must supervise their charges rigidly, taking care not to become obsessed with mistaken ideas of humanitarianism or swayed by personal feelings toward prisoners that might grow over a long incarceration.

Tōjō made an occasional visit to prison camps in Japan itself. And very occasionally an army ministry official would take a trip to one part or another of the occupied territories to see if camp administration was up to snuff.

Aside from that, area commanders and local commanders had the say over what happened to prisoners. And in the camps, day by day, it was the commandant who decided what life was going to be like. Anything in the regulations was the commandant's to interpret. Anything not in the regulations was his to allow or disallow. He could make prisoners stand at attention for hours if he felt like it, all day or all night if he wanted to, and then slave them all through the next day and into the next night. He could forbid religious services. He could decide whether prisoners would be allowed to meet in groups of more than five, or more than two. He could make them shave their heads. He could have blankets issued, then taken away again. He could make sure that food got into camp in quantity, or make sure that it did not. He could have the water turned on, then turned off. He could withhold medicine. He could make whistling a crime. He could keep his guards on something of a tight rein, or let them loose with their boots and rifle butts. The commandants and guards had the prisoners in their hands; they had the power of life and death.

In the Japanese armed forces, a prison camp posting was no plum job. There were good, conscientious commandants, but the odds against that were great. The Japanese running the camps ranged from careful men to average men, to outright incompetents, slovens, drunks, sadists, and homicidal maniacs.

::

ONE OF the things the Japanese did early on was to make prisoners sign a non-escape oath. This was against the Geneva convention, but the Japanese did not care. Everywhere the prisoners objected to signing; everywhere the Japanese applied heavy duress; and everywhere the prisoners ultimately signed, on the instructions of their officers, in the moral understanding that signing meant nothing.

The Japanese were quick to torture and kill men caught trying to escape. They made an example of them in front of the other prisoners, tying them to a stake and bayoneting them, or hanging them from a wire and beating them to death.

And the Japanese said that for every man who escaped, they were ready to kill ten. There were times when they did this, times when they did not, but very few times either way, because there were very few escape attempts.

For American, British, and Australian soldiers there was a duty to escape. It was in the military regulations. Of course not all enlisted men knew this. Officers were more likely to know, senior officers more likely than juniors—and to know that the Geneva convention recognized the duty. But should an officer try to escape if it meant abandoning his men, as of course it would? What about a medical officer? Should he act on his soldier's duty to escape, or his doctor's duty to help save lives? Should officers stay, but encourage their men to escape? All men or only some? If only some went, what if this laid the rest open to reprisals from the Japanese?

Officers did a variety of things, from talking about duty and doing nothing themselves, to encouraging others, all the way to punishing men for trying, or threatening them that if they made it back to friendly territory they would be instantly court-martialed there. In isolated cases, officers even gave names to the Japanese.

The Dutch were situated differently from the Australians, the Americans, and the British. The Dutch army in the Indies, KNIL, had no regulation specifying a duty to escape. But there was a pull from outside the wire. The white Dutch in the Indies were much more on their home ground than Americans at Woosung or O'Donnell or Bicycle Camp, or Australians and British at Changi in Singapore. The Dutch had been in the Indies for centuries. Many of the white Dutch who were in uniform when the Japanese invaded were born in the islands. So they would have had familiar places to go, and educated ways of getting there. But the practical arithmetic of escape worked out about the same for the white Dutch as for everyone else, because against whatever pluses the Dutch might have been able to calculate, they had the decisive minus of the Indonesians. In the Philippines some helpful Filipinos might have been ready to harbor Americans. In Malaya and Singapore some Malays and Chinese might have been ready to do the same for Australians or Britishers. And Chinese Communists in the jungle might want to recruit white prisoners with technical skills. But in the Netherlands East Indies the Indonesians—overwhelmingly—were not about to help Dutchmen get away from the Japanese. The Dutch arithmetic was that a white Dutchman on the loose on Java or Sumatra had only about a 2 percent chance of happening upon a friendly brown face, meaning a 98 percent chance that the Indonesian who found him would turn him in to the Japanese—or kill him on the spot.

The biggest sustained escape operation was run out of Hong Kong, by an Australian officer fighting with the British, Lindsay Ride, who had escaped himself early on. One way and another, Ride got hundreds of prisoners out, some of them military, more of them civilian. The number of escapers from other places was minute. The biggest single successful American escape from the Philippines was by ten men. The biggest single attempted British escape from Thailand was also by ten men; it did not succeed. The Dutch got a few dozen men out of Burma and Thailand, and probably more than that out of the Indies. A few dozen Australians made it back to Australia from Ambon and Borneo. The total number of prisoners who attempted escape would only have been some few hundred, and only a small percentage of attempts were successful.

Any white captive was a prisoner not only in a Japanese camp, but in Asia. His skin was a prison uniform he could never take off.

So where was sanctuary—especially with the Japanese offering bounty money? The prisoners had no way of knowing. On top of all that, most men were physically down from malnutrition and disease, and getting lower all the time. So where was the strength going to come from to make a dash for it and keep going for as long as it might take?

Of all white prisoners, something approaching one in three died in captivity at the hands of the Japanese, starved to death, worked to death, beaten to death, dead of loathsome epidemic diseases that the Japanese would not treat. From the beginning, what the Japanese did to their prisoners, body and soul, was humanly appalling. Even so, the prisoners stayed and took it. For them the stakes were: try to escape, with the chances of suffering and dying almost a hundred percent, or stay, with what turned out to be a two-to-one chance of surviving. The final gross score was: died trying to escape, next to none; died as prisoners, tens of thousands.

::

THE Japanese ran their prison camps by the same clock as their army, on Tokyo time. To them it made no difference that, by the sun, Wake Island was two hours ahead of Tokyo, Manila, Hong Kong, and Shanghai an hour behind, Singapore an hour and a half, Bangkok and Batavia two and a half. Everywhere in what the Japanese called their Greater East Asia Co-Prosperity Sphere, from Manchuria and Korea and Formosa to the Philippines, Burma and Thailand, Java, Sumatra, Makassar and the Lesser Sundas, the bugles blew reveille at exactly the same moment, even though in time zones west of Japan this pushed wake-up well back into the dark before the dawn.

In the prison camps, reveille was Japanese guards stumping through the huts in their split-toed boots, hefting rifles and clubs, rousting the prisoners, kicking and thumping and cursing them up and out. Japanese roll call was called *tenko*. Count-off was *bangō*. From 1 to 10 the numbers went *ICHI, NI, SAN, SHI, GO, ROKU, SHICHI, HACHI, KŪ, JŪ*; 11 was *JŪ-ICHI*, ten-one; 12 was *JŪ-NI*, ten-two; 21 was *NI-JŪ-ICHI*, two-ten-one; 22 was *NI-JŪ-NI*, two-ten-two, and so on. For white men, this alien counting system was hard to learn. Bangō among Americans was uproar, all those numbers being shouted out, hit or miss, in Japanese, in accents from the Bronx to the West Coast. And in big camps where different nationalities were herded together, it was even worse. Morning after morning the count would get fouled up. *ICHI, NICHI, SON OF A BITCHI!* And the moment anything went wrong, the Japanese would scream, and this would set the monkeys in the trees to screaming. In a big camp, on a good day, getting the grand total absolutely straight could take an hour, on a bad day two. And the longer tenko took, the more likely it was to bring on beatings before breakfast.

KI O TSUKE!—Attention. *KEIREI!*—Salute. *ATSU-MARE!*—Line up. *KASHIRA NAKA!*—Eyes front. *KASHIRA HIDARI!*—Eyes left. *KASHIRA MIGI!*—Eyes right. *KASHIRA NAKA!*—Eyes front. *MAE SUSUME!*—Quick march. *TO-MARE!*—Halt. *NAORE!*—As you were. *YASUME!*—Stand at ease. Everything in close-order drill had to be done the Japanese way, and the roughest drill sergeant at home was nothing compared with a Japanese *gunsō*. To the eye of the prisoner, Japanese soldiers did not look military. Even the officers thought nothing of walking around with the crotch of their pants down around their knees, and their sword dragging in the dirt. But on parade everything about the body had to be correct to the millimeter. To the limit—all dicks had to hang the same way at attention, to the left. That was the story Forrest Knox got, anyway. At least he could be thankful the guards did not teach him the lesson personally.

The Japanese were forever beating prisoners. Forrest made a study of the theory and practice of it. One school of thought said: Forget dignity, at the first hit go down and stay down, it proves you are weak and contemptible, not worth a second hit; that way you save yourself more damage. The other school said: Don't go down, or if you do, get up again, it will show the Japanese that despite your being a disgusting white prisoner there is some remnant of you still soldierly, worthy of respect; and a guard might give you points for it. But maybe not. And which guard would do what? Forrest never cracked the puzzle.

When they were beating prisoners, the Japanese were shameless about being short; they would stand on a box to bring themselves up to a white man's height, or they would make him stand in a ditch so they could get at his face. Somebody somewhere was always taking a beating. A section of prisoners might be sitting in their hut after dark, chewing on their evening handful of rice, and the night detail of guards would take it into their heads to creep up silently in their rubber-soled boots so as to be able to peek in unnoticed and pick out a man to beat for eating with his feet at the wrong angle. Or they would burst in and bash the man nearest the door for not shouting *KI O TSUKE!* quickly enough, and then beat everyone else for not jumping to attention instantly on his call. Or they would come stumping in one after the other, so that the prisoners would have to jump up and bow seven times in fifteen minutes. Or, half an hour before lights-out one guard would come in and order everyone into bed, and three minutes later the other guards would come in and beat everybody for being in bed before the regulation time.

Every so often, out of nowhere, the guards would grab some prisoner and put him in a cage where he could not stand and could not sit. Or they would put him on exhibit outside the guardhouse, where the other prisoners could not help but see, forcing him to stand with his face up to the glare of the sun for hours, eyes open and no hat; or make him hold a big rock over his head till his arms were about to drop off; or make him kneel bare-legged on sharp stones with a log behind his knees to cut off the circulation. Or they would truss him up like a pig with signal wire or barbed wire pulled tight. When the guards changed shift they would pretend to give him a drag on a cigarette and then shove it down his throat, or stick it in his nose or his ear, or grind it out on him. Or beat him. Then every prisoner going by had to beat him too or get beaten himself. It was nothing for the Japanese to beat a man for days and leave him hanging from the wire; he could die hanging.

Mass punishment was against the Geneva convention, but the Japanese did not care. They did not see anything out of scale in keeping a whole section standing at attention, or a whole barracks, or the whole camp, in the heat of the sun, without food or water, for hours, all day, all night too. Or they would make them pair off and hit each other, and if they looked as if they were faking their punches, the guards would beat them.

Or else the guards would take the beating to the limit themselves. On the island of Ambon in the Moluccas, the Japanese had prisoners at Tantui, Dutchmen taken on their home ground, plus Australians and a few Americans. Some of the Dutch were caught trying to smuggle messages out of camp to their wives. These were not military secrets, just personal notes, but it was enough for the Japanese to take thirty-four men and stand them in the sun all day. Tantui was a Japanese Navy camp, so there were marines around. The camp commandant turned two truckloads of them loose, drunk, packing baseball bats and iron pickets. The commandant

refereed the event with a whistle, like rounds of heavyweight boxing, with the rest of the Japanese crowded around cheering the
knockdowns. The marines beat the Dutchmen until the last one
stopped screaming. No one ever forgot that day. The Australians
named it the Dutch Garden Party.

That was early on, in the Netherlands East Indies, but it could
happen anytime, anywhere—prisoners being beaten to death,
other prisoners forced to watch.

No one could imagine anything worse than a Japanese guard until
Korean guards began turning up in the Southeast Asian camps.
The Japanese had had Korea under their thumb since early in the
twentieth century. They ran the country as a military colony and
treated the people like dirt. They made them take Japanese names
and learn the Japanese language, but never for a moment did they
let them imagine they were real Japanese. Coming up to World
War II, the Japanese conscripted Koreans in huge numbers as
forced labor for heavy industry. By 1941 they had the better part
of a million and a half in Japan. There were Koreans toiling to
exhaustion down coal mines, bending their backs on the wharves,
slaving in the steel mills. Korean females were rounded up—many
of them girls pulled out of school, some as young as eleven or
twelve—and shipped off to be prostitutes for the emperor's soldiers
all over the Co-Prosperity Sphere. *Comfort women,* the Japanese
called them; a hundred thousand, it might have been two hundred
thousand—the Japanese never gave a true count. Tens of
thousands of Korean men were drafted into the Japanese Army as
service troops. Three or four thousand wound up as prison camp
guards in Southeast Asia.

Japanese guards treated Korean guards no better than prisoners,
like another breed of mongrel dog to kick. One Korean who
learned a bit of English in the camps used to say on the quiet, *Japan
no pucking good.* The prisoners christened him George Pucking, and
he preferred that name over the Japanese name he hated. But he
could not bite back at the Japanese; no Korean could. One said to
an Englishman, *Inggeris-korean samo, all prisoner nippon.* Another said
it to an Australian: *You me samo.* But for every one miserable Korean who saw life in the camps that way, there were all the others,
Hatchet Face, Shadrach the Shitbag, and the rest, taking out their
rage against the Japanese on the prisoners. *Samo?* said the Australian, with feeling. *Like hell.*

The Undertaker was Korean. Doctor Death, the one with three

long hairs growing out of a mole on his chin, was Japanese. The Lizard and The Mad Mongrel were Korean; so were Rubberlips and Pig's Vomit. The Big Pig and The Blind Boil were Japanese. So was The Lavatory Brush. And on and on, Japanese guards, Korean guards, *samo*. The Boy Bastard and The Boy Bastard's Cobber (named by the Australians and known as The BB and The BBC for short). Joe Louis, Babe Ruth, Pickhandle Pete, Plugugly, Poxy Paws, Storm Trooper, Battlegong, The Bodysnatcher, The Wolf, Bloodhound One and Bloodhound Two, Big Misery and Little Misery, The Yellow Express, The Orang Utang, The Bombay Duck, The Black Adder, The Iguana, The Maggot, Captain Bligh, Simon Legree, Edward G. Robinson, Mussolini, Little Caesar, Napoleon, Frankenstein, The Mad Mullah, Ming the Merciless, Mephistopheles, Scarface, Dillinger, Damme, Five O'Clock Shadow, The Magnesium Flame, Make Me More Beautiful, Shit San, Hot Shit Harry, and The Blue Arse Fly. The Silver Bullet was violent and syphilitic with it. And there was a matched pair, Mori Masao, a Japanese, known as Bamboo Mori for the way he laid on the stick, and Kasayama Yoshikichi, a Korean. They were a plague condition, like dysentery. The prisoners called the two of them together Blood and Slime.

The only protection the prisoners had was their own officer class, and that turned out not to be enough.

From the start, the Japanese segregated and isolated the most senior officers. Generals and full colonels were sent to a special camp at Karenko on Formosa, along with high-level colonial civil servants—governors, chief justices, and so on. It was intended to chop the head off the body of prisoner organization.

At Karenko everyone had to bow. And everyone was ordered to work. That was against the Geneva convention; officers were supposed to be exempt from labor, even growing vegetables, which was what the Japanese wanted to make them do. They balked. The commandant put it to them another way. They could volunteer; those who did would enjoy the fruits of their labor, and those who did not would go without. Some generals argued that they should be excused from menial work on the grounds that it would damage their prestige; some colonels thought the generals were damaging their prestige by trying to get out of work. In the end, just about all of them voted with their stomachs and swapped their convictions for a hoe.

In letting go of principle like that, the senior officers were behaving like their own enlisted men—and unlike the Japanese. The Japanese way, in its purest expression, was to die rather than be taken prisoner, or if captured, die rather than knuckle under. The overall way of the Allied prisoners, officers and enlisted men—and it was essentially the same with all nationalities, American, Australian, British, Dutch—was to do anything to survive, even if it meant doing things that were humanly degrading.

It was not dishonorable, though. Allied prisoners could think of themselves as salvaging honor by the way they endured and survived degradation. And certainly no prisoner thought there was anything dishonorable about being determined to survive to see the emperor's army defeated, Japan in ruins, and Japanese hanged by the numbers for war crimes against prisoners. But—as a hypothetical question—what would have happened if the senior prisoner officers had refused from the beginning to put up with shameful treatment? The Japanese were contemptuous of the Western world's moral judgment. But they had sensitive practical issues to negotiate with the Allies, such as the safe repatriation of high-level Japanese nationals trapped abroad at the start of the war. So, all things considered, would the Japanese have gone to the limit with the senior officers and high-ranking civilians on Formosa? Meaning to the death?

Take the conjecture further. If POW generals and colonels had resisted from the first day of captivity, it would have been the command-level equivalent of the enlisted-man POW getting up after being knocked down, a marker of soldierliness in the eyes of the Japanese. If the senior officers had led with this example, might it have resulted in the Japanese treating enlisted men better everywhere in the camps?

These questions remained moot. By the time of Karenko, meaning months into captivity, very likely it was too late to make a difference. In any case, the generals and colonels, average age mid-fifties, each with much of his life and most of his military career already on the scoreboard, never put the ultimate question to the ultimate test.

In the winter a cold wind out of Siberia blew across Formosa. The Japanese issued work pants, of an ersatz material with wood fiber in it that flaked off and blue dye that ran; gray shirts, also of wood pulp; and cotton sweaters, one size that fit no one. When summer came back it was hot in the sun, and the generals working the vegetable gardens were sweating in conical Asiatic coolie hats of split bamboo with corn husk covering and underwear made from corn sacks.

The sickest of them were set to herding goats. So were the most senior, by age and by rank, among them Jonathan Wainwright from the Philippines; Sir Shenton Thomas, governor of Singapore; Sir Mark Young, governor of Hong Kong; and A. I. Spits, governor of Sumatra. The high-ranking goatherds had to graze the animals exactly where the guards ordered them to, or get flipped on the nose.

One day Wainwright was on an urgent run to the latrine, the *benjo*. Before he could make it, a guard called The Toad hauled him up for not bowing. Wainwright was cavalry, he had bandy legs, and he was skinny; his legs looked like badly warped bamboo. When he stood at attention, daylight showed between his knees. To a Japanese, that should not have been an item of special note, they being a bowlegged people themselves. But The Toad poked at Wainwright's legs with his bayonet and roared. Wainwright put his knees together and his heels came apart. The Toad played around, pushing Wainwright's knees together, letting go, watching them bounce apart, grinning at the sight, fooling with the knees of an American general struggling to hold on to his bowels.

Also herding goats was a British general, Edward Heath. He had a bad left arm from World War I, and he carried his left hand in his pocket for support. He saluted a Japanese in that position and was mauled for it. One American colonel was bashed at tenko seven days in a row, kneeling with his hands behind his back. The American interpreter, a captain named Bob Hoffman, had a terrible life. He was the only American officer on Formosa with enough Japanese to qualify for the assignment. He was an intelligent, capable, useful man, a good camp diplomat. His reward was to have the Japanese shouting after him day and night, *HOH-MAN! HOH-MAN!* They hectored him, beat him, and finally drove him to a nervous breakdown. The American mess officer, another colonel, was forever in line for a bashing from the Japanese cooks. It went with the job. One day he took three or four beatings in an afternoon and wound up insensible.

There were other camps on Formosa much worse than Karenko. These were straight labor camps, enlisted men plus NCOs, with a skeleton administrative staff of officers. The worst was at Kinkaseki. The Japanese ran a copper mine there, the biggest in the Co-Prosperity Sphere. They had the prisoners working alongside

Chinese and Formosans, coolie labor, women as well as men. The mine was hell, six levels underground at two-hundred-foot intervals, temperature at the bottom one hundred thirty degrees, streams of sulfurous water flowing even hotter, too much humidity, not enough oxygen, no ventilation, next to no lights, no safety, rockfalls all the time, blasting routines careless of life, and no medical aid, only mine police with clubs, and *hanchō,* gang bosses, coolie pushers, bashing prisoners with their geological hammers.

The officers were the ones who surrendered to the Japanese, and for enlisted men that was powerful grudge material. Early in the captivity, some men came up with a new doctrine: Rank meant nothing anymore; a prisoner was a prisoner was a prisoner. They would bow to the Japanese because the Japanese had the boot and the rifle butt and the bayonet. But no more did they have to pay respect to officers merely out of respect for rank. At the Jaarmarkt camp on Java, a lieutenant of E Battery of the 131st Field Artillery reserved himself a good sleeping place and a thick straw mattress, and some of the enlisted men were about to kill him for it. At Bandoeng, when the Japanese called for a parade of officers—Dutch, British, and Australian—the enlisted men, all nationalities, stood up and booed them. In the first days and weeks of captivity this sort of thing happened everywhere. And there were men who kept up the booing all the way through prison camp. Oklahoma Atkinson was one. A marine major jumped on him for sassing a noncom: *What's your rank? Don't you recognize stripes?* And Oklahoma said, *I don't give a damn if you've got stripes on your underwear, it don't mean nothin' to me.*

The officers' first argument for the privileges of rank was the age-old one: Things had always been that way. The second was specific to prison camp: Internal discipline was essential, and officers were essential to internal discipline. If enlisted men insisted on bringing officers down to their own level, they would have nobody to stand between them and the Japanese. In prison camp that was the working definition of a good officer, and really the only one that mattered.

Every enlisted man could point unhesitatingly to good officers. The trouble was that for every one officer who met the test, the enlisted men could count fifty who fell short, who were more title than quality.

At Cabanatuan, the biggest camp in the Philippines, part of the problem was that there were just too many officers. There were not only officers from American units, but American officers who had been with Filipino units, who had been separated from their men as early as the march out of Bataan to Camp O'Donnell. Those officers turned up later at Cabanatuan, with no men from their old units to look after and believing this freed them to look after themselves. Cabanatuan at its high point had more than three thousand officers, more than one to every five men, and the product of that arithmetic was not strength in numbers but self-absorption and inertia.

At North Point in Hong Kong, some of the British officers wired themselves off in a separate compound; the other ranks could see them in there eating better food, playing bridge, making petty complaints to the Japanese about not getting their supply of gin.

At Tanjong Priok in Batavia, and other camps all over Java, the Dutch officers were notorious for their mattresses and blankets and steamer trunks full of canned food and liquor and humidors full of cigars, and for their unwillingness to share.

At Bilibid in Manila, there were American officers continually moaning about having to live at close quarters with lower grades and civilian internees. These officers petitioned the Japanese to let them set up by themselves in the city, say at a hotel, where they could live in a style befitting their station as gentlemen under restraint. The Japanese laughed. That did not stop officers in Bilibid from looking after themselves, devotedly. An army clique, led by a colonel from the veterinary corps, got a lock on medical supplies, which were critically short, and sold them to the enlisted men at black-market prices. *He and his cohorts,* said another American, *should be tortured to death.* One army medical officer, a colonel, set himself up in a private room, known as The Sallyport; the men could see him in there, sitting up in bed, surrounded by footlockers and furniture, an exalted person, looking for all the world *like a fat pasha.*

Some months into captivity, the Japanese began paying the prisoners, a rare bow in the direction of Geneva. They set the pay scales heavily in favor of officers. Enlisted men had to work to get paid, but officers did not. The ratios were much the same everywhere. At Cabanatuan it was 220 pesos a month for a lieutenant colonel, down to 85 for a first lieutenant. A working private got 3 pesos.

The officers had enough money to set up welfare funds for sick enlisted men who had none, each officer contributing so much per month. At Cabanatuan the officers used screening committees, medical and financial, to allot welfare money. And here was a serious moral question. Take an officer in reasonable health, with no physical work to do, the only energy he consumed being to stroll around camp. Morally, how much did such an officer and gentleman owe a sick enlisted man who had no money and no chance of getting any, not even the miserable pay of a working prisoner, 10 centavos a day, because if a man was too sick to work the Japanese cut off his pay?

Welfare funds or no, never was there anything like equality in the distribution of money—and therefore of food. Transpose that into the arithmetic of survival, and an officer's chances of staying alive were multiples better than an enlisted man's.

The officers took this to be their right. Forrest Knox's considered opinion was that if the Last Supper were held in prison camp, a general would be sitting up above Jesus, not enough so that people could criticize him for being ostentatious, just enough to let everyone know who was God.

Many enlisted men came to the view that—a few great and good officers aside—they would have been as well off, even better off, with no officers, just WOs and NCOs. But there was no prison-camp revolution to overthrow the officer system, or even bend it constructively to the circumstances of captivity. Most officers got away with what they could; the best officers let them, and the men let them, too. The rules favoring officer prisoners had been written at international conferences; privileged men, the officer class of society, had written them. The system held. Even so, officer privilege was a running sore, never to be healed in camp, in fact never to be healed for life.

The naked evidence of officer privilege—meaning money and no work—was flesh on the bones. Officers were uncomfortable about enlisted men seeing that privilege nakedly displayed. So officers as a caste bathed separately from the lower ranks, at specially reserved times. For the enlisted men, that said it all.

::

THE word from Tōjō in Tokyo was that prisoners must work hard at labor useful to Japan. A prisoner who did not work was a prisoner who did not deserve to eat.

On the food side of the equation, the Japanese did not get around to drawing up official prison camp ration scales until October 1942, months into captivity. When they did, they fixed the basic daily ration for a prisoner of enlisted-man rank at 570 grams (1 pound 4 ounces), plus 220 grams (7 ounces) for working.

In the peacetime United States Army, when an enlisted man's physical workload was by no means heavy, his daily food ration was set at 4 pounds 7 ounces (2,013 grams), and the combat ration was set much higher. The Japanese scale for a prisoner doing hard labor—790 grams—was about 60 percent less than the American peacetime ration. And that was only numbers on paper. Food actually delivered to the camps was less again. So the working enlisted man's ration was chronically short weight.

For a nonworking enlisted man, meaning a man too sick to work, the scale was slow starvation. At the big American camp at Davao in the southern Philippines, the food handlers used different-sized rice scoops for workers and nonworkers, and the nonworkers' was known as the Death Dipper.

Work or die. On the Japanese ration scale a prisoner might work *and* die. Some men calculated that a hard day's labor under boot and whip would use up more energy than they would ever get back from the extra grams of food in the work ration. So by their figuring it was smartest not to work, and a camp doctrine of malingering began to develop.

But at the maximum, only about five prisoners in a hundred would have tried that kind of professional malingering, and not one in five hundred managed to make a career out of it. The rest calculated that it was better to go out on work detail. For Forrest Knox in the Philippines, Slug Wright on Java, Harry Jeffries and Oklahoma Atkinson in Shanghai, and just about everyone else, it was no contest: If a man got himself properly situated at work, he would be in a position to score himself extra calories.

The cookhouse detail was the top. *No one ever saw a thin cook—* that was universal doctrine. But cookhouse jobs were scarce, no more than one or two per hundred men, which meant that only the quickest and most political prisoners scored.

Failing the cookhouse, find another strategic location along the food chain. The best detail outside of camp was on the food trucks, riding around all day, with opportunities always offering for the quick and the cunning, smuggling messages and money out and scrounged food and other contraband back in, taking a cut both ways. Jobs on the trucks were as scarce as cookhouse jobs, and as political. Truckers ranked with cooks—at Cabanatuan they were called kings.

After cooking and trucking, waterfront details in big cities like

Manila or Batavia or Singapore could be the best work. Or the worst. The worst was heavy lifting of war materials for the emperor. Prisoners had to learn to hoist weights heavier than themselves. They became intimately familiar with the coolie yoke, a length of wood or bamboo laid across the shoulders with a bucket on each end, or another version with a man on each end and a bigger load in the middle. They called it the *Asiatic pickup truck,* the *yoyo pole,* the *yoho pole,* the *yahoo pole.* Once they learned the coolie trot they could yahoo anything.

The best waterfront work was yahooing bulk food, because of the opportunity to scrounge. Scrounging from the Japanese was called *liberating.* Anything and everything in cans was liberated, especially white man's food—beef stew, pork and beans, tomato soup, sweet corn. And sugar—stick a sharp-pointed bamboo tube into a burlap sack without being spotted, run it out, gulp down huge amounts, lick the last grains from around the mouth, and smuggle some more back into camp.

The best smuggling clothes were coveralls with pockets and long legs that could be tied at the cuff. The Americans in the Philippines called them *lootin' suits.* Next best were British tropical-issue shorts, known as Bombay bloomers, baggy around the bottom and with wide legs buttoning at the knee. Next best, hand-sewn cloth sacks to hang concealed under the armpits of a shirt or down the inside leg of trousers. Next, hats, the empty space under the crown, or a double-deck inside. Last and least, but still handy, oversize boots and hollowed-out heels.

For men with no pants—and as time went on that came to be as many as one in four, in some camps one in three—there was the Japanese-issue G-string, the *fundoshi,* known to the Australians as the *jap-happy.* Everybody used the fundoshi crotch method for smuggling canned goods. There was an American known for his ability to carry duck eggs safely, and an Englishman who brought in a radio transformer. The Australians took the crotch technique to the ultimate. They had their own pronunciation for it, *crutching.* Some of them went around with a pouch in their jap-happy, like a kangaroo. They had a man who crutched a revolver; a man who crutched a live chicken; and a man who crutched a fresh pineapple, prickly skin and all, a mile and a half, finishing with the official Japanese goose step past the guardhouse into camp.

Beyond survival, scrounging had a second drive powering it—to get away from a diet of rice and nothing but rice.

The Japanese loved their rice. To them rice was life itself. They believed it controlled history. There were guards who told the prisoners that the Japanese were winning the war by rice; the emperor's armies had captured all the rice on earth, and without rice the rest of the world would starve. *There is no more rice in London!*

The Indies Dutch might have been brought up on *rijstafel,* but the other prisoners were meat-and-potatoes men. To them rice was miserable Asiatic glop. And prison-camp rice was the worst, floor sweepings riddled with sand, stones, bits of broken glass, nuts and bolts, straw, rat droppings, worms, weevils. What a thing it was for white men to be counting weevils as animal protein. But they were prisoners of rice, so they had to make the best of it. A rice joke turned up: *Rice is the greatest food there is—anything you add to it improves it.*

Rice was a carbohydrate. Everything else needed for a balanced diet was seriously lacking—fat, sugar, salt, a balance of vitamins and minerals. And protein. Especially red meat. Under the Geneva convention, prisoners were supposed to be fed according to their national and cultural background, but no POW ever got enough red meat to make him feel like a white man.

Red meat was a dream. At Bilibid Prison in Manila an American dreamed he sliced a piece off his right thigh and ate it. It was not bad, and in his dream he was childishly delighted at discovering this new food source; it seemed quite natural to suppose it would replenish itself in a few days and be ready for another cutting.

Nutrition aside, there was nothing in the Japanese camp diet to leave a prisoner feeling content after eating. Getting hold of extra food became an obsession. It took time and trouble, cost a lot, and meant a great deal. It turned into a ritual. It even developed its own language. The Australians and the British had a made-up word for extras: *doover,* probably from *horse's doovers,* a prison-camp version of *hors d'oeuvres.* The Dutch word was *snerken.* The Americans in the Philippines took over a Tagalog word, *kuwan,* which they spelled *quan.* It started out as a catchall noun, *whatchamacallit, thingumajig.* Then at O'Donnell it came to mean anything eatable over and above the Japanese ration. Then it became a verb as well: To quan was to cook a personal meal. It became another kind of noun as well: a group of men who got together in a group to cook a private meal. It was an adjective too, meaning delicious. By the time of Cabanatuan, there were quans quanning quan quan.

Quan came to be the high point of life. Quanning in private, alone or with close friends, was the warm heart of the ritual. For intensity, the only thing in life to compare with it was sex. And because sex was long gone, quanning turned into the very sex of existence.

Before the war, at Malaybalay on Mindanao, a Filipino girl known to all as Goldie used to sell herself to the Americans, short time three pesos, or one and a half dollars. In the middle of 1942, Goldie was still selling, and she had all the business she could handle; but now the Americans were prisoners, on Japanese rations, and what Goldie was peddling by the piece was candy, at ten and twenty times the old unit price of her body—her quan was her fortune.

Quanning was everything the pursuit and seduction of a woman used to be. The prisoners said they would turn down a naked starlet for a piece of chocolate pie; they would crawl over Betty Grable to get to a steak. They had quan on the brain. It happened to Harry Jeffries. He would never have believed it of himself. Back in San Francisco, aged twenty-six, six feet one and one hundred ninety-five pounds of ironworker, he was Hollywood Harry and there was no such thing as enough sex. Coming up to his twenty-seventh birthday at Woosung he was one hundred twenty-nine pounds of prisoner, sex was just a memory, and there was no such thing as enough food.

What drove men craziest, even worse than no red meat, was no sugar. Prison camp on zero sugar was like the locked ward in a lunatic asylum. Black-market sugar commanded top dollar. A can of sweetened condensed milk was gold. Eagle Brand was scroungeable in the waterfront warehouses. A man who managed to crutch a can of Eagle back into camp past the guards might take it to bed at night and tease himself with it, hold the can in his hands in the dark, rub it across his skin for the pure pleasure of the smoothness, keep it intact for as long as he could stand to before he punched into it. Men were turning into sugar misers, sugar molesters, food perverts of all kinds; they took to swapping recipes like dirty stories.

Then there was smoking. In camp it turned into a kind of quanning raised to the *nth* power by the power of nicotine.

At the time of World War II, three out of four young men were smokers. Forrest Knox smoked, as did most of Company A of the 192nd, and most of MacArthur's army. Harry Jeffries was a smoker, though mostly for effect—Hollywood Harry and his perfect smoke rings. Oklahoma Atkinson was the one with the real habit; southern boy that he was, he smoked, chewed tobacco, and dipped snuff. Slug Wright's unit, being out of Texas, was full of smokers who chewed and dipped. Slug himself only smoked cigarettes. He was a pack-a-day man. On his travels from Texas to the Netherlands East Indies he went from Camels to Capstans, in Australia Woodbines and Craven A, and on Java he came across a Turkish-American brand called Davros Rondos.

As for smoking in prison camp, it was considered important enough to be authorized under the Geneva convention. Not that the Japanese paid any attention to that, but they did let in their own kind of cigarettes. To a white man, though—an American, say, with his taste formed on Virginia leaf—the first Japanese smoke was a terrible shock. Japanese cigarettes were built proportionate to the Japanese, small and stubby, so short that when a white man lit up he was in danger of scorching the end of his nose. One brand name was Kyōa, supposed to be short for the Japanese words for Co-Prosperity Sphere. Another was Kinshi, meaning something like Golden Bat. Oklahoma Atkinson considered Kinshi well named, the taste coming onto his tongue had to be bat guano.

Still, smokers needed their nicotine fix. Many times, even Japanese cigarettes were not to be had, and that meant going to raw native tobacco. In Southeast Asia the prisoners' generic name for the stuff was *wog*. It went by all kinds of individual names. Mountain Madness. Monkey Fur. Sikh's Beard. Sheik's Beard. The Beard of the Prophet. Wog's Armpit. Tamil's Armpit. Granny's Armpit. Hag's Bush, coarse enough to stuff a sofa. And Maiden's Bush, fine enough to be teased out, the real sex of tobacco. It came in different colors, from orange to black, the darkest so strong it left the inhaler feeling as if he had been scalped. *Whoo,* said Ray Robinson, Headquarters Battery of the 131st Field Artillery, *you realized you had encountered Mr. Tobacco.*

Cigarette papers were scarce in camp. After they were all gone, any kind of paper was rolled. Japanese paper occupation money. Toilet paper—the Japanese issue had more value as cigarette paper, so it got promoted from the latrine run. Yellow quarto stolen from the Japanese camp office, message pads, old laundry slips, writing paper, especially airmail, newspaper, wallpaper, cement bags. Even a Japanese light-duty chit, and that was something, a prisoner wanting a smoke worse than he wanted to stay off work.

Books were rolled: bits of Charles Dickens's *Pickwick Papers;*

ten pages of *David Copperfield* (sold for five cents); the collected works of Shakespeare (*Titus Andronicus* was smoked early and noted as burning with a blue flame); *Gone with the Wind* (any amount of smoking there). Reference works got rolled: a Los Angeles phone book a long way from home; a medical textbook—one doctor smoked his tropical manual disease by disease, holding back only the cholera pages.

The rolling paper of true choice was Bible paper, because it was the thinnest. The Dutch Army pocket Bible was excellent. The American Army–issue New Testament went three cigarettes a page. Rolling with religious paper had a whole theology attached to it. A Dutch Jesuit chaplain on Sumatra said the word of God was sanctified, not the paper, so roll away. Sick men smoked their Army-issue Bible after reading it. Or they smoked without reading, and about this the chaplains had nothing to say except that it was better for men to get the Word into them by inhaling than not at all. For those who were willing to read before rolling, where should they start? An English chaplain said Revelation, which no one understood anyway. The Dutch Jesuit said the Old Testament, then the Acts of the Apostles because they were only practicalities, then the Gospels; leave the Sermon on the Mount for last, and learn it before smoking it.

Matches were mostly gone, lighters and fluid too. So it was tinderboxes, or a rope end kept burning, or a long walk to the cookhouse fire. A percentage of wicked smokers would hang around with nothing but an empty tube, bum a light from someone else's cigarette, and before the other man caught on they would sneak a free puff. And the moment a man lit up legitimately, there would be instant hopeful shouts claiming butts. Buttsniping was serious business. Buttsnipers staked out territories; they competed to get on the detail that policed up around the huts, for the chance of butts. The Australians and the British called it *bumpershooting* or *bumpersnatching*. The Dutch had no word for it, they just did it without definitions, and there was one Dutchman who cut out part of the sole of his rubber shoe so he could pick up butts with his toes.

Oklahoma Atkinson had his own cigarette hustle. He turned it into a business, the way he meant to do with everything in camp. He would raffle a loaf of bread, a cigarette a chance, ten chances. To start with, he cut a little slice off the end of the loaf and ate it, as the first slice of his business edge. He had his ten raffle tokens in a bowl, and to make everything look perfectly fair he would hold the bowl over his head and shake it, and an impartial man would draw the winning token. Except that the impartial man was really a silent partner, coached by Oklahoma. The winning token was a special one, heavier than the others; all the educated partner had to do was reach to the bottom of the bowl and the right token was there every time, so the correct person always won the bread, he being another man in on the hustle. Then Oklahoma would take his ten cigarettes and cut one tenth off the end of each one, roll the ten one tenths into a whole cigarette, trade the cigarette for another loaf of bread, cut a little slice off the end of the loaf and eat it, walk around to another hut and start raffling all over again.

Cigarettes were the standard of value and the main medium of exchange in camp. Black-market prices would be quoted in cigarettes: *Corn beef is 5 today.* A man with cigarettes could get smokers to sell him anything. Or do anything for him: cut hair, wash mess kits, hone knives, make sandals out of old tires, launder clothes, patch and sew. If a prisoner had something of value on the black market—a watch, a fountain pen, VD pills—he could make a guard pay in cigarettes. With cigarettes a man could buy his way off a bad work detail. One of the Catholic chaplains in the Philippines used to hand out smokes to get men to come to confession. Nicotine trumped religious prejudice—he could draw Protestants, and even an atheist like Forrest Knox would go to service if the Word came with cigarettes. And at Changi, if a prisoner had any sexual energy left and any appetite for a different kind of service, there was an old British sergeant, regular army, who would take out his false teeth and blow a man for smokes.

Forrest was a smoker, but he could take it or leave it. He was never more happy about this than when he saw a guard with a cigarette. Let the guard light up and blow smoke, and every nicotine hound would come to a sniffing point like a bird dog. The guard could go any of three ways with his butt. One, grind it under his boot and watch those white faces fall. Two, flick it in the air still burning, and watch the prisoners leap like mongrel dogs after a bone. Or three, drop it at his feet and wait. Which white man would be shameless enough to come after it? Or stupid enough, knowing he was being lured in for the guard's delight, to mash a white man's fingers with his rifle butt. For sordidness, Forrest had never seen anything to match this nicotine madness, not in the gutters of the worst slum block in the worst city in the worst year of the Depression. It made him feel a long way from home.

:

NOT one in ten camps in Southeast Asia or the Philippines had water on tap. There were no pipes or spigots, much less showers. In most places, running water meant some stream, near or far, clear or dirty, and it was the camp commandant who decided when prisoners could go there to wash up—once a day, once a week, or not at all.

Soap was another scarce item. Oklahoma Atkinson and Harry Jeffries had been prisoners for twenty-one months when finally they got to a camp with Japanese-style community bathtubs, big ones, but they were allowed only one dunking every two weeks. This camp was yet another one where the Japanese did not issue soap, so the prisoner's bath was only a rag and a rubdown, among bodies crammed together in the tub, like cattle in a pit, filthying up the water.

Toothpaste was rarer than soap—some prisoners used soap for toothpaste when they could get it, or salt when they could get that, or ash. Toothbrushes were rare, too. There was a market for used ones, but only a nicotine addict would sell his toothbrush. Slug Wright's outfit had a Texas solution. Back home, the old folks dipped their snuff with twigs of black gum or mesquite, and the grandmas would get kids to break the twigs and chew the ends into a little mop. So the 131st in captivity were always on the lookout for the right kind of Asiatic twigs, for mop toothbrushes.

Shaving gear was husbanded. One Gillette blade would be honed for years on a curved bit of broken beer bottle; or a sharpened mess kit knife, or a bayonet smuggled into camp, kept hidden from shakedowns, would be shortened and shaped for shaving. For hair cutting, a camp here and there might have a barber with real tools. Cecil Minshew, E Battery of the 131st, managed to sneak his electric clippers through shakedown after shakedown. The first camp he was in on Java happened to be one of the few with electric power. But his equipment was American, 110 volts, and the Dutch current was not, and when he plugged in, his clippers took off like a Zero.

The Japanese made the prisoners shave their heads. Japanese soldiers had shaved heads, by regulation. But with prisoners, head shaving would be on and off and on again, no one could ever tell when or why. The first time it happened on Java, one of the Americans came to tenko with a big *US* carved out of his hair. The Japanese did not respond favorably to that kind of wit. Or to the Australians who bleated and jumped around under the blades like sheep being shorn. Where Slug Wright was, at Bicycle Camp in Batavia, no prisoner was allowed to have hair longer than the commandant's. And on top of that, a Japanese senior officer used to turn up at midnight, drunk, to roust everyone and inspect heads in the dark for hours. If a scalp had hair long enough to be pulled, it got a beating with the flat of his sword. The least of evils was for the prisoners to shave their heads themselves, with or without soap and water, mostly without. Yet another humiliation, and it hurt. The only thing was to try to summon up a laugh about it afterward. At that, the shaved heads were funny-looking. One of the lieutenants with Slug was doing a head count at tenko the morning after a shaving. He took in all the different bare scalps, nicked and scarred, grayish ones, bluish ones, pink ones, pale white ones, ivory knobs, cue balls, and when he got through saluting the Japanese and giving them the numbers, he shouted: *Rack 'em up!*

The shaved head was the cleanest part of the prisoner's body. The dirtiest was the butt. It could not help but be so, with no soap, no certainty of water, and the Japanese stingy about latrine paper. Tissue was not the word for the Japanese standard issue. It was like Grade 00 sandpaper, it rubbed the ass raw; all by itself it was enough to explain why the guards were so foul-tempered.

If there was one thing that made everyone else want to separate themselves from the Dutch, it was that they were not paper users. Their method was a bottle of water and their fingers. *A boot full of water and a hand full of shit,* the Australians said. *Trink wasser for arsen waschen,* the British said, and that made the Dutch too dirty for them. At the same time the British were too dirty for the Dutch. The Dutch used to stare in amazement at British officers ordering up a bucket of water from their batmen, dipping a rag in the water, wiping themselves body part by body part—when a complete bath in the river was only a short walk away. The British were too dirty for the Australians too. It was well known among Australians that in winter the British sewed themselves into their flannel underwear and piled coal in the bathtub. Of course the British were too dirty for the Americans. The Australians were not clean enough for the Americans either. Nobody was. Consider the standard army issue of toilet paper by nation before captivity—Americans 22.5 sheets per man per day, 3 for the British, 0 for the Dutch.

Whatever the paper issue used to be, in the camps the prisoners got down to a personal shitrag that they had to use and wash over and over. Or a corncob for a scraper. Or a little length of bamboo. Or grass, if there was grass. Or leaves—every time the Japanese moved prisoners around, the trees by the latrines at the new camp-site immediately started looking autumnal.

From the latrine to the cookhouse to the sleeping huts and back, the camp flies went buzzing. They walked all over the filthy floors of the sick bays. They settled on men's faces at tenko. At feeding time they dive-bombed into the rice. Forrest Knox worked out a defensive style of eating—every prisoner did—hand covering the mess kit, face ducked down, mouth right into the food. From the start in the camps dysentery was the big killer. At Cabanatuan, in the first months, following directly on O'Donnell, 90 percent of all deaths were from dysentery.

Malaria was all over the camps as well. The biggest quinine factory in the world was on Java, but the prison camps got hardly any pills. So Slug Wright and the 131st at Batavia developed work detail doctrine for quinine: Get on a waterfront gang loading bagged quinine powder, and inhale the dust. Other than that, the only thing the prisoners could do was keep an eye out along the way for cinchona bark, and pound it into powder with stones. Pills, bulk factory powder, or pounded bark, there was never enough quinine, never enough mosquito nets either, and so malaria was a killer.

Other medical conditions got out of hand in a way they never would have done in civilized life, everything from hemorrhoids to hernias. And tinea. At home tinea just meant athlete's foot; in the tropical camps it was ferocious. It would attack the hands as well as the feet, get under the nails and invade. It was savage on the scrotum. Generically it was called rice balls, place by place Changi balls, Hong Kong balls, Java balls, Bandoeng balls, Shōnan scrotum. At sick call the tinea scrotums would line up in a row; the medical officer would paint them with whatever he had, iodine or potassium permanganate or Formalin; the sufferers would buck and holler; and the medical corpsman would be following along, fanning with a hat to soothe the sting. The worst place for a tinea attack was the penis itself, under the foreskin; fungus fulminating inside there would drive a man mad. There were prisoners who had to be circumcised because of it, and it was odds on that they would have to take the cut without an anesthetic, because the

Japanese were not letting enough ether or chloroform or novo-caine into the camps for it to be squandered on minor operations.

If it was not tinea rotting the crotch, it was scabies. The infestation started on the testicles, and it could spread to cover the whole body. The only part spared was the head. Alum on scabies was another scream-producer.

Then there was the oculo-oro-genital syndrome. It started with scrotal dermatitis, and went on to stomatitis, glossitis, erythema, conjunctivitis, optic atrophy, corneal ulcers, ulcers in the corner of the mouth, fissures in the tongue. Prisoners all over the Co-Prosperity Sphere came down with it. They looked vague and wasted, they walked slowly and uncertainly, spraddle-legged, and their jap-happies were sopping with blood.

What triggered this affliction was a vitamin deficiency. Deficiency diseases of all kinds were predictable: scurvy, pellagra, protein edema, beriberi. Beriberi among the prisoners at Bilibid in Manila had an irony to it. Bilibid was an old Spanish colonial jail, and at the turn of the twentieth century it was one of the main places in the world for experimental work on beriberi. In fact, prisoners in jails all over Asia had been used in beriberi experiments. Coolie laborers, too. Lunatics in asylums. And military units: Philippine Scouts, Dutch sailors in the East Indies, Japanese sailors on long cruises in the North Pacific. And, in different parts of the world early in the century, prisoners of war. Captive subjects all.

Well before the war the Japanese knew as much as anyone did about beriberi, in fact more than most. A deficiency of vitamin B_1 would bring it on, and within a diet high in carbohydrates—for example, a rice diet—extra B_1 was needed. The Japanese had it substantially beaten in their own armed forces. But when they turned their white prisoners into rice eaters, aside from the fact that they did not feed them enough rice, they did not feed them anything like enough extra B_1.

There were two main kinds of beriberi, wet and dry. The dry kind was terribly painful. The wet kind did horrible things to the look and feel and functioning of the whole body. It caused men to swell up with the fluids of edema. It turned them into blobs, with distended belly and huge puffy chest and the head resting on the shoulders, neck invisible. Their arms and legs were like bags of suet or baker's dough; poke a finger into a thigh and it would leave a dent. The doctors told them to sleep sitting up, or with their feet up, but either way the fluid drained back to the middle of their body, so the sack of their balls swelled like a water balloon. The longer they were deprived of B_1 the worse they filled up, until fluid began to accumulate in their lungs and suffocate them from inside. They were immobilized, puffed up and swallowing like frogs. Everyone could tell when they were going to die by the choked noise that came out of them—in the camp at Muntok on Sumatra it was called the beriberi song.

In the Japanese Army, the number of doctors and medical corps-men per unit was lower than in any of the Allied armies. In the prison camps, they did not even bother to allot prisoner medical officers and corpsmen in proportion to the number of men, and they did not care if the prisoner doctors had to go short of equipment, supplies, drugs, and food supplements. The medical specialty of Japanese doctors was standing upwind from the dead and dying, lecturing the prisoner doctors about how worthless they were: *Those who fails to reach objective in charge by lack of health and or spirit is regarded in Japanese Army as most shameful deed.*

Japanese military doctrine was that illness was a weakness of the spirit. *Health follows will.* No Japanese soldier was allowed to become attached to the thought of illness; he had to lie at attention on his sickbed. Prisoners were not allowed to get sick either. They had this beaten into them, to strengthen their weak spirits. Despite all, they got sick, by the scores of thousands. But very few ever saw a Japanese doctor. If they did sight a senior Japanese medical officer, it would be momentarily, as he was going through the motions of inspection in his white mask, rubber gloves, and rubber boots, making speed past the sick prisoners, with one of his corps-men preparing the way for him, spraying disinfectant everywhere he might tread or breathe.

Japanese medical enlisted men, though—the prisoners saw them every day, close up. For a Japanese soldier, being forced to deal with sick prisoners was the lowest of dirty work. Prisoners were foreigners, white men, and that made them dirty by definition. They were soldiers who had surrendered, which made them dirtier. In prison camp they obstinately refused to keep their bodies clean. Dirtier still. And because they were weak in spirit, they let themselves get shamefully sick—the ultimate in dirtiness. So disgusting to the Japanese that by preference they had Koreans working around the sick huts, the dirtiest of their own army doing the dirtiest of work in the dirtiest of places.

Koreans or Japanese, these medical enlisted men knew little

and cared less about the serious practice of medicine for the benefit of prisoners. They did not care whether sick prisoners lived or died. What they cared about was filling the day's quota for workers. It was rare to come across a knowledgeable and conscientious medical orderly. Overall they were as idle and corrupt as they were ignorant. They would make the prisoner doctors sign receipts for drugs written in Japanese, and then deliver short weight. The doctors would slip them welfare fund money to buy specific drugs on the black market, and they would come back with worthless patent medicines. They would tear up prescriptions rather than go to the trouble of filling them. They would put down false causes of death in their clinical records—to go by Japanese records, in the prison camps there was never a single death from malnutrition. Japanese medical enlisted men were a cause of death in themselves, a plague upon the prisoners.

After the workday came the evening meal, evening tenko, and then lights-out. Nights in the huts should have been a relief, but they were only more dirty primitiveness in the dark. The Japanese packed the prisoners in on their sleeping platforms, only a couple of feet per man. Always there were men tossing and turning in bad dreams, shouting out terrible things. Other men would be up all night with a condition called *burning feet, electric feet, happy feet*. This was yet another vitamin deficiency problem, so painful to the nerve ends that there was no rest from it. The sufferers moaned and soaked their feet in cold water, if they had water, if they had a bucket; or they stood for hours shifting their weight from foot to foot, wincing and muttering and cursing; or they shuffled up and down like zoo animals in a cage. If it was not happy feet shufflers disturbing sleep, it was dysenteries on the endless benjo run, stumbling in blind haste out of the huts, treading on bodies in the dark. And all night the rats went charging around on the floor, playing football with the mess kits, or up in the thatch roof, scuttling along the rafters, shitting down. *Never sleep with your mouth open.*

There were rats, and there were roaches, and an assortment of other vermin that most mid-twentieth-century white men had never seen and never expected to see, let alone cohabit with, skin to skin. For Harry Jeffries it was hard to take. He was a dandy, Hollywood Harry, fastidious about his grooming, and now here he was, coming back from the benjo with his legs black with fleas. Lie down on the sleeping mat, turn over, and the lice would run footraces to get out from underneath. And bedbugs—one night they would be biting a man so fiercely it was like having a perpetual blood transfusion taken, waking torment. The next night he would be so weary he could sleep through the hours of bites and never feel a thing. Turn all the bedding over every day, and so many bedbugs would pour out they looked like peppercorns spilled on the floor. Squash them and the stench was appalling—take a vote among prisoners, and of all the terrible smells of camp they would elect that one the worst. Some Dutchmen in a Java camp had a special chicken that ate bedbugs off bunks and mosquito nets; they used to rent her out by the quarter-hour, and they did nonstop business. But nothing could beat the bedbugs.

So men would shuffle out to morning tenko bitten all over, in a jap-happy or underpants polka-dotted with blood. Standing at Japanese attention, they would see vermin on the back of the neck of the man in front, lice trooping down from his hairline and disappearing into his shirt. Tenko was not the time for lice picking; that would bring on a beating. In the chow line, though, or waiting to go out on work detail, prisoners would groom each other, sociably, like monkeys. Everybody did it. But as one American said, he just could not be nonchalant talking with people picking bedbugs off his jacket.

::

PRISON camp time was slave-labor time. Time off was rare and precious. It was called *yasume,* the same word as for standing at ease; but even on a yasume day the Japanese could choose to make the prisoners improve their close-order drill, or do camp fatigue work. With whatever yasume was left, if any, they had to make time to wash their clothes, turn over their bedding for bugs, take care of their sick friends. After the miserable evening meal, they could check their butt tin to see if they had the rollings of a skinny smoke, then sit down and shuffle the cards, or imagine some higher grade of entertainment, like a stage show.

Out in the jungle there would be no stage, perhaps just a giant anthill with the audience squatting around the base, no stage lights, just a big fire in the night, and the boniest prisoner, singing solo in a G-string, to the melody of a devotional song: *There's fuck all left of me, Of what there used to be.*

The big camps were more cultured, and the British most sophisticated of all. Slug Wright and the other Americans who were with the British at Bicycle Camp in Batavia and Changi in Singapore were amazed at what they came up with, everything from variety shows to grand opera with orchestral accompaniment, costumes put together out of nothing, and wonderful stage effects, sets decorated with paints made in camp, red from powdered brick, beautiful greens, yellows, and browns from bullock and buffalo dung.

And here was a strange thing—not unique to the British, but they were the ones who raised it to the highest art—male prisoners taking female parts. In prison camp, to be able to feast the eyes on something that looked like a woman was a powerful thing. And complicated. Back in the real world, the touring entertainment companies of the armed services featured soldier boys in drag; and in prison camp the female impersonators were the stars of the show. Not the ones who left their army boots on and made sure their false tits looked false, those were comedians. It was the others, the attractive young men who could look like attractive young women. They drew wolf whistles, stage-door Johnnies, even Japanese guards bringing gifts, cigarettes, candy, perfumed soap.

No one had numbers for homosexuals in the service. The official figure everywhere was zero, which of course was not to be believed. Naturally each nationality said the other nationalities had the most. In prison camp, however many or however few homosexuals there might have been, they were on the same ration scale as heterosexuals, which meant next to zero possibility of energetic activity for anyone. But there were wistful longings, heterosexual, homosexual, or just confused by captivity. Everyone liked looking at the stage ladies.

Mosquito-net gowns, mercurochrome wigs, breasts of coconut shell or the fruit of the pomelo—it did not do to look too closely. In the footlights the chorus girls were glamorous, but there were times when they danced with their legs all over scabies, and other times when the female star could not go on because he was down with Changi balls.

Every camp was a branch of what the prisoners called the University of the Far East, with compulsory classes in life and death. In the bigger camps, the prisoners went in for education of their own choosing, up to the limits of what the Japanese allowed. At Cabanatuan there were classes in Greek philosophy, wine tasting, astrology, banking, beekeeping, cheese making, and languages (German, Russian, Spanish, Tagalog, as long as there were also classes in the Japanese language). Changi at its high point had two institutions of British learning, 18th Division University and Southern Area University, with books from the library of Raffles College in Singapore, and classes in agriculture, mathematics, engineering, law, medicine, science, business, history, French, German, Dutch, Spanish, Italian, and Malay. Hundreds of men took elementary reading and writing. An Australian officer even had some Australian enlisted men improving their Australian vowel sounds—hairy, uncouth Diggers sitting on logs, chorusing in round tones, *How now brown cow.*

The early months in the big camps were the best for education, before work forces were drafted away, and before hunger and disease drained energy out of the body and took the edge off the mind.

After the universities faded, or in places where they never existed—meaning most places—individual prisoners had to keep trying to keep their minds active and functioning. It was important; it was a way of staying human.

They played mental games: backgammon, acey-deucey, all kinds of card games, chess or checkers on a board drawn in charcoal on the back of a khaki shirt, with pieces made out of bark. Harry Jeffries played poker every minute he could find someone to go up against him. Not that he was in it for the sake of his humanness; he was in business, second-carding from his own deck. Others made decks out of pages from magazines or book jackets, all fifty-two cards differentiated by color and suit. Poker players took up bridge; bridge players took up poker, more of the prisoner's education in the customs of other cultures.

They took up arts and crafts. In the six months Slug Wright was on Java, the best six months of the 131st's time as prisoners, Bicycle Camp turned out enough for an exhibition: jewelry made of glass and bone and Bakelite plastic, model ships and airplanes, chessboards, inlaid coins, leatherwork, patent rat and mouse traps, and cigarette-rolling machines. Jack Kenner of F Battery scrounged a saw, a pocket knife, and a bit of broken glass that made a good carpenter's plane, and built a car engine out of wood, about sixteen inches long, a straight four-cylinder. Preston Stone, also of F Battery, had the ambition to go up a step in horsepower and class, to a V-8 in teak, but he overestimated his yasume, and never finished it.

Any number of POWs designed themselves a dream home in

their head. They would give mature consideration to the rear-view prospect, and whether the living room should be finished in knotty pine, then reconsider and start over—they could keep it up forever. A man the Japanese threw into solitary brought in consulting architects in his mind, built his house, chose the wallpaper, polished the floors, put down rugs and furniture, moved in, ate the breakfast of his choice, and enjoyed the running water in his bathroom, for months, all in a filthy black hole.

An Australian who watched this kind of thing going on all around him decided that the most contented POW was the one who could build himself the most perfect microcosm for mental escape and disappear most effectively within it.

Forrest Knox was not about to disappear into a mental escape microcosm. He was curious about everything—including tattoos. Of course he was too smart to get himself tattooed, but in camp he educated himself on the subject, mostly by talking with sailors and marines, to the point where he could tell where a tattoo had been done. Different places had different styles. There was stateside east, and stateside west, mainly San Diego, around the navy base. And there were different levels of art. To Forrest's eye, India had poor design and poor color. Hotel Street in Honolulu was good. Manila, too. And for amazing all-over skins, the China coast. He came to be a connoisseur; he could tell when the needle artist was sloughing off—for example, the naked lady on the biceps, with huge tits but short, wizened-looking legs.

Tattooing was a big thing among the Japanese in their home islands—certain kinds of Japanese anyway, *geisha* girls and criminals—so the camp guards were primed to take an interest. Where Forrest's brother Henry wound up, there happened to be a Japanese doctor, and whenever he came across a prisoner with a tattoo he made a color copy on paper. In some camps, if the Japanese sighted an Englishman with a Union Jack tattoo they would threaten to cut it off him. But it all depended. One Englishman had the royal coat of arms on his chest, the Battle of Trafalgar on his back, the rest of him covered in dancing girls and snakes; and when high Japanese officials came around, the commandant would call him to headquarters and give him extra food for exhibiting himself.

Then there was the Englishman with an entire soccer team on his chest, done from a photograph, sitting in their striped jerseys, arms folded, names printed underneath. The trouble was, in camp he lost so much weight that his skin went loose, and the team went all saggy and scrunched, to the point where it was impossible to read their names anymore.

Nothing recharged a prisoner's mind like the thought of contact with home, the chance to send a message. The opportunity came randomly, at long intervals. The standard message was a printed card, preworded in English, along these lines: 1. *I am interned at . . .* 2. *My health is—excellent; good; fair; poor.* 3. *I am—injured; sick in hospital; under treatment; not under treatment.* 4. *I am—improving; not improving; better; well.* Finally: *Please see that . . .* with space for an individual message, ten words, or twenty-five, or in the de luxe version, fifty. Circling the less sunny options did not improve a man's chance that the Japanese would forward his card.

Outgoing messages from the Asian camps might eventually turn up on the other side of the world, via proper channels. Or they might not. The Japanese might take it into their heads to drop sacks of cards from the air into enemy territory, with a polite note expressing hope that letters would be delivered. Or whole batches of cards might never leave camp. A prisoner might come across them in a crate being used as stuffing to protect bottles of Japanese beer.

Incoming mail came the long way: Letters from the United States went across the Atlantic to Europe, then to Teheran in Persia, then north into the Soviet Union, east by the trans-Siberian railroad to the Asian coast of Russia, and from the port of Nakhodka near Vladivostok to Tokyo. And from there, sooner or later, out into the Co-Prosperity Sphere, and by one means or another, at one time or another, some percentage of them, into the camps. Perhaps.

Every prisoner was hungry for letters. Mail was special, rare, the sweetness of home. It was quan for the mind and the soul. A man with just one letter would read it over and over. Some men hid their letters, hoarded them for solitary pleasure, like condensed milk. A man who got no mail would read surreptitiously over someone else's shoulder, a guilty pleasure. True generosity was sharing mail. But not many prisoners would allow a letter out of their sight—letters were paper and paper got smoked.

The Japanese permitted a few prisoners to send a spoken radio message. The messages were recorded onto disks, with an English-speaking Japanese sitting by the microphone to cut the prisoner off if he said the wrong thing, and sometimes a guard with a gun. Then the approved disks were played over the Japanese shortwave propaganda stations.

The message senders were chosen by lot, and meanly—one prisoner calculated that if the Japanese kept to their monthly rate, it would take twenty-four years to get through every man in camp.

There were nicotine addicts who would sell their message chance for cigarettes. Oklahoma Atkinson bought a chance that way. He spoke his message in plain English but at the same time in code. He wanted his father to know he was the same weight as Jimmie—Jimmie Sue being his sister, who weighed sixty pounds less than Oklahoma used to. He said that when he got home they would kill the fatted calf. In the meantime, prison camp was just like living in the Buford Hotel—Buford being the name of the sheriff, the Buford Hotel being the jail.

Oklahoma's message got through, by way of Harry Jeffries's mother. All over the world the families of prisoners were sitting down to shortwave receivers, tuning in on the longest of long shots, to hear the living voice of their missing man far away; and they took on the duty of copying down every name and home address they heard, then writing or phoning to make sure the messages were received. Harry's mother knew Oklahoma's name from Harry's San Francisco days, and she got in touch with Oklahoma's father. So did eighty-three other people listening to the voices of prisoners in the night.

As much as anyone on earth, the prisoners needed to know how the war was going. To hear the guards talk, it was *Washington boomboom! London boomboom! Sydney boomboom!* It did not matter what imaginary place a prisoner named, it was *boomboom.*

Secret radios were the answer. Every work detail was on the lookout for radio parts—resistors, capacitors, transformers, valves, flashlight batteries and car batteries for power, dynamos, magnetos scavenged from Japanese trucks, telephone earpieces, bits of gear from crashed planes. Copper wire for coils came into camp wound around waists; flashlight batteries in bamboo yoyo poles or walking sticks for lame men; valves in false hat crowns or false-bottomed canteens or thermos flasks; bigger parts in Red Cross boxes; complete sets in wagonloads of vegetables. At Changi a Highlander crotched in a whole radio under his kilt.

Hand-built receivers by the number were sealed into the bottom half of canteens, the top half full of water. There were radios in false-bottomed chairs and tables and bed frames. On Java there was a set made to look like a set of surgical instruments, and another that walked around inside a one-legged American's tin leg. At Bicycle Camp in Batavia, an Australian built a succession of sets, smaller and smaller as he went along. The first one he kept in a tin trunk in a wooden box buried in a camp garden with a removable flower bed on top. The second was in a false-bottomed kerosene can; the third, in the seat of a stool; the fourth, in a hollowed-out book; and the fifth, in a pair of wooden clogs, transformer in one, receiver in the other at the toe, earphones at the heel. At Changi a man built a set into the head of a broom; he led the power and the aerial in through the bristles, tuned it with a screwdriver, and listened through a stethoscope.

There were bigger sets in hut walls behind loose boards. There was a set in a slit trench in a box waterproofed with tar scraped off the road by a one-armed prisoner. There was a set in a little cavern dug under a quartermaster store, the operators squeezing in at news time and a man on top keeping watch with a bottle of booze, *arak*, to offer to any Japanese guard who happened by. There were sets hidden behind cookhouse stoves, in sacks of rice, or in the big rice cookers. There were sets in the benjo, hanging down on a rope over the trench, the operators squatting like any other dysentery, but with an earphone.

For an operator there was nothing like the excitement of news time, lookouts in place, aerial hooked up, earphones on, power on just before the hour, fine-tuning through the shortwave static, to bring in Chungking, or All-India Radio from New Delhi, or Sydney, or the BBC direct from London. Tokyo Rose was another option, and some Americans rated her as offering better news value than William Winter on KGEI, San Francisco.

Who should get to hear the news, when, and in what form? The perpetual worry was that the Japanese would be able to pick up signs around camp that the prisoners were getting war news from outside—extra misery at bad news, waves of joy at good, even some fool (and every camp had them) stupid enough to go around baiting the guards with a military fact that did not jibe with Japanese propaganda. And always there was the possibility of the Japanese planting informers, especially in camps with Eurasian-Dutch prisoners, men with brown skins and alien ways of speaking and thinking.

The British, especially in the big camp at Changi in Singapore, had the most complete answers to security questions. Their doctrine was, first, to keep all the news to themselves—they were not even sure how reliable the Australians and Americans were, let alone the Dutch, let alone the Eurasian Dutch. And second, even among the British, to limit direct access to news to the officer class, letting it out in measured quantities, over time, through cells or news trees, so as not to frighten the Japanese horses.

A good case could be made for the British way. The case against it was a good one too—it was yet another display of rank and its privileges.

Radio officers were against unauthorized operators. They called them pirates. But ordering pirate radios out of existence did not get rid of them. They just went deeper underground. Pirates were in double jeopardy; they had to keep their sets secret from the official radio officers as well as from the Japanese. So there were men who never told anyone—not even the men who slept beside them—that they were operating a crystal set.

The Japanese military police, the kempeitai, were always after radios. Their worst suspicion, their deepest hatred, was of subversion, sabotage, uprisings, based on information secretly passing this way and that, with radio reception and transmission at the heart of the conspiracy. Whenever they came upon evidence of a radio, or just the suspicion of one, they would torture, interrogate to the death, and execute. They did it everywhere, to POWs, internees, and local civilians. In Singapore, fifty-seven internees were arrested and held for months, fifteen of them tortured to death. In Hong Kong, thirty-two men and one woman were executed. At Rabaul on New Britain, a whole family was executed. In Saigon, fifteen Chinese were executed. At Palembang on Sumatra, a radio got some white doctors and nurses tortured; one doctor had his head chopped off, and hundreds of natives were killed.

Yet the news kept coming in—about Europe, the Russian front, Burma—and it was by no means all bad, nothing like the awfulness of the first months of 1942.

News was like the food ration. There was never enough of it, for quantity, quality, or variety. So the prisoners filled up their emptiness with rumors.

The busiest place for generating and spreading rumors was the latrine. At Changi the word *borehole* meant both latrine and rumor. At Davao there were three enormous latrines, as big as Hindu temples, and someone painted letters on them, KGEI, the San Francisco station of William Winter, famous for spreading shit on shortwave.

A man could hear a rumor at one end of camp, walk to the

other, and it would be there ahead of him. Some men deliberately started rumors for sport. F Battery of the 131st had two doing that, Jennings Pitts and Roy Jordan; they were known as Rumor and Rumor Junior. At Cabanatuan the daily greeting was *What are the rumors?* An army officer kept a cumulative list that rose to two thousand, without running into a word of truth.

There were rumors for every taste and for all occasions. The pope had moved to Florida and was taking a special interest in POWs. Tōjō was in London. Hitler had been assassinated. The Americans had sunk the Japanese fleet. Then they sank it again. The *Queen Mary* had been sunk, or else Queen Mary was dead. Deanna Durbin was dead. Miss Topeka was Miss Universe. Good prisoners were going to be allowed to have their wives and children join them and farm peacefully. All prisoners were going to be sterile from malnutrition. The Russians were in Greece—an Englishman spent a whole day tracking this one to the source, it was shouted out by someone going by on a truck, and actually it was *Rations are increased,* and of course that was empty noise. The Americans had retaken an island in the Pacific, and who should they find living there but Amelia Earhart and her copilot, Fred Noonan, making babies. But no, Amelia Earhart was really Tokyo Rose.

The most powerful and persistent rumor was about going home. The prisoners had become an embarrassment, the Japanese did not have enough food for them, they were going to repatriate them all. No, only the blind and limbless. No, only the medical officers. The point of exchange was going to be Lourenço Marques on Mozambique. No, Ecuador, the United States was transferring ships to Ecuadoran registry. No, it was Manila, an exchange ship was there already, at Pier 7, being painted white ready for the voyage home, direct to the United States.

And back home, every prisoner had a new car waiting for him in the garage, free. Fords. No, Fords for enlisted men, for NCOs a Mercury, for officers a Lincoln. Plus, free to everyone, a house and land, a Frigidaire, a General Electric radio, a bicycle, a Mix-master, a railroad pass, a transcontinental trip by Greyhound bus, a month in a hotel in Pennsylvania, three months in a hotel in Florida, free magazine subscriptions, a year of Budweiser beer, five years of Acme beer, cigarettes for life.

The Australians would be getting a square mile of land. They were going to be swapped for bales of Australian wool. No, seventeen thousand Australians for fourteen thousand Japanese. With the Americans it was one American to fifty Japanese. Or else US$10,000 per American. Rumor had it that a fund of $10 million was available. Rumor had it that the reason why the exchange never seemed to come any closer was that the Japanese kept raising the rates.

A few thousand white civilians did get sent home by ship, exchanged for Japanese civilians marooned in the West. This was a highly political exercise, and very limited. Among the tens of thousands of white internees stuck in Asia the exchange ships were known as *Wangle Marus*. In the Philippines some loose women managed to wangle themselves on board with one shipment. There were rumors about how they made their way to the head of the line, and the respectable women left behind called that ship the *Puta Maru*. In a women's camp on Java the most wonderful rumor was that a volcano had erupted, the whole island had broken in two, and the part the women were on was drifting toward Australia.

As for repatriating military prisoners—even the sick, disabled, or untreatable, as provided for in the Geneva convention—the Japanese never gave an inch. So in prison camp, from beginning to end, all the repatriation rumors amounted to nothing more than a South Sea bubble.

Anywhere from six to nine months into captivity—the date varied between camps—each prisoner got a permanent number. The Japanese had finally got around to making them official prisoners of war, *horyo*.

Horyo numbers were recorded against names at the commandant's office. In some camps each man had a wooden tag with his number on it, painted, stenciled, or branded. If he left his hut to go to the benjo, he had to move his tag from one nail on the wall to another, and when he came back he had to move it back. The guards knew where he was by his number; and which prisoner he was, by the matching number on his jacket. Every POW had to learn his horyo number in Japanese. No one ever forgot it. The guards called him by that number, in Japanese. To them he was not a white man with a white man's name, not even a human being; he was a thing with a Japanese number.

Man by man, horyo by horyo, the POWs had to face the fact that they had not the faintest idea how long they were going to be captives. At least a common convict knew when his sentence would be up; he could count the days, do the arithmetic that connected him with the free world. But POWs of the Japanese had to scratch their days on the prison wall one at a time, and for all they knew the scratches would add up to all the days of their lives.

An English doctor named Cyril Vardy kept a diary, the way any number of prisoners did, to have a secret private part of his life where he could still be a person. Vardy used to write about the sweet things he missed from life in the real world—the sound of a distant train, ice tinkling in a glass, a bath being run, the sight of a woman putting on her makeup, the swish of a dress, a waft of perfume. At about the time he became a horyo he made an entry that read in its entirety: *Did nothing all day except be a prisoner.*

::

FROM the moment they were taken, all prisoners were united against the Japanese, in the fundamental brotherhood of captives against captors.

Early on in the camps, a higher sort of unity was talked about, a brotherhood of man among POWs. Sometimes it sounded like socialism, sometimes like New Testament Christianity.

It was a noble vision, but a prisoner brotherhood of man had two strikes against it from the start. First, prisoners of one nationality could never bring themselves to agree that all prisoners of all other nationalities were truly their brothers. Second, within any given nationality, the officers as a high caste could never bring themselves to concede that the low caste of enlisted men deserved to be equal to them in brotherhood; they were sure God intended officers to be more equal. So, on the large scale, all for one and one for all did not work all the time; in fact, hardly any of the time.

Harry Jeffries and Oklahoma Atkinson were not subscribers to any doctrine of human brotherhood. They way they saw things, they had to look out for themselves, and not just against the Japanese but against every other POW. There were eyes everywhere, prisoners' eyes like rats' eyes, sharp and cunning—the others were rats looking to live off them. The only way to survive was to be the sharpest and the most cunning of all. Their doctrine boiled down to one line: *The strong beat the weak and the smart beat the strong.*

Harry was smarter than Oklahoma, Oklahoma was stronger than Harry, and both were smarter and stronger than most. And they both felt the same way about life, which was why they had clicked originally, back in San Francisco. They recognized themselves in one another. Each of them, and the two of them together, believed they owed the world nothing; the world owed them. In camp they were a tribe of two against the world.

Between universal brotherhood and Harry and Oklahoma against the world stood POW tribes of many different sizes, shapes, and styles.

The Geneva convention recognized nations as tribes. POWs were supposed to be assembled in camps by nationality, each nationality separate from the others. The Japanese observed that part of the convention as well as they did the rest. At the same time, they did not want their prisoners drawing sustenance from nationality. They would not so much as let POWs sing their national anthems. So British prisoners at church service in Hong Kong used to stand, looking as if they were praying, for the length of a silent "God Save the King." Australian POWs religiously observed their national day, Anzac Day, April 25, 1915, dating from World War I, when Australian troops were blooded in battle. Any number of American prisoners kept a Stars and Stripes hidden from the Japanese. Patriotism was strong all the way to the death—when the Japanese tied a Dutchman to a stake for bayoneting, or beat him to his knees to chop his head off, the last words he shouted were *Leve de koningin!* Long live the queen!

Within the nation, another natural basis for brotherhood was branch of service, then regiment or battalion. United States Marines in POW camps were still of the brotherhood of the Corps. Dutchmen from the Indies were soldiers of their queen, serving her in KNIL. The same went for men from the historic British named regiments, like the Northumberland Fusiliers, who tried in captivity to wear a red and white flower every year on St. George's Day, the way they had done with roses for a century and a half. Australian units were often raised from a particular district. Boys who grew up together joined the army together, fought together, were captured together, and in POW camp they tried, against whatever Japanese odds, to stay together. That was just as true, for the same reasons, with an American unit like Forrest Knox's— Company A of the 192nd Tank Battalion was a hundred men from Janesville, Wisconsin.

And it was true for Slug Wright's unit, the 2nd Battalion of the 131st Field Artillery, a brother-in-law outfit from Texas. They were not one hundred percent pure state-of-origin Texans. Just before they were shipped overseas, some late additions from other parts of the country were transferred in, *Damyankees*. The *Houston* men with the 131st were in a strange position; their ship was named for a Texas city, and they were with the Texas tribe, but not necessarily of it. Otto Schwarz was from New Jersey; he and three others like him were a little alien subtribe that the Texans called the Dead End Kids. But essentially the 131st was a Texas tribe. In camp they talked Texas day and night, hometown talk, how long to the minute it took in a souped-up V-8 from Decatur or Wichita Falls or Lubbock or Jacksboro to Camp Bowie, every side road and back track, where to turn and go down to get to somebody's house, old John Farley's barn, everybody's girlfriend and her sister, women and watermelons, the world according to Texas.

A Texan was likely to be of the opinion that he did not need anyone for his tribe and his subtribe except more Texans. For most other prisoners, though, it felt good to be able to hook up with different kinds of men for different occasions and purposes. It helped break the terrible monotony of being stuck in the sewer of the world, under duress, locked into a miserable life in one hut with one everlasting set of bodies, and not so much as a three-day pass until liberation or doomsday, whichever might come first.

Especially in the big camps, with thousands of men from any number of units jumbled together, there were all kinds of subtribes. In the biggest of the American camps, Cabanatuan, they formed up by point of origin (Missourians or South Carolinians) or point of origin plus occupational specialty (former Ohio National Guard instructors) or a shared interest (miniature golfers, members of the Carabao Country Club, a glee club, a vocal quartet). There were religious subtribes, Catholic and Protestant, and Mormons were particularly strong. The Jews had no synagogue and no rabbi, but one of the carabao drivers, Aaron Kliatchko, a Russian Jew with a big beard and a voice like a cantor, did the funeral wailing when a Jew died. There were Knights of Columbus, Knights of Pythias, Kiwanis, and Elks from all over the place—Manila, Olongapo, Shanghai, Panama. And, before the days of the big drafts for work details, as many as three hundred Masons, including one of the chaplains and a civilian who used to manage the Manila Hotel. They met every week, and they were able to connect secretly with Masons in Manila and get things smuggled into camp for needy brothers, money and medicine and food.

In the life of every subtribe, food was a major item, almost a sacrament. The Cabanatuan Combine was a little group of officers who were writing a secret book about the camp. One of them, looking forward to his birthday, saved up to buy a duck, special quan to share with the combine. It would have been a great tribal occasion, only the duck died. POW camp ducks were malnourished, too. Still, it was the thought that counted.

On the other side of the ledger, food could cause tribal wars, raids, and retaliations. Bill Delich and three of his friends at Cabanatuan had not eaten cake since before the war. They volunteered for extra work, wood detail, fatigue, anything to make enough money to buy the fixings, including a pineapple. It took them days. When they had everything together, they held off eating rice for another two days, drew their rations raw, scrounged a bottle and a board and ground the grains into flour. It took them hours. They were a little subtribe deep in the rituals of quan. They dropped everything off at the central kitchen for cooking. But when they came back to pick up their cake, all they found was a miserable thing made of nothing but rice flour, no pineapple, and *small,* only about eight by six inches by a half inch deep. One of the cooks told them a chaplain had come by and claimed a pineapple cake. He named the chaplain. Delich's tribe knew him by sight, a carp-faced individual. They tracked him down in the chaplains' quarters and found him and his tribe, officers and men of God, with a four-inch square of pineapple cake and crumbs on their lips. The carp-face had the gall to say he would let them have what was left, *out of Christian charity.* It took them a month to get even. They kept their eye on the carp-face. Finally they spotted him on his way to the cookhouse with four ducks. They waited till the ducks were ready, then talked the cook out of them, ate them, and threw the pan and the bones in the benjo; and forever after that when they saw the carp-face, they quacked at him.

A stolen pineapple cake, a birthday duck that died, shared quan that worked out just right, tribes and subtribes building up their history around food—this kind of thing was central to the annals of the camps. And day by day, just the act of eating together was humanly nourishing. All over the Co-Prosperity Sphere, at feeding time twenty or thirty or fifty men would pack in under the roof of a single hut; and within that aggregation little regular eating groups formed—three, four, or half a dozen men to a cluster— each with its own little tribal territory.

* * *

Charley Pryor and Lloyd Willey were two *Houston* marines, in camp on Java with Slug Wright and the 131st. They had come out of the sinking with next to nothing, not even mess kits. Along the road to Bicycle Camp they picked up a helmet, and that was what they ate out of. They went through the chow line together and had both their rations dealt into the helmet. Pryor had a little demitasse spoon. Willey made a spoon out of bamboo, twice as big. Their agreement was that Pryor would get two spoonfuls to Willey's one, and they kept their agreement. Close feeding and close living, mutual sustenance. But, at that, not as close and mutual as two men, civilians, caught on Bataan and dumped down among the military prisoners at Cabanatuan: They were old, they had none of their own teeth, and the misfortunes of war had left them with only one set of uppers and lowers between the two of them, so one would eat, wash the dentures, and pass them to the other.

To be a loner, a man without a tribe or a subtribe, meant long odds against surviving. To come across a loner who looked certain to survive was the longest of long shots. Forrest Knox only once spotted one, an amazing man who never seemed to need anything from anyone, not help, not conversation, not even quiet company, and yet he was doing fine. Forrest was curious about him, as he was about everything. He started putting himself unobtrusively in the man's way, with the thought that finally the man would speak. He did. He turned out to be a Basque from northern Idaho, Wild Horse Heaven. He was a sheepherder; he had logged thousands of hours on his own before his first hour of prison camp. When Forrest asked him his secret, this is what he said, and all he ever said: *My father taught me how to make a fire. And how to make a fire that doesn't make any smoke.*

By Forrest's observation, perhaps one man in 200 or 300 was a loner. And as time went on, fewer still—Forrest figured the odds against a loner surviving to be at least 500 to 1.

Forrest and the others in Company A, everybody in F Battery of the 131st, and Harry Jeffries and Oklahoma Atkinson in their own way—in fact prisoners everywhere—were strong believers in the doctrine of a durable little subtribe. Preferably it would exist within a larger tribe that was also durable. But if push came to shove, and with the Japanese it was bound to, they could struggle along without the larger tribe as long as the subtribe held together.

As for how subtribes formed, it might start with an order from the Japanese—for example, in some camps it was forbidden for more than three or four or five men to congregate. Or it might start on work detail, with two men the same height on either end of a long yoyo pole; or two on either end of a stretcher, carrying the dead to be buried; or three on a crosscut saw, trading off the cutting and carrying; or three smokers with only one cigarette to share, and a fourth, a nonsmoker, who could be trusted to hold it for them until work break.

Another basic starting place was the sleeping arrangement. A man had to be able to get on with the men who slept either side of him, or at least be able to tolerate them, their habits, the state of their mind and soul and the way they expressed it, and the sounds and smells of their bodies, because they were going to be crammed together night after night, maybe for years.

At Bicycle Camp, the setup of the old Dutch barracks practically guaranteed that the standard number would be four: There were four 131st or *Houston* men to a two-man cubicle. In another camp, on Celebes, where the Japanese were as stingy with space in the huts as they were with food, three big white bodies had to fit between the five-foot gaps in the duckboards.

By chance those duckboards and cubicles served a purpose, because it turned out that the best size for a subtribe was between three and six. With more than six there was a tendency to split up (although at one time or another Forrest Knox was in groups bigger than six that did well). Some Australians thought five might be too many: A scrounged can of food split five ways was slicing things too thin. At the low end, fewer than three did not give enough depth, or backup. Harry Jeffries and Oklahoma Atkinson were a team of two, and twos had their strengths; but there were risks as well. The best number was probably four. If one man was sick (and one man sick out of four was virtually guaranteed), the three others could look after him. If the Japanese kicked the sick man out onto work detail, the others could cover for him on the job, meet his labor quota. If he was down so far that the Japanese gave him sick hut time, meaning that his ration would be cut, the three could pool their food so that he would have a bit extra, try to scrounge him a duck egg, take turns visiting him, wash his clothes, look after his belongings back in the sleeping hut, and do all of the hundred little things that went into the one big project of keeping him alive. And when the sick man was well again and any of the others fell ill, he would do the same for them. Up to the power of four, all for one and one for all could be relied on, and in a Japanese prison camp that was a blessing beyond words.

Everywhere, work detail by work detail, hut by hut, little clusters of men were finding ways to hold on to humanity, at whatever cost, together, day by day, month by month, for as long as it took. An Australian doctor went to the heart of it in one sentence: *There's quite a lot of God in the ordinary bloke.* This was the true brotherhood of the camps, and in it was the meaning of life.

III

LEARNING ON THE JOB

OKLAHOMA ATKINSON AND HARRY JEFFRIES WERE HORYO 193 and horyo 194, two among twelve hundred American prisoners inside the electric fence at the Shanghai War Prisoners Camp at Woosung.

They had come off the *Nitta Maru,* from Wake, out of the tropics in their ragbag hot-weather clothes, straight into the Chinese winter. An icy blast blew out of Siberia, chilling the soul, shriveling the scrotum. The guards were not about to fire up the Japanese bath, the *furo,* just so white prisoners could have hot water. All they were allowed was cold-water wash racks, with never a sliver of soap. The barracks had electric light, but no heat. Men would stand shivering, reaching their hands as close as they could to the bulb for the warmth, twenty-five watts at fifteen degrees below. The speedy scroungers came up with bits of unburned coal from the Japanese ash rakings, and scraps of sheet metal and old cans, to make little stoves. Stoves made little tribes, three or four men huddled close, with a blanket over their heads, breathing in the fumes. Of course the Japanese had regulations against stoves. The prisoners cut trapdoors in the floor, so that if a guard made enough noise coming, they had time to lower the stove out of sight onto the freezing ground underneath, risking a burn to save a beating. After lights out the only heat was body heat, men sleeping as close as they could under the worthless Japanese blankets, bundling together; that made little tribes, too.

The Wake marines and the CPNAB contractors were not the only Americans in camp. There were some North China marines as well, legation guards who had surrendered at Tientsin and been brought to Woosung. The Wake senior officer was J.P.S. Devereux, a major. The Tientsin marines had a major too, Luther Brown. Devereux and Brown wanted military discipline, of course. Devereux had his Wake enlisted men saluting their own officers, and the Tientsin officers too, for military courtesy. And he had his men out exercising—J.P.S. bound and determined to maintain discipline even at the cost of burning precious calories in the cold. Luther Brown went by the book, too. The marines called him Handbook Brown. The contractors called him Pork Chop Brown, for the extra officer's rations he was always eating. Brown tried to make the contractors march like marines, but that was never going to happen. Just as the marine noncom was set to shout, *Right step!* some contractor in the ranks would shout it ahead of him and ruin everything. That was Oklahoma's invention. The contractors were forever taking potshots at Brown and his dignity. He had the perfect career officer's look, striding out clean-scrubbed, with his Ronald Colman leading-man moustache, dressed in the full North China, greens and a polished Sam Browne belt. He would be up at the far end of the compound, they could pick him at a distance by the shiny shoes, and they would chant so he could hear: *What color is horseshit? Brown!*

Brown never could get the contractors to behave like marines. Neither could Devereux. Their fallback position—and for two marine majors this amounted to surrender—was to discourage their men from mixing with the civilians.

In the contractors' barracks, discipline was supposed to be in the hands of section leaders and barracks adjutants, on up to some sort of civilian camp head office, at the level of marine headquarters. But even if the barracks bosses were foremen or office managers from Wake, they did not have the boot and the bayonet. So as far as Harry and Oklahoma were concerned, it was open season; they were going to do whatever they could get away with.

The Woosung POWs were on short rations: a scoop of rice three times a day, or cracked wheat for breakfast, no sugar or salt to go with it but plenty of weevils. Plus scraps of vegetable. Plus something liquid that did not deserve the name of soup—Tōjō Water, they called it, or Whangpoo, after the filthy river running down to Shanghai.

Harry and Oklahoma wangled themselves onto a detail unloading bread—at least a Japanese version of bread: it had wood fiber and sawdust in it, and when it was toasted it burst into flame. They had another contractor with them, John Cowalski, known to them from the fighting on Wake. Quietly they set some loaves by a window in the storeroom, and later they broke the glass and reached through. They were stealing from their own kind, but that did not stop them. They lifted six little loaves each. Harry and Oklahoma each took three to eat in the benjo. The rest they hid in the rafters. Another prisoner spotted them. He was going to turn them in, and Oklahoma had to fight him to persuade him to change his mind. When they came back for the rest of their loaves, everything was gone; some other prisoner, maybe the one Oklahoma fought and beat, had sniffed them out.

Cowalski got caught eating too. Someone ratted on him to his barracks leader, who was supposed to act as a kind of sheriff with a kangaroo court. When this sheriff came to take Cowalski to be tried, Cowalski knocked him down and went out the window, and that was the end of the sheriff system in Cowalski's section.

Cowalski was not a camp bull, but he would not take anything from anyone. Oklahoma and Harry were not camp bulls, either. They had no ambition to be. Oklahoma would fight anyone who needed fighting. But being a bull for the sake of being a bull—that might be strong, but it was not necessarily smart.

Anyway, they had a territory of their own. They commandeered the food serving table in their section, for gambling. Anybody who wanted the table for a game had to ask them. Anybody who wanted to use their cards paid a percentage. No one awarded them the table rights, they took them, and anyone who wanted to take them away would have to fight Oklahoma.

They set the house rules. If a man bet a dollar and won, give him a dollar. If he bet a cigarette and won, give him a dollar and keep the cigarette. If he bet a cigarette and lost, keep the cigarette. One dollar was the rate for a Chinese or Japanese cigarette. Top-quality American smokes like Luckies went for three dollars, Chesterfields and Old Golds somewhat less, Raleighs the lowest.

The Japanese allowed card playing, but not for money. So Oklahoma always had a man keeping watch, paid with a cigarette to give a shout when he saw the guards coming: *Air the blankets!* One night the lookout was asleep at the switch, and the guards caught Oklahoma with cards, cigarettes, and money in plain sight on the table. The other players scattered like quail, but Oklahoma was trapped. He managed to scoop up most of the bills and cigarettes, and along the way to the guardhouse he dropped them. If Harry could not get to them, the others would pick them up. Oklahoma would lose some for sure, but maybe get some back, and that was better than losing everything to the guards.

In the guardhouse they beat on him. He turned over a five-dollar bill he had taken out of the game because it was torn. They knew he was worth more, and they tried to beat it out of him, but that was all he had on him, and anyway they hit like girls, roundarm.

Then they stood him to attention outside the guardhouse and left him for hours. He was freezing. This one night of all nights he was not wearing his greatcoat in the barracks; it was crawling with lice, he was sick of it, and he had his stove stoked up. Jess Bowers came by, another contractor, a small man with a big red beard. Bowers was in trouble himself. He had stolen some rice and cooked it in a little can with a handle. He would reach down into the can and secretly pinch up a bit into his mouth, but a few grains got stuck in his beard, and the guards saw. They hung the can on his neck and made him walk around beating on it and calling out *Rice thief,* as if this would embarrass him. Bowers was smoking, which was against the rules for rice thieves, but he had his greatcoat on, sizes too big for him, and he had his cigarette hidden up the sleeve, with smoke coming out of the cuff. When he was through with his punishment and the guards said he could go inside, he lent Oklahoma his greatcoat. If it was far too big for Bowers, it was far too small for Oklahoma. Still, it was something.

He was shivering, but no money was shaking loose and dropping off him, so the guards got tired of him. They sent him back to his barracks and let him keep his cards.

Oklahoma's section leader said the barracks adjutant would not allow any more gambling. Oklahoma told the two of them to go fuck themselves, they were politicians and kiss-asses, and he kept on gambling.

Everybody played cards. They would take Chinese cigarette packs, the hard kind, and draw suits and face cards on the underside of the label. They would mark the cards, bending them a bit or giving them a little snick with a thumbnail, deluding themselves that nobody could tell. Harry and Oklahoma could see them at it; nothing could have been more obvious. Everybody did it, everybody knew everybody was doing it, so everybody dealt off the bottom and everybody covered their cards with their hands.

Harry's brain was as sharp as it had ever been. On nothing but dirty rice and Whangpoo he could still count the cards at blackjack, and to him it was amazing and rewarding how many men would go up against him, time after time, betting their rations against his mind. Once he played a man checkers all night, eight hours, and next day Harry was eating double and the other man was going hungry.

Oklahoma and Harry played singly and together. They pooled their winnings. When they won themselves a food bowl, they carved both their sets of initials on it. They loosened a board under the straw mat on the sleeping platform to hide their stash. If one of them was asleep on the mat, the other was awake.

The section leaders and the adjutants were running their own rackets. One of the contractors in Oklahoma's barracks was quick enough and smart enough to get the job of official bread man. He happened to fall sick, and for his replacement he tapped Oklahoma, as someone smart enough to know which end was up, also smart enough not to talk about what he knew. Oklahoma took private instruction on certain secret share-outs that were made before the bread was dealt to everybody. One of these distributions was legitimate, to take care of the sick. The Japanese were doing what they always did, cutting the rations of sick men, to inspire them to get well and go back to work. The bread man showed Oklahoma how to fake the numbers and get the sick men their full loaf—including the bread man himself for as long as he was sick. Another piece of faking, not legitimate: The bread man's friends were getting extra loaves, and Oklahoma learned who got how much and why. Also, news to Oklahoma but really no surprise—the section leader and the adjutant were in for their cut, too. These were the same politicians and kiss-asses who had crossed him before, so he took their extra for himself and Harry and hid it under their loose board. The adjutant threatened to report him for stealing. Oklahoma looked him in the eye and said, *Go ahead, we're all here and we're all going to be here.* The adjutant never did report him, just waited till the sick man got better, then bounced Oklahoma, and the old firm was in business again. Except that the bread man added Oklahoma to his secret list.

Everyone was in business for himself, American-style—after the war, that bread man became a banker in Los Angeles. Oklahoma used to watch the barracks economy, and it was like looking at an ant farm under glass. One man would be sewing for money. One would cut hair. One would repair shoes with anything he could find for the soles. One would take in shirts for washing. One had a bit of a mirror; he charged a quarter-cigarette to shave in it. One would wash food bowls and take his pay in fishbones to crunch on.

Ants by the hundred laboriously gathering crumbs. And rats, snouting the cage, sniffing the wind, pouncing on scraps.

One day the Japanese said the camp was being moved, from Woosung to Kiangwan, about a ten-mile march. They said Kiangwan would be a much better place. Of course it was not. The Japanese went in for that sort of pointless deception all the time.

Kiangwan was flat land, and the prisoners were ordered to raise a mound, six hundred feet long, two hundred feet wide, forty-five feet high. The story was that it was going to be a playground for children from Shanghai. Or a monument to the glorious Japanese war dead. More pointless deception—it turned out to be a rifle range, more labor directly against the Geneva convention. They had to work from scratch, by hand power, breaking rocks with Asiatic tools, hauling the breakings up the slope. The Japanese made them start on the anniversary of Pearl Harbor. The POWs christened it Mount Fuji.

Once in a great while, Red Cross food arrived from overseas. The Japanese were brazen about looting it; they would take as much as a third, even a half. The only item likely to be left strictly alone was cheese, because it offended the Japanese nose, smelly white man's food. Still, enough Red Cross boxes did get to the prisoners to make a difference, body and soul.

A Red Cross delivery was a red-letter event. Canned milk, canned butter, canned fruit, dried fruit, chocolate, coffee. Something new, a kind of canned meat called Spam that the prisoners had never seen before, wonderfully fatty. And the spaces in the boxes were stuffed with American cigarettes. It was like Christmas, and that was about how often it came around.

Harry and Oklahoma had their own reasons for looking forward to Red Cross parcels. Men would bet on them at cards. A Red Cross box was rated at seventy-five packs of American cigarettes, meaning big money; it was far and away the biggest bet in prison camp. It was also the longest bet on credit. The financial year for gambling began in January. If a man got in the hole, Harry and Oklahoma would carry him. If a man was fool enough to get in so deep that he was down the equivalent of seventy-five packs of smokes, he would have to forfeit his next Red Cross box.

That was a gamble on both sides of the table. The next Red Cross delivery might never come. Or it might not get past the Japanese. If it did, the loser might be gone, transferred, or dead. The same went for Harry and Oklahoma. Or—the longest of long shots—the war might be over, and all bets would be off. Anything was possible. The certainty was that enough men would keep gambling to keep Harry and Oklahoma running their game.

Everybody who gambled was playing for food, anything from a handful of rice to a Red Cross box. Those calories added up. In the end they could be the difference between life and death. Harry and Oklahoma made sure they were on the plus side. They were the house; they were ahead of the game. Even if they were big men, meaning that they needed more calories to service their bodies, they were better fed than the others, meaning they were that little bit less likely to get sick.

Away from the card table Oklahoma had a strength trick that he bet on, the standing broad jump. He had been doing it all his life. At home there were not many boys who could beat him. In camp he had a tout on commission, working the other barracks, suckering men into betting against him. It was a straight contest, not fixed, except that Oklahoma's food edge gave him just that bit more spring in his legs. He always won.

He had another winning hustle going for him every yasume day, the best timing being when there was a cigarette issue and men were flush enough to bet some of their smokes. The rice paddies around camp were full of frogs. The prisoners would put them inside a circle and bet on which one would jump out first, entry fee one cigarette, winner take all. Oklahoma had a personal frog wrangler, a Mexican named Rudy Flores, on a cigarette butt retainer, scouting the paddies for likely-looking competitors. Before the race meet, Flores would make a stop at the benjo with the frog of the day. He would secretly rub its behind close to blood-raw on a special piece of stone. Then he would dip a finger into the lime that was sprinkled in the benjo to keep the maggots down, just a small pinch, under a fingernail that he kept long for the purpose. At the start of the race all he had to do was poke the frog's sensitive rear end with that fingernail, and the sting galvanized the frog. It was a sure thing.

One day Harry was out on work detail, building Mount Fuji, shoveling away, and he came across a grave—Chinese graves were everywhere—and buried with the skeleton he found a cigarette holder, ivory, with characters carved into it. He got one of the Chinese mess boys from the Pan Am Inn on Wake to translate for him, and what it said was *The less you smoke the more you enjoy it.* Harry never had to test that one; he was a winner at the card table, he had plenty of smokes, and he enjoyed every one of them. But he never had enough food. Certainly not enough of the right kind, American food, white man's food. Even with his food edge from winning at cards, he always felt starved for the sensation of plenty to eat, wild for the sensation of too much.

Yet in a strange way he found that being perpetually hungry kept his edge at its sharpest. He felt like a hunting animal. His senses were fine-tuned. Especially smell. He could smell smells within smells. The benjo and the filthy bodies in the barracks were universal stinks, but he could separate out the particular smell that came when some prisoner on a maintenance fatigue on the other side of camp opened a can of Japanese paint. He could smell smoke from a riverboat, out of sight in the distance along the Whangpoo. He could pick the feeblest of cooking smells off the wind, the very moment the cookhouse gang dumped some pitiful vegetable stalks into hot water for the day's Tōjō water.

He developed another prison camp talent—he could look at a man he had never seen before, the hair would rise up on his arms and on the back of his neck, and he would know the man was going to die. And he could sit down across from a man at poker and smell what the man was thinking about the hand he was holding. Not really a smell, but Harry could pick up the whiff of it.

All of this made Harry the leader and Oklahoma the follower. Harry was the one with the nose, the intuition. The judgment calls were his. And with Oklahoma backing him, fast enough to be his shadow, he did not need anything else or anyone else. Outside of

Oklahoma, Harry asked nothing from any man in camp and gave nothing either. If a man wanted something from Harry, he had to come to Harry, and Harry would make him meet his price.

Harry did not operate on the black market. That was too much in the open for him. At Kiangwan he sniffed out something more private, a storehouse with food in it, kept for show, in case of camp inspections by neutral nations (called protecting powers), which meant it was never going to be eaten. The storehouse had a hot wire around it, but Harry found a way under. One night he and Oklahoma went in and came out with canned milk. They drank it in the benjo. They went in a second time and got soybean curd, for the vegetable protein. A third time it was jam, for the sweetness of the sugar.

Harry called the shots on the operation. So far so good. But there were rats' eyes everywhere. Someone from another barracks saw how they were doing it, and next thing they knew there were rats all over the place. Harry was disgusted; the others had no sense, they were going in with yoyo poles. Of course the Japanese caught them, and someone ratted and gave up Harry and Oklahoma as the ones who started it all.

The real power in camp was not the commandant but the head interpreter, Ishihara Isamu. He had spent time in Hawaii before the war; the story was that he had been a taxi driver or a truck driver or a teacher in Honolulu. He hated America and Americans. He used to say that when Japan won the war he was going to shit on the Stars and Stripes. That did not stop him from speaking with an American accent. When he was having trouble understanding a British prisoner he said, *You British really fuck up the English language.* But then he was not really on top of the language himself; especially when he was crossed, he would go crazy and the words would come out wrong. If a prisoner did not salute him he would scream, *Why you not giving me SOLUTION?*

Ishihara was a civilian, not a soldier, but he had delusions of grandeur about being an officer. His story was that when he became an interpreter he was promised officer status, and with his outstanding intelligence and ability he was entitled to it. But when he got to Woosung the officers made him salute the guards, enlisted men. He never got over that. He wore a sidearm and a sword like an officer. He would beat POW officers with the sword till he was frothing, tell them they should kill themselves for being prisoners, and offer them his sword to do it. No one took him up.

The British governor of Hong Kong, Sir Mark Young, was in camp before he was sent to Formosa. Ishihara tried to make him salute, and when he would not, Ishihara whipped out his sword; he was going to chop his head off. No white man was safe from Ishihara. He was so bad that the Japanese themselves took his sword away. Then he went to a leather riding crop with a loaded handle. Short of chopping heads off, he was pretty much allowed to run wild. Ishihara was a believer in the water cure as a wonderful way to get truth out of prisoners. Prop a ladder on a slope, tie the prisoner to it, feet higher than head, pound something into his nostrils to break the bones so he had to breathe through his mouth, pour water into his mouth till he filled up and choked, and then it was talk or suffocate. The prisoners called Ishihara The Beast of the East, for cause.

Now he had Harry and Oklahoma cold for breaking into the storeroom. They would not admit to anything. He put them in the guardhouse and beat them. He broke Oklahoma's nose and smashed his front teeth. Then he stood him and Harry up in front of the whole camp, the two of them and two men from the other barracks, with everyone at attention until they confessed. It was summer, stinking hot. The four of them were stripped to the waist in the sun, with no hats, and the mosquitoes were feasting on them. If they moved, the guards bashed them. If they fell, the guards kicked them back onto their feet. One of the men from the other barracks was old. He reached the point where he could not stand. Ishihara had him tied to a pole.

If Harry and Oklahoma kept refusing to admit anything, they would suffer for it, and the whole camp would suffer as well, everyone at attention in the heat, rations cut off, more than a thousand men who had not done anything suffering for two men who had—that was the Japanese way, and it could go on forever. They were both in bad shape, their eyes bulging, bloodshot as plums. The old man hanging from the pole beside them died. When that happened Harry and Oklahoma said yes, they had stolen from the storehouse.

Ishihara put them in the camp brig for a week, no talking, and beatings every time the guards changed shifts. Then a dump truck came for them, with armed guards. They thought they were being taken away to be killed.

They were not. They wound up in prison in Shanghai, at Ward Road, a huge jail built by the British before the war. Thousands of Chinese were locked up there, thieves, murderers, and syphilitics. The cells were cages, raised off a narrow walkway, with iron bars and a bare concrete floor with a benjo hole in it, and once a day everything was hosed down with a fire hose, prisoners and cages at the same time. If a man was looking out of his cell with his hands clasped around the bars, a guard would break his knuckles. Harry saw a guard kill a Chinese with a rifle butt, smash his skull, and the body was left lying for days.

Harry came down with amoebic dysentery and raging malaria. After about a month, the Japanese shipped him back to Kiangwan. Ishihara said he had not been punished enough and put him in solitary in the camp brig.

Oklahoma got out of Ward Road three weeks later. His broken nose was healing, but crooked, and his smashed teeth were not going to grow in again. Back at Kiangwan he was put in the brig with Harry.

Harry was just about unrecognizable. To Oklahoma he looked to be dying. By chance the Japanese camp doctor made a stop at the brig. And by chance he was a good man. His name was Shindō Yoshihiro. Measured by the professional standards of the POW medical officers, Shindō was not much of a doctor, but at least he was one Japanese who did not hate white men. He had trained in Germany. By chance Harry had a grandmother who was German. When he was a kid she taught him some German words. Now in his delirium he called out in German. Shindō heard him and had him taken to the sick bay. Shindō saved Harry's life, and Harry would never have laid odds on something like that.

Oklahoma was not in good shape himself. A mosquito bit him on the foot, he scratched it and it got infected, a redness running all the way up his leg into his groin. Shindō looked after him, put a cold compress on the swelling and gave him some Japanese medicine to take. Shindō found him a razor too, so he could shave his pubic hair and deny his crabs their cover. Forever after that, Oklahoma never had anything but good words to say for Shindō; he called him the only white Jap he ever ran into.

When Harry was a bit better, Ishihara made Shindō send them both back to the brig. They had to stand in their cell all day. Shindō wrote a note saying they should not have to. Sometimes the guards let them sit, sometimes not. Either way the windows were closed all day, then opened at night, and they had to take all their clothes off.

The cell had no screens against mosquitoes, and no such thing as a bath. And no mattress; they had to lie on filthy straw. Their entertainment was catching flies—they would stick a little splinter up the fly's rear end, which paralyzed the wings; put the flies inside a circle; and bet on which one would crawl out first, bets to be settled later, with cigarettes.

Some of Oklahoma's contractor contacts, the ones who were in on his hustles, would sneak over at night, crawl under the brig and push bread and cigarettes up through cracks in the floorboards. Oklahoma hid the bread behind a straw hat of Harry's from Wake that he had hanging on a nail—the guards never looked there— and Oklahoma fed himself and Harry in the dark. He unraveled some thread from his shirt and tied the cigarettes to it and lowered them through a knothole in the double wall, and at night he pulled them up and he and Harry smoked lying on the straw and blew the smoke down through the cracks in the floor.

Other than a bit of bread and a cigarette or two, they were on the Japanese jail ration of rice and salt, plus soup every once in a while. Oklahoma was barely maintaining. Harry started losing ground again, and Oklahoma could see him failing. But they did not talk about it. With them, that was doctrine. Part of their smart-ness was knowing that all they had to offer each other was their strength. If one of them was feeling down, why let on? There was no help in talking about such things, in fact it was worse than useless, it would only make the other one feel down too; their combined strength would be less, and that was not smart. It was like talking about food. They would do anything to get their hands on more food, up to and including taking it from other men, gambling or stealing; but they would never talk about how they felt about food they did not have. Or how they felt about anything. They never talked about feelings. Feelings were weaknesses. Once weakness was out in the open, confidence leaked, strength slipped away, grip was lost.

Harry had seen prison camp turn any number of men weak. He preyed on their weaknesses. He bought their rice for cigarettes and made them pay and pay. His name for them was *weak sisters*. He could not abide them. And now he was turning into a weak sister himself. Finally he broke; he told Oklahoma he was finished. He wanted Oklahoma to help him outside and drop him on the hot wire, the electric fence.

Oklahoma would not do it. He had made up his mind that he was in it with Harry for keeps, for the duration. They had gone to Wake together, and they would make it back home together. Oklahoma knew Harry was more selfish than he was; he put it down to Harry being an only child, spoiled by his mother. He had to wonder to himself what Harry would have done for him if he had been the one who turned into a weak sister. But he let Harry have the most of the food. *Eat my soup, I can make it.*

Gradually Harry came back from talking about the hot wire. Neither of them ever mentioned it again.

The question then was, who was the leader and who was the follower? They never talked about that, either.

::

AT THE time Forrest Knox decided he had to get out of Camp O'Donnell he was carrying dysentery, dengue fever, severe malnutrition, and general exhaustion. But at least he was up and walking and he still knew who he was, and that qualified him as a worker. He was taken to Manila with about three hundred other men, a fair number of them tankers from his battalion. The Japanese herded them into a big recreation hall at Grace Park and set about parceling them out for labor all over southern Luzon. Forrest was tagged for bridge building, terrible work. Then a *gunsō*, a sergeant, came by, making signs with his hands like a steering wheel. He was looking for truck drivers. Sandy Sandmire from Forrest's company was the quickest to pick up on it—he was tall, he could see over the crowd. He flagged down the gunsō and cut the deal, and of course he pulled in as many Janesville boys as he could, Forrest included.

It was their lucky day. Truck driving was better than bridge building—no contest—and the gunsō was a bonus. He turned out to be a human being. His last name was Nakamura. They never found out his first name. They called him The Bull, all five feet and a hundred pounds of him. Forrest never got the impression that Nakamura wanted POWs to kill themselves for the shame of being prisoners, or for being loathsome white men. The way Forrest put the story together, The Bull had been in the service for years in China; he was locked into the system, and he had found a way to live with it. He was efficient; when he spoke his own men jumped. Still, he did not beat them and slap them the way a Japanese sergeant was entitled to. And he did not beat his prisoners. His guards did not beat them either, at least not when The Bull was around, though when he was somewhere else it might happen: One day an orderly smashed Forrest in the face for nothing; another time a bunch of guards went after Alva Chapman with their rifle butts. Forrest classed them as pet rattlesnakes; you could play with them, but you had to be careful.

The Bull and his guards took to sitting around with their prisoners at night, and once everyone got past sign language and grunts to where they could talk to each other somewhat, they swapped stories. The Japanese loved to hear about dating in America. A movie or a dance, then into the car, down a side road, work the girl into the backseat and tell her to put out or walk home. The Bull just about fell out of his chair laughing at that one—where he came from, a fishing village in the north of Japan, it was *samo samo:* Take the girl out in a boat and tell her to put out or swim home.

The truckers called the dumbest guard Harvard. When Harvard judged that he had come to know Forrest well enough, he asked him confidentially if it was true that American girls were built crossways, and Forrest just about fell out of his chair laughing.

The truck detail's big project was ferrying logs to rebuild bridges all over Luzon. Along the mountain roads most of the villages were empty, because the Filipinos did not want to be anywhere near a Japanese, so at night the truckers could throw their blanket down in any hut they wanted. On one of Forrest's jobs the Filipino riding with them found two village girls who had stayed, and they were willing to put out, no charge. Forrest went for it. The next day the guards said Knocky was too weak to drive, he should ride in the back of the truck and rest. It was a good joke.

Except it was true. In the energy budget of food and work and sex, Forrest was better off than anybody starving back at O'Donnell. Once he got on the truck detail and onto something like a livable amount of food, the sap rose in him again, dysentery and dengue or no. But just one night's worth.

The only man with sex on his mind every day was Aaron Combs, known as Curly. He was back in Manila cooking for the truck detail, eating well enough to be inspired to polish up some of his old ladies'-man moves. He would make eyes at a woman who worked across the street, blowing her kisses, and she would send a street vendor over with ice cream for him. She was no vision of loveliness, in fact she was known to the truckers as Scabby Legs, but then Combs had sores on his legs, too. Combs had another thing going, trying to get close to a married Chinese woman who lived along the street. With her he had language trouble; he never could get her to comprehend what he was interested in. She, in her innocence of his intentions, offered to get her husband to interpret, but Combs thought best not.

Combs never did wind up bedding her, but he did trade her and her husband a lot of scrounged rice for a little pig; and in the seven months of the truck detail, that pig was the outstanding meal.

No one was dying of malnutrition and only one man came down with beriberi, the same man who vomited a lot of worms one day. But even so, no one was properly nourished; the inside of the body was never in good shape.

No more was the outside. Everyone had fungus infections. Goosie the Japanese medic would stand the prisoners up on a little table and brush iodine on their testicles and they would buck and holler and the guards would laugh; it was their entertainment.

Forrest was sure he had the perfect cure. In the confusion at Grace Park he had liberated a field medicine kit, and in among the medicine was crystals for foot powder, super-strength. He applied the stuff liberally to his crotch, and instantly regretted it. It was like putting a blowtorch to himself. But it burned out the fungus.

So it went on, life with the truck detail, only about a fiftieth of a standard white American life, but bearable, and for Forrest, with his fungus-free crotch and his one night of joy in the mountains, maybe a twentieth.

The Company A men were the basic tribe of the detail, about ten of them. They stayed; other men came and went. Joe Erington looked after the Japanese officers' stables and was known as Horse-cock in three languages, English, Japanese, and Tagalog. (*At last,* Erington used to say, *I am getting the respect I deserve.*) Dick Walker got on the detail because he was a class tennis player before the war. He had played in Japan with Bill Tilden. On Luzon he was recognized and picked out of the prisoner herd by a Japanese officer who was a tennis player himself. And there was a man named McKnight, from Pennsylvania, no particular friend of Forrest's, but he taught Forrest something interesting. Before the war McKnight worked in a lunatic asylum, and he knew how to kill a man with a towel, in no time and making no noise. Forrest had his tanker's neck towel, the one that Herb Durner wetted down with water on the march out of Bataan to keep Forrest alive. How to kill a man with a towel—that was the kind of curious information Forrest loved to pick up, to be filed in his mind along with little-known facts about tattoos and other subjects of interest.

McKnight showed him the towel trick one night before lights

out, over a cup or three of mango-leaf tea with P-40 juice, pure industrial alcohol liberated from the truck depot.

Fuel of any kind was so short that pure gasoline was as precious as blood. So there was a black market. The Bull ran it out of the truck depot. The kempeitai were in on it, too. They were forever turning up at midnight, ordering a POW driver out, to load five barrels for a rendezvous in the dark with some cash customer who was supposed to be their enemy. The kempeitai were stealing cars, too; they had Forrest and the others doing repaint jobs for them on the quiet, in between driving them to the cathouse. The whole operation made Forrest wonder about the kempeitai's spirit of bushidō, torturing all day for the emperor, then off at night screwing around and trading hot cars.

The truckers never got anything extra for helping out with the black market, but on the other hand they never got bashed for siphoning off P-40 juice. They made sure they kept their scrounging small-scale enough to be inconspicuous, setting the best of the brew aside one barrel at a time in a safe place, and tapping it into quart bottles. For certain, the Bull knew what they were up to. But for him it was not a big deal, just a small silent part of the bigger deal he had going.

One day Forrest was out on the road with Chipper Chapman. They were not far from Lumban, standing up in the back of the truck, the way the Japanese made them do, the theory being that if the Filipino guerrillas saw white American faces they would not blow them up.

That day there were Filipinos by the side of the road, crowds of them, watching the truck go by, looking stricken. The Bull was riding in the cabin with the driver. When they came to a checkpoint, he got out and talked to the guards. It was a long conference. Then he ordered the truck turned around, straight back to Manila, and he would not tell them why.

Forrest collected the facts in dribs and drabs, and he never did get them all, just enough to know that something terrible had happened. It was this: At Lumban, the Japanese had something like 150 prisoners repairing a bridge that had been blown in the retreat into Bataan. They had to work naked in the river all day driving piles, and at night they had to flop in a little Filipino movie house, the strong taking the benches and balcony steps to sleep on, no mattresses, the weak lying on the dirt floor, and a hole in the corner for a latrine.

The day before Forrest saw all the Filipinos on the road, the

Japanese had raided a little store in the *barrio* at Lumban and found a radio. They beat the storekeeper; they kicked his pregnant wife in the stomach. And this nastiness brought on a guerrilla raid that night.

In the dark the guerrillas shot three or four Japanese. Their plan was for the prisoners to run off with them in the confusion. Out of 150, only 1 went.

The next day the Japanese bashed the mayor of the barrio and the head policeman. Then they marched all the prisoners to the Japanese headquarters at the schoolhouse, set up machine guns to keep them in line, and started picking men out.

There was a lot of milling in the ranks. These were prisoners off the terrible march out of Bataan and the killings at O'Donnell for having Japanese things. No one wanted to be picked out for any reason by Japanese with guns.

For working on the bridge, the Japanese had the POWs broken into three squads of about fifty each, with different-colored arm-bands, red, white, and green. The man who escaped was a green. So the Japanese were looking for greens. They picked and chose, fingered three men who turned out not to be greens, pushed them back, and fingered three others. The ones they picked out were all supposed to be men who slept near the escaper. When they had ten, they shot them in front of everybody.

Japanese officers from all over were there to watch, and the one giving the orders was the colonel of engineers from Manila, The Bull's boss, a notorious son of a bitch. He put a harmless guard from the truck detail on the firing squad. This poor guard did not want to shoot anyone. He told Forrest afterward that he fired over the prisoners' heads, and so did some of the others. Meaning that not every one of the ten got killed in the first volley, they were screaming and groaning, and it took a sickening number of shots to kill them all.

In among the greens were two brothers, sticking together the way brothers did. One got picked out and the other had to watch him die.

When the butchering was over, the senior POW officer realized he had torn out a clump of his hair. He had to collect the dog tags off the bodies, one private, three PFCs, three corporals, three sergeants.

Terrible arithmetic, but would it have been better if they had all gone with the guerrillas? Or worse in the end? Who could ever know?

The prisoners took to calling each other *blood brothers,* because if one escaped, the blood of the others would be spilled. The Janes-ville truckers agreed that if one of them went, everyone would go, the whole tribe. It became doctrine to trust everyone in the tribe, but suspect everyone else. The Company A tribe kept their eyes on any new man transferred in among them from somewhere else. Why had that other tribe gotten rid of just this one man? And why should the Company A tribe take the least chance with him? So, whenever there was the slightest doubt about the look in a new man's eye, they talked to Sandy Sandmire. Sandmire would tell The Bull the man wanted to leave, and The Bull had him shipped out. The way the Bull was placed, an escape would bring his own son-of-a-bitch colonel down on him. So he went by the old army system, the one that worked in every army on the face of the earth: Transfer trouble out before it makes trouble for you. In their tiny part of the big war, The Bull and the prisoners of Forrest's tribe were on the same side. They had a good thing going.

What broke it up was the way the big war was developing, a long way from the Philippines. The Bull and his men got orders for the southern front, New Guinea or somewhere. It was bad news for them, and bad news for the truckers, too. The Bull made the best of it. He threw a party for guards and prisoners, with lots of food, plus green-looking wine made out of dried fruit with a couple of bottles of some sort of imitation Scotch mixed in. The morning after, The Bull lined everyone up for a picture. He sat himself in the front row with his sword, guards on either side, and behind them the prisoners lined up in their best clothes, meaning their only clothes; some of them even managed to smile through their hangovers. The Bull had prints made, and gave them to For-rest and the others; then he and his men went away to war.

The truckers had no idea what was coming up next. What they drew was a few weeks at old Bilibid prison in Manila, and then Cabanatuan.

At Cabanatuan, no sooner had Forrest set down his one miserable sack of belongings than he was drafted for hard labor on the grave-yard detail. It was the old army system yet again—the first men into camp scored the best jobs, the last ones in had to take the worst. For Forrest it was a long way down from the truck detail.

Cabanatuan was originally a big Philippine Army barracks, reg-iment-size. By the time Forrest came in, the Japanese had had it operating for a little over six months as Cabanatuan Concentration Camp. It was the biggest single herding of Americans in the Philippines, one of the largest camps anywhere in the Greater East Asia Co-Prosperity Sphere; at the peak it held more than fifteen thousand men, survivors of Bataan and Corregidor.

Camp 1 at Cabanatuan was where the Japanese sent their white prisoners when they closed down the American side of O'Donnell. At first it was nothing but O'Donnell continued. In six months the graveyard went from nothing to more than twenty-five hundred bodies, meaning that a man was dying about every one and three-quarter hours.

When Forrest got there, in January 1943, seventeen men from Company A were buried in the Camp 1 graveyard. He did some asking around and some calculating, going back to the start of the war: two dead in the fighting on Bataan, two dead on the march, twelve dead at O'Donnell, five dead on outside work details that he knew about, and now seventeen dead at Camp 1. In just over eight months since the surrender, thirty-eight men from Janesville were dead as prisoners already, more than one in three. For Company A up to that point, less than a year into captivity, being a prisoner of the Japanese had been 17.5 times more lethal than fighting them.

By the time Forrest reached Cabanatuan, the worst of the worst was over. June and July of 1942 were the bottom of the pit, with deaths totaling more than 1,150. Somebody worked it out that at that rate everyone would be dead in ten weeks. Then in August the Japanese let some quinine into camp, and the malaria eased somewhat. There was a diphtheria epidemic, but by September it was burning itself out. The hygiene situation changed for the better, not because the Japanese improved the water supply but because there were fewer men to overtax what water there was—deaths plus drafts for outside work details took the numbers in camp down below 10,000. An engineer colonel named Freddie Saint designed septic tanks, and that reduced the number of dysenteries. Soap turned up, made in camp out of lard and ashes, it was rancid-smelling, but soap. In November the food improved a little, for a while. That same month more medicine came into camp, from Japan—it was not supplied by the Japanese, but came off an exchange ship from the West. Then in December, also via Japan, the first Red Cross boxes arrived at Cabanatuan, and to the prisoners it felt like every Christmas of their lifetime coming at once. They had white food by the pound: corned beef (actual meat!) evaporated milk, cocoa, sweet chocolate, sugar—and American cigarettes.

* * *

Forrest liked the fact that Cabanatuan was a big camp. There were all kinds of different lives for him to take an interest in, quan to feed his mind. At the wash tap he could look at some hillbillies, a strange little tribe of spooks with skin that never tanned. They never spoke to Forrest or anyone else. Forrest was just the opposite, he would talk to anyone who would talk to him. A rodeo rider. A used-car salesman. A pool shark. A card sharp from Phoenix. A Salt Lake City Mormon. A New York Jew. The only prisoner Forrest ever met who did not want the war to end was a man wanted back home for murder; he had joined the service to get away to the Philippines under another name.

Forrest knew Ted Lewin the gambler by sight. Lewin was very visible. He survived O'Donnell—if anyone was going to, Lewin was—and when he came over to Cabanatuan he kept up his Manila connections. He had his own black market pipeline, and Japanese guards in his pocket. One of the sayings at Camp 1 was that if you could pay for it you could get absolutely anything—you could order a Cadillac and it would be delivered, smuggled in in pieces. Lewin would be the one to arrange that deal. There were all sorts of Lewin stories: Lewin making donations to the officers' welfare fund; Lewin hustling extra food for the sick; Lewin going to all kinds of trouble for a man he liked, using the Manila pipeline to get a pair of prescription eyeglasses made up for him. It paid to be on the right side of Lewin—the other story about him was that he stamped on the eyeglasses of a man he did not like.

Lewin would do business with anyone. But first and foremost he was looking after Number One. It showed. One of the doctors at Cabanatuan used to make sketches on some school notepaper he had scrounged, and the only prisoner he ever drew with a spare tire was Lewin.

Forrest did not see any need to envy the rich at Cabanatuan—not Lewin, and not the senior officers, for all their rank and privilege. He knew the way they operated, but it was not a sore point with him, because his lucky number came up again. He got off the graveyard detail and into the cookhouse, and not just any cookhouse, the Japanese cookhouse, where the best food was.

This came about because one of the Bushaw brothers of Company A, Delmon, was a wheeler-dealer. He got on the right side of the POW officer in charge of making out work details, and the officer gave Bushaw the Japanese cookhouse. Bushaw kept the job, partly because he developed a knack with rice—he could cook it to Japanese satisfaction—but as much or more because he was paying off the work detail officer with extra food. As part of the deal, Bushaw was allowed to name some of his own cookhouse crew, and of course he picked Janesville men: Sandy Sandmire, Chipper Chapman, Herb Durner, Bob Stewart, and Forrest.

They had to be on the job before dawn, Cabanatuan time. Bushaw was the butcher. He killed a pig a day for the Japanese. The guards used to come around to watch. They liked the sound of the squeal when the knife went in. They liked the blood, too; they would catch it in little pans full of rice, let it coagulate, then cut it up in squares and deep-fry it. Every so often the Japanese mess sergeant let Forrest's cookhouse crew keep some blood in a bucket and pass it over the fence to their friends, their *tomodachi*. Anything to do with pig was top-quality quan. One pig of the day was a pregnant sow, and the womb and the unborn piglets went into the bucket and over the fence. Forrest and the rest were always scrounging for the Janesville tribe. He and Bob Stewart made false bottoms in their water canteens and smuggled out duck eggs, which were like gold for protein, three or four a day. They could have sugar in their Japanese tea, and every chance they got they stole more. They smuggled it out bagged and stuffed into their socks, in their trousers, in their G-strings. The Japanese watched the level in their sugar sacks going down. They took to smoothing the surface and writing Japanese characters on it so they could see when it was disturbed. That worked for a while, but Bushaw practiced copying the characters and learned to write them in the sugar with his finger. Not that he ever knew what they meant, but it confused the Japanese; they could not figure out how the level could still be going down, which made for a small extra sweetness in the life of the tribe.

All things considered, if Forrest had to be a prisoner—and he had to—the cookhouse was the place to be.

Then one day a *tōban,* a Japanese dog robber, came storming in out of the blue and beat Forrest up. It was Chipper Chapman who brought on the beating. One of Chapman's jobs was to wash the Japanese officers' mess kits, and his work was not measuring up to the emperor's standards. The Japanese officers gave the tōban grief. So the tōban had to give a prisoner grief. Chapman was not to be seen. Forrest was visible, checking on the bean sprouts. He was the dog that got kicked.

It was Forrest's observation that, as a species, the Japanese tōban was likely to be effeminate. This one was, and hysterical with it. Forrest was a POW who could never make up his mind whether to stay down under a beating or get up. This time, with the effeminate tōban beating on him, he discovered that he could not make himself stay down. He kept getting up, and the tōban kept knocking him down again. He used his fists, then a heavy wooden sandal, escalated to a cookpot, and burst Forrest's eardrum with it.

That did it. Forrest got himself transferred; he made a swap with a man on the detail that cut wood for the cookhouse fires.

Forrest liked his new job fine. The woodcutters got out of the stinking camp into the jungle, twenty-five axes between fifty men, each man working for fifteen minutes, wearing nothing but a G-string made out of the liner of a sugar sack, sweating a river, but then resting for fifteen minutes. The wisdom was never to go after trees so big that the butt trunk pieces were too heavy to carry to the truck. The Japanese set only a perimeter guard, no one ever got beaten up, and on top of that they got an extra ration for heavy work. Plus the occasional chance to rob a beehive for the honey. And every so often native quail for quan. Other than the one time a guard swung his bamboo club at a hornet's nest out of curiosity, the most uproar was the day hundreds of head of cattle came stampeding through the jungle. They were from an old government experimental farm, gone wild in the war. Forrest heard them coming and went up a tree. The guards should have been shooting into the herd for the meat, but they were all up a tree too. Still, if that was the worst thing that happened, Forrest would not have minded if the wood detail went on indefinitely.

It did not. He was taken off woodcutting and put to work on the Farm, and that was a drastic turn for the worse.

The Farm was started before Forrest came to Cabanatuan. It was sited on ground about a mile outside the fence. The carabao caravan hauled rocks from a streambed; the prisoners made a human chain and laid down the rocks for a cobblestone road. Then they dug a ditch to bring water; a job so big they called it the Panama Canal. Then they broke ground for planting. The soil had not been worked for years. It had gigantic old anthills, with the ants long gone. When the prisoners chopped the hills down, out came baby cobras.

The reward for prisoner labor on the Farm was supposed to be that Cabanatuan would be self-sufficient in vegetables. It never happened, although probably it could have. At its biggest, the Farm was about a square mile of garden being worked by more than twenty-five hundred men, and it grew all kinds of good things: beans, carrots, peppers, corn, onions, radishes, okra, eggplant, cassava, camote. But the prisoners did not get a fair return on their work. They were worse off than sharecroppers. The Japanese skimmed the crops for their garrison troops on Luzon. The Cabanatuan guards ate off the top, too. Then they took a lot of what was left and—so they said—traded the vegetables in Cabanatuan City for rice for the prisoners. The prisoners never saw that much of an increase in their rice ration. And anyway they would have preferred vegetables. They never got nearly enough vegetables. In fact, one of the great ambitions on the Farm detail was to eat a vegetable raw without being spotted by a guard, be weeding along and in one swift pass pull a carrot or an onion or a radish, bolt it down, dirt and all, then stick the green top back in the ground.

In Forrest's time, the first half of 1943, the Farm was growing month by month, until it became the biggest call on the prisoners' labor, far bigger than everything else at Cabanatuan put together: camp fatigues, honeybucket detail, road work, airstrip construction, ditchdigging, gravedigging, truck driving, the carabao caravan, hay carters to feed the carabao, mechanics for the power plant, cobblers and tailors, duck wranglers, on and on, all the way to the field-grade POW officers' barber and bathroom orderly.

The Japanese wanted more and more workers on the Farm. To make up the numbers, *officers* were going to have to work, on a quota basis: Every work party must have 12.5 percent officers.

This was a fierce disturbance to the way the camp had been running. It was like chopping into an old anthill; it threw the resting cobras into a fit.

Until then the officers had not had to work directly for the Japanese. They tried to stand on the Geneva convention. But they had no chance.

Naturally, the first ones to go were the company grades, captains and lieutenants, because the field grades above them had the most privileges. The POW camp commander, a marine lieutenant colonel named Curtis Beecher, was one of those senior officers who would take bedding away from incoming junior officers. Beecher and his field grades were not about to take the lead in working on the Farm, long days in the sun, stooped over with a native hoe and a high probability of contusions on the skull.

Another thing—the field grade officers had personal orderlies, and the company grade officers could not see why these dog robbers, nothing but enlisted men, should be allowed to stay comfortably inside the fence doing body service for field grades, when the company grades, who had no orderlies of their own, were out breaking their backs. So the company grades protested. They wanted field grades to work as well as company grades, the field grades' dog robbers to work too, and no sick man, enlisted man or officer, to be sent out to work.

The protest made its point, more or less. But there was still a lot of defensive scurrying around camp, a lot of wangling to get on what was called the overhead—the staff supposed to be necessary to keep the camp functioning—and once on the overhead to stay there.

The only good job on the Farm was pollinating. It went by the name of *flower fucking*. For some reason the area around Cabanatuan lacked bees, so the Japanese had prisoners going along on their hands and knees among the vegetable plants and bushes—press the flower-fucking pistil in until the pollen was used up, throw it away, and repeat.

The flower-fucking guards took their work seriously, but they did not carry clubs. The other Farm guards did. They made the prisoners work in rows; if they strayed out of line, it cost them a beating. They had to work bent over, head lower than ass. If they raised their head they would get clubbed. If they did not raise their head they might get clubbed anyway.

The guards on Forrest's detail had a game they loved to play. They would creep up behind a prisoner and see how far they could whack his hat with their club. It was like golf. Top the hat, no distance. Swing too fat, take too much of a divot, the prisoner would be knocked out cold. Sandy Sandmire was working with Forrest. Even properly bent over, Sandmire was a tall man, and the guards used to like teeing off on him. He wound up with great welts and bumps all over his head, concussed so often that he developed memory loss, and after a while he could not remember anything.

Coming back into camp, the guards shook the prisoners down. When they caught a man with vegetables stuffed in his G-string, they would take him into the guardhouse and break his arm. Find two men and they would make them stand and slug each other till they bled. Forrest judged these Farm guards to be no better than animals. Big Stoop, Big Speedo, Little Speedo, Air Raid, Laughing Boy, Many Many, Beetle Brain, Fish Eyes, Web Foot, Hammer

Head, Hog Jaw—Forrest hated them. And he hated the American officer who thought up the Farm in the first place, a lieutenant named Henry Jones, known as Farmer Jones.

Forrest wanted out. There were always details being formed for work away from Cabanatuan, every kind of work, airport construction, road building, bridge building, stevedoring, in all kinds of places, Caloocan, the port of Manila, Clark Field, Nichols Field, details big and small, all the way from a couple of dozen men up to the twelve hundred who were shipped away, off Luzon altogether, to the south, to the big island of Mindanao, to the Davao Penal Colony, Dapecol, to work alongside Filipino murderers on a southern version of the Farm.

Forrest was of two minds about an outside detail. The truck detail was his best time ever, but what were the odds of hitting the jackpot a second time? He had seen prisoners come back to Cabanatuan from bad details, young boys with their hair gone white, Carl Nickols of Company A with beriberi and just about blind. And five others from Company A never came back at all; they died out there.

Forrest did not want anything such as metal scavenging among unexploded bombs. Or bridge building, as at Lumban. But the Farm was getting to him badly. An airfield construction detail came up. Forrest talked it over with Bob Stewart, who had been with him in the cookhouse, and they decided to give it a try.

::

AT BICYCLE Camp in Batavia, where Slug Wright was inside the fence with the 131st and the *Houston* survivors, the gut issue day by day was the same as in any POW camp, food. At chow time the lines formed as quick and buzzing as flies. Some men had mess kits; some did not, especially the *Houston* men. The ones without improvised, using anything that came to hand: empty condensed-milk cans, a sardine can with a length of bent wire for a handle, pieces of tin beaten into shape, a hubcap off a little English Ford, a baby's potty from Serang. O. C. McManus had the container with the most cubic content, a lampshade with a plug where the bulb used to be; he hung on to it all the way through prison camp and was forever being accused of getting more rice—as if a big bowl would attract a big serving.

At Bicycle Camp the officers, army and navy together, formed a high-caste tribe for eating, separate from the enlisted men, behind a wire fence, with the Chinese mess boys off the *Houston* to cook and serve them. The officers claimed to be eating no better than the men, but that was not how the men saw it. From where Slug ate, sitting on his bunk on the veranda, he could see the officers behind their fence. They took their meals at tables in the open, as if it was nothing to them who saw them. One day their mess gang served them something that looked like apple pie and smelled like apple pie. An enlisted man called them on it through the fence, and all they said was *It's amazing what those Chinese boys can do with rice.*

The top noncom of the 131st, a Headquarters Battery master sergeant named Jack Shaw, started standing at the fence at feeding time, making notes. The officers court-martialed him, busted him to private and set him to cleaning out ditches. Shaw offered, come the end of the war, to throw the colonel of the 131st overboard on the way home. Some of the other men suggested all officers down to lieutenants. After Shaw was busted, the enlisted men took to crowding the fence every feeding time, banging on empty mess kits, until the officers moved their eating inside, out of sight.

The officers were not getting their extra food free. They were buying on the black market, by way of Javanese in Batavia pleased to be making a quick guilder from white men, then through Japanese guards bribed at the gate.

This raised the whole question of money. Who was holding, who was spending, and for whose benefit?

Coming up to capitulation, most of the 131st men had not been paid for quite a while, and after the surrender some of them decided that white money was going to be worthless under the Japanese anyhow, so they gambled away what they had, or lit cigarettes with big bills for the flourish. But right before the surrender, some officers had gone to a Dutch bank in Bandoeng and drawn out a hundred thousand guilders, in fives and tens, barracks bags full of bills, which they dealt out among the battery captains and sergeants, the idea being that if the 131st scattered and took to the hills as guerrillas, at least every man could pay for food and favors. After the surrender, some of this money was buried to hide it from the Japanese, but then it was dug up and brought to Bicycle Camp, one sergeant coming in with ten thousand guilders stuck in a Mennen talcum powder can, another with a stash wrapped in a T-shirt to look like a pillow, and so on. The officers told them to turn the money in so it could be pooled. They did, but it was only pooled among the officers.

And that was not even all the money in camp. The men kept hearing stories about a lot more, connected with a lieutenant named Roy Stensland.

Stensland was not from the 131st. There were all sorts of stories about him. He came to Java on a ship; on a plane; he was from the Philippines; he was AWOL from Honolulu; he was from Borneo. He was a mystery man, and the word was that he had as much as a quarter of a million dollars.

The true story about Stensland was that he was on the same convoy with the 131st from the West Coast via Hawaii to Australia, but with a different field artillery battalion on a different ship. In Australia he was detached for special duty, as part of a plan to ship food from the Netherlands East Indies to Luzon, for the Americans starving on Bataan. The war had not reached the Indies yet. Washington wanted bold and resourceful men—that was the official description—to go there with money, buy food, charter ships, and sail through the Japanese blockade to the Philippines.

Stensland flew to Celebes in a wobbly Beechcraft with a letter of credit for four hundred thousand dollars, about eight hundred thousand guilders. Nothing worked out; the situation was hopeless. Stensland wound up on Java, at Soerabaja, just as the war hit and the 131st were getting ready to go into combat. He was field artillery himself, so he went with them, and after the surrender his money came with him into Bicycle Camp.

The enlisted men never saw it. But they knew about it, and they saw the officers eating well. Banging on their mess kits got them nowhere, so they proceeded to choose representatives to put their case. They did not go through the chain of command; they elected spokesmen—something that would never have happened in the service before prison camp.

The *Houston* men picked two representatives; the 131st, two, and one of them was Slug Wright. Slug did not know the honor was coming. But of course he was pleased to have his chosen tribe think so well of him.

They voted for him because of something he did before Bicycle Camp, at Tanjong Priok. Out on a detail he bought some food. The others did, too. They ate theirs on the spot, their beginning prisoner's wisdom being that the Japanese would shake them down at the guardhouse. Slug managed to sneak three small bags of food back into camp: bread, bully beef, coffee, and canned sweetened cream. In a flash the officers were all over him, the very ones who had been keeping their distance at the far end of the hut, with cash offers. Slug would not sell to them. He gave the battalion doctor a sack and a half for the sick, especially the sweetened cream. The rest he shared among his F Battery tribe. That was what got him elected at Bicycle Camp.

Under the new food system, Slug drew five thousand guilders at a time from the officers. He doled out five guilders to every man going out of the camp to work. They bought food on the black market and smuggled it in. Slug pooled everything for the mess and accounted for the funds.

The food was kept in a concrete basement under the officers' quarters, and that was a prickly point, but Slug was down there. He took his job so seriously as to sleep on the food.

Once Slug had the routine up and running well, the battalion supply captain came and took over. He said Slug had not turned in proper receipts, claimed he was short ten thousand guilders, and threatened to have him court-martialed. Before the war, Slug's paperwork was good enough for Standard Oil of California. In camp he had the services of an intelligent accountant from the *Houston*. And he was honest. It made him mad enough to want to have the captain court-martialed after the war, and he told him so. The captain backed off. Slug got the feeling that the captain could not account properly for all the money on his own side of the books and he was giving Slug a bad time to cover for that.

The captain was not about to sleep in the basement. He brought in men from his own Service Battery tribe. Their security was slack. They put the food up in the rafters, as if that would keep it safe. A man from F Battery found out in the course of turning into a prisoner that he was a born cat burglar. One night he and two other F Battery men sneaked into the basement. They scored Eagle canned milk and canned beef. Some they kept for themselves, the rest they shared with their subtribe. An F Battery sergeant who was not in on the deal turned them in to the officers. The three of them were busted to private and were ordered to hand the food over. They gave back some of it, but not all, and the officers never found the rest. They ran a shakedown, just like the Japanese, but they did not find anything. Their conclusion was that the Australians must have thieved it away across the border into their part of the compound.

Only one officer came out of the food wars with the full respect of every enlisted man: Roy Stensland, and he was not even from Texas.

Stensland was the lowest grade of officer, only a second lieutenant, and lacking the looks of a gentleman. He was built low to the ground, with short legs, long arms, and a big barrel chest like a wrestler, actually more like an ape.

He was afraid of nothing and no one. Slug saw him in combat, on forward fire control, standing on the dike of a rice paddy with his binoculars, directing fire as though he did not care what happened to him, and nothing did happen to him.

It was the same at Bicycle Camp. Stensland was an officer— just about the only one—who would go out regularly with the men on work detail. He did not have to, but he did. Stensland would take a beating to save a man from getting beaten. Once he wrestled a rifle loose from a guard who was bashing a man. For anyone else that would have meant a bad beating, if not death, but Stensland got away with it. Another time a guard was beating a Dutch woman who had been trying to slip the prisoners food and smokes. Stensland took off his shirt and said, *Over my dead body,* and the guard folded. Stensland had the respect of the Japanese, and for a white POW that was supposed to be unthinkable.

One story about Stensland was that he was drunk a lot of the time. This was not an impossibility. Stensland would have been well able to look after himself for liquor, as for everything else— the army had ranked him in the top 1 percent for resourcefulness and entrusted him with a lot of money. And certainly there was booze to be had in Batavia. The Dutch did the same as the British in Singapore, tried to get rid of all hard liquor before the Japanese came in, except that at Batavia many bottles were not smashed, just thrown in the harbor, and the work details at the docks could salvage them and smuggle them back into camp, with Stensland leading them through the gate, bold as brass.

One major thing to be said in favor of outside details at Bicycle Camp was that the Japanese were not slaving the prisoners to death. The work day was not dawn to dusk, but more like eight to five, Tokyo time. And they could make their own luck. They cannibalized a car, and a truck that ran out of gas near camp. Headlights went for mess kits, door panels for frying pans, windows for tabletops, mirrors for shaving, seats for sitting and sleeping, tires for soling shoes, sump oil for lamp oil—they left nothing of the truck but the frame and the sound of the horn.

The star scrounger was a marine off the *Houston,* James McCone. He brought in whiskey. The guards caught him and beat him up, which only made him more cunning. He brought in canned cream, canvas and bamboo for a sling to sleep in, a hammer and saw set, a different hammer plus tacks and bits of tire rubber for half-soling shoes, and two five-gallon cans, one at a time— McCone was the only man who could make five-gallon cans invisible to the Japanese. The item that made him truly famous was shower heads from the old Royal Tire plant in Batavia.

McCone did not show this talent before the war, it just came to him at Bicycle Camp. Weigh everything he smuggled in and it would have added up to one hundred fifty pounds, more than his body weight. He was known to all as Pack Rat.

McCone went into the tobacco business. He was not a smoker himself, but he would supply smokers, which was a sure money-maker, and then he would lend out the money and never ask for it back. That was his way. He was more a pack rat than a businessman, more a philanthropist than a capitalist.

Lester Rasbury, Headquarters Battery, was a real capitalist. He was in the fudge business. His first recipe was just cooked-up canned milk that he scrounged at the docks. Then when others went into competition with him, he bought up whatever chocolate and cocoa the miserable camp canteen had for flavoring. When the others caught on, Rasbury added peanuts, and in a couple of months he had so much demand he was paying men to shell for him after work.

Rasbury's Finer Fudge. The best people ate it, including Ben Dunn, Headquarters Battery, one of the Damyankees. Dunn was a boxer, ring name Dynamite. One of the boys who was a good artist made up a poster, with Ben's face looking over his gloves: DYNAMITE DUNN EATS RASBURY'S FINER FUDGE.

Dunn held the gloves for the boxing team. The Americans fought the Australians and won, mostly by knockouts. The Japanese watched and were appalled at this white man's cruelty. In volleyball, the *Houston* team played the Australians in fierce competition. And everybody went to the camp stage shows, Saturday and Sunday nights in an old mule stable the Japanese let them use.

There were female impersonators, like everywhere else— Poodles Norley, an Australian sailor off the *Perth,* looked remarkably like a woman. But, also like everywhere else, the appetite for sex was fading; food was taking over. O. C. McManus—the man with the breast-shaped lampshade mess kit with a plug where the nipple would be—was a good artist. He painted a mural in his cubicle, a beautiful native girl, and gave her eight breasts, two breasts apiece for each man in the cubicle. Men from other cubicles came by to look at her, and it was even money that what she brought to mind was nourishment rather than sex.

Outside camp there were women to look at. One day Slug Wright was on work detail, sneaking a quiet smoke, when a girl rode up on a bicycle, a Eurasian, Javanese-Dutch. She talked to Slug in English and gave him some money and some oranges. She told him to be there the next day and she would bring him cigarettes. So Slug had to make a point of getting on the same detail again. Like a fool he told a lieutenant back in camp why, and the lieutenant did everything he could to move Slug off the detail and move himself on, for a chance at the nicotine. Slug held out, and the girl brought him his smokes. He asked her how she came to have enough to give away, and she said she was shacking up with a Japanese major. Slug asked her how she could bring herself to do it, and she said, *I want to live. And how can you do what you're doing, working for the enemy?* That was something to think about. Slug never saw her again; not that she went away mad, she was sure to be off on her bicycle with money and oranges and smokes for some other prisoner.

The Americans held to their opinion of Dutch men as not worth much, but Dutch women they ranked as outstanding. They would take trouble over prisoners even if they were not Dutch; they did not limit the tribe of humanity to their own kind. And they were not frightened of the Japanese. Some of them were as fearless as Roy Stensland. They would throw food and smokes over the fence into camp. They would pass things to men out working, right under the noses of the Japanese, and risk a beating to do it. The prisoners blessed them for it. Out of the special goodness of her heart one young Dutch woman on a bicycle raised up her skirt a bit, her fingers making an inverted V for Victory sign, and that was inspiring, a little flash of something to live for.

In September, the Japanese came around looking for what they called *technicians,* men with a trade or a craft, or with some education. Among prisoners everywhere there was conflicting doctrine on whether to tell the Japanese the truth about skills. Some did, some did not. It amused the Australians to put themselves down as amateur jockey, banana straightener, beer tester, brothel inspector, centenary bell-ringer; and that was only the Australians, and only the first three letters of the alphabet. One British officer put down dilettante. Some Americans put peach-fur picker. Most of the Jacksboro boys said they were farmers, whether they were or not. And some actually did tell the truth.

In the end just over two dozen of the Americans were formed

into a group under Captain Lundy Ziegler of D Battery. The word went around that they were going to be shipped to Japan, along with some Australians and Dutchmen.

Jess Stanbrough was in Ziegler's group. He had told the truth. He had a college education and radio skills. He was the communications chief of Headquarters Battery, a tech sergeant with a radio instructor's rating.

Stanbrough had been a ham operator all his life. When he was a boy he built a set for three dollars that could transmit from Wichita Falls to Australia. At Camp Bowie he had a ham station, W5GTJ, to talk to Wichita Falls.

What he did not tell the Japanese was that he had a radio with him in Bicycle Camp. It came to him by way of Jack Karney, the motor sergeant of D Battery. Karney could not persuade the set to work, so he brought it to Stanbrough. Stanbrough knew a good thing when he saw one—a GE portable, small, about fourteen by ten and a half by four inches, running off a rechargeable wet-cell battery with built-in copper rectifiers. It was a regular AM broadcast set. Stanbrough tried everything between 500kh and 1700kh and got nothing. It turned out that Karney had tightened the intermediate frequency padders out of alignment. Stanbrough adjusted them. He picked up electrical storm noise. Then at the low-frequency end of the dial he got 500HZ CW code, ships at sea. He adjusted the high-frequency padders, and he had a working set. He wanted to be able to receive shortwave over long distances, so he had to rewind the oscillator coils. It took him several nights, winding on a fountain pen. On one of the hookups, with Karney watching, he did not even have to touch the dial; out of the blue a voice said: *This is KGEI, San Francisco, with the latest news of the world.* The reception was not perfect, he went to adjust it, and Karney said: *Touch that and I'll kill you.*

Stanbrough kept the radio under his bed. At night he could listen to the voice of Dinah Shore, and the orchestra of Guy Lombardo, the sweetest music this side of heaven. He heard the result of the Joe Louis-Abe Simon heavyweight championship fight at Madison Square Garden, Louis in six. And the war news.

In June, the headlines were about a big naval battle at a place called Midway, and no matter what the Japanese in camp said, *boomboom* here, *boomboom* there, the radio said Midway was bad news for Japan, good news for the United States.

There was no British-type officer-class news-tree exclusiveness

about Stanbrough's radio operation, in fact the 131st officers had
nothing to do with it. It was Stanbrough's show entirely. One of
the Headquarters Battery sergeants he was sharing his cubicle with,
Pat Patterson, had a job typing at the Japanese camp office. He
would take the news in shorthand late at night and type it up next
day under the nose of the Japanese. Then he would trade it off to
the Australians for food. Stanbrough was aware that running a radio
was a form of insanity. Wilson Reed of Headquarters Battery got
caught smuggling in some antenna wire for him, wound around
his waist. Reed was only a boy, still short of his seventeenth birthday. The Japanese gave him a bad beating in front of the guardhouse. There were sensible men who would not sleep anywhere
near Stanbrough. Frank Ficklin, the third Headquarters sergeant
in the cubicle, was sure Stanbrough was going to get everyone
killed. One night Stanbrough was recharging the battery with a
cord hanging down from the light socket, when a guard came in.
His bayonet touched the cord. He did not see it for what it was,
so nothing happened, but afterward Ficklin was ready to strangle
Stanbrough.

When Stanbrough was drafted to leave with Ziegler's group,
the radio went too. Jack Karney carried it out of camp under his
jacket, and made it through shakedown. It was October 1942, and
the Pacific war news was that the Americans were in heavy combat
with the Japanese on an island named Guadalcanal.

The Ziegler draft was not the only one. The Japanese were starting
to drain Bicycle Camp. Another draft of Americans was put together, no technical specifications, just bodies, about 190, including most of the F Battery enlisted men, under Captain Archie
Fitzsimmons of Headquarters Battery. And a third group, pretty
much all the rest of the 131st and the *Houston* men, 450 or so, left
under the command of the colonel of the 131st, Blucher Tharp.

One after another these groups were shipped from the port of
Batavia at Tanjong Priok, no one knew where for sure. The senior
officers of the *Houston* were long gone. They had been culled out
at Serang, sent to an interrogation camp in Japan. E Battery of the
131st had done their fighting separated from the rest of the battalion, in another part of Java. They were captured there, and they
were only at Bicycle Camp in transit. Then, with the big moveout
in October, the other batteries began getting separated one from
the other, and within batteries the little subtribes of friends and
bunkmates were in danger of being broken up, too.

Slug Wright wound up separated from his old F Battery gun crew. By the luck of the draw they were with Tharp and Slug was with Fitzsimmons.

Slug had skills, from his Standard Oil days. But he did not want the Japanese to know that. He was afraid they would set him to cleaning out oil storage tanks that the Dutch had sabotaged with sticky resin. So he put down that before the war he was a farmer, and his only skill as a soldier was camouflage.

At Tanjong Priok he was loaded onto a merchant ship, a rust-bucket. The Japanese stacked Australians and Dutchmen on shelves, and the Americans below them, at the bottom of the bottom hold, where there had been a load of rice, no eatable grains left, just the residue, and horseshit, the air thick with a hot fermenting stink.

Their food came down into the hold in buckets, swinging on ropes, slopping over. It was mutton, which was horrible enough to Americans, especially Texans, even when it was served fresh to them in Australia; and this stuff was old and green and awful. It blew their stomachs out. The line to the benjo had no end. And on top of everything, the ship ran into a typhoon. Slug was so seasick that his memory of the voyage was never any better than flaky.

He came up into the fresh air again at Singapore. The harbor was busy. War or peace, Singapore was one of the great ports of the world. Among all the ships, a special one caught everybody's eye, a passenger ship, painted shiny white, clean-looking, a vision from the real world. Slug was sure it had come to carry the prisoners home, and he was not the only one with that certainty. In the last days at Bicycle Camp one of the stories circulating was that the outgoing drafts were for exchange with Japanese prisoners. Repatriation was the word; it had a much better sound than capitulation.

Right after they tied up, a bizarre thing happened. Japanese medical corpsmen made everyone drop their pants and bend over to have a glass rod stuck up their rear. No one had ever had anything so atrocious done to them before, and some of the boys were so goosy they could hardly stand still for it. But obviously the Japanese were testing them for dysentery, to make sure they were in good shape before they went on board the white ship. That was the only possible explanation.

So it was a shock, worse than the glass rod, when they were off-loaded and trucked away from the harbor, away from the white

ship, to the east end of Singapore island, to a huge prison camp
called Changi.

Before the war Changi had been a big British barracks complex
for the defense of Singapore. Now it was Bicycle Camp multiplied.
At the time the American drafts came in, late in 1942, there would
have been something like fifteen thousand prisoners there, some
Dutch, most British and Australian.

The Americans had been educated about the Dutch on Java,
beginning before combat and continuing through capitulation. For
Australians they had an affection dating back to Christmas in Brisbane, and at Bicycle Camp the more they saw of them the better
they liked them. Of all the other Allied tribes the Australians
seemed to be the most like Americans, in fact almost like Texans,
more of them from the country than the city, hardworking stock,
plainspoken, tough, but easy to get along with. And entertaining—
great storytellers, great characters, even the thieves and con men
among them had a style that the 131st could appreciate. And they
had the good sense to respect the United States for coming to the
aid of Australia in the war.

Now Changi was the place for the Americans to be educated
about the British. The British were responsible for POW administration. The Japanese stayed pretty much outside the fence. Inside, they had Indian guards working for them, Sikhs who had
gone over to the Japanese for the pleasure of ordering the British
around. One of the few sights of Changi that amused the Americans was to see little Japanese with their shaved heads trying to
teach big Sikhs in their turbans how to bow like little Japanese
without sticking their big Sikh behinds out. The Americans were
not amused at the British officers. They acted as if they had not
lost the war. They went strutting around with swagger sticks, demanding military courtesy and formal salutes. They even had their
own men doing pack drill for punishment. In a Japanese prison
camp. The Americans could not believe it. The British officers
treated their own enlisted men like dirt, and in their loftiness they
assumed they could treat Americans the same way—they called
the transit groups coming in from the Indies *Java rabble*. The Australian enlisted men had no time for British officers, that was plain
to see. Neither did the Dutch. Even if it was only a Dutchman
saying so, he was right: At Changi everyone was a double prisoner,
of the British as well as the Japanese. So when a British officer
came by, with his nose in the air and an expression upon sighting

an American as if he smelled something bad, the American would make as though he was going to salute, and then instead scratch his head or pretend to be swatting a fly, and let the British officer shift for his own dignity.

The British camp administration was in charge of organizing work details, and the Americans were sure they were getting the wrong end of the stick: dirty work and long hours. The British would even try to make American enlisted men do things like move British officers' personal gear. The Americans drew their line in the sand; they refused to be ordered around as if they were British *other ranks*. And if there truly was work that had to be done, they wanted a fair share of the good tools, not the junk the British tried to foist off on them, keeping the best for themselves. This was what caused one of the Hensley brothers, John, a sergeant in F Battery, to come to the end of his tolerance with a British officer. He cracked him in the face with his junk shovel and laid him out.

In POW camp, whoever held the kitchen held the high ground of life. At Changi the British had the kitchen, hogging whatever food there was. That kind of thing had shown up earlier, on Java after the surrender. When the Americans came to their first prison camp at Tanjong Priok, the British told them to turn everything in to them or else the Japanese would take it. The Americans were new to being prisoners, still naive enough to believe what other prisoners of other tribes told them. Then the British turned around and tried to sell the Americans their own stuff back. At Changi they tried the same flimflam. The first time the Americans ever heard about Red Cross boxes was at Changi. The story was that they came off the white ship in the harbor. They were from the International Red Cross, but nothing ever got as far as the Americans. The British hogged it all—which caused Zip Zummo of the American boxing team to knock some Englishmen down.

That was satisfying, but it was not food, so they went after the Changi coconuts, and this brought the British down on them again. If it happened once it happened twenty times—the Americans would be chopping away at a coconut palm and some Britisher would appear, an officer or an officious noncom, shouting: *You can't do that! Those are the King's coconuts!* Not that it stopped the Americans chopping, but it was an irritation.

Coconuts were food, but they were not meat. There was mutton at Changi, but it stank so horribly that it could only be eaten holding the breath. So the Americans started to eye the sparrows that came to the latrine trenches after the maggots. They brought them down with slingshots, made from scrounged inner tubes. In Texas in those days a slingshot was called a niggershoooter. At Changi it was a sparrowshooter.

Compared to latrine sparrow, monkey meat was appealing. At Bicycle Camp the Americans were in the city, there were no monkeys around, and anyway, thinking back on it, they were not eating so badly. But after a week or two at Changi on mutton and latrine sparrows, monkey began to appear desirable. A crowd of monkeys used to hang out by a big iron garbage can where the British threw their leftover rice. Griff Douglas off the *Houston* made a snare. He was a sailor, supposed to be knowledgeable about knots. He scrounged a length of rope, looped it around the top of the garbage can, trailed it back behind a hut, and hid there holding on to the end. A monkey came. Douglas jerked the rope and caught it around the waist. The theory was that it would run off and the rope would tighten. But instead it ran toward Douglas, loosened the loop and hopped out. Douglas saw it go off and tell the other monkeys, and they never would come back.

After that it was back to slingshots. Douglas and the others fusilladed a dozen or so monkeys and put them in cages; they were going to boil them and eat them. They had a mother monkey and her baby, the mother bleeding, the baby holding on to her, scared. Douglas started to have second thoughts, and he was glad enough when a 131st captain came up and said: *I'm giving you an order to turn them loose! We're not going to eat monkeys at this stage. Too much like a human being!*

So then they used their niggershooters on British officers, for sport. They caught a fat colonel shaving with his suspenders down and let him have it, not meaning to hit him, just rattle his shutters. He stuck his head out his window and abused them, so next morning they came back and let him have it again, every American in camp who had a slingshot, about a hundred of them.

That was highly satisfying, but not nourishing. So they organized raids on the British officers' chickens. The British had MPs guarding their coops at night. The Americans had a man who was a track star. They put him in big boots, and they all crept up, quietly but with loud whispers, so the MPs would challenge them, *Halt! Who goes there?* The track star took off, clumping away, the MPs after him, at the bottom of the hill he shucked his boots and disappeared, and by then the others had the chickens.

Dempsey Key, Headquarters Battery, was an excellent chicken thief. Key and some of the others had a doctrine of theft, fitted to the various tribes in camp. Theft from the Japanese was no theft. The same went for the Dutch, they were fat pigs. The same for the British, they were horrible snobs. There was hesitation over Australians, because they were so like Texans, but absolution from guilt because the Australians were remorseless thieves themselves. One American enlisted man stealing from another—that was something else, not so much a Texan stealing from a Damyankee, but the closer to Texas the more it was a worry. Hardest of all was to contemplate stealing from someone who came from north Texas, 131st territory. And within a battery, one enlisted man stealing from another was next to impossible to imagine. Though for a man to think of stealing from an officer of his own battery was little of a worry, at least since Bicycle Camp, because the officers had kept all that money to look after themselves.

Frank Fujita, E Battery, ate a British dog. A dog of another nationality and he might not have eaten it, but he felt the same way as everyone else about the British, and that went for the dogs they rode in on. He and Dan Rafalovich off the *Houston* saw a British dog romping around trying to catch a bird. It was something like a beagle, only half a dog high but a dog and a half long. They flipped to see who would have to catch it. Fujita lost. He grabbed it and hid out with it down at the swill pit, and Rafalovich answered for him at evening tenko. When Rafalovich came back, they flipped again for killing it. Rafalovich lost. Fujita got the fire going, but Rafalovich still had not done a damn thing to the dog: *I can't kill him, you do it.* Fujita got as far as picking up an iron bar, but he could see doggy eyes looking at him and a doggy tail wagging, and he had to wait until dark before he could bring himself to knock it on the head. Then, come to skinning, Rafalovich had not the least idea, he was a city boy. Fujita was from Texas, that was supposed to qualify him, but it was nothing like a rabbit, a couple of quick passes with the knife and pull the skin off like a glove. This dog's skin had to be cut into strips, and even then Fujita did a poor job, he left a lot of the hair on.

He and Rafalovich boiled some meat to keep for later, some they fried to eat right away. They had red palm oil for the frying, hijacked off a British supply detail on the road outside camp. The smell drew a crowd, men standing around to see if dog was actually going to be eaten—for the 131st and the *Houston* it would be a first. Fujita and Rafalovich tried it. It tasted good. Some of the others made disgusted noises and went away, but there were plenty more who wanted a piece.

The next day a Britisher turned up, Royal Air Force with a

bristly moustache, asking about the dog in his British voice. Rafalovich was not impressed; at home in the USA an accent like
that just by itself would have got a man his ass kicked. Fujita said,
yes, he had eaten the dog. He was not going to say he was sorry,
because the dog was British, and the British were feeding their
dogs ahead of feeding Americans. The Britisher went so red in the
face Fujita thought he was going to explode. It turned out that
not only was the dog British, and therefore superior to Americans,
it was a mascot dog, it had been in combat with the RAF over
Dunkirk and on Crete, *it had 200 hours of flying time.*

The Britisher said Americans were cannibals. Fujita and Rafalovich did not offer to give him back the boiled part of the dog.
They never did eat it either, but not out of respect for the hallowed
remains; when they looked in the pot it had gone bad overnight,
and anyway it had too much hair on it.

The Britisher threatened to come around again with his friends,
but he never did.

Some of the 131st could bring themselves to admit that some individual Limeys were all right. It was the tribe as a whole, and
outstandingly the officers of the tribe, that graveled them so badly.

They did learn about an interesting distinction, between Englishmen and Scotsmen, both from Great Britain but all the difference in the world, like Yankees and Southerners. At Changi they
would get up in the morning and shout insults at each other—
Bannockburn! Flodden Field!—the names of battles hundreds of years
ago, before there was any such thing as Great Britain, just warring
tribes, north and south.

The Americans liked the Scots, and the Scots liked the Americans. But as for the English, and especially their officers, one of
the *Houston* marines brought it down to this: *After we found out their
mutton wasn't any good and their chickens was gone, we didn't have much
to do with them.*

E Battery left for Japan, Frank Fujita and the rest. Ziegler's
group of technicians left for Japan too, Jess Stanbrough and the
secret radio with them. Fitzsimmons's group left. No one knew
where they were headed, except that it was not Japan. Tharp's
group left, also for somewhere unspecified, not Japan. The Scots
piped them out of camp, which was an honor. Some British officers were looking down their noses at the departing Java rabble,
and Dempsey Key yelled at them in his big Texas voice, *You Limeys
can unlock your chicken pens now!*

* * *

Slug Wright was on the *Maebashi Maru* out of Singapore, with about eighteen hundred other bodies, more Australians than Americans. For fifty-six hours they went nowhere, stuck at anchor in the harbor, heat building up, the men in the sweatboxes of the holds feeling the water in their bodies boiling off.

Finally the ship moved off, heading north up the west coast of Malaya and Siam. Slug was completely dried out. By the fourth or fifth day his tongue was huge in his mouth. He was not in the bottom hold; there were other men from Bicycle Camp below him. One of them was Pack Rat McCone. Being McCone, he had packratted water on board in his five-gallon cans. Slug got some fluid into himself that way, but not enough. He was desperate. He found a steam pipe with a leaky joint dripping water, put his mess kit under it, and collected about half a pint not too fouled with oil, but a guard caught him and beat him up. Slug had been beaten up enough to know to snatch off his glasses and hold them so the guard could not knock them to the ground and stamp on them. He tried for water two other times. Both times he got caught and bashed. He finished up with a broken nose and some ribs smashed in. He had no doctor to put his nose back into shape; he had to form it with his fingers. He could not breathe freely and his glasses did not sit right. He was gasping for breath, with broken ribs, a broken nose, and a swollen tongue plugging up his mouth. He could not eat and he had nothing to drink. He went into hallucinations, crazy dreams of meadows and spring water and flowing fountains. Off he floated in his mind and soul, all the way to the twilight of life and death; he felt himself wishing he could just go over the edge and be in heaven.

The *Maebashi Maru* was headed for Burma. One of the *Houston* sailors, Donald Brain, had been to Burma as a boy with his father, who was in the oil business, and he recognized the port of Rangoon coming up. An Australian with a good voice sang the famous British song, by Rudyard Kipling, "On the Road to Mandalay."

At Rangoon they were put on a smaller ship and crossed the bay to Moulmein, to the pagoda in the song, beautiful-looking with all its gold leaf. They did not bed down there, though; they were herded into the town jail.

Somebody loaned Slug a number three peach can, fitted with a wire handle the Australian way, and he found a long piece of string to let the can down into a well. The water was not safe to drink, it needed to be boiled. Slug thought it was never going to cool. He could not wait. He drank it hot, down over his swollen lips, burning his swollen tongue. Then someone got hold of some concentrated soup stock and gave him some; it was delicious, it brought strength back to him.

At night, lying on the jail floor in the dark, he could hear the wind chimes from the pagoda, a nice sound. It put him to sleep. But then around four or five in the morning the wind began to blow harder, making a weird noise, and every dog in town started barking. Slug woke up, and in the dawn light he found that he and the others were in the leprosy section of the jail, stretched out on the same dirty floor where lepers slept.

That was the way Slug came to Burma. He could not imagine anything worse. Then the Japanese moved his group out. Slug was barely functioning. The best he could say for the march was that the Burmese cried for him and the others as they went by, and tried to give them food. Slug had to put one foot in front of the other for something like twenty-five miles, to a place called Than-byuzayat, and neither he nor anyone else had the least idea of what was waiting for them there, except that it was something to do with a railroad.

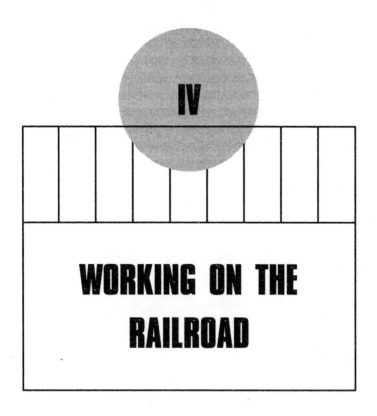

IV

WORKING ON THE RAILROAD

THE JAPANESE HAD A BIG FIGHTING FORCE IN BURMA, AND they had their eyes on India. But they could not supply or reinforce their armies in that region just by land; they needed the oceans. To service the Burma campaign, their ships had to cross the South China Sea, all the way to Singapore, head through the Strait of Malacca, and then turn north along the west coast of Malaya and Siam and up the coast of Burma to the port of Rangoon. A long, long way, part of it exposed to air attack and at risk from submarines. And after June 1942, when their navy ran into disaster at Midway, things at sea were only going to get worse for them.

If instead of Rangoon they used the port of Bangkok in Siam, that would cut sea distances by hundreds of miles, and danger by days. But then everything for Burma would have to be hauled overland from Bangkok to Rangoon, and there was no railroad connection. From Bangkok the track went only 40 miles west to a place called Ban Pong. From Ban Pong, northwest across the border into Burma, and northwest again to Thanbyuzayat, the rail link to Moulmein and Rangoon, the gap was something like 250 miles.

A Siam-Burma railroad had been thought about as far back as the nineteenth century, but the country it would have to cross was fearsome. From lowlying plains in the south, at the Siam end, it rose to mountains more than 5,000 feet high, with ravines and twisting riverbeds that would have to be bridged again and again. Tropical jungle, dank and rank—it could rot a dead elephant down to tusks and bones in fourteen days. There were tigers, pythons, cobras, kraits, and giant scorpions; monsoon storms and floods; malaria and cholera. Clearing a 250-mile swath and laying a level railroad track would take years, and it was guaranteed to cost many lives.

But the Japanese in 1942 were doing their sums by the arithmetic of war. To turn the Burma campaign in their favor they had to have a railroad. Their engineers said that even a single line of track would take two to five years to build. The military ordered it ready for use by the end of 1943, in less than eighteen months. It was going to be the worst work in the world, but the Japanese had scores of thousands of prisoners of war; they could work them like slaves, work every one of them to death, if that was what it took.

Along the 250-mile stretch of track, the total number of POW laborers was more than 61,000. About 30,000 were British; about 18,000 Dutch or Indonesian-Dutch; about 13,000 Australian; and about 650 American—the 131st Field Artillery and the *Houston* survivors. About 45 percent of all prisoners of the Japanese worked on the railroad. It was the biggest single use of POWs.

A huge project, and yet the Japanese brought in next to no heavy construction equipment. So the prisoners were condemned to build the railroad by hand.

Not one POW in a hundred ever sighted a bulldozer or a steamroller; not one in a thousand had so much as a jackhammer or a circular saw to work with. Prisoners broke up the ground along the track with pickaxes and shovels, or the hoes the local villagers used, *chunkels*. For earth moving they did not even have wheelbarrows, just buckets, bamboo-and-burlap litters, and yoyo poles. Stonecrushing for ballast was done by prisoners with hammers, chain-gang work. For boring holes in hard rock for dynamiting it was iron drills and sledgehammers, a long day of hard slog for a two-man team to make a single hole for blasting powder. The Japanese cannibalized a big steel bridge from Java, dismantled it, and shipped it in sections, eleven spans of twenty-five feet each, to Tha Makhan, at the Siam end of the railroad, not far upcountry from Ban Pong, where the track had to cross the Mae Khlong River. It was the only steel bridge on the Siam side. The Burma side had six. The rest were wood, six hundred eighty-plus, some of them higher and longer than the steel one at Tha Makhan. The Japanese used logs of teak and kapok, cut from the jungle, barged upriver or floated down, beached, then hauled to the site by elephants, or more often—most often—by prisoners. The Japanese railroad arithmetic was that eight prisoners equaled one elephant. They had to hoist twenty-foot logs to their shoulders, hundreds of pounds of weight and carries of hundreds of yards. Prisoners in gangs drove the piles for the bridges, naked to G-strings in the river, covered in leeches, hauling on ropes to a Japanese chant, with guards hurling iron rail spikes at them to keep them up to the count. *ICHI-NI-NESSAIYO, SEND THE BASTARD HIGHO! ICHI-NI-OH-SAI-OH, OH-SAI-OH, BUMP!*

Slug Wright and the rest of the Americans with Fitzsimmons got a welcoming speech from a Japanese lieutenant colonel wearing trousers with bull's-eye patches on the seat. He was Nagatomo Yoshitada, Chief of the War Prisoners, Number 3 Branch. *Nobody is permitted to eat and do nothing at the present,* said Nagatomo. *There are also countless difficulties and suffering, but you shall have the honor to join in this great work which was never done before.* There will be many of you, he said, *who will never see your homes again.* We will build the railroad, he said, *if we have to build it over the white man's body.*

The white men with Fitzsimmons started work at Beke Taung, south of Thanbyuzayat. The Japanese measured in kilometers. At the Burma end of the railroad, Thanbyuzayat was the base camp, 0 kilometers. Beke Taung was at 40 kilometers; the prisoners called it 40 Kilo.

Slug got there in terrible shape. His broken ribs and broken nose had not mended, he was not breathing well, his glasses were never going to sit right again, he was still not all the way over his bad dehydration, and it was on his mind that he had likely caught leprosy off the floor of the Moulmein jail. Then beriberi took hold of him, and he went into terrible spasms of dysentery, on the benjo run twenty-four hours a day.

He needed a doctor, but Fitzsimmons's 190 prisoners from Bicycle Camp did not have one, not even a medical orderly. Tharp's 450 had 3 doctors and 14 orderlies. In Burma the Japanese said this was a waste of prisoner manpower, and they turned most of the orderlies out to work on the railroad. They did not think to send some over to Fitzsimmons's group, even though they were only a few kilometers away.

Fitzsimmons was never going to get medical staff by asking. He had to trade. Before the war he was a jeweler. He had an eye for things such as watches. At 40 Kilo he still had some that he had been able to keep hidden through all the Japanese shakedowns. And a lieutenant from F Battery, Jimmy Lattimore, still had a wristwatch, a family graduation present. He put it up, Fitzsimmons threw in a pocket watch, and gave both to an interpreter with the Dutch, Cornelius Punt by name, to trade to the Japanese for a doctor.

This deal could have gone wrong any number of ways. But by good luck or good management, it went through without a hitch. And that was how Fitzsimmons's bunch got Dr. Henri Hekking.

He was a medical captain in KNIL, the Dutch colonial army in the Indies. He was on the same *maru* to Burma as Fitzsimmons's men, and after Thanbyuzayat he wound up not far away. Three other doctors were there, an Englishman and two Australians. They had no tropical experience. Hekking did. But they were not about to take advice from him, because he was a Dutchman, meaning that by definition they knew better about everything than he did. Besides which, Hekking was junior in rank. They had huts for sick call; Hekking was out under a tree. They put him in medical charge of the cookhouse, as something beneath them. Actually it turned out to the prisoners' advantage, because Hekking knew what British and Australian doctors did not, that washing rice before cooking took away as much as half the Vitamin B_1. He knew that their prescribing of coarse greens for dysentery was a bad idea; food went through a man so fast it was better to chop greens fine, it gave the body more chance to absorb the nutrients. And so on. The enlisted men started coming to him at sick call, Britishers and Australians as well as Dutchmen. This did not sit well with the majors. When the trade to Fitzsimmons's group came up, the name they automatically floated to the Japanese was Hekking. He was happy to go. He did not know about the wristwatches.

Fitzsimmons never made a better trade. The railroad was the worst thing that ever happened to his men but Hekking was the best. Even if he was a Dutchman, he turned out to be the difference between life and death, and all he cost was two watches.

When Hekking turned up at 40 Kilo, Slug Wright came to him. He looked no better than a marginal bet to survive, so bad that Hekking was able to talk the Japanese into sending him back to Thanbyuzayat, where the Japanese had something they called a hospital for prisoners.

He was bounced around on the back of a flatbed truck for hours, and then the section of the hospital that he wound up in was nothing more than fourteen filthy huts, with hundreds of disastrously sick men laid out in rows, a body in pain every three feet, not enough doctors, and hardly any medicine.

Slug was in bad enough condition to be sent to a hut called the Death House. He was down from about 145 pounds to 85, and he had beriberi balls the size of grapefruit. All he could think was: *This is depressing and it stinks, and I am a miserable human being and I'm going to die. But I am trying to live.*

He managed to talk his way out of the Death House by lying to the doctors about his dysentery, how many times a day he was going. In his new hut he was still flat on his back, in a hammock made of bamboo poles and a rice sack. His salvation was a cheerful skinny redheaded Australian called Blue—all redheaded Australians were called Blue—who sprinkled ashes on the floor under the hammock to cover Slug's mess, brought him fried things to eat, and generally kept him encouraged. After a while Slug managed to get up and about somewhat. Then another Australian, an old reprobate from World War I named Jimmy, took him into his business, cooking doovers, rice deep-fried in flour, with *shindagar* on top, the local dark sugar. Slug's pay was one Burmese rupee a day for looking after doover sales while Jimmy was off gambling.

Then, miracle of miracles, the senior medical officer, also an Australian, a major so hard and unforgiving he was known in the sick huts as Der Fuehrer, put Slug on a special diet, three eggs a day. For a sick man one hut up from the Death House, that was like inheriting a million dollars.

Slug loved Australians. He trusted them enough to leave his three eggs on his bunk while he went out to get himself a bamboo full of water. And that was when the hospital got bombed. The Japanese had a little red cross on the roof of the dispensing hut, and another one on the far side of the camp; but apart from that the hospital huts looked the same as the rest of the base, and the Liberators let go everywhere. There had been a raid a few days before, and the prisoners, the ones not too sick to move, had been practicing getting out of the huts and into the slit trenches. Slug had dug himself a personal trench. He ran for it, but his beriberi legs were not up to speed, and his hole was full of quicker men. So there he was, sticking out under the bombs in nothing but shoes, eyeglasses, and a piece of towel. *You sons of bitches,* he said, *make room for me! I dug that damned thing!*

He was in luck. He came through without a scratch, better than if he had been inside—his hut took a hit, a man from D Battery of the 131st was killed, and Slug's bunk was blown to smithereens, all his worldly goods with it, blanket, mosquito net, kapok pillow, British shorts, and his three eggs. He was in luck again, though, courtesy of the Australians. Old Jimmy gave him two gunny sacks for bedding and a Chevy hubcap to eat out of, and Slug made himself a coconut-shell spoon.

The raid killed about fifteen prisoners and injured forty-five. The Japanese let Slug and the others draw a big cross on the ground in red sand, but the Liberators came back and laid a bomb right in the middle of it, and at that the Japanese decided to abandon the place and move the prisoners, sick as they were, back along the railroad.

The Japanese stood them at tenko for an hour and then moved them out on foot, a thousand sick prisoners hoisting their own bedding and gear, men with high fevers who had no idea what was happening to them, men gone blind who had to hold on to other men, dysenteries who could not walk half a mile without having to go, beriberis who for months had not been able to walk more than a hundred yards, men with their feet in bloody bandages who could not walk at all.

The nearest camp was at 4 Kilo. That was the distance by rail. By road it was six miles. And the next camp after that, at 8 Kilo, was another six miles. From the first step, Slug could see men collapsing and dying around him, but not a thing could he do for them; it was all he could manage to stay on his own two feet. At 4 Kilo, the worst cases were allowed to stop. Slug did not qualify; he had to walk to 8 Kilo. He got there in the dark and the rain, plopped himself down in the mud, and lo and behold, there were two Australians he knew. One pulled out a rusty can of condensed milk he had been saving since Bicycle Camp, and the three of them demolished it.

That was the only good thing about 8 Kilo. A chance came for Slug to hitch a ride back to the Americans, and he jumped at it.

The Japanese were using Fitzsimmons's men as part of what was called a mobile force. In the space of six months they were moved from 40 Kilo to 25 Kilo to 35 Kilo to 14 Kilo to 25 Kilo to 45 Kilo to 18 Kilo, and they were at 30 Kilo when Slug came back.

He was hardly any fitter than before. The Japanese set him to bridge building; he lost his footing and fell into the river, and if he had not fetched up against a sandbank he would have drowned.

He was still badly ill, but his good luck was holding. Hekking found space for him in the sick bay. And because Slug could walk, though barely, Hekking gave him something to do. Hekking had already finagled himself—he was a great finagler—a personal orderly, a Welshman, plus three other men to work with him: an Australian; an Englishman from Manchester with a heavy accent and only two teeth; and an American off the *Houston,* Robert Hanley, so slow-moving that Hekking christened him Torpedo. None of the three were trained medical orderlies. Hekking taught them from scratch. He started Slug at the bottom too, cleaning mess kits. Then Slug took on the bedbugs, working his way along the rows of sick men, moving them off their bamboo bunks onto the floor so he could pull the slats and run them through a flame. Then he took on keeping the men clean, bathing them, scrubbing their clothes and bandages.

It was filthy work—no soap, no disinfectant, diseased bodies, horrible messes, evil smells. Slug was never one for bad smells, but there he was, the whole world smelled bad, he smelled bad himself. Neither was he one for living close up with masses of bodies. He liked a bit of privacy; at Bicycle Camp he preferred bunking out on the barracks veranda. But he had come a long way since then. He had seen the Death House at Thanbyuzayat; he had helped bury the dead. He was alive only because when he was in bad trouble himself, men with their own bad troubles had taken care of him. They were from a different tribe, Australians, but they had looked out for him like one of their own. Now he was back with his Texas tribe, and there were sick men from all the other tribes who needed looking after. Slug was still badly ill. He could not do his share of his own tribe's work on the railroad. But Hekking had a way of making him feel he was not a dead loss. Hekking was Dutch, yet he had orderlies of different nationalities. So to Slug, feeble as he was, it seemed only right and proper that he should

work for Doc Hekking, doing what he could for men too sick to
do anything for themselves, regardless of tribe.

The Japanese drafted Torpedo Hanley away. One morning he was
gone, just like that; Slug never knew where or why. Slug took his
place, and that was the beginning of his real education with Doc
Hekking.

Hekking was born in the Indies, at Soerabaja on Java. His family were white Dutch, three generations in the islands, and Henri's
grandmother on his mother's side lived in a mountain village
named Lawang. When Henri was small he caught malaria, and for
the sake of his health his parents sent him to his grandmother. She
was not a doctor, but she knew native medicine. She kept a big
herb garden for remedies, and on Sundays she treated poor people.
They came to her in crowds. Henri stayed with her from age four
to six. She taught him about the forest, with all its plants useful for
food and medicine; he saw what she could do for poor sick people;
and he decided that when he grew up he would be a doctor.

He went to the Netherlands for his medical degree, by way of
a Dutch government arrangement that committed him to come
back to the Indies after he graduated and serve ten years with
KNIL. Junior medical officers drew the jungle. Hekking was based
for four years at Kolonodale, on Celebes, an island as big as South
Holland. His job was to look after the KNIL garrison, and the
native population as well, which meant treating malaria, beriberi,
all sorts of parasites, obscure strains of dysentery, dengue fever,
yaws, and tropical ulcers.

When the war broke out he was on the island of Timor, a
captain, married, with a son and a daughter, living in a big house,
with servants, and driving a Packard. When the Japanese invaded,
they took his wife and children away. A general moved into his
house and commandeered his car. Then the general got sick. The
Japanese doctors had no tropical experience. They put Hekking
on the case. He did a good job, and the general was grateful. He
asked Hekking if he needed anything. Hekking said yes, a case of
quinine for the POWs. What about himself? Hekking said he
would like some photographs of his family from his house. The
photographs were gone, but an oil portrait of his wife done before
the war was still there, May in a white halter dress with a waist
sash, looking extremely attractive. When the Japanese moved the
Timor prisoners to Java, Hekking carried the portrait with him,
rolled up in a big hollow bamboo. The Japanese who shook him

down thought he was trying to hide a machine gun, and when he finally got it across to them that it was his wife inside, they thought it was her ashes—it amazed them to think what a huge white woman she must have been. Hekking had no idea if May was alive or dead, his children either, but at least he had May's portrait, and it went with him to Batavia, then Changi, then Burma.

Hekking had learned the basics of tropical medicine in a six-month course at Batavia, taught by Dutch doctors with experience in the Indies, using a textbook by de Langen and Lichtenstein, Dutchmen writing on the spot specifically for the purpose. The standard world textbook was *Tropical Diseases,* by Sir Patrick Manson, an Englishman. White doctors everywhere in the tropics swore by it, especially the British. But when Hekking was out on patrol on Celebes, practical experience taught him that there were medical conditions in the jungle that did not get into the textbooks.

Not in any medical text, but something Hekking took as an article of faith from his grandmother, was his belief that if there was a disease in a given area, nature had the cure for it. So on the railroad he foraged for medicinal plants. He was not an admirer of the Burmese jungle. Compared with Java or Celebes or Timor it struck him as poor, meaning sparse in useful plants and herbs. But he gathered what he could, whenever the Japanese would let him, which was not often. He collected anything that resembled what he had used in the Indies, *daon inggu* for headaches and fevers, *kumis kutjin* for urinary problems, *temu lawa* for intestinal problems. He took Slug with him and taught him to see what was before his American eyes. They brought back eatable greens. They could not harvest much in the way of bamboo shoots, because the elephants ate the young growth, but from the villages they could get pumpkins and shindagar, raw sugar, to make yeast. And salt, and cow's blood and cow's eyeballs. In deserted villages they looked for the spot where the natives used to pound rice, they scraped up the husks and made cookies for the sick, terrible-tasting, but good roughage, and with some Vitamin B_1 in them.

After all the Japanese shakedowns along the way to Burma, Hekking's entire medical kit was a stethoscope, a blood pressure machine, a rubber hammer, and two syringes, one of them a big horse needle that a man from the 131st found. For surgery he had a good razor with a whetstone and strop. Anesthesia was him yelling louder than the patient. He had to do dental work too. For pulling teeth he stole a pair of pliers from a Japanese truck. For fillings he used scrapings from an empty sack of cement, mixed with beeswax; he had read—he was a great reader—that in prehistoric Turkey they used beeswax for a disinfectant, because it stayed sterile. For medications he had some quinine, though never enough, some iodine, some salicylic acid, some creosote pills, and two sulfa tablets. For bandaging open sores, he used leaves as wrappings and latex from rubber trees to hold them in place. For dysentery, his all-purpose oral prescription was ground-up charcoal and sieved clay—not a cure, just to soak up mucus. His dysentery lab work was to have the sufferer shit on a leaf and show him.

Doc's working day started before dawn, at sick call, with the Japanese breathing down his neck, harassing him to get the work details out. A man might be so sick that work would kill him, but if he did not look awful, the Japanese would send him out anyway. Slug looked more awful than most, so Doc used to show him to the Japanese as a hopeless case; it was a way to finagle another body onto the sick count.

With sixty or seventy men at sick call, the Japanese gave Doc half an hour to examine and diagnose the lot. If he did not classify enough men as fit to work, he got a beating. There never was a morning when his numbers came up to the Japanese quota, so they beat him every day.

The same guards who would kick him in the crotch before breakfast wanted him to treat them. They came to him on the quiet, after dark, with VD. The Japanese Army did what most armies did to men with the pox or the clap—fined them and busted them. So the sorry guards would buy an ampule of black-market Salvarsan and bring it to Doc to inject them. Doc had his own use for Salvarsan; it was good for certain kinds of malaria. Getting ready to inject his first syphilitic guard, Doc told him what was true: The ampoule held 900 milligrams, the standard dose for syphilis was 450, and once the ampoule was broken the drug was only good for another half hour; it spoiled in air, actually turned to poison. Considering that, would the guard mind if Doc used the leftover for his malarias, 150 milligrams each for three of them? The moment Doc finished giving the shot, the guard grabbed the ampoule, threw it down, and stamped on it. So, from the second Japanese syphilitic on, Doc did not say a word, just stuck him, and finessed the rest of the ampoule for the three malarias Slug had waiting for him.

Doc was forever finessing and finagling. The Japanese engineers ordered him to make house calls at their huts, and while he was there he would lift some of their vitamin pills. Sulfa tablets, M&B 963s, were a great black-market item. Doc had none, so he made up counterfeit batches out of rice powder with a fake May & Baker identifying mark on them, and traded them to the Japanese for other drugs.

Doc always had prisoners stealing for him, liberating for the sick. His best scrounger was Eddie Fung, F Battery of the 131st. Fung was small and slight to begin with. By the time of the railroad he was down to almost nothing, and at night he was invisible. Once he came back with eggs from under a Japanese cook's bed. Another time, from under an engineer's bed, a five-gallon can of something that turned out to be seaweed. Another time, a huge sack of refined sugar that weighed more than he did.

Fung was not the only one scrounging for Doc. Doc could always persuade people to do helpful things for him. And he could always get his patients to help themselves. He enlightened Slug about the body and the mind being one unit, and how a doctor had to treat both. He had practically nothing to treat the body with, so he had to be a master mind doctor. Slug would hear him talking to an amoebic dysentery down so low he appeared to be dying. Doc would tell the suffering man he had the very thing for him, creosote pills, guaranteed efficacious. Slug would give the man the pills every three hours, knowing, as Doc knew, that creosote was next to useless for amoebic dysentery; but the man would come around because Doc told him he would. Doc would tell a man in atrocious pain that he was going to administer morphine, saved especially for him. The injection was really nothing but boiled water, but the man's pain would be eased and he would sleep. Doc could cure the worst malaria headaches; he had a silver coin that he would rub around a man's face and temples and the pain would disappear. Doc was available every day, from sick call before dawn to lights out and after. He believed in closeness with his patients. Slug saw Doc a thousand times touching sick men, and he came to believe in the power of the laying on of hands, Doc's hands, anyway.

Doc was an educated man. He spoke many languages. Spanish he learned on the railroad, from Refugio Medina, one of the Mexican-Americans in F Battery. Medina was paralyzed from a bad beating. Doc's treatment was to have him sit in a barrel of hot water while he talked to him, and in a couple of months Medina was up and walking and Doc was speaking Spanish.

As for English, Doc considered his understanding to be good, and so it was, good enough for him to read an English military-issue Bible that he bought from his Welsh orderly before the orderly could smoke it. Spoken English was another matter. Doc had to learn three different tribal versions, American, British, Australian.

The children in the villages along the railroad listened to the prisoners and learned to say English words in an amazing variety of accents. After *OK, very good,* and *no good,* the words most indelibly impressed upon them were obscenities. On the Siam side of the border, the children would say the words and laugh. On the Burma side, the Japanese issued an instruction that the use of such words must cease, because Japanese soldiers were being contaminated.

No power on earth could stop the Australians from swearing. Their expressions astounded Doc. He took to writing them down and trying them out in his Dutch accent. *Unbebloodylievable. Fanfuckingtastic.* A British officer had a novel that he read with Doc page by page. He would take minutes explaining and exploring each new word for Doc's benefit. Doc loved to say them. *Luscious. Snifter.* Fitzsimmons told him he must be spending too much time with the British, he was developing a British accent. Doc practiced Texas talk, and at the same time he practiced sounding like Otto Schwarz, one of the Dead End Kids from New Jersey. The British told him he must be spending too much time with the Americans, he was developing an American accent.

Doc knew American history, better than any American in the sick hut. At night he took them through the War of Independence, which only confirmed them in their view of the British. Then he went on to the Civil War, and the Yankees and Rebels lying ill and exhausted in the godforsaken dark in Burma got their juices flowing; some of them were even moved to try to get up off the floor and fight. To Slug this was pure Doc, treating the mind as well as the body.

Doc was old, at least old for a POW. He was forty when Slug first ran into him, almost of an age to be the father of the young enlisted men of the 131st and the young sailors and marines off the *Houston.* He took endless trouble over them. And he was positive. He always had optimistic things to say about how they were coming along, and they believed what he said. He was a father to them, far more than any senior officer of their own ever was.

Slug thought Doc was a great man. He would do anything for him. And it was true with Slug, as it was with all the others, that

Doc could get him to do things he did not think he was capable of. Doc pushed Slug, but without ever making a fuss about it. In all the time Slug worked for him on the railroad, through all the nerve-racking battles Doc had with the Japanese, starting the morning with a beating at sick call, struggling twenty-four hours a day to keep sick prisoners alive on less than nothing, and all through his private worries about his wife and children, he never once lost his temper with Slug, never so much as raised his voice at him.

For his own part, Slug turned out to be a quick study. Soon enough Doc did not have to tell him what to do, Slug could figure out the day's work around the sick huts for himself. Sick as he was, he could persuade his legs to carry him from the sick huts to the railroad. He had a red cross on his G-string, and that improved the odds that the guards would not bash him for not having a chunkel. So Slug could look after the men on the job. He was not a dead loss. Helping to keep other men alive was a reason and a way for him to stay alive himself.

One day Slug did something medical of a major kind; something that not even Doc ever did on the railroad. He delivered a baby. He was out along the track and some Japanese in a boxcar ordered him over. They had a Burmese woman with them, she was in labor, and there was Slug with a red cross on his G-string. All Slug knew was from the movies: *Quick, bring me a sheet and plenty of hot water,* and he never knew what for. He would have appreciated help. There were prisoners watching, but all they did was kibitz. Slug panicked, but he managed. The baby came out the right way, a boy, a tiny thing, no bigger than a double handful. Slug bit through the umbilical cord and tied it off. For lack of sheet and hot water, he cleaned everything up with a burlap sack and some Japanese tea.

::

IN BURMA, 95 percent of POWs had malaria. Most malarias had something else serious too, most often dysentery, and many malarias-plus-dysenteries had beriberi as well. Malaria kept knocking them down; dysentery meant they had to keep trying to get up to run for the benjo; beriberi meant they were never going to make it. On top of all that, there was pellagra, dengue fever, and scrub typhus. And then they ran into tropical ulcers.

Ulcus tropicum, tropical sloughing phagedena: A disease of food, filth, and friction, Manson called it, apt to attack half-starved malaria-stricken pioneers in jungle lands, soldiers campaigning in the tropics, and over-driven labor gangs. That amounted to a textbook description of POWs.

All it took to start an ulcer was a break in the skin. Doc Hekking had had years of experience with the problem, beginning on Celebes. Not so much among KNIL soldiers; on patrol they covered themselves top to toe, especially their legs, with long trousers and puttees. But the villagers went barefoot, and on the coast at Kolonodale, where Doc was based, the fishermen on the reefs were always cutting themselves on the coral, and a cut from old coral made for a vicious ulcer.

The treatment according to Manson was to anesthetize the patient, curette the dead flesh, apply a strong cauterizing disinfectant such as carbolic and a dusting of iodoform powder, then bandage. POW medical officers had no such medicines. In the Philippines they used a salve of margarine, or burned the bad flesh out with picric acid from unexploded bombs. On Ambon they tried copper sulfate, which the Japanese used for toughening horses' hooves. On Haruku, near Ambon, the Japanese had prisoners busting coral for a runway—rock chips flying everywhere, perfect for ulcers. An air raid blew up the airfield. The Japanese military brothel went up too. The POWs were the ones who had to clean up the brothel mess, so they scrounged the Korean comfort women's white face powder to dust on their ulcerated legs, and liberated condoms to cover their ulcerated toes.

The worst ulcers in the world were on the railroad. Sixty thousand-plus prisoners were laboring barefoot, in shorts or G-strings. A slip with the chunkel, a scratch from a rock chip or a sharp bamboo, a guard heightening productivity for the emperor by raking his boot down a man's shin, something as insignificant as an insect bite—and overnight a sore appeared, about the size of a nickel. With some men it went no further. With others the ulcer grew by the hour. In a matter of days it could eat a hole in a leg the size and depth of a saucer, a yellow, moist, stinking slough, expanding at the edges, leaving dead flesh. It could grow to the size of a dinner plate. It could eat its way down to the tendons and expose the bone. In under two weeks it could kill a man.

The slightest touch on an ulcer could make a strong man scream, and having an ulcer cleaned out was more than a touch— it meant cutting dead flesh away to expose live flesh. The doctors had no anesthetics. So, a wog cigarette for a stupefier, or a hard right to the jaw, or just a length of bamboo to bite on and four men to hold the patient down while the doctor went at the ulcer with a spoon sharpened to a knife edge. A hideous business. There were men who would try to hide their ulcer, even from friends, because the friends might turn them in to the doctor for their own good. Ulcer huts were stinking butcher shops, and there were doctors who came away from this dreadful work sweating and shaking. The worst human sound on the railroad was ulcer patients screaming.

Doc did not have a curette; he had to use the sharpened spoon method. Paul Leatherwood, F Battery of the 131st, who did some barbering in camp, kept the edge on the spoon for him. Doc had no iodoform either. The Japanese were not issuing it. The only way to come by it, other than scrounging, was to trade for it, and the black-market price was sky-high. Doc had no anesthetics either, so he had to use holders, big marines.

After the Japanese took Torpedo Hanley away, Slug graduated to ulcers. Doc taught him how to spread axle grease on the live flesh of the spooned-out crater, zinc oxide if there was any, which was rarely, and cod-liver oil for the vitamins, if a bottle happened to turn up out of nowhere, which it did once. Then a leaf-and-latex bandage against the flies. After two or three days, clean with gasoline siphoned out of Japanese trucks on the sly, wipe the crater down to bright live flesh, raw like a steak, and start again with the axle grease.

Without iodoform the body had to heal the ulcer from its own resources, and a starved and exhausted body could not heal well. Tropical ulcers were dreadfully persistent. The word Manson used was *intractable,* requiring lengthy hospitalization, and what Manson meant by the word *hospital* did not exist on the railroad. An essential part of the treatment was rest, and on the railroad rest did not exist either. The Japanese sent far more men with ulcers out to work than they allowed to stay in camp, and any time a guard sighted an ulcer, on the job or on the floor of a sick hut, he might kick it, just because it was there.

Men with ulcers could not always find a doctor, and a doctor could not always get to them. They had to look after themselves. They made shin guards out of bamboo, like hockey players. If they had no bandages, they used torn-up clothes. If they had no clothes to spare, torn-up mosquito net. If no mosquito net, mud packs. The sharpened spoon was a horror—every prisoner heard the screaming and thought to himself, *Anything but that.* There was POW doctrine on how to keep an ulcer cleaned of dead flesh, and how to start it healing. Some men tried the Burmese way: heat a rock over a fire, hold the rock over the ulcer and knock the soot into it. There were Englishmen pissing into the hole in their own leg. B. D. Fillmore, who used to talk philosophy with Slug, thought he remembered this from reading *The Seven Pillars of Wisdom* by T. E. Lawrence, Lawrence of Arabia—Lawrence was an Englishman, so maybe that was where they got the idea. The British were strong for rice poultices too. The Dutch said no, a hot mash of rice on an ulcer was a disaster, guaranteed to breed infection. There were Americans who poured on gasoline, if they could scrounge it. Or boiling water—agonizing, but no more agonizing than the pain of the ulcer, and if nothing else a change. There were Australians using rock salt, pounding it to powder, heating it, and packing it in. Men would collect latrine maggots and poke a dozen into their ulcer to eat the rotten flesh away. They counted carefully and made sure they pulled every last one out. If they missed one it would keep burrowing into their live flesh and they would have to dig it out, and the pain of that was unearthly. They put leeches in to suck the bad blood. A leech was good for two suckings; it would fill up once, vomit, and suck again until the toxic blood killed it. Men would drag themselves down to the river, dangle their ulcerous leg in the water, and little silvery fish the size of minnows, with sharp teeth, would come and nibble away. Those fish would nibble at anything; there were stories of men who went in for a swim and came out circumcised. That was an unearthly thought, but the most unearthly feeling was being eaten alive by fish so as not to be eaten alive by ulcers.

Either an ulcer got better or it did not. A relapse of malaria, a bad attack of pellagra diarrhea, or the body sinking into protein edema, and the ulcer could get radically worse. According to Manson, beyond a certain size and a certain stage, the effective treatment was excision and a skin graft.

But in the work camps on the railroad there were not many POW doctors with the professional training for skin grafting, and next to no sick huts with the equipment. So ulcers went beyond the skin-graft stage to being life-threatening. Then it was amputation or death, the bone saw or the burial detail.

The greatest surgeon on the railroad was an Australian named Albert Coates. He knew the history of amputations: The ancient

Romans amputated, and in Europe, battlefield amputations with saw, forceps, and ligatures went back to the sixteenth century. Coates had done wartime amputations himself. He was on Sumatra when the Japanese invaded. It was medical chaos. Coates was down to next to nothing in the way of surgical instruments; he had to take off legs with a chopper.

Coates had the chance to be evacuated ahead of the surrender, but he chose, as a doctor and an officer and gentleman, to stay with the sick and wounded, and go into prison camp with them.

When the Japanese moved him to Burma, they told him he would have a fully equipped hospital. That was a standard Japanese lie. Coates had thousands of sick men to look after and next to nothing to work with. For several months he was moved up and down the railroad. Looking after the sick, he got sick himself, with amoebic dysentery and scrub typhus. When he was down in weight from 168 pounds to 98, the Japanese sent him to 55 Kilo, an abandoned work camp, a cluster of filthy bamboo huts that they called a hospital camp, but really nothing more than a dump for the worst sick off the railroad.

At any serious hospital in the civilized world, Coates would have been admitted as a patient. At 55 Kilo he was the senior medical officer. He did his early rounds on a stretcher.

Among eighteen hundred sick, Coates counted something like five hundred with ulcers. Mornings he spent curetting—his curette was a gynecological one, given to him by a Japanese doctor as a kind of joke. Badly ulcerated toes he cut off with scissors, without anesthetic. He had to deal with seventy or eighty men screaming before midday. Morning was his time for morale-building, telling funny stories in between the screams coming down the row. He did his serious amputating in the afternoon, some days nine or ten legs before dark.

Coates had seen a railroad hospital camp for Japanese soldiers. It was well equipped. But all the Japanese let him have for an operating room was an open bamboo lean-to. For hygiene he had no surgical mask, and no rubber gloves, just some alcohol distilled from Burmese brandy to disinfect his hands. He had no iodoform, and next to no other supplies or equipment. But he did have a helper, an Australian sapper named Edward Dixon, who was a genius at improvising useful things. For general anesthesia he had nothing, but he had a Dutch captain, C. J. van Boxtel, who was a genius at chemistry. Coates came by a small bottle of dental cocaine tablets, and van Boxtel worked out a way to make the cocaine up into a 2 percent solution that could be injected as a spinal anesthetic. So when Coates amputated, the patient could not feel his leg being cut off. But he could see it and hear it. For amputating, Coates had a scalpel, some sharpened table knives, three or four artery forceps, and some bent forks for retractors. And to cut through the bone, he had the loan of a tenon saw that the butchers in the cookhouse used when the camp carpenters were through with it.

When to amputate, or whether to amputate at all—this was a judgment call for the POW surgeon. Coates was for action, for intervention. If anything, he was for early amputation, and on this crucial point of medical doctrine he would not have heard much argument from most other Australian doctors on the railroad, British doctors either. In their thinking, with a long delay the patient was a dead man anyway. Amputate, and at least he had some chance. Even if a man died after the operation, at least he would be leaving life in less pain, and with more dignity, his leg a clean-cut stump instead of a foul gangrenous horror.

Coates and Doc Hekking were known to each other by reputation. More than once they were in camps only kilometers apart, and finally they met. The Japanese were showing their favorite propaganda movie, the one that starred them bombing Pearl Harbor to bits. Doc had seen it more than enough times, so he took a walk along the railroad track. Someone came walking the other way. They stopped to pass the time, two POWs in the dark, one tall, with a Dutch accent, one short, with an Australian accent. It turned out that they were both medical officers. On a hunch Doc said: *Dr. Coates, I presume?* And Coates said: *Dr. Hekking, I presume.*

They sat on a railroad tie and talked. Coates told Doc about all his amputations at 55 Kilo, how many he had done, how fast he was, stumps stitched up in under thirty minutes, and his excellent survival rate, one in two.

Then Doc told Coates that on the railroad he had never amputated, and he had never lost a man to ulcers. Coates was amazed. But it was true. Doc Hekking was of a different medical tribe from Coates. He was an Indies Dutchman who all his life believed in fundamental Dutch medical doctrine: *No cutting, healing.* No prisoner with Doc in Fitzsimmons's group died of ulcers, and no man had to have a leg taken off.

The Americans with Tharp's group were not so lucky. When they started out on the railroad, one of their doctors was Hugh

Lumpkin of the 131st. He had never practiced tropical medicine, any more than any other American doctor from Amarillo, Texas, would have done in the 1930s. He was not blind to what this was going to mean on the railroad. He used to say that in the jungle one Dutch doctor was worth more than the whole American Medical Association. Lumpkin died on the railroad himself, at 100 Kilo, of dysentery. After that the main doctor with Tharp was William Epstein, off the *Houston*. Epstein took lessons about ulcers from the Dutch every chance he had. He learned the spoon method, but he was only a learner. Things got away from him. He could see he was going to have to start amputating. He was not a surgeon, so he was reluctant, and sometimes he left it too late. In a four-month period forty-eight of his Americans died of ulcers. Epstein was not a bad doctor or a negligent one. On the contrary, he was like Lumpkin, he always tried his hardest, and he saved lives. It was just that he was an American doctor.

On the railroad it was obvious to everyone that the colonial Dutch, and not only Eurasians but white Indies Dutch as well, got fewer ulcers than other POWs, and fewer really bad ulcers. When a Dutchman in a work camp did come down with a serious ulcer, no Dutch doctor wanted him sent to a hospital camp with Australian or British doctors, because they might take his leg off.

Coates had Dutch doctors with him in Burma, and he got on well enough with them. When he was badly ill with scrub typhus, it was a Dutchman who nursed him. The Dutch chemist van Boxtel was invaluable to him. The night Coates sat with Doc on the railroad track, Doc's best advice to him was to get more Dutch doctors at 55 Kilo. But Doc was only a Dutchman. Coates was an Australian, and an Australian with very British ideas. Doc was only a captain. Coates was a lieutenant colonel. Doc was only a doctor. Coates was a doctor, and a good one too, but first and foremost he was a heroic surgeon, in direct line of descent from the great battlefield amputators.

No POW doctor was more skilful or more experienced at amputating than Coates. After the war, and for the rest of his life as a surgeon—and he had a long and distinguished career, he rose to the top of his profession in Australia and was knighted—he always looked back on his work in POW camp as probably his best. This was his record with ulcers at 55 Kilo: He did 114 leg amputations, all but 25 above the knee. About one in ten of his patients died directly after the operation. And by a couple of months later one out of every two was dead.

::

THE Americans were shipped to the railroad early, and to the Burma end. That passed for good luck. The worst of bad luck was to be on a late draft to Siam, overland by train from Changi to Ban Pong and then north on foot.

On every march the prisoner doctors, never enough of them, had to keep ranging through the lines to do what little they could with what little they had. Behind them came the Japanese and Korean guards, always too many of them, with their clubs and bayonets. If it was not fear of the guards pouncing on fallen men it was fear of tigers; and if it was not fear of tigers it was the fact of Siamese bandits, scavenging.

The transiting prisoners turned into scavengers themselves. The further they were marched the weaker they got, until to keep going they had to lighten their packs. Then when they found a camp they would fall upon anything left lying loose and unguarded: blankets, towels, water canteens, shoes, shaving gear, cigarettes. They never knew where their next meal was coming from, or if there was going to be a next meal. So they stole camp food, and for their cooking fires they tore down the bamboo fences or stripped the bamboo bedding from the huts. They were nomads, alien marauders on the ragged margins of life, plague locusts. Once, some Australians turned up at a camp in the dark. The guards herded them onto the parade ground and left them. After a while they started to howl like dogs. A lamp was lit in one of the huts and some Dutch officers came out. An Australian sergeant said: *Any of you blokes speak English?* The head Dutchman, a kindly-faced elderly man, said: *Ja, I do, just a leedle.* And the Australian said: *Good, you can get fucked for a start.* Nothing and nobody was sacred. An Englishman found a place where for once he could move his bowels in what passed for privacy, behind a canvas screen at the end of the camp compound; but while he was squatting at the trench a hand came under the canvas and tore his trousers off him. So much for gentility. The custom of tribes roosting in transit was to crap on the ground and take off.

The farther upcountry, the farther food had to be shipped from the base camps, and the more it was pillaged and ratted along the way. There were times and places in the mountain camps where men were doing slave labor on less than an ounce of white rice per hour.

And the deeper into the jungle, the fewer the villages, meaning fewer chances for the POWs to trade for food on the side. Any kind of fresh fruit was a luxury. A duck egg was dream food, protein in its own container. Along the rivers there were traders on boats and rafts. Sometimes they had shindagar, dark sugar in a sticky brick shape, wrapped in leaves—also dream food. But with some traders, what they palmed off at speed and under wraps was not sugar at all, it was caked mud. The prisoners were caught so often by this that they gave the stuff a name, *Burma real estate.*

Honest merchants or real estate salesmen, the farther upriver and upcountry the fewer traders there were, and the higher their prices. The prisoners had trouble paying. Their Japanese pay did not always make it all the way from base camp. And anyway they were being paid in Japanese paper invasion currency, the Japanese were printing the stuff nonstop, and it kept losing value. With nothing but banana money, and sometimes none of that, the only thing of real value the average prisoner could trade for food was a pair of shorts or a shirt. By the time of the railroad most of them had only the shirt on their back, and every month more of them were down to no shirt at all; either they sold it or the jungle rotted it, and then they were of no interest to the traders. The formula was simple: no shirt to trade, no extra food. So their bodies were being run down to nothing. All they could do was look around them with longing. The classic railroad joke was the one about the lovely native girl going by, balancing a big bunch of bananas on her head, and not wearing a shirt. The prisoners' eyes bugged out at the view, and every last one of them had the same instantaneous lustful thought: *What . . . a . . . beautiful . . . bunch of bananas.*

Any beef that turned up on the hoof was likely to be scraggy or sickly or both. Oxen, water buffaloes, yaks—they might be so emaciated they could not walk any distance, meaning they had to be trucked into camp. It came down to sick starving men killing sick starving animals to stay alive. The cattle were feeble, but the prisoners were too, and the sick white-man smell of the camps unsettled the animals; so pinning an ox for a railroad sledgehammer between the eyes turned into a malnutrition rodeo event.

The Japanese way of dividing a cow was: the best half to them, the other half to the prisoners. There were five prisoners to one Japanese, and the Japanese took all the steaks.

One night when Slug Wright was sleeping, someone threw a leg over him. That was always happening in the crowded huts. Slug woke up, grabbed the leg to throw it back, and it was a python. He yelled, *Snake!,* and the noise of men hitting the bamboo floor was like machine guns. A Dutchman caught the serpent, took its head off, and got it ready for cooking—pleasurable to watch, the skin peeling down the white meat like a stocking down a woman's leg. They ate it fried on a skillet made from a Chevy fender.

Down in size from python, there were other reptiles. Iguana on a skewer was good eating, like chicken, with a dried persimmon flavor. A chameleon tail pulled off would cook up like a sausage. With other lizards, it was a matter of observing what they ate, eating that, then eating them. With ants, root them out of the anthill and throw them on the fire, and they would go off like popcorn. The Eurasian Dutch knew about a particular grub that lived in rotting trees, white with a dark head; twist the head off and a brown string came out, spit the body on a wire or a sliver of bamboo, cook it like a wiener till it popped, and it had a taste between chicken and strong cheddar cheese. The Eurasian Dutch were experienced about strange plant foods too: eatable ferns, bamboo shoots, all kinds of herbs. The 131st came across jungle plants looking just like things that grew in Texas: chile peppers, sassafras for tea, Johnson grass that gave boiled water a lemony flavor, wild tomatoes, wild figs, good enough for the railroad birds to eat, therefore good enough for the 131st, and a wild spinach that sprouted up powerfully around the latrines.

But there was never enough to eat, never such a thing as a full and satisfied belly. The Eurasian Dutch were by far the best foragers; they had the know-how, they were always quickest up the palm tree after the coconut, but even they were losing weight badly. So were the next best, white Dutch who had grown up in the Indies, and a few of the British who had been planters in Malaya before the war. Some Gordon Highlanders were famous for lassoing food off trains in the night—sacks of sugar, baskets of vegetables—but one time as the flatcars were going by in the dark they roped a coolie by mistake and lost their lariat, jerked away. Australian country boys at home in the Depression could go all day on one meat pie, but on the railroad there was no such thing as a meat pie, and what used to be a big heavily built Australian looked like a drought-stricken horse—you could hang a hat on him anywhere. It was the same with the Americans, all the way to Sid Matlock, F Battery of the 131st, lying awake at night contemplating cutting the tops off his shoes, if only he could think how to cook them.

* * *

Eight months after the Japanese made their decision to build the railroad, they concluded that just holding the fort in Burma was not enough. They had to go on the offensive. So they set a new deadline for finishing the railroad, August 1943. From then on, everywhere along the track, the Japanese word, first, last and always, was *SPEEDO!*

From the beginning, the Japanese used to say that as soon as a *kumi,* a squad of prisoners, met their daily earth-moving quota, they could quit and go back to camp early. It was a big incentive, and there were men who dearly wanted to give it credence. They started out working hard and fast, which only demonstrated that the Japanese could still make fools of white men in their second year of captivity. If a kumi met the quota early, the Japanese raised the workload, and if the kumi managed the higher figure, the Japanese raised it again. In Burma, the first earth-moving quota was 0.6 cubic meters per man per day, which was just about tolerable, at least for prisoners not too sick, working in soft soil, with a short carry. But the Japanese kept raising the quota, to 1, to 1.2, to 1.5, to 2, to 3—five times the original workload. And they made no allowances for hard rock or a long carry, or for both together. *SPEEDO!*

By Japanese medical arithmetic on the railroad, only 15 percent of prisoners were allowed to be sick, and a prisoner was allowed to have only one disease at a time. So every day the POW doctors, Doc Hekking and all the rest, fought the battle of sick call, and every day they lost.

The moral sums they had to do were agonizing. One British doctor and his work detail officer had a private formula: Take two men, one classified as sick, the other as sickest. Send the sick man out to work and he would probably die. Keep the sickest one in camp and he had only a small chance of surviving. Send the sickest one out, he would certainly die. But keep the man who was merely sick back in camp and he had a better chance of surviving. That was medical ethics under the Japanese.

The Japanese took the fit, so called, then the light sick, so called, and if that was not enough they beat the heavy sick to their feet and out onto the job. Mephistopheles the guard used to make the dysenteries squat in a circle and demonstrate. If they could not show him blood, he kicked them. Along the march to the work site, if a man looked like falling the guards would throw him down with judo to inspire him to get up and walk. If he could not, the others in his kumi had to carry him, and up-country the carry might be a mile or more of mountain mud, all before the start of the workday. On the job, if a man collapsed under the weight of the yoyo pole, or if he was too weak to keep a grip on his chunkel, the others had to make up his share of the quota. There were men with foot infections so bad they could not walk another step after they got to the work site. The guards made them stand barefoot in the mud. There were malarias with 105-degree fevers. The guards made them stand in the river. A wet beriberi was lucky if the guards let his friends lay him down to drain with his legs propped up against the embankment, his hat over his face to keep the rain off him, if he had a hat.

The bandmaster of the *Houston,* a trumpeter named George Galyean, known as Bandy, was with Tharp's group. He took it upon himself to blow a call in the morning as a signal that the Japanese were about to come blitzing through the sick huts to get more bodies up and out to work. Galyean's call was not familiar to the Japanese. They wanted to know what it was. He told them, "Fall Out the Sick." But really he was playing a song called "Bless 'Em All." It was known in enlisted men's barracks all over the world as "Fuck 'Em All," and that was Galyean's comment on the Japanese and their sick-hut blitz.

At the end of the day, the bodies of the prisoners who had dropped dead at the work site were carried back to camp. Of all the long carries on the railroad, that was the most heartbreaking; men had to reach deep into themselves to find the fortitude for it. And the final wrench was hearing Bandy Galyean blowing Taps yet again, the saddest sound on earth, with the mountains sending it back as Echo Taps.

Burma and Siam were monsoon territory. The monsoon came at midyear, the dry season ending with what were called *mango showers.* Then heavy clouds settled over the mountains, down to tree level, so that the air itself was drenched. And then fierce storms broke, with cracking thunder, terrifying lightning, and rain in torrents—for months, all the way to October.

The monsoon rain blew in through the open sides of the huts and soaked through the *atap* roofs; it swamped the latrines and flowed under the huts. There were fish swimming around in it. Men could drop a line through the bamboo floorboards and catch any number, bony specimens that tasted like mud if they did not taste like something floating downstream from the latrine. The river was up so high and running so fast it was scouring its banks, tearing loose great chunks of the land. Stands of trees still rooted in earth went sailing off downstream with birds and monkeys screeching in the branches; and other floating islands were going by too, massive rafts of bamboo cut for the railroad by villagers at the order of the Japanese, with the families who lived in little huts on the rafts caught in the flood now, swept away down-current. In the racing river, fierce whirlpools formed, sucking everything down, bananas in bunches, pumpkins, dead pigs, dead water buffaloes, and dead men.

The monsoon turned the prisoners' known world into a mudslide. Ballast was torn away from the railroad bed, bridge pilings came loose, bridges crashed down. Just for a man to stay upright in the wind, he had to lean at forty-five degrees. Just for him to hoist his body around was slave labor. It could take a sick prisoner classified fit thirty minutes to climb a hundred yards up a hill; it might take a gang of men all day to drag a cart five kilometers to pick up a camp's rice and beans.

Who could believe that the Japanese intended to keep the prisoners laboring through the monsoon? Surely they would have to let them stop until it passed. But it was never in the mind of the Japanese to call a halt.

They even turned POW officers out to work in the speedo, *shōkō* as they were called. That had not happened before on the railroad. The officers protested. And if the protest failed, they tried to see to it that the Japanese did not get value out of shōkō labor. By one version of Japanese railroad arithmetic, enlisted-man labor was eight men to one elephant, for officers it was *One elephant same as twenty shōkō.*

But even with every officer who could not talk his way out of manual labor working, and every enlisted man who could move a muscle working too, and even with the Japanese cutting camp administration to the bone, raiding the cookhouses and sick huts— even with all the stops out, a workday from *can't see to can't see,* and then at night men sweating at hand-cranked generators to power arc lamps, or bonfires lit against the dark so work could go on—even with all this, the slave labor of sixty thousand white men was not going to be enough to get the railroad finished by August.

The Japanese were going to have to pile on more labor, in fact multiples more, meaning they had to find many times more working bodies than they had white POWs.

They were using Asian civilians already. Now they started rounding up more, in great numbers.

When the Japanese first came down upon Southeast Asia they said they were racial liberators, Asians freeing their Asian brothers from the white man's yoke of colonial slavery. A year later they had hundreds of thousands of Asians yoked to slave labor, and eventually millions. The name for them was *rōmusha*.

The railroad was not the only project where the Japanese used rōmusha labor, but, as with the POWs, it was the biggest. The Japanese never kept an accurate count, but by the middle of 1943, speedo time, there were probably something like a quarter of a million rōmusha, four for every one white POW—and the Japanese were beating them, starving them, working them to death, just like white prisoners.

In fact, the rōmusha had it worse than the POWs. They were of many different tribes, thrown together or torn apart by the Japanese. They were not trained soldiers with discipline. They did not have even a semblance of military unit organization, and once they were set to slave labor they had no chance to develop camp organization for putting up huts, digging useful latrines, and so on. They came to the railroad with their families, and the Japanese had no intention of feeding them or their children any better than POWs were fed. And as for medical help, the rōmusha had no doctors or medical corpsmen of their own, and the Japanese gave them next to none. The Japanese had no compunction about leaving POWs fatally short of doctors, orderlies, drugs, and equipment, and they left the rōmusha shorter still; they would herd thousands of them into a camp with only one POW doctor, or no doctor at all.

All of which led to another railroad disaster, a cholera epidemic. The breeding place for the cholera bacillus, *Vibrio cholerae,* was in the big river deltas of India and Burma, the Ganges and the Brahmaputra and the Irrawaddy. Cholera was a disease that attacked the poor and destitute, human beings forced to subsist crammed together in hordes, who could not afford the modern luxury of good community hygiene, and whose drinking water was contaminated. The war, the POWs, the rōmusha, the river, the filth of the work camps, it all added up—the cholera chapter of Manson's *Tropical Diseases* could have been written along the railroad.

Everyone in Asia knew about cholera. In the Japanese home islands, the government's cholera regulations were stricter than any other Asian nation's. In their army, every division had an epidemic

prevention unit, with equipment for purifying water. Their soldiers overseas got cholera shots every six months, boosters every
three. Even so, the Japanese had cholera among their troops in
China in 1937, and again in 1940–1941. In 1943 cholera was being
carried across their Co-Prosperity Sphere, from Shanghai to Formosa to Singapore to Makassar to the Philippines.

They knew specifically about the risk of cholera in the territory
of the railroad—they had cholera among coolies laboring for them
in other parts of Burma in 1943. When they drafted POWs to
Burma and Siam, they put them through a glass rod test and gave
them shots. But not all POWs on all drafts. Besides which, the
Japanese did not follow up everywhere with boosters. As for the
rōmusha, the Japanese never had a plan, not even a real intention,
to give all of them shots; and so it was the rōmusha who brought
cholera to the railroad.

Cholera was sudden and dreadful. Dizziness, a ringing in the
ears, then nausea, fierce vomiting, and violent diarrhea, gallons of
it, a gray-white color like rice water. The attack seized a man by
the gut and twisted his body in agony, wringing all the fluids out
of him from both ends. Cramps, delirium and derangement, then
a rapid falloff, voice down to a raspy whisper, eyes rolled up, face
cadaverous, washboard ribs, washerwoman's fingers, body temperature dropping, pulse fading, gone, in seven days, five days, as
little as three days—it could happen overnight, nothing left of a
man but a pinched bag of bones, with his guts shriveled and stuck
together like old inner tubes.

Cholera seized the attention of the Japanese like no other disease on the railroad. They did not care—never had cared—if their
slave labor died, but they did not want slaves' diseases killing them.
Cholera above all—one case in the labor huts today, and tomorrow
it was in the Japanese lines.

To keep the infection away from them, the Japanese cordoned
themselves off. They put on masks and gloves and white coveralls
and rubber boots. They doused themselves prodigally with potassium permanganate. They ran around with backpack sprays of
phenyl. They made the prisoners and the rōmusha do the horrible
close work, moving cases to isolation, care and feeding and cleaning, the burning of infected huts, the handling of the dead.

The Indies Dutch and their doctors knew more about cholera
than any of the other prisoners on the railroad. KNIL soldiers
before the war were given regular cholera shots and boosters. On
the railroad the Dutch knew to abide by the strictest of cholera

discipline—never drink unboiled water, never stand in the river above the waist, never let river water touch the lips, all the way to never drying hands in the huts because someone else might brush up against a wet towel in the dark. They had cholera squads enforcing the rules by physical punishment. The Dutch doctors were the quickest and best at diagnosis, and the most confident about excluding doubtful cases so as to hold down panic. The essential treatment was replacement of fluids by intravenous injection of saline solution, quickly and in quantity, pints a day. The Japanese were not about to supply equipment. The Dutch doctors were the quickest and best at improvising.

The cholera epidemic raced up and down the railroad for six months. The Dutch lost men by twos and threes and tens. The British and the Australians lost hundreds. At first, British and Australian doctors did not always understand what they were seeing; they might misdiagnose colitis or dysentery, and that put them behind from the start. They called for rigorous hygiene—no bathing in the river, boil all drinking water and all mess kits and spoons, all food to be served covered with leaves against flies, keep hands away from mouth, clean teeth only with boiled water, *do not lick cigarette papers.* For saline solution they had to improvise stills, lengths of stolen gasoline pipe in bamboo jackets, river water or spring water boiled and filtered, plus rock salt or kitchen salt, stored in containers made from beer or sake bottles scrounged from the Japanese, attached to rubber tubing from stethoscopes, and fed into the vein through needles cut from fine copper tubing or bamboo. The epidemic got on top of them. They segregated the choleras in isolation huts, and called for volunteers to take care of them. Volunteering meant being willing to go in harm's way, to the ultimate, and there were always men brave enough, even though some of them caught the infection and died, and other volunteers had to carry their bodies to the cholera graves.

The Japanese drafted some POW doctors and orderlies from Changi specifically for rōmusha camps, but far too few and far too late. The rōmusha had no medicine. Their only epidemic control was to throw the sick on the fire. One case, then ten, then hundreds, and the rest would take off into the jungle, not enough guards to keep them corraled, the epidemic spreading at the speed of their flight to the river, the river carrying contamination downstream. A POW might be bathing, splashing water on himself, and he would find stuck in the reeds the big bloated body of a dead Tamil.

Corpses were rotting in the jungle, eaten at by rats, left on the side of a hill, dirt thrown over the body but the head out in the open so the soul could depart, worms at work on the body under the dirt, so many that the corpse appeared to be trying to move. Bodies were left by hundreds to lie in camp until the Japanese sent POW burial details. They found one with a Malayan dollar in its mouth, and scrawled on the tent wall in red: *All I have is for family look my family. Ghant.* Not likely. For the rōmusha it was mass graves, men, women, and children.

What the Japanese should have done was to keep whole camps quarantined off from one another. But the height of the epidemic was at the height of the speedo, and the railroad was all that mattered. The Japanese kept moving prisoners up and down the track in thousands, marching new drafts into old camps, onto the same parade grounds where day after day the guards maximized work numbers by making men show blood on the ground, on command, to prove they were not malingering.

Cholera or no cholera, if a rōmusha camp was where the Japanese called the day's halt for transiting groups, that was where the POWs had to take their rest, with corpses in the huts, the air black with flies, the ground covered with the droppings of dysentery. At Konkuita a British officer asked the Japanese for spades to clear away the filth and they said, *Use your hands.*

The Japanese did not allow funeral services for dead rōmusha. They begrudged the time it would take to bury the bodies; it was work time taken away from the speedo. At Takanun a coolie gang of British officers took a whole day to bury 161 rōmusha, and after that the Japanese made them build the corpses into the railroad embankment.

Dead POW choleras were burned, so many of them that cremating turned into a labor of hell, like everything else on the railroad. At morning sick call, the first thing the doctors did was tally the number of cholera dead, so that the cremation squads would know how much bamboo they had to cut. The longer the epidemic lasted, the farther the cremators had to go for bamboo; in bad camps it might be a mile's march out and a mile dragging it back. Burning the bodies was afternoon work. That way the cremation gang could get the fire going in the morning, use it to make tea for their midday meal, toss a snake on the coals to cook, and when it was ready rake it out with some cremated cholera's rib saved for the purpose, being prepared for an occasional toe joint or wristbone to turn up in the ashes. Once they were through eating they would turn to stacking the corpses of the day: teak logs with the bodies laid across, or a layer of bamboo, a layer of bodies, more bamboo, more bodies. With wet beriberis, they speared the bodies first to drain them so that they would not burst and put out the fire.

If the bamboo was green, the water in it turned to steam and exploded. When the bodies started to char, their arms and legs twitched, and they sat up as if they were alive. Smoke came out of their burned-out eyes. Their mouths opened, and licks of flame came out; their lungs were full of steam, and noises came out.

The way to stop a dead cholera sitting up was to lay him on his stomach. The cremation gangs learned that one quickly.

If ever there was a place to be away from, it was the railroad. Some men tried to escape, but not many; and few succeeded, dozens only. Prisoners on the railroad were like POWs everywhere: prisoners of Asia, prisoners of their failing bodies, and prisoners of the jungle, too.

The only other escape from the railroad was death, and one way of dying was suicide. No one will ever know exactly how many prisoners on the railroad took their own lives. But it was very few, certainly fewer than the few who tried to escape. There were fewer than a hundred escape attempts, and probably no more than a dozen or so suicides.

Some men did not kill themselves but gave up and let themselves die. That was more common. It had been happening since the first days of captivity, and it kept on happening along the railroad. No one had the numbers. It was not epidemic, but every prisoner saw it.

Swede Ecklund, F Battery of the 131st, had Doc Hekking and Slug Wright looking after him, but he was slipping; he had beriberi, dysentery too, and barely strength enough to make it to the benjo. One day Preston Stone asked him how he was. Ecklund said he had fooled them last night, he did not have to go. He did not know he had fouled himself. He started putting all his belongings in his ditty bag. He told everyone he was going home. *There is a ship right out there in the harbor! It is a beautiful ship! It is most wonderful to behold!* He caught the ship the next day. He sat up, the way a beriberi sometimes did right at the moment he went into cardiac arrest, and fell over dead.

* * *

The deaths were too many to keep up with. Every fit man was on work detail, and most of the sick, too. Gravedigging had to take its chances. In the worst camps it fell behind by days. Even where there was no cholera, funerals came down to no coffins—too much work, not enough wood. So men were buried in their blanket. Then in the mountains, where it was cold at night, and especially during the monsoon, blankets became too valuable to be buried with the dead, so it came down to bamboo matting. Or rice sacks over the head and feet, tied in the middle—if the Japanese would let them have rice sacks. If not, it was down to the clothes the man died in. But then dead men's clothes were too valuable to bury; there were living men who needed them. So the dead were buried naked. In the worst of the camps, the only way to get men to go on burial detail was to promise them they could divide up the belongings of the dead.

Where were the decencies? Not one camp in ten had a chaplain to say a prayer. Whoever was closest to the graveside had to say the words, if he could think of anything to say. It might not even be friends laying the dead man down; they might be out on the line under Japanese boot and whip, burying dead rōmusha in the embankment. Swede Ecklund had friends, no coffin but at least friends. The first shovelful was going to be a hard one, until finally Snuffy Jordan said: *Well, Big Swede, I hate to do it, but here it goes,* and shoveled dirt right on his face.

::

THE entire length of the railroad there were secret radios, the product of a clandestine POW export industry, based mainly on Changi. Parts scavenged from a Chinese school in Singapore went, hidden in Red Cross boxes, to the British at Chungkai, enough to make two shortwave receivers. Tarsao had six. F Force had a radio in a flashlight. The same man who figured out how to fit a receiver inside a broomhead at Changi built one inside an accordion that traveled with some Australians, and the accordion was playable. In the nature of things, no one had an accurate count of every set on the railroad, but the total would have been well into the dozens.

Tom Douglas, an Englishman who was a BBC engineer before the war, built nine radios in all. A water-canteen set he helped to make was operated at Chungkai by two British brothers, Donald and Max Webber. They kept the batteries in a bamboo bed frame in their hut, and at night they ran an aerial out around the roof. In the interest of security they moved the set every so often, to a clump of bamboo near the Japanese sentry post, to an atap toolshed in the cemetery, to a quartermaster store. Beginning in February 1943, they operated through the entire time the railroad was being built, and beyond. They put out seven hundred-plus news bulletins, distributed up and down the line.

The Pacific war news in 1943 was more good than bad. The Americans had control of Guadalcanal. Admiral Yamamoto Isoroku, commander in chief of the Japanese Combined Fleet, the man who had planned the attack on Pearl Harbor, was dead; the Americans had shot him out of the air over Bougainville in the Solomon Islands. United States marines had landed on Tarawa and Makin in the Gilbert Islands in the central Pacific. Any educated news analyst in camp could tell that this was an arrowhead aimed ultimately at the Japanese home islands. And President Roosevelt announced that it was known, on good evidence, that the Japanese were executing POWs, an atrocity. When the war was won the guilty would be brought to justice.

Give or take an occasional alarm—shakedowns, or a guard patrolling in the night and snagging his bayonet on an aerial without realizing what it was—the war news was received and distributed steadily, all the way to within a month of the completion of the railroad.

Then at Kanchanaburi, a big base camp in southern Thailand, the Japanese found a radio.

The August date for finishing the railroad had not been met. Looked at rationally, it was an impossible deadline, but the Japanese put the delay down to sabotage, and to wrong spirit on the part of their prisoners—the POWs kept saying the Allies would win the war. Which meant they must be getting war news. Which meant there must be a radio.

At Kanchanaburi there was. Going up-country, one of the men who went on to run the radio in the cholera camp at Songkurai had handed off some equipment to a British sergeant major. It was this set that was found, hidden in a coffee can.

The Japanese bashed the sergeant major unrecognizable. It was not the kempeitai doing the bashing; it was the camp adjutant, a captain, drunk; plus a civilian interpreter with lieutenant rank, a lame leg, American-style rimless glasses, and an American accent; and some Korean guards, one of them known as The Undertaker. They beat the sergeant major on his back and thighs with bamboo clubs and teak poles, and on the face with wooden clogs. He was black and blue all over. His jaw was beaten out of alignment, his nose twisted to one side; one of his eardrums was burst, and one eye was suppurating. They stood him in the sun by the guardhouse. He was not allowed to kneel or sit down; he had to stoop to the food they left on the ground. When he fainted, the guards brought him around and stood him up again. They kept him standing for five days. Then they turned him over to the kempeitai.

The sergeant major had been giving the news to his officers. The Japanese took two majors and three lieutenants to the guardhouse, beat them and left them lying all night, one of them almost dead from shock, another unconscious in a ditch, another with both forearms broken. Then they put them in a cage so small they could not stand; they had to go on all fours. They were so badly injured that they could not feed themselves. One of the majors died later.

They took four more officers, two captains and two lieutenants. They beat the two lieutenants unconscious. They threw buckets of water on them to bring them round. When one came to they beat him; when the other came to they beat him. They beat them for hours—beat them to death. They threw the bodies in a swill pit behind the Japanese latrines. Some prisoners found a Red Cross-issue hat in there, and the next morning one of the guards was walking around in a pair of British suede shoes.

Word of the disaster traveled up and down the railroad with the truckers. After that, who would want to be in the radio business? Some sets went into the latrines. But the Webber brothers did not ditch theirs, even though they were only a few miles from Kanchanaburi, at Chungkai; they kept listening and putting out bulletins, through the end of the construction of the railroad and beyond.

::

WORKING to finish the railroad put the prisoners between a rock and a hard place. Pushing the track through the jungle was helping the Japanese war effort on the largest scale, at the strategic level. So, early on, the POWs did everything they could to slow it down. But if they set a tie crooked in the ballast so that it had to be reset, or laid track a fraction wide so that it had to be realigned, what were they accomplishing? They were condemning themselves to do the work all over again. No matter what they did or did not

do, the railroad was going to go through; the Japanese kept telling
them that. The longer the railroad took to finish, the more prisoners would die. So if the POWs wanted to survive—and the
overwhelming majority did—they had to get the job done.

If a kumi did not make its quota, the Japanese would be on
everyone's back. So if one man did not pull his weight for any
reason other than sickness—if he was a goldbrick, what the Australians called a bludger—all he was doing was dragging down his
kumi, his tribe, the men he would be depending on if he ever
needed help himself.

If a senior POW officer dug in his heels about how much work
his men had to do, he might be dicing with death, his own and
his men's. A British lieutenant colonel, H. H. Lilley of the Sher-
wood Foresters, was a POW for the second time. The Germans
had captured him in World War I; now it was the Japanese. Lilley's
men were being marched up the line, and they were exhausted.
He demanded rest for them. The Japanese said they would kill
him. Lilley told them to go ahead; after they killed him they would
have to kill every man in order of seniority until there were none
left to work on the railroad. The Japanese did not kill anyone.
Lilley did the same thing again in one of the work camps. He said
his men would not work the next day because they were too cut
up. He stood there, not looking anything like his rank, shirtless,
in a civilian trilby hat and a pair of shorts made out of an old kit
bag, and faced the Japanese down. Not many senior officers of any
nationality could have done that, and fewer tried. But of course
in the end Lilley's men had to go out to work.

Another British lieutenant colonel, Philip Toosey, had a different style. Toosey was the POW commander of the big camp at
Tha Makhan, at the southern end of the railroad, where the steel
bridge crossed the river. The way Toosey saw his job, it was to
maintain human dignity and at the same time bring as many men
as possible out alive. Toosey was a camp diplomat, a successful
POW businessman, an endless schemer for the good of his men.
He would do anything to keep the Japanese off his back and off
his men's backs. He used the Changi gambit, talking the Japanese
into letting him and his own officers look after discipline and organize the work force—in the interests of efficiency, which meant
getting the railroad built and finished.

The way Toosey calculated, refusing to work might get men
killed or badly punished. He was even in favor of officers doing
manual labor. He would go out on work detail himself, a lieuten-

ant colonel laboring alongside enlisted men, if that would keep the Japanese happy. The Japanese were happy enough with Toosey to give his men a yasume one day in seven, and on the railroad there was no better deal than that. Toosey had the admiration of everyone in his camp. Beyond that, he was known up and down the track in Siam in the same admiring way that Albert Coates and Doc Hekking were known in Burma. In fact, Toosey was judged to be the greatest of British officers on the railroad.

Finally—finally—on the Siam side of the border, about thirty kilometers south of Three Pagodas Pass, at a place called Konkuita, on October 16, 1943, toward the end of the monsoon, after the worst of the cholera, the two ends of the railroad were joined.

According to Japanese figures, the POWs and the rōmusha had shifted 3 million cubic meters of rock, built 4 million cubic meters of earthworks, hauled 60,000 cubic feet of bridging timber and 650,000 cubic feet of timber poles, and built 688 bridges with a total length of 14 kilometers. They had laid 415 kilometers of track, almost 258 miles, at the rate of 890 meters a day.

For the great day, the Japanese had trains bringing important personages in cattle trucks with atap roofs—*flying kampongs,* the prisoners called them, flying villages. An antiaircraft battery and a military band were brought in for the ceremony. A propaganda film was made of prisoners laying the last rails, starring the least starved-looking men, hand-picked, specially dressed. After they were filmed, the Japanese took their good-looking clothes away and they went back to their G-strings. The commanders of the two Japanese railroad regiments, the 5th from Thanbyuzayat and the 9th from Kanchanaburi, were filmed driving special gunmetal spikes into a special ebony tie. On their first try they missed. The Japanese engineers were given a bronze medallion, struck in the base camp workshops at Nong Pladuk in Siam, with an inscription on one side, *To commemorate the opening of the railroad connecting Thailand with Burma,* and on the other, in relief, a map of the Greater East Asia Co-Prosperity Sphere, featuring a stretch of track and a palm tree. Comfort girls on traveling brothel trains were making forty-eight-hour stops along the line, with the guards waiting for them, cleaned up, even the Koreans, holding army-issue Attack No. 1 brand condoms, everyone shaved, eyebrows trimmed, circumcised men to the head of the line.

The prisoners were given a yasume day and *Tōjō presentos:* cigarettes according to the number of days they had worked without

yasume, or rice, margarine, canned milk, canned fish, or fish dynamited from the river, or cheap cotton shorts and rubber boots.
The day after the ceremony was the first anniversary of Nagatomo
Yoshitada's No. 3 War Prisoner Branch in Burma. To mark that
occasion, all the POWs who had started out on the railroad at
Thanbyuzayat and were still alive and together a year later were
issued, between them, two pigs, two bags of dried green peas, and
a third of a bag of rice polishings, cost deducted from their pay.

::

THE POWs were still slaves. The Japanese had more labor lined
up for them. They shipped them back to southern Thailand.

Riding the railroad they had built was an experience. They had
come around to wanting to get the railroad finished, but that was
not to say they wanted the Japanese to be able to ride it safely. So
they took every chance to sabotage it. There were ways to tip
rubbish into the embankment instead of making it all solid fill, or
roll logs into the fill and leave them to rot. There was a skill in
driving dog spikes that looked fit to pass inspection, but at an angle,
so that the weight of a locomotive would separate the rails, the
best place for this being on a high curve with a steep drop. It was
possible every so often to smuggle a balsa log into a bridge support
instead of a teak log, balsa being a soft, light, fragile wood, ideal
for children's model airplanes. The Australians had a specialty of
filing a bolt off between the head and the nut and screwing in the
worthless ends. And everybody enjoyed seeding bridge timbers
with termite eggs.

So when a prisoner on a train passed over a stretch he had
worked on, he had a tendency to hold his breath, and any smoker
with the makings would light up to steady his nerves. Two days
or more north to south, switchback curves and rickety bridges,
steep grades, at ten miles an hour or less—the prisoners had all the
time in the world to look down into the ravines at the derailed
rolling stock lying there smashed.

The Americans had gone north to Burma by ship. They had
never been on the ground in Thailand. Coming south by train,
they could see that northern and central Thailand would have been
much worse than Burma. The Burma section of the railroad was
only 152 kilometers, the Thailand section 263, with steeper mountains, jagged peaks with valleys falling away below the embank-
ments to fantastic depths, meaning more bridges, higher and

longer, and deeper cuttings. Between Tamajao and Takanun there were three huge cuttings in less than ten kilometers, backbreaking work. Cholera Hill, Death Valley No. 1, Death Valley Number 2, and Shit Creek, all living up to their names. The Pack of Cards Bridge, one of the biggest and craziest Japanese wood constructions, 400 yards long by 80 feet high, green timber held together with wooden wedges and dowels and rattan and cane rope ties. Two thousand men built it in seventeen days, it collapsed three times, thirty-one men were killed in falls (as many as were killed building the Golden Gate Bridge), and twenty-nine were beaten to death. At Konyu the cutting was huge, in two sections, one about 500 yards long by 25 feet high, the other about 80 yards long by 80 feet high, and every piece of blasted rock had to be hauled away by hand. The Japanese had their prisoners slaving into the night, by the light of carbide lamps and bamboo bonfires. The shadows of guards swinging their clubs were huge; they beat 68 men to death. The Australians called the place Hellfire Pass, and said they could have given Dante lessons about infernos.

Some of the most hopelessly sick prisoners—meaning barely functioning bodies worthless for work even by Japanese standards— were sent down off the railroad to the base camps ahead of the rest. Some were dead on arrival; others collapsed and died before they could get to the sick huts. The rest were walking skeletons, the whites of their eyes gray, pupils just a splotch in the middle, like broken eggs. They stank to high heaven. The men in the receiving camps could smell them hundreds of yards off. They came crawling in like frightened rats; if they were offered food and help they would burst into tears.

What was left of F Force was sent from northern Thailand all the way down to Singapore, not nearly as many boxcars needed to bring them back from Ban Pong as it took to ship them up there eight months before. From Singapore station one night, some Australians, the tatters of the 2/30th Battalion, were trucked out to Changi. Along this last short stretch a couple of men died. The others laid them on the ground, then formed ranks in the moonlight: malarias with the shakes, their friends holding them up, others leaning on sticks, all hanging on to life, skeletons in bits of rags trying to look like Australian soldiers still. The sergeant major dressed them off, reported to the commanding officer, and the CO reported to the senior Australian officer at Changi, Lieutenant Colonel Frederick Galleghan. Galleghan was a hard man, known as Black Jack. He had never been on the railroad himself, but his was the human responsibility for sending all the Australians into the speedo and the monsoon and the cholera. He was closest to the 2/30th. They were his own men, he had trained them at home, marching them far and fast, until they were called Galleghan's Greyhounds, and he had led them in combat. The CO saluted Galleghan and said, *Your 2/30th all present and correct, sir.* Galleghan, unbelieving in the dark, asked, *Where are the rest?* The CO said, *They're all here, sir.* And Black Jack, the hard man, the old man of the Australian tribe, broke down and wept.

According to Japanese figures, 20 out of every 100 POWs on the railroad died, and 30 out of every 100 rōmusha. The Allied figures for POW deaths were about the same, but for rōmusha deaths more like 50 per 100, and by some estimates even higher. The Japanese figure for their own deaths was 7 per 100.

To hear the Japanese tell it, this radical difference in their favor was not because the Japanese were slavemasters and the prisoners and the rōmusha were slaves being worked to death. Not at all. The railroad was a labor of peace; the world would be filled with admiration for it. The prisoners should be proud to be participating in such elevated work. They should take an example from the Japanese farmer, the healthiest man in the world. Fresh air and sunshine were enough for him. His work in Japan was much harder than the work of a Malayan rubber plantation coolie or an Australian on a ranch or a Dutchman in the Indies; and on the railroad a Japanese soldier worked two hours longer per day than a prisoner.

Also, in this Japanese version of things, Japanese soldiers did not eat any better than prisoners. And they had less medical support. Japanese figures were: for 12,000 Japanese soldiers, only 6 medical officers, 20 NCOs, and 20 orderlies. As against, for 45,000 to 52,000 POWs, 150 of their own medical officers, 150 NCOs, and 700 privates—much better ratios (even applying the Allies' correct figure of 61,000-plus POWs). And hospital accommodation for POWs was the same quality as for Japanese, so the Japanese said. Yet the Japanese did not die in numbers anything like the POWs, let alone the rōmusha.

According to the Japanese, they survived better because they were Japanese. As one of their senior officers said: Push men of different kinds into a river, some would not be able to swim, some would not be able to endure hardship. The Japanese could, because they were rice eaters. They were physically strong. They could handle jungle diseases and jungle weather. They had discipline. And good spirits. The senior Japanese were forever making speeches to the POWs about this. It was necessary for prisoners to have high spirits, like the Japanese. If they put spirit into their work they would not become sick; they would be better able to meet the arduous physical task imposed upon them.

All this well-meant advice the senior Japanese urged upon their prisoners with affection, or so they said after the war. The experience of building the railroad bound Japanese and prisoners together. A certain friendship naturally developed from sharing pains and pleasures. They could be seen sharing work, washing their clothes together. As for themselves, the senior officers said, they were like parents to the prisoners, looking upon them as sons.

Whatever happened on the railroad that might have been *wrong,* so these senior Japanese said, had nothing to do with them as officers, and nothing to do with the way the Japanese as a people did things. It was a matter merely of individuals. Not all prisoners were good, so the senior officers said. They were even prepared to concede that not all individual Japanese were good.

Though, to go by Japanese figures, next to no Japanese were bad. At least not bad enough to be court-martialed. There were 12,000-plus Japanese on the railroad, and for every one of them there was a dead POW. Yet the total number of Japanese court-martialed for mistreating prisoners was only two. (And for every dead POW, there were as many as ten dead rōmusha. But of course there would never have been a thought among the Japanese that mistreatment of rōmusha was a punishable offense.) Calculating by the simplest of arithmetic, a total of two Japanese court-martialed could not have included the Japanese whose complete course of treatment for POWs with cerebral malaria was a slap in the face and an order to shut up; plus the Japanese who hit a malaria on the head with an eight-pound sledgehammer and killed him; plus the Japanese who went around injecting sick rōmusha with chloroform for the pleasure of watching them die in convulsions; plus the Japanese who crucified rōmusha on the branches of trees and dropped them in the river; plus the Japanese who threw a British interpreter in a hole and left him there till he went out of his mind; plus the Japanese who tied another British interpreter to a tree and set him on fire; plus the Japanese who beat the Kanchanaburi radiomen to death; plus all the other Japanese who beat prisoners to death at Pack of Cards Bridge and Hellfire Pass and anywhere and everywhere else along the railroad. By Japanese moral standards, none of those Japanese were sufficiently bad to be punished by court-martial, and neither were any of the other 12,000 Japanese on the railroad, excepting only two.

Furthermore, in the Japanese version of things, if indeed there were bad individuals in their army, they were certain not to be true Japanese. According to the Japanese senior officers, the greatest problem was staff who were not from Japan proper. Meaning Koreans. The Japanese were sure all Koreans were bad—both inferior and evil. In Japanese thinking that was a given. And yet no Japanese group commander ever reported to his superiors that he had punished a Korean for mistreating a prisoner.

After Koreans, the big problem, according to the senior Japanese, was their own army's Siam-based administration—not enough trucks, no proper commissary service. *With inadequate preparation sad results are inevitable.*

Beyond that, there was disease. As for disease among prisoners, they said they could do nothing about it—though of course they did things to protect themselves. Beyond that again, there was the monsoon. The Japanese railroad officers could do nothing about the weather except stop work, and they were never going to do that. What it all added up to, in the Japanese senior officers' arithmetic of life and death on the railroad, was that not even loving Japanese military parents could do anything for their POW sons.

When the Allies tried to put together an exact figure for POWs dead on the railroad, they came up with a tally of 12,399.

On the Burma side of the border, with between 11,000 and 12,000 POWs, the overall death rate in a period of roughly a year was something like 15 percent. On the Thailand side, with more than four times as many POWs, the death rate was far higher. Northern Thailand was the worst: In eight months or less there, F Force and H Force between them lost more than 45 percent, more than double the overall railroad average of about 20 percent. And one section of F Force lost 1,175 out of an original strength of 1,602, or 73 percent.

F Force had more than 7,000 men, half of them Australian, half British. The Australian death rate was 29 percent, the British 61 percent. Here were prisoners of two different tribes pushed into the river together. Why such a difference in death rates? Basically, a greater number of the British drafted onto F Force were seriously sick already when they left Changi for the railroad. That went back to their general poor level of fitness when they were sent to Singapore to fight the war in the first place. And that went back even further—to Britain in the 1930s and the generally poor level of health and nutrition among boys in the British lower classes of the Depression years, who became the conscripted British other ranks in World War II.

Hardly any Dutchmen wound up in F Force. That was the luck of the draw. But no matter where Dutch prisoners worked on the railroad, no Dutch group ever had a death rate anything like as high as F Force. Take H Force: Only 6.64 percent of Dutch enlisted men died, as against 37.3 percent British. And that went back to the composition of KNIL, with many Eurasian Dutch, and *indische jongens,* white Dutch born in the Indies.

Of total railroad deaths, 6,318 were British, 2,815 Australian, 132 American, 2,490 Dutch (the nationality of the rest unknown). In gross terms, about 1 in 3 British died, about 1 in 4 Australians, about 1 in 5 Americans, and about 1 in 6 Dutch.

With all the more or less random variables factored in—who drew which particular camps on the railroad, who was farthest from the food or closest to the cholera, who drew the best interpreters or the worst commandants and guards, which enlisted men drew the best or the worst prisoner officers and doctors, and so on—there is one other thing to be considered: what the Japanese thought of their prisoners by nationality, and what they did with what they thought. As they saw things, the English were the best-disciplined POWs, with blind faith in their own superiority, and many of them had good heads for technical work. Australians were the exact opposite of the *English gentleman,* very rough types, not well educated, but they had great working ability. Americans were like Australians, despising the English. Also Americans were arrogant; they had a very high opinion of themselves. The Dutch were very individualistic, not very nationalistic. The mixed-blood Indonesian Dutch lacked the ability to control themselves. In order of working ability: Australians 1, English 2, Americans 3, Dutch 4. That was an official ranking. Some of the Japanese on the railroad had an unofficial saying: *One Aussie, fifteen Englishmen, four hundred Dutchmen.* In another official Japanese ranking, the Dutch scored as the stupidest. The most interesting thing about all this is that the Dutch were the best survivors, by far. The Dutch would not have been the first slave tribe in history to cultivate the appearance of stupidity as the most intelligent way of handling an impossible situation.

*   *   *

The Americans of the 131st and the *Houston,* like all other prisoners, were at the mercy of where the Japanese happened to push them into the river.

For example, no American died of cholera, or even so much as got cholera. That was the luck of the draw—where the Japanese pushed them in happened not to be where the cholera was worst.

Two out of every three Americans who ended up dead died in the sixty-five miles between Thanbyuzayat and 105 Kilo. In that relatively small space there were more than a hundred American deaths in less than twelve months, not as heavy a death rate as the Australians had, much less heavy than the British, but heavier than the Dutch, and certainly a heavy loss for one small national railroad tribe of something like 650.

Between Fitzsimmons's men and Tharp's men, the death rates were very different. Often enough the two groups were only a camp or two apart. Yet of Tharp's 450 or so, well over 100 died, a higher death rate than the overall average for all nationalities, whereas of Fitzsimmons's 190 or so, only 9 died, much lower than the overall average.

If the two groups had been lined up side by side for inspection just before they went onto the railroad, they would have looked much the same—the 131st, mostly Texans, plus a few Damyankees, and men off the *Houston* (some of whom were Texans, too). So what were the differences?

First, a considerably higher percentage of *Houston* men died on the railroad than men from the 131st—61 out of 268 as against 65 out of 381. That was probably because, after the early disaster of the sinking, the sailors and marines went into captivity much less fit, so that when they were drafted onto the railroad their health was already closer to the breaking point.

Most of the *Houston* men were with Tharp. By contrast, a big percentage of F Battery men were with Fitzsimmons, and the Jacksboro boys were a close subtribe—they would have said none closer on earth, they lived by that doctrine, and they had no doubt that it helped keep them alive. (Even so, there were Jacksboro boys with Tharp, and some of them died.)

Then again, Roy Stensland was with Fitzsimmons's group. Stensland had been an outstanding officer at Bicycle Camp, and he was the same all the way to Burma and back. On the miserable transports from Tanjong Priok to Singapore and from Singapore to Rangoon, Stensland was a tower of strength, taking care of the sick, keeping morale up. On the railroad he was everywhere. On

Men of 131st Field Artillery, 2nd Battalion, F Battery—the Jacksboro
Boys—setting up camp at the Louisiana Maneuvers, 1941

Houston Tom "Slug" Wright, F Battery, 2nd
Battalion, 131st Field Artillery, 1940

Frank Fujita, E Battery,
131st Field Artillery, 1940

FRANK FUJITA

Dan Rafalovich, U.S.S.
Houston, who ate the British
dog with Frank Fujita at
Changi POW camp,
Singapore

DAN RAFALOVICH

U.S.S. *Houston* with crewmen on deck, at Darwin—probably the last picture taken before she went down in Sunda Strait during the Japanese invasion of Java

The Janesville tankers outside their National Guard Armory in 1938, the year Forrest Knox joined the company

The world of Western Empire in Asia turned upside down—big white
prisoner, little yellow conqueror

JOHN STEPHAN

The Fall of Bataan

The Bataan Death March

The living carrying
the dead—Filipino
POW burial detail
at Camp O'Donnell

The end of the road

The Zero Ward at
Cabanatuan, drawn
by Medical Officer
Eugene Jacobs

EUGENE JACOBS

The cemetery, Cabanatuan, July 1942

EUGENE JACOBS

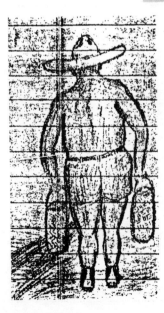

Ted Lewin the hard trader—one of the few at
Cabanatuan carrying excess baggage and a
spare tire

EUGENE JACOBS

Forrest Knox and the truck detail, early 1943, the best time of Forrest's life as a POW. The day after The Bull's farewell party. Note that the prisoners appear reasonably well nourished and in reasonably good spirits. The Bull is front row center with sword. Forrest is center row, third prisoner from left in white cap. Sandy Sandmire, center row, fourth prisoner from right. Curly Combs, center row, second prisoner from right. Chipper Chapman, back row, third from right. McKnight, back row, second from right in white cap.

"Blood and Slime," a matched pair of guards, one Japanese, one Korean—Mori Masao and Kasayama Yoshikichi

The Burma-Siam railroad—bridge building

Working on the railroad. The Japanese have classified these men fit for heavy labor. They are aged 19 to 23. POW George Aspinall took the picture with a secret camera and kept the film hidden till liberation.

Doc Hekking before the war—with wife May, son Fred, and daughter Lukie, at Kolonodale, Celebes, 1933

HENRI HEKKING

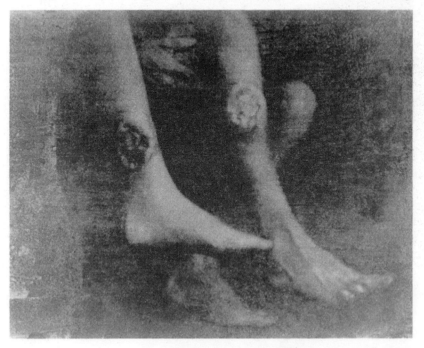

Tropical ulcers. Another secret-camera photo by George Aspinall.

TIM BOWDEN

Operating on tropical ulcers. No anesthetic—the sufferer must be held down.
The scene as recorded by POW Murray Griffin.

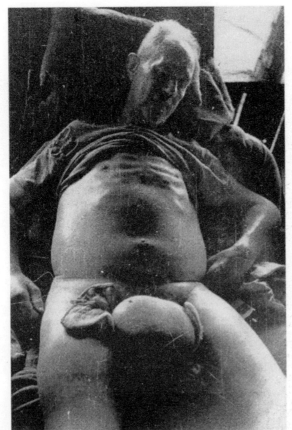

Wet beriberi

Burning the cholera dead, northern Thailand. Drawn on packing
cardboard by POW Charles Thrale.

Riding the railroad—note men perched on tops of boxcars.

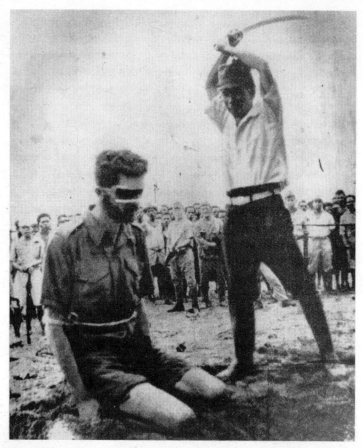

Death of a POW

Oil-soaked survivors of the sinking of the hellship *Rakuyō Maru*,
about to be taken aboard an American submarine

The last stretch. Japan, spring 1945.
Photo taken by POW Terence Kirk
with a pinhole camera he made
secretly in camp. Note that the
man in the center is being
supported from behind
by another man.

TERENCE KIRK

The final stages of starvation,
Mukden, Manchuria

CHARLES BALAZA

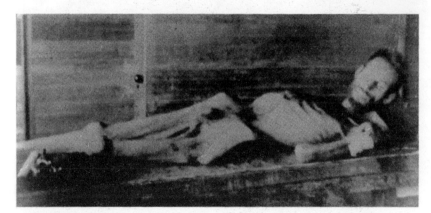

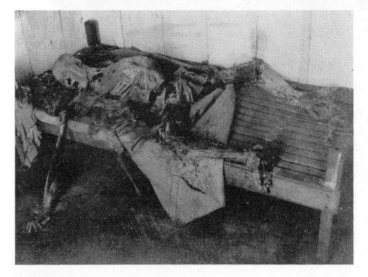

Left for dead by
the Japanese at
Davao, southern
Philippines, 1945

MAC ARTHUR
MEMORIAL ARCHIVES

Airdropping food—the view from the B-29

Liberation—prisoners wearing airdropped clothes, with some
flesh back on their bones

Blood and Slime under arrest for war crimes—Mori Masao (*right*), Kasayama Yoshikichi (*center*)

LESLIE POIDEVIN

Victor's justice—the Americans hang a C Class war criminal, by the book.

U.S. NATIONAL ARCHIVES

The Janesville tankers. Two out of three did not make it home. Forrest Knox
(*standing on tank, second from left*) keeps seeing dead men on the streets.

ROCK COUNTY HISTORICAL SOCIETY

Captivity recollected in tranquility—Slug Wright (*left*) and Doc Hekking, old
friends, best friends, revisiting the Southeast Asian camps in retirement

HOUSTON TOM WRIGHT

the march between work camps, when some British prisoners broke to the river for water, Stensland raised himself up in front of the Americans and said he would beat the hell out of the first one who drank that foul contaminated stuff. Stensland was the one officer who always went out with work details, the way he had done at Bicycle Camp. He stood between his men and the guards and took his beatings. He was one of those prisoners who stuck to the doctrine of never falling down. He was a bull, a bull reduced in weight and strength but still a bull. He had all the self-confidence in the world. He had a loud voice. And he had a gift for bullshitting the Japanese. He talked them into believing he knew more about engineering than they did, and indeed he was a true technician, able to secretly shave the meter stick and shift the quota peg.

He even managed to keep getting hold of booze. For Stensland, liquor was like spinach for Popeye; it gave him strength. At Christmas, 1942, when the POW workers got a day off and their officers were given a shot of brandy, Stensland dressed himself up in his prisoner's best, went over to the Japanese lines, and came back with four bottles. Every so often the Japanese invited him to drink with them. One day they found him in a warehouse, working his way through the liquor. They did not beat him, just made Slug Wright and some of the others carry him out.

Another time the Japanese took him pig shooting. They let him have a gun, he shot a pig, and after that they shot at him for sport. They missed. That was a life-and-death difference for Stensland. And, truly, Stensland was a life-and-death difference for the men in Fitzsimmons's group.

The other two officers with Fitzsimmons were Jimmy Lattimore and Dave Hiner, second lieutenants, the same rank as Stensland. They were average to good human beings, neither one overselfish about RHIP. Lattimore was the one who put up his wristwatch to trade for Doc Hekking. But neither he nor Hiner was a Stensland.

Fitzsimmons himself actually improved on the railroad, at least the way Slug Wright and Doc Hekking saw him. At Bicycle Camp he ate well with the other officers. In the hold on the way from Tanjong Priok to Singapore, he was more noticeable for protecting his own blanket space than for looking out for his men. In Burma, Fitzsimmons did not even take on the responsibility of making up the work parties; he left that to one of the F Battery noncoms. But then during the speedo, when the Japanese were forcing officers to do manual labor, Fitzsimmons had to go out and slave in the monsoon mud up to his belly, and Slug and Doc were pleased to see him come in with a different attitude.

And of course, if Fitzsimmons had never done another thing, he was still the one who organized the greatest trade on the railroad, two watches for one Doc Hekking. Tharp's men did not have Doc, and more than 100 out of 450 of them died, 48 from ulcers. Fitzsimmons's men did have Doc, and out of 190 only 9 died, none from ulcers.

Regardless of nationality, there were some categories of POWs who survived far better than the average. Cooks for one. Truck drivers. And doctors. Of all POWs, doctors were the best equipped to keep themselves alive. In addition, they were doing essential work. To be sure, they were radically overburdened, and the Japanese went after them at sick call every day. But, by way of compensation, POWs had the strongest interest in seeing that their doctors were taken care of—favors of all sorts, food, black market drugs (for the sick, of course, but for the doctor too, if he needed them).

For officers considered as a caste, the survival rate was hundreds to one better than for enlisted men. It was the same old story, the arithmetic of food and work, with officers making sure they scored to their own advantage. Officers coming down off the railroad were likely to weigh in twenty or even thirty pounds heavier than enlisted men: *RHIP.*

And then there was the *spijkerploeg,* a group of Dutch prisoners on the Thailand side. After the roadbed was cut, ballast laid and leveled, ties wrestled into place, and rails settled on top of them, the spijkerploeg came along and spiked the rails to the ties.

The spijkerploeg was formed at Ban Pong—about four hundred men, of all ages from eighteen to fifty, in reasonable condition. They were from all parts of the Dutch military: infantry, cavalry, artillery, engineers, marines, reserves, home guard, plus several academy cadet officers. So, going in, they were not a close tribe. But something like seven out of ten were born in the Indies, and of those a big percentage had some Indonesian blood. Meaning that they had the makings of a tribe well suited to surviving in the jungle.

They had good discipline; perhaps the cadet officers were an extra help in this. They were willing to put not just some of their pay, but all of it, into a central fund, which was very unusual. Half was spent on extra food for the sick, also an unusually high percentage; a quarter was for workers' food, the rest for necessary luxuries like sugar and tobacco. They smuggled a strain of baker's yeast into camp and cultured it on pumpkins enriched with sugar, which gave them extra thiamine, vitamin B_1.

They had three medical officers, an unusually high number for only a few hundred prisoners, and the three among them had years of tropical experience. Teunis Stahlie was in charge of clinical work; Henri de Monchy, of hygiene; and Frits Wolthuis, a regular in the medical corps, was senior medical officer. In practice each doctor did anything that was necessary. By great good luck, the Japanese officer in charge of them (not a career military man—in civilian life he had been a geography teacher) turned out to be a reasonable human being. He came to trust Wolthuis. He let de Monchy go ahead of the group to each new camp site and set things up—cookhouse, swill pit, latrines, fly control system. He allowed the prisoners to forage for food, and for medicinal plants. The men were under strict orders from their doctors not to drink river water; to keep the temptation down they had a two-man detail boiling tea for them at the work site. When they shifted camp, which was often, their food was delivered to them. Because they were always on the move, they did not have much contact with other prisoners, or with rōmusha. Their Japanese officer could see the good sense in letting them set up camp away from other camps whenever that was possible, with their own latrines. This helped them keep their distance from the cholera, even though there were times when it was all around them. As well, they had been getting their cholera shots in KNIL, the Japanese gave them boosters, and above all they had their Dutch cholera discipline.

By railroad standards they were well looked after, because they had a special value. They were not going to be slaved to death. They could only do their work after all the other gangs had done their part, which meant that every so often they might get a rest. They had to eat their share of lizards, but no one starved. They had to take their share of beatings, but no one was beaten to death.

The spijkerploeg worked the length of the railroad from Ban Pong in southern Thailand to Three Pagodas Pass at the Burma border, start to finish, through the speedo, the monsoon, and the cholera, and they did not lose a man.

That was a great exception to the rule. If the Japanese had cared, there were any number of ways they could have kept death rates down all along the railroad. But they did not care. They were driven by their rage to finish the railroad. This rage was authentically Japanese. It was not in Japanese tribal thinking to consider that the railroad might be finished sooner if they looked after their white prisoners better.

By the time the railroad was completed, Doc Hekking was sick. He was worn out, ground down. A six-foot Dutchman, and he weighed only 110 pounds.

Slug was still with Doc. They were at a camp close to the Thai border. Slug was taking care of a clump of sick huts on his own because Doc was not strong enough to walk up and down a hill. An F Battery man died. He was not a Jacksboro boy, not even a Texan, just a transfer from somewhere else before the 131st went overseas. Still, on the railroad he qualified as a member of the tribe. Slug rolled him onto his back and tied his hands together. Shouldering the bamboo litter uphill to the graveyard was heavy work, and the corpse was a wet beriberi. Slug was on the down end, the body burst, and an awful stinking wetness ran out all over him.

That was the ceremony of Slug's farewell to the railroad. It was a great thing to be riding away on the train, crossing the border south into Thailand, seeing the backside of Three Pagodas Pass.

Slug rode down looking after his sick men. They were on open flatcars, and Slug started out thinking it was pleasanter traveling than standing up jammed in boxcars; but the Japanese had the steam locomotive burning wood, and the smokestack was belching sparks and red-hot cinders, clouds of them, blowing back onto the sick men, setting their raggedy clothes on fire, singeing their bare skin, and Slug had to be forever scrambling around with a bucket of water and a gunny sack, dousing the flames and beating out the smolders on the scorched bodies.

Before the railroad was finished, Slug and all the others along the line had seen Japanese troops being moved up to the Burma front on the miserable dirt service road beside the track. There were tens of thousands of them, mostly on foot, with mules and mountain guns. Some of the soldiers from the railroad regiments had to go and fight. Now there were Japanese wounded coming down from the front by train. Slug and his sick POWs were stopped at a siding when a trainload of Japanese pulled up, boxcars full of exhausted men, their wounds untended, stinking of gangrene. By no means did they appear to be in good Japanese spirits, the way their senior officers said Japanese soldiers always were; by no means were they lying at attention, the way sick Japanese soldiers were supposed to. So here were two trainloads of men from enemy tribes, both chewed up and spit out by war, and in Slug's estimation there was not much to choose between them for misery. The Japanese had a nurse. She saw the red cross on Slug's G-string, and she spoke to him—in perfect English. Slug had some water and some bananas, and that was more than she had. He gave them to her. To thank him she sang for him in her perfect English, "Columbia, the Gem of the Ocean." Slug could not help himself, he bawled like a baby.

::

THA Muang, Chungkai, Kanchanaburi, Tarsao, Tha Makhan, Nong Pladuk—after the up-country work camps the base camps in southern Thailand were like paradise. Comparatively speaking, of course. At Tha Muang the POW administration took a clothing inventory that produced these figures: Of 4,804 men in camp, including 567 officers, 1,670 had no blanket, 3,414 no towel, 2,546 no shirt, 1,899 no shorts, 1,595 no hat, 3,193 no long trousers, 3,264 no leather boots, 4,127 no rubber boots, 4,387 no jacket, 3,909 no underpants. But a base-camp latrine might very well have an atap roof, and that made it a palace. And the food—Doc and Slug drew Kanchanaburi, and the first meal Doc organized for the two of them there was fried fish with an egg on top, dinner at the Savoy.

The Dutch were turning out *sambal,* doovers with hot chile peppers, big sellers because they actually had taste. The Australians were peddling coffee, or something they called coffee, with sugar in it, advertised as *Hot, Sweet and Filthy.* At Tha Makhan there was a little distillery, officially producing medicinal alcohol, and on the side a man was running a bar, selling mixed drinks.

Men were selling cigarettes, made in camp, every style, even filter tips. A little tribe of sick men invented rolling machines, using bamboo and strips of rubber. They had a truck driver going as far as Ban Pong to buy tobacco in bulk at the best price and bring it into camp under the seat or the tailboard or in a crate of vegetables. They bought Australian-made rolling papers, which were the best. One man cured the tobacco, one man got the papers ready with rice paste, two men rolled—the tribe of four at work. They advertised on a placard at the end of their bed space. Their prices were moderate, they were doing well, but soon other firms were in business, each with its own trademark, and salesmen hustling customers. The Dutch put together a cartel of experts who could get twice as many cigarettes out of a *kati* of tobacco, and squeezed the little men out of business; they had to go back to being salesmen or paperstickers.

All kinds of other small businesses were thriving. Charley Pryor, off the *Houston,* scrounged some canvas, twenty-four-ounce tarpaulin ducking. When he was out on cow detail a Thai girl gave him a needle. For an awl, he scrounged a piece of stiff wire, shoved one end into a stick, and sharpened the other. He unraveled thread from the canvas and rubbed beeswax on it to give it body, and he was set to sew. He specialized in shorts, so sturdy they would stand up by themselves. Two Dutchmen with a mallet and hatchet were in the business of splitting bamboo bedding into narrower springier strips and shaving off all the knobbly bits, at fifteen cents a bunk. Some other Dutchmen, sailors, started a little laundry they called *Sneeuwwitje,* Snow White. They made good money, kept some of the profits, and gave the rest to the hospital. Men were coming around to the sick in the wards, offering to boil their egg for one cent or fry it in oil for two and a half. Others were greasing boots or descaling and polishing mess kits, for a price. And all the old rackets were flourishing, plus new ones—one man found some copper tubing, made rings out of it, and sold them to the natives as gold.

In base camp a POW could feel as if he had some margin of life again. At Kanchanaburi, Eddie Fung, F Battery of the 131st, threw a party for his twenty-second birthday. He had turned twenty-one on the railroad, no party then, but at Kanchanaburi he had some Japanese pay to his name, he was still a master scrounger, and lumping everything together he managed to assemble enough edibles to invite guests.

The base camps were in the egg belt of Thailand. So the prisoners did not have to think about eating monkey for protein anymore. In fact, life was luxurious enough for men to be able to afford pet monkeys. Mick the Yank was a monkey at Kanchanaburi. He used to belong to the Japanese, but they beat him up, broke his tail and burned some of it off, so Bill Yarbrough, D Battery of the 131st, took him over to the hospital and got what was left of the tail properly amputated. That was the only amputation Slug Wright was ever close to among the Americans (and it was done by a Dutch doctor).

Mick the Yank liked to snatch hats, and he gave every evidence of enjoying crapping in his paw and throwing it at POWs passing by, but his biggest thrill was to sit on a man's foot and pull hairs out of his leg with delicate fingers, or fasten on a single hair with his teeth, lick it for the salt of the sweat and splutter it out. That was entertainment, for Mick and the man both.

For a higher class of entertainment, the theater groups formed up again and put on shows at night. Toward the end of 1943, Tom Douglas, the BBC radioman, started hearing a song on shortwave that was new to him. It was called "White Christmas," and it was sung by Bing Crosby. It must have been a big hit back in the world, because it was played often enough for Douglas to copy the words and another man to write down the music, and that was how it got into the Christmas show.

Any stage ladies still alive and kicking after the railroad could start shaving their legs again in base camp. Some fierce fighting men among the British did not like seeing brother officers mincing around with their hair up in curlers. But the ladies were a big hit, as they always had been—Bobbie and a chorus line of three high-kicking girls, and the star of a Dutch show, a ravishing beauty who stepped out of a big unfolding flower and danced with the devil.

Yasume—the word had some meaning again. There was a chess champion, Eurasian Dutch, who would play ten men at a time. There was a sporting life. The arithmetic of work and food was favorable enough for some men to play baseball, basketball, and volleyball. At Tha Muang the prisoners organized a race meeting, with bookmakers and bettors. The horses were prisoners big and fit enough to be ridden by other prisoners light enough to be jockeys and strong enough to hang on. On the railroad there had been race meetings here and there, but only among the crazed Australians—most often the action up-country was frog races, or betting on a praying mantis and a stick insect fighting to the death in a bottle.

POW horse races were entertainment for the Japanese, too; and they had a practical use for the event. It showed them the fittest prisoners in camp, and the Japanese could note their names for drafting away on new work details.

A terrible rumor was circulating: The Japanese were going to build a canal across the Kra Isthmus in northern Malaya. The POWs did not want to think about that; the Japanese pharaohs had just got through making them build the pyramids, and now they were ordering the Panama Canal dug. It turned out to be only a rumor.

But at the same time, shipments of POWs were being put

together by the thousands to be sent to Japan. For once the Japanese were being systematic, at least in their own categories of thinking, culling the oldest men, the worst dysenteries, recurrent malarias, badly scarred ulcers, dark-skinned Eurasian Dutch, Australian aborigines, and men of any nationality with red hair or freckles.

Here was yet another stage in the breakup of POW tribes. It was happening in every base camp. For every small reunion after the railroad, there were major separations and reorganizations. The drafts for Japan amounted to new compulsory tribes being formed, their new tribal names nothing more than new kumi numbers, their new tribal dress no more than a Japanese clothing issue for the voyage north out of the tropics, green tunics from KNIL—too small for white men because they were Eurasian-size—or cotton shorts from who would ever know where, blue, red, green, pink, mauve, spotted, striped, flowered.

It was happening to the 131st and the *Houston* men along with everyone else. There would not have been as many as a hundred Americans in one place anymore. As always, the thing to do was to try to stay with the tribe—and with the big tribes being broken up more and more, try all the harder to stay with the subtribe, the little group of three or four or five men who could be the difference between life and death.

Doc Hekking and Slug Wright were not picked to be drafted away. They were allowed to stay where they were needed, with the tribe of their sick.

For all that the base camps were a big improvement over the railroad work camps, they were hospital camps, too. The Australian doctor Edward Dunlop had a phrase for them: *cities of the sick.* Every hospital had thousands of sick men, filling whole sections of camp, Red wards and Blue wards, rows and rows of huts sectioned off by disease. The British doctor Cyril Vardy still had to do rough sick-hut triage. His method was to line his patients up on their hands and knees with their bare bottoms pointing at him, and go along the row sighting at anuses like a drill sergeant inspecting rifle barrels. A shrunken behind like the back end of a cow was diagnostic of a man too far gone to recover. *I did a bum inspection this a.m. and counted 33 cow bums staring at me off the platform beds, all doomed men.* And there was not a thing Vardy could do but kid them along a day at a time, and, when one man died, give another his egg. The base camp graveyards were bigger than any along the railroad. *Chungkai, Chungkai, the place where the Englishmen come to die.*

All the diseases that had traveled up-country with the railroad traveled down again to the base camps. Tropical ulcers, too. A doctor with the British at Chungkai, Jacob Markowitz, had 2,000 ulcer cases, 500 of them bedridden. He was an amputator on the scale of Albert Coates; he took off more than 100 legs at the thigh, with a mortality rate of one in three. When Edward Dunlop came down to Chungkai, he was astonished to see so many men he knew from up-country standing by the road without a leg. Tarsao had an artificial leg factory run by a prisoner who had trained as an automobile engineer at the Austin motor works in Britain; he knew about assembly-line mass production. And at Tha Makhan one of the concert acts was a twenty-man chorus, all of them amputees, 'Arry's 'Appy Amps.

Doc Hekking and Slug had brought their ulcer patients out of Burma, and at Kanchanaburi they inherited some more, Americans from other camps where they had been using the hot saltwater method, which in Hekking's view was a serious mistake. So Doc and Slug had a hut full of ulcers to work on.

Then the Japanese moved them all to Tha Muang—Doc, Slug, and the ulcer patients too, some of them with only a paper-thin tissue of skin over the crater. And there, of all things, a British officer ordered them out to work, on heavy duty, at a brick factory.

On the railroad the Americans and the British did not get on any better than they had at Changi. Early on, when Fitzsimmons's group came to 35 Kilo, a British battalion out of Sumatra was there ahead of them. The two groups were pushed up close against one another, against the will of the British. For a short time they fed together, but they argued, and the Americans split off. After the railroad was finished there was no improvement. Preston Stone of F Battery was court-martialed over a difference of opinion with a British sergeant major. Stone told the court that America had settled its differences with Britain in 1776. The British fined him his weekly egg, but some Australians shared theirs with him. Ray Robinson and Charlie Whitaker of Headquarters Battery executed a Fujita-Rafalovich maneuver on a British colonel's dog. The colonel kept it chained to the leg of his bed; they sneaked in while he was sleeping, slipped the chain, got away with it, and gave the dog to the Australians. On July 4, 1944, at Kanchanaburi, Dynamite Dunn of the 131st boxing team was going to make a speech about how the United States won its independence; then after the speech the Americans were going to fight the British behind the latrines. There was a sign posted in advance: *The Australians are with the Yanks.*

Now at Tha Muang it was Slug versus the British. He had ulcer cases on the line, men of his own tribe, and it could come down to their lives. Ulcers needed rest to heal. Slug told the Britisher what was right: leave them on camp duty. The Britisher ordered Slug to stand at attention and say *Sir* when he was addressing an officer. Slug called him a son of a bitch. The officer charged him with insubordination and had him put under close arrest.

An Australian officer took Slug's case and got the charge dismissed, yet another reason for Slug to love Australians. But the British got their own back. Doc Hekking had put in a word for Slug, of course; and in revenge, the British officer had Doc transferred.

Slug did not find out about the shanghai until he came upon the Japanese shaking Doc down for transfer; they had his kit laid out on the ground, tossing his medical kit, his wife's portrait in the bamboo tube, everything.

Doc signaled to Slug to take his water canteen. It was an Australian one, bigger than the American kind. Slug had never seen Doc with it before. *Benjo,* said Doc out of the side of his mouth, meaning dump it down the latrine. Slug could not figure out why; it looked like a good one, and he wanted to keep it. But Doc muttered, *Slug, do what I tell you.* Finally Slug caught on. The canteen had a radio in it.

Some Australians being drafted away to Japan had given it to Doc ahead of their own shakedown. It was battery-powered. Doc had a flashlight, authorized by the Japanese for his medical work, and he used the batteries to listen to the news in his little shack, pretending to take his siesta but actually tuning in to the BBC from New Delhi. When Doc passed the news to Slug, he always said it was an Australian truck driver who told him—that way if the Japanese caught him with the radio he could truthfully say that Slug did not know about it.

Slug took the canteen away unnoticed and dropped it in the benjo. By the time he came back Doc was gone, and the Japanese had dumped his wife's portrait and his medical records in the trash pit.

From what the Australian truck driver told Doc, the war was going badly for the Japanese. Not that it took a BBC report to deliver that level of news analysis to the base camps. The Allies were bombing bridges all along the railroad, which was one main reason why the Japanese had to keep drafting work details back up the track, to repair damage. As well, the bombers were hammering the big railroad workshops at Nong Pladuk, and the big steel bridge at Tha Makhan; and for good measure they were bombing the base camps too, without knowing they were POW camps.

The bombers used to key off a paper factory with a big smoke-stack at Kanchanaburi. They would come roaring in over the camps, so low the prop wash lashed the huts and lifted the atap roofs like a whirlwind. For the prisoners it was joy and terror and disbelief all at the same time. Here were the Allies taking the war to the Japanese, but the POWs were under the bombs too; they could see the bomb bay doors opening, the bombs spilling out, and they could plainly see the belly gunners and the tail gunners, men of their own big tribe, looking down, happy to see them being blown to bits without any idea who they were, then flying blithely back to base and sitting down to a beer and a steak dinner.

Slug was out one day when a Liberator came over low and dropped something that whistled and whacked down beside him as if it was intended for him personally. It was a gallon can of peaches, but it was empty. Those free Americans flying about up there had eaten the lot and tossed the can. All that was left was some syrup around the edges. Slug dipped his finger in and sucked; it was cold and sweet, and it tasted of America. That was how close he felt to home, and how far away he still was.

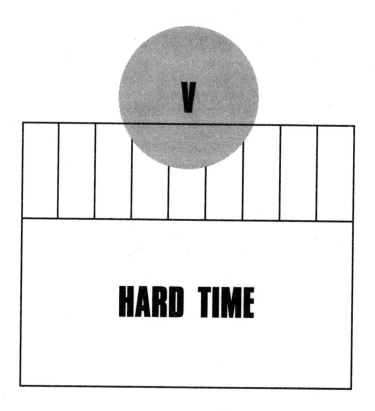

V

HARD TIME

A T T H A M A K H A N T H E J A P A N E S E C A U G H T S O M E A M E R I C A N S
smuggling Thai newspapers into camp. Mel Forsman off the *Hous-
ton* was one. The Japanese shipped him away to serve a sentence
at Outram Road jail in Singapore.

The Japanese threw prisoners into Outram Road by the hundred: men captured escaping, the ones they did not kill on the spot;
downed bomber crews (the Japanese classed them not as POWs
but war criminals, and at Outram Road they gave some of them to
Japanese airmen to kill); three officers from the Kanchanaburi radio
atrocity, including the lieutenant with the broken arms; Australians
from another radio disaster at Sandakan on Borneo, badly knocked
about, one of them with a kempeitai skewer driven through his
eardrum; white civilian internees supposed to be involved in resis-

tance work (some were, most were not); Malays; and Singapore Chinese in droves, their crimes unknown to the POWs.

Before Outram Road got overcrowded, the prisoners were mostly in solitary. They could tap on the wall with a stone or a button, talking in Morse code to whoever was in the next cell, hoping the guards would not hear. The only times they saw each other were at taisō, and when they were taken for their once-a-week twenty-second wash. Anyone with scabies—and that was everyone—was run through a disinfectant bath. The smart money tried to line up ahead of the Indian syphilitics. One man balked at going in after them, and a guard kicked him in the crotch. That was Outram Road hygiene.

Someone somewhere was always screaming under torture, or deathly ill and in agony, or going insane. The prisoners could try to stop their ears against the noise and blank out what it meant. They could spend their days figuring endless mathematical problems to keep their brain turning over, or try to recall everything that ever happened to everyone in their family—one Australian took himself all the way back to when his mother was breast-feeding him. Or they could give up on family, tribal memory, the sustaining power of human reason, and any hope for a life beyond Outram Road. Time passed unbearably slowly and yet they had no memory of it. They were existing as caged carcasses, nothing more. They chewed their fingernails off and ate them. They tried to see how long they could go without scratching their scabies raw. They squashed cockroaches and bedbugs, then squashed some more, or made friends with a mouse and then stamped it to death, or pulled the wings off a fly to keep it with them for company, or fed their body lice to a spider, and watched the spider fattening up while they wasted away.

Their food came to them through a slot in the door—hardly anything to eat and hardly any time to eat it, ten seconds in the morning, other feeding times twenty seconds. Every so often the guards ordered them out to empty the Japanese honey buckets, and that was a sight, white men panning Japanese shit, prospecting for an undigested black bean to salvage and eat.

To be a prisoner of the Japanese, then to be accused of whatever the Japanese took it into their heads to call a crime, then to fall into the hands of the kempeitai—that was triple jeopardy.

The Japanese had kempeitai all over the Co-Prosperity Sphere, trained torturers, tens of thousands of them at the peak: Japanese

officers and enlisted men, all volunteers, plus Korean and Formosan auxiliaries and native recruits, willing and less willing, with
buckets and soaked facecloths for the water cure, kendō sticks, iron
bars, knotted ropes, wooden clubs, baseball bats—the Japanese
loved baseball—thumbscrews, and needles and bamboo slivers for
sticking under fingernails. No POW ever had enough rice to eat,
but the kempeitai always had rice to spare for torture—they would
force it down a prisoner's throat by the fistful, pour water into him
by the gallon until he swelled up inside to bursting, then jump on
his belly. POWs were forever short of cigarettes, but the kempeitai
always had enough for burning ears and noses and eyes. And they
had dynamos and batteries for electric shock, wired up with alli-
gator clips for grabbing onto nipples and testicles.

The kempeitai liked to make their arrests in the black of night,
0300 hours Tokyo time. And any place they took over for their
torturing was a black hole: Bridge House and Jessfield Road
in Shanghai, the music conservatory in Manila, the law school in
Batavia, the Chamber of Commerce in Saigon, the YMCA in
Singapore. Kempeitai or not, any Japanese jail in the Co-Prosperity
Sphere was a black hole: Outram Road, the military jail in Nanking, Fort Santiago in Manila, the Rangoon city jail, Pudu jail in
Kuala Lumpur, Palembang jail on Sumatra.

The big city jails were as bad as any place could get. As for
the POW camps themselves, size did not necessarily mean anything for better or worse. But the farther a camp was from a big
Japanese administrative base, the worse it might be. That was not
necessarily so in the Philippines. But it was true enough on the
railroad. And certainly it was true in the Indies. The Java camps
were bad. The Sumatra camps were as bad, if not worse. And
then there were places like Haruku in the Moluccas, the end of
the earth.

On Haruku the Japanese had prisoners building an airstrip
against a deadline. They had natives laboring too, sad starving rōmusha. At the noon break the natives would huddle together for
comfort and whistle "Silent Night"—they had been missionized
before the Japanese came. The Japanese hated whistling, they hated
Christianity, and they hated natives. The natives hated being rōmusha, so the Japanese shot a few dozen of them to encourage the
others. The prisoners had to slave at crushing white coral rock,
which was blinding in the sun—to keep their sight they had to
make eyeshades out of rings of bamboo and cellophane and string.
There were dysentery and ulcers everywhere. Haruku was where

the Japanese military brothel was bombed and the POWs liberated condoms for their ulcerated toes; for ulcer surgery the doctor had one blade razor salvaged from a dead man. There were no American POWs, only Dutch and British and some New Zealanders, about two thousand in all. Only one out of two came away alive. Haruku stank of rotting bodies. It was such a terrible place a Korean guard shot himself.

Early in the war the Japanese took New Britain, a big island off the coast of New Guinea. They shipped their captives away and brought in more than a hundred thousand of their own troops. When they moved six hundred British from Singapore to work in the Solomon Islands, more than eighty were off-loaded sick at Rabaul; the rest were worked to death or starved or massacred. Of the eighty at Rabaul, only eighteen were alive at the end of the war. The other POWs around Rabaul were shot-down aircrew, almost all of them American, and an Australian coast-watcher. The Allies started bombing Rabaul heavily. The Japanese herded the prisoners into a tunnel. Even by Japanese standards it was too small. They moved the prisoners out in batches. One batch got caught in an air raid that killed some Japanese, and out of revenge the Japanese killed them. Later on the rest, by then only twenty-three, were moved to another site. They were not worked or beaten to death, just kept penned like chickens in a coop and not fed enough. They died of slow starvation and disease in a small place, a waiting room for hell. Of that last twenty-three only seven came out alive, one Australian and six Americans.

So it went—New Britain, Haruku, Ambon, Celebes, Borneo, Sumatra, Java, Singapore, Malaya, Hainan, Hong Kong, China, Formosa, Manchuria, Korea, the Philippines from Luzon in the north to Mindanao in the south, camps by the score up and down the Burma-Siam railroad, permanent camps and transit camps, base camps and work camps built, used, and abandoned; camps of thousands of prisoners and camps of only a few dozen bodies; camps all across the Co-Prosperity Sphere, hundreds of camps in all, wretched and more wretched.

::

IN 1944 some scientists in the United States recruited thirty-six military-age men and put them on a monitored exercise program, walking up stairs, carrying suitcases for weights, doing timed stints on a treadmill, thirty minutes on a 3.5 percent grade at 3.5 miles per hour, air temperature 78 degrees, humidity 50 percent, and so on; and at intervals the exertion was stepped up to the maximum. The subjects were fed two meals a day, mostly vegetables, very little meat or dairy products. Their intake was reduced until they reached semi-starvation, and then they were held there.

They were not prisoners; they were free men, volunteers. They were not crowded; they were housed reasonably comfortably, in the stadium at the University of Minnesota. They were not isolated from each other; the buddy system was encouraged. They had plenty of time off. They could take college classes if they wanted to, or read, or keep a diary. They could go out on dates. They knew the experiment was only going to take twenty-four weeks.

Even so, four of the thirty-six could not make it. The thirty-two who stayed the course finished down in weight 25 percent on average. Their clothes hung off them. Their hair was starting to fall out. Their level of fitness had dropped almost 75 percent, their work capacity almost 85 percent. Their coordination was bad. They were wobbly on their feet, clumsy and accident-prone. The education program collapsed. The buddy system turned sour. Their sex drive wasted away. They were fixated on food, talking about it, collecting recipes. They turned angry when the meal servers were slow, possessive about their rations, torn between hogging and hoarding. They wanted something in their mouths all the time, so they chewed gum; one man went through forty packs a day. And they smoked and smoked. Even though they had plenty of soap and hot water, they went around dirty. They bit their nails. They turned irritable, to the point of hysteria, and at the same time apathetic and antisocial. And devious—they squirreled away food; they secretly ate everything from candy to garbage and lied about it. One of them got a cold. He thought how good it would be if the cold turned into tuberculosis, so he could eat and rest. Late in the experiment he collapsed on the treadmill, and after that he tried to mutilate himself. He was going to cut off a finger, but he lost his nerve. Then he got hold of an ax and chopped three fingers off his left hand.

When the Minnesota experiment was being designed, POWs all across the Co-Prosperity Sphere had been in captivity more than two years—four-plus Minnesotas back to back in Japanese prison camp, and for almost half of them a year on the railroad, subsisting on the Japanese regimen of rice and slave labor, and with no end in sight.

*   *   *

The Japanese had any number of captive subjects for scientific study. In one camp on the far side of the world from Minnesota they set some POWs to lifting weights, running a hundred yards carrying fifty kilograms, breathing into a machine. At Saigon they had men peeing into flasks for metabolic tests. At Cabanatuan they took the physical measurements of some POWs from New Mexico, men with American Indian blood. They looked at the shape of their skulls, poked around in their ears for wax samples, and told them they were Asians. At Moji on Kyushu they measured prisoners of all nations, to see which tribe had the biggest penises. No results were recorded in the erect column. In Tokyo the Army Medical College did epidemiological investigations of malnutrition among POWs and made recommendations about food—not that this resulted in POWs actually being fed any more. At Nichols Field near Manila, some doctors came to look at prisoners going blind from malnutrition—three or four doctors, more than the prisoners had ever seen, photographing them, talking among themselves and taking notes, but not prescribing special diets for nutritional blindness or anything else.

Nothing stopped Japanese doctors experimenting on POWs, or on civilians, or on natives. The doctor at Rabaul on New Britain took blood from Japanese guards with malaria and injected it into POWs, to prove—contrary to accepted medical doctrine—that there was such a thing as immunity to malaria. He told the POWs he wanted to go to the United States after the war, to *the New York clinic,* and that if his experiment was successful he might become *a very famous man.* At Shinagawa, the head doctor did operations and gave injections no Western doctor would have approved: caprilic acid, soybean extract, sulfur and castor oil, serum from malaria sufferers, urine. He enjoyed seeing pain; he bled men to death for plasma. At Tantui on Ambon, the camp doctor took nine groups of ten prisoners each, ranging from men classified fit to hospital cases, and injected them with something supposed to be vitamin B_1 and caseine. About fifty of them died. The commanding officer of a naval hospital, a fleet surgeon, killed eight prisoners experimentally: tourniquets for hours, followed by shock death when they were removed; injections of streptococcus bacteria to cause blood poisoning; death by dynamite and bamboo spears. The bodies were dissected, the heads cut off and boiled.

In other places doctors did anatomical demonstrations on native criminals and POWs. At Khandok, for the benefit of some Japanese medical students, a POW was tied to a tree, his fingernails were torn out, his body was cut open, his heart cut out. On Guadalcanal two prisoners were caught trying to escape, and to stop them trying again the Japanese shot them in the feet. Then a medical officer dissected them live, cutting out their livers. One of the Japanese watching wrote in his diary: *For the first time I saw the internal organs of a human being. It was very informative.* On the Japanese home island of Kyushu some doctors used prisoners as guinea pigs to see if they could live with parts of their brain and liver cut out. In China doctors shot living men in the stomach for practice at taking bullets out of wounds. They amputated arms and legs, sewed intestines together, and took out teeth and appendixes and brains and testicles, all for practice. A doctor with two prisoners to practice on used one, then chopped the head off the other to test his own strength.

In Manchuria, at Pingfan, outside the city of Harbin, the Epidemic Prevention and Water Supply Unit of the Kwantung Army, known as Unit 731, had a compound of 150 buildings. In Ro Block they did experiments on human beings. The kempeitai brought them prisoners for guinea pigs: men, women, and children, Asians and Caucasians. They were called *maruta,* meaning logs of wood. Some were infected with disease: cholera, typhoid, anthrax, plague, syphilis. Others were cut up alive to see what happened in the successive stages of hemorrhagic fever. Others had their blood siphoned off and replaced with horse blood. Others were shot, burned with flamethrowers, blown up with shrapnel and left to develop gas gangrene, bombarded with lethal doses of X rays, whirled to death in giant centrifuges, subjected to high pressure in sealed chambers until their eyes popped from their sockets, electrocuted, dehydrated, frozen, boiled alive.

Two were put on a diet of water and biscuits and worked nonstop, circling in the compound loaded with twenty-kilogram sandbags on their backs till they dropped dead. One lasted longer than the other, about two months. This was research into malnutrition, like the Minnesota experiment, but done the Japanese Army way, to the death.

Ro Block at Pingfan was where the Japanese kept killing human experimental subjects under scientifically controlled conditions; but the book of starvation could have been written on the bodies of prisoners in Japanese camps anywhere.

Their bodies were stalling out. Their hair was growing so

slowly they only had to cut it back to Japanese shortness once every few months. At Cabanatuan their fingernails had transverse grooves, like the annular rings of a tree. They could read the grooves as a nutritional chart of their bodies, little spurts of growth showing good times for food, no growth showing bad times. Each groove marked a Red Cross food shipment, and there were only three of them.

In the eternal food lottery of the camps, whenever anything extra remained in the cookpots after everyone was served, there was a system for doling it out. This system for seconds developed early and everywhere, and the prisoners monitored it obsessively.

In the Southeast Asian camps the word for it was *lagi,* Malay for more. Every man got a lagi number. If there was only enough lagi today for numbers one through ten, then next time lagi would start at number eleven. No POW ever forgot his lagi number. There were camps with lagi numbers for garbage.

The prisoners watched their food servers with an eagle eye. Servers were forever suspected of packing the rice in their friends' mess kits, or dipping down to the bottom of the soup to serve them the substance of the sediment instead of the thin dirty water on top. As a kind of performance bond, some servers put their own food portion on display; if a man did not think his portion was fair, he could swap. In one camp the servers were forbidden to raise their eyes to see whom they were serving; in another they had to serve with their backs turned.

Who could be trusted? And not only about food, but about anything? That was becoming the question of all questions in the camps. As time went on, more and more the universe of trust, the moral community, came down to just the little subtribes, handfuls of men trying to stay human together in a world turning more and more inhuman.

The Texans of the 131st prided themselves on the closeness of their tribe. With them it was an article of faith, and they put the faith into practice.

The Offerle brothers, Oscar and Roy, were in D Battery. Oscar was the older, known as Big. Roy was Little, or Junior. When they were on the railroad Roy had bad diarrhea, and an ulcer. To get to the benjo he had to crawl backward on his feet and hands. One day he did not make it, and he messed himself. He was disgusted and disheartened, feeling so sorry for himself he was sitting there crying. His friend Zeke Naylor came in from work. *Junior,* he said, *what in the world is the matter with you?* Roy told him he had just dirtied his pants. And Zeke said, *Take the blankety-blank things off, and I'll wash them for you.* Roy thought that was one of the finest things a man could do for him. He never forgot it.

Big Offerle had an ulcer too, so bad he could not walk. The Japanese sent him to 80 Kilo as a heavy sick. Little went with him, on crutches. Zeke Naylor and another friend, Ed Bruner, had some money saved up, and even though they were sick themselves they gave it all to Little, a dollar and a half. At 80 Kilo, Big got worse. Every day his blanket was saturated with blood and pus. Little had to keep taking the filthy thing down to the river to wash it out. Late one afternoon, he found Big only semiconscious, running a fever. He was dying, and he died with his head in his little brother's lap.

In another camp, not on the railroad, there were two Americans, one blind, the other legless. They had a buddy system. The legless one sat on a makeshift mover's dolly and used his eyes so the blind one could tow him. Then the camp doctor took a good look at the blind man's eyes and found nothing wrong: The blindness was hysterical. The doctor hypnotized him and brought his sight back. And the moment he could see for himself he dumped the legless man and left him to dolly himself to the chow line.

The moral of that last story—and by 1944 there were many like it—was that men who had been turned into POWs were turning more and more into convicts. The doctrine and wisdom of the camps was turning into the ratlike cunning of yardbirds.

Watch out for thieves. Never leave laundry on the line: A pair of socks or a towel stolen at one end of camp would set off catchup thefts all the way to the other. Learn how to hide quan in the blankets or up in the catwalks. Sleep on your valuables. (And even that might not be theft-proof. One camp had a little subtribe of thieves who preyed on men asleep. The way it worked, one man crept along outside the tents, feeling through the canvas for a skull; he would give it a rap that jolted the sleeper upright, and inside the other thief would snake the valuables out from under his head.)

Another scheme was to keep an eye out for a truly sick man without a friend, fake concern, bring him his food and hope for him to be too sick to eat it himself—or convince him that he was. Another way was to keep an ear out for the sound of a man dying in the night, steal his pants off him before his bowels let go, and then not declare him dead until after the next meal, keep him on the hut count for his food until the smell got too bad. And, before the burial detail came to cart him away, pry the gold out of his teeth with an ice pick.

It was smart to get on the right side of the doctor. A little tobacco could go a long way, an unobtrusive hand in the medical orderly's pocket, *This is for the doctor, take a drag for yourself.* Five cigarettes and the right orderly would fake a high temperature for you. If a labor draft sounded bad, give blood, because men who had just given blood were not drafted. Or buy a live dysentery sample. There were men in the business of selling hot stools, and other men in little subtribes sharing a single hot stool. It was a medical amazement how the dysentery numbers went up whenever the Japanese ordered a draft.

A POW doctor had to have eyes in the back of his head, constantly watching that the men were not playing him for a fool. He had to hope his orderlies were not black-marketing drugs, or stealing the food from the sick and the clothes from the dead. (The British had a name for orderlies in the Royal Army Medical Corps: *RAMC,* Rob All My Comrades.)

At the same time the doctors were always playing the Japanese. They faked VD pills to sell to the guards. Doc Hekking finessed Salvarsan ampoules. Gerrit Bras, another Dutch doctor on the railroad, kept a supply of liver flukes from diseased animals to wave under the noses of the Japanese so they would gag at eating the slaughtered beast of the day, and the prisoners could have healthy liver soup. In the Philippines the American doctor Paul Ashton put a nasty Japanese on a faulty course of VD treatment that kept him sick and in pain. The British doctor Stanley Pavillard made sure that whenever he injected a Japanese with antisyphilis arsenicals he did not find a vein on the first try. He always aimed for maximum inefficiency and maximum pain—the arm would swell, the elbow would not work, the Japanese could not even salute properly, which would put him in trouble with his own officers, and he would still be syphilitic. The Australian doctor Les Poidevin built up a specialist side practice, circumcising Japanese. He did dozens; he was the *potong* doctor. To a Japanese guard a circumcised penis was a prize; with that and a gold tooth he was a made man, so let him pay top dollar, in pain and cigarettes.

The average prisoner's yardbird war against the Japanese went on nonstop. The first man to spot a guard sneaking up would call out *Air raid!* Or *Butch!* Or *Joe!* Or *Tallyho!* Or *Flag eight!* (the British navy signal for enemy in sight). Or *Rood voor!* (the Dutch warning for unsafe conditions on the target range). Or *A tisket, a tasket, a little yellow bastard!* Or *Cockroaches!* Out on work detail, the plan was to puncture gas barrels, loosen nuts on engine heads, switch electric wires, put iron filings in oil boxes, pour sand in gas tanks or pee in them. Imitate the doctors: Sell the guards fake VD pills made out of aspirin or sodium bicarbonate or chalk. Sell them fake Parker pens and fake Omega and Rolex watches—all over the Co-Prosperity Sphere, master engravers were faking trademarks. Put lice in the guards' clothes. Spit in their soup. Crap in their applesauce, give them dysentery for dessert. The Indies Dutch knew that the tiny sharp hairs on the inside of peeled bamboo were lethal—so, harvest them, drop them in the guards' drinking water and hope. Keep repeating the well-known story about the local whores, poxed by the Japanese, fighting the war on their backs, infecting as many as they could. And rejoice in the sight of the loincloths on the guards' laundry lines, all those fundoshi showing stains from the gonorrhea drip.

In a big camp like Changi or Cabanatuan a lot of money came in from outside, on the quiet. At Cabanatuan a lieutenant colonel named Harold Johnson was in charge of central purchasing for the POWs for more than a year. During his time on the job, calculating by legitimate income—meaning the Japanese pay scale—about five hundred thousand pesos should have been circulating. But actually, with the money the prisoners had managed to keep hidden from shakedowns, plus what they got from trading with the guards, plus counterfeit Japanese occupation currency being run off on secret presses by the Luzon Chinese, plus major amounts that came in along the secret pipelines from Manila, rolls of notes in hollow bamboos in the framework of the carabao wagons— putting all this together, it came to something like a million and a half pesos. The Japanese knew that something was wrong, but they never found out what. Harold Johnson had a secret audit committee cooking the camp books—one set of accounts for the Japanese, another for the truth. It was useful work, and Johnson was good at it. After the war he rose to be Army Chief of Staff.

Another perpetual part of the prison camp war of deception was scrounging. Bring a dead snake out on work detail, create a commotion "killing" it in front of the guards, and behind their backs the scroungers would be liberating food. At shakedown, learn to pass a full pack of contraband through the ranks invisibly.

Imitate the experts, like Pack Rat McCone of the *Houston*. He had evolved scroungers' feet; he could dig a hole with his toes, drop his contraband in, stand on it, and get away with it.

One classic scrounging story was told all over the camps. It went like this: A Japanese guard is haranguing his work detail for stealing. He knows all POWs are thieves, he even knows how they steal. *You think I know damn nothing. You are wrong, wrong. I know BUGGER ALL!* Those are his words at Jaarmarkt on Java. In other camps he says: *You think I know fuck nothing. Ha! I know FUCK ALL!* In Saigon he says: *You Americans think that you're smarter than the Japanese, but we watch a lot of your gangster movies, and we know just how you operate.* He demonstrates. He takes the hat off a prisoner's head, pantomimes looking around to check that no one is watching, then palms a can of condensed milk and sets the hat down on top of it. Then he mimes nonchalance, waiting for the chance to sneak off with his prize. The moment comes. He lifts up the hat—and the can has vanished. A prisoner has stolen it out from under his nose.

A second punch line: In a rage, the guard shakes the POWs down, but he finds nothing. His loss of face is terrible. He marches the prisoners back to camp, apoplectic. He halts them at the camp gate for guardhouse shakedown. And with every prisoner standing at rigid Japanese attention, out of the ranks rolls the can, right to his feet, empty.

Sometimes the thief in this joke is an American, sometimes an Englishman. Most times, though, he is an Australian, and that sounds right; the Australians had the best kind of hat for the story, and in the POW camps they were the internationally ranked number-one thieves. The day the railroad was completed, it was supposed to be an Australian who stole the gold spike. That was not a true story; the Japanese were not stupid enough to leave a ceremonial gold spike to be stolen. But it was a good story, and it sounded Australian. All Australians were thieves, so Simon Legree said. He was a guard with a heavy hand, but he had a sense of humor too, and after a day on work detail with Australians he would laugh and make a performance of searching himself to be sure he still had his wallet and his cigarettes.

::

A JOKE like the one about the condensed milk could hold its flavor indefinitely. But great jokes did not come around every day, and there were so many, many days to get through. There was always the old standby, the food fantasy, to pass the time: *I'll have a Hershey bar factory, I'll have Hersheys all over me, I'll swim in them, they will cover my head, I'll step in them barefoot, sleep in them, and I'll eat a hundred per day after every meal.* But food talk was like everything else about prison camp, it got old and irritating. Oklahoma Atkinson reached the stage of threatening to thump anyone who talked about food where he could hear. Some huts posted rules: after the meal, ten-minute talks on anything *except* food. But then a man would start talking about the great football game he saw, beginning with how he was walking along the street to the stadium, and by minute two he was passing a restaurant, and by minute three he was inside and ordering. If a prisoner was sick of all that, what could he do but climb up to the top bunk in the farthest corner and sit with a wet towel wrapped around his head to block his ears.

There was too much talk about food and not enough food; bodies were getting scraggier and scraggier; life was getting mangier and mangier. Clothes were wearing out or rotting away, and this led to revelations. About tattoos, for example. There was one particular skin that Forrest Knox would have loved, but he was in the wrong camp to see it—it was on a British officer in Southeast Asia. This officer had butterflies and bowls of flowers on his arms, on his chest an enormous windjammer in full sail, and on his back The Hunt: at about north center a mounted huntsman in a top hat, and from all directions hounds converging on the fox, which was retreating southward toward the only really safe cover, with nothing but its tail showing. Early on, this work of art had not been visible in its entirety, but with the slow disintegration of the clothing heightening the thrill of the chase it showed itself more and more, until there was the fox disappearing up the officer's fundamental orifice.

How could a prisoner do his time under the Japanese when he did not know how much time he had to do? At Changi, quite early, some men started using the Bible to predict the day of their liberation, manipulating words and numbers, constructing mathematical proofs from the Book of Daniel and Revelation. In the Philippines the Americans bet on when they would be out, with food for stakes (of course), the wagers to be settled at home. As of April 1942, men were laying odds on eating at the Bay City Grill on the Fourth of July. The pessimists were saying not till December, but even that was wonderful to look forward to: *Christmas turkey in Albuquerque.* Then it was *Forty-three and we'll all be free.* Then *No more war in Forty-four.* Then *Forty-five if you're still alive.* Or *Forty-seven if you're not in heaven.* Or *The Golden Gate in Forty-eight.* Or *Everything nifty by Nineteen-fifty.*

Some did their time in six-month stretches. Some did it by the hour. At Cabanatuan the navy men rang a bell in their barracks on shipboard time, as if they were still standing watch. Forrest Knox could hear it from his hut. At Davao there was an old American officer with a beard. He was sick but he still had a watch that worked, one of the few timepieces in camp, and his duty, his only duty, was to ring a bell for morning tenko and then on the hour through the day. At Siringoringo on Sumatra the Dutch had a bedridden sergeant who every morning called out the day and date, and an eighty-year-old Catholic priest who called in response, *Thank the Lord!*

Men who used to have nine-to-five jobs in the city and a home in the suburbs were out in the jungle doing slave labor on Tokyo time, dawn to dusk, and they did not know for sure what day it was, they were down to living like savages, cutting notches in sticks, existing by the phases of the moon.

One Minnesota, two Minnesotas, three Minnesotas, four—on the Japanese ration scale, the brain was starving along with the belly. Keeping the mind sharp and focused was harder and harder. Men tried boxing the compass, memorizing the keyboard of a type-writer, recalling every stop on the Sydney-Liverpool line, or every London street along the No. 11 bus route to Victoria Station. Early on, half a dozen men from the 131st started reading *Gone with the Wind.* They had the book torn into sections, fast readers going on ahead, slow ones coming along behind, moving their lips on the big words. It was two years before the last one got to Rhett telling Scarlett, *My dear, I don't give a damn,* just ahead of the smokers salivating to roll the final pages. Men without enough mental stamina left for reading would fall into long and bitter arguments about which state was the worst for illiteracy, whether it was *reafforestation* or *reafforestRation,* whether Kraft made a bulk cheese without the brand name on the package. Men without the mental strength to argue would bet on whether a dysentery struggling along the benjo path would make it to the trench or do it all over himself. They would watch the tinea balls and the scabies getting painted—always amusing as long as it was someone else. They would go to the pigpen and poke the hog in the balls with a stick to see if they could get him to shoot off. They would have a contest to see who could pop his bedbugs the loudest. Or just lie around trying to ignite fart gas, if they had a light.

Or, on the way to the river in the morning to wash up, they would go by the dead shed and count the bare feet sticking out and divide by two. If it came up an odd number, either a one-legged man had died or they had lost the power to do simple mental arithmetic.

Concentration wavering, memory fading—men were beginning to forget the names of people at home, friends, even family, and this caused them to panic and make lists. One man lost his mother's given name and it was months before he got it back. There was an Australian with a piece of paper, blank except for squares he had drawn, and under the empty squares he had written the names of his children, *Billy,* and *My Little Jan,* and he would stare at it as if it was a priceless treasure, with big tears rolling down his face.

In the evening after their miserable chow, the prisoners would mill around and around inside the fence. At Changi jail this was called *the goldfish parade.* The way the men moved was turning spavined and stereotyped, like animals in a zoo. One man in a Hong Kong camp made up his mind that he never wanted to see caged beasts again.

In a big camp a prisoner was never more than a hundred yards away from a thousand men, and in the huts never more than inches away from the same everlasting bodies. The way a man held his spoon, played with his moustache, whistled through his teeth, pulled at his earlobes, picked his nose, scratched his backside—and someone's hairy backside was always in someone else's face—anything could cause temper to flare up, fiercer than a runaway fungus.

If a man could still raise his eyes and look, there was some solace to be taken in nature. Frank Fujita of the 131st had an artist's eye; he could even find fascination in being able to study the anatomy of prisoners, how the muscles worked in a man down to eighty pounds. And he always saw beauty and wonder in the world outside the fence.

It was there for anyone who could still see. The hushed silence of the tropical dawn, the lovely ceremony of the sun gilding the coconut palms. Or butterflies along a river in the jungle, flights of dazzling whiteness, sheer black, green and orange, mauve, pink wings threaded with black, old gold with splashes of emerald on black tracery, gorgeous things, even if what attracted them to the camps was diarrhea and dysentery.

Changi was a different case: no doves, no flying foxes, no beautiful golden orioles, no croaking bullfrogs after the rain—all the wild life was gone, eaten.

::

FORREST Knox was a student of survival. He managed to survive, and from his own experience and observation this is what he came up with in the way of wisdom:

Good physical condition was something, but not enough by itself. Champion athletes might not survive; they might worry too much about what was happening to their bodies. Big heavyset men had a hard time. That was easily understood; a big body needed more fuel to power it, and as early as Camp O'Donnell even small slight men were running on a lean mixture. Boozers had it extra hard, because the Japanese were not about to issue liquor (and the Philippine Department of the Army was famous for heavy drinking, from Jonathan Wainwright down to the *dhobie* soldiers of the 31st Infantry, an outfit that used to be known as The Thirsty-First).

O'Donnell was hard on old men, old by POW standards, meaning forty. Strangely, though, being very young could be hard too. A young strong body was not enough. Some young POWs were still growing boys, and the Japanese ration scale was bound to be punishing for them. Experience of life seemed to be important, too, and that was something that could only come with the years. It brought a tempered discipline, or at least it might; whereas if a boy was too young he might be overwhelmed by what was happening to him, and this might cause him to fold.

It also began to appear to Forrest as if country boys might do better overall than city boys. Of course there were city rats who learned how to run the POW camp maze in seconds flat. But overall, the country boy seemed to be able to make do better than most. Growing up on the farm in the Depression years, the average country boy had never had anything in the way of luxury, so he never expected much out of life. He did not harp on fancy food. He knew about hard work and sweat and dirt, and he could do things with his hands.

Forrest himself was in his middle twenties, neither too young nor too old. He was small and stringy. He was not a country boy, but close enough for POW purposes, a small-town boy whose work before the war was roofing and rough carpentering. He was not educated, but he had any amount of native wit; he could take in what was happening around him and make sense of it. So he was smart enough to see that in prison camp intelligence was like physical strength, not enough by itself. Take the case of one sergeant major in the 192nd. Forrest knew him personally. He was an experienced soldier, supposed to be the smartest tanker of all, IQ 160; he could quote army regulations word for word, from memory. But he died early, because he would not eat rice. Forrest watched him die, and made up his own mind that he would eat anything, as a matter of stubbornness; and from then on stubbornness seemed to him to be more to the point than intelligence.

A strong philosophy could be a help. It did not necessarily have to be a religion. Some men held on to their faith in camp, some lost it; a few found it, but not many. There were ebbs and surges in faith, just as there were variations among the chaplains. In camp the men of God ranged from towers of strength to weak reeds; from Robert Taylor, who turned out to be the one chaplain at Cabanatuan who could be trusted to carry milk to the sick without nipping at it on the way, down to the carp-faced individual who stole Bill Delich's pineapple cake. If not religious faith, then a man needed at least something to sustain the idea that life was worth living. Even hate would do. That was what Forrest used, and he was not the only one. There was an Englishman who knew shorthand; he used it to note atrocities—dates, places, Japanese names. An Australian used to do portrait sketches for the guards, the way he did for his friends, except that with the guards he always held back a copy to identify them as war criminals. And another Australian kept himself alive by sharpening his knife every day against the time when Tōjō might visit his camp.

The survival wisdom that came early to Forrest came to others in season, and was added to as time went by. Single men might have an edge because they had no wife and family to fret over. On the other hand, married men with children might have the edge because they had something to go home to. Men who made themselves too obvious for any reason were buying trouble. Trying to stay invisible made better sense. Do not attract attention, do not stand out in the crowd.

Plan carefully. Husband energy. Be considerate, but at the same time be determined to survive. Good thoughts all, but no real explanation for who lived and who died. Strong men died and weak men lived, good men died and the orneriest of characters lived. In the end survival in POW camp was a great mystery. *Faith and digging in garbage cans*—maybe that said as much as could be said. Maybe even that was not to the point. Maybe the will to live was a gift, like having a good voice, and everything else was luck, or fate.

There might have been no atheists in foxholes, but in prison camp there were plenty of fatalists. The famous phrase about atheists and foxholes originated on Bataan, coined by William Cummings, an army chaplain, a Catholic, as fervent a believer as there ever was, a true servant of God in the camps. Yet God did not see fit to bring Cummings out of captivity alive.

In the face of dark mysteries like that, and coming up against the terrible things the Japanese did to their prisoners every day, it was easy to lapse into apathy or depression, and that condition was something that neither doctors nor chaplains could cure. Men who gave up trying to keep themselves clean were putting themselves in the way of decline. Men who traded their rice ration for cigarettes were putting themselves in the way of death. Forrest saw this for himself in Company A. The Madison brothers, Harold and Ralph, known as Curly and Dimples, made it to Cabanatuan, but Curly had a bad nicotine habit, and he started trading off his food for smokes. There was a camp saying about men who did this: *He is smoking his way to Group Four,* there being no Group Four. Curly had the offer from some of the Janesville tribe that if he would eat his food they would steal smokes for him, but he was too far gone, and he died.

In the sick bays, and especially among subtribes, most men would make a big effort to keep a sinking man afloat and swimming for himself—they would joke with him, or insult him, even slap him and kick him, anything to keep his vital juices flowing. After a certain point, though, there was wisdom in knowing when to stop. When a man truly gave up, if he would not help himself, there was no help for him.

In the Shanghai War Prisoners Camp where Harry Jeffries and Oklahoma Atkinson were doing their time, there were so many rats that the Japanese set the prisoners to catching them. They did not turn them in alive. They would drop them in a bucket of water and bet on how long they could swim, how long they would last before they drowned. Harry and Oklahoma did not bet on this game, because they had not figured out a way to fix it. The camp was never going to run out of rats. For unlimited resupply, the huge city of Shanghai was just down the road, with its deep and horrible drains and sewers—more rats than humans. Beyond Shanghai there was the rest of China. And beyond China the whole Greater East Asian Co-Prosperity Sphere, teeming with rats, enough to last till doomsday. The POWs were trapped like rats in the Japanese bucket. The question was how to keep swimming. And for Harry and Oklahoma, the same question in the same breath was how to fix the game so as to be the ones who swam the longest.

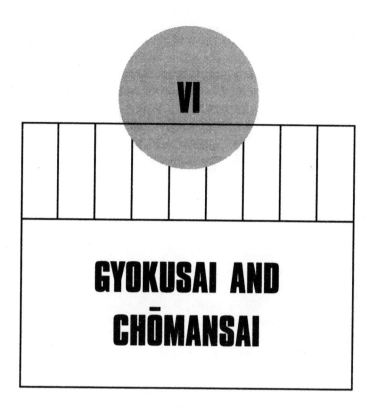

VI

GYOKUSAI AND CHŌMANSAI

THE OUTSIDE WORLD HAD ALMOST NO INFORMATION ON what was happening to the prisoners. The most basic things about them, and about civilian internees too, were not known: their names, how many of them there were and where they were being held, much less their condition and what they had suffered.

The Japanese would not let observers from neutral powers or the International Red Cross into camps in the war zone, and they defined most of their Co-Prosperity Sphere as the war zone, so that nine out of ten prisoners were never officially sighted.

Even away from the war zone, the Japanese selected which camps could be visited. Official visitors were not allowed to turn up unannounced. They could not walk about unescorted. Prisoners were not allowed to talk freely to them. And of course the

Japanese always dressed up the camp—with good-looking clothes for selected prisoners to wear and extra food trucked in to make the storehouse look lavish, then trucked away afterward, and so on.

It was not unknown for local Red Cross people to be thrown in jail for being conscientious about their work, or even killed by the kempeitai on suspicion of being underground agents. So, out of prudence, official Red Cross reports were light on discouraging words. Japanese food figures were never openly disputed. Red Cross boxes came into the camps and the POWs only received what was left after the Japanese were through looting. From the prisoners' side, everything else about official visits was either a charade or simply an unknown.

One European official observer, a well-nourished individual, did not bring food on his only visit to one camp. He did bring his young son. The boy was well fed too, in fact perfectly round. The prisoners stared at him, seventy pounds of plump white piglet, visibly high in fat content, and the only nourishment they could draw from the occasion was to imagine him served roasted on a big platter with an apple in his mouth.

From start to finish, the Japanese stonewalled about what they were doing to conquered peoples in their captured territories. Specifically concerning POWs, the Japanese government issued an early all-purpose announcement: In the generous spirit of bushidō, all captives were being accorded the best possible treatment, and they were unanimously expressing appreciation of Japanese magnanimity. From then on the Japanese kept saying either that abuses were nonexistent, or that allegations were being looked into and no response was appropriate until more was known, et cetera.

Stories came out early in the war about atrocities in Hong Kong, and mass murder and rape after the fall of Singapore. And on and on. Official Allied protests piled up—British, Australian, American. By the turn of 1943–1944 the United States alone had a backlog of eighty-nine protests unsatisfied.

But what should be done with information about atrocities? It could be a two-edged sword. It could hurt morale at home, especially while the Japanese still appeared to be winning the war. There were other serious considerations as well. The earliest first-hand reports of the Bataan death march came from a handful of escapers in the spring of 1943, but the terrible facts were held back from the newspapers for many months, till early 1944—long enough for a Red Cross shipment to reach the camps and be distributed, for fear that the Japanese, out of spite, might renege on letting the prisoners have the food and medicine.

Looking ahead: Once the Japanese were definitely, irreversibly, losing the war, what might happen? Making more of their atrocities known might provoke them to more of a killing rage.

In fact, the Japanese were losing the war. They had lost control of the air and the sea. Their planes were being shot out of the sky faster than they could build new ones; they were hemorrhaging experienced pilots. And their shipping was suffering: In 1941 it was Allied ships being sunk, but in 1942 the Allies were sinking one Japanese ship approximately every three days, in 1943 one a day, and in 1944 American submarines alone sank more Japanese ships than in 1941, 1942, and 1943 combined. The Japanese could not get raw materials for their war industry back to Japan from the Co-Prosperity Sphere. And they could not get food to their troops in the field. In 1942 the official daily rice ration of a Japanese soldier was 850 grams; by late 1944 it was 400 grams.

Those material statistics were decisive facts of war. But in Japanese military doctrine, material things did not signify. Spirit was crucial. A white soldier might be twice as big as a Japanese soldier, but that meant nothing, because the white man's heart was small. A tiny Japanese pursuit plane could bring down a huge American bomber—a specimen was on exhibit at Hibiya Park in Tokyo to prove it. Western materialism was gross, overblown, corrupt. The Japanese spirit was pure and spare. And unconquerable. That was what the emperor's military leaders kept telling the Japanese people, and everyone in the occupied territories, and the world—even after the war began to turn against Japan. In fact, the worse things became, the louder they said it.

Japanese fighting men would be human bullets. But what if the enemy had a thousand guns to one Japanese gun? Ten thousand? A hundred thousand? There were figures to show that, at the peak, every American fighting man in the Pacific was backed by four tons of equipment, as against two pounds for a Japanese soldier. Still it would be indomitable Japanese flesh against enemy steel. *If your arms are broken kick the enemy; if your legs are injured bite him; if your teeth break glare him to death.*

* * *

For a Japanese fighting man, death in victory was supposed to be glorious. In defeat—not that the word *defeat* was ever spoken— death rather than surrender was insisted upon. And to become a prisoner was unthinkable.

On the Allied side of the war, from beginning to end, doctrine and practice were against taking Japanese prisoners, at least beyond a bare minimum for interrogation. In China, if such and such a number of prisoners was specified for questioning, many more had to be collected at the front line, because not all of them were going to make it back to headquarters alive—that was understood. The United States came into the war in the Pacific by way of Pearl Harbor. The Japanese had not declared war. Their opening state- ment was a sneak attack. Considering that, the Americans did not think they needed to feel unduly constrained by conventional bat- tlefield honor. There were written instructions about the treatment of prisoners, but the reality was: *Take him back to G2. If he tries to escape, get him. Don't be gone more than five minutes.* There were American bomber pilots and submarine commanders who would sink a Japanese ship and then be just as happy to machine-gun the survivors in the water as leave them to drown. As for Australians, the opening statement of the Japanese in the Malaya campaign, at Parit Sulong, had been to truss captured Australian soldiers with barbed wire, bayonet them, pile them up dead or alive, machine- gun them, and then set them on fire with gasoline. There was another massacre at Tol on New Britain, and another at Laha on Ambon, all in the first weeks of the war; and after that the one ambition of the Australians was to exterminate all Japanese, kill them like snakes. If they did take prisoners, they might shoot them once they were through with them—*We had one, but he tried to get away*—or throw them out of a plane and call it *harakiri*.

The Japanese massacred when they were winning, and when they were threatened they massacred, too. In April 1942 the war was going all Japan's way. Wake, Guam, Hong Kong, Singapore, the Netherlands East Indies, and Burma had all surrendered, Bataan had just fallen, and only Corregidor was still hanging on. Then, out of nowhere, a force of carrier-based American B-25 bombers led by Lieutenant Colonel James Doolittle appeared over Japan in daylight, at low altitude. It was the first time in history that the home islands had been attacked from the air. The damage was not severe, and there were no follow-up raids. But American bombs falling close to the emperor's palace—to the Japanese military that was an obscenity. Doolittle's raiders flew away, heading for landing fields in free China. Eight crewmen fell into the hands of the Japanese. They were tortured, strung up, beaten, given the water cure, and tried by the military under a new law passed specifically to punish captured airmen as war criminals. Five were sentenced to life; three were executed. The Japanese sent a hundred thousand troops into the Chinese province of Chekiang, where most of the bombers had come down, and into the neighboring province of Kiangsi; and for three months they ravaged and burned, destroying airfields, wiping out whole villages and towns. They killed something like a quarter of a million Chinese—an atrocity on the scale of the rape of Nanking.

Later, when the Japanese began losing the war, their troops expected to be massacred in turn. They had been fed a steady diet of atrocity stories. Both sides had—stories absolutely true, only partly true, or not true at all, it did not matter. For their part, the Japanese were told that the British in Burma hung Japanese prisoners on trees for target practice, and that they ran over them with tanks and squashed them into road fill. When the Sittang River flooded and Japanese soldiers were swept downstream, the British had a Bren gunner firing bursts at them, and their screams and convulsions were recorded with check marks on a slate, for sport. The Australians in the Pacific bayoneted their prisoners. They gouged the gold teeth from their jaws, dead or alive. The Americans took Japanese ears, boiled heads too, and sent the skulls home as souvenirs—and indeed *Life* magazine ran a photograph of an all-American girl with a skull her fiancé had sent her. To the Japanese, who were scrupulous about the bones of their dead, that was the ultimate barbarism—that and the story about President Roosevelt using a bone from a dead Japanese soldier for a letter opener.

So Japanese fighting men were told to be ready for death in battle. Kill or be killed—those were the choices their army always put before them. And, as the war turned more and more against Japan in 1943 and 1944 they were told to kill themselves rather than be captured.

On the island of Attu in the Aleutians, the Japanese had a garrison of about twenty-five hundred. In May 1943 the Americans invaded in force. When it was obvious to the Japanese that they were doomed, more than a thousand of them made a *banzai* charge. *Japanese drink blood like wine!* They were mowed down. When the battle was over, the Americans found Japanese dead in heaps, blown up with their own grenades held against their stomachs. The Japanese doctors had shot their own wounded, or killed them with morphine injections. The total number of prisoners taken by the Americans was a couple of dozen.

The word the Japanese used for what happened on Attu was *gyokusai,* meaning the smashing of the jewel, heroic death as supremely valuable, with a special Japanese beauty and poetry to it.

For the rest of the war they kept on using the word. They had to. They were being smashed.

By mid-1944, Saipan in the Marianas was under threat. It was a big island, strategically important, less than thirteen hundred miles from Tokyo. It had been in Japanese hands since the time of World War I, with something like 20,000 Japanese civilian settlers living there, plus Korean and Okinawan laborers. It was heavily fortified and strongly garrisoned. In June 1944 the Americans attacked at division strength. To go by Japanese figures, between June 16 and July 9, 41,000 of 43,000 Japanese troops died in battle. By American figures it was about 30,000 Japanese dead, against 14,000 Americans killed or wounded. Only 921 prisoners were taken. Of the 20,000 civilians, 8,000 to 10,000 were killed, and about 4,000 killed themselves rather than allow themselves to be captured. They blew themselves up with grenades, ran into the sea to drown, and threw themselves off cliffs, mothers with babies, whole families. The Americans had never seen anything like it.

(As for what happened after that, the Saipan Japanese would never have seen anything like it either: From the time the Americans secured the island to the end of the war, Seabees were cruising around in boats decorated with Japanese skulls skewered on stakes like shish kebabs.)

Next, two other important islands in the Marianas—Guam and Tinian—were invaded. There was no mass civilian suicide to match Saipan. But on Tinian there were five thousand Korean laborers and so as not to have hostiles *at their back* when the Americans invaded, the Japanese killed them.

At their back the Japanese had hostile POWs, more than a hundred thousand. What might happen to them when the time came?

When Tarawa in the Gilbert Islands was invaded late in 1943, there were no Allied prisoners being held there. But a year earlier there had been. In October 1942 American planes bombed some Japanese ships, and the Japanese chopped the heads off all their prisoners, twenty-two of them. The same thing happened on Nauru, in the equatorial Pacific: The night after the first Allied air attack, the Japanese killed their prisoners. It was the same on Ballale, in the Shortland Islands: When the Japanese heard that Allied ships were coming, they bayoneted all their prisoners, about ninety. And it happened on Wake. In the first week of October 1943, American ships bombarded the island. All ninety-six prisoners still being held there were rounded up. They were tied, blindfolded, and machine-gunned, and their bodies were thrown into a long grave at the water's edge.

Ballale, Nauru, and Wake were tiny islands with small garrisons, not central to the war as it was shaping up through 1943 and into 1944. In those out-of-the-way places the Japanese massacred their prisoners. And, as they had done at Tarawa in 1942, they killed them well ahead of actual invasion, killings triggered by nothing more than a threat.

So, what might happen when the great thrust of the war, driving toward the ultimate objective of the Japanese home islands, brought the Allied advance closer to where more than a hundred thousand POWs were being held, not to mention another hundred thousand civilian internees?

At the big POW camp at Davao in the southern Philippines, the senior officer was convinced that, come the invasion, the Japanese would kill them all. He started working up a plan to break everyone out ahead of that day and make for the mountains.

The timing would be life-and-death. If they went too early the prisoners would not be able to survive long enough in the wild to be saved. But if they left it too late the Japanese would mow them down inside the fence. He had to have accurate advance information. For that he needed a shortwave radio receiver.

Russell Hutchison was the man to put one together. Hutchison had been building radios since he was five or six, real sets that worked, assembled from whatever came to hand around the house, including the insides of his mother's telephone. In junior high he had a portable set on his bicycle, with batteries behind the seat, the receiver in an orange crate on the handlebars, earphones, antenna, and all. Before the war he was a radioman in the National Guard. He came to the Philippines in a coast artillery unit, and on Bataan he built himself a little shortwave set so he could listen to KGEI.

His radio did not survive the march out of Bataan. He did. He stayed alive through O'Donnell and the first months at Cabanatuan. Then, late in 1942, he was sent on a big labor draft to Mindanao. At Davao the Japanese camp commandant put out a call for a prisoner who could fix radios. Hutchison got the job, plus a commission from the senior POW officer to build a secret short-wave set.

The camp machine shop was a happy hunting ground for him. He fixed the commandant's personal radio, an American Zenith. The other Japanese brought in their looted sets, Sears, Roebuck and Montgomery Ward brands, also a 35-millimeter Simplex movie projector with a sound amplifier that needed work. Every chance Hutchison got, he liberated parts. From a broken-down car radio he lifted a couple of tube sockets. He scrounged capacitors and condensers and resistors and a voltage meter, a headset that had survived a fire, everything up to four new tubes still in their packages. He used the shop lathe on the sly to wind some Japanese wire for his power supply. He wound coils and wrapped them in friction tape, rubbed them in mud to make them look old, and dropped them in the trash can for safekeeping.

The shop was outside the main camp. Hutchison had to get his parts back in. He arranged to be the one to pick up the midday meal from the cookhouse, because the midday inspection was loose, the best time for getting by the guards. He would bow to them with radio bits and pieces tucked in his armpit or covered up in the buckets of his carrying pole.

When Hutchison had everything inside the gate, the senior officer suggested that he go to work at the hospital pharmacy, living and running his radio from there. Hutchison did not want to put the hospital at risk. He used a building where the Japanese had prisoners repairing shoes and watches.

At night for a month he and two of his friends watched the guards, timing every step they took: so many seconds to the first gate, to the next gate, to the company street, halfway down, between the buildings, out to the back, past the latrines, every hour on the hour.

He kept his set disassembled, buried in sections in canvas wraps. At night he had his friends pick up the parts, and keep watch outside in the dark while he put the set together, plugged it in, and listened. They had a routine rehearsed for when the guards were coming. One lookout would cross his legs, which was the signal for the other to tap on the window, whereupon Hutchison would start breaking up the set. Then they had fifty-five seconds to get the parts to the benjo and be sitting with their pants down like all the other dysenteries, ready to dump. One night the guards were off schedule, it threw the timing out, and Hutchison was making for the benjo with the headset under his jacket when the guards halted him. He patted his stomach woefully and said, *Tak-usan byōki,* very sick, and got away with it.

Late at night, after the radio was disassembled and buried again, Hutchison would stay up with the news analysis group. They had a navy commander who knew the China coast and all the main Pacific islands by heart, and that was how they followed the war, on a map drawn on the inside of his raincoat.

In better days for the Axis powers, the Davao Japanese would post their version of the world news, bulletin board *boombooms* to impress the prisoners. The last one of those was in the fall of 1943, some story about a big German victory at a place called Salerno—which the analysis group interpreted to mean that the Allies must have been successful in North Africa and then gone on to invade Italy.

From then on the news was all Hutchison's. In May 1944 he heard about an American naval victory near the Palau Islands. The Palaus were only 600 or 700 miles from Mindanao on the raincoat map.

The Japanese started winding the camp down. They did not send the prisoners out working the rice paddies anymore, or re-planting the vegetable gardens. Next thing, orders came that everyone was going to be moved away.

Hutchison meant to take his radio with him. Shakedowns were the big threat, so he scattered the parts. The chassis and a piece from an old alarm clock that he used for changing stations went to the watch repair people to carry. He got his friends to sweat the top and bottom off some corned beef cans. His headphone fit that size can nicely. So did some other parts, packed in kapok, ballasted with sand. He made a scale and weighed the packed cans against the real things, then soldered everything together again, aged the seams, pasted the labels back on, and dropped the cans enough times to make sure they did not always land same side up. He put two radio cans and one real can of corned beef in among his personal stuff in a musette bag that had belonged to a major the Japanese had shot, and he was ready to go.

Move-out was set for June 6, 1944. The prisoners were loaded for transport before dawn. The Japanese made them take off their shoes, then blindfold themselves with strips of white cloth; then they strung them together, forty or fifty roped bodies to a truck.

They were driven standing up to Lasang and herded onto a freighter, the *Yashu Maru,* jammed into the two forward holds, so crushed they could not sit.

For days the ship did not budge. They had to sleep in shifts, making space for one man at a time in each little group to lie down. They were fed rice, and amazingly they got a Red Cross box; but the holds were stinking hot, and everything was filthy, so bad that some men went out of their minds and had to be tied up like dogs.

Finally, on June 12, the ship moved out, in a shaky convoy, under air cover, hugging the coast, stop and go, south and then west to Zamboanga City. Then to Cebu, where they were off-loaded, stuck dockside for three days, some sweltering inside a metal warehouse, some cooking outside in the sun. Then they were loaded onto another ship. All their bags were dumped in the hold. Hutchison crept down to find his musette bag. As an iden-tifier, he had stuffed some dried okra in the side pocket, and amaz-ingly, feeling with his fingers in the pitch dark among the jumble of hundreds of bags, it was the first one he laid his hands on. It had been ratted; the cans had been opened. But whoever did it was only hungry, only a rat, not a white mouse, an informer—the can of corned beef was gone, but the two cans with the radio parts were still there, opened but untouched. Hutchison had to disguise everything again, working in blackness in 120-degree heat. He hollowed out bars of soap, put the parts inside, then peed on the soap to wet it and seal it against shakedown.

The second ship was smaller and even more crowded, and no one was allowed on deck. They headed north, and on June 25 they docked at Pier 7 at Manila. They had been nineteen days covering eight hundred miles.

Half of them were held in Manila. The other half were sent to Cabanatuan. Hutchison was in the Cabanatuan half. There was a Cabanatuan radio already operating, and the POW com-mand did not want two. Hutchison's set was to be used as a backup. When it was needed, he went to the senior chaplain and asked if he could plug in at the chapel altar. *Okay,* said the man of God, *but if the Japanese come in, you get down on your knees and pray like hell.*

In July, Hutchison plugged in, and found he had missed the invasion of Europe. The very day he left Davao, June 6, was D-Day, and now there were more than a million Allied troops in France. Then he heard about a naval battle in the Philippine Sea, a great victory for the Americans. Then that the Americans had taken Saipan. Then that General Tōjō Hideki, premier of Japan, war minister, and army chief of staff, had been dismissed. And he heard about a huge new American bomber called the B-29, the

Superfortress, the biggest thing in the air, capable of raiding the home islands of Japan from amazing distances.

::

THE Japanese had been moving prisoners around by sea in thousands since the earliest months of the war.

For Americans taken in the Philippines, Manila was the big port of embarkation, to Japan via Formosa. In Southeast Asia, for the British, the Australians, the Dutch, and the Americans of the 131st Field Artillery and the *Houston,* the main port was Singapore. It was one of the great ports of the world, and the Japanese used Keppel Harbor to transship prisoners along with everything else for their war. From Singapore, drafts went to Japan via Saigon and Formosa. And prisoner transports were in and out all the time, to and from Java, Sumatra, Burma, Borneo, Ambon, Haruku, Timor, New Britain—wherever the Japanese called for labor. This way or that, more than one in every three POWs found himself on a prisoner sea transport.

POWs were shipped the way animals were, in the hold, loaded along with all kinds of other freight: rice, coal, sugar, rubber, cinchona bark, cigarettes, steel tubing, gasoline, bombs.

On the upper decks, where the humans traveled, were all kinds of Japanese: Co-Prosperity Sphere administrators, educators, economists, agricultural specialists, often with wives and children. There were also comfort women and, many times, all over the ship, Japanese soldiers.

The Japanese always claimed they did not treat POWs being transported by ship any worse than their own fighting men. Their troops certainly did not have things easy at sea. When Lieutenant Colonel Tsuji Masanobu was planning the invasion of Malaya, he subjected infantrymen to days on end in holds as hot as steam baths, preparing them to be shipped into the tropics to fight. After that, Japanese soldiers going to war in the southern zone were often shipped on what were called banana transports, so named because the troops were supposed to subsist on raw fruit, without cooking facilities. And they were crammed in. By the time the Japanese were trying to reinforce Saipan ahead of the American invasion in mid-1944, they had troops traveling by thousands on small ships, packed in with their gear, sweating, on stacked shelves in hot-box holds—like broiler chickens, as one of them said.

This went by the name of *chōmansai,* a word coming to be used more and more, the way *gyokusai* was, as part of the language of a war turning worse and worse. *Mansai* meant full capacity, or a loaded condition, *chō* meant super or ultra. In practice, *chōmansai* meant extreme overload.

Going back as far as the Russo-Japanese War, the Japanese military calculated space for shipping troops by one of two rules of thumb: so many bodies per gross ton of ship's weight, or so many per *tsubo* (3.95 square yards). The recommendation was one man per three gross tons, or about one per tsubo. But within the first twelve months of World War II it was up to one man per two tons, then one per ton; and by 1944 it was two per ton, or six times the recommended density. That meant less than one square yard per man, with men sleeping in shifts, rotating for deck time and latrine time, for as long as the transport took, days or weeks. Chōmansai was one index of rising desperation in a losing war.

The Japanese said they did not overload POWs just for being POWs; they did it only because circumstances forced them to. But the POWs were foreign, they were white, they were prisoners of war, *disgraced individuals,* miserable objects. It was always POWs who were packed the tightest—bigger bodies, more per tsubo. When Japanese troops had to share the same ship with them, it was the POWs who were down lowest, deepest in the holds, parched for water, gasping for air, in the filthy leavings of fermenting rice and sugar and coal dust and horse droppings, trapped in their own shit with the Japanese shitting down on them.

POWs were not assigned priority shipping value over any other kind of war material. If they were extremely lucky, they might draw a civilian Japanese ship captain who could find it in himself to take some human trouble over them, or a crew of merchant seamen who had seen something of the world beyond Japan and were not absolutely hostile to white men. Or even a guard commander who saw it as his duty as a conscientious soldier to land his full tally of prisoners alive on Japanese soil. But for every one guard commander like that, there were any number just as happy to make up their final count from the dog tags of the dead.

In the early months of the war, while the Japanese still had control of the seas, prisoner transports were at least safe from attack; and if the ship could make any kind of speed, the POWs would be only days on the water.

The first big batch sent to Japan traveled on a fast passenger ship, the *Argentina Maru*, out of Guam, early in January 1942. They were down in the hold, but only for six days, no attack, no deaths. Also in January, the Wake marines and CPNAB contractors were in the hold of the *Nitta Maru*, another fast passage, less than two weeks Wake-Yokohama-Shanghai, no attack, and no deaths except the five men who had their heads chopped off.

Most other POW transports, though, were freighters, old, disreputable, and cranky. The prisoners christened them the way they christened guards. *Hotsy Maru. Byōki Maru*, meaning sick. *Stinko Maru. Diarrhea Maru. Dysentery Maru. Benjo Maru*, meaning floating shithouse.

And the *Mate Mate Maru*, which took sixty-one days from the Philippines to Japan. Mate Mate meant Wait Wait, and that could have been a generic name for the freighters. Even at top speed and with a free run from point A to point B, they would take forever. And from the second half of 1942 on, with the seas not safe anymore, they were condemned to go slower still, coast-hugging, harbor-hopping. That meant multiples more elapsed time for prisoners in the hold, and even without the ship being attacked it could mean the difference between life and death.

Before the end of 1942, there were deaths that could be blamed on slowness. The *Tottori Maru* left the Philippines on October 2 for Formosa, then the port of Pusan in Korea. That took thirty days, and Japan another twelve, finishing with more than a dozen dead bodies thrown overboard and hundreds of men off-loaded sick. The *Dai Nichi Maru* left Singapore on October 30; by November 11 men were starting to die, and by the time the ship reached Japan on November 25 there were something like 80 dead.

Those deaths were from starvation, suffocation, and disease. Death in bulk quantity came from submarine attacks. In July, the *Montevideo Maru* out of Rabaul was sunk off Luzon by an American sub. It was carrying more than a thousand Australians—840 POWs, the rest civilians. None survived. On October 1, between Hong Kong and Japan, the *Lisbon Maru* was torpedoed, also by an American sub. Out of more than 1,800 British POWs, almost 850 were lost.

Early in the war the Japanese were not in favor of sending merchant ships out in convoy, their thinking being that convoys were nothing but concentrated targets. By 1943 the facts of war had converted them to using convoys with armed escorts. But that was no guarantee of security either. Convoys traveling by day were exposed to air attack, and night was the best time for submarine torpedo attacks.

Nineteen forty-three was worse than 1942, and 1944 was worse again. The worst single time for a POW to be on the water was September 1944.

Early in the month the *Shin'yō Maru* was coming up from Mindanao, headed for Manila with American prisoners from an airstrip detail at Lasang, 800-plus men in the hold. On September 7 it was torpedoed by an American submarine. Only 81 made it to shore.

On September 12 two ships, the *Rakuyō Maru* and the *Kachidoki Maru*, zigzagging in convoy from Singapore to Japan with Australian and British prisoners in the holds, were torpedoed by American submarines off the island of Hainan. The Japanese lifted some hundreds of survivors out of the water and left the rest to the sharks. The two subs picked up 72; two other subs picked up 42. Out of 2,200-plus POWs, more than 1,500 were lost.

On September 18, off Sumatra, a British sub sank the *Jun'yō Maru*—the total deaths were 5,620, of which 1,377 were Dutch and Indo-Dutch, 64 British and Australian, and a handful American, mostly merchant seamen; all the rest were rōmusha; there were only 723 survivors.

Between the Moluccas and Java, little ships crammed with POWs were island hopping, or lying at anchor for fear of air attack out on the open sea. The *Maros Maru* was on the water from July through September to November, 127 days. Packed on deck were 500 Dutch and British from Haruku and Ambon, and another 150 loaded from a ship sunk by a Liberator. For 40 days they were stuck off Makassar, with men starving, parched for water, hallucinating, going insane, dying by the scores, by the hundreds; the dead were thrown overboard, their bodies floating, turning purple and yellow, bloated—a man was detailed to row out among them and weight them down with rocks or slit them open with a knife, to let out the gases of putrefaction so they would sink. Two of the guards on this transport were Mori Masao and Kasayama Yoshikichi, Blood and Slime. Both of them made it to Soerabaja. Fewer than one in two prisoners did, and the POW doctors thought they were the worst-looking human beings they had ever seen.

On September 21, off Manila Bay, the *Toyofuku Maru* was sunk by American torpedo bombers. It had left Singapore as far back as June, heading for Japan, carrying British and Dutch POWs. Its engines kept failing. In the holds men were dying of starvation, and disease broke out. The Japanese thought it was cholera, so they put in at Manila. Dozens died there, still in the hold, and dozens of others were taken to Bilibid, alive but looking worse than anything the American doctors had ever seen. The *Toyofuku Maru* sailed again in convoy. Three days out it was sunk. It went down in three minutes. Something like a thousand prisoners were lost. Less than two hundred made it back to shore.

For a POW trapped in the hold of a sinking ship, the odds were worse than fifty-fifty that the Japanese would open the hatches so that he could get out. Then the odds were less—much less—than fifty-fifty that the Japanese would leave a life belt for him when they abandoned ship. If he did make it over the side and into the water, it was less than fifty-fifty that a Japanese in a lifeboat or on a raft would let him climb on—some POWs from the *Jun'yō Maru* had their hands hacked off by the Japanese when they tried. If Japanese ships came back for survivors, it was to pick up Japanese; again, the odds were less than fifty-fifty that they would save prisoners. Some were pulled from the water and then thrown back in, or killed on deck. The rescue ships for Japanese on the *Lisbon Maru* used prisoners for target practice. POWs from the *Shin'yō Maru* were machine-gunned in the water.

A few prisoners on their makeshift rafts could find it in their hearts to pull a guard out of the water; but far more would kill every struggling Japanese they could get their hands on, swimming after them and drowning them like rats.

Then it was the devil and the deep blue sea. Day after day of scorching sun, madness rising, hallucinations, *Come over to that island, my old man owns it, plenty of water, plenty of rice,* swimming for it, swimming to nothingness. In the last days, dehydration, raging thirst, drinking seawater and going crazy, men turning crazed enough to drink their own piss or other men's piss, dead bodies slipping off the rafts, sharks in the water, blood in the water, men still on the rafts looking for a throat to slit, for blood to drink, men without a knife going for the throat with their teeth, men gone mad who had to be killed before they killed others.

By September 1944, Forrest Knox had been gone from Cabanatuan for a year. He had wanted to get away from the Farm, and he did, but what he drew was airfield construction at Las Piñas, in the Manila district, and that turned out to be the Philippines equivalent of a year on the Burma-Siam railroad.

Forrest was on an eight-hundred-man detail digging ditches, draining rice paddy land, knee deep in mud in the wet season and the air boiling with mosquitoes. Then they had to level the ground for runways, break down dikes, push dynamited rock and dirt along narrow-gauge rail tracks in ore carts, dump it, and spread it with flimsy hoes and shovels made out of sheet iron from fifty-five-gallon drums. They were working to a deadline, and of course the Japanese did what they always did on their rush construction jobs—raised the work quotas, lengthened the hours, and cut yasume to nothing.

Las Piñas was a new camp, dating from September 1943. In less than twelve months it was down from its original 800 men to about 450.

The wet-season mud sucked the soles off Forrest's shoes. He had to go barefoot, and he developed hookworm. His clothes rotted away with sweat. He worked in a G-string and a straw hat. Where his arms chafed his sides from shoveling, he got a bad case of Guam blisters. Some men from his hut scrubbed them off him under the kitchen hose, and it felt like he was being set on fire. That was the only time he was hot. The rest of the year, especially in the wet months, he could never get warm. He was forever shivering. His chattering teeth were coming loose in his head. He started losing sensation in his legs; it was like walking with stumps of wood below his knees. And his eyes were going. He had a deficiency disease called *central scotoma*. What it did was to make a hole in his vision, literally. When he looked straight ahead there was a blank spot in what he saw.

On the morning of September 21, Forrest looked up at the sky and something caught his eye, little black specks. He thought that something else had gone wrong with his sight, but in seconds the specks turned into American planes, carrier-based navy fighter-bombers and fighter escorts, hundreds of them filling the sky over Manila.

Suddenly the whole world looked different. MacArthur was returning, getting ready to land on Leyte. As part of the softening up, he was pounding Luzon, especially the port of Manila and the airfields around the city, including Nichols and Las Piñas. Forrest was no fan of Douglas MacArthur, but for MacArthur's return he could swallow his distaste.

He was out on the job when the planes came swooping in, laying bombs along the airstrip, and he found out he could still run, even on his legs like stumps of wood.

That was the end of work for the day. The Japanese let the prisoners dig slit trenches between the barracks. They dug them at angles, to spell a big *PW* that would be seen from the air, and next day when the planes came back Forrest thought he saw one pilot give a wing waggle.

The barracks were boiling with excitement. No one slept. A note came into camp, smuggled in, from guerrillas, telling the prisoners to form themselves into squads of ten and wait for an attack on the guards. But ahead of that the Japanese moved everyone out.

It did not take Forrest long to pack. He had managed to keep two things since Bataan: a toothbrush, which by 1944 had many miles on it, and his neck towel, the one he used in the tank to stop getting burned by hot machine-gun shell casings, the same one that kept him from dying of heat stroke on the death march. With the rest of his worldly belongings thrown in—pillow, canteen, mess kit, knife, spoon, and fork, in a little burlap sack—he would have weighed in at under a hundred pounds.

He was trucked to Bilibid. Nichols Field was being emptied out, too. It was an evil place, bigger and even worse than Las Piñas. And there were details coming down from Cabanatuan. There was no room in the cells; little tribes of prisoners were clumped everywhere on the ground. Forrest ran into Janesville men he had not seen for a year, but that was the only good thing. They were all going to be shipped to Japan.

::

MANILA Bay was full of Japanese ships, scores of them, strafed and bombed, blown apart, sunk or drifting in flames. But there were ships still in commission, and the Japanese were bound and determined to load them with their own civilian refugees and wounded troops and point them toward Japan, send them out in convoy into an ocean filled with American submarine wolf packs under a sky controlled by American bombers. It was the flight by sea from Singapore in 1942 being replayed at Manila in 1944, in Japanese—chōmansai and gyokusai on the upper decks, and the holds jammed with POWs.

Forrest, in 90-degree Manila heat, wearing Japanese-issue cold-weather clothes—a winter trench coat with English buttons and a pair of hobnail boots—and with his burlap sack over his shoulder, had to go shuffling on his woodstumps of legs up the gangplank of the *Harō Maru,* a rusty little freighter that looked to weigh not much more than a thousand tons, overloaded already, with Forrest and a thousand other white men staring down into the black hole of the holds.

There were two holds, forward and rear. The floor of one was covered with horse droppings, the other with loose coal, sharp and dusty. Forrest drew the coal. He could not believe how many bodies the Japanese kept cramming in on top of him. The heat was fierce, tropical sun beating down on the steel plates of the deck and no air circulating below. A POW doctor in Forrest's hold still had his clinical thermometer, and the mercury shot straight up to 108 degrees, the highest it would register. If it had been a cooking thermometer it would have gone up past 120. Everybody shucked their cold-weather greatcoats and got down to G-strings. Forrest tied his towel around his head, the way the Japanese did, for a sweatband.

After two days the *Harō Maru's* convoy still had not moved. The Japanese were not sending down anything like enough drinking water. The prisoners were raining sweat, and the sweat was starting to give off the stink of fear and madness.

A man next to Forrest was making a scratching noise with his knife. He was working away at the hull. His plan was to get at the water outside. He had gone crazy, and he was driving Forrest crazy. He kept scratching all one day and into the next, and somewhere in those two days Forrest lost track of time.

It was not that his memory went. What happened to him in the hold he remembered moment by moment for the rest of his life. It was only that he could not remember what happened when. He was curled up trying to sleep, but the man asleep next to him had long, lanky grasshopper legs that he kept throwing over him, until Forrest took off his belt and tied the legs together. Awake, Forrest had a raging thirst; everyone did. A boy near him would not stop talking about water, some place up in the mountains where he came from, with clear trout streams, pure springs bubbling out of the ground; it reached the point where if Forrest had had a full canteen of water he would have smashed him with it to shut him up. Then Forrest let out a scream—his canteen was gone, stolen. If he did not get it back he was dead. For the better part of a day he kept his eyes glued to a rope the Japanese had hung down into the hold, because everything went up and down that rope: food buckets, slop buckets, canteens. The canteens were supposed to be numbered by owner. That did not last. But Forrest was sure he could recognize his. Finally he saw it coming down. And he saw a man pick it off. He struggled to get at him, wading through a swamp of bodies; men were passing out from the heat all around him and sliding down out of sight, other men were standing on bodies, and he had to step on the bodies, feeling with his bare feet for the next step, and the space he opened up would suck closed behind him like human quicksand. He cornered the thief. He could see the canteen was his, it had his etchings on it, done with a nail at Cabanatuan. He was ready to kill the bastard. The thief could see it in his eyes; he backed off and held out the canteen, still full. It was all Forrest could do not to bash his skull in with it.

Then he saw a man from Las Piñas sitting slumped with his skull bashed in, dead. And suddenly there were men going mad, charging at the bulkhead, trying to smash their own skulls. A navy chief tried to talk them down; a chaplain tried to pray them down. They would cower, but then they would run some more, crashing into other men, howling like dogs. A colonel safe on deck shouted down the hatch that the Japanese were not going to put up with the howling; if it did not stop they were going to cover the hold. Meaning everyone would suffocate. Forrest had no intention of dying because of some howling madmen. No officers or doctors were doing anything. So men with guts were going to have to shut the howlers up, meaning kill them. Forrest summoned up the guts. He used his sweat towel, the way McKnight on the truck detail had taught him, the way it was done in the lunatic asylum. The only sound Forrest could hear while he was killing was a roaring in his own ears. When the hold was quiet, he was sick to his gut.

The bodies were tied to the rope and hauled up, twirling. They were thrown over the side, and the ship's screws made chum out of them.

In the Luzon Strait, at night, the convoy came under submarine attack. Some ships close to the *Harō Maru* took bad hits. The jarring of the explosions came up through Forrest's feet like jolts from giant sledgehammers pounding the hull. There were a few men on deck, in line to use the box benjo hung over the side. They could see big splashes of phosphorescence heading their way. It was a torpedo that had lost gyro and depth control. It was porpoising. In the hold Forrest could hear it, making a noise like a speedboat; he knew what it was, and he was about to break his own rule and drink the last of his water—*why die thirsty?*—when it dived. Nothing happened; it must have gone right underneath the hull.

The Luzon Strait was a shooting gallery. The convoy had started out at eighteen ships. It was down in numbers already. The rest were never going to make Japan in a single run. Eleven days out from Manila, they put in at Hong Kong.

Bombers came over, working the harbor. Forrest was up on deck. Bombs were falling all around, every time one went off, he could feel the ship jump. A tanker right alongside took a direct hit; there was a huge explosion, a giant waterspout, and before the water came down, the tanker had disappeared, like a fish taking a bobber.

They were ten days at Hong Kong, with only one feeding time per day and half a canteen of water, and more men dying in the holds. On the eleventh day they sailed, eleven ships in convoy; it was a short hop to Formosa but it took a long four days, with no water at all and more men going insane. They came in at Takao with the madmen tied up on deck.

The Japanese kept them in the hold for twelve days, with the guards standing over the hatches eating mangoes, throwing rotten ones down for the sport of watching the prisoners fight for them. One night a rat fell in; it ran around on men trying to sleep, only a tiny disgusting thing in the middle of terrible things the size of life and death, but the hold did not quieten down for two hours, so many men were so close to the end of their tether.

The next day the hatches were battened down, lashed into place with steel cable, weighted with heavy timbers. Who could tell why, other than that the Japanese wanted to be sure the prisoners would drown if they took a hit. The ship got under way, but then it turned and came back, and who could tell why, except that it must have been too dangerous to even try for Japan.

On the thirteenth day the Japanese opened the holds. They were wearing face masks against the stink. They offloaded the prisoners at the end of rifle butts and boathooks, sprayed them with disinfectant, broke them into small groups, and trucked them away.

Thirty-nine days out of Manila, thirty-nine dead, many more dying, and the rest still had the sea leg to Japan ahead of them.

In fact, they were lucky, if that was the right word. At Manila the detail after them drew the *Arisan Maru*. It was supposed to leave on October 11, but did not get away until October 21. Three days later, about 225 miles off Hong Kong, it was torpedoed. The Japanese cut the forward hold rope, slammed the rear hold hatches down, and abandoned ship. Hundreds of POWs were dead already, killed in the explosion. The living built pyramids of corpses to climb up and out. Some made it; most went down with the ship. The convoy's escort destroyers did not pick the swimmers out of the water; the crews pushed them under with poles. In the end, out of 1,802 prisoners only 8 survived: 5 found an abandoned lifeboat and made it to the coast of China; 4 were picked up by Japanese ships and taken to Takao, and one of them died.

After that, in November, one Manila transport made it safely to Japan. And after that there was only one more shipment, in December.

Not many POWs were left on Luzon, at least not many enlisted men with much life in them, let alone useful work. But by then the Japanese were drafting walking skeletons.

At Bilibid there were mainly hopeless beriberis and pellagras and cerebral malarias, blind men and amputees. They stayed. But almost all the medical officers and corpsmen had to go. And the medical staff from Cabanatuan. Plus, in great numbers, officers.

At this late date, with nine out of ten enlisted men drafted to Japan, one out of every three officers was still in the Philippines. In Forrest's time at Cabanatuan he had seen how the system worked. Officers had the best of it right where they were, inside the fence. They would do anything to get out of laboring on the Farm, let alone be drafted away, especially to Japan. It put Forrest in mind of a flock of penguins on the ice, none of them wanting to be first into the water, in case of sea leopards. The smart ones would push the dumb ones in. If they got eaten, the smart ones would not go in.

Officers did not even have to be smart penguins; all they had to do was pull rank, and with them that was basic instinct. But now the Japanese were pushing them in. So it came about that on the last transport out of Manila, the *Oryokkō Maru,* loading at Pier 7 on December 13, of the 1,619 prisoners in the holds almost two out of every three were officers: the senior officer from Cabanatuan, Lieutenant Colonel Curtis Beecher; most of the combat unit commanders from Bataan and Corregidor; medical officers from Bilibid and Cabanatuan; and 92 lieutenant colonels, 5 commanders, 14 lieutenant commanders, 170 majors, 261 army and marine captains, 36 naval and 400 army lieutenants, 12 naval lieutenants JG and 31 ensigns. And 16 chaplains. Noncoms and enlisted men totaled about 500.

Plus 47 civilians, including Ted Lewin the gambler, the

smartest of prisoner penguins, odds-on to be the last to have to risk the sea leopards.

The *Oryokkō Maru* had a crew of about 100, plus 30 guards, plus about 700 civilians, plus about 1,000 seamen from ships sunk in Manila harbor—numbers roughly even with the POWs.

By late-1944 chōmansai standards, a seven-thousand-ton ship with a total of something like 3,300 bodies aboard was not extreme. But of course the Japanese were traveling on deck and in the passenger cabins, and the POWs were packed into the holds.

They were not evenly spaced. The midships hold had fewer bodies per square foot than either the aft or the forward hold, which were both heavily overloaded. Forward, men started fainting, and by the middle of the night it was chaos; men were screaming for water, lashing out with their canteens at other men, using up air screaming for air, suffocating. It was the same in the rear hold. And that was before the ship had even got under way. In the morning they counted something like thirty dead.

They left the harbor before dawn. Off Subic Bay, before midmorning, navy planes attacked them with bombs and rockets and machine-gun fire. The planes came back time and again, all day. The deck was a killing ground, with hundreds of Japanese left dead; and in the holds that night it was madness, men crawling around naked in the dark, stealing canteens, killing for water, slashing throats to drink blood.

The next morning the Japanese wounded and the civilians were offloaded at Olongapo. Only the guards and the gun crews were still on deck when the planes came back. The aft hold was hit. About 150 prisoners were killed, and fire broke out. The ship was finished. The Japanese got themselves off the best way they could. The prisoners had to swim for it. The Japanese laid machine-gun fire on them in the water. As they staggered onto the beach they were herded away, and when a head count was taken it added up to only 1,333 which meant that 286 were dead or missing.

On December 20 half of them were taken to the town of San Fernando; on December 21, the other half. Fifteen of the worst wounded were trucked away, supposedly to hospital at Bilibid, but actually to a cemetery, where the Japanese bayoneted them and chopped their heads off.

On December 27 two ships were loaded, the *Enoura Maru* with 1,070 in the hold, plus hundreds of wounded Japanese on deck, the *Brazil Maru* with the rest. They made Formosa in four days. On the way, 5 dead bodies were thrown overboard from the *Brazil Maru*, 16 from the *Enoura Maru*.

At Takao they were kept in the holds until January 6. Then the men from the *Brazil Maru* were moved to the *Enoura Maru;* again bodies were crammed in on top of bodies. Takao was bombed on January 9, and the *Enoura Maru* was hit. In the forward hold two hundred were killed. The corpses were loaded into cargo slings and hauled up by crane, to be buried in a mass grave. The survivors were transferred to the *Brazil Maru.* On January 14 it sailed in convoy for Japan.

The prisoners were down from the original 1,619 to only 1,000, and between Formosa and Japan they kept on dying. The Japanese ordered head counts, but a true count was impossible; there were men so weak their voices could not be heard, and men who answered to their name and then died.

It took two weeks more to reach Japan. In that time more than half of them died. The bodies piled up in the holds. Less than 500 were alive to be unloaded, and in the first month ashore 150 more died. The original 1,619 were down to well under 400.

That was the last POW ship out of the Philippines—there were hardly any more prisoners left to transport, and no more time for the Japanese to transport them. MacArthur had returned. By February 1945, Cabanatuan and Bilibid were liberated.

At Singapore the Japanese still had POW transports moving out in convoy, but not many. A few ships made it to Japan, others got no farther than Saigon, and others were sunk. For the prisoners that was the last of chōmansai.

According to Japanese figures, about twenty-five ships carrying POWs were bombed or torpedoed. Which raises an obvious question: Why were POW transports not marked? Why were those ships out on the ocean in the war zone, some armed, some not, looking no different from any other targets for attack?

There is a simple answer: for the same reason that the Japanese did not mark POW camps on land, even camps sited near obvious military targets like railroads and airfields and ammunition dumps. But that in turn raises another question: Why not? And to that question there is no clear answer. It might be thought that marking POW camps close to military targets would be to the advantage of the Japanese; presumably it would lessen the chances of those targets being bombed. But the Japanese did not reason along those lines.

On the specific question of POWs being moved around by ship, though, no other belligerent power looked much better.

Since the beginning of the war in the Atlantic theater and the Mediterranean, the International Red Cross had been trying to persuade the Allies to agree with Germany and Italy on some way of guaranteeing the safety of POWs at sea. The two sides answered letters from the Red Cross. No more than that, but at least that. The Japanese, when they came into the war, did not bother even to make that gesture. And the United States decided on unrestricted submarine warfare.

Prisoners in the Pacific had no way of knowing anything about all those distant non-results. They had a more pressing concern, and particularly for American POWs being shipped out of the Philippines it was dire: They were being killed at sea by their own forces.

Why did the United States Navy task forces—submarines and carrier-based planes—appear to know nothing about which Japanese ships in which convoys were carrying American POWs?

By the time MacArthur was planning his return to the Philippines, and certainly by the time the softening-up bombings began, the locations of POW and civilian internment camps on Luzon were accurately known; they were even marked on pilots' maps, for avoiding. The movements of POW drafts from the camps would have been easy for the Luzon underground to follow—train or truck to Bilibid and from there to the Manila waterfront. At Pier 7, the POWs could be seen loading, ship by identifiable ship. The convoys could be seen forming up and leaving. There were underground workers on the waterfront, and guerrillas in the hills. They were in radio contact with the guerrillas on Mindanao, and Mindanao was in constant radio contact with MacArthur's headquarters; the saying was that MacArthur knew every name on the Manila Hotel guest list.

At MacArthur's headquarters, intelligence summaries were circulated, daily, weekly, and monthly, to a wide distribution list, interservice, meaning army and navy, including detailed information about POW movements. And by September and October 1944, without question MacArthur personally knew what was happening to POWs on the water. After the *Shin'yō Maru* was sunk off Mindanao in September, several dozen men who survived to be picked up on shore by guerrillas were taken off by an American submarine to Australia and debriefed there, and MacArthur immediately issued a warning to the Japanese in the Philippines that they would be held responsible for bad treatment of POWs. So—at every level up to and including MacArthur himself, it was known that the Japanese were transporting POWs in unmarked ships, and it was known what that could lead to.

About all this the prisoners knew nothing. The Japanese went on shipping POWs out of Manila the way they always had, and the U.S. Navy went on sinking POW transports until there were no more to sink.

According to Japanese figures, of the 50,000 POWs they shipped, 10,800 died at sea. Going by Allied figures, more Americans died in the sinking of the *Arisan Maru* than died in the weeks of the death march out of Bataan, or in the months at Camp O'Donnell, which were the two worst sustained atrocities committed by the Japanese against Americans. More Dutchmen died in the sinking of the *Jun'yō Maru* than in a year on the Burma-Siam railroad. The total deaths of all nationalities on the railroad added up to the war's biggest sustained Japanese atrocity against Allied POWs. Total deaths of all nationalities at sea were second in number only to total deaths on the railroad. Of all POWs who died in the Pacific war, one in every three was killed on the water by friendly fire.

So the POWs, who suffered so much on land, suffered again at sea. They died in the holds, of starvation, suffocation, dehydration, and disease. They were killed by bombs and torpedoes aimed at them by their allies, their countrymen. The Japanese killed them in the water, or they drowned, or they died on the rafts. Or, most terrible of all, they killed each other.

Madness and murder after shipwreck are as old as the history of seafaring. Murder in the holds of POW transports, though, raises one question in particular. POWs of every nationality had to go through long and hazardous voyages in the worst conditions imaginable. Yet only Americans killed each other in the holds. Why was that?

Who could ever say with certainty? The POW transports were not part of Unit 731; they were not controlled laboratories for experiments in suffocation, starvation, and dehydration, with the nationality of the prisoners a deliberate variable in the experimental design. Still, in the way men of different nationalities behaved in the holds and in the water there were observable differences.

The British were British to the end: When a torpedoed ship started to go down, the British were the ones who lined up in an orderly fashion to get out of the hold. And in the water they sang "Britannia Rules the Waves."

Australians were Australians. On the *Byōki Maru*—proper Japanese name *Rashin Maru*—a draft of Australians were seventy days on the water from Singapore to Japan in 1944, in the same convoy as the *Toyofuku Maru*. The *Byōki Maru* was a traveling wreck, with one of its holds burned out and a jury-rigged bridge. The Australians were in for more than two months of rotten rice, a typhoon, and a submarine attack that blew a tanker out of the water behind them and a freighter in front of them. They sailed through the wreckage. In between times they sang, tore books into sections and passed them around for reading, shifted positions at set intervals, and when they were allowed on deck they sat in circles to pick the lice off each other. What they were doing was exactly what good Australians did instinctively, in peace or war, in prison camp or on a POW transport: they worked together to preserve the tribe.

Again, when the *Rakuyō Maru* went down with seven hundred Australians and six hundred British aboard, it was the Australians who tried to preserve the biggest prisoner tribe. On the third day in the water, some Englishmen who were almost finished sighted a mass of black shapes. *As we drew nearer we saw there were about two to three hundred men gathered on a huge pontoon of rafts. They had erected a couple of lofty distress signals, coloured shorts and other bits of clothing fixed to spars of wood. As we paddled up we saw there was a large outer ring of rafts linked to each other with pieces of rope and the attachment tapes of life-jackets. Inside the circle were other rafts, unattached but safely harboured. They seemed organized compared with the disintegrated rabble we had become during these last two days. They may have been drifting as aimlessly as we had; but at least they all drifted together. A lot of them still wore those familiar slouch hats. We had caught up with the Aussie contingent. One of them looped us in with a dangling end of rope. "Cheers, mate," came the friendly voice. "This is no place to be on your lonesome."*

None of this is to say that other nationalities on POW transports did not try to preserve individual lives by preserving the tribe. Of course they did.

And it is just as true that, at one time or another, Australians found they could not hold themselves together. On the water it was only a matter of time before men started going mad. The time would vary, sinking by sinking, circumstance by circumstance, man by man, but it was only a matter of time, once the only water to drink was salt water and men started drinking it. That was a certainty about the human brain and body; it was beyond nationality, inexorable.

Some men struggled to stay alive; they fought against their own failing strength, or fought others. Some did not fight death, but let themselves die. Some decided to commit suicide; that happened among all nationalities on the water.

It happened in the holds, too. Yet in the holds, Americans—and only Americans—killed each other.

On the *Harō Maru,* Forrest Knox knew he had to kill. And equally he knew he would not have had to kill—no one would have—if the POW officers had lived up to the responsibilities that went with their privileges. But all the colonel on deck did was shout safely down the hatch, and the officers in the hold did nothing but look out for themselves.

Then there was the *Oryokkō Maru,* the POW transport with the highest number of officers in the holds, more than a thousand, more than one in four of them field grade, and by far the highest proportion of officers to enlisited men, two to one. Yet of all ships, the *Oryokkō Maru* was the one where the worst, most uncontrollable madness broke out, and broke out earliest, starting on the very first night and turning into killing by the second night. More than a thousand American officers could not, or at any rate did not, summon up discipline enough to stop Americans from killing each other.

Was it simply that the *Oryokkō Maru* had the absolute worst level of unbearable heat, the worst lack of water, the worst lack of oxygen, prisoners in the worst shape when they were loaded aboard, and the worst stress from being attacked? In other words, was everything simply over the human physical edge? Who can say? No one could possibly have been keeping exact figures on nutritional and health status, ounces of water per man per day, maximum temperature in degrees Fahrenheit, and the relativities of oxygen and carbon dioxide in the air, in every hold of every POW transport. Short of verifiable and verified facts, and conceding that neither Unit 731 nor anyone else set up those prisoner transports as controlled experiments in national behavior, it does appear that POWs of all nationalities were subjected to essentially the same dreadful stresses in the holds. Yet only Americans killed each other.

Between the Philippines and Japan all kinds of men died horrible deaths. All kinds of little tribes were decimated. On Formosa, Forrest Knox talked to one of the handful of men who had survived off the *Arisan Maru.* Forrest went through the roster of Company

A with him. It turned out ten men from Janesville were on that transport, and none of them made it, including Fay Balden, the second of the Balden twins to die. And both the Luther twins, John and Henry, sticking together the way brothers were meant to.

Forrest was on Formosa two months. Then he and the others from the *Harō Maru* were shipped to Japan. They went out on the tail end of a typhoon. Bad traveling for prisoners in the hold, but bad weather for submarines too; that was why the transport left when it did, and that was how they made it.

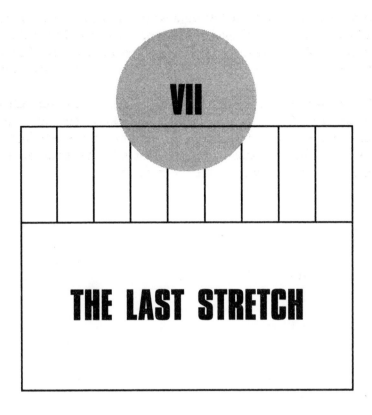

VII

THE LAST STRETCH

THE BIG JAPANESE PORT OF ENTRY FOR POWs WAS MOJI, ON the island of Kyushu, across the Straits of Shimonoseki from the main island of Honshu. The men on the last transports in 1944 and 1945 came out of the tropics, from ninety-degrees in Manila or Singapore to the Japanese winter, zero and below, up out of airless, waterless holds into snow and sleet. The dead bodies were trucked away from the docks with the sick who could not walk. The prisoners still standing were stripped naked, shaken down, glass-rodded, hosed with cold salt water, sprayed with disinfectant, ordered to dress, counted off, formed into new kumi, and marched through the streets to be loaded for transport to their assigned camps, with Japanese children spitting at them.

All over northern Asia, that winter was the coldest in forty years. In Japan, Hong Kong, Shanghai, Korea, Manchuria—wherever the POWs were, they froze. Before work they huddled in the snow like cattle, the men on the outside of the huddle trying to burrow in, and gradually the whole mass would start revolving in a slow, shivering circle. At night, huddling inside, they could see their breath in the air like frosty vapor in a cold store, clusters of shaved heads like so many chilled melons. And out at the benjo, shit stalagmites were forming under the squat latrines, frozen spires building up until they reached floor level and had to be chipped away with a crowbar.

Where Forrest Knox came from in Wisconsin it snowed, but never had he felt cold as severe as in Japan. Prisoners in their second winter already, and even more so their third, with the fat long gone from their bodies, were struck to the marrow with the freezing certainty that they would not make it through another. *Frisco live in Forty-five or stiff as sticks in Forty-six.*

The Japanese were cold too, hungry and deprived. By 1944–1945 rice was drastically short. Sugar had just about disappeared. There was almost no gasoline for private cars. The shops had no tobacco; for smokers, it was either pay black market prices, or roll persimmon leaves in the pages of pocket dictionaries. Trains were crammed, chōmansai on rails, with special military police patrolling the cars to make sure that all passengers with a *bento,* a box lunch, ate every bit and did not throw anything away.

The official daily calorie count for civilians was below two thousand. The zoos had hardly any animals left; they had been eaten. The last survivors were a few starving elephants, feebly doing the tricks that used to get them fed. There were no grossly fat *sumo* wrestlers anymore. Babies were being born smaller, and growing boys and girls did not weigh as much. Everyone was wearing austerity clothes; women were not in *kimono* anymore but *mompei,* working trousers. By 1945, children aged ten and older were in the work force, along with more women than ever, college students (if they had not been drafted already), Korean and Chinese conscript laborers, and convicts.

The POWs were at the low end of the work force, meaning they were condemned to be bottom feeders. When they were first captured they had had trouble getting used to rice. In Japan they had even more trouble with the rest of the Japanese diet: seaweed, strange roots, pastes and gelatinous substances made out of soybean, what they called *snotty gobbles* and *elephant semen*. And even if it had been to their taste, there was nowhere near enough. The POWs had to scavenge—for stingray, rotting beans, old horse, black-market zoo monkey, chicken bones toasted on a shovel, dog deep-frozen in the snow, slaughterhouse bones, fertilizer made of ground bones and fish scraps graded unfit for human consumption, cattle fodder, grasshoppers. At Hakensho, a work detail down a coal mine found stalactites in the tunnels, underneath some tidal river; they broke them off and smuggled them back into camp for the salt taste.

On this kind of nourishment the prisoners had to labor, working long shifts with next to no yasume, mining coal, copper, lead and zinc, stoking furnaces in steel mills, unloading ships, loading boxcars in railroad switching yards—the heaviest lifting in the last stretch of a losing war.

In the camps the losing was obvious. More and more of the guards now were soldiers maimed in combat, One-Armed Bandits and Peglegs. Little Glass Eye at Mitsushima. Burnt Ears at Habu Innoshima, one side of his face incinerated in the Malayan campaign. At Futase, Joto Nai, meaning No Good, had many scars; he said they were American. Nelson at Kobe House wore an eye patch and he was short a hand; so was Wingie. There was more than one Scarface. The one at the military hospital at Moji used to practice his judo on sick men. And at Hakodate, a snowbound northern camp, a guard named Chalky used to beat the prisoners with his artificial arm.

::

HARRY Jeffries opted for Japan over China the way Forrest Knox went for Las Piñas over Cabanatuan, choosing an unknown devil over a known one. Harry still had amoebic dysentery from his time in the Ward Road jail, and his chronic malignant malaria kept rising up to bite him. He came out of Ward Road with only a fingernail-hold on life, with black thoughts of the hot wire. Men around him were slipping toward dying; he could see it in their faces, and he was afraid it was himself he was looking at. Anywhere else had to be better.

Oklahoma Atkinson was easy. He was of the opinion he could make it anywhere. If Harry wanted to try somewhere else, he would go too.

It arranged itself. A draft came up, to be filled by the numbers, so many from this barracks, so many from that. The old army system—transfer trouble out—was applied to contractors. Harry and Oklahoma were put on the list, first thing. Also John Cowalski, who had been in on stealing bread with them at Woosung and then punched his barracks leader.

On the way across the China Sea to Osaka, Oklahoma got in a cribbage game with a contractor, for cigarettes, payable whenever the next issue might be. By the time they docked, Oklahoma was ahead seven smokes. But he never collected. A Japanese who spoke perfect English split up the shipload by numbers, so many for this camp, so many for that, and Oklahoma had to go one way, the loser another.

The camp Oklahoma and Harry drew was Kawasaki 5, known as Dispatch Camp, on Honshu, between Tokyo and Yokohama. It was an enormous steelworks: acres of blast furnaces and rolling mills, the anvils of hell, with thousands of workers, Japanese and Korean, men and women both; plus prisoners, Americans from the Philippines and a ragbag from Wake—marines and contractors, Chinese mess boys and Guamanians from Pan Am—and later on some Javanese Dutch.

Oklahoma and Harry were big men, so the Japanese put them on heavy labor, in an all-American gang, lumping steel billets, turning them with giant tongs, looking for imperfections, chipping away the flaws with an air hammer or grinding them down with a huge emery wheel.

They worked twelve-hour shifts, breathing metal dust with no face masks, and the racket was so loud they could not hear each other talk. For work that absolutely had to be done they used hand signals, and for the rest they were in silent agreement—with everyone thinking of the tribe, they could bear down together on the heavy grinder, hard enough to break the belt, and then they would have to sit and wait until it was fixed. That was their contribution to the emperor's military productivity. All over Dispatch Camp, and every other camp in Japan, prisoners were winding electrical coils backward, bolting cylinder heads on too tight or not tight enough, pouring emery dust into axle grease, mixing concrete with too much sand and then throwing small machine parts into the mix, shaking iron filings into generators, taking the cotter pins out of the wheels of ore carts, driving rivets crooked into the hulls of ships, shuffling the destination markers on freight cars in the marshaling yards. It was their constant study.

One day Oklahoma was sitting down at the end of his twelve hours at the grinder, which he was entitled to do, when a guard came up behind him the way guards always did and shouted, *Ki o tsuke!* Oklahoma was not quick enough to his feet, and the guard hit him. Before Oklahoma could think what he was doing he jumped up and hit the guard back, knocked the cigarette out of his Japanese face. The guard marched him off to the punishment room, and all the other guards went after him with their four-foot clubs. *Stick fools,* Oklahoma called them. But he was the fool, and he knew it, he had been a prisoner long enough to know better.

What saved him was that he had something going with a Japanese interpreter. One of the first things a POW businessman routinely did in a new camp was look for some Japanese or other to corrupt. It gave him leverage, and it worked this time for Oklahoma. He and the interpreter were in a regular card game; Oklahoma always won, and the interpreter had to pay him in rice. The interpreter was military age, and he knew that if Oklahoma told the guard commander he was gambling with prisoners, he would be shipped to the front line. So he got the stick fools to ease off, and finagled an easy job for Oklahoma, inspecting.

Oklahoma and Harry decided to work alternate shifts. That way they could each have two blankets, and one of them could always be keeping an eye on their stash. But as it happened, this brought on their first big fight ever, in the fifth year they had been close friends, their third year as two against the world in prison camp. They had some salt that they made from Tokyo Bay seawater boiled in a coffee can. It was dirty, it looked like rust, there was not enough to fill a bottle cap, but it was all they had. For once they were not pooling their wealth, not the salt, anyway; they had separate stashes. They were each convinced someone was getting at their stash, and they came to suspect each other. They made accusations, and eventually they were so mad at each other they stopped talking. It reached the point where they were thinking murderous thoughts.

The truth was that everybody was stealing. Harry and Oklahoma had a pile of Red Cross food, gambling winnings, hidden in the ceiling. Someone—they never found out who—sniffed it out, crept in there like a rat, and got away with it. John Cowalski was stealing rice from the Japanese storehouse. He built himself a hiding place in the benjo. One of the other contractors spotted him at it, and every time he went to the benjo he would rat a fistful of Cowalski's stolen rice and eat it raw. The guards were stealing rice by the sack, selling it to civilians over the back wall on the sly, then stirring up a commotion—*No food tonight, Amer-*

icanu he steal—standing everyone at attention for hours in the dark to make it appear as if they were serious about getting a confession.

Harry was always hungry for taste. He hated tasteless dirty hot water pretending to be soup in the morning and tasteless dirty rice at night, the only variety a bit of Kafir corn or horse barley mixed in. Once, desperate for something with taste—anything—he drank motor oil. It made him sick. Another time he bought a bag of ground red pepper from some Koreans, put it all in a coffee can, boiled it up at the steam pipe, drank it straight down, burned himself all the way, and did not feel hungry for four hours, a record.

He was like every working prisoner; he had sabotage in mind all the time. He would be turning steel billets with the big tongs, and when he saw a flaw, instead of fixing it he would seal it in with the air hammer. One day a guard caught him, grabbed the heavy tongs, and clubbed him across the spine. Harry went down like an axed tree, and when he tried to get up his legs were paralyzed. The grinder gang had to carry him back to camp, and from there he was taken to something called a hospital at Shinagawa. It was an evil place; there were stories about medical experiments, spinal injections, prisoners going in and never coming out. Harry got no treatment, no medication. He had to pull through on his own, and he always believed that what brought him out alive was willpower. Some movement came back to one leg and then the other, and that was enough for him to make it to camp again. But on the job he was next to worthless. He and Oklahoma were speaking, their salt war was over, but they never talked about Harry's weakness. Oklahoma just switched shifts and did Harry's work as well as his own, so Harry could keep drawing full working rations and get better sooner.

Oklahoma was having troubles of his own. One of his trading deals was with an old gray-whiskered navy man who used to limp around looking pathetic to get out of work. Oklahoma was fronting him cigarettes, and the old man was supposed to be paying him back in barley. But he kept stalling. It was bad for Oklahoma's business credibility. Finally he told the old man, *Get your ass outside;* he was going to beat the barley out of him. The old man turned out to be faking the limp, and he turned out to be a fighter; he used to carry the navy belt. He punched Oklahoma bloody. A guard caught them. They said they were sparring. The guard told them to get to the guardhouse and keep sparring, and the old man bloodied Oklahoma some more. Oklahoma never fronted him another cigarette. The old man never paid him what he owed either. And the moral of this story was right out of Oklahoma's own book of life: *The strong beat the weak and the smart beat the strong.*

Oklahoma and Harry were not the only ones in business at Kawasaki. All kinds of hustlers were operating, from the gray-whiskered old navy man on up. As for Harry and Oklahoma, their own biggest hustle was with the cards; they were gamblers first, but they were serious traders as well.

Japan brought out the truly hard traders. That was bound to happen. By the time the POWs were unloaded at Moji, they had been shaken down so often the average man had practically nothing left to trade with. And Japan itself, the whole country, was being shaken down—that was what losing a war meant, being stripped of everything. So in the Japan camps there was nothing like the big black market of places such as Changi or Bicycle Camp or Cabanatuan or Bilibid early in the war, or even the railroad base camps in Thailand in 1944. In Japan it took smart men to come out ahead in trading, and more and more it took hard men.

Serious trading started with a man so hungry he could not stand it, he had to have more rice. If he had nothing to pay with, and no collateral, he would go to a trader and borrow the rice, and the trader would charge him interest: one rice now for rice and soup later, or one and a half rices, or two rices.

This kind of deal had a history in the United States Army. Before the war, if a man developed an urgent need for a few beers or a woman or both, but he was strapped for cash between paydays, he would go to the barracks moneylender. Every barracks had a moneylender, as often as not the paymaster in business for himself. Six for nine was common, meaning six dollars now for nine on payday. It was outrageous interest, 50 percent in ten days or even a week, but it was either that or not go to town.

This was called borrowing *on the jawbone*. There were different stories about where the expression came from. One version was that in the Philippines before the war, the native women who did the American soldiers' laundry used to ask for extra money for soap, *jabon*. Everybody knew the extra was not for soap, it was squeeze, graft, cumshaw, but everybody paid it, and along the way the word got attached to borrowing at heavy interest on a verbal contract, on the jawbone.

Jawbone rice dealing was around as early as Cabanatuan. It traveled with the transports to Japan, and that was where it really came into its own.

A trader could start out in the morning, lending a breakfast against the evening meal. The evening meal traded at two breakfasts, 100 percent interest in one day. Then men would come back from work at dark, cold and so hungry that for an extra dinner they would trade two breakfasts. The next morning the trader would trade those breakfasts against the evening meal. A man might be so down he was willing to go even further into debt for the sake, just once, of a full belly.

Everybody needed rice. Serious smokers had to have their nicotine. Some of them in urgent need would even trade away all their next cigarette ration for a single smoke, meaning that for one cigarette now they would be paying back five or even ten later.

In the extreme, smokers were even known to trade their rice for cigarettes, one rice ration for one cigarette. Those were terrible odds for the smoker, but for the trader it was good business. *Nicotine for protein* was the trader's call. That was not accurate nutritionally, but it rhymed and it worked.

Cigarettes would keep, but cooked rice would go bad, so a trader could not maintain a big physical inventory. He had to be able to think ahead, juggle rice going out with rice coming in. What he was doing was trading in commodities futures.

Some men could not tell a good trade from a bad one, not even to save themselves, and the hard traders were certainly not going to be looking out for anybody but Number One. There were men trading their rice away for cigarettes and smoking themselves all the way to serious malnutrition. Or borrowing so heavily against future rice that when their debts came due they could not pay in full. They would be bankrupt in food, they would have nothing to eat, less than nothing.

Forrest Knox never had those problems; he was not a hooked smoker. He saw it happen, though, as early as Cabanatuan, with Curly Madison, and far more often in Japan later on. By Forrest's observation in his Japan camps, as many as one man in twenty, maybe more, got himself in bad trouble over rice trades; and of those in trouble, at least four out of every five were smokers.

Harry and Oklahoma would have confirmed those figures and those consequences. They did business on those terms every day, and they had no trouble looking the situation in the eye. They did not see trading at interest in rice and cigarettes as any different from gambling, where the man on the other side of the table was trying to take their rations just like they were trying to take his. No one forced anyone to borrow. For every winner there was going to be a loser, and if a man came out badly on the wrong side of trading—if any number of men did—those were the breaks. The wounds were self-inflicted.

But take the extreme case: If a man smoked away his next week's rice in advance, or borrowed rice until he owed more than he could pay back without starving, then he was futures trading on margin with his own life on the line. Trading could go all the way to the death.

Harry and Oklahoma watched men on the wrong side of their trades die, and so did other traders. Of course a trader was never willing to think of himself as straight-out killing other men. There were hard traders—Oklahoma and Harry for two—who would say that the losers really wanted to die, but they were weak sisters, they did not have the guts to kill themselves, so they would eat up big on the jawbone until they got cut off, and die that way, or go out smoking.

When POWs of other nationalities came to Japan and ran up against these hard American rice traders, they were staggered. The Dutch were supposed to be a nation of traders, but they would have nothing to do with trading to the death. The Australians were horrified. They had nothing like it in their Southeast Asia camps, and when they first laid eyes on it in Japan they could not believe what they were seeing. Charging interest on rice—it was simply beyond their tribal comprehension. Australians would cheat and lie and steal without blinking an eye, at least outside their own tribe; they were famous for it. Some of the biggest racketeers at Changi and in the railroad base camps were Australians. But Australians could not imagine doing men to death by charging interest on something as basic to life as rice. That was bloodsucking; it was murder. Within little tribes of Australian enlisted men, rice went back and forth all the time, but this was not trading in commodities futures, it was sharing, it was Australian tribalism. And the British—even if they were called a nation of shopkeepers, they stuck to moral principles. Late in the war, some British were in a camp in northern Honshu when a draft of Americans came in. One of them was a rice trader. He had been in five camps already, in every one he traded rice, and he had nothing against branching out among the British. The senior British officer gave him a stern lecture. *This,* he said, *we do not tolerate.* The trader just laughed his

American laugh and said, *Boy, you've got a lot to learn*. But he never could make any headway with the British.

: :

DAN Rafalovich, the *Houston* man who ate the British dog with Frank Fujita of the 131st at Changi, wound up in the worst of all rice-trading camps in Japan, at the worst time.

Fukuoka 17 was a coal mining camp at Ōmuta on Kyushu. Rice trading had been bad there since the first draft of Americans from Cabanatuan opened the camp in mid-1943, and it grew worse and worse.

In January 1945 some survivors from the *Oryokkō Maru* were trucked in, almost a hundred. Rafalovich was terribly sick himself, but these men were worse than he was; they were zombies. One of them did nothing but walk around camp with eight canteens full of seawater tied to his waist. It was hard to get them to talk. When they did speak, horror stories came out of them. One man told how he was sleeping on his canteen to keep it from being stolen. Someone tried to sneak it, and he bashed the thief's head in with it. The thief was a colonel, and that was a double satisfaction. Another man (a Czech, and how he turned up on an American draft out of Manila no one knew) told about drinking the blood of a dying man, eating the fingers off a dead man. Even the Ōmuta camp commandant was taken aback by the awful look of them. He issued them an egg each, and some good-quality rice from the Japanese cookhouse. And in an instant the traders were all over them, trying to trade their rice away.

One of the *Oryokkō Maru* men was Ted Lewin the gambler. He was not dying. He was not even thin. All the way from Manila to Moji he had been rice-trading. The senior POW medical officer at Fukuoka 17, Tom Hewlett, saw the terrible procession come stumbling into camp, *ninety-five skeletons and a fat man,* and the fat man was Lewin, well dressed, looking as if he had called ahead for reservations. The first time Lewin was named to a work detail he waved a thousand-yen note. He never worked at Fukuoka 17, any more than he had at O'Donnell or Cabanatuan.

Lewin had everything. Hewlett heard he even had morphine. Hewlett had none. At the hospital, men were forever being brought in from the mine in agony—hurt by a rockslide or a cave-in, a slip with a jackhammer, a runaway ore car, or beaten by a gang boss with a temper and a two-by-four. For two weeks Hewlett had had a man in improvised traction, screaming. Hewlett asked Lewin for morphine. Lewin said Hewlett would have to pay. Hewlett told him, *Okay, keep your morphine, but for as long as the war lasts you won't get any medical treatment, your friends either, and you don't know how long the war is going to last.* And Lewin came across with the morphine, five vials, unopened, the government seal still on them. That was one of the few times anyone beat Lewin.

Lewin moved in on the rice trade. Compared to him the other traders were nothing. All the same, they had been busy enough for long enough to get men in trouble. By the winter months at the end of 1944, with Lewin yet to come, there were more cases than ever before of trading for rice at interest. And cigarette trading, all the way up to trading away future rights to cigarettes, commissary privileges, Red Cross packages, for the duration of the war—anything for nicotine. Men were going downhill, more of them every week, sliding fast—so many that the hospital was backed up for bunk space. From what Tom Hewlett could see, part of it was rice trading pure and simple, another part was trading rice for smokes, and the third part was more and more gambling, men betting their rations and losing. Add Lewin and his gang, and it brought on a business crisis: bankruptcies looming, losers with so much rice debt to pay off that they were down to one meal a day—meaning they going to die.

This was the end product of classic American free-enterprise capitalism turned loose in prison camp on a thousand calories a day. The method that evolved to halt things short of death was classic American business practice as well: declaration of bankruptcy and reorganization of affairs, so that the debtor could trade out of difficulties. Any man owing more than three meals had to sign up and list his creditors. The creditors had to waive interest payments. Then they were issued IOUs for the rice principal, postdated so that a bankrupt man would not have to go short more than one meal in ten days. An officer saw the bankrupt through the serving line, so that the traders could not strongarm him out of rations he owed along the way. Then a noncom walked him to the bankrupt table, and he had to sit and eat his ration, every grain, in plain view, under supervision.

To make this work, there had to be a trustee in bankruptcy, someone trustworthy. The men on both sides of the bankruptcies, creditors and debtors, were all Americans, but no American was judged to have the qualities for the trusteeship. Carel Hamel was the choice. Everyone could see that he was an outstandingly good man, even if he was a chaplain, even if he was a Dutchman. Before the war he had spent years in the United States, so he could speak English, and that took some of the curse off his Dutchness, even if his man-of-God accent did come out sounding like south-side Chicago. As a POW he had been on the Burma-Siam railroad, and it had not killed his faith. Or his sense of humor. One day the Japanese were getting ready to weigh him, naked like any other prisoner. Hamel still had his G-string on. They made him take it off and prodded him onto the scales. He jumped down again, whipped off his glasses, jumped back on, jumped off again, whipped out his false teeth, and jumped back on.

Hamel was a Protestant, but he was not a narrow tribesman of religion. Working among all the tribes of prisoners on the railroad had turned him into a Christian who crossed hostile frontiers between creeds as if they were not there. He was the only chaplain at Fukuoka 17 until William Duffy came in. Duffy was a Catholic. He was one of the *Oryokkō Maru* skeletons, and he was flat on his back; he could not go around to the dying faithful and hear their confessions. Hamel said to him: *I will be your ears.* He would listen to the dying Catholic, carry the message to Duffy, whisper it to him, and carry absolution back. Then Hamel got the idea of carrying the dying man to Duffy, on his own back. No load was too heavy for Hamel.

He was such a good man that he even had Ted Lewin's admiration. When Hamel wanted to do something extra for all the sick men shivering with cold in the hospital, Lewin volunteered to bring them hot water bottles from the cookhouse.

At the peak, Hamel had about fifty bankrupt men to look after. The system worked, but not quickly enough to turn things around for everyone—about a month after the bankrupt table was set up, the first bankrupt died.

Outside the fence at Ōmuta the Japanese people were eating miserably. Inside the fence the prisoners were hardly eating at all. Gerrit Bras, the Dutch doctor, was a highly experienced POW medical officer—he had been up and down the Burma-Siam railroad, some of the time with Carel Hamel. At Fukuoka 17 he kept track of malnutrition. Deficiency diseases came on early: In the first year of the camp 25 percent of the men had protein edema; in the second, up to 50 percent; and going into 1945 almost everybody was showing symptoms, from mild to severe. Mild was a man with edema up to his knees trying to goosestep past the guard-house after a day's labor in the mine. Moderate was edema up to mid-thigh, with circulatory problems. Severe (and Dan Rafalovich would have qualified) was a prisoner who could hardly stand.

One night a man fell into a sewage ditch in the dark and broke his leg. He would not have to go down the mine again till it mended. To a sizeable number of prisoners that sounded like a good deal; in fact it struck them as a revelation. It was the beginning of self-mutilation at Fukuoka 17.

Self-mutilation had begun about the same time as rice trading. There had been some of it before Japan. Forrest Knox had seen it at Las Piñas, and it had been around on the other terrible airfield detail near Manila, Nichols Field. It happened on the Burma-Siam railroad, too. In the railroad camps there were men desperate enough to cultivate ulcers. But only a few. Japan bought out a more advanced stage of the pathology, and nowhere worse than at Fukuoka 17.

Men down in the mine put battery acid from their head lamps on their working sores, or they used benjo lime, or they went to a Dutchman who would bring in an alkaline chemical from the zinc smelter and rub it into a sore for a price. Men would stare at a welder's torch to flash-burn their eyes. A man working in the mine set off a detonator in his hand. There were men breaking arms and legs for their friends, as a favor, the way it had been done at Las Piñas and Nichols. And, as at Las Piñas and Nichols, there were professionals set up to do it with a jackhammer or a drill. Ōmuta had two professional bone crushers—one offered a cheaper rate if he did not have to carry the customer out of the mine, and night calls were more expensive.

Men saved up to have it done. They comparison-shopped options the way they would on a new car, figuring costs, calculating what would be the best value, an arm or a leg.

There was more and more of it all the time, dozens of cases, to the point where the head medical orderly at the camp hospital had to do traffic control, spacing out admissions. Almost all the self-mutilated were Americans. And so were the bone crushers. The doctors never found out who the crushers were, but they could figure out what was happening, because the fractures were being mass-produced and they did not look like mine accidents. Tom Hewlett saw any number of arms broken straight across, mostly left arms because men wanted to keep the use of their right hand. And straight leg breaks. Yet another man would be carried in on a stretcher with the pitiful question in his eye, *Will I ever dance again?* and Hewlett would say to him, *You got it done wrong, try the other one.*

Then there was the Dog Man, also an American. He decided he was never going down the mine again. If he got his leg broken, it would only mend. So he turned himself into a dog. There was a real camp dog called Peace who did not believe him, even though he went around on all fours, lifted his leg to pee, and slept curled up on the floor. When the guards tried to make him stand on his hind legs he barked at them; when the commandant came around he snarled and bit him on the boot.

More strangeness: something like twenty-five homosexual couples were getting counseling from one of the American doctors. This doctor was not without problems of his own. All prisoners had to have their heads shaved, medical officers not excused, and even though this doctor was only young his scalp turned out to be outstandingly wrinkly. He was obsessed by it. He traded nonstop on the black market for creams and ointments. Every night he would sit for hours massaging his scalp. And once a week while he was massaging he would lecture the homosexual couples on how to get along in camp among standard-issue military homophobes.

Then there was the American in such bad trouble from rice trading that he went to hang himself in the benjo. Another American came in, saw him kicking at the end of the rope, did not even break stride, just said *Good riddance,* strolled on by to a vacant stall and settled himself for a leisurely dump.

All through this, Dan Rafalovich was present and accounted for at Fukuoka 17, but he did not know about any of it. He was a number in the tenko head count, but beyond that, nothing. It was a long, long time on from Changi, eating the British dog with Frank Fujita. Rafalovich was into his third Japan winter and so sick he hardly knew he was alive.

: :

ON NOVEMBER 21, 1944, Fujita marked an anniversary in his secret diary. *Three years ago left the USA, two years ago ate a dog in Singapore, today I ate some cat.* It was a month after his twenty-third birthday, and he was in a Japan camp even stranger than the one where Rafalovich wound up.

He was there because of his last name. When he was captured on Java with the rest of E Battery of the 131st, some of his friends wanted him to change it, for fear of what the Japanese might do if they caught a Japanese in an American uniform. Why not turn himself into a Texas Mexican—he had the skin color, and there were others in the battery. He did not want to. What if he died under a wrong name? His folks would never know what became of him. He risked it and stayed Fujita, all the way from Soerabaja to Bicycle Camp to Changi to Japan.

His first Japan camp was Fukuoka 2 on Kyushu, in the Nagasaki district. That was where his father was born. What a strange feeling it was for a Fujita to be returning to Japanese family territory as an American POW.

And even stranger, not be recognized as Japanese. After four changes of camp—two of them by ship—any number of shake-downs and sick calls, hundreds of days of morning and evening tenko and work details, he had still not been spotted.

It was hard to believe. But it was a fundamental piece of POW wisdom, validated time and again by experience, that the Japanese saw only what they were looking for, and the last thing they would be looking for among white POWs was a Fujita.

Then at Fukuoka 2, in June 1943, a guard was showing off his English language skills, reading the names on the hut roster out loud, very pleased with himself, and in among all the white names he read out *Fujita,* and suddenly he registered what he had heard himself saying.

An American Fujita, captured in uniform—the only one of his kind in Japan—could have great propaganda value. The Japanese immediately tried to turn him their way. The commandant took him on as his *tōban,* his dog robber, meaning no hard labor in the shipyard. Then they offered him the rank of captain in the emperor's army, plus some land, plus as many women as he wanted. Fujita turned it all down. He was an American, and he said so in his Texas voice. He could not even speak Japanese. They gave him a tutor, a corporal, with a book, *Japanese in Thirty Hours,* but the thirty hours went by, then a hundred hours, and still he was not speaking a single Japanese word. The corporal could tell Fujita was acting stupid. He stood him up and swung his samurai sword at him, so close Fujita could feel the swish of the blade, but that did not cause him to speak Japanese either, and the corporal put up his sword and quit.

Fujita got orders to pack. He was being transferred to Tokyo.

The word *propaganda* was mentioned. He wrote in his diary: *I sure don't like the look of things.*

He wound up at a place called Bunka Gakuin, only a few blocks away from the imperial palace, with a few dozen other prisoners, all picked to work on radio propaganda. They were told that if they cooperated, life would be easy; they would have more food, blankets, a fire, et cetera. If they did not cooperate, life would not be guaranteed. One man, a Britisher, refused point-blank. The Japanese took him away, and they told the others he had been killed. No one else refused, including Fujita, not that he felt easy about it: *Have wound up in one hell of a mess. No choice.*

The radio prisoners were a mixed bunch. There were some Australians, some British, and some Dutch; but most were Americans, several of them from Wake Island, including the contractor who had brought Oklahoma Atkinson in on the bread distribution racket at Woosung. Their enthusiasm for propaganda work ranged from zero, as with Fujita; to cool; to warm, as with another Wake contractor who was so anti-American he might as well have been a Communist; all the way to hot, as with John David Provoo. Provoo was an American enlisted man on Corregidor. He had been a student of Japanese language and culture before the war. When Corregidor surrendered, out came Provoo in a kimono, speaking Japanese; and within days he was responsible for the killing of an American officer.

The more Fujita got to know about the others, the stranger it felt. *Intelligence ranges from ignorance to genius; we have traitors, confirmed, suspected and potential; education from grammar school to university graduates; erotics, erratics, queers, mental cases, cowards, brave men, good men, no accounts, artists, writers, playwrights, actors, typists, journalists, newsmen, typesetters, farmers, cotton pickers, Americans, English, Australians, Scotch, Dutch, soldiers, sailors, marines, airmen, suck asses, dog robbers, and civilians—Wow! If that's not a hell of a lash-up to be connected with, I throw in.*

The radio station had another lash-up on its staff—English-speaking Japanese writers, reporters, and announcers. Some of them had lived in the United States before the war. Some were women, and over time their voices—plus others like them broadcasting in English from other cities in the Co-Prosperity Sphere—were lumped together by the Allied troops listening to them around the war zone. They called them all by just one name, Tokyo Rose.

Fujita wanted no part of any of this. He did what he had done at Fukuoka 2, played dumb. Early on, everyone had to write an essay, to Japanese specifications, as an aptitude and attitude test. Fujita turned in a miserable piece; he was at the bottom of the class, and from there he worked his way down until he was reduced to looking after the bathhouse and then cleaning the latrines— Fujita the benjo boy.

Even so he was on the air occasionally, against his will, and he was around the station and around war news every day. Once in a while he even heard news of his own tribe, the 2nd Battalion of the 131st. Sometimes it was bad news, about enlisted men from one battery or another who had died at sea on a transport to Japan. Once in a great while, a man from his old camp at Fukuoka 2 was picked to record a message for broadcast, and Fujita would hear a familiar E Battery Texas voice. And he got to send some messages of his own.

He heard the Japanese propaganda news going out, the Japanese navy sinking the American navy for the tenth time, et cetera. The Allied version of the war was available, too, picked up at the station off shortwave, and it filtered down to him—from the fall of Saipan in mid-1944, through the end of the year and into 1945, to the taking of Iwo Jima in February.

In April a terrible thing happened—President Roosevelt died. Even some of the Japanese seemed to think of FDR as a great man. No one had ever heard of the new president; his name sounded like True Man.

Then, in May, a red-letter day—the war in Europe was finished: Germany had surrendered and Hitler had killed himself in his bunker in Berlin. Now it was Japan alone against the world. Fujita marked it down in his diary: *Jubilation in camp.*

He kept the diary hidden under a loose board under the tatami mat under his bunk. Some entries he made in code. He had been constructing codes since he was a boy. He had one based on mixing up the letters of the alphabet, another based on tic-tac-toe, and another one, uncrackable, that he had worked up in prison camp, using Javanese script. And he used a set of symbols—stars, crosses, numbers in circles, partially filled in squares—to record air raid alerts, minor raids, large raids, and major raids.

Fujita was using his coded symbols more and more. By the spring of 1945 the war was right on top of him.

The plane doing the damage was the B-29, the Boeing Superfortress. There had never been anything like it in the sky—length

98 feet, wingspan 141 feet, weight close to 100,000 pounds, designed to fly at well over 300 miles per hour for well over 3,000
miles, carrying a bomb payload of 4–5 tons.

Against Japan, the B-29 was used at first for high-altitude daylight precision bombing of strictly military targets. But that did not
do damage fast enough. By the early months of 1945 a different
method was being worked up, based on experience in Europe:
area bombing using incendiaries.

Japanese cities, even the big modern ones, were 90 percent
wood. They were made for burning. If incendiaries were dropped
by the thousands, they would set fire to the industrial districts,
square miles at a time, and Japan's war-making capabilities would
be burned up in the blaze.

Because industry was concentrated in heavily populated districts, the civilian population was going to be burned up, too.
Once, it had been a point of principle in war to spare civilians, but
by the last year of World War II this was obsolete thinking. Killing
civilians had come to be figured as a plus rather than a minus; the
goal now was to kill as many of the enemy as possible, civilians as
well as soldiers, as frightfully as possible—not just to reduce a nation's war machine to wreckage but to mangle the bodies of its
people as well, not only to destroy its capability but to crush its
will, to make it impossible to go on fighting, unbearable to go on
resisting.

That had been happening in Europe. Now with Japan, the
justification for fire-bombing civilians was of a piece with the rest
of Allied thinking on the Asia-Pacific war. The emperor's government, by its own acts, had put itself outside the pale of humane
consideration. The Japanese armed forces were guilty of dreadful
atrocities across vast stretches of the globe, against not only soldiers
and POWs but whole civilian populations. So now if Japanese
civilians in their own home islands were going to be *scorched and
boiled and baked to death*—the words of Curtis LeMay, the American
air force general who came from Europe to organize the area
bombing of Japan—then so be it.

The key to the burning was Tokyo, the capital, the biggest
city, with a population as of early 1945 between 5 million and 6
million, more than 1 million living and working in a twelve-
square-mile area at its industrial center.

The key firebombing raid was on the night of March 9–10,
when 279 B-29s unloaded magnesium cluster bombs and another
type of bomb using gasoline with a thickener of aluminum sulfate,

naphthenic acid and palmitic acid, forming a sticky jelly called *napalm*.

Just after midnight the pathfinders came in, at five hundred feet, marking out a big fiery X in napalm. They were followed by the bombers, in groups of three, dropping five-hundred-pound clusters of incendiaries every fifty feet.

It was the biggest air raid in history to that date, and it kindled the most devastating man-made fire ever, a huge terrifying thing, leaping like a solar flare. By ordinary human scale, the heat and fierceness were unimaginable, with temperatures as high as 1,800 degrees Fahrenheit, whole city blocks going up at once, cars on the street consumed like crumpled paper, the shells of big buildings roaring like blast furnaces. Japanese by the scores of thousands ran for their lives, but the fire was too quick for them. Mothers fled the inferno with babies strapped to their backs, and the babies burst into flames. The bombers kept coming in to unload. Huge thermal drafts hit them, powerful enough to flip a Superfortress like a paper plane; some of the bombers went out of control and crash-dived into the roaring fire their bombs had made. The sky was full of whirling debris, smoke, and flying ash. The raid went on for three hours, and long after the fire-bombers had turned for home and were a hundred miles out over the Pacific, the tail gunners could still see a huge and terrible red flower blooming in the black night sky. Their planes were filled with smoke, and even after the sight of Tokyo burning was gone, below the curve of the earth, their nostrils were still clogged with the stink of burned human flesh.

In the fire-bombed city, corpses were piled on the streets, a mile of corpses on one stretch of road by Tokyo Bay. The Meiji Theater was full of corpses, twisted like piles of human-size ginseng roots. On the bridges over the Sumida River, the dead lay in tangled heaps, and the river was choked with blackened bodies like charred logs of wood.

That was the work of only one night, with only fourteen planes lost—and, on the other side of the balance, almost sixteen square miles of Tokyo burned, including 63 percent of the commercial district razed, 18 percent of industrial capacity destroyed, a quarter of a million buildings gutted, at least 80,000 Japanese dead, possibly as many as 100,000, plus another 40,000 injured, and a million-plus homeless.

Fujita's camp at Bunka Gakuin—Bunker Hill, the prisoners had taken to calling it—was not directly beneath this raid. But fires were burning in a complete circle around it, and there was smoke to the horizon. The radio-station Japanese kept coming in with amazing statistics of destruction. Fujita could not comprehend such figures. Eight days later, he had to go out on a truck to get supplies, and then he saw it for himself, fires still burning, square miles of smoldering ruins.

In April the B-29s came back, bombing close enough to Bunker Hill to knock out some windows, Tokyo burning to within one block north and south, three or four blocks east and west. Just about everything between the camp and the emperor's castle was gutted.

Times were as hard and dangerous as they could be, but Fujita was like every other prisoner; he did not want the bombing to stop. *Rations small as hell—bread molded—greens rotten—no water— no cigarettes for four days (completely out); no laundry soap: and face soap is seven months overdue—and no big raids in days— Woe is me!*

On the night of May 24–25 there was another big raid—still no direct hits on Bunker Hill, but fires everywhere, water and gas and lights kaput, everyone in camp gasping, eyes smarting; they could not see across the courtyard for smoke.

That raid was the biggest single bombing mission of World War II, 558 planes. Half of Tokyo was burned now, 56.3 square miles. Yasukuni Shrine, the place where the spirits of dead Japanese soldiers gathered in honor, was damaged. Nothing was sacred anymore—inside the walls of the imperial palace grounds some buildings were set on fire, and the emperor and his family were reduced to hiding underground until the fire-bombers went away and they could poke their heads up into the world again. It was the end of Tokyo as a war target that meant anything.

Fujita was trucked out of camp to get coal. The Japanese made him bow to the palace as he went by, and that was all there was to bow to. Everything around it was burned out, leveled, square miles of the city looking like a giant graveyard, with smokestacks rising out of the ashes like headstones.

In that raid 62 POWs died at a military jail. The commandant's explanation was that in the bedlam of the firebombing his guards were too late to let them out of the cells. Perhaps, but there were 450 Japanese prisoners in the jail, and the guards got them out. Then too, not all the POWs had just burned to death; some of the corpses showed evidence of bayoneting, and there were bodies with broken legs and smashed skulls.

Those dead prisoners were downed airmen. Of all their white enemies, the Japanese hated airmen worst, particularly bomber crews. From the time of the Doolittle raid in April 1942, the Japanese called them war criminals, and flyers coming down in Japanese-held territory were marked men.

Terrible things were done to them. In the overseas war zone they were likely to be tortured, if they were not killed on the spot. During the naval battle of Midway, two months after the Doolittle raid, three airmen were picked out of the water; two were thrown overboard again, weighted down, and the third was killed with a fire ax. At Bicycle Camp in Batavia, four flyers were kept for months, their beards growing long, until one day they were taken away and shot standing in their graves. In Singapore some B-29 crewmen were paraded through the city naked; then they had their heads chopped off in public. At Outram Road jail, Japanese airmen did the head-chopping. In China, at Hankow, three men were tortured, then burned alive. At Beo, on Talua Island, four men were bayoneted at a ceremonial parade. Near Buin a man had boiling water poured all over him. At Kendebo the kempeitai chopped the head off a fighter pilot; then his body was cut up, fried, divided among about 150 Japanese, and eaten, after a speech by a major general. On Chichi Jima in the Bonin Islands, a Japanese general issued orders that captured airmen were to be killed and eaten; he and other senior officers ate the flesh at private parties, and an admiral put in a request for the liver of the next airman.

In the Japanese home islands, civilians were told that any white man coming down in a parachute deserved to be killed. One flyer who parachuted into a river was pulled out by fishermen and beaten to death. Another who came down on the roof of a Mitsubishi factory was thrown off and killed. Another was buried alive. Another was tied up in a schoolyard with a sign on him, WREAK YOUR VENGEANCE. Another was about to be burned at the stake when some soldiers turned up and took him away. It was luck— if that was the word—to wind up in prison camp, segregated, fed on half rations, refused medical treatment. It was luck for a man to be brought in at Niigata and only have his fingers broken, all ten, one after the other. In Tokyo a man was interrogated for sixty-seven days by the kempeitai, then moved to a zoo and locked naked in the monkey cage to be stared at. In the interrogation camp at Ofuna, men were beaten and tortured. Sometimes there was what was called a trial, most times not, and either way there were executions, in batches—at a rifle range in Nagoya or a maneuver area near Osaka. At Hakensho on Kyushu men had their heads chopped off in front of a big crowd. At Fukuoka it was soldiers demonstrating sword cuts and judo strikes, training civilians how to fight white invaders, showing how white men looked when they were shot with bows and arrows, before they had their heads chopped off.

The Western Japan military command gave some medical professors at Kyushu Imperial University eight B-29 crewmen. The professors cut them up alive, in a dirty room with a tin table where students dissected corpses. They drained blood and replaced it with sea water. They cut out lungs, livers, and stomachs. They stopped blood flow in an artery near the heart, to see how long death took. They dug holes in a skull and stuck a knife into the living brain to see what would happen.

The human arithmetic of the raids over the home islands was this: something like two hundred POWs dead, killed in the firebombings, and something over a hundred downed flyers killed horribly—as against hundreds of thousands of Japanese dead and millions homeless.

In not much more than a month of night raids, all the major industrial cities were in ruins. By the end of June, thirteen million Japanese were homeless. In another few weeks fifty-eight smaller cities had been hit. The B-29s were dropping bombs at the rate of forty thousand tons a month. On July 10, two thousand planes were in the air, fighters as well as bombers, over targets all the way from the island of Kyushu to the area around Tokyo on Honshu. By the end of July, leaflets were being dropped in thousands, telling which cities were scheduled for bombing and burning the next day. The biggest remaining targets were relatively minor: Toyama, Hachiōji, Mito, and Nagaoka. The only cities of any size left essentially undamaged were Sapporo on the far northern island of Hokkaido, and five on Honshu: Kyoto, the cultural capital; Niigata; Kokura; and two others, Hiroshima and Nagasaki.

::

WHEN MacArthur returned to the Philippines and it came time to retake Corregidor, five thousand Japanese fought for eleven days, to the death, the final hundreds of them killed in the Malinta tunnels when tons of explosives were detonated. Only twenty were taken prisoner.

In Manila twenty thousand Japanese troops held on for weeks. *If we run out of bullets we will use grenades; if we run out of grenades, we will cut down the enemy with swords; if we break our swords, we will kill them by sinking our teeth deep in their throats.* They blew up square miles of the city. They blew up what used to be MacArthur's penthouse suite at the Manila Hotel. And they massacred Filipinos, raping, bayoneting, machine-gunning, burning. *When killing Filipinos, assemble them together in one place, thereby saving ammunition and labor. The disposal of dead bodies will be troublesome so either collect them in houses scheduled to be burned or throw them into the river.* Civilian deaths totaled something like a hundred thousand, and among them were whites from neutral nations, killed for being white.

In the battle for Iwo Jima twenty-one thousand Japanese soldiers were killed in combat, the last of them in a banzai charge. Their commanding general committed harakiri. About three thousand refused to surrender. They holed up in caves to die. Only about two hundred were captured.

On Okinawa it took more than two months to reduce seventy thousand Japanese to cave holdouts, suicides, and prisoners, and in that time something like ninety-five thousand Okinawans were killed, mostly civilians.

Okinawa was less than an hour by air from Kyushu, so close to the home islands that the Japanese people had to know an invasion was coming. The same Japanese draftees who had been firing bolt-action rifles at B-29s overhead were training with ten-kilogram backpacks of explosives; when an enemy tank came they were to throw themselves under the treads and blow themselves up. Children were being trained to do that, too. Men up to age sixty-five and women up to forty-five were formed into volunteer squads, drilling with old muskets, bows and arrows, and bamboo spears. They were told to expect massacre, rape, and pillage from the white invaders, and they were told that the emperor expected them to resist to the death. *One hundred million die together!*

The war was so near now that Frank Fujita, only eight blocks from the imperial palace, could look up at the sky and see not just Superfortresses, long-range strategic bombers, but fighters too, operating from short range. And there were American warships standing so close in that he could hear them shelling the bases at the entrance to Tokyo Bay.

* * *

Other than in the drive to the Japanese home islands, the fighting in the Pacific–Asian war hardly mattered anymore, strategically or tactically. But far away from Japan, Japanese soldiers were still being wiped out in combat; and every month in 1945 still more were dying from disease and starvation. It was Bataan, 1942, being played out again in reverse, on a much bigger scale, all over the war zone. In the midst of it, what was going to happen to the prisoners?

Tokyo policy as of late 1944 was *to prevent prisoners of war from falling into the enemy's hands.* That policy was tested in the Philippines. On Palawan, in the southern islands, the Japanese herded 150 prisoners into air raid shelters, poured on gasoline and lit it, and when the prisoners came rushing out in flames, they machine-gunned them and went at them with clubs and bayonets. At Davao the last prisoners were not killed, just left for dead. At Cabanatuan, down by then to a few hundred living skeletons, the Japanese killed no one—in a surprise raid, American Rangers and Filipino guerrillas got everyone out alive. In Manila, in the midst of the mass slaughter, the guards at Bilibid just left. So the picture was mixed.

By the time the Philippines were retaken, POWs in other parts of the war zone knew things were coming to a critical stage for them. In April the prisoner officers were culled and moved into separate camps, away from enlisted men; the most senior—including the generals and colonels from Formosa—were moved the farthest, to Manchuria. In some of the camps the commandants were in a perpetual rage now, and some of the guards, too. Other guards acted depressed, almost stunned. Some turned pleasant and helpful without saying why. Some were open about the fact that Japan was finished. They told the prisoners as much; and in the same breath they wanted them to know that despite all the beatings they had always been the prisoners' secret friends, so could they have a note of recommendation to show to the Allies when they came? And the few guards who really were friends, most of them quiet Christians, told the prisoners they were all going to be killed: *Oru men die.*

This had the ring of truth. The Japanese were ordering large-scale digging of ditches, moats, trenches, and tunnels. It could have been preparation for a last-stand defense, getting ready to go underground the way they did on Iwo Jima and Okinawa. But it could also have been getting ready to do what they did on Palawan. They were building pillboxes like the one at Davao, facing inward; they were bringing in machine guns and drums of gasoline and power alcohol.

Sometimes the word was that the Japanese were going to fight to the last and then kill themselves; sometimes, that they were going to drive the prisoners ahead of them onto the battlefield, to be killed first; other times, that they were just going to massacre them. At Taihoku on Formosa, an entry in the Japanese head-quarters journal recorded *extreme measures* to be taken against POWs in *urgent situations: Whether they are destroyed individually or in groups, or however it is done, with mass bombing, poisonous smoke, poisons, drowning, decapitation, or what, dispose of the prisoners as the situation dictates. In any case it is the aim not to allow the escape of a single one, to annihilate them all, and not to leave any traces.*

At Miyata on Kyushu the word the prisoners got was that they were going to be taken down into a disused mine and killed. At Fukuoka 17 it was going to be a tenko with no advance warning, then machine guns. At Tha Muang in Thailand, a Korean called Red Balls said that if the Allies invaded, the prisoners were going to be killed in the big ditches around camp. At Kanchanaburi, a guard on the goat-herding detail told Ilo Hard, F Battery of the 131st, that if paratroopers came down, he should not get in the holes that had been dug, they were for machine-gunning.

The prisoners could sit still for whatever was coming, or they could take action. Camp by camp, they started working on plans to rush the guards and break out, *frontally toward a machinegun post in the wall which can be approached with visual cover to either side from enfilading fire, by parallel hutments up to the last fifty metres.* They were hiding knives, piling up rocks to throw, and making Molotov cocktails with sake bottles and gas stolen from trucks. In one of the Osaka camps they smuggled in dynamite and fuses from the mine. At Bunker Hill, Frank Fujita had his own one-man plan. He had a kempeitai captain picked out, about his size; he was going to knock him off, take his uniform, get out of camp, commandeer a taxi, and go.

At the same time, in remote areas, places with no war value, POWs were being worked to death as if there was still some military point to it. And some camps went over the edge into madness, with the Japanese hounding prisoners to death as if death *was* the point.

On Sumatra the Japanese had POWs building a railroad. From Pakenbaroe on the northeast coast the track ran inland, south across the equator, then west to connect up with an existing railroad. It was supposed to be for transporting coal and moving troops. Thousands of slave laborers being shipped over from Java never reached Sumatra: First the *Van Waerwijck* was sunk, then the *Jun'yō*

Maru, the worst of the war's sea transport disasters. Construction did not start until after the Burma–Siam railroad was finished. Then Pakenbaroe was like Burma–Siam all over again, Japanese engineers, Korean guards, rōmusha, and POWs of all nationalities, the great majority Dutch, with some British and Australians and a handful of Americans. Something like five thousand POWs were used, and about thirty thousand rōmusha. The work went on for more than a year, more and more irrelevant to the war every month. Men were dying of malaria and malnutrition, beriberi and ulcers. For POWs the death rate was about 12 percent, not as bad as Burma–Siam, partly because most of the Pakenbaroe prisoners were Dutch, meaning better survivors, but more because the Japanese had rōmusha doing the heaviest work. The rōmusha death rate was terrible, about 80 percent. There were well over a hundred deaths per kilometer for more than two hundred kilometers. No Japanese troops were ever transported.

One of the ways POWs were told they were going to be killed was by being marched to death. At Bicycle Camp in Batavia the story was that they were going to be taken on a *long walk;* men who dropped out would be killed, and it would go on until they were all dead. In Manchuria it was going to be a forty-mile march into the mountains, anyone falling out to be shot. In Batavia and in Manchuria the long march did not happen. On Borneo it did.

At Sandakan, the Japanese had between 2,000 and 3,000 prisoners—mostly Australian, the rest British—building an airfield and service roads. They were in the last stages of disease and starvation. In January 1945 the Japanese began moving them out in batches of 50, on foot, to Ranau, in the interior of the island, 175 miles into mountainous rain-forest country. Those who fell were shot. Those who made it to Ranau only just made it; men started to die there straightaway. The ones who could still walk were turned around to carry rice back to feed the oncoming drafts; they hauled the forty-five-pound sacks, half their body weight, up to 20 miles a day, up mountains, down cliffs, across rivers full of leeches. Those who fell were bayoneted or shot. Those still on their feet had to hoist the dead men's rice load on top of their own. Then in June, more than 530 men were marched out of Sandakan; fewer than 140 reached Ranau. The men too sick to be moved from Sandakan were left to die, or taken on stretchers to the cemetery and killed, or had their skulls bashed in on the spot, and the Japanese burned most of the camp. Late in July the last remaining sick were herded to the air raid shelter and shot. When there was only one man left alive, the Japanese pushed him into a trench with the dead.

The first forced march out of Sandakan, in January, had been in anticipation of an Allied invasion. The second big move, in June, was after the Allies bombed the airfield. In between those dates, the Australians planned a landing to rescue the POWs. Early in March they actually put an advance party ashore, less than thirty miles from Sandakan. But there was no follow-up. Borneo was under the supreme command of Douglas MacArthur, and MacArthur refused to release planes to bring the prisoners out.

A month before, MacArthur had given the highest priority to finding and freeing POWs and civilian internees—in the middle of fierce large-scale fighting, and with no expense spared. But that had been in the Philippines; it was part of the grand gesture of MacArthur returning, and the prisoners to be rescued were Americans. The POWs at Sandakan were many times the number at Cabanatuan and Bilibid, but they were not Americans. With unlimited resources at his disposal, MacArthur could not find it in himself to spare a few DC-3s, for a few days, far from any front line that mattered, for the sake of any other tribe.

If the March rescue operation had gone ahead, well over a thousand prisoners would still have been alive to be lifted out of Sandakan, with no serious Japanese opposition to be concerned about—on the northeast coast of Sumatra there were only about fifteen hundred troops, at the camp itself only a handful of guards.

The final arithmetic of Sandakan-Ranau, from mid-1944 to August 1945, was this: Only six prisoners survived Sandakan-Ranau, all of them Australians, and only by escaping. Almost twenty-four hundred Australian and British prisoners were dead, many times the number of Americans who died on the death march out of Bataan. One Formosan guard at Ranau could not stand what was happening; he tried to kill the Japanese captain and three other Japanese, then blew the top of his own head off.

::

IN THE middle of the fire-bombing of Japan, Harry Jeffries and Oklahoma Atkinson were drafted away from the steelworks at Kawasàki. This was happening with almost all the industrial-city camps. So much productive capability was bombed out that there was not enough work for prisoners. Many were shipped out to labor in the country; and as well this would put them farther from the beachheads of the invasion that was looming.

Harry and Oklahoma, with a hundred or so others from Kawa-saki, drew the Sendai area of northern Honshu. Up there the camps were small and scattered, mostly at old mines, copper, lead, and zinc, brought back late into desperation production. Harry and Oklahoma were at Sendai 7B, near Ōdate. It used to be a working copper mine, but the shaft had fallen in on itself. The story was that 250 prisoners were buried alive. Harry and the others were set to clearing the debris, turning it into an open-cut operation. They had to push ore cars of rubble on a narrow-gauge rail loop from the mine to the dump and back, three quarters of a mile. That was animal work, but all the horses and mules had been eaten.

There was one friendly Japanese at the mine, an old man with a dried-up face and a limp, rugged up against the cold in corduroy pants and black leggings, a fur cap with a visor, and a dog skin over his back. He had no love for the war. And there was one little guard who treated the prisoners halfway decently; when the other guards were around he would not act friendly, but on his own, any chance he got he would slip a man an egg.

Except for those two, the camp was humanly miserable, and not just because of the Japanese, it was the other prisoners as well. Fifty Australians had been moved from Zentsuji, all officers; they did not have to work, and they would have nothing to do with anyone who did. A hundred-plus Americans, originally from the Philippines, had come in ahead of the Kawasaki draft. Not by much, only a couple of months, but they called themselves The Old Bunch and looked down on the Kawasaki men.

The captain of The Old Bunch was the camp commander. The way Oklahoma heard it, in the Philippines he was no great shakes as an officer—he used to command a garbage scow or some-thing—but at Sendai 7B he lorded it over the Wake men. Espe-cially the civilian contractors. He gave them a bad time, he treated them like dogs, he would turn them over to the Japanese, and he would kiss Japanese ass to eat better and get cigarettes.

That was Oklahoma's judgment of him. Of course, Oklahoma never met an officer he did not hate, but this captain he hated personally. Oklahoma had a lot of little soap bars, hotel-size, that he had traded for at Kawasaki, and the captain cockroached them. Someone had stolen something, the Japanese had everyone stand-ing at attention while they searched the huts, and the captain went along with them and stole Oklahoma's soap bars.

Oklahoma and Harry got themselves sent to Sendai 7B from

Kawasaki the same way they got sent to Japan from Kiangwan, transferred as troublemakers. John Cowalski was drafted with them both times. They were three of a kind, and there were others like them. The Old Bunch had nothing but bad words for contractors—they were the ones who talked back at the guards, they climbed the fence and went over to the Chinese labor camp and stole, which got everyone stood at attention for hours. And on and on.

Harry and Oklahoma were still running their card game, for cigarettes and Red Cross futures, with the same house rules and the same limit: If a man lost enough in cigarettes he owed his next Red Cross box, and he was out of the game. Except—and this was a new wrinkle they introduced—if he could find a sponsor. If he had a buddy who did not gamble, and he could talk him into risking his next Red Cross box, he could get back in the game.

Ōdate was the same as every other American camp; there were men fool enough to get themselves on the wrong side of rice trading. One Wake contractor was borrowing across tribal lines, from the Philippines Americans, The Old Bunch. He was in over his head, 103 cigarettes. Sendai 7B had no bankrupt table, no reorganization schedule. They were threatening to kill him. He came to Oklahoma. Oklahoma thought that was ballsy of him, because he was the very man who had turned Oklahoma and Harry in at Woosung for stealing bread. But he was frantic, so Oklahoma, out of the goodness of his trader's heart, made him a deal: He would front him the 103 cigarettes, throw in a month installment-free so he could get himself together, eating full rations, and then he could start paying off in rice at interest. The man was pathetically grateful to Oklahoma for saving his life. And the very next thing he did was to go to the camp commander, the Philippines captain, get all his debts wiped off, and smoke all 103 cigarettes. When Oklahoma found out, he lost patience with the sorry son of a bitch, took him behind the benjo and worked him over.

Up in the mountains in the far north of Honshu, Sendai 7B was a cold place. Even in the summer it felt like winter. The only good thing was the wonderful views—a prisoner could see forever, out to where there was no camp, no mine, no guards, no gang bosses, no Japanese at all, no Japan, no captivity. Oklahoma and Harry convinced themselves they could see all the way west across the Sea of Japan to Russia. No matter that Oklahoma had been having trouble with his eyes, he was sure he could see Vladivostok, over the curve of the earth to freedom. Harry had not been anything like fit ever since Ward Road. Sendai 7B was a year and a half on from there and he was still carrying bad dysentery and bad malaria. But he saw what Oklahoma saw. They started talking about escaping.

John Cowalski was up for it, and so were four other men, a total of seven. They began putting together an escape kit. They scrounged a meat cleaver. They said they could repair watches, and the Japanese believed them. One watch had a little built-in compass, and they liberated it.

Their plan was to make for the coast, pirate a fishing boat, terrify the crew into working for them or throw the lot of them overboard, and sail for Vladivostok. They were not much of a pirate gang, just bags of bones. Oklahoma was the heaviest, in fact the second heaviest man in camp, and he was only 136 pounds on a six-foot-one frame.

They kept their plan to themselves. The only people they told were men they could trust, meaning hardly anyone, and yet the POW commander found out. Oklahoma had no doubt that if that soap-stealing captain knew when they were going to make their break, he would tell the Japanese and they would have a machine gun set up. So when the captain braced him, *I hear you boys are going over the hill,* Oklahoma said, *First I heard about it,* and decided then and there that they should go soon rather than late.

Harry came down with a malaria relapse. He could not walk a hundred yards. Oklahoma had to decide whether to stay with him or go. He decided to go. He left all his business collectibles with Harry, promised that if he made it he would get in touch with Harry's mother, and took off into the dark.

The camp fence was fifteen feet high, with spikes. The plan of escape was for each of the six to get himself over the top separately, then rendezvous outside. Oklahoma was waiting, Cowalski turned up, then two others, and that was all. The other two had puddled out at the last moment.

So it was four of them on the run, with something like fifty miles to cover to the coast, mountain country, cold and rough, and all they had was Japanese split-toe rubber shoes with a useful life of less than two weeks, and shaggy Japanese peasant rain capes of grass that let the wet in after about ten minutes.

They traveled by night and hid by day. For two days and nights it rained, and they holed up in a charcoal burner's shack, eating fish that Oklahoma had scored from where they were drying on a line, maggoty things—they had to burn away the maggots with hot charcoal and eat what was left with weeds for greens.

Oklahoma could make good time, Cowalski too, but one of the others came down sick. The original plan was to stay off the beaten track and go over the top of the mountains, but with a sick man to carry they had to take the pass that all the Japanese used.

On the fifth day they were resting up, three of them sleeping and the fourth keeping watch, and the next thing Oklahoma knew, he woke up with the watchman kicking him on the foot: *They've got us surrounded.*

It was farmers, with hoes and scythes. The question was, who was the most scared, and it turned out to be the farmers. Oklahoma and Cowalski let out a roar and charged them with the meat cleaver; they scattered, and the four all made it away. But they got separated, Oklahoma and Cowalksi with the compass, the other two with the food.

Oklahoma and Cowalksi were creeping through the pass in the dark, looking for the others, when they ran into Japanese soldiers looking for them. The Japanese stripped them, tied their hands behind their back and made them stand at attention all night. In the morning they made them call out to the others; it was that or get bayoneted, so they called, and in about two hours they heard gonging noises, a signal that the others had been caught.

The Japanese trucked them back to Sendai, kneeling with their arms tied. Every town and village along the way one of the guards yelled out, *We've caught them! We've caught them!* and they had to get out and kneel and be hit and kicked and spit at and pelted with stones.

At the Sendai guardhouse the Japanese dry-shaved them—head, chin, eyebrows, and nose—put them in solitary, and made them kneel at attention fifteen hours a day.

They had a story ready for the court-martial: They were hungry, they went over the fence after food; so what if the guards shot them, they were being starved to death anyway.

Oklahoma was sentenced to three years solitary confinement for being the leader. The others only got two years—even Cowalski, despite the fact that when he was asked who was going to win the war, he said the United States.

The Japanese on the court said: *We cannot shoot you, and we cannot give you more food,* and that was when Oklahoma figured the war must be just about over.

There was some kind of public address system near the guardhouse, for early air raid warnings, telling which direction the bombers were coming from. They had only been in their cells a few weeks when B-29s hit Sendai in a night raid. The Japanese prisoners were taken out to a shelter; Oklahoma and the other three were left. The bombs kept falling, closer and closer, in tighter and tighter circles. A near-miss blew the cells open. The doors had spring locks, the guards ran in and slammed them shut, but Oklahoma's did not catch. He could see a bunch of keys, and he slipped out and opened the others' doors, so that if the place caught fire they could get away. Back in his cell he lay flat, holding his nose and ears shut against the concussion. On the seventh pass the roof blew off. They crawled out and sheltered by a wall while the bombers kept strafing and dropping incendiaries.

The next day the guards moved them out, walking them along the road tied up. They were in among thousands of Japanese, bailing out, heading for the mountains with their belongings. One made a rush at Oklahoma with a long knife, and the guard lieutenant had to fend him off with his saber.

They wound up in a big civilian jail—hundreds of Japanese prisoners, most of them ordinary criminals, about ten of them politicals, and in among them the four white POW escapers, separated from each other.

Oklahoma was crammed in with four Japanese, in a cell so small that if one man turned over all the others had to. He was handcuffed so tight it hurt. He complained. The guards squeezed the cuffs tighter, and left them on till sores formed on his wrists. Food came in through a hole in the door, dirty-water soup and rice mixed with barley. Oklahoma roughed his way closest to the hole. He was the biggest, and he was going to get the biggest serving.

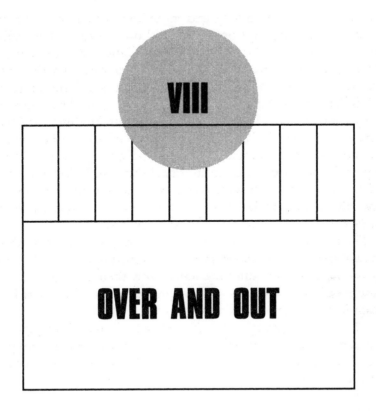

VIII

OVER AND OUT

IN MID-JULY THE LEADERS OF THE MAJOR ALLIED POWERS MET at a conference code-named *Terminal,* to force an end to the war and dictate surrender terms. On July 26, Japan was told to give up or face *prompt and utter destruction.*

Japan's response was not quick enough or clear enough. Prompt destruction followed. On August 1, 836 B-29s raided Honshu and Kyushu, the greatest number over Japan in a single day, dropping the biggest one-day tonnage of bombs.

Then came utter destruction. On the morning of August 6, a single B-29 at 31,600 feet over Hiroshima dropped one parachute bomb, code-named Little Boy, armed with a warhead of uranium 235. The explosion created a huge fireball, millions of degrees centigrade at the bursting point. It leveled Hiroshima for over a mile around the hypocenter, and more than a hundred thousand Japanese were dead, roasted, gutted, flayed, shredded, brains boiled, eyes melted out of their sockets, bodies burned to instant ash, or simply vaporized, dematerialized, reduced to atoms.

The working assumption of the Americans, based on the scraps of intelligence available, was that no POWs were being held in the city, which was one reason why Hiroshima was the first choice for Little Boy. But in fact there were prisoners, a couple of dozen, all downed airmen, in different locations, all close to the center of the blast. Some survived—a miracle, if that was the word. Then in the hours after the blast, three of them were killed by Japanese in the streets, two beaten to death, one tied to a stake and stoned to death.

With the smoke of Little Boy still in the sky, Harry Truman issued a statement saying Japan must give up *or face a rain of ruin from the air, the like of which has never been seen on this earth.*

Japan did not give up. On August 9, a B-29 over Nagasaki dropped another atomic bomb, Fat Man, armed with plutonium 239.

It was known that there were POWs in and around Nagasaki. But that did not qualify the city to be crossed off the target list, because other than Hiroshima all possible targets were known to have POWs.

The total of Nagasaki prisoners, not known then, was about 350—some American, British, and Australian, most Indonesian-Dutch. A little over a mile from the hypocenter, the camp at Saiwaimachi, Fukuoka 14, was destroyed. Between 60 and 80 men were killed. About five miles farther away from the hypocenter, on the islet of Koyagi, at Fukuoka 2, Frank Fujita's first Japan camp, 4 men were killed.

In a bowl of earth formed by the hills of the city, something like 40,000 Japanese were killed. And out of the devastation poured refugees, tens of thousands, desperate for shelter, fighting to get into the mines where POWs had been slaving underground, foul and hazardous black burrows that passed now for sanctuaries.

Atomic bombing did not mean the end of area bombing. After Hiroshima, on a raid over Yawata, a B-29 crew had to bail out into the ocean. They floated for almost a week before they were picked up and taken to Hiroshima. They were being trucked through the city to prison when their guard pulled their blindfolds off and made them look at the world laid waste around them. *One bomb! One bomb!* he said. *Look there. That blue light is women burning. It is babies burning. Is it wonderful to see the babies burning?*

On the truck were two other airmen from Hiroshima Castle. When the bomb went off, they were outside on benjo fatigue. They saw the blast up close, but it did not kill them—a miracle, again if that was the word. They dived into a cesspool and stayed alive while the city burned. But they had been poisoned by radiation. Without understanding what had happened to them, they knew they were dead men. Running sores covered their bodies; there was green stuff coming out of them, mouth and ears; they were in agony, begging to be put out of their misery. It took them eleven days to die, the way thousands of Japanese were dying in the city around them.

Americano joto nai, said a young Japanese to a prisoner at Hakensho on Kyushu, not far from Nagasaki. *Tuxan gasu, gasu joto nai, ichi bombu.* He mimed a parachute. *Go acker, boom. Ichi bombu ema tuxan bombu, gas bombu, radioka, telephonu gasu, boom, boom.* He pointed to himself—eyes, arms, legs, body—and shook his head. This is what he was saying: The Americans are bad, they are using very much gas. One bomb dropped by parachute explodes at five hundred meters and then becomes many bombs, all gas bombs, the gas comes out of the radios and through the telephones, and unlike a bullet which hits you at one spot, this gas travels to your eyes and all parts of the body.

Stories about the terrible bomb were coming out of shortwave radios in all parts of the war zone: Japanese radios, civilian radios, and the secret radios of prisoners. In Saigon a boy on a bicycle passed a note to a POW; it was in French, and it translated to something about an *automatic bomb.* In other places the word was that the bomb was a huge land mine. Or else small, only the size of a grapefruit. Always it was—unbelievably—just one bomb. And whatever it was, it had set off a primal cosmic explosion. *Genshi bakudan,* some Japanese called it, "original child bomb," or "fundamental element bomb." In the Hōten camp at Mukden, Manchuria, the word for it was *adam bomb.*

At noon on August 15, Japanese national radio announced a broadcast of the gravest significance, so important that listeners were told to stand. The national anthem was played, and over radio sets everywhere in the country a voice spoke, like no other voice ever heard, high and strained, using ancient formal words, next to impossible for ordinary Japanese to comprehend.

In all the history of Japan the invincible, as far back as the sun god, this was the first time commoners had ever heard the voice of their emperor. And the first words of this first emperor to speak directly to his people were about catastrophic humiliation. The unconquerable Japanese empire had been terminally crushed in war, forced into abject surrender. The voice of the Son of Heaven went out into the poisoned air of Japan, out by shortwave to his empire in ruins, and World War II was over.

For months, the Imperial Japanese Army at Osaka had been killing downed American airmen, poisoning them, shooting them, chopping their heads off. After the emperor spoke, the last five were taken to a military cemetery. Three were shot, two beheaded. The same day, hours into the peace, Japanese officers at Fukuoka on Kyushu took their samurai swords and chopped sixteen airmen to death, with the squad commander's girlfriend along to watch. On Celebes, well after the war was over, two Australian airmen were chloroformed and strangled. And it was twelve days after the emperor's broadcast before the Japanese at Ranau on Borneo killed the last thirty of their surviving prisoners.

In Manchuria, at the Unit 731 laboratories at Pingfan near Harbin, the Japanese machine-gunned six hundred Chinese and Manchurian laborers, and killed all the human experimental subjects, the maruta. They were gassed to death with toxic chemicals, or poisoned with potassium cyanide in their food. Their bodies were stuffed in incinerators, or dumped in a pit in the courtyard and burned. Then the bones were sunk in the river; all the laboratory specimens too, a charnel heap of tortured and infected and vivisected human flesh so big that it would not burn.

The Japanese general in charge of Unit 731, Ishii Shirō, the man directly responsible from start to finish for what went on at Pingfan, wanted all his staff and their families to commit suicide. They were issued poison. Of course Ishii was not about to take poison himself. And hardly any of his people took it, either. Instead they bailed out of Pingfan at top speed, about two thousand of them, Ishii too. The parting gesture of Unit 731 was to turn thousands of infected rats loose on the world.

Elsewhere, camp by camp across the war zone, the war did not end on the stroke of noon, August 15. It had begun to wind down before that moment, and it went on not quite ending for days afterward. Work details were sent out and brought back in again, and the guards gave explanations that made no sense. It was too rainy. There had been a cave-in at the mine. The mill had no more raw materials. The equipment was broken. All men were byōki, sick—of course they were, but no sicker than the day before. Cholera had broken out—when obviously it had not. The prisoners were being given two days off while the guards negotiated permission for them to have a vegetable garden of their own. It was a holiday, all men could rest. Also they were allowed to whistle or sing.

There were gunsō, sergeants, who used to holler and scream so loud they made the leaves quiver on the trees; now they were talking in whispers. There was no shakedown at the gate. There were officers burning papers by the armload. There were guards sitting around stunned. Finally someone said it. *Sensō owari.* The war is over.

Even when a camp commandant spoke those words officially and stepped down off his parade-ground soapbox for the last time ever, the prisoners had to strain to take the measure of the astonishing fact that they were free men. They shouted and went silent, wept with bewilderment and fear that it might not be true, then laughed and shouted again. They sang their national anthems. They broke out flags that they had kept hidden all through captivity, or they made new flags, iodine for red, a miner's shirt for white, and mosquito netting or hospital trousers for blue. They stayed up all night talking nonstop, chain-smoked, ate the precious food they had been hoarding, drank anything and everything from guardhouse sake to power alcohol, snake-danced drunk around camp, and flung their filthy bedding out the window and set fire to their disgusting huts.

An urgent Japanese Army telegram had gone out, instructing guards who had mistreated prisoners to vanish. Some guards stayed, and whether they were mistreaters or not, the free white men who were not their prisoners anymore felt free to take it out on them. They marched them up and down, ordered them to *Ki o tsuke!* and *Keirei!*, made them work on the double, police the grounds, honeybucket the vegetable garden, scrub the benjo, and here and there they pushed one into a cesspit and did not care if he never surfaced. The Japanese colonel at Ōmori made an official complaint to the senior POW officer that someone had urinated in one of his boots and defecated in the other. An evil mine boss was force-fed horse dung; and at the same camp some men, one of them without legs, went after the commandant and beat him unconscious. Next day his door was nailed shut, with a sign, DIED OF PNEUMONIA, the same strain of Japanese pneumonia that had been killing prisoners for three and a half years.

This kind of thing went on for a few days. In the home island camps, over the same few days, Japanese civilians were showing up inside the fence, humble and more than willing to work for food. One of them was in his kimono, bowing, and an Australian recognized him as a mine boss who used to beat up his friend. He dropped him with a terrific punch to the jaw. He said, *Get up and fight, you bastard.* But the Japanese would not get up; he lay cowering, and the Australian found he could not go on with it. *I planned to give that bastard a proper hiding, but when he wouldn't fight, I had to give up. It was like kicking a kitten.*

Of all the strange things about liberation, surely this had to be the strangest. Two weeks back, ninety-nine prisoners out of a hundred would cheerfully have skinned any Japanese guard. A rage for personal physical revenge had been smoldering in them for three and a half years, forcibly banked down. After the emperor's broadcast it flared up. But only here and there, and only briefly. In a matter of days it burned itself away to next to nothing. It was hard to believe. The prisoners themselves shook their heads over the strangeness of it. But for ninety-nine men out of a hundred it was true.

The chemistry of this strange change of heart and mind was basic and simple—freedom plus a full belly. Freedom was official as of August 15, and after that the filling of the belly took only a couple of weeks at most.

Camp by camp a plane would appear overhead, a fighter or fighter-bomber, carrier-based or Okinawa-based. The pilot would fly back and forth, do some wing waggles, and be off. Soon more planes would turn up, and the pilots would drop seabags packed with their own personal stuff—shoes, socks, skivvies—and messages, magazines, chocolate bars, chewing gum, and packs of cigarettes with lighters.

The next drop was leaflets with instructions: Put a sign on the roof in big letter, PW, with the number of men in camp. And next thing the skies were raining food and clothes and medicine, manna from heaven by the ton.

Air-dropping was a science that had been perfected on a small scale in the European theater, pinpoint night drops behind the lines to resistance fighters. In the China-Burma-India theater it was taken to the largest scale and the highest level of efficiency, tens of thousands of tons dropped every month, month after month.

For the Japan camps, the airdrop planes were from Curtis LeMay's 20th Air Force, B-29s out of the Marianas, the same huge Superfortresses that had firebombed everything from southern Kyushu to northern Honshu and then parachute-dropped Little Boy and Fat Man.

The crews had flown thousands of sorties in war. Airdrops in peacetime were new to them. They made practice runs and decided on parachute drops at 165 miles per hour, the bombardier doing the targeting and sighting, picking the moment to let go.

The benevolent intention from the air was precision bombing in the spirit of peace, a blessing from the B-29s. It turned out to be low-level area scatterbombing—huge bombers roaring in low and slow over the mountains, wheels down for drag, weaving through steep narrow valleys at five hundred to a thousand feet, unloading in a frantic rush, then wheels up, stick back, gun the engines to a scream, out over the peaks again with treetops scraping the underbelly and props shredding leaves.

Down came the drop packs, forty to a plane, totaling ten thousand pounds, crates and bales on pallets and fifty-five-gallon drums welded together—and with one out of ten, in some places more, especially in the first few days of the operation, the chute did not open, or else the load broke loose, and the crates and bales and barrels came hurtling down like cluster bombs, landing anywhere and everywhere, inside camp or out, crashing through roofs, smashing into barracks, cookhouses, sick bays, mortuaries, villagers' houses, village streets, bringing down power lines, rupturing water pipes, bouncing off coal dumps, burying themselves in fill land, splashing into rice paddies, slamming into hillsides, exploding, geysers of ketchup, avalanches of cigarettes, dry streambeds running with Lucky Strikes, bundles of boots hanging off trees like bunches of giant black and brown grapes, a chocolate-flavored duck pond, sugar and cocoa and swamp mud in equal parts, sudden farm lots of fruit salad, mountains of cornflakes. A camp going up in flames, firebombed by matches that ignited on impact. Bales of cigarettes thumping in, the impact compressing them to an inch long. Acre lots of canned ham a millimeter thick. A cow grazing, a direct hit, instant hamburger. A direct hit on a Japanese farmer, buried under a burst bale of American boots, one foot sticking out with a Japanese sandal on it. A prisoner at Fukuoka 26 thought he was all over blood, but it was just a big splash of tomato puree. At another place, they thought the big splash was tomato, but it was a Japanese woman pureed. At Nakama it was a Japanese miner, hit square in the kidneys, they scraped him off the barrel and rolled it into the cookhouse. An old Japanese woman was in the benjo— down came a barrel and hammered her in like a flathead nail. At another place it was two Japanese girls dismembered by a cigarette drop, a cut-off hand was lying on the floor, a free prisoner came bustling in and shook it, *Glad to meet you, ma'am,* and went ahead and scooped up cigarettes and smoked the bloody things.

Men on wobbly legs were sprinting every which way, trying to get out from under the scatterbombing and score on the food all in the same stride. It was something to think of POWs surviving Japanese starvation for three and a half years, and then in their first days as free men getting themselves killed by American food. But it happened, a head cut off by canned peaches, brains knocked out by fruit cocktail, Spam as an instrument of violent death—the last Wake marine to die in prison camp, and he might well have been the last marine casualty of the war in Asia, was killed by Spam.

In less than a month, from the last week of August through the third week of September, 1,066 planes flew 900 effective sorties over 150-plus camps, in Japan, China, Manchuria, Formosa, Hainan, and Korea. Parachutes requisitioned: 63,000. Tons of supplies dropped: 4,470. Freed prisoners eating like kings: upwards of 35,000, plus thousands of civilian internees. Planes lost: 8, aircrew casualties: 77. Many days into the peace, Soviet fighters attacked a B-29 over northern Korea, forcing it to crash-land; and the excuse the Russians gave was that they thought it must have been hijacked by desperate Japanese. And—not in the official report but a fact—in and around the camps, there were more deaths on the ground than there were POWs killed by the Hiroshima A-bomb.

The leaflets with the food drops said DO NOT OVEREAT. Too much white man's food too soon was going to play hell with POW bodies, and in fact there were men who died of sudden excess. But prudent advice had no force in the face of unlimited beef stew and fruit cocktail and Pet milk and ketchup and Campbell's soup— and white bread, fresh-baked in the ovens of great aircraft carriers equipped to feed crews the size of a small American town or a big POW camp, loaves by the hundred cascading from the sky with the yeasty smell still on them. And butter, and jam. And sugar candy. A man with a clean new air-dropped shirt could stuff his shirt with candy, then stuff himself. Men everywhere were wolfing it down, Harry Jeffries for one—he was drooling, he was slavering, he could feel the sugar firing up his body, his blood coming to a roiling boil, and still he could not stop.

Everywhere in the camps there was instant weight gain, a pound per man per day, two pounds. In a week the aggregate weight of white men in Japan was up by tons. Not that it was healthy weight. It was bloat. Still, for the first time in three and a half years men were looking and feeling something like human, the juices of food and freedom were flowing in them, and it stirred them to get dressed up in their air-drop shirts and trousers and shoes and go out into the world.

The best advice from camp commanders and cautious friends was not to. *Stay in camp; you've done been through too much crap to go out and get your butt shot off.* But the constraint of sensible advice or officers' orders could never prevail against the joy of slipping the leash and running free.

It was sport to wave a VD medical form at a Japanese officer and tell him that if he refused to hand over his samurai sword he had to sign the form and MacArthur would get him. Forget the VD form, it was sport to strip him to his baggy underpants and snap his sword off him. It was sport to commandeer a fire wagon and race around winding the siren. Or drive a tram—one man bought a tram from the conductor for ten cigarettes; another was drunk-driving his tram through Moji. It was sport to jump a train and roust the kempeitai, then sit tossing chewing gum down onto the tracks and watch Japanese kids bobbing for it. Best of all—flag down a trainload of Japanese soldiers, order them to get out and stack their rifles, slap the officers and take their swords, then drive off with the train.

It was sport to rob a bank. A bunch of Australians had always wanted to do that at home, it was their life's ambition, so now they did it in Japan, and threw paper yen in the air for the Japanese to fight over.

The chemistry of food and energy was turning so positive that there were men ready to try themselves out in the brothels. Would they have lead in the pencil again? It was a momentous question. Sometimes the answer was yes, sometimes not yet. And sometimes it was not even a question of the flesh still being weak. Some Australians descended on the second-best geisha house in Nakama, and of all things, the Japanese women would not lie down for them, not even with their whole beaten country rolling over, paws up. The Australians took this as a terrible insult. It caused them to throw a radio through the window.

Some Americans out carousing wound up so far from camp they decided to lay over at a country inn. No Japanese would have had the effrontery to refuse them entry. In the middle of the night they woke up hearing little pattering sounds like rain. It was the Japanese sprinkling salt to ward off evil spirits, meaning them.

At midnight on August 8, two days after Little Boy and only hours before Fat Man, the Soviet Union declared war on Japan. The two nations had had a neutrality pact But late in the war Russia denounced Japan as an aggressor, and in the last days Stalin sent mechanized divisions racing into Manchuria and northern Korea, scooping up resource-rich territory.

The Americans dropped leaflets to say liberation was coming. The Russians had a different style—at the big POW camp at Hoten in Mukden, their opening announcement was to run a tank through the wall. They gave the Japanese five minutes to stack arms and their cooks five minutes to start serving better food or get shot, and in the same breath they offered to take care of any guard the prisoners nominated.

Mukden was crawling with drunk Russians, looting, shipping away trainloads of stuff, everything from industrial machinery to carpets from rich homes. They were shooting other looters, hanging them from chimneys, driving over their own people with tanks and not stopping, shooting horses, and raping anything that moved—a POW reported suffering one of the last war crimes, or perhaps it was an early peace crime, rape by a truckload of huge Russian women soldiers. The Russians were the ones who shot at the food-drop B-29 over Korea; and at Hōten one drunk Russian, days after peace was declared and for reasons utterly unknown, bayoneted the tires of a plane that was set to lift out the sickest POWs.

When the first American torpedo boats and landing craft into Tokyo Bay came cruising down the channel off the POW camp at Ōmori, hundreds of men climbed up on the pilings of the wharf, in jubilation. Frank Fujita was there. He could not stand to wait. He dived in and swam out, thrashing along, but his free man's eyes were bigger than his prisoner's arm muscles, and after fifty yards he was done for. He could have drowned himself; but his fellow

Americans, coming to carry him home, managed to lift him out of the water, though with his prisoner's shaved head his hair was too short to grab and they had to pull him up by the ears. Within three weeks of the emperor's broadcast, he was on his way back to the United States.

Forrest Knox was, too. He was at Toyama on Honshu. In the last few months he had bad hookworm. And bad beriberi. He was nothing but a human balloon full of fluid. If he lay on one side his face would swell up, and the guards would point at him and laugh and turn him over so they could laugh at him swelling up on the other side. He heard the emperor on the radio and had no idea what it was about. Food fell out of the sky and he was given the right things to eat, which changed his body chemistry for the better, which caused him to pee gallons, which brought him down again from a beriberi balloon to more or less human shape. But he was still not properly back in the world. Even when they loaded him on a liberation train there was something strange and disconnected about it all, remote, not real, like watching a movie out the train window, devastated cities flicking past one after another, Toyama to Tokyo, and every mile the film seemed to be cranked faster. Then he was at the port of Yokohama, blinking at huge crowd scenes, a thousand freed prisoners a day pouring in, two thousand, out of a Japanese daze into an American delirium.

The same thing was happening at other ports, Wakayama and Sendai on Honshu, and Nagasaki on Kyushu; at Dairen on the coast of Manchuria; in Korea; and on Formosa and Hainan. Brass bands. Speeches from generals. Coffee and doughnuts and ice cream and Coke from Red Cross girls. White hospital ships, shining bright, with wonderful names, *Samaritan, Hope, Rescue, Relief, Consolation, Benevolence, Sanctuary, Haven, Tranquility*. Filthy prison camp clothes stripped off for burning, stinking bodies into the hot shower, the clean sweet scent of American soap, a delousing with DDT, penicillin for whatever might ail them, fresh new clothes—and suddenly they were white men again in a white world.

But they were still a tribe separate from the white men who had come to liberate them. These men were wearing strange new uniforms and different helmets, they were carrying different guns, and they all looked huge, seven feet tall and unbelievably well-fleshed—they could have been from another planet.

And at the railroad stations and the ports and on the hospital ships there were white women, Red Cross girls and nurses. They were so big, so full of confidence, there was just so much of them, and they were so *white*—at the sight of them some of the men rushed up and gave them huge hugs, some just dropped everything and stared, paralyzed.

The moment Forrest stepped on board ship he started eating nonstop. The mess lines were open to the prisoners twenty-four hours a day. There were tables, chairs, knives, forks, napkins, and everything was *clean*. Salt and pepper shakers, sugar bowl, hotcakes and eggs and bacon and toast and coffee—if they wanted ice cream with chocolate topping for breakfast they could have it. They could not believe it.

There were men too timid to pick up knives and forks; one boy would wait for someone else to finish so he could use theirs. Others were stealing the eating irons and squirreling them away; they just could not stop themselves scrounging. There were men who would not give up their old mess kits; they hung on to them like grim death. There were men hiding food in their pajama pockets and their pillowcases. There was one POW doctor who ate thirty-two poached eggs and threw them all up.

Forrest did not have any problem behaviors with food; his eating regulated itself. As his body filled out, his mind started coming back to him; he was hungry to fill it up too—and suddenly he was the original Forrest Knox again, energetic and curious, talking a mile a minute to any man who would talk to him, asking a thousand questions and getting a million answers, gorging on information.

Everybody was. They had a hole in their lives as big as three and a half years of prison camp. To them everything military in 1945 was new—radar, bazookas, rocket launchers, flamethrowers, recoilless weapons, DUKWS. There was something called electronics. There was something called a jet plane—it could fly without a propeller. Seabees were new. WACS and WAVES were new—women in the services, incredible. DDT was new. Penicillin was new. KILROY WAS HERE, written all over the place, even in the shower on the hospital ship, what did it mean? And what had been happening at home? Who had been winning the World Series? What was a zoot-suiter? What was a bobby-soxer? Someone named Frank Sinatra was supposed to be as big as Bing Crosby, if that could be credited. And the wildest story of all—*Shirley Temple was engaged*. There was no end to the wonders; the pictures in the *Life* magazines were as extravagant as the Arabian Nights. Forrest could not get enough of the world of home, no one could. They were Rip Van Winkles in their twenties, waking up.

*   *   *

Officially they were not called POWs anymore; now they were *RAMPs,* Recovered Allied Military Personnel.

The United States took on the responsibility of moving them out of Japan, Manchuria, Korea, Formosa, and Hainan, all nationalities, Australians, British, and Dutch as well as Americans.

They had come to Japan on hellships. The return leg by ship was one more packed voyage, but it was heaven. And for the men who went out by air, in bombers and cargo planes, everything was free and easy. The pilots slept by their planes, under a wing, and got up in the morning to fly them out, just like that. Those pilots were relaxed about load factors; they would take on more than the authorized body count because so many RAMPs were still underweight, stack them in and trust to the laws of physics or the grace of God that there were enough inches at the end of the runway to get airborne. And up in the air they would put the plane on automatic pilot and come back and make coffee and shoot the breeze.

Of all dreadful things to happen, some prisoners of war died as free men on their way home, the same kind of absurd deaths as in the food drops. In the middle of a typhoon, a mine blew out the side of a ship and killed some. A couple of planes flew into the same typhoon and crashed. Another flew into the side of a mountain. And—a real horror story, one that everybody heard—there were men in a bomber, no seats, sitting wherever they could find space, and somehow, somewhere over the Pacific, the bomb-bay doors opened and out went a cluster of live bodies like a scatter-bomb food drop.

Those were terrible things to prey on the minds of men still waiting for transport, especially the story about the bomb bay. But, overall, the RAMP operation was a success on the order of the food drops, and the speed of it was amazing. The forecast had been that to find everyone, process them, and lift them out of Japan—plus Korea, Manchuria, China, Formosa, and Hainan, bringing out civilian internees at the same time—would take months, possibly a year. But, in fact, less than six weeks after the day of the emperor's broadcast, by the official count there were effectively no POWs left in Japan and the rest of northeast Asia, and 32,624 RAMPs were on their way home.

They were beginning to live in their bodies like white men again, and in their minds they carried the confident expectation that they were never going to have to look at another Japanese.

All by itself that was a delousing of the spirit. But not a complete disinfecting. They were not clean of the Japanese yet. On the way home they kept thinking about them all the time.

One thing every RAMP was asked about, either before he left Japan or in transit through Okinawa and the Philippines, was war crimes in the camps. Sorting back through three and a half years of guards and commandants, everybody could come up with personal candidates for hanging. Speaking strictly legally, not every one of those Japanese would have qualified as a war criminal. But in the POWs' book of life, just being Japanese qualified them as nasty and vicious.

The POWs had physical stripes and mental scars; and even though they were not prisoners anymore and never would be again, Japanese brutality was a sore they could not stop picking at.

White men and Japanese—science would define them both as human, *Homo sapiens,* the same species. But they were different races, on opposite sides of a fierce and ugly race war, and in the prison camps they were tribes of hate, each seeing the other as unspeakably alien and repulsive. The POWs had had to look at the guards from the underside, disgustingly close up, for years on end, and for many prisoners that was the only way ever to think of the Japanese, as animals. To the Japanese, white prisoners were just as disgusting.

In the early days of captivity a Japanese officer was taking tenko, holding a handkerchief to his nose. A POW sergeant asked him if he had a cold. *Baka! Stupid!* said the Japanese. *You smell bad, you smell very bad.* In another month the prisoners had to be smelling worse, because the Japanese were not issuing soap. But the officer was not using his handkerchief anymore. The sergeant asked him if he had gotten used to the smell. *I have not,* said the Japanese. *Now you smell OK. You no eat meat since you become pu-ri-so-na.* This story could be read another way: The Japanese liked their white prisoners to be starving.

The officer with his handkerchief was at Changi, the biggest POW camp of all, in mid-1942, when Japan was still riding high. In mid-1945 on Hokkaido, the butt end of the home-island POW camp world, the Japanese were down to using teenage boys for guards and interpreters. One boy interpreter at Hakodate was lost and wandering, struggling to make sense out of what he was seeing, and failing. He had no love for the emperor's war. His own people in uniform, and all those white men in rags, were both alien tribes, as foreign to him as they were to each other, guards walking like monkeys, with O-shaped legs, prisoners too skinny, with X-shaped legs, sticklike. The prisoners were worn out, faltering between life and death. When they were silent they were frightening. When they spoke, their words were grotesque, almost insane. They were forever asking the boy questions, about how the Japanese saw things, how the Japanese thought. They never stopped asking, and the boy got sick and tired of answering them.

White POWs could not comprehend anything Japanese—not even after three and a half years of intensive instruction, boot and fist and bayonet and club.

Then—and this was yet another thing the POWs would never be able to understand—the moment the war ended the Japanese changed, like traffic lights turning from red to green. Just one instance was enough to make the case for incomprehensibility. For three and a half years the guards kept holding back food and medicine, right up to the last day of the war, and what earthly sense did that make when everyone was starving, Japanese along with prisoners? Then as soon as the emperor spoke, the Japanese said, *Now we are friends,* and broke out warehouses of food, vitamins, drugs, bandages, no limit. At Ohama they came up with big wooden cases of stuff labeled Detroit Branch, Red Cross Society of USA, Yokohama Earthquake Fund 1923. What POW could ever hope to fathom that mind?

At Saganoseki on Kyushu, in the summer of 1945—in the middle of months of B-29 firebombings, with hatred of white men never stronger—a prisoner on a work detail was being marched through town, and a small boy, only a tot, came up and put an orange in his hand. *I studied his face—bland, impassive, Oriental, and old beyond its years. Compassion? I don't know. But I often think of him. . . .*

That was the haunting part. Every POW on his way home could bring to mind a good Japanese, a real human being. At Singapore early on, one of the guards came around at night and tucked his prisoners into their mosquito nets. In Hong Kong, Uncle John, an interpreter, smuggled stuff into camp; it would have cost him his life if he had been caught, but he kept doing it. On one work detail at Kobe a guard nicknamed Charlie Chaplin would keep an eye out while the prisoners stole oranges, and buy them plates of noodles. Little Tateyama used to talk to Griff Douglas off the *Houston* and give him his own cigarette ration. Smiley, a three-star private with a mouthful of gold teeth like the sun coming up, had a brother who lived in the Sacramento Valley.

Smiley was with some *Houston* men. At night he would slide a little tin of water or rice under the hut door; when he was off duty he would still come around and lay down three or four cigarettes for them to pick up. Kanemura was a Korean on a ship transport to Burma; he fell into conversation with Big Oscar Offerle, D Battery of the 131st, about Shakespeare, and they became friends.

At Niihama on Shikoku, the guards would take the prisoners out picnicking in the hills; those were happy times. And the farm people treated them kindly. When a storm damaged the prison barracks, some old women came and mixed clay and straw and slapped it on the walls and whitewashed everything until it was as good as new.

Late in the war, at Senju on Honshu, there was a widow with two children living next door to the camp. The prisoners, 131st and *Houston* men, would hear a rap on the wall of the barracks, and that would be the old woman outside, poking one bean at a time through a hole. They never knew her name, but when they were liberated they left her their blankets and a big bag of rice, and told the local kempeitai it was hers by order of the United States government.

So some prisoners were prepared to look back and give the Japanese points. Some Japanese anyway. But very few. *You can't hate them all. Perhaps only nine hundred ninety-nine out of a thousand.*

Harry Jeffries and Oklahoma Atkinson had one nominee for a good Japanese: Shindō Yoshihiro, the doctor at Kiangwan who looked after them when they came out of Ward Road jail. Aside from Shindō, if every other Japanese dropped dead they would not have shed a tear. Ishihara, The Beast of the East, they would have killed, cheerfully.

Harry and Oklahoma left Japan together, along with John Cowalski. At the end of the war, Oklahoma and Cowalski had liberated themselves from jail. They walked back to Sendai 7B and joined up with Harry again. Harry was still alive, but he was out of business. Peace plus the food drops had done it. A ration of rice had no trade value anymore, it was garbage. A Red Cross box was a puny thing, of no account when stacked up against crates of canned food and pallets of cigarettes. Anyone who owed Harry could have paid him a hundred times over.

Leaving Japan by ship, they had the same joyful expectation as everyone else, never to have a Japanese foul their sight again. But they were routed via Guam, and when they put in there it was as if they were back on the wrong side of some kind of distorted looking glass. There were Japanese all over the place, prisoners of the Americans, but they were ambling around loose. They were wearing clean American clothes, they were doing as they pleased, giving a lazy imitation of work or not even bothering with that, smoking American cigarettes, lining up for chow in the same line as Americans, for American food, going back for seconds. They had plenty of flesh on their bones. One of them was leaning on a shovel, grinning in Cowalski's face. Cowalski grabbed the shovel and smashed his Japanese skull.

Not one official word was said about it. They shipped out, from Guam to Hawaii, then from Hawaii to the West Coast.

And one fine morning, there they were sailing in through the Golden Gate—through the looking glass again, for the final time, and this time they wound up on the right side.

From Golden Gate to Golden Gate, they had been gone four years and one month, and they had been prisoners of the Japanese 1,332 days. Now they were home. Nothing in life ever looked better to them than the sight of the great bridge sliding overhead. The ship docked, and they raced down the gangplank and kissed the ground.

America the beautiful—some other Wake men who got off together at San Francisco, a little tribe of four, booked themselves a great big room in a great big hotel, called room service for an enormous container of ice cream, gallons, spooned it all out on the bed, took off their clothes, and rolled around in it.

∷

SLUG Wright came home the other way, out of Southeast Asia. The overall operation there was called RAPWI, Recovery of Allied Prisoners of War and Internees. For every one POW to be repatriated through Japan, there were more than two in Southeast Asia, from more than twice as many camps, more than 250 in all. And multiples more civilian internees than in Japan and the Philippines combined: men, women, and children by tens of thousands, most of them Dutch, but other nationalities mixed in. Plus hundreds of thousands of stranded rōmusha. Plus more than six hundred thousand Japanese troops, not all of them necessarily convinced that the war was really over. And on top of everything else, revolutionary wars of independence were breaking out—the

colonies of French Indochina and the Netherlands East Indies starting to turn themselves into the nations of Vietnam and Indonesia,
brown people struggling up from under the boot of yellow empire
and determined not to go back under the boot of white empire.

Out through all of this came the POWs, by the campful from
Java and Sumatra and Borneo, by the trainload from the far reaches
of the Burma-Siam railroad, gaunt, hollow-eyed, in rotten rags,
skin flaking off in dirty brown patches, the stink of the jungle and
the stench of dysentery upon them. And civilian internees from
the Indies camps, including women with their children. Many
of the youngest boys and girls had not seen a white man for the
better part of their life. They would not have recognized their
fathers. And their fathers would not have recognized them, little
boys and girls grown older but no taller, with stick legs and the
distended bellies of malnutrition, hardly knowing where they were
or who they were. When the food drops came down over those
camps there were children, starved on rice, who did not know
what to do with bread—they tried to peel it.

· This was the stuff reprisals were made of, more serious in
Southeast Asia than in Japan. And in the universal fashion of reprisals, it was not always the sufferers themselves taking revenge.

Some British troops had a bunch of Japanese, about a hundred,
cooped up on a swampy little island at the mouth of the Irrawaddy
River in Burma. The Japanese were from a railroad unit, meaning
from atrocity country; they had watched thousands of POWs and
rōmusha die. The British were not actively killing them for being
war criminals, just watching through binoculars and doing nothing
as they turned hungrier and hungrier, hungry enough to have to
catch crabs from the river. They had no firewood, so they ate the
crabs raw; they got amoebic dysentery and died.

On the island of Bougainville, off New Guinea, some Japanese
were lined up at a small airstrip to surrender. In came the victorious
Allies, two men in a reconnaissance plane. They landed, taxied
close, and machine-gunned the Japanese where they stood. A
planeload of Australian POWs were coming out of Java, badly ill,
five of them blind. They put down at Balikpapan on Borneo, and
the Australian troops on the ground there were so appalled at the
sight of them that they shot two Japanese. On the little island of
Labuan, off Borneo, heavy POW traffic was coming through; the
Australians in charge on the ground were holding Japanese prisoners, and the sound of gunfire was in the air, regularly.

Another Borneo story had surrendered Japanese being force-marched for miles, thousands of them to start with, only hundreds at the finish. Not that there was bayoneting and shooting along the way, like Sandakan-Ranau, just that the forced march was deliberately through headhunter territory. At least that was the story.

There were Korean guards being shot on the grounds of the hospital at Nakom Pathon in Thailand. Korean guards everywhere were going after Japanese guards; the Koreans had been kicked like dogs for years, now they were biting back. On Java there were kempei, Japanese jailers and torturers, in jail themselves now, with Indonesians torturing them. Other kempei, plus regular Japanese troops, were dragooned to help the Allies keep order in the Indies. Indonesian nationalist uprisings were breaking out; there were riots, natives massacring Dutch civilians, attacking internment camps, raping Dutch women. Whites in uniform, Dutch or not, were being killed from ambush, and there were not enough white forces to get on top of it all. So the Japanese were made to help. That was a strange spectacle—yellow skins and white skins, enemies yesterday, fighting together against brown skins today. And it was complicated still more by some of the Japanese turning their arms over to the revolutionaries, some even joining them.

Slug Wright had the good luck to be off to one side of all the turmoil and violence. His way out of Asia was like a walk through the park.

After the railroad, he had been drafted from base camp at Tha Muang into northern Thailand, on a detail with some other 131st men and some Dutchmen, digging tunnels and building airfields. The moment word came that the war was over, his homing instinct cut in and he began heading for Texas. Some of the Dutchmen on the airfield detail had worked for American firms in the Indies before the war, and they made up a Stars and Stripes for Slug out of handkerchiefs they found in a warehouse, using Mercurochrome for red, a mixture of zinc oxide and cow's blood for white, and for blue, Japanese mosquito netting. Slug mounted the flag on a bamboo pole, and with a little 131st tribe under this American banner, he hitched everyone a ride on a rice truck to a railroad station. From there they rode an empty freight car to a town with a big modern hotel, where they had drinks on the house. They told a dapper Japanese major they wanted to go to Bangkok. He said he would be happy to arrange it. He took some chairs from the hotel lobby and put them in the back of a truck, and off they went, sitting up there taking their ease, with Slug still flying the Stars and Stripes, all the way to the Bangkok kempeitai headquarters. They were directed to a big warehouse across town, and who should be there but more men of the 131st, some of them old ulcer cases of Slug's from base camp. That night the Thais threw them a party, with food and booze unlimited and a Victrola playing "Yes, Sir, That's My Baby" over and over. Next day, up came an American in coveralls, galoshes, and a beard. He was OSS; he had been undercover in Bangkok for months. He asked Slug, *Have you got a roster?* Slug said, *No, if I had a roster I would have smoked it.* The OSS man said, *Can you get all the guys together?* Of course Slug could, and he did. The OSS man told him, *You've got the green light.* Out to the airport they went, and piled into C–47s, and just like that they were off.

Flying north and west, they were looking down on the railroad. It was a mess: whole stretches bombed out, base-camp sites turning back into jungle already. Good luck to the rōmusha who were still trying to get themselves out of there, and peace to the rōmusha thrown dead into the river—all that was left of them was middens of bones exposed on sandbanks. On up to Burma. Farewell to the thousands of prisoners buried along the track, men from the 131st and the *Houston* among them, dead and moldering in their graves in the hills where Bandy Galyean blew Taps. Over Moulmein, Slug could see the pagoda. Then came a shock. The plane was fired on from the ground, a Bofors ack-ack gun. What on the peacetime earth that was about no one could imagine, and the pilot did not linger to ask. He made for Rangoon. They stopped there for refueling, and for something to eat, coffee and a smoke, and they were gone again, to Calcutta.

Ambulances met them at the airport, to take them in for hospital tests. They wanted to be on their way home. So if they judged a question about a medical problem was likely to hold them back, they answered no. To everything else they said yes. *Do you have malaria?* No, said Slug, even though he did. *Do you still like girls?* There were white women all around the hospital, and they looked very white, except for some who looked yellow. Slug and the others thought privately that they must have been in Asia too long, but then they found out about Atebrin, the antimalaria substitute for quinine, and how it made the skin turn color.

The Calcutta hospital was a strange place. An army captain was taking his psychological tests in full uniform, except that he was barefoot, curling his toes around stones and carefully placing them in a neat little pile. Blucher Tharp was there, the colonel of the 2nd Battalion of the 131st, carrying letters from the family of a man who had been dead a long time. Of course the family had no way of knowing that. Tharp was going to have to be the one to tell them when he got home. He was sitting reading the letters, and down the ward there were men playing a record over and over to learn the words, something ridiculous about one meatball.

It came to Slug that he was alive and more or less well and on his way home without any idea of what had happened to Doc Hekking. He had not seen Doc since the British had him shang-haied away from base camp at Tha Muang. If ever there was an honorary American, Doc was the man, and Slug was seized with the urge to carry him to the United States. He found a pilot who was flying to Bangkok, and asked him to see if he could locate Doc. Amazingly, the pilot managed to track Doc down. He brought back a message: *You tell my friend Slug I would love to come with him, and if I was single I would.* But Doc had a wife and children, he had no idea where the Japanese had interned them, or even if they were still alive, and he had to stay and search for them.

So Slug had nothing holding him back. He got himself up and away again the first chance he had, on a big, beautiful C-54 with seats. It was a long haul to Cairo, then Tripoli, then Casablanca— with a stopover there to clean up at a wonderful hotel, supposed to be the one where Roosevelt and Churchill had met in 1943— and then across the Atlantic to New York.

It was the thing for planes bringing Americans home out of captivity in Asia to do a figure eight over Broadway and around the Statue of Liberty, to announce their touchdown. Slug stepped out onto American soil waving his Mercurochrome-and-cow's-blood Stars and Stripes.

His first day on the loose in New York, he went looking for new eyeglasses. It was a miracle that he still had a pair of lenses intact. He had been beaten up from Bicycle Camp to Burma, all the way along the railroad, down to base camp, and up again into northern Thailand; but he always managed to protect his glasses, snatch them off and hold them. When his frames got broken he taped them, and on the railroad a man did a soldering job for him. Then he had some tin frames made, and they served, even if everyone said they made him look like a Model T Ford with headlights. Those were the headlights he was navigating by when he hit New York.

He went into an optometrist's shop on Fifth Avenue and they said, *My god, what have you got on?* He told them, and they were more than happy to fix him up with new frames, for free. The only payment they wanted was a picture of him wearing the old ones, so they took a snapshot, and away Slug went in New York tortoiseshells.

He decided he wanted new shoes, too. He saw a sign for Florsheims, and they had a pair of loafers, his size, 9½ AAA, the best-looking things he had seen in years. But it turned out that to buy shoes, a serviceman had to have a stamp and his commanding officer's signature. Slug had never heard of the stamp arrangement, and his CO was still in Calcutta.

So he took off for home in his old shoes. At the railroad station he asked for a ticket to Texas. They said, *Are you kidding? Don't you know there's a war on?* Slug was not unaware of World War II, but it was his understanding that it was over. So he did not bother about a ticket, just got on a train for St. Louis and sat down. Some ladies came in. Slug could tell he had one of their seats. He told them where he had come from and where he was going, and they said, *Be our guest, sit right there.* The ride was a long one, and on the way he had a malaria attack. The ladies called the conductor and they looked after him. By St. Louis he was fine again. He got off and did the same thing again, all the way to Dallas; and then to San Antonio, reporting in at Fort Sam Houston, only a hop, step and jump from the Wright home. A nephew of his, who was a night editor with Associated Press, came out, and they took a picture of him in front of the Alamo with his Asian-made POW's Stars and Stripes—Slug Wright, 2nd Battalion of the 131st Field Artillery, part of the 36th Division with its T for Texas patch, Houston Tom Wright of the Texas Ranger Wrights, back on tribal ground.

From beginning to end of the war, no one at home in Texas knew for sure what had happened to the 131st. After they were captured on Java they disappeared, they were called The Lost Battalion, and the *Houston* survivors disappeared with them.

John Harrell kept a record of *Houston* men as prisoners, where they went and what happened to them, keyed to numbers indicating camps on Java, then the railroad in Burma and Thailand, drafts, transports, deaths. He wound up with thirty-one different numbered destinations and destinies, and that was only up to April 1944, when he was drafted away from the service record book.

After that there were *Houston* men shipped to Japan, between five and six dozen of them. Some did not make it; they were on hell-ships that were torpedoed. Some only got as far as Saigon. One of those was Otto Schwarz, an original New Jersey Dead End Kid at Bicycle Camp. On the railroad he was separated from his own little tribe. He wound up with some Australians who were named to a Japan draft. He wanted to go along. He and an Australian who did not want to go swapped identities, but the Japanese found out, so instead of seeing out the war as an Australian in Japan, Schwarz finished as an American in French Indochina. By 1945 there were three *Houston* men on Borneo, five on Sumatra. And close to the end of the war, two escaped in Thailand and were picked up by the OSS.

With the 131st it was the same story: move after move, separation after separation; Tanjong Priok, Bicycle Camp, Changi. E Battery and the technicians' draft were shipped to Japan early. On the railroad, in camp after camp, men were left behind sick and dying; after the railroad, there were drafts to Japan, and deaths on the water. In the Japanese home islands, some were shuffled around, others moved as far as Manchuria. Frank Fujita was in Tokyo, eight blocks from the emperor's palace. Dozens from E Battery were in the Nagasaki area when the bomb went off. And Slug's original tribe, F Battery, the Jacksboro boys, were scattered from hell to breakfast.

Now, by different routes from Asia back across the Pacific, then at different speeds across the United States to Texas, and at last along two-lane blacktops and down dirt roads, the Jacksboro boys were coming home. For a bunch of country lads, most of them still in their early to mid-twenties, they had gone the long way round in life. Take Sid Matlock. He was one of the majority being sick over the side of the *Republic* on the way to *PLUM*. He was in the hotel at Malang on Java the night the sergeant shot out the chandelier. On the railroad he was the one who thought he was going to have to cook his shoes and eat them. He came out of Asia through Burma, and at Rangoon he ran into, of all possible RAPWI nurses, two sisters raised in Jack County. As of the moment he got off the bus in Jacksboro, he had not seen the town and the town had not seen him for more than four years. It was late in the day, in the dusky dark, and he still had to get out to his folks' farm. A pickup truck going by jammed on its brakes, the driver stuck his head out, and called, just as if he had spotted Sid coming out of the soda fountain, *Matlock, you want a ride to Ante-*

lope? I don't have room up front, but if you don't mind riding in the back, get in back there. When they came to the Antelope crossroad, Matlock gave a knock, climbed down with his suitcase, hollered *Thank you,* and the pickup went on. That was all their conversation, and Matlock never did know who the man was. He dropped his case over the fence in a field so he would not have to carry it, and walked on in the dark, a mile and a half to home. There was no light burning in the house; his mother and father had gone to bed. The door was open, the way it used to be. He did not knock, just went on in. Before the war his folks had no electricity, and with everything as short as it was, they were not going to have it still. Matlock knew where his mother kept the lamp setting, and he knew just where the matches would be in the cabinet, so in the dark he went and got a match and came back and lit the lamp, and his father called out, *Son, is that you?*

In October the 131st held their first reunion, in Wichita Falls. There was a parade, speeches, a barbecue in the park, and a great time was had by all. Not quite everyone was back home yet, so the next month they had another one, in Abilene, after which some of the boys went on to party for ninety days. The thing to do was to buy big cars—Frank Fujita went for a twelve-cylinder Lincoln—and drive around in high-speed convoys, and drink, and chase after pretty girls, and drink and drive around some more; and if a red light halted them, and if there was a pistol in the glove compartment, why, then, the red light was at risk for reprisals.

While Slug Wright was at home with his family in Floresville, he went through all the *Life* magazines his mother had kept for him since he went away, and that was an amazement. There were pictures of the Louisiana Maneuvers of 1941, and then the war, from start to finish, all the way to the A-bombs.

After a time he felt himself to be back in the world securely enough to think of picking up where he had left off in life, and to go to work again for Standard Oil of California. He went out to San Francisco. The big wheels at Standard had him to lunch. They asked him to tell about being a POW, and by the time he finished some of them were in tears and they said they would fix him up with a service station. To Slug that sounded perfect, sitting around, getting up every thirty or forty minutes to put gas in a tank—better than the railroad and a poke in the eye with a sharp stick from a Japanese guard.

He still had Doc Hekking on his mind. As it happened, across the way from the Standard of California office on Bush Street was a Dutch business house. Slug talked to the people there and they could not do enough for him; they sent cables everywhere they could think of. Slug sent one of his own, to the *Bangkok Chronicle*. Back came an answer: Doc had just left for Celebes. Slug tried to send a cable to Makassar. No good— the cable company said their connection was still down from the war. But the Bangkok paper printed an article, which was reprinted in a Dutch paper, which happened to be read by a Dutch merchant captain headed for Celebes, and at Makassar this captain looked for Doc and found him.

Doc wrote to Slug to catch him up. At the end of the war they had missed each other in Bangkok by a couple of days. After that it took Doc months to find his wife and children. They were in an internment camp near Makassar, sick with pellagra. They were getting better, but things in general were still nowhere near back to normal. They were living in one house with four families, Doc the only male, and their only furniture what the Japanese had left. They were short of everything. Slug made up a big package, food, stainless steel knives and forks, and medical journals to bring Doc up to date on his profession. Slug tried to send it direct to Makassar, out of Long Beach, but that did not work; the package had to go around the world the other way, to Amsterdam and from there to the Indies. It took months, but it got there. And the important thing was, Slug was back in touch with Doc. He did not want to be out of touch ever again. Anything he could do for Doc he would do, for the rest of his life.

Standard of California made good on their service station offer. Slug picked Oceanside, a little town on the coast between Los Angeles and San Diego, and he was in business.

He still had some way to come back in strength. He walked on the beach, and drank a lot of chocolate malts, and the day dawned when he found he was used to the sound of a woman's voice; it did not unsettle him anymore, and he felt like dating again. He tried church, and he tried the bars, but the marines from the base outside of town had all the girls. Then he met a WAC, a little girl from Brooklyn: They got on well, and when she was going to relocate to San Francisco, Slug was moved to propose.

A wife, a home, a business—Slug was assembling a life after prison camp. He was a positive thinker, putting being a POW behind him. Except when the movie he went to see happened to be about the war and a fighter plane flew across the screen; then he hit the deck under his seat and it was minutes before he could get up. And he had nightmares all the time; in one of them he fought a tiger all around the bedroom and woke up with big marks on his arms where he had bitten himself.

::

PUT *it behind you*—that was the military doctors' prescription, and it was exactly what every freed prisoner wanted to hear. Medical officers and POWs were together in a well-meant conspiracy, all wanting to believe that it was just a matter of saying the words. The doctors ran the men through their checkups double-quick. *They looked down my throat and couldn't see bottom, looked in the other end and couldn't see daylight, and that was that.*

In their tens of thousands, the POWs were officially stamped by their government as liberated from the past. And then at home on their own they ran into themselves again as prisoners.

Forrest Knox had it worse than Slug. For a POW trying to put things behind him, Janesville, Wisconsin, was a bitter place, because of the hundred men who went away with Company A of the 192nd only thirty-five came home.

The rest—meaning two out of three—died as prisoners of the Japanese, horribly, all over Asia. Two dead on the march out of Bataan. More than a dozen dead at Camp O'Donnell, of dysentery, malaria, beriberi, and diphtheria. Seventeen dead the same awful way at Cabanatuan. Half a dozen dead on work details. Fourteen dead on hellships. One last seen on the docks at Moji. One dead on Formosa, one dead in Korea, one dead at Mukden. And five machine-gunned and burned to death in the massacre at Palawan.

Of all the brothers in Company A, only the Knoxes, Forrest and Henry, both got back alive.

They were the ones who drew the duty of talking to the families of the dead, and they had to carry that load for years, because bodies kept being found, identified, and brought home for burial, one at a time.

Forrest took it upon himself to be in on every funeral, a pallbearer, or firing the salute. Some of the coffins he shouldered were empty, he knew that, but a Gold Star mother needed a grave and a marker for her mourning place. Gold Star mothers—there were so many of them around Janesville, and they all wanted to know every detail of what happened to their boys. Or they thought they

did. Forrest knew terrible things about the way men died as prisoners of the Japanese, and he could not bring himself to tell their
mothers. He lied a lot, and was sure it was for the best.

Some of the others who came back would simply say, *I don't
remember.* They took to saying it even to other Company A men.
Even to themselves. They believed they were putting things behind them.

Sandy Sandmire truly did not remember. He was the one who
got Forrest onto the truck detail in Manila. They were on the
Farm together at Cabanatuan, and that was where the guards
bashed Sandmire on the skull until he developed memory loss.
Back home, he did not remember anything between capture and
liberation. Otherwise he was fine; he was holding down a good
job at Oscar Mayer in Madison. He even liked to hear about prison
camp. Forrest would tell him stories, and Sandmire would say, *Is
that right!* Then straightaway he would forget.

But Forrest—walking down the street in broad daylight, not
thinking of anything in particular, he would see someone from
Company A coming his way, he would have a sudden happy feeling, starting toward his friend to greet him, and then a sick shock,
because he was seeing a dead man.

This happened so often that he stopped wanting to go into
town. He had bad physical problems as well. Hookworm from Las
Piñas. An ulcer. Eyes so bad he could not read a sign across a room,
a residual of vitamin deficiency. And a crazy eardrum; when he
had a cold and blew his nose, air would come out his ear, from
getting bashed in the cookhouse at Cabanatuan. He checked himself into the big army medical center at Battle Creek, Michigan,
and did not come out for a year. In among the amputees and the
paraplegics he would have nightmares and wake up drenched in
sweat. He would sleepwalk and come to in some terrible Japanese
camp in his mind. Or he would have waking flashbacks to the
Harō Maru, the black hole, the madness and the killing.

::

IN THE terrible arithmetic of POW deaths, Forrest's tribe had it
far worse than Slug Wright's: 65 percent of Company A of the
192nd Tank Battalion dead compared with 21 percent of *Houston*
men and 16 percent of the 2nd Battalion of the 131st Field Artillery, and 12 percent of F Battery, only eight out of sixty-five Jacksboro boys.

The 131st and the 192nd were both small units. One drew the railroad and wound up with a death rate only half as bad as the overall American average; the other drew the Bataan death march, O'Donnell, and hellships, and wound up with a death rate twice as bad as the American average.

As for the men from Wake Island, 16 percent of contractors died in Japanese hands, compared with only 3 to 4 percent of marines. The differences was not hard to understand. The marines were younger and fitter than the contractors; and as a disciplined tribe of POWs, marines were the ultimate.

Taking Wake marines and Wake contractors together, their survival rate was much better than the overall American average, and better than the average for POWs of all nationalities. That could be attributed to the fact that the Shanghai camps, Woosung and Kiangwan, miserable as they were, were above average for food and health. And the Wake men did not have to contend with the major killers: the death march out of Bataan, the Burma-Siam railroad, the hellships. In the black book of POW life and death, though, half the Wake men who died as POWs were outright slaughtered by the Japanese.

For all nationalities of POWs together, the death rate was 27 percent. The American rate was higher, 34 percent; so was the Australian rate, 33 percent; and the British, 32 percent. What brought down the all-nationalities average was the much lower figure for the Dutch: under 20 percent. The Dutch were scorned in the camps for being Dutch. But whatever it took to be a POW, the Dutch were the best at it, by far.

The war in the Pacific was not on the scale of the war in the European theater. Especially on the Russian front, the fighting was of a much greater order of magnitude, and a much higher percentage of prisoners wound up dead—possibly 45 percent of Germans captured by the Russians, 60 percent of Russians captured by the Germans, and bodies by the million.

Something else to note: Whatever the barbarism of the Japanese in occupied territory—and their atrocities against civilians were massive in China, the Philippiness, and Southeast Asia—they did not aim at total extermination of whole categories, of civilians the way the Nazis did with Jews, Slavs, and Gypsies. When POWs of the Japanese like Slug Wright and Forrest Knox saw the *Life* magazine photos of the ovens at Auschwitz and the bodies at Belsen, they had no way of coping with the hideous scale of it, any more than any other ordinary human being did.

Still, the POWs of the Pacific war saw huge piles of their own dead. The piles of POW dead on the eastern front in the European theater were bigger, and the piles of Nazi concentration camp dead were bigger and more awful still; but the POWs of the Japanese were not in competition over the size of piles of dead, they were in sympathy.

They had one special irony to reflect upon. The Nazis, who did such terrible things to Russians in the east and to Jews everywhere, nonetheless observed the Geneva convention for military prisoners taken on the western front. The Japanese, who did such terrible things to Asian civilians everywhere, did not observe the Geneva convention for white POWs. So—take two brothers in uniform, American, Australian, or British, and assume that one was captured by the Japanese, the other by the Germans on the western front. In German prison camps, the POW death rate was only 4 percent. In Japanese prison camps, it was 27 percent. The Japanese camps were seven times more lethal. To be a prisoner of the Japanese was like being caught in a twentieth-century version of the Black Plague, a Yellow Death.

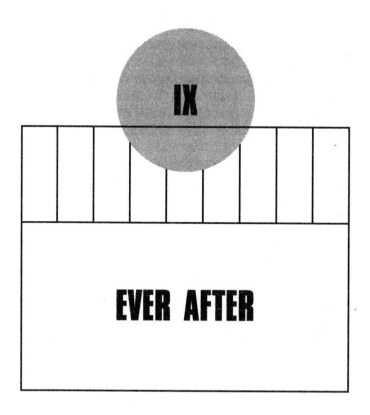

IX

EVER AFTER

Asia under the Japanese was a charnel house of atrocities. As soon as the war ended, evidence of war crimes began piling up, in mountains. POWs, civilian internees, and Asian natives starved, beaten, tortured, shot, beheaded. The water cure. Electric shock. Vivisection. Cannibalism. Men strung up over open flames or coiled in barbed wire and rolled along the ground, nails torn out, balls burned with cigarettes, dicks cut off and stuffed in mouths. Women dragged naked behind motorcycles, raped and ripped open, babies skewered on bayonets. Cities in China and provinces in the Philippines laid waste, mass murders in the Indies, towns and villages wiped out, all the way to the remotest of small places in the Pacific, the island of Nauru, where the thirty-four sufferers in the leprosy hospital were taken out to sea and drowned, and Ocean Island, where days after the war ended all the native laborers were pushed over a cliff.

The Japanese were responsible. But which Japanese? And how should they be made to pay?

The Allies defined three classes of war crimes and criminals. A Class referred to top men like Tōjō, policymakers who conspired to wage aggressive war. B and C Class referred to men who ordered atrocities, allowed them to happen, or actually committed them.

To try A Class criminals, the International Military Tribunal of the Far East, IMTFE, was established in Tokyo. For B and C Class criminals, each Allied nation held trials in the area where the crimes had been committed.

In Japan itself, the name at the top of the war criminal list was Tōjō Hideki. Tōjō had been prime minister, war minister, and home minister. He was the one who said a POW who did not work should not eat. He knew that this led to barbarous treatment: sick men being driven out to slave labor that would kill them. He knew about the Bataan death march and the Burma-Siam railroad, the terrible rates of sickness and starvation and death, and he did nothing.

Less than two weeks after the formal surrender on September 2, an arrest order was issued for Tōjō. He had made preparations. He was going to shoot himself. He got a doctor to mark the exact position of his heart on his skin in black, with the soot that was used for Japanese brush painting, *sumi-e*. The American military police came for him, with a crowd of reporters. His house was surrounded. A voice shouted, *Tell this yellow bastard we've waited long enough. Bring him out.* Tōjō had an American service-issue handgun, probably taken from a downed airman. His son-in-law had used it to commit suicide at the end of the war. Tōjō aimed at the mark on his chest and pulled the trigger. The MPs broke in. He was alive; he had missed his heart. The press photographers took pictures of him lying bleeding from a sucking, frothing chest wound, and everyone dipped pieces of paper in the blood for souvenirs. He was taken to an American military hospital and kept alive with transfusions of American blood and units of American penicillin. He recovered; and on December 8, 1945, four years to the day after Pearl Harbor, he was transferred as an accused A Class war criminal to Sugamo Prison in Tokyo.

The day before, Yamashita Tomoyuki had been sentenced to death by an American military court in Manila. In the first months of the war Yamashita was the Tiger of Malaya, the general who took Singapore; and at the last he was the Japanese Army commander in the Philippines, standing off Douglas MacArthur to the bitter end. Yamashita was not being accused as an A Class criminal, but his trial was historic just the same: He was the first ever high-level officer of a defeated army to be tried by the victors for command responsibility, specifically for atrocities committed by his troops in the Philippines. His trial was an American showpiece, held in the ballroom of the old United States high commissioner's residence; the grounds were overrun by reporters and cameramen, the streets outside were packed, with ice cream vendors working the crowd.

Massacres in the city of Manila, massacres in the guerrilla country of Batangas, the massacre of POWs at Palawan—the testimony was overwhelming and appalling. But there was no evidence that Yamashita had ordered atrocities, and little evidence that he even knew about them at the time. Specifically concerning POWs, Yamashita had not set out to kill them; in fact, he had made positive moves to get them out of the way of the war.

The betting in the press room was that Yamashita could not be convicted. But he was. He was sentenced to death by hanging—the ultimate ignominy for a professional soldier—and buried in an unmarked grave.

Then came the trial of Homma Masaharu. He was charged with command responsibility for crimes in the Philippines at the beginning of the war: bombing Manila after it was declared an open city, refusing quarter to the American troops on Corregidor, and—specifically concerning POWs—allowing the massive atrocities of the death march out of Bataan, and the disgusting atrocities at O'Donnell and Cabanatuan that followed. Homma was found guilty. In April 1946, four years to the month after the fall of Bataan, he was executed by firing squad; not allowed to wear his general's uniform, he was killed by a ragged volley from fifteen paces, only three bullets through a white patch sewn over his heart.

Homma and Yamashita were the two Japanese generals who had given Douglas MacArthur the most offense in the place dearest to his heart and most essential to his ego, the Philippines. They were done away with rapidly.

For the rest, the war crimes trials were going to be a long haul. The investigators and prosecutors started out with several hundred prospects for A Class criminals, and wound up with just over two dozen actually tried and sentenced. As for specific crimes in the B and C categories, the Allies developed a list of more than three hundred thousand, and they stopped only because they had to stop somewhere. If they had had inexhaustible investigative and prosecutorial resources, they could have brought scores of thousands of Japanese to trial. They wound up trying only fifty-seven hundred-plus.

Even at those low numbers, the work load was immense. It was eased by trying defendants in job lots, taking a batch of atrocities in a given camp or in a given area and prosecuting a batch of Japanese together. That was Allied military justice, and it could be speedy: an accused C Class criminal arrested Saturday, before the court Monday, executed inside a week.

High-priority cases, though, involving large numbers of victims and big batches of defendants, could take months. And with the A Class criminals, the trial took years: The indictment was ready in April 1946 and it was November 1948 before the verdict was handed down.

From arrest to conviction and sentencing, Tōjō and the other accused generals and politicians spent their time in Sugamo Prison, along with hundreds of B and C Class criminals tried and sentenced close by at Yokohama.

This was not as prolonged a captivity as the POWs had suffered in Japanese prison camps. Sugamo was a modern jail, not a jungle dung heap. And it was not a place of atrocities, not an Outram Road. But still it was a prison; it was where Japanese war criminals, from generals and cabinet ministers to camp guards, learned what it was like to be a prisoner.

They were stripped and body-searched coming in. There were surprise inspections; they had to stand naked in their cells while the guards tossed everything—they called this The Sugamo Storm. The guards eyed them while they were bathing and shaving, and did body cavity searches in case any war criminal had hidden a bit of razor blade to kill himself with later. When they were allowed outside to exercise, they had to walk in circles, and they wore a stereotyped prisoner's path inside the fence, going nowhere. Their minds emptied out. They came down to meditating on the social life of cockroaches and peeing on ants' nests for a pastime. They turned into buttsnipers. They had to put up with each others' meannesses and bad habits, cabinet ministers bribing the cooks with cigarettes, senior officers snatching the biggest slices of bread and jumping the bath line, the man who sang too loud, and the old man with a white beard that shed; he was saving the fallout and making a hairball. Such was the life of the jailed war criminals, all the irritations and exasperations of confinement, with an underlay of atrocity. One man waiting to be tried was cooped up with a medical officer responsible for atrocious deaths and a major who shot the crew of a B-29, and his main complaint about them was that they were constantly farting.

The higher class of Japanese war criminal found the American guards uncouth. They were young, many of them under twenty. They were forever talking through the barbed-wire perimeter fence to Japanese whores in the street, negotiating prices. Around the cell they were noisy, singing, clapping hands, playing the harmonica, practicing dance steps. They had a dance hall just beyond the barbed wire, and at night the music would penetrate into the cells. That and the awful noise from the upper floor of the jail, B and C Class criminals sentenced to death, some of them out of their minds, shouting at the top of their lungs.

The execution block at Sugamo was in Building 5-C, and it was busy. The standard method of execution for Japanese war criminals there was hanging. The firing squad was used much less, at Sugamo or anywhere else. The Chinese way was a bullet in the back of the head, in public. The Dutch shot some behind prison walls. Most of the time the others used the noose, at Changi in Singapore, Manila, Rabaul, and Hong Kong.

At Shanghai the British had a hangman, a jailer himself before the war, then interned by the Japanese in his own jail, at Ward Road. For hanging Japanese, he used the classic British method of calculating the drop: inspection of the condemned for weight, height, age, and body condition. At Changi another British hangman did more than just look through the death cell spy-hole; he would go in, give the subject a warm sympathetic hug for the purpose of feeling his neck, and speak in a warm confidential British voice right into the subject's Japanese ear: *I'm going to rip your bloody head off.*

The United States Navy had hanged fewer than a handful of men in more than a hundred years: a few mutineers in the 1840s, then no one until a Samoan in the 1930s, and no one since then. Now on Guam they had all kinds of Japanese to try and sentence to death, from high-ranking cannibals who ate the flesh of downed airmen in the Bonin Islands, to the admiral who ordered the massacre of the ninety-six prisoners on the beach at Wake and killed one of them personally. They had to requisition an Army executioner to show them how to hang. He was a lieutenant with silver-rimmed glasses, a leading-man moustache, and a paunch. He used the traditional British drop formula, but he was an innovator as well: He invented a method of lowering the dead body to the stretcher without having to cut the rope.

As for the U.S. Army in Japan, ex-POWs volunteered their services, with specific Japanese from specific camps in mind. *If you need me to find them I could show you the exact place free of charge. I will gladly pay for the ammo to shoot them. Just get me there, gentlemen . . . I assure you I am very serious.* John Cowalski, who carried out one execution with a shovel on Guam, made an open offer: *I am at complete liberty, available any time.* His offer was not taken up. At Sugamo a hangman came in from the provost marshal's office at Yokohama. His routine was to report a couple of days early, go straight to the officers' club and get blind drunk; and the guards would put him in a cell in the hospital area to sober up ready for work.

Hangings at Sugamo were always in the middle of the night. They were never announced to the other prisoners. One day a batch of condemned men would be out on the exercise walk, barefoot and handcuffed; the next day they would be gone. On the gallows they shouted *Banzai,* like true Japanese soldiers. One of the hood and lever men who sent them off volunteered for the job because he had a brother who was a POW at Fukuoka 17. It was his hangman's sport to spring the trap before they could get out a third banzai.

All through 1946, 1947, and 1948, while the B and C Class criminals were being sentenced and executed, the A Class criminals were being tried before the International Military Tribunal of the Far East.

What with the endless litany of charges about conspiracy and aggressive war, it took until December 1947 for the tribunal to come to crimes against POWs, and after this evidence was heard, the rest of the trial on other counts took until November 1948.

Of the twenty-five accused who were brought to judgment, nine were identified as being heavily involved in running the POW system, nineteen as responsible for breaches of the laws and customs of war against POWs. Those were not their only crimes, and not the only basis for sentencing: In the overall IMTFE judgement, crimes against POWs took up only about one tenth of the 1,445 pages. Of the eight men convicted of crimes against POWs, four were sentenced to death—four of the total of seven A Class death sentences.

Tōjō was one of the seven. From the day of sentencing, he and the rest of the condemned men were under twenty-four-hour surveillance at Sugamo. They were manacled to guards every time they were moved in or out of their cells; they had to do their walking exercise manacled to MPs. They were watched every second while they ate and bathed and used the john. They were made to sleep with the light on, head toward the doorway, face and hands always in view.

They had a Buddhist priest to prepare them for death, helping them with final statements and wills, recording their posthumous names, taking hair and fingernail clippings for their family shrines, collecting personal effects—books, papers, prayer beads, eyeglasses, false teeth. Tōjō had trouble with his teeth during his trial. The American chief of dental surgery at Sugamo, a U.S. Navy reserve officer, made him a new upper denture, and Tōjō was so pleased with it that he gave him his old three-unit gold bridge to remember him by. What Tōjō did not know was that on the new denture the dentist had engraved a message in Morse code: *Remember Pearl Harbor.* Those words were in Tōjō's mouth all the time he was testifying, until the story leaked out by way of loose lips in a bar, and the dentist's superior officer made him erase the message. Tōjō never knew about any of this. The dentist told him the denture needed cleaning, the cleanup job was done, and the message was erased, long gone by the time Tōjō took out his teeth to be hanged.

He was sixty-five. He weighed 130 pounds, and he was short. His hanging drop was seven feet six inches.

He was executed with the others, seven old men, bald and toothless, shuffling to the scaffold in GI salvage clothes, to be hooded and noosed and hanged in the first frost-cold midnight minutes of December 23, 1948. Four, including Tōjō, were hanged together, then the other three. The bodies were trucked in the dark to a crematorium outside Yokohama, burned to ashes, and the ashes were scattered—no Japanese was ever supposed to know where.

As for B and C Class death sentences, war-zone-wide, there were two for command responsibility for the Bataan death march. The commandant of Cabanatuan got death, the commandant of O'Donnell life. For the Burma-Siam railroad, there were thirty-two death sentences in all, from senior officers to guards. For Out-

ram Road jail, a couple of officers were hanged; for
Sandakan-Ranau, one. For the *Oryokko Maru,* two. For the *Nitta
Maru,* the ship that took Harry Jeffries and Oklahoma Atkinson
from Wake to Shanghai, none. The guards who had chopped the
heads off five Wake prisoners on the way got life. The guard officer
who gave the orders was never brought to judgment—the story
was that he killed himself when Japan surrendered. Ishihara Isamu,
The Beast of the East, who beat up Harry and Oklahoma at Kiangwan, got twenty years—not for beating them, not even for the
death of the old man who died hanging off a stake beside them,
but for water-cure tortures. The doctor at Shinagawa, where Harry
was sent when the Kawasaki guard hit him with the tongs and
paralyzed his hips, got death for using POWs for medical experiments. When he heard the verdict he went catatonic, and they
had to feed him through a tube in his nose. Then the sentence
was commuted and he came back to life; in two weeks he was
asking for his medical books. Blood and Slime, Mori Masao and
Kasayama Yoshikichi, a plague upon POWs from Java to the Moluccas and back, were caught and tried. Blood was hanged, Slime
got life. And in Batavia, Sone Ken'ichi, commandant of Bicycle
Camp in Slug Wright's last weeks there, got death from the Dutch.
Not for Bicycle Camp, though—Sone was put in charge of a big
women's internment camp later on, and he turned into a sadistic
madman. The Dutch doctor at his execution was Gerrit Bras, a
POW himself. While Bras was suffering on the railroad and then
at Fukuoka 17 in Japan, his wife was suffering under Sone. Bras
pronounced Sone dead, took his brain out, and used it as a specimen in his pathology classes.

What percentage of Japanese war crimes and criminals were accounted for by the trials is impossible to determine. It can be said
with certainty, though, that justice was nothing like complete, not
even substantive.

The percentage of all sentencing that was directly for crimes
against POWs cannot be precisely calculated. Besides the POWs
who suffered and died atrociously there were the white internees,
roughly as many of them as there were POWs, and multiples more
Asian civilians. In any of those categories only a small percentage
of victims had their cases heard.

Twenty-five A Class criminals were convicted and sentenced,
7 of them to death, 16 to life. Five thousand seven hundred-plus
B and C Class criminals were brought to trial, about 3,000 were
convicted and sentenced, 920 were executed.

Leaving white civilians and Asian natives out of calculations, and imagining that every one of those sentences was for crimes against POWs, that would still work out to only 1 Japanese sentenced to prison for every 50 POWs who spent three and a half years in prison camp, and only 1 Japanese executed for every 250-plus POWs who died atrociously. Far short of an eye for an eye.

The way the Japanese looked at things, though, the whole operation was victor's justice, meaning no justice at all, merely the all-powerful Allies taking bloodthirsty vengeance, consigning powerless Japanese to death and calling it morally right.

The Japanese judged the war crimes court system to be arbitrary and peremptory, trying the accused in batches and hustling them off to execution. True enough, those military commissions worked fast, and they did not go by strict rules of evidence or meticulous rules of procedure. There were chronic difficulties in identifying defendants. To white men, all Japanese looked alike. Their names were hard to pronounce, much less spell, much less decipher in Japanese writing. And, often enough, guards were only known to POWs by nicknames. And what if the prosecution's evidence was not given by eyewitnesses who could be cross-examined in court, but instead taken from affidavits written by POWs thousands of miles away about things that allegedly happened years ago. How could defense lawyers contend with that? Especially considering that, more often than not, the defense lawyers were not even Japanese, but white men assigned by the court. So, accused Japanese were being tried for life and liberty in a language they did not understand, struggling to make their case through lawyers they could not speak to directly, dependent on interpreters, and at the mercy of a bench of military officers who might or might not have any legal training—but who were in a hurry, under orders to be speedy.

And then, what about the other weighty questions raised by the fact that race and culture were being forced in the roughest manner through the coarse mesh of military law? What was the true moral situation of a Japanese soldier being tried for doing things to white prisoners? In the Japanese Army, and to a Japanese prison camp guard, a slap on the face was nothing—but in a war crimes trial it was blown up into something huge. *Five years a slap:* That was the arithmetic the C Class criminals put on it among themselves—there were even those who rated one slap at ten years, two slaps twenty years, three slaps death.

And what about violent deaths in the camps? Say a guard killed a prisoner. In one camp or another, that happened every day. But what if the guard was only carrying out orders? Would an Allied soldier have done any differently?

In fact, orders or no, did Allied soldiers do any differently from Japanese soldiers? From beginning to end of the war, the Japanese saw Allied troops committing atrocities. But after the war only the Japanese were called war criminals. And a Japanese guard jailed for trial as a war criminal could get the same abuse from his white guards as he was accused of having dealt out to his white prisoners: humiliation, intimidation, threats, beatings, torture under interrogation. The Japanese wanted to know where the justice was in that, let alone the morality.

Above all, what was a war crime and what was not? What kinds of acts were justified in war and what kinds were not? If the Bataan death march and the Burma-Siam railroad were crimes against POWs, what about the dropping of the A-bombs as crimes against humanity?

Accept for the sake of argument that there really was something called command responsibility, and then imagine that the Allies had lost the war. Would Truman and MacArthur have been hanged? And should they have been? These were unanswerable questions, unresolvable moral problems.

Each of the Allied nations had its own style and approach to prosecution, with different rates of conviction and execution, and so to this extent defendants were at the mercy of chance. The Australians were especially fierce. An Australian soldier being tried before an Australian military court would not have been subject to the death penalty even for murder, but the Australians in their war crimes trials set about hanging and shooting Japanese in job lots.

They wanted to hang Hirohito. They were not the only ones who wanted this, but the emperor was never brought to trial. Douglas MacArthur was among those against trying him, and that was how the agreement was struck, at the highest level of national and international policy.

There was another class of Japanese that MacArthur did not want to see tried: the men who ran Unit 731 at Pingfan. In fact, he made sure they were never brought to court. If ever there were Japanese war criminals, they were the ones. Their lethal medical experiments on living prisoners were atrocities as morally disgusting as anything in the twentieth century. But the American military had a use for advanced research in biological and chemical warfare. So MacArthur cut a deal with General Ishii Shirō: immunity in return for information. For MacArthur, the lives and deaths of the maruta, those thousands of suffering prisoner bodies, were worth nothing, legally, morally, humanly.

The only nation to bring any Japanese from Unit 731 to trial was the Soviet Union. The Russians convicted twelve, from a lieutenant general down to a private: no death penalties, two years for the private, twenty-five for the general—plus a loud public accusation that Ishii and the rest of the morally guilty were safe in hiding under the wing of MacArthur. Which was true.

The reasoning behind MacArthur's deal with Ishii was that World War II was over and done with and the Cold War was beginning. World War II had been the Allies versus Japan. Now the Cold War was the Soviet Union versus the United States. Even if the Japanese were the implacable enemies of the United States only a few years before, now it made sense geopolitically and strategically to have them in place as a barrier against the Russians, the new enemy. So, with the war crimes trials still nowhere near complete, a new kind of haste overtook the old—haste to wind things up and sign a peace treaty with Japan.

Immediately after Tōjō was hanged in December 1948, a large group of other A Class criminals were released from Sugamo, and that was the end of A Class trials. At the same time, the Americans began winding down their B and C Class trials, and the other nations did too. Every month made it easier for war criminals to evade being brought to trial at all, and not nearly so likely that any brought to trial would be hanged. After April 1950 no one was hanged at Sugamo. By then there was a push for general commutation of sentences, for parole, for clemency. By April 1952, when the peace treaty went into effect, the Allies were emptying their war-crimes jails in the Asian region, sending criminals to serve the rest of their sentences at Sugamo, where the prison administration was turned over to the Japanese. Year by year the numbers in the cells at Sugamo dwindled: more commutations, more clemency. The longest sentence any Japanese war criminal served—A, B, or C Class—was less than thirteen years. As of December 1958 the last war criminal was a free man again.

And by 1958 there were war criminals back in big business, and in national politics. Sasakawa Ryō'ichi, an accused A Class criminal held in Sugamo but never tried, was freed. He was working with the CIA and the *yakuza,* the mafia of Japanese organized crime, against the Japanese left wing, and he was on his way to making multimillions out of a gambling monopoly. Kodama Yoshio, another Sugamo prisoner freed without trial, was also making money playing both ends against the middle, politically, commercially, and criminally. Any number of Unit 731 civilian scientists were back doing academic research at prestigious universities. Lieutenant Colonel Naitō Ryō'ichi, the 731 officer who brokered the immunity-for-information deal with the Americans, was in partnership with another high-ranking 731 officer, Lieutenant General Kitano Masaji, and on his way to becoming a millionaire in the business of commercial blood—and a member of the New York Academy of Sciences.

Outside of Unit 731, if ever there was a Japanese war criminal it was Lieutenant Colonel Tsuji Masanobu. He was everywhere in the war, trailing atrocities. He was in China in 1937, massacring. At the fall of Singapore in 1942 he was responsible for the massacre of thousands of Chinese, and for the killing of scores of white prisoners, doctors, nurses, and patients at Alexandra Hospital. He was on Bataan when the death march began, telling everyone the emperor wanted all prisoners killed, and out on the death march road there were sightings of an officer who looked like Tsuji, killing. He was in Burma in 1944, saying his body carried bullets from five countries, that no bullet could kill him, and eating the liver of a downed airman. Tsuji was never brought to account. At the end of the war he disappeared from view. But by 1948, before the end of the A Class trials in Tokyo, and while B and C Class crimes everywhere were still being investigated, he was back in Japan. He was never so much as questioned. By 1952 he was visible in national politics, highly so—elected to the Japanese parliament.

Shigemitsu Mamoru, who had been tried with Tōjō as an A Class criminal and sentenced to seven years, was foreign minister again by December 1954, and by 1956 he was negotiating with the American secretary of state for the release of the remaining A Class prisoners still serving time at Sugamo. And Kishi Nobusuke, arrested as an A Class criminal in September 1945, held at Sugamo, never tried, and released after the A Class executions in 1948, went into national politics in 1952. By 1957, while there were still war criminals in jail, he had risen to be prime minister of Japan.

With every year in the postwar period, the clearer it became to the POWs that though the Japanese might have lost the war they had won the peace. Time went by. Harry Truman died, Churchill and Stalin and Chiang Kai-shek too, and MacArthur, but Hirohito lived on. In the 1970s he made a world tour. The queen of England restored the royal decoration the British had taken away from him at the beginning of the war, and the only ones who saw anything wrong in that were POWs. They demonstrated, the demonstrations were reported on the inside pages, and life went on; the world kept spinning, and the Japanese kept spinning it their way.

By the 1980s they were all over Asia again, and not only that, they were invading America; there were Toyotas and Hondas everywhere. The Japanese were *the* world economic superpower; they had the old Allied powers bowing like prisoners.

To the POWs it looked as if Japan owned the future. As for the past, as early as the 1950s an association of kempeitai started meeting to keep alive the memory of the great old days, and by the 1970s and 1980s they were congratulating themselves on being the most active veterans' group in Japan. The Unit 731 scientists were an active group, too. They called themselves *Seikonkai,* Refined Spirit Association. In a cemetery in Tokyo they had a 731 memorial tower, dedicated not to the maruta but to the memory of their own kind.

As early as 1960, the hanged A Class war criminals had a public monument, inscribed *Tomb of the Seven Martyrs.* And it turned out that the night they were hanged and their bodies were burned, some of the ashes were secretly spirited away from the crematorium for their private family shrines.

In 1971 Sugamo Prison was razed, cleared for high-rises and a park; and on the spot where the gallows stood a stone was placed with an inscription, a hope that the tragedies of war would not be repeated—which tragedies not specified.

Then in 1979 the executed A Class criminals were enshrined at Yasukuni, close to the emperor's palace, where the spirits of Japan's glorious war dead were gathered. Yasukuni Shrine had public exhibits, from the blood-soaked uniforms of heroes of the Russo-Japanese War to World War II memorabilia of the *kamikaze,* the suicide pilots, and the *kaiten,* the human torpedoes. On the grounds was a locomotive from the Burma–Siam railroad, present at Konkuita the day the two ends of the track were joined, and kept polished at Yasukuni over the years by a preservation society of old railroad regiment soldiers, the ones who had forced the work through the jungle in the speedo, leaving POWs and rōmusha dead by the tens of thousands. In the inner sanctum of the shrine, behind the sacred sword and mirror of the emperor's cult, was the written register of the spirits, with the names of Tōjō and the other war criminals, in the company of Japanese soldiers who had died by the millions fighting for the emperor. High-ranking Japanese politicians made official visits to Yasukuni—on Hirohito's eighty-fifth birthday the prime minister made a point of it. Whenever the day came for Japan to rise again in war, the spirits at Yasukuni would rise with the emperor's armies.

::

IN THE immediate postwar years, when Japanese war criminals were learning how to be prisoners, the POWs were having to relearn how to be free men, and it turned out to be a life sentence. Home was supposed to be perfect, exactly the way it used to be. But it was not, nothing like it, and a lot of men could not reconnect, body or soul.

On the way home sex was high priority. *The second thing I'm going to do is take my pack off.* But it did not always happen right away, and it was by no means exactly the way it used to be. There was an ex-POW joke: *If I don't do it every day I'm miserable, and I'm miserable every day.* Sometimes the problem was physical. Or it might be another kind of devastation. The girlfriend might have gotten married. Worse, the wife might have gotten a divorce. Or worse still, she might have come to believe her missing husband was dead and married someone else. Of all people for that to happen to, it fell upon the senior chaplain at Cabanatuan, Robert Taylor. Or, just as terrible in a different way, and something that happened much more often, a husband coming home and the wife waiting for him found they had turned into strangers. Or a child might not recognize its father or want to accept him. That happened to John Nardini, a medical officer captured in the Philippines. His son would not hold his hand. Nardini had to train him to it by stages, persuade the little boy to hold on to the end of a stick and inch his way up.

At the POW's end of the stick, any kind of intimacy could be a problem. Glenn Self, F Battery of the 131st, came home to Texas and found he had no heart. He had been on the railroad; he was an ulcer case with Doc Hekking and Slug Wright in base camp afterward; he had seen friends die horribly, skeletons buried naked, with the burial detail cursing the chore of cutting the tendons in the bent legs to straighten them out. The only way Self could get himself through it was to go dead to feeling, and at home he was like that for months. It was not until an uncle of his died and he went to the family funeral that he finally felt something stir in his heart again.

So, close to home it could be difficult. And around town it was hard to reconnect, too. People had moved away. Or if they were still there, they had been living their own lives. They had no conception of a Japanese prison camp. And either they did not want to know, they rattled on about the horrors of gas rationing, or they asked ridiculous questions, *Didn't you get bored eating rice every day?*

That kind of thing made the POWs strangers among their own hometown folks; it pushed them back into themselves, among their own isolated kind, prisoners of the prisoner tribe.

In Janesville, Wisconsin, before the war, Company A of the 192nd used to drink at Wellenkotter's, across the alley from the armory, and after the war there would always be some of the boys huddled at the bar, not nearly as many as before, because for every one who came home alive two were dead, but at least some company.

In Jack County, Texas, the meeting place for F Battery of the 131st was the Jacksboro courthouse lawn. Jacksboro boys turned up there every day, sometimes several times in a single day. They went from the courthouse to home and back to the courthouse, and this went on for months. It took them the longest time to wind down again to anything like Jack County speed.

There were POWs everywhere who could not stand to be around for long in the place where they were born. On the spur of the moment they would bail out, Englishmen heading for the woods, Australians going fishing, staying away for however long it might take before they could bring themselves to come in from the wild, then disappearing again somewhere else—with no certainty even that they would be back for their first family Christmas. Mel Forsman, home by way of the sinking of the *Houston,* Bicycle Camp, the Burma–Siam railroad, and Outram Road jail, would go to football games by himself and sit in his car drinking Four Roses; and then one day he went out for a drive and did not stop till South Dakota.

There was an Australian boy who had been a cobbler on the railroad, fixing boots for the workers and the Japanese, too. Compared with laying track in the speedo, it was a soft job. But he did not rest easy; he did his work in front of the dysentery hut, and all day he would carry dysenteries who could not walk to the latrine, getting filthy himself. Not many would have done that. Back home at his mother's house he killed himself. A boy from D Battalion of the 131st lasted less than last six months before he shot himself. And there was a little American tribe out of the Philippines, eight men, who had an agreement that if they were not making it at home they would kill themselves. By 1947 six of them had done it.

Death by gunshot wound. Death from cirrhosis of the liver, far more than there should have been among young men. Fatal one-car accidents. Year after year men went that way. It was hard to talk about.

Better to concentrate on how the living were doing. And, all things considered, most were doing well, the way Slug Wright was: a steady job, marriage, normality. Or at least they were able to give a working imitation of normality. Inside, they were not normal. At home or out at a restaurant, if they saw someone leaving food on the plate they might be seized by the urge to shove it in his face, or her face. After a while, though, they could bring themselves down to quietly cleaning their own plate, or at most being the one who made sure the leftovers got saved for the dogs. A man honest in every way before the war would catch himself shoplifting. For a POW it was so easy it was irresistible, it happened without thinking. But given time, the ratlike scrounging impulse could be brought under control. Just back from the war, a respectable smoker would find himself lurking by the butt can in the foyer at the movie theater, or squirreling butts away in his pockets, and even when his wife chastised him he could not stop himself. Nicotine still had the power of the camps. Monroe Woodall, E Battery of the 131st, smoked his free man's American cigarettes—unlimited quantities, pennies a pack—as though each one was going to be his last. And nearly every ex-POW was a hoarder. To feel secure they needed months of provisions in the house. Hoarding went beyond food, to the ridiculous: keeping stacks of old magazines in case they ceased publishing, pack-ratting all manner of things until the basement was crammed to bursting. Kelly Bramlett, Headquarters Battery of the 131st, used to do that kind of thing. His wife would get mad at him, and he would dutifully start piling junk on the truck to dump it; but before he had a load he had it back in the basement.

That was one kind of POW extreme. Overplanning was another; making ready for a day trip was like an expedition to Tierra del Fuego. Or hair-trigger touchiness. Not being able to take orders on the job. Or hating loud noises. Or not being able to handle standing in line, especially at a buffet loaded with food, but even waiting for a ride at Disneyland. Or hearing about someone trapped in a well, or a cave-in, and being upset for weeks. Or not being able to bear the constriction of tight clothes. Or not being able to go to sleep without socks (this one was from the Japan camps in winter). Or having to start the day with a thirty-minute shower, get dressed in clean clothes, then go straight back for another shower.

If a POW did not have one of these behaviors he had another, and many men had more than one: private madnesses of all shapes and sizes. The best they could do was keep their most extreme and inexplicable weirdnesses to themselves.

Whenever Frank Fujita turned on the tap for drinking water he always poured just a little extra, for the private luxury of not needing it; and who else but another POW would ever imagine that in his mind Fujita was back in the hold of his hellship, Singapore to Japan, the guards doling out half a canteen of water in ten days, men going crazy from thirst.

::

HARRY Jeffries and Oklahoma Atkinson never talked about their POW days. They had a silent agreement. They were back on the town in San Francisco, and the pressing questions of life were the same as before the war, whether the steaks were rare enough, the hotel beds soft enough, the blondes on the barstools classy enough. Of course those were POW questions now as well, just not talked about as such.

They had never stopped planning on their gambler's version of the POW's dream house, their club with class and a game upstairs, the one they had gone to Wake to bankroll. Four years of their lives had gone down a filthy drain, and they came out with nothing but the clothes they stood up in. But it did not take them long to get into the game again. They put a proposition to a knowledgeable man about town; he checked out the way they dealt the cards, and he staked them—lease, liquor license and all, protection included—against a percentage of the take from the game.

It worked out perfectly, until their knowledgeable man crossed a man more knowledgeable and got himself killed. They lost their protection, and they were out.

Not out in the cold; they could still do well with a deck of cards, operating as a team the way they used to. But for some reason they were never as tight in the postwar peace as they had been in prison camp.

If Oklahoma bought a diamond ring, Harry had to have a bigger one. If Oklahoma bought himself a new car, a straight-eight, Harry had to have the next model up, the convertible with the twin smitties.

Going into his mid-thirties, Oklahoma was losing some of his appetite for the game, at least the remorseless way Harry wanted to play it, so he quit and went back to being an ironworker on civilian contract jobs with the military. The only gambling he did was on the side. Harry kept playing professionally. Then, just before Oklahoma went out to a long job, which happened to be on Guam, Harry borrowed a chunk of money from him. While Oklahoma was away he fell seriously ill, with a burst appendix. He had to come back. He was in bad shape, down to 130 pounds, POW weight. He was down in funds too, and of all things, Harry would not give him his money back. Harry was wearing a big diamond ring and driving a Cadillac, but he just looked down his nose at Oklahoma, the friend who had given him his soup in prison camp to keep him alive, and talked him off the hot wire. Oklahoma went up into the mountains and got in shape, walking miles, swimming, doing sit-ups. He came down, found Harry in a fancy restaurant wearing a tuxedo, and swung on him. The two of them wound up in jail overnight, and the brawl was an item in Herb Caen's column. After that they did not have much to do with each other.

Oklahoma was always on the move: Guam again, Alaska, Thailand, anywhere, living rough in work camps with hundreds of other men, into his middle age. He was still gambling on the side. One time he was in Las Vegas, waiting for a friend to come in from Houston; the friend was a day late, and in that twenty-four hours Oklahoma dropped $12,000. Another time he worked for twenty-nine months on Kwajalein in the Marshall Islands; he came back with $100,000 and spent it all. It struck him that he was old enough to know better. He said to himself, *I believe I'll quit these big casinos.* He stayed in contract work for the military, gambling at night on base, until he started feeling too old for that as well. The young boomers were faster and better with the cards than he was. A strange change came over him as he got older, something he would not have predicted: he developed an aversion to swearing. He had heard a lifetime's worth of cursing in prison camp, and he did not want any more. So he quit construction work. In his fifties he came to rest, semi-retired, married to the widow of a Wake contractor from the old days, living in Reno. The air agreed with him and the big casinos were just down the way, but the most gambling he did anymore was a flutter on the football cards.

If the mood caught him right, but only if, he might take off for a day or two and drive to a Wake contractors' reunion. The committeemen were never all that enthused to see him turn up, because he never paid the registration, just bellied up to the bar and the buffet. He would have a beer or two, show the boys how he used to work the cards with his educated finger, the one missing a joint, and that was enough for him, he was gone. He knew everyone's POW stories by heart; he had no interest in turning into one of those old farts sitting on the dead-pecker bench gumming over the same tired stuff year after year.

Harry never went to reunions, and he never joined a single ex-POW organization. He wanted nothing to do with organizations or institutions. That was how Harry had been before he was ever a POW, and he was even more so afterward; and it applied across the board, all the way up to the United States government.

He came back from prison camp believing more strongly than ever what he had always believed, in fact he was consumed by it: The world owed him, and now it owed him double for being a POW. His way of recovering was never to pay taxes. He gambled, kept a hundred cents on the dollar, and called it a matter of principle.

He would go crossroading, hit a small town, get into the game over the barber shop, clean out the local sharpies, and take off at speed in his convertible. He would walk into a little gambling spot in Nevada after midnight, quiet except for a single table with some poker action, and sit at the bar, nursing a beer, listening to the fall of the cards; and his ears were so sharp he could pick up the sound of the dealer second-carding.

Harry and Las Vegas were made for each other. He was there from the early days of the big casinos. He knew everyone, up to Bugsy Siegel. He did exceptionally well, until management realized he was counting the cards at blackjack. He was one of the first in Vegas to be banned for being smart enough to beat the system. He stayed around, though, through the years when the Nevada desert was being used for nuclear testing, because he liked nothing better than a private poker game with atomic scientists, superbrains who thought they were supersmart. They would play for high stakes and Harry would take all their money, the super-smartest beating the supersmart.

He had safe-deposit boxes of cash everywhere. He could afford the best class of blondes, any number. And over the years he got married seven times, chorus girls and starlets. He was Hollywood Harry; one time he honeymooned on Errol Flynn's yacht.

In bed he did fine. Besides working a deck of cards, screwing was his special skill, and he figured that one of the things he was owed from being a POW was three and a half years of sex his way, with compound interest. That entitlement was part of his appetite for women, part of his potency.

But he was sterile from prison camp. He never had any children after the war, just the one from before, from his first wife, and he never saw anything of that child.

He got older, the wives got younger, the marriages shorter. Oklahoma came to the seventh wedding. It was years since he and Harry had seen each other, and now they were not against getting together again for old times' sake, even if some of the water under their bridge had turned muddy. Harry still had his Hollywood hair and Hollywood moustache, but he had gone gray. Not that Oklahoma had anything on him for youthful good looks, he was bald and a bit paunchy himself; but he laughed and told Harry, *You look like an old gray rat.* Harry was pushing sixty, his seventh bride was seventeen. *Goddamn,* he said to Oklahoma, *this is the first time I ever had to drive my wife to school.* Oklahoma told her he had slept more nights beside Harry than she was going to. He was right. This marriage was the shortest one of all. She was quick to leave Harry, for a man thirty years younger who owned a high-class dress shop.

Harry never talked to any of his wives about being a POW. Even married to a woman, he could not trust her enough. In fact he trusted no one, man or woman. He never wanted anyone too close to him. His way of putting it was that he had lost his relationship with the human race in POW camp and never got it back.

He was like every other POW; he had a front for the world. He was always Hollywood Harry, spending any amount on clothes and grooming. He had a closet full of dark suits and white-on-white shirts, and a bathroom cabinet full of hair oil and aftershave and deodorant. On the dark side of the looking glass, though, that cabinet was the warehouse for his POW behaviors. He was forever in the bathroom, washing his hands.

And he had nightmares, filled with the smell of rotting flesh, the Japanese beating him bloody. For a long stretch in his late middle age he was addicted to tranquilizers. He went to psychiatrists. But he could never bring himself to tell them the truth about what he had done in prison camp, trading to the death.

He was at the end of his seventh marriage when he had a stroke. He was not disabled; looking at him, no one would ever know. With only half the brain he used to have, he could walk and talk and think better than most, and he was still a snappy dresser. But it was the end of his edge for gambling. He was not the smartest anymore.

He lived by himself with a deck of cards and time on his hands, but solitaire was not his game, there was no gain to it. He still had the strength of his one unshakable conviction, that he was *owed*. The stroke did not disconnect that part of his brain. He spent the rest of his existence not paying taxes and at the same time going after the government for compensation. Even though technically he was a civilian, he had fought in combat, and he wanted proper veteran status. And a Purple Heart. And 100 percent entitlement to medical benefits for POW-related disabilities.

::

CONCERNING compensation, Harry was the most extreme of extremists. With him it amounted to a pathology. But one way or another every POW had the question on his mind, and not unreasonably so.

In prison camp the most wonderful rumors were the ones about all the things a grateful country was going to shower upon the POWs once they got home; free this, all you can eat of that, a lifetime supply of the other.

The reality was next to nothing. The only thing a POW of any nation ever got was his back pay, plus, years later, some miserable pittance per day of prison camp.

The Allies sold Japanese business assets they had seized at the outset of the war, and distributed the proceeds among their POWs. The Thais bought their end of the railroad, the proceeds to be split among the prisoners who built it. It was a slow process, taking years, and out of it no POW received more than a couple of dollars per day of captivity.

Insult piled upon injury, the countries they had suffered for were letting it go at that. The peace treaty of 1951 was deliberately worded to tie off the issue of Japanese liability. Of all nations,

Canada did the best by its own POWs, or the least poorly. By the mid-1960s, the Canadian government was automatically granting a POW 50 percent disability, and the POW was entitled to prove more, up to 100 percent. That had taken twenty years, and no other country was close. POWs of other nations made their own calculations about governmental meanness. Canada had had only two battalions of POWs taken by the Japanese to begin with, so the Canadian government could look after the survivors on the cheap; whereas in the other countries there were tens of thousands of POWs, meaning a far larger money commitment, and the politicians were fobbing them off, doing what politicians always did, putting pork barrel ahead of life and health, even the life and health of men who had suffered for their country.

If one tribe of POWs was treated worse than the others, it was the soldiers from KNIL, the Dutch colonial army in the Indies. They had had the hardest time of all—three and a half years as prisoners like everyone else, and then straightaway they had to put on their uniform again and fight the Indonesian national revolutionaries. The Indonesians won. Which meant that the Indies Dutch did not have a country anymore. For them home was not Holland but the Indies, yet Holland was where they were forced to resettle, or else try to migrate to the United States or Australia. The Hague had a big tribe of them. Their saying was, *The Hague is the widow of the Indies.* The Dutch home government disowned them, left them orphaned. They had been soldiers of the Dutch queen, but when they applied for compensation as POWs, the queen's government refused them. They were told that KNIL had ceased to be a Dutch army the day of the surrender in 1942. If they believed they were entitled to compensation for what happened to them in the Indies after that, let them apply to the government of Indonesia. Unbelievable. It took them (and the Dutch civilian internees) the better part of forty years to squeeze a token payment out of the country they had suffered for.

Physically, the POWs never stopped suffering. In the first ten years after the war, while most of them were still young, only moving out of their late twenties into their thirties, their death rate was higher by far than that of civilians of their age, and considerably higher than for war veterans who had not been POWs. By age forty, proportionately far more of them were dead. After that, somewhat surprisingly, the differential in death rates narrowed. But life was hard for them. They had to hoist themselves through middle age in damaged and disabled bodies. There were men who could not see well, hear well, walk well; their bones creaked, their feet hurt, or their legs went numb; they were harboring tropical parasites, and their guts were constantly in spasms, not to mention that their minds were still in uproar just under the surface. Stand them together for sick call once more, and the lineup would show mental pathologies—high rates of anxiety, depression, and insomnia—and all sorts of physical pathologies, cardiovascular, gastrointestinal, respiratory, urogenital, oral, ophthalmic, spinal and paraspinal, lingering parasites and infestations of worms. And all this they could trace straight back to prison camp.

The best they could hope for was to have a high percentage of their disability recognized for benefits and pension purposes. And this meant battling the bureaucracy for every percentage point. The United States was no different from anywhere else. The onus was on the POW to prove that his disability was service-related, meaning prison-camp-related. The Veterans Administration was not the POW's friend; in fact, the VA operated more like an adversary—unresponsive, skeptical, not ready to take a man's word about the beating on the Farm that ruined his back, not recognizing the aftermath of an ulcer from the railroad, simply not knowing and therefore not believing that beriberi and all the other deficiency diseases of the camps had long-term residuals.

The POWs grew older and the VA doctors got younger, until there were doctors who were not even in school when the POWs were captured. What did those beardless boys know, what could they know? They had barely heard of World War II; they had no idea of a Japanese prison camp, the things that could happen to a POW's body and mind, and they were not interested to take time to listen and learn.

Surviving POWs were just that, survivors. They were sentenced to a long carry with a heavy load. It weighed on the body and it preyed on the mind, and only another POW could ever understand how much.

Dear Charles, . . . we can sure count our blessings that we are alive today and nor murdered like many of us were by those slant eyes baboons as I always called them. I am hoping that you and yours are in the very best of health. I have not been feeling that since I have leukemia, cancer, blackouts, nerves are play tricks on me and I get flash backs and I do not get much sleep for I seem to see the beatings and tha murder of our pals and I seem to hear thoes men crying for water and food that we seldom got and

I just get to sleep even if I take sleeping medications from the doctors at the mental health clinic and they said that my nerves are so bad—that I am subject to pass out and I have a letter from the doctors saying if the police see me stagger or pass out not arrest me for being drunk but to take to a veteran hospital for treatment.

∷

FORREST Knox was one more POW who could never bring himself to love the VA. He spent a year in the hospital at Battle Creek. He knew what was wrong with him physically and psychologically, and yet they discharged him with everything stamped *Denied*.

At least back in Janesville the dead men were not walking the streets anymore. But he never stopped seeing live men from Company A half-dead, turning old and worn out before their time. One man had gone blind in camp from vitamin deficiency; he wore a sign in Japanese on a string around his neck so the guards would not beat him for not bowing, and back home it took the VA doctors twenty-five years to translate that sign into American. Another man was deaf, blind in one eye, and diabetic, with one dead leg. The VA awarded him 40 percent disability. Another man, an alcoholic who screamed in the night, was given 10 percent, raised to 40 when a senator leaned on them. Forrest had seen better-looking corpses; he thought 110 percent and the VA to pay the liquor bill would fit the case. Another alcoholic, with lung cancer, was just hanging on. Two were dying of emphysema. Another had been dead below the knees since 1944 from beriberi; at home he fell over a lot and they said he was drunk, which much of the time he was, but he fell when he was sober, too. The VA ruled that none of his falling was POW-connected. And all of the above was happening well before any man from Company A was old by the calendar.

Forrest had his own load to bear. He managed to hold up under the weight. He settled down and found steady work as a mechanic, twenty-six years at the one shop. He had a first marriage that turned out bad, then a second one in middle age that turned out much better. He was a member of the Veterans of Foreign Wars, and the American Defenders of Bataan and Corregidor. And the Janesville target-shooting club, not that he could sight well enough to see a target, much less hit one. He liked to go hunting, not that he could see well enough to put a deer in any danger; mainly he was there for the cooking and the lying. He went to reunions, and he was the opposite of Oklahoma Atkinson; he liked hearing all the old stories. And telling them. It helped with his mental pain.

Not that the pain healed altogether, but some, enough that the memories did not smart so much and he did not have so many nightmares. It was as if the wounds to his mind were not so open and bleeding anymore; they were closing. He was marked by them for life, but at least they were forming scar tissue.

The problems that finally got on top of him were physical: bad eyes, heart, diabetes. He had to retire before he was sixty, and he died at sixty-eight.

Oklahoma Atkinson did not make it to seventy, either. He stayed in Reno, except when he had to check into the VA hospital in San Francisco. Once in a while he had the feeling that he would like to go back to Wake, to Woosung and Kiangwan, and Kawasaki, and up to Sendai, just to look things over. He never did; he had too many miles on him already. But even staying put in one spot, things kept coming back to him, from more than halfway around the world, more than halfway back in his life. Strangely enough, most times it was something funny, like fixing the frog races at Kiangwan; and remembering would make him smile. One day he was out puttering around in the garden, smiling, and he just fell over.

Harry Jeffries was another who did not make it to seventy. After his stroke he was more alone than ever. On his shelves he had a year's supply of everything, canned goods, matches, flashlight batteries, toilet paper, deodorant and disinfectant, soap, and creams for keeping his hands immaculate. His apartment had to be spotless; he had cleaners in every week, and he rode them about their work like a prison camp guard. He still had nightmares, loathsome with the smell of rotting flesh. And the Japanese were still coming to get him. He took to sleeping with a pistol under his pillow.

He kept going after the government for his 100 percent disability, writing his congressman, hiring lawyers; and every year he was closer to needing the 100 percent. More and more parts of him were malfunctioning: heart, brain, belly, bowels. After his stroke he was impotent, and that hurt him; he was miserable every day. He was turning into nothing but a sick old man. He reached the point where he had thirteen different medications on his breath. Then he was diagnosed with emphysema. He was certain that it was from breathing copper dust in the mine at Sendai 7B.

He had to go onto medical oxygen. Then he had some chest X rays taken, and lung cancer showed up.

He decided not to go on living. He made up his own mind when to go, and how he meant to go. He wanted to be buried as a veteran, in a military cemetery, with a flag on his coffin and two buglers for "Echo Taps." When he had everything taken care of, he unhooked his medical oxygen, lay down on his single bed, and took an overdose of pills. He left a tape cued up on his stereo with a message telling the person who found him to play it—the country song about the gambler, winning and losing, and the best way a man could hope to die, in his sleep.

Harry gone, Oklahoma gone, Forrest gone—for ex-POWs it was getting late in the day, forty, forty-five, fifty years on from when they were captured. Even boys who had lied about their age to join up at sixteen or seventeen were getting on in years. And on the clinical evidence, three and a half years in a Japanese prison camp aged a man physically ten to fifteen years. A POW coming up to his seventieth birthday was eighty or eighty-five years old in his body.

For those who were left, the last chance in life to square accounts with the Japanese came with the fiftieth anniversary years of World War II in the early 1990s.

Their own governments were not going to do it for them. So they got together, led by the Canadians, and put their case to the United Nations, asking for compensation in money, but—far more important to them—an acknowledgment by Japan that what had been done to POWs was humanly atrocious.

Compensation and a formal apology—the POWs were not the only ones wanting this, because they were by no means the only war victims still unrecognized and unrecompensed. Some slave prostitutes of the Japanese Army, comfort women from Korea, Formosa, the Netherlands East Indies, and the Philippines, sued Japan. Formosan men drafted into the Japanese Army sued. Chinese civilian laborers sued. Korean conscripts sued, among them prison camp guards claiming they had unjustly been made to carry the load of war crimes guilt. There was even a suit brought by some Japanese soldiers, men taken prisoner by the Russians at the end of the war and held as slave laborers in Siberia for years—they believed they were owed by their own government.

The comfort women were asking for $150,000 each, and who would have begrudged them twice or even ten times that—the

Japanese had forced them into the foulest of slave labor. The Chinese government in Beijing raised the ante, with the National People's Congress asking for $236 billion as reparations for what civilians had suffered. By comparison, the money bill the POWs presented was modest, amounting to only $10 per man per day. The apology was what they really wanted.

But they did not make any real headway with the United Nations. And the Japanese—of course—would give an inch only if they were absolutely forced to.

What made it all the more galling for the American POWs was that their own government made big payouts to other Americans who had been held prisoner in other places for other reasons. A handful of hostages held by Iran for four hundred forty-four days got $22,000 each. And more than a thousand anti-Vietnam war demonstrators who had to spend a weekend in jail sued their own government and were awarded $10,000 each.

Then there were the payments made to large numbers of Japanese for *their* suffering on American soil during the war—payments bigger by many multiples than the POWs had received or were ever likely to receive in their lifetime.

In the early months of the war, Japanese who were resident in the United States—aliens, naturalized citizens, and citizens by birth; men, women, and children—were rounded up and interned. They lost their liberty and their property. They were held in miserable camps under military guard. Without question their human rights were grievously abused. It took them close to fifty years to force the United States government to acknowledge this and to make restitution.

When restitution did come, though, it was on a scale that amazed POWs who were still waiting for Japan to compensate them, and who felt like they would be waiting till hell froze over.

The number of Japanese interned in the United States was one hundred ten thousand-plus, not all that many fewer than the number of white POWs of the Japanese, or the number of white internees of the Japanese in Asia.

So on the face of things there was a kind of comparability. But no matter how harsh conditions were in internment camps for Japanese in the United States, objectively—by death rates and disease statistics—there was no comparison with white civilian internment camps under the Japanese in Asia. And no matter how harsh those white civilian camps in Asia were, by the same rates of disease and death, and not even counting beatings, there was no comparison with the POW camps.

Yet now, fifty years on, with American POWs having to turn to the United Nations because their own government would not give them much more than the time of day, here was that same government taking all kinds of trouble over the Japanese internees: congressional hearings, federal legislation, a separate office with staff to handle the operation, fast-track paperwork, three short forms, even a toll-free number to call—even, of all things, special provision at the United States embassy in Tokyo for Japanese who had chosen to live in Japan after the war. It was less hassle than what a POW had to go through with the VA to make a claim for an additional 5 percent disability, with no guarantee of collecting. And the federal appropriation was $1.25 billion, amounting to a payout of $20,000 to any Japanese of any age, from infancy up, who had had to spend as little as one day of the war interned on American soil.

Liberals, and not necessarily only liberals, would say that the Japanese internees had been badly used. That was incontrovertibly true. The restitution program recognized as much. But with that said, compare the American government's treatment of the Japanese internees with its treatment of its own POWs, and what would be the correct thing to say?

On this subject there were not many liberals among the POWs themselves. Part of the bad feeling—in fact a large part, the most ferocious part—was racial. To most POWs, a Japanese was a Japanese was a Japanese. Not many POWs were willing to concede even that Japanese internees who were United States citizens deserved to be treated as citizens. Or that Japanese aliens were still entitled to certain constitutional protections, certain rights as humans. To most POWs, the Japanese had been and always would be the enemy in a race war. Now here were all these Japanese getting sizable benefits from the United States, while white American POWs were getting the short end of the stick from their own government, a government that was too craven to go after the Japanese government and force it to pay its moral debts.

And, on top of everything, in all the publicity, the internment camps for Japanese in the United States were being called *concentration camps*, making it sound as if they were an American version of Nazi death camps. Which, quite simply and objectively, they were not. Far from it. The death rate for interned Japanese, ages one to seventy-five, was no different from that of the American population at large. Objectively, comparing disease and death rates and beatings and torture, the POW camps in Asia were orders of magnitude worse.

Along the way, the site of the internment camp for Japanese at Manzanar in California was officially named by the federal government as a national historic landmark, significant in commemorating the history of the United States of America. It had a California state marker too, for tourists to read and believe, calling it a concentration camp. One old POW with a lot of miles on him—Bataan death march, O'Donnell, Cabanatuan, hellship, Japan, the VA wars—saw the story on the evening news, and it was too much for him. He got in his car, drove two hundred miles, his longest trip in years, and pissed on the plaque.

::

As THE POWs grew older, and especially after they retired, they went touring in Asia, traveling in memory. But, as one of them said, sometimes it was hard for memory to find a place to stand.

For a POW it was strange to land at Singapore at an airport called Changi, on top of the old prison camp. It was the same in the Philippines; it was eerie to set down at the Manila international airport and know that it was on top of Nichols Field, where one of the unluckiest details on earth had to slave for The White Angel, a homicidal dandy who killed with his own hands. Under the Manila tarmac, under the wheels of the plane as it taxied to the terminal, were POW skeletons.

Jess Stanbrough, Headquarters Battery of the 131st, who ran the secret radio at Bicycle Camp, traveled back to Batavia with his friend Wilson Reed. Stanbrough had done well for himself in military high tech; Reed had done well for himself out of Texas oil. Batavia was called Jakarta now, and where Bicycle Camp used to be there was a five-star hotel. The swimming pool was where Stanbrough's barracks had stood, where he would give his friends the news. The Brown Bomber would come in and beat the hell out of any man who did not *ki o tsuke!* quick enough, and Stanbrough would freeze and stare at a tree. A bit of the old tree was still growing in the hotel grounds. Stanbrough could make a right by the pool, to some gate pillars overgrown with vines; to the right of that again was where the guardhouse used to be, and Stanbrough could see Dub Reed at sixteen, hands tied, kneeling, bamboo be-

hind his knees, taking a bashing for getting caught smuggling copper wire in for the radio.

Slug Wright and Doc Hekking took a tour of their own. They
had stayed in close touch. Slug kept his vow never to lose contact,
and he was proud that Doc considered him his good friend. When
Doc's son Fred wanted to emigrate to the United States, Slug
sponsored him and looked after him till he got himself set up. Not
that this took long. Fred was a talented engineer; he wound up
doing important work in the space program. Slug was a good cit-
izen of Oceanside. He got elected to the city council, and served
as mayor. He was in on the development of the port. And the
hospital—one expression of the feeling for the human tribe that
was Doc's gift to him in the sick huts along the railroad. Slug was
a hard worker. He wore out two Standard of California service
stations and his heart. He had two coronaries, and after the second
one he retired, just shy of sixty. Doc retired too, in his late sev-
enties. They both liked the idea of traveling back together to their
POW days, so they did it. They took their wives, and Slug introduced his to wog tobacco, not that she thanked him for it.

The railroad was changed beyond recognition. The Burma end
had gone back to jungle. At the Siam end there were only seventy-
five miles of track, from Kanchanaburi to Tarsao, and Tarsao was
not called that anymore; now it was Nam Tok. Beyond there the
line was cut up for scrap, and up in the direction of the Thailand-
Burma border, north of Kinsayok, where the monsoon had washed
the cookhouse into the river during the speedo, everything was
going to be under water permanently, a dam for a big hydroelectric
scheme.

Kanchanaburi had a vast POW cemetery, and the whole area
around it was being turned into a tourist attraction, featuring something called the Bridge on the River Kwai. To POWs like Slug
and Doc this was hallucinatory. A Frenchman who had never been
on the railroad, a fiction writer, had written a novel about prisoners
of war forced to build a bridge for the Japanese. Then a Hollywood
film had been made, a wonderful movie that did huge box office,
only it had hardly anything to do with the novel, and less than
nothing to do with reality. And the steel bridge over the river at
Tha Makhan that the tourists kept photographing had nothing to
do with the wooden bridge in the movie; it was the one the Japanese had brought in in sections from Java. The river there was
not even properly called the Kwai; it was the Mae Khlong. Nothing had anything to do with anything except tourism. Every year

there was going to be more and more River Kwai tourism—River Kwai train rides, River Kwai boat rides, River Kwai air-conditioned bus rides, a River Kwai sound and light show with the noise of ack-ack guns, a River Kwai festival, River Kwai T-shirts, River Kwai souvenir stands, big Coke signs and hot dog stands, genuine railroad spikes for sale, fake Rolex watches and Gucci bags. Kanchanaburi was turning into a River Kwai zoo, and there were Japanese cars everywhere.

Slug and Doc could see this beginning to happen already when they were there. What could they do but pay their respects to the dead lying quietly in the cemetery, and be gone.

In 1990, a Thai who lived at Kanchanaburi started having bad dreams. He saw bodies in mass graves, and ghosts haunted him, begging him to help them. Near the railroad track bodies were found, close to the surface, hundreds of skeletons, some tied with wire, some in contortions as if they had been buried alive, one crouching with hands stretched up, trying to climb out. They were rōmusha.

The horrors surfaced in POWs' dreams, too. Even after forty or fifty years it did not take much to bring on a nightmare: a phone call from a friend who had been out of touch, reading a book about the camps, even something as trifling as a particular sound or smell. There were men who had bad dreams every night the first year after they came home, then no more. Over time, most were able to bring their nightmares down to one a month. There were lucky men able to sleep well the rest of their lives. But there were others who were never free, suffering a nightmare a month for fifty years, meaning six hundred nightmares, going on for two years of nights back in the horror of the camps. And there were men condemned to bad dreams every night, eighteen thousand nightmares and rising—a life sentence for being a POW.

In a trailer camp in the Midwest lived a prisoner from the Philippines, alone, with a whiskey bottle for company and a sawed-off pool cue for protection against whatever might be about to come through the door at him. Along the march out of Bataan he saw men die by the hundreds. At O'Donnell he saw them crawling under the huts to die by the hundreds. At Cabanatuan he saw them dying by the hundreds, in the Zero Ward, in agony. He could do nothing to save them, and it came to him that the best thing, the right thing, the merciful thing, was to help them die. So at night he would go over to the death hut and listen in the dark. He would pick out a man by the horrible rasp of his breathing, and take a pillow, and gently, out of terrible compassion, hush his moaning, calm him forever, and hope he was bringing repose to the soul. He was twenty when he did that. For forty-five years he never talked about what he had done; and when he finally spoke, it was as if he was still there in the dark in the Zero Ward, holding merciful death in his hands, and after he finished telling about it he banged his pool cue on the floor and said in his sixty-five-year-old whiskey voice, *Who nominated me to be God?*

He never went to reunions. There were a lot like him. Not that they had done what he did; but if they went, they would have prison camp nightmares in the king-size bed in the air-conditioned room. They suffered from post-traumatic stress syndrome. They felt guilt for having been captured, guilt for not having fought the war through like real soldiers, guilt for things they did in the camps to survive. They felt guilty just for surviving. They suffered the intimate and awful companionship of the dead, making eternal claims on them that they could never satisfy.

There were little tribes who got together only once in a lifetime. One such was from the *Arisan Maru,* the handful of men who made it away from the sinking and washed up on the shores of China. In 1983, after thirty-nine years, the four living survivors had a reunion. With the Rabaul prisoners, the handful of survivors of the prison tunnel, it fell differently. One of them, Jose Holguin, had gone back trying to find the wreck of his plane, and the bodies of his crew. He went to Japan too, to talk to the guards from Rabaul, and to an officer who had been good to him. Holguin came to the reunion in the early 1980s. So did three of the other four Americans still alive, John Kepchia, James McMurria, and Joseph Nason. The fourth one did not come. He had given up on life among his own kind, and had gone to live in the desert among Indians.

In Amarillo, Texas, a little tribe of men from the Philippines camps got together once a year, to eat a pot of what they called prisoners' sukiyaki: rice, millet, maize, dried fish, grasshoppers. There was another little tribe from the Philippines whose members lived in different parts of the country. They might not see each other from one year to the next, but they marked birthdays. They had an old khaki undershirt from prison camp that they mailed round and round among themselves for years.

There were men whose minds and bodies went off like pagers at certain times. Doc Hekking, the master treater of mind and body as one, had a back that gave him a wake-up call every year on the anniversary of his worst beating on the railroad, a bashing for not sending enough men out to die working in the speedo. One man from the *Houston* clocked four days every year when he had to tell everybody things they did not want to hear; he physically *had* to. Otto Schwarz put out a *Houston* newsletter regularly, several times a year, from his home in New Jersey. His basement was full of *Houston* documents; he was the walking memory of the *Houston;* and his wife used to say it was all he remembered anymore, the ship and the camps. Not true, but the lost *Houston* was freighted with the meaning of his life, and of course his wife understood.

Otto had been back to Asia several times. He went to Australia for the fiftieth anniversary of the sinking of the *Perth* and the *Houston*. And every year, barring illness, he went to the annual reunion of the 131st and the *Houston* survivors.

Their tribe was the world champion for POW reunions. Since 1945 the string had been unbroken. They always met in mid-August, the anniversary of the end of the war in the Pacific, when they ceased to be POWs and started being ex-POWs; and they always met in Texas.

Many of them still lived in Texas, and for the gathering of the tribe the others came in from all over the country. The hotel parking lot was full of out-of-state Winnebagos with special POW license plates, and never a Toyota among them.

The tribal ritual repeated itself, growing richer by the year. Days together with old friends, nights staying up late over a beer or several, telling the old stories. Formal sessions with solemn moments: the blessing, the salute to the flag. The election of officials for the next year. With other tribes, it might have been officers running the association as a matter of course, but not with this tribe, not beyond the very earliest reunions. Every name on the list of presidents called up the special history of the tribe. Lieutenant Roy Stensland, the enlisted men's officer—voted president two years in a row. Luther Prunty, Slug Wright's first gun sergeant—chosen two separate times. Onis Brimhall, who played "Deep in the Heart of Texas" on his guitar the first day at Bicycle Camp. Lester Rasbury, of Rasbury's Finer Fudge. Frank Ficklin, who shared bunk space with Jess Stanbrough and his secret radio. Zip Zummo, who punched the Englishman at Changi flat over the Red Cross food. Frank Fujita, who ate the British dog. Jimmie

Gee, one of the marines who held the ulcer patients for Doc Hekking on the railroad. Big John Owen, another holder. And Little Roy Offerle, whose brother died of an ulcer at 80 Kilo. Otto Schwarz, his mind with the *Houston* in memory-washed waters. And Jesse Bumpass, F Battery of the 131st—legally blind, but he kept putting out the battalion newsletter on his computer, faithfully updating his roster of the living and dead, the annals of the tribe on hard disk.

Every year the reading of the roll of the dead took longer. At the 1993 reunion an item came up once more that had been hanging fire for years. The old men of the tribe had been trying to get a plaque placed honoring their dead who died young. The problem was the language. The words they had chosen for the inscription spoke only the truth, and nothing but the truth, cast in bronze. But fifty years on, the world could not find it in itself to offer a place for the memories of the tribe to stand. Kanchanaburi, at the foot of the railroad, was the right place. But the Thai government backed and filled, for fear that the honest words of the plaque would offend the great trading partner, Japan. And the British who administered the huge war graves cemetery said an American plaque was not suitable for admission to a hallowed British Commonwealth site. Finally, in mid-1994, a spot was found, at the National War Cemetery of the Pacific in Honolulu, a green and pleasant place of dappled sunshine, high on a hill, with a clean wind blowing.

For POWs, memory was all-important. *We can forgive but we can't forget.* All prisoners of the Japanese said that. It was the special chant of their tribe, their password, the first article of their faith that what they had been through meant something. Forgiving was hard. Forgetting was impossible. It was humanly impossible to forget what the Japanese had done. It was humanly necessary—essential—to hold the dead in mind and heart. There were some other words spoken like an oath by POWs all over the world, as part of the one big tribe of living soldiers who lived with their dead, had to live with them, could not be free of living with them, and when all was said and done would not have wanted to be free of the bondage of comradeship: *They shall grow not old, as we that are left grow old, Age shall not weary them, nor the years condemn; At the going down of the sun, and in the morning, We will remember them. . .*

SOURCES

INTERVIEWS

The personal testimony of prisoners of the Japanese is the heart and soul of this book.

Between 1982 and 1993, I did interviews in the United States, Australia, Great Britain, the Netherlands, and Canada, often preceded and/or followed by phone conversations, correspondence, and a questionnaire which started small and simple (and ignorant) but grew over the years to almost four hundred questions asked worldwide. In addition to military prisoners I spoke to a number of civilian internees, and to family members. In the notes that follow, my interviews and other direct contacts are cited simply as: Interviewee/Daws.

I was fortunate to have access to records of interviews carried out by others. Tapes and transcripts of Ronald Marcello's interviews with the men of the Lost Battalion and survivors of the sinking of U.S.S. *Houston* are in the Oral History Collection at the University of North Texas, Denton, Texas; I cite them as Interviewee/UNT. Tapes and transcripts of Donald Knox's interviews for his book *Death March* (San Diego: Harcourt Brace, 1981) were kindly made available to me by Kathleen Rucker; I cite them as Interviewee/Knox. Transcripts in the Marine Oral History Collection, Marine Corps Historical Center, Washington Navy Yard, Washington, D.C., are cited as Interviewee/MCHC. Tapes and transcripts of Conrad Wood's interviews for a project on Far East Prisoners of War, 1941–1945, and other separate POW tapes and transcripts in the Department of Sound Records, Imperial War Museum, London, are cited as Interviewee/Sound/IWM. Tapes and transcripts for a project on the Japanese Occupation of Singapore, 1942–1945, in the Oral History Department, Singapore National Archives, are cited as Interviewee/SNA. Tapes of interviews by Tim Bowden, Margaret Evans, and Hank Nelson for the Australian Broadcasting Commission's radio documentary series *POW: Australians Under Nippon* (and for Nelson's book of the same title, published by the ABC, Sydney, 1985) are at the Australian War Memorial, Canberra, in the Keith Murdoch Sound Archive of Australia in the War of 1939–1945; I cite them as Interviewee/AWM.

The names of interviewees follow. By no means are all of them directly quoted or even identified in the text of the book, but the sound of their words has shaped every sentence.

Peggy Abkhazi, Bill Adair, Frank Adam, Geoffrey Pharaoh Adams, George Adams, Bob Adolphson, Robert Aitken, Shirley Akin, Billy Allen, Louis Allen, Peter Allen, Roy Allen, Charles Almond, James Anderson, Austin Andrews, Garry Anloff, Andrew Aquila, David Arkush, Dick Armstrong, Stan Arneil, Berry Arthur, Paul Ashton, George Aspinall, Oklahoma Atkinson.

Johan Baijens, Eric Bailey, Stuart Bailey, Frank Baker, Guy Baker, Tom Baker, Charles Balaza, Jim Ballinger, Carl Bamsch, Arthur Bancroft, Willi Banens, J.A.H. Bange, Dato Haji Mohamed Yusuf Bangs, Syd Barber, A. Bartholemew, Leland Bartlett, Sam Bass, George Batros, Wes Becher, Leon Beck, Leroy Becraft, William Bee, Willie Benton, Ross Berryman, Harvey Besley, Loutie Besters, Theodore Bigger, Harry Blackham, Tom Blalock, Lord James Blears, Rex Blow, Jack Boardman, Roy Bodine, Hayes Bolitho, Fred Bolt, H.A. Boon, Keith Botterill, James Boyce, Russell Braddon, Jack Bradley, J. B. Bradley, Lindy Bradley, Jack Brady, Richard Braithwaite, Kelly Bramlett, Loren Brantley, Gerrit Bras, Puck Bras, Des Brennan, Art Bressi, Colin Brien, Burt Briggs, Geoff Boreham, Fred Brightfield, Douglas Broadhurst, Theodore Bronk, Alf Brown, Arthur Brown, Charles Brown, Herbert Brown, Ken Brown, Lawrence Brown, Robert Brown, Herbert Bruce, J. Buck, Pat Bullamore, Vivian Bullwinkel, Jesse Bumpass, William Bunch, Jack Burge, Volney Burk, George Burns, John Byrnes.

Lloyd Cahill, James Caire, Steve Cairns, Owen Campbell, J. Caplan, Wayne Carringer, J. J. Carter, Tom Carter, Uell Carter, Charles Cates, James Cavanaugh, Lewell Chandler, Graham Chennells, Lee Ngoe Chew, Graham Chisholm, Horace Chumley, Vic Ciarrachi, J. D. Clark, Hugh Clarke, Blaine Claypool, Onnie Clem, Ralph Clifton, Jim Collins, Joe Colvin, Bill Cook, Charles Cook, Ishmael Cox, P. Cranefield, T. G. Crews, Gene Crispi, Eldon Crow, W. Crozer, Ferron Cummins, Adrian Curlewis.

M.L. Daman, Alex Dandie, Jack Daniels, E. E. Dann, Ted Date, Melvin Davidson, H. Davis, Lee Davis, Paul Davis, R. G. Davis, Stan Davis, Clarence Day, Kenneth Day, L. de Bruijn, Leon De Castres, Dimmen de Graaff, Slim De Grey, Willem de Man, Hubert de Monchy, C. De Souza, Leonardus de Vos, Bill Delich, Douglas Denham, A. L. Denholm, L. H. Denny, George Detre, John Devenish, J. W. Doherty, Griff Douglas, Tom Douglas, Thomas Drake, Robert Drukker, Alex Drummond, Donald Duff, J. J. Duizend, Frans Dumoulin, Ian Duncan, Edward Dunlop, Ben Dunn, George Dunnington, Herb Durner.

C. Eber, Lewis Elliott, Eric Endacott, Robert Erdwin, Ed Erickson, Ewart Escritt, W. R. Evans, William Evans.

Kevin Fagan, John Falconer, Harold Feiner, Jack Feliz, Melvin Felton, Frank Ficklin, Colin Filkins, Benjamin Fillmore, M. Fletcher-Cooke, Bill Flowers, William Foley, Mel Forsman, George Fox, C. A. Frances, Dale Frantz, Bertram Freedman, Nicholas Fryziuk, Frank Fujita, Eddie Fung.

George Gaboury, Frederick Galleghan, William Galos, Jack Garcia, William Garleb, J. B. Garrison, Leona Gastinger, Hubert Gater, James Gee, John Gibson, Lance Gibson, Fred Gifford, Ross Glover, Bryghte Godbold, William Godfrey, Joe Goicoechea, Samuel Goldblith, Louis Goldbrum, Jim Goodman, Crayton Gordon, Monique Gordon, Richard Gordon, H. Goulding, Claude Green, J. H. Greenwood, Robert Gregg, Colin Grey, Murray Griffin, Franklin Gross, Benson Guyton.

Ben Hackney, A. L. Halbrook, Neal Harrington, Douglas Harris, Roy Harris, Courtney Harrison, Fred Hauner, William Hauser, Herschel Heimann, J. B. Heinen, Fred Hekking, Henri Hekking, May Hekking, E. Henderson, Roy Henning, Joseph Hepworth, Mark Herbst, Thomas Hewlett, Antonius Heyne, King Hiebert, Alan Hobbs, C. Hodge, F. Hodgson, W. Hodson, Ron Holberton, Jose Holguin, C. W. Holtham, Max Hoogvelt, Gary Hooper, Eric Horton, Preston Hubbard, William Hubrecht, A. L. Humphreys, J. Hundscheidt, E. B. Hunter, Russell Hutchison, Charles Hurley.

William Ingram, Neil Iovino, John Isaacs.

Calvin Jackson, Eugene Jacobs, Herb Jaffe, Max Jagger, Reginald Jefferies, Betty Jeffrey, Harry Jeffries, Bill Jinkins, T. Jones.

Otto Kafer, Gerald Kasner, Harold Kent, James Kent, Larry Kent, John Kepchia, Woodrow Kessler, Frank King, Terence Kirk, J. Kirkwood, Douglas Knight, Freddie Knightley, Forrest Knox, Henry Knox, George Koury, John Kuslak.

Thye Mee Lam, Fred Lanzing, Sjoerd Lapré, C. Larkin, Eddy Laursen, George Lawley, Marion Lawton, Kermit Lay, Victor Lear, C. Lee, John Lee, John W. Lee, Ralph Levenberg, Stanley Levine, Patrick Levy, Wayne Lewis, Seng Lim, Lucas Lindeboom, Harry Liskowsky, Eric Lomax, H. Lüning, Kenneth Luton.

Ian Macrae, Mel Madero, John Mamerow, Leo Manning, Victor Mapes, Bob Maple, P. Marcus, Linus Marlow, H. J. Marsh, Kai Martin, Robert Martin, Robert Martindale, Jack Masefield, Norman Mathews, William Mattson, Gordon Maxwell, John May, Dean McCall, Charles McCartin, James McCone, Bill McCure, George McDaniel, Jerome McDavitt, Derry McDonough, Frank McGovern, Peter McGrath-Kerr, Sylvia McGregor, Al McGrew, John McInerney, Bob McKelvey, Michael McMullen, James McMurria, George McNeilly, Max McQuinn, Refugio Medina, Harry Medlin, Sheldon Mendelson, Nancy Merlo, Paul Metzler, Alf Michell, A. Michielsen, Loyd Mills, Harry Mock, Samuel Moody, Don Moore, Charles Morgan, Glen Morgan, Tom Morris, Ken Mosher, Cliff Moss, Jack Moss, Stanley Mroz, Annie Muijser, Alan Munro, John Murphy, Ray Myors.

John Nardini, Joseph Nason, Keith Naylor, Arthur Neijndorff, Chris Neilson, Lloyd Nelson, Henk Neumann, Clive Newnham, Charles Newton, Ken Newton, Reg Newton, Gustave Nichols, Don Noble, Dirk Nooij, Ernest Norquist, Daniel Nugent, Chaim Nussbaum.

Robert Obourn, John O'Brien, Geoff O'Connor, Roy Offerle, Jerome Okonski, Humphrey O'Leary, John Olson, Alias Osman, Cletis Overton, John Owen.

Jack Panaotie, Ray Parkin, Ken Parkyns, E. Parrish, Glenn Pace, Harold Payne, J. Pearce, Snow Peat, John Perkowski, Fred Perrin, Ed Perry, C. Petrowsky, Sydney Piddington, Henry Pitcher, L.O.S. Poidevin, Samuel Pond, John Posten, T. Pounder, Alvin Poweleit, Rita Powning, M. D. Price, Charles Pruitt, Charley Pryor, Luther Prunty, Albert Puckett.

Tom Quilliam.

Mary Radner, Dan Rafalovich, R. Ramsay Rea, F. W. Rappard, Lester Rasbury, M. Rea, Louis Read, E. S. Readwin, Raymond Reed, Wilson Reed, Seldon Reese, Rowley Richards, Jim Richardson, John Robe, Sandy Robertson, Blair Robinett, Frank Robinson, Lloyd Robinson, Lee Roland, Fred Roth, David Runge, Philip Ruth, Dick Ryan.

Frank Samethini, Paul Sarno, Bernard Saunders, Marjoke Schepel, C. Schnerr-de Haas, Alfred Schreiber, Sol Schwartz, Otto Schwarz, C. W. Scott, G. Scott, E. Scully, Glenn Self, Roscoe Sellers, W. H. Seward, J. C. Sharp, Arthur Shepherd, Ted Sherring, Robert Shoobridge, Earl Short, Nelson Short, Sam Silverman, C. Simon, Chas Skarda, Zoeth Skinner, Reuben Slone, George Small, P. J. Smallwood, Bob Smetts, Keith Smith, Ray Smith, William Sniezko, Wilburn Snyder, Stanley Sommers, C. H. Sosvielle, John Spainhower, O. R. Sparkman, Lionel Speller, Thomas Spencer, George Sprod, C. H. Spurgeon, James Stacy, Fred Stahl, Teunis Stahlie, Jess Stanbrough, Henry Stanley, Robert Stannard, W. L. Starnes, Frank Stecklein, Ray Steele, J.B.W. Steen, Jacoba Steltenpool, Bryant Sterling, Keith Stevens, Leonard Stevens, Bob Stewart, J. A. Stewart, James Stewart, John Stewart, J. H. Stitt, C. J. Stolk, Preston Stone, Daniel Stoudt, Desmond Stratton, Fred Stringer, John Stroud, Donald Stuart, Jack Sue, E. Swanton, Walter Swope, Micky Syer.

Cheng Hwee Tan, Kim Ock Tan, Norman Tant, E. Tanzer, Jim Taylor, Robert Taylor, Daya Teding-van Berkhout, Foster Templon, Alec Thompson, Claude Thompson, David Thompson, Kyle Thompson, Charles Thornton, Clarrie Thornton, Marvin Tilghman, Wiley Tipton, Vern Toose, Herb Trackson, Walter Tucker, Ray Tullipan, Houston Turner, Michael Tussing, H. G. Tyson.

Joseph Upton.

George Vafiopolous, Barend van Dam, Albert van Geffen, Mies van Gerrevink, Gus van Gorp, Cornelius van Heekeren, E.A.A. van Heekeren, L. R. Vanhove, Regy van Iterson, J. H. van Kempen, John Van Nooten, C. van Rooy, I. Meualda van Witsen, Joe Vater, Stan Vaughan, E. S. Virgo, Derk Visker, F. Voges, Gottfried Voll.

Gerald Wade, Earl Walk, Bob Wallace, William Wallace, Karl Wampler, Willem Wanrooy, Cliff Warn, S. Warren, Hadley Watson, Ian Watt, J. C. Weigling, Bill Weissiger, Daniel Weitzner, L. Wellard, Rod Wells, Glyn White, Harold White, Roger White, Roy Whitecross, Thomas Whitehead, G. Wilkinson, R. B. Wilkinson, Ted Williams, George Williamson, John Williamson, J. R. Williamson, Jack Willis, Bob Wilson, Ian Wingfield, C. Wise, Donald Wise, Mark Wohlfeld, Robert Wolfersberger, D. Wollraven, D.J.B. Wolterbeek, Monroe Woodall, Beryl Woodbridge, Eric Woods, Tom Woody, Gene Wooten, Charles Worthington, Anton Woudsma, Houston Tom Wright, William Wright, J. Wyatt.

Robert Yates, Arthur Young.

Ed Zimmerman, Tom Zivic.

DOCUMENTS

Among thousands of file boxes of documents worldwide, the most useful to me were the following:

Record Group 389 at the National Archives, Washington, D.C. (cited as NA), and Record Groups 153 and 331 at the Washington National Records Center, Suitland, Maryland (cited as WNRC). I cite by the name of the person making a statement or the title of the document, then record group number, box number, and repository, thus: U.S. v. Homma, RG 331, B 1671, WNRC.

Other frequently cited American repositories are identified by the following abbreviations: Operational Archives, U.S. Naval Historical Center, Washington Navy Yard, Washington, D.C. (NHC); Marine Corps Historical Center, Washington Navy Yard, Washington, D.C. (MCHC); Center of Military History, Washington, D.C. (CMH); U.S. Army Military History Institute, Carlisle Barracks, Pennsylvania (MHI); MacArthur Memorial Archives, Norfolk, Virginia (MMA).

Typescript summaries based on thousands of written statements by liberated American POWs were prepared by the Liaison and Research Branch, American Prisoner of War Information Bureau: "Prisoner of War Camps in Japan and Japanese Controlled Areas as Taken from the Reports of Interned American Prisoners"; "Prisoner of War Camps in Areas Other Than the Four Principal Islands of Japan"; and "Reports on American Prisoners of War Interned by the Japanese in the Philippines." Copies of these summaries are in NA, WNRC, and CMH, among other places.

A number of American POW diaries and other documents originally held in the National Personnel Records Center (Military Personnel Records) in St. Louis are on microfilm in NA; they are cited thus: Name, reel number, NA. (POW diaries and memoirs in private hands or in scattered institutions are cited by name and repository.)

British manuscript diaries and unpublished memoirs in the Department of Documents, Imperial War Museum, London, are cited thus: Name, Documents, IWM.

Australian documentary material in AWM is identified by major file number. File 55 has a complete run of documents of NEFIS, the Dutch intelligence service for the Indies, based in Australia during the war. POW documentation is also held in the Australian Archives, Melbourne (AA).

In Amsterdam, the Rijksintituut voor Oorlogsdocumentatie (RIOD) has much documentary material, which formed the major source of a comprehensive published compilation by E. van Witsen, *Krijgsgevangenen in de Pacific-Oorlog, 1941–1945* (Franeker: Wever, 1971). At The Hague, in the Dutch ministry of foreign affairs, Ministerie van Buitenslande Zaken (MBZ), file 322.191 was especially useful. There is also a good deal of material (though, as it turned out, much less directly useful for my purposes) scattered throughout the Londens Archief of the Algemeen Rijksarchief, The Hague (ARA).

The trials of Japanese war criminals generated mountains of documentation. The proceedings of the International Military Tribunal of the Far East (IMTFE), which tried the A Class criminals, can be found in several archives, but no single repository has a complete set of papers plus a complete set of supporting exhibits. The best initial approach to the records of IMTFE is through the published version: R. John Pritchard and S. Zaide, eds., *The Tokyo War Crimes Trial,* 27 vols. (New York: Garland, 1981–1987).

Trials of B and C Class criminals were held under separate national jurisdictions. For American trials, most useful are the already-cited RG 153 and RG 331, WNRC, and RG 389, NA. British trial proceedings are in the Public Record Office, Kew (PRO), in the series WO/235. For Australian trials, see file 1010, AWM. For Dutch trials, see the already-cited file 322.191, MBZ. An overview is: Philip Piccigallo, *The Japanese on Trial* (Austin: University of Texas, 1979).

Documents of the Allied Translator and Interpreter Service Section (ATIS) show Allied intelligence in the process of gathering and assessing information about the Japanese as military enemies, including their treatment of POWs. ATIS reports and other documents are scattered across many archives. They have been collated on microfiche, with a published guide: *Wartime Translations of Seized Japanese Documents: Allied Translator and Interpreter Section Reports, 1942–1946* (Bethesda, Congressional Information Service, 1988). Comparable useful material can be found in the bulletins (scattered, uncollated, unpublished) of the Southeast Asia Translation and Interrogation Centre (SEATIC).

A large published collection of useful contextual information put together soon after the war is the multivolume United States Strategic Bombing Survey, which covers a range of topics far broader than the title suggests. See Gordon Daniels, ed., *A Guide to the Reports of the United States Strategic Bombing Survey. II. The Pacific* (London: Royal Historical Society, 1981).

See also the compendium by Van Waterford, *Prisoners of the Japanese in World War II* (Jefferson, McFarland, 1994).

OFFICIAL HISTORIES AND RELATED MATERIAL

The Japanese official history is Bōei-chō [Self-Defense Agency], Bōei Kenshūjo [National Institute for Self-Defense Studies], Senshishitsu [War History Room], *Senshi Sōsho* [War History Series], 102 vols. (Tokyo: Agasumo Shimbunsha, 1966–1980). For compilations of Japanese regulations concerning prisoners of war and other official material on POW camps in Japan and in the overseas territories, see Chaen Yoshio, ed., *Dainihon Teikoku Naichi Horyo Shūyōjo:* [POW Camps on the Japanese Mainland of the Japanese Empire] (Tokyo: Fuji Shuppan, 1986), and *Dai Tōa Senka Gaichi Horyo Shūyōjo* [POW Camps in Outlying Areas During the Great East Asian War] (Tokyo: Fuji Shuppan, 1987). Chaen has also collected documents on B and C Class war crimes trials in the Philippines, China, and Japan. Utsumi Aiko has published a collection of Allied documents protesting the treatment of POWs: *Furyo Toriatsukai ni kensuru Shogaikoku kara no Kōgishu* (Tokyo: Fuji Shuppan, 1988); she has published as well on the situation of Koreans in the Japanese Army. See also Adachi Sumio, "Unprepared Regrettable Events: A Brief History of Japanese Practices on Treatment of Allied War Victims During the Second World War" (Yokosuka: National Defense Academy, 1982).

For military context on the American side, useful volumes of the official Army history, *United States Army in World War II. The War in the Pacific* (Washington, D.C.: Department of the Army), are Philip Crowl and Edmund Love, *Seizure of the Gilberts and Marshalls* (1955); Philip Crowl, *Campaign in the Marianas* (1960); and Roy Appleman et al., *Okinawa: The Last Battle* (1948).

Useful volumes of *History of U.S. Marine Corps Operations in World War II* (Washington D.C.: Historical Branch, U.S. Marine Corps) are Frank Hough et al., *Pearl Harbor to Guadalcanal* (1958); Carl Hoffman, *Saipan: The Beginning of the End* (1950); Henry Shaw et al., *Central Pacific Drive* (1966); G. Garand and Truman Strobridge, *Western Pacific Operations* (1971); and Benis Frank and Henry Shaw, *Victory and Occupation* (1968).

Useful volumes of Samuel Eliot Morison, *History of United States Naval Operations in World War II* (Boston: Little, Brown), are *The Rising Sun in the Pacific, 1931–April 1942* (1948); *Aleutians, Gilberts and Marshalls, June 1942–April 1944* (1951).

Air Force involvement in postliberation food drops to POW camps is described in Wesley Craven and James Cate, eds., *The Army Air Forces in World War II* (Chicago: University of Chicago), vol. 5, *The Pacific to Matterhorn, 1944–1945* (1958).

Much officially gathered detail, variously American, Australian, and British, is in Louis Morton, *The Fall of the Philippines* (Washington, D.C.: Department of the Army, 1953); Lionel Wigmore, *Australia in the War of 1939–1945,* vol. 4, *The Japanese Thrust* (Canberra: Australian War Memorial, 1957); S. Woodburn Kirby, *The War Against Japan* (London: H.M. Stationery Office), vol.1, *The Loss of Singapore* (1957), and vol. 5, *The Surrender of Japan* (1969). The official Dutch version of the fall of the Indies and what happened to POWs (and civilian internees) is L. de Jong, *Het Koninkrijk der Nederlanden in de Tweede Wereldoorlog,* vol. 11b, parts I and II, *Nederlands-Indië* ('s Gravenhage, Staatsuitgeverij, 1985); a separate, heavily documented edition was published by Martinus Nijhoff. Strangely, New Zealand, with very few prisoners taken by the Japanese, has given them, relatively speaking, a lot of space on the official page; see David Hall, *Prisoners of Japan* (Wellington: War History Branch, Department of Internal Affairs, 1949), and W. Wynne Mason, *Prisoners of War* (Wellington: War History Branch, Department of Internal Affairs, 1954).

NONOFFICIAL SOURCES

Differing nonofficial national perspectives on the war, with attention to POWs that ranges from some to very little, can be observed and compared in Ronald Spector, *Eagle Against the Sun* (New York: Vintage, 1985); John Toland, *The Rising Sun* (New York: Bantam, 1971); John Costello, *The Pacific War* (New York: Rawson, Wade, 1981); Edwin Hoyt, *Japan's War* (New York: McGraw-Hill, 1986); Ienaga Saburō, *Japan's Last War* (Canberra: Australian National University, 1979); David Bergamini, *Japan's Imperial Conspiracy* (New York: Pocket Books, 1972); Haruko Cook and Theodore Cook, *Japan at War* (New York: New Press, 1992); Gavin Long, *The Six-Year War* (Canberra: Australian War Memorial, 1973); D. Clayton James, *The Years of MacArthur* (Boston: Houghton Mifflin), vol. 2, *1941–1945* (1975); and William Manchester, *American Caesar: Douglas MacArthur, 1880–1964* (New York: Dell, 1979). A comprehensive work on civilian internees with a great deal of useful comparative context for the experience of POWs is D. van Velden, *De Japanse Interneringskampen voor Burgers Gedurende de Tweede Wereldoorlog* (Franeker, the Netherlands: Wever 1985). And very much worth looking at for a modern Japanese point of view is a massive documentary film using archival footage, costing more than $16 million, with twenty reels and a running time of more than four and a half hours, produced by Kodansha Ltd., directed by Kobayashi Masaki, released in 1983, distributed worldwide under the English-language title *The Tokyo Trial.* An English-language script was published by Kodansha in 1985.

There is no comprehensive up-to-date bibliography of published works on POWs. Useful within defined limits of time, space, and subject are Janet Ziegler, *World War II: Books in English, 1945-1965* (Stanford, Hoover Institution, 1971); and

Morton Netzorg, *The Philippines in World War II and to Independence (December 8, 1941–July 4, 1946): An Annotated Bibliography* (Ithaca: Cornell University Press, 1977). MHI has prepared brief working lists of titles on "POWs in WWII," and on "Allied Prisoners of the Japanese." Charles Roland of McMaster University in Canada is assembling a computerized bibliography of POW titles from both the Asian and the European theaters.

Individual published POW memoirs number in the hundreds. They range widely in scope, from the Australian enlisted man Stan Arneil's *One Man's War* (Sydney: Alternative Publishing, 1980), a secret diary, plain utterance that still makes for wrenching reading, to the American medical officer Paul Ashton's *Bataan Diary* (1984) and *And Somebody Gives a Damn* (1990), huge volumes with the heft of Tolstoy novels. Ashton's books are self-published. Many memoirs are. Very few POWs would pretend to be stylists, and their small-town print jobs are not necessarily state-of-the-art. Their books may not always have complete publication data or a copyright notice. Most often there is no ISBN number, or Library of Congress catalog data. And no mention in *Books in Print*. This makes coming upon such memoirs pretty much of a researcher's lottery. And it also makes for incompleteness and apparent inconsistency when citing in footnotes. But none of the above matters at all. These books are not "vanity press" self-indulgences. They are the product of the POWs' painful effort to make sense out of their lives.

Many POWs tried to write about their experiences soon after they came home; and now, forty-five and fifty years on, late in life, many more are trying. For every memoir in print there must be a hundred written but never published, most of them never meant for publication, just for the family to read, or as a private attempt at exorcism, driving the demons out of the mind and onto paper, to be locked in the attic or the basement.

With these POW memoirs and equally with every other kind of document, in the notes that follow I cite only a very small percentage of what I have read. If I were to document fully every page of this book, the documentation would run longer than the text. Not practical. Not by orders of magnitude.

Book prices keep spiraling upward and every author has to be concerned with the rigorous cost constraints of publishing. With this in mind, I have prepared a separate set of notes for readers who might want to see a fuller representation of my overall documentation, or who might want to pursue a specific subject further on their own. I began this practice with a book of mine published a good many years ago. That first time around, my educated guess was that readers in the need-to-know-more category would add up to no more than 1 percent; and in practice this turned out to be almost exactly right. So—seeing no reason to run up the cost of this book unnecessarily for 99 percent of readers, and at the same time wanting to take care of the legitimate interests of the other 1 percent, I continue to favor a separate set of notes. For this book, I have lodged notes under my name in two places: one in the Northern Hemisphere, in the Pacific Collection, Hamilton Library, University of Hawaii, 2550 The Mall, Honolulu, HI 96822, the other in the Southern Hemisphere, in the Division of Pacific and Asian History, Research School of Pacific and Asian Studies, Australian National University, Canberra ACT 0200, Australia, with the title *Prisoners of the Japanese: Notes*. Anyone interested can write for a copy.

In doing the severe triage necessary to limit the selective notes that follow directly below, I have given most attention to documenting subjects that might seem surprising, alarming, or even hard to credit for readers coming across such things for the first time: the scale of atrocities on Bataan during the death march, on the Burma-Siam railroad, and in other places; the *kempei* at work; Unit 731; the Japanese dissecting POWs live; what was done to downed airmen; American POWs trading to the death among themselves; the ferocious friendly-fire death rate among POWs on ship transports to Japan; the lengths to which POW officers would go to maintain their privileges of rank at the expense of their own enlisted men; the extreme and unaccountable variation in postwar compensation as between Japanese civilians interned in the United States and Allied POWs of the Japanese held in Asia; and so on.

I. SITTING DUCKS
Notes for pages 31–50

Harry Jeffries, Oklahoma Atkinson, and Wake Island. Principal interviews: Daws with Jeffries, Atkinson, Crow, Davidson, Green, Maple, L. Nelson. Also McDaniel/UNT, Venable/UNT.

Wake Island, 1941. Daws interviews with Nye, Pitcher, Williamson. Woodrow Kessler kindly made his manuscript memoir available. Florence Teters: H. Brown/Daws; David Woodbury, *Builders for Battle* (New York: Dutton, 1946), 256. "Sucker": Atkinson/Daws. "Just Plain Shit": Gregory Urwin, "The Defenders of Wake Island," Ph.D. dissertation, Notre Dame, 1983, 40.

The Japanese Attack on Wake. Much detail in Urwin, "Defenders of Wake"; and Robert Heinl, *The Defense of Wake* (Washington, D.C.: U.S. Marine Corps, 1947). See also Kessler, "Report on Wake Island Operations 7 Dec. to 24 Dec. 1941, 11 Oct. 45," MCHC; James Devereux, *The Story of Wake Island* (Philadelphia: Lippincott, 1947), and the Devereux interview in Oral History Collection, MCHC; W. Scott Cunningham, *Wake Island Command* (Boston: Little, Brown, 1961); Duane Schultz, *Wake Island* (New York: Jove, 1983). Also Joseph Astarita, *Sketches of P.O.W. Life* (Brooklyn, n.d.); Walter Bayler, *Last Man off Wake Island* (Indianapolis: Bobbs-Merrill, 1943); Hans Whitney, *Guest of the Fallen Sun* (New York: Exposition, 1951); J. Darden, *Guests of the Emperor* (Clinton, 1990); Rodney Kephart, *Wake, War and Waiting* (New York: Exposition, 1950). "SOS. ISLAND OF OAHU ATTACKED": Urwin, "Defenders of Wake," 101. "I see boats!": Urwin, 167. "ENEMY ON ISLAND": Urwin, 208. "Stay under cover!": Jeffries/ Daws. "Do you speak English?": Devereux, *Story of Wake,* 190.

Race Hate in the Pacific War. John Dower, *War Without Mercy* (New York: Pantheon, 1986) is an indispensable treatment of this difficult subject. "Well, thank the son of a bitch": Urwin, "Defenders of Wake," 236. The airstrip: Atkinson/ Daws, Jeffries/Daws; Venable/UNT; Kessler memoir.

The *Nitta Maru.* See testimony and affidavits in the war crimes trial U.S. v.

Hida, RG 153, Case Docket 260, WNRC; many statements in RG 331, Box 986, 987, WNRC; IMTFE 13, 248ff., PX 2037, 2038.

Notes for pages 50–60

Slug Wright, the 2nd Battalion, 131st Field Artillery, and U.S.S. *Houston.* Principal interviews: Daws with Wright, Schwarz, Stanbrough, Forsman. Ronald Marcello's invaluable interviews with 131st Field Artillery and *Houston* survivors are excerpted in Robert La Forte and Ronald Marcello, eds., *Building the Death Railway* (Wilmington: Scholarly Resources, 1993), and in La Forte, Marcello, and Richard Himmel, eds., *With Only the Will to Live* (Wilmington: Scholarly Resources, 1994).

Published memoirs: Hollis Allen, *The Lost Battalion* (Jacksboro: Leigh McGee, 1963); H. Robert Charles, *Last Man Out* (Austin: Eakin, 1988); Clarence Day, *Hodio* (Merrillville: ICS, 1984); Benjamin Dunn, *The Bamboo Express* (Chicago: Adams, 1979); Clyde Fillmore, *Prisoner of War* (Wichita Falls: Nortex, 1973); Frank Fujita, *Foo* (Denton: University of North Texas, 1993); Reuben Slone, *The Light Behind the Cloud* (Waco: Texian, 1992); Horace Teel, *Our Days Were Years* (Quanah: Nortex, 1978); Thomas Woody, *The Railroad to Nagasaki* (privately published, 1992); Kyle Thompson, *A Thousand Cups of Rice* (Austin: Eakin, 1994).

Louisiana Maneuvers. Daws interviews with Wright, Prunty, Stanbrough, Worthington; *Life,* October 5, 1941. How the 2nd Battalion went overseas: Clark/Daws, Tilghman/Daws; Matlock/UNT.

Eddie Fung and Frank Fujita. Fung/UNT; Fujita/Daws; Fujita/UNT; Fujita, *Foo,* 15ff., 328.

Republic. Wright/Daws; UNT interviews with L. Brown, Matlock, Offerle, Reichle. Brisbane: Wright/Daws; UNT interviews with Minshew, Knight, Slate.

Java. "Macmac OK!" Dunn, *Bamboo Express,* 12; Fujita, *Foo,* 58. Corky Woodall and the siren: Dunn/Daws; Evans/UNT. Capitulation: Stanbrough/Daws; Henderson/AWM; UNT interviews with Armstrong, Hard, Offerle, Rasbury, Stone, Whitehead; Rogers diary, RG 389, B 2178, NA.

U.S.S. *Houston.* Daws interviews with Forsman, Schwarz, Weissinger, Wilkinson; UNT interviews with Burge, Detre, Pryor, Reese; Day, "Saga of the USS *Houston,*" MS, Command File, World War II, Navy, NHC. See also Duane Schultz, *The Last Battle Station* (New York: St. Martin's, 1986); Walter Winslow, *The Ghost of the Java Coast* (Satellite Beach: Coral Reef, 1974); Walter Winslow, *The Ghost That Died at Sunda Strait* (Annapolis: United States Naval Institute, 1984). Serang: Douglas/UNT; statement of Smith, Command File, World War II, NHC; S. Stening, "Experiences as a Prisoner of War in Japan," *Australian Medical Journal,* Vol. 1 (June 1946), 773. "This is not the way": Schultz, *Last Battle Station,* 220.

Bicycle Camp. Dunn, *Bamboo Express,* 39. *Houston* prisoners: Rasbury/UNT; Fillmore, *Prisoner of War,* 19. "Deep in the Heart of Texas": M. Robinson/UNT.

Notes for pages 60–72

Forrest Knox and Company A of the 192nd Tank Battalion. Principal interviews: Daws with Knox, Durner, Stewart. Adaline Knox kindly gave me access to Forrest Knox's private papers.

Company A. The Rock County Historical Society, Janesville, Wisconsin, has a newspaper clipping collection and other documents. See also Tom Doherty, "Too Little, Too Late," *Wisconsin Magazine of History,* Vol. 75, No. 4 (Summer 1992), 243–283; Dale Dopkins, *The Janesville 99* (Janesville: privately published, 1981).

The Japanese Invasion of the Philippines. In addition to official sources, detail in: John Whitman, *Bataan* (New York: Hippocrene, 1990); Donald Young, *The Battle of Bataan* (Jefferson, McFarland, 1992); Jonathan Wainwright, *General Wainwright's Story* (Garden City: Doubleday, 1946); Duane Schultz, *Hero of Bataan* (New York: St. Martin's, 1981); John Beck, *MacArthur and Wainwright* (Albuquerque: University of New Mexico Press, 1974); Carol Petillo, *MacArthur* (Bloomington: Indiana University Press, 1981); Michael Schaller, *Douglas MacArthur* (New York: Oxford, 1989); John Coleman, *Bataan and Beyond* (College Station: Texas A&M, 1978); Allison Ind, *Bataan* (New York: Macmillan, 1944); and especially the oral history by Donald Knox, *Death March* (San Diego: Harcourt Brace, 1981). Kathleen Rucker kindly gave me permission to use Knox's interview transcripts and research papers.

One-Horse Shea: Knox/Daws. "What do you think?": Knox/Daws. "This is as far as I go": Knox/Daws.

Food on Bataan. In addition to official volumes, see Charles Drake, "No Uncle Sam," MS, CMH; James, *The Years of MacArthur,* Vol. 2, 32–33; Mariano Villarin, *We Remember Bataan and Corregidor* (Baltimore: Gateway, 1990), 93–94; Stanley Falk, *Bataan* (New York: Jove, 1983), 34; R. Jackson Scott, *90 Days of Rice* (Pioneer: California Traveler, 1975), 38.

"Ladies and gents": Ernest Whitcomb, *Escape from Corregidor* (Chicago: Regnery, 1958), 52. Japanese propaganda: Bob Reynolds, *Of Rice and Men* (Philadelphia: Dorrance, 1947), 32. "Don't wait to die": Ward Rutherford, *Fall of the Philippines* (New York: Ballantine, 1972), 112. "You too can enjoy": Coleman, *Bataan and Beyond,* 36; see also Fidel Ongpauco, *They Refused to Die* (Gatineau: Levesque, 1982), 91; Ambrosio Peña, *Bataan's Own* (Manila: 2nd Regular Division Association, 1967), 174; Eric Morris, *Corregidor* (New York: Stein and Day, 1984), 357. Leaflets for wiping behinds: Ralph Hibbs, *Tell MacArthur to Wait* (New York: Carlton, 1988), 78.

"You have already cut rations": Morton, *Fall of the Philippines,* 269. "Use this ticket": Rutherford, *Fall of the Philippines,* 112–113. "Battling bastards of Bataan": Toland, *Rising Sun,* 325. "Dugout Doug": Manchester, *American Caesar,* 269. "I am going to the latrine": John Toland, *But Not in Shame* (New York: Ballantine, 1974), 306.

"Shucks, I got proof": Knox/Daws. Ranking animals for taste: see detailed notes. Sugar: see detailed notes.

Hospitals, Hygiene, and Disease. Wibb Cooper et al.: "Medical Department Activities in the Philippines," MS, CMH; J. Gillespie, "Recollections of the Pacific War and Japanese Prisoner-of-War Camps, 1941–1945," MS, CMH; Eugene Jacobs, *Blood Brothers* (New York: Carlton, 1985); Alfred Weinstein, *Barbed-Wire Surgeon* (New York: Macmillan, 1961); Paul Ashton, *And Somebody Gives a Damn!* (Santa Barbara: privately published, 1990), 53ff. Malaria: Falk, *Bataan,* 65–66. Quinine: Whitman, *Bataan,* 448; Hibbs, *Tell MacArthur,* 83.

Homma's Message. Morton, *Fall of the Philippines,* 418. Effectives: Richard Mallonee, *The Naked Flagpole* (San Rafael: Presidio), 128. Tired hair: Garleb/Knox. Human flesh in trees: Coleman, *Bataan and Beyond,* 53. Arms and legs: Alvin Poweleit, *Kentucky's Fighting 192nd Light GHQ Tank Battalion* (Newport, Ky.: 1981),

70. Japanese in the night: Coleman, *Bataan and Beyond,* 56; Stephen Mellnik, *Philippine War Diary* (New York: Van Nostrand, 1981), 81. The 192nd destroy their tanks: Daws interviews with Knox, Durner, Stewart. White flag: Dopkins, *Janesville 99,* 13.

Surrender. Morton, *Fall of Philippines,* 457, 466; Whitman, *Bataan,* 583ff.; Toland, *Rising Sun,* 333; Calvin Chunn, *Of Rice and Men* (Los Angeles: Veterans', 1946), 5–13.

Notes for pages 73–84

The Bataan Death March. Principal interviews: Daws with Knox, Durner, Stewart.

A basic source is the thirty volumes of testimony and exhibits in the war crimes trial U.S. v. Homma, RG 331, B 1671, WNRC. In addition to books already cited for Bataan, and other sources in detailed notes, see Bergamini, *Japan's Imperial Conspiracy,* 955ff.; E. Bartlett Kerr, *Surrender and Survival* (New York: Morrow, 1985), 49ff. See also papers of Moore, Johnson, Mallonee in MHI.

Japanese Infantrymen March. Meirion and Susie Harries, *Soldiers of the Sun* (London: Heinemann, 1991), 141. Japanese treatment of officers: Johnson papers, Mitchell papers, MHI; Cooper, "Medical Department Activities," CMH; Wainwright, *General Wainwright's Story,* 94; Falk, *Bataan,* 129. "Dear friends": Ongpauco, *They Refused to Die,* 97; Combat History Division, Manila, *Triumph in the Philippines* (Manila: Philippine Historical Association, 1972), 110–111; U.S. v. Homma, Vol. 8, 1011ff. Ten American bodies a mile: Poweleit, *Kentucky's Fighting 192nd,* 87; Alvin Poweleit, *USAFFE* (privately published, 1975), 50. Twenty-seven headless bodies: Toland, *But Not in Shame,* 351; see also U.S. v. Homma, Vol. 7, 834. Hospital 2: Poweleit, *Kentucky's Fighting 192nd,* 84; Cooper, "Medical Department Activities"; U.S. v. Homma, Vol. 7, 763, 823.

Killing on the Death March. U.S. v. Homma, Vol. 8, 945, Vol. 9, 1105; William Evans, *Kora!* (Rogue River: Atwood, 1986), 12. Hit from trucks: Knox, *Death March,* 141. Water: Dick Bilyeu, *Lost in Action* (Jefferson: McFarland, 1991), 74, 77, 78. Shot for water stains: Knox, *Death March,* 128. Falling back through the ranks: L. Reed/UNT. Buzzard squads: Knox/Daws; U.S. v. Homma, Vol. 7, 733ff.; Samuel Grashio and Bernard Norling, *Return to Freedom* (Tulsa: MCN, 1982), 43. Filipinos killed for helping: Ashton, *Bataan Diary,* 161–162; Bilyeu, *Lost in Action,* 89; Villarin, *We Remember Bataan,* 107. Hospital No. 2: U.S. v. Homma, Vol. 7, 763, 823; Poweleit, *Kentucky's Fighting 192nd,* 84; Poweleit, *USAFFE,* 51–52; Chunn, *Of Rice and Men,* 120ff. Sun treatment: Grashio and Norling, *Return to Freedom,* 39; Falk, *Bataan,* 133. "Where the hell": Knox/Daws. Lubao: Poweleit, *Kentucky's Fighting 192nd,* 93.

Iron warehouse: Grashio and Norling, *Return to Freedom,* 44. Bayonet game: Knox, *Death March,* 146. Train: Grashio and Norling, *Return to Freedom,* 44.

Professional Japanese Military Hardheads. Bergamini, *Japan's Imperial Conspiracy,* 957. Tsuji Masanobu: Hoyt, *Japan's War,* 153; Arthur Swinson, *Four Samurai* (London: Hutchinson, 1968), 65ff.; Ian Ward, *The Killer They Called a God* (Singapore: Media Masters, 1992), 247.

My discussion of issues raised by the death march is based on the voluminous evidence in U.S. v. Homma, both prosecution and defense, especially testimony of

Homma and other senior Japanese officers. For a different assessment, see Falk, *Bataan,* 225ff. See also Harries and Harries, *Soldiers of the Sun,* 357–358, 411–412.

Notes for pages 84–90

Camp O'Donnell. Principal interviews: Daws with Knox, Durner, Olson, Stewart, Tant. Also UNT interviews with Bunch, Halbrook, L. Reed.

A basic source is the war crimes trial U.S. v. Tsuneyoshi, RG 331, B 1607, WNRC, and related documents in B 1061, 1640, 9640, 9771, 9787. Camp O'Donnell also figures prominently in U.S. v. Homma, previously cited. Books already cited for the Bataan death march also describe experiences at O'Donnell, especially Knox, *Death March,* 153ff. See also the papers of Johnson, Moore, and Wohlfeld in MHI. John Olson, *O'Donnell* (privately published, 1985), is the most detailed inventory of factual information on any single POW camp.

Shakedown. Olson, *O'Donnell,* 42–43. Killed for having Japanese things: U.S. v. Homma, Vol. 10, 1145–1148; statement of Drummond, prosecution exhibit in U.S. v. Tsuneyoshi, Vol. 2; Dorothy Cave, *Beyond Courage* (Las Cruces: Yucca Tree, 1992), 181. The Japanese fan: statement of Limpert, prosecution exhibit in U.S. v. Tsuneyoshi, Vol. 2. Filipinos marked with a red *X:* Ongpauco, *They Refused to Die,* 149. Tsuneyoshi and his speech: U.S. v. Tsuneyoshi, Vol. 1, 82; U.S. v. Homma, Vol. 11, 1509; Olson, *O'Donnell,* 44–47.

Water and Food. Extensive testimony in U.S. v. Tsuneyoshi and U.S. v. Homma; Olson, *O'Donnell,* 85ff. "Would you eat the dog": Tant/Daws. "You talk too much": U.S. v. Tsuneyoshi, Vol. 1, 503. "I got bleeding hemorrhoids": Knox/Daws.

Dysentery Ward, Death and Burial. Extensive testimony in U.S. v. Tsuneyoshi and U.S. v. Homma. See also Olson, *O'Donnell,* 109ff.; Cooper, "Medical Department Activities in the Philippines"; Gillespie, "Recollections of the Pacific War"; Kary Emerson, *Guest of the Emperor* (privately published, 1977), 22; Weinstein, *Barbed-Wire Surgeon,* 68ff.; Evans, *Kora,* 36–37.

Company A deaths, including One-Horse Shea: Knox/Daws; death lists, RG 331, B 1640, WNRC; exhibits in U.S. v. Tsuneyoshi, Vol. 2.

Ted Lewin. See detailed notes.

Work Details. Anloff/Daws; Skinner/Daws; McCall/UNT; Olson, *O'Donnell,* 61, 145–146.

II. IN THE SACK
Notes for pages 91–96

Recriminations. The drunken Dutchman: Matlock/UNT. Dutch defense of the Indies: Rayburn/UNT; Rohan Rivett, *Behind Bamboo* (Sydney: Angus and Robertson, 1946), 131ff.; Fujita, *Foo,* 78. "Dutch courage": see the multivolume *Oxford English Dictionary,* and any substantial American dictionary. "Huns with their guts ripped out": Nelson, *POW,* 63. "Green on the outside": Braddon/AWM. Cursing MacArthur: Robert Haney, *Caged Dragons* (Ann Arbor: Sabre, 1991), 38; Hugh Myers, *Prisoner of War* (Portland: Metropolitan, 1965), 122; William Brougher, *South to Bataan, North to Mukden* (Athens: University of Georgia, 1971), 32, 36. Cursing Wainwright: Nugent/Knox; Ernest Miller, *Bataan Uncensored* (Long Prairie: Hart,

1949), 250ff.; Emerson, *Guest of the Emperor*, 5; Poweleit, *USAFFE*, 10.

Combat Ratios. Figures are drawn from Allied and Japanese official military histories, and other sources including Adachi Sumio, "Unprepared Regrettable Events," 261; and H. Zwitser, "Enkele Gegevens over Krijgsgevangenen en Gesneuvelden onder de Europese Militairen van het Koninklijk Nederlands Indische Leger Gedurende de Oorlog in de Pacific (1941–1945)," *Mededelingen van de Sectie Krijgsgeschiedenis Koninklijke Landmacht*, Deel 1 (1978), 5–23. See also George Kanahele, "The Japanese Occupation of Indonesia: Prelude to Independence," Ph.D. dissertation, Cornell University, 1967, 251–256.

"Sub-human specimens": Dower, *War Without Mercy*, 99. This sort of statement was endemic; see detailed notes. For a Japanese view of the Malaya campaign, see Tsuji Masanobu, *Singapore 1941–1942* (Sydney: Ure Smith, 1960). See also Susie Harries, "British Army Perceptions of the Imperial Japanese Army, 1941–45," in *Aspects of the Allied Occupation of Japan, Part II*, Suntory-Toyota International Centre for Economics and Related Disciplines, London School of Economics, Discussion Paper IS/91/229 (September 1991), 1–24.

Notes for pages 96–99

The Japanese and Prisoners of War. Japanese policy and practice are discussed at length in IMTFE. See the many index entries for Prisoners of War in the published transcript, especially entries for 14,295ff., where numerous exhibits are referenced, 27,117ff., and 31,749ff. See also the tribunal's judgment, at 49,699–49,751. See also documents in RG 200, B 1020, NA; ATIS Enemy Publication 321; Adachi, "Unprepared Regrettable Events," generally; Aiko Utsumi, "Prisoners of War in the Pacific War," in Gavan McCormack and Hank Nelson, eds., *The Burma-Thailand Railway* (St. Leonards: Allen and Unwin, 1993), 68–84; Charles Roland, "Allied POWs: Japanese Captors and the Geneva Convention," *War and Society*, Vol. 9, No. 2 (October 1991), 83–101; van Witsen, *Krijgsgevangenen*, 49ff.; I. Brugmans et al., *Nederlandsch Indië Onder Japanse Bezetting* (Franeker: Wever, 1960), 333ff.; Marcel Junod, *Warrior Without Weapons* (New York: Macmillan, 1951), 234–245.

Russo-Japanese War. Louis Seaman, *From Tokio Through Manchuria With the Japanese* (New York: Appleton, 1905), 60ff.; Peter Calvocoressi, Guy Wint, and John Pritchard, *Total War* (New York: Pantheon, 1989), 626–627; Shigemitsu Mamoru, *Japan and Her Destiny* (London: Hutchinson, 1958), 343–349. Siberia: George Montandon, *Deux Ans Chez Koltchak et Chez les Bolcheviques* (Paris: Felix Alcan, 1923), 15; Olive Checkland, *Humanitarianism and the Emperor's Japan, 1877–1977* (London: Macmillan, 1994), generally.

Notes for pages 99–101

Escape. Duty to escape and nonescape oaths: M. Foot and J. Langley, *MI9* (Boston: Little, Brown, 1979), 261; A. Lodge, *The Fall of General Gordon Bennett* (Sydney: Allen and Unwin, 1986), 254; Lewis Bush, *Clutch of Circumstance* (Tokyo: Okuyama, 1956), 82; Oliver Lindsay, *At the Going Down of the Sun* (London: Sphere, 1981), 59ff.; Wigmore, *Japanese Thrust*, 385, 535, 539, 546–547, 631. For information on Dutch regulations, I thank Dr. H. Amersfoort of Sectie Militaire Geschiedenis Landmachtstaf, The Hague. See also Hank Leffelaar and E. van Witsen, *Werkers aan de*

Burma-Spoorweg (Franeker: Wever, 1982), 264ff.; Brugmans, *Nederlandsch-Indië*, 340ff.

Killing Ten. Daws interviews with Besley, Bigger, Knox, Murphy, Sellers, Smetts; UNT interviews with R. Allen, Bolitho, Fung, Stone; Caire/Knox, Turner/Knox; Cook/AWM; G.P. Adams, Sound/IWM; Cranefield, Sound/IWM; Turner, Documents, IWM; IMTFE, PX 3133; U.S. v. Homma, 1545ff., 2171ff.; statement of McComas, U.S. v. Tsuneyoshi, RG 331, B 1061, WNRC; Cabanatuan Log, Microfilm 88, NA; documents on Bilibid and Palawan in Command File, WW II, NHC; Mitchell papers, MHI; Owen papers, MHI; Jackson, MS memoir, MCHC; Michael Quinn, *Love Letters to Mike* (New York: Vantage, 1977), 143; Bert Bank, *Back from the Living Dead* (Tuscaloosa, 1945), 31; A. Feuer, ed., *Bilibid Diary* (Hamden: Archon, 1987), 190–191; Edward Dunlop, *The War Diaries of Weary Dunlop* (Melbourne: Nelson, 1986), 14–16; John Barnard, *The Endless Years* (London: Chantry, 1950), 18; Charles McCormac, *You'll Die in Singapore* (London: Robert Hale, 1954), 35–36; Jack Edwards, *Banzai, You Bastards* (Hong Kong: Corporate Communications, n.d.), 70; Virgil Vining, *Guest of an Emperor* (New York: Carlton, 1968), 75–77; William Berry, *Prisoner of the Rising Sun* (Norman: University of Oklahoma, 1993), 149–150; Reynolds, *Rice*, 92–95; Haney, *Caged Dragons*, 91; Mellnik, *Philippine War Diary*, 175; Grashio and Norling, *Return to Freedom*, 61; Weinstein, *Barbed-Wire Surgeon*, 89; Knox, *Death March*, 180–189; Kerr, *Surrender and Survival*, 96–97, 157; Urwin, "Defenders of Wake," 320; Allen, *Lost Battalion*, 78; Poweleit, *USAFFE*, 70–71, 91; van Witsen, *Krijgsgevangenen*, 31.

Lindsay Ride: Edwin Ride, *B.A.A.G.* (Hong Kong: Oxford, 1981). What I say about escape attempts, successful and unsuccessful, was put together from many scattered sources; see detailed notes. For Japanese soldiers captured and escaping, see Arnold Krammer, "Japanese Prisoners of War in America," *Pacific Historical Review*, Vol. 52, No. 1 (February 1983), 67–91; Charlotte Carr-Gregg, *Japanese Prisoners of War in Revolt* (New York: St. Martin's, 1978); Shinya Michiharu, *The Path From Guadalcanal* (Auckland: Outrigger, 1979).

Notes for pages 102–110

Beatings. Every POW has opinions on the subject; see detailed notes. Japanese standing on boxes: Bras/Daws; Medlin/Daws; Armstrong/UNT; J. Coombes, *Banpong Express* (Darlington: Dresser, n.d.), 111. Somebody always getting beaten—a sampling: AWM interviews with Almond, Botterill, Devenish, Short; UNT with Matlock, McCall, Schwarz; Wright papers, MHI; C. Blackater, *Gods Without Reason* (London: Eyre and Spottiswoode, 1948), 158–159. The Dutch Garden Party: Macrae/AWM; Panaotie/AWM; Joan Beaumont, *Gull Force* (Sydney: Allen and Unwin, 1989), 88–89; Nelson, *POW*, 88.

Korean Guards. I thank Utsumi Aiko for information. For more, see detailed notes. For guidance on comfort women I thank Sekiguchi Noriko, producer of the film "Sensō Daughters." "Japan no pucking good": John Coast, *Railroad of Death* (London: Simpkin Marshall, 1946), 208. "Ingerris-Korean": Barnard, *Endless Years*, 29, 70. "You me samo": H. Nelson/Daws. Guards' nicknames: collected from many sources. Blood and Slime: van Witsen, *Krijgsgevangenen*, 89; Cook and Cook, *Japan at War*, 113ff.

Senior Officers at Karenko. Bunker diary, CMH; papers of the following officers in MHI: Beebe, Gard, Lawrence, Mallonee, Mitchell, Moore, Peck. See also Quinn, *Love Letters to Mike;* William Braly, *The Hard Way Home* (Washington, D.C.: Infantry Journal, 1947). The Toad: Mallonee papers, MHI. Heath: Wainwright, *General Wainwright's Story,* 195; Braly, *Hard Way Home,* 103–104. "Hohman!": Mallonee papers, MHI. The American mess officer: Mallonee papers and Beebe papers, MHI; Wainwright, *General Wainwright's Story,* 203. The mine at Kinkaseki: Edwards, *Banzai,* 92ff.

Officer Privilege. Daws interviews with Adair, G.P. Adams, Bange, Ciarrachi, Drukker, Goodman, Hundscheidt, Luitsz, McInerney, Neumann, Olson, Poidevin, Samethini, Self, van Heekeren, Voll, Woodall, Wright; UNT interviews with Armstrong, Bolitho, Chambers, Hard, Heinen, Lawley, Slate; AWM interviews with Bailey, Braddon, Drummond, Morris, Newton; Marsh, Sound/IWM; the following in Documents/IWM: Boddington, Innes-Ker, Murphy, Pringle, Woodhouse, Thompson, "Into the Sun," MS; papers of Montgomery and Owen in MHI; Jackson MS memoir, CMH; "Diary of a Medical Officer", MS, CMH; Gillespie, "Recollections of the Pacific War"; Peart, MS journal, Library of Congress; Joan Beaumont, "Rank, Privilege and Prisoners of War," *War and Society,* Vol. 1, No. 1 (May 1983), 67–94; Samuel Stouffer et al., *The American Soldier,* Vol. 1, *Adjustment During Army Life* (Princeton: Princeton University, 1949), 367ff.; John Barrett, *We Were There* (Ringwood: Penguin, 1987), 205–206. For many other published sources, see detailed notes.

Jaarmarkt: Fujita/Daws; Allen, *Lost Battalion,* 76. Bandoeng: Dunlop, *War Diaries,* viii. "What's your rank?": Atkinson/Daws. Hong Kong: Bush, *Clutch of Circumstance,* 43. Cabanatuan: Hewlett/Daws; Beecher diary, MS, Douglas County Historical Society—I thank Lee Bendell for permission to see the diary; Chunn, *Of Rice and Men,* 20–21; Weinstein, *Barbed-Wire Surgeon,* 123. Bilibid: Gillespie, "Recollections of the Pacific War"; John Vance, *Doomed Garrison* (Ashland: Cascade, 1974), 175; Ashton, *And Somebody Gives a Damn!,* 302; Chunn, *Of Rice and Men,* 96. "Fat pasha": Skinner/Daws.

Pay, Food, and Welfare Funds. Hayes, Bilibid notebooks, MS, Command File, World War II, NHC; Millar, MS, Command File, World War II, NHC; statement of Morris, RG 339, B 2177, NA; Urwin, "Defenders of Wake," 393ff.; Adachi, "Unprepared Regrettable Events," 300; Walter Rundell, *Military Money* (College Station: 1980), 195; N. Beets, *De Verre Oorlog* (Amsterdam: Boom Meppel, 1981), 210ff.; J. Carel Hamel, *Soldatendominee* (Franeker: Wever, 1975), 65; Leslie Poidevin, *Samurais and Circumcisions* (Burnside, 1985), 67–68; Dunlop, *War Diaries,* 102–103; Blackater, *Gods Without Reason,* 147; Barnard, *Endless Years,* 69. Separate bathing: Daws interviews with Perrin, Stratton, van Heekeren; Leffelaar and van Witsen, *Werkers aan de Burma-Spoorweg,* 29.

Notes for pages 110–114

Work and Food. No work, no food: IMTFE, 14,708–14,709. Japanese and U.S. ration: IMTFE, 10,591; see also Nelson, *POW,* 51. Death Dipper: Alan McCracken, *Very Soon Now, Joe* (New York: Hobson, 1947), 46. "No one ever saw a thin cook": Every POW says this. Malingering percentage: This is my educated guess based on interviews. Drivers as kings: Vince Taylor, *Cabanatuan* (Waco: Texian, 1985), 95.

Crotch Method. Cabanatuan log, microfilm 88, NA; Tisdelle diary—I thank Ash Tisdelle for access to his father's diary; Don Peacock, *The Emperor's Guest* (Cambridge: Oleander, 1989), 133–134. Australian crutching: K. Smith/Daws; White-cross/Daws; Panaotie/AWM; Peat/AWM.

Rice. "There is no more rice in London!": Reese/UNT; Stewart, *To the River Kwai* (London: Bloomsbury, 1988), 114. Dream of slicing the thigh: McCracken, *Very Soon Now, Joe,* 167–168. For more, see detailed notes.

Doover, Snerken, Quan. Ruurdje Laarhoven tells me there is a version of snerken in books and documents about the Netherlands East Indies in the seventeenth and eighteenth centuries. For doover and quan, see detailed notes. Goldie: Malaybalay MS, microfilm 15, NA. Sugar: Fujita/Daws; UNT interviews with Kenner, Matlock, Pryor; Boddington, Documents, IWM; Benjamin Proulx, *Underground from Hong Kong* (New York: Dutton, 1943), 192. Recipes: Knox/Daws; Schwarz/UNT; Taylor/UNT; Hew Crawford, *The Long Green Tunnel* (London: Michael Joseph, 1967), 53; Denis Russell-Roberts, *Spotlight on Singapore* (Douglas: Times, 1965), 229–230. "Food has taken the place of sex": Vardy, Documents, IWM.

Notes for pages 114–118

Smoking. Among POWs a whole smoking culture developed, a vast and intricate subject that was an eye-opener for me; see detailed notes. "Whoo": Robinson/UNT. Oklahoma's cigarette hustle: Atkinson/Daws. "Corn beef is 5 today": McCracken, *Very Soon Now, Joe,* 96ff. The old British sergeant: Stewart, *To the River Kwai,* 104. Guards and cigarette butts: Knox/Daws.

Notes for pages 118–124

Hygiene. See detailed notes. The Texas toothbrush solution: UNT interviews with Chambers, Pryor, Stone, Whitehead. Clippers take off like a Zero: Minshew/UNT. Shaved heads at Bicycle Camp: Searle papers, diary no. 4; I thank Ian Sayer for access. "Rack 'em up!": Wright/Daws; Day, *Hodio,* 61–62.

"A boot full of water": H. Nelson/Daws. "Trink wasser": Payne/Daws. Dutch too dirty for the British: Richard Gough, *S.O.E. Singapore* (London: William Kimber, 1985), 171. British too dirty for the Dutch: Daws interviews with Bras, Hekking, Hundscheidt; also Duff/Daws. Others too dirty for Americans: Fujita, *Foo,* 131. The toilet paper index: Lee Kennett, *G.I.* (New York: Scribner's, 1987), 96. Paper substitutes: Stone/UNT; Mario Machi, *The Emperor's Hostages* (New York: Vantage, 1982), 60; Stanley Pavillard, *Bamboo Doctor* (New York: St. Martin's, 1960), 182.

Rice Balls. Daws interviews with G.P. Adams, Erickson, L. Nelson; Fujita/UNT; Rea/UNT; Arneil/AWM; the following in Documents, IWM: Vardy, Pringle, Springer; WO 235/975, PRO. See detailed notes for more; also for scabies, oculo-oro-genital syndrome, deficiency diseases, etc. The Japanese and beriberi: Baron Takaki, "The Preservation of Health Amongst the Personnel of the Japanese Navy and Army," *Lancet,* May 19, 1906, 1370–1374, May 26, 1906, 1451–1455, June 2, 1906, 1520–1523; Louis Seaman, *The Real Triumph of Japan* (New York: Appleton, 1907), 220ff. Beriberi song: William McDougall, *By Eastern Windows* (London: Barker, 1951), 205ff.

"Those who fails": Basil Peacock, *Prisoner on the Kwai* (London: Blackwood,

1966), 191. "Health follows will": Dunlop, *War Diaries,* 259. Japanese medical officers: As an introduction, see "Prisoner of War Journals in Hospital Corps Archives Files," and "List of Documents, Personal Papers, Diaries, Official Records, and Other Items Recovered From the Bilibid Hospital for Military Prison Camps of the Philippine Islands," NHC. See also Poidevin/Daws; statement of Gaskill, RG 331, B 957, WNRC; statement of Hagan, Prisoners of War, World War II, NHC; Philps, Documents, IWM; WO 235/963, PRO; ATIS Research Report 76, iv, 18–19; USSBS 12, "Effects of Bombing on Health and Medical Services in Japan," 16ff.; Geoffrey Adams, *No Time for Geishas* (London: Leo Cooper, 1973), 103; John Howell, *42 Months of Hell* (Muskogee: Hoffman, 1971), 28; Dunlop, *War Diaries,* 242, 324, 367–368; Ashton, *Bataan Diary,* 260; Weinstein, *Barbed-Wire Surgeon,* 119; Coombes, *Banpong Express,* 137; Bilyeu, *Lost in Action,* 292; Alex Dandie, *The Story of J Force* (Sydney: 1985), 45–49.

Burning feet: Pryor/UNT; Montgomery papers, MHI; J. Page, "Painful-Feet Syndrome Among Prisoners of War in the Far East," *British Medical Journal,* Vol. II, No. 4468 (1946), 260–262; Kenneth Harrison, *The Brave Japanese* (Adelaide: Rigby, 1966), 98.

Rats. Malaybalay MS, microfilm 15, NA. "Never sleep with your mouth open": Roy Bulcock, *Of Death but Once* (Melbourne: Cheshire, 1947), 110. Vermin: Burke/UNT; Stone/UNT; statement of Hinkle, RG 389, B 2132, NA; statement of Gilles, RG 331, B 957, WNRC; "To Victory, Joe," MS, microfilm 15, NA. Bedbugs: Daws interviews with Knox, Mroz, L. Nelson; Robinson/AWM; Chambers/UNT; Pryor/UNT; Pringle, Documents, IWM; C. van Heekeren, *Het Pannetje van Oliemans* (Franeker: Wever, 1975), 14. The Dutch chicken: van Heekeren/Daws. Picking bedbugs off the jacket: Owen papers, MHI.

Notes for pages 124–134

Yasume. Entertainment, homosexuality, and stage ladies: Daws interviews with Becher, Bras, Harrison, Luitsz, Mock, Poidevin, Samethini, van Heekeren; Chisholm/AWM; Drummond/AWM; Turner, Documents, IWM; Wim Kan, *Burmadagboek 1942–1945* (Amsterdam: Arbeiderspers, 1986). This is another subject of great fascination to POWs; for more, see detailed notes. See also Allan Berube, *Coming Out Under Fire* (New York: Free Press, 1990), 3, 70ff. "There's fuck all left": Fujita, *Foo,* 152.

University of the Far East. See detailed notes. "How now": Nelson, *POW,* 26. Mental escape: Wigmore, *Japanese Thrust,* 515.

Tattoos. The Japanese doctor copying tattoos: H. Knox/Daws. Soccer team tattoo: Wallace/Daws.

Mail. "I am interned": Norman Gruenzner, *Postal History of American POWs* (State College: American Philatelic Society, 1979), 68. Outgoing mail: Luitsz/Daws; documents in RG 389, B 2120, NA. Incoming mail: Gee/UNT; Pryor/UNT; Korteweg, Documents, IWM; Hodge, Sound/IWM; Wright papers, MHI; David Nelson, *The Story of Changi* (Perth: Changi, 1974), 123; Chunn, *Of Rice and Men,* 140; Feuer, *Bilibid,* 212–213. Reading over shoulder: Knox/Daws.

Radio Messages. Daws interviews with Atkinson, H. Brown, Dandie; Curtis, Oral History Collection, MCHC; Kessler memoir; Innes-Ker, Documents, IWM; Earl Fitzgerald, *Voices in the Night* (Bellingham: Pioneer Printing, 1948).

Secret Radios. Another big subject. A sampling: Daws interviews with Banens, Besters, Briggs, Ciarrachi, R. Davis, Denham, Denholm, Douglas, Duizend, Duncan, Hutchison, Maple, Price, Readwin, Stanbrough, van Iterson, Visker, Wise, Woudsma; UNT interviews with Godbold, McDaniel, Pryor, Reichle, Sparkman; S. Davis/AWM; Scott/SNA; Kessler memoir; IMTFE, 13,403ff.; M. Price, "Communicators in Far East Prisoner of War Camps, 1942–1945," *Journal of the Royal Signals Institution* (Summer 1981), 89–95. For more, see detailed notes.

Kempei and Radios. IMTFE, 12,935–12,945, 13,404–13,419; Pringle, Documents, IWM; Nelson, *POW,* 102ff.; Wigmore, *Japanese Thrust,* 594ff., 598ff.; van Witsen, *Krijgsgevangenen,* 56. Singapore: Colin Sleeman and S. Silkin, eds., *Trial of Sumida Haruzo and Twenty Others* (London: William Hodge, 1951). Hong Kong: Lindsay, *At the Going Down,* 131ff.

Rumors. See detailed notes. "Rations are increased": Charles Fisher, *Three Times a Guest* (London: Cassell, 1979), 47–49; Adams, *No Time for Geishas,* 35. Amelia Earhart: Chunn, *Of Rice and Men,* 108–109. Davao latrines: McCracken, *Very Soon Now, Joe,* 43, 107. Rumor and Rumor Junior: Matlock/UNT. Whores repatriated: Royal Gunnison, *So Sorry, No Peace* (New York: Viking, 1944), 138ff. White civilians exchanged: Paul Corbett, "Quiet Passages," Ph.D. dissertation, University of Kansas, 1983. Wangle Marus: Abkhazi/Daws. Volcano on Java: Banens/Daws. For rumors in war generally, see Paul Fussell, *Wartime* (New York: Oxford University Press, 1989), 38ff.

"Did nothing all day": Vardy, Documents, IWM.

Notes for pages 134–140

Brotherhood and Tribes. "The strong beat the weak": Atkinson/Daws; Jeffries/Daws. Damyankees: Dunn/Daws. Dead End Kids: Schwarz/Daws. Texas talk: Burge/UNT. The Cabanatuan Combine's duck: Chunn, *Of Rice and Men,* 172. Pineapple cake: Delich/Daws. Pryor and Willey: Pryor/UNT. One set of uppers and lowers: Chunn, *Of Rice and Men,* 24. "My father taught me": Knox/Daws.

Subtribes Forming. Every prisoner interviewed has strong opinions on this; see detailed notes. See also Tisdelle diary; Price, Documents, IWM; Murphy, Documents, IWM; Thompson, "Into the Sun," MS, IWM; E. Hall, *The Burma-Thailand Railway of Death* (Armadale: Graphic, 1981), 130; Bilyeu, *Lost in Action,* 112–113, 251; Hibbs, *Tell MacArthur,* 183; Preston Hubbard, *Apocalypse Undone* (Nashville: Vanderbilt University Press, 1990), 115ff.; Knox, *Death March,* 265–266; McCracken, *Very Soon Now, Joe,* 45, 75, 196–197; Vining, *Guest of an Emperor,* 26; Lindsay, *At the Going Down,* 182; Beaumont, *Gull Force,* 84; Emerson, *Guest of the Emperor,* 75, 117ff.; Blackater, *Gods Without Reason,* 125ff., 153; Russell-Roberts, *Spotlight on Singapore,* 229; McDougall, *By Eastern Windows,* 197–198; Peacock, *Prisoner on the Kwai,* 52–53, 130–131, 223; Reginald Burton, *Road to Three Pagodas* (London: Macdonald, 1963), 57–58; J. Veenstra, ed., *Als Krijgsgevangene naar de Molukken en Flores* ('s-Gravenhage: Martinus Nijhoff, 1982), 168; Hamel, *Soldaten-dominee,* 96–97. Stewart, *To the River Kwai,* 83, 105–106; John Glusman, "Heroes and Sons," *Virginia Quarterly Review,* Vol. 4, No. 4 (Autumn 1990), 703.

Best Size for a Tribe. Every POW has an opinion. A sampling: Daws interviews with Bange, Duizend, Forsman, Goodman, Nooij, Wallace; Mapes/Knox; Nelson, *POW,* 94; Ernest Gordon, *Through the Valley of the Kwai* (New York: Harper, 1962), 102. "There's quite a lot of God": an observation by Edward Dunlop.

III. LEARNING ON THE JOB
Notes for pages 141–153

Shanghai War Prisoners Camp. Principal interviews: Daws with Atkinson, Jeffries, Brown, Ciarrachi, Crow, Davidson, Foley, Green, L. Nelson, Nye, Williamson. Also: UNT with Sparkman, Venable, McDaniel.

For background on Woosung and Kiangwan, see statement of Brown, RG 389, B 2176, NA; Kessler MS memoir; Urwin, "Defenders of Wake," 282ff.; Cunningham, *Wake Island Command,* 163ff.; Quentin Reynolds, *Officially Dead* (New York: Random House, 1945), 35ff.; Terence Kirk, *The Secret Camera* (Cotati: La Bohème, 1983), 40ff; Chester Biggs, *Behind the Barbed Wire* (Jefferson: McFarland, 1944).

"Right step!": Atkinson/Daws. "What color is horseshit?": Atkinson/Daws. Bread and Whangpoo: Kessler MS memoir. Tōjō Water: John White, *The United States Marines in North China* (Millbrae: 1974), 31. "Air the blankets!": Atkinson/Daws. "Go ahead": Atkinson/Daws. Mount Fuji: Urwin, "Defenders of Wake," 345ff. Red Cross packages: Atkinson/Daws. "The less you smoke": Jeffries/Daws. Ishihara: Urwin, "Defenders of Wake," 340ff.; White, *United States Marines,* 69ff. "You British really fuck up the English language," and "Why you not giving me SOLUTION": testimony in U.S. v. Ishihara, case 119-19-2, B 1662, RG 153, WNRC. Weak sisters: Jeffries/Daws. "Eat my soup": Atkinson/Daws.

Notes for pages 153–165

Forrest Knox and the Truck Detail. Principal interview: Knox/Daws. "At last I am getting the respect": Knox/Daws. Lumban escape and shooting: Knox/Daws; Bigger/Daws; Caire/Knox; U.S. v. Homma, Vol. 12, 1545ff.; Knox, *Death March,* 181–184.

Cabanatuan. A basic source is the Cabanatuan log, microfilm 15, NA. See also Beecher diary; Chunn, *Of Rice and Men,* generally; Knox, *Death March,* 198ff. Ted Lewin: Daws interviews with T. Carter, Herbst, O'Leary, Skarda; Lawton/Knox; Beecher diary; Moore papers, MHI; Wright papers, MHI.

The Farm. The Cabanatuan log has details. See also Galos/Daws; Burns/UNT; the papers of Wright, Owen, and Moore in MHI; Jackson memoir, MCHC; Knox, *Death March,* 229ff. Officers working: Beecher diary; Chunn, *Of Rice and Men,* 44–45, 51ff., 149ff.; Weinstein, *Barbed-Wire Surgeon,* 152. "Flower fucking": Knox/Daws. Airfield construction detail: Knox/Daws, Stewart/Daws.

Notes for pages 165–181

Bicycle Camp. Principal interviews: Daws with Wright, Stanbrough. The UNT interviews are full of detail. See also Harrell papers, courtesy of Otto Schwarz; Tharp papers, courtesy of Roger White; Day, "Saga of the USS *Houston,*" MS, Command File, WWII, NHC; Lost Battalion and *Houston* memoirs already cited; Arthur Bancroft and R. Roberts, *The Mikado's Guests* (Perth: Paterson, n.d.) 22ff.; Rivett, *Behind Bamboo,* 111ff.

"It's amazing": Wright/Daws. Jack Shaw taking notes: Bramlett/UNT; Dunn,

Bamboo Express, 60. Guilders brought into camp: Kelley/UNT; Slate/UNT.

Roy Stensland. For background, see Robert Underbrink, *Destination Corregidor* (Annapolis: United States Naval Institute, 1971), 29, 34, 59, 60–74. "The hell you say": Wright/Daws. For another version of the food system, see La Forte and Marcello, *Building the Death Railway,* 68ff. Stensland and Japanese guards: UNT interviews with Douglas, Pryor, Spencer, Stone; Dunn, *Bamboo Express,* 62. Liquor in camp: Rivett, *Behind Bamboo,* 116.

Pack Rat McCone: Every American from Bicycle Camp has McCone stories; see UNT interviews. Rasbury's Finer Fudge: Rasbury/UNT. Dynamite Dunn: Dunn, *Bamboo Express,* 31, 50, 54. Poodles Norley: Rivett, *Behind Bamboo,* 121. McManus's mural: Schwarz/UNT.

Dutch women: Every Java POW has a story; see Bulcock, *Of Death but Once,* 121ff.; Peacock, *Emperor's Guest,* 39; Fujita, *Foo,* 102.

Stanbrough's radio: Stanbrough/UNT; Ficklin/UNT; Devenish/AWM; Spurgeon/AWM. "Touch that": Stanbrough/Daws.

Technicians. Australian lies: C. Harrison/Daws; Harrison, *Brave Japanese,* 124–125; Clarke, *Last Stop Nagasaki,* 72. Peach-fur pickers: Pryor/UNT. Shipped to Singapore: Harrell papers; Pringle, Documents/IWM. The white ship: This vision turns up in POW stories everywhere. The glass rod: Every POW has stories about this, too.

Changi. Nelson, *Story of Changi;* Nelson, *POW,* 24ff. British officers: UNT interviews with Detre, Rasbury, R. Robinson, Pryor, Stone; Turner, Documents, IWM; Dunn, *Bamboo Express,* 67. "Java rabble": Schultz, *Last Battle Station,* 232. Food and Red Cross packages: Pryor/Daws. "You can't do that!": Dunn, *Bamboo Express,* 68C. Niggershooters and latrine sparrows: Fujita/Daws. "I'm giving you an order": Douglas/UNT. The fat colonel: Detre/UNT. Chickens: Rasbury/UNT. Dempsey Key: Dunn/Daws; Dunn, *Bamboo Express,* 71; Day, *Hodio,* 71. Eating the British dog: Fujita/Daws; Rafalovich/Daws; Fujita, *Foo,* 120–123. "Bannockburn!": Dunn, *Bamboo Express,* 70. "Their mutton wasn't any good": Burge/UNT. "You Limeys can unlock your chicken pens now": Dunn, *Bamboo Express,* 78.

"On the Road to Mandalay": Rivett, *Behind Bamboo,* 166. Recognizing Rangoon: Brain/UNT. Moulmein jail: Every POW coming to Burma through Moulmein has a jail story—for a sampling, UNT interviews with Armstrong, Hard, Rea, Taylor, Whitehead; Bancroft, *Mikado's Guests,* 51.

IV. WORKING ON THE RAILROAD
Notes for pages 183–195

Burma-Siam Railroad. Principal interviews: Daws with Wright, Hekking, G.P. Adams, Bras, Forsman, Wallace. Many UNT interviews are excerpted in La Forte and Marcello, *Building the Death Railway.*

A major documentary source is testimony from British war crimes trials. Transcripts in PRO run to thousands of pages. The principal trial is WO 235/963. See also SEATIC Consolidated Interrogation Report 83, January 22, 1945; SEATIC Bulletin 246, October 8, 1946.

For more railroad background and detail, see Ewart Escritt, *Beyond the Three Pagodas Pass* (privately published, 1988). Escritt's papers, in Documents, IWM, include a translation of Y. Futumatsu, *Santogē wo Koete* [Across the Three Pagodas

Pass—The Story of the Burma-Siam Railway] (Tokyo: 1985). Futumatsu published two other works: *An Account of the Construction of the Thai-Burma Railroad* (1955), and *Recollections of the Thai-Burma Railway* (1980). T. Yoshiwara, ed., *Santari Tetsu-dōhei no Kiroku* [Radiant Record of Railroad Troops] (Tokyo: 1965), contains a Burma-Siam section. See also Frank Trager, *Burma* (Philadelphia: University of Pennsylvania Press, 1971), 231–236; Charles Fisher, "The Thailand-Burma Railway," *Economic Geography*, Vol. 23, No. 2 (April, 1947), 85–97; Clive Kinvig, *River Kwai Railway* (London: Brassey, 1992); Leffelaar and van Witsen, *Werkers aan de Burma-Spoorweg*. "ICHI-NI-NESSAIYO": Donald Smith, *And All the Trumpets* (London: Bles, 1954), 86–87.

"Nobody is permitted to eat": Every POW from the Burma end of the railroad remembers Nagatomo's speech; for example, Gee/UNT; Roy Whitecross, *Slaves of the Son of Heaven* (Sydney: Dymock's, 1953), 47ff.; Hall, *Burma-Thailand Railway*, 51.

Trading for Hekking: Wright/Daws; Hekking/Daws. The interpreter who made the trade, Cornelius Punt, published a memoir under the pseudonym Cornel Lumière: *Kura!* (Brisbane: Jacaranda, 1966).

"This is depressing": Wright/UNT. "You sons of bitches": Wright/Daws; for another version of what Slug said, see Rivett, *Behind Bamboo*, 243.

Doc Hekking. Daws interviews with Henri Hekking, May Hekking, Fred Hekking, Wright. Hekking stories are like Stensland stories; they are everywhere in UNT interviews. See also Poidevin, *Samurais and Circumcisions*, 11; Hall, *Burma-Thailand Railway*, 54.

Dutch Colonial Military Medicine. Daws interviews with Bras, de Monchy, Hekking, Stahlie. Medina's paralysis: Medina/Daws. Language on the railroad: Clarke/AWM; Strongg, Documents, IWM; Rivett, *Behind Bamboo*, 184; Coast, *Railroad*, 89; Philippa Poole, *Of Love and War* (Sydney: Lansdowne, 1982), 207. Delivering the baby: Wright/Daws.

Notes for pages 195–201

Tropical Ulcers. Philip Manson-Bahr, ed., *Manson's Tropical Diseases*—especially the tenth through the thirteenth editions (1935–1951). Ulcers on Timor: G.P. Adams/Daws; Hekking/Daws; Poidevin, *Samurais and Circumcisions*, 15, 44, 50. Philippines: Cooper, "Medical Department Activities"; Carlos Quirino, *Chick Parsons* (Quezon City: New Day, 1984), 34. Ambon: Hunter/Daws; Edward Weiss, *Below the Horizon* (privately published, 1992), 176. Haruku: the following in Documents, IWM: Hodson, Philps, Springer. All POW doctors agree that ulcers on the railroad were the worst.

POW Doctrine on Ulcers. Daws interviews with Bras, de Graaff, van Dam, Whitecross; many UNT interviews (see detailed notes); Coast, *Railroad*, 118–119, 141; Cornelis Evers, *Death Railway* (Bangkok: Craftsman, 1993), 56–57; Harrison, *Brave Japanese*, 200. Fish the size of minnows: Bolt/Daws; T. Douglas/Daws; Offerle/UNT; Michell/AWM; Frank Foster, *Comrades in Bondage* (London: Skeffington, 1946), 140; van Witsen, *Krijgsgevangenen*, 139; Ray Parkin, *Into the Smother* (London: Hogarth, 1963), 230; Ray Parkin, *The Sword and the Blossom* (London: Hogarth, 1968), 11–12.

Albert Coates. Albert Coates and Newman Rosenthal, *The Albert Coates Story*

(Melbourne: Hyland House, 1977). Coates's testimony in IMTFE is at 11,403ff. 55 Kilo camp: Schwarz/Daws; Turner, Documents, IWM; Gavan McCormack and Hank Nelson, eds., *The Burma-Thailand Railway* (St. Leonards: Allen and Unwin, 1993), 30ff.; Hall, *Burma-Thailand Railway*, 92ff.

Doctrine on amputation: Kevin Fagan, "Surgical Experiences as a Prisoner of War," *Medical Journal of Australia*, Vol. 1 (1946), 776; Alan Walker, *Clinical Problems of War* (Canberra: Australian War Memorial, 1952), 669; Dunlop, *War Diaries*, generally; Daws interviews with de Graaff, Drukker, Duizend, Hundscheidt, Luitsz, Neumann; G. Douglas/UNT; van Witsen, *Krijgsgevangenen*, 136–139. L. Robertson, *The Gap* (Sydney: 7th Division Engineers Association, 1982), 228–229; Rowley Richards and Marcia McEwan, *The Survival Factor* (Sydney: Kangaroo, 1989) 155ff.; J. Cannoo, *Bushidō* (Leiden: Slijthoff, 1947), 107; van Witsen, *Krijgsgevangenen*, 136, 142; Leffelaar and van Witsen, *Werkers*, 8, 190.

"Dr. Coates, I presume": Hekking/Daws. Hugh Lumpkin and William Epstein: UNT interviews with Brown, Douglas, Reese Taylor; statement of Smith, Command File, World War II, NHC; Dunn, *Bamboo Express*, 107, 117, 120–121.

Coates's death rate with amputations: Albert Coates, "Surgery in Japanese Prison Camps," *Australian and New Zealand Journal of Surgery*, Vol. 15, No. 3 (January 1946), 150–155. See also Coates, "Fundamental Principles in Medical Practice," *Medical Journal of Australia*, Vol. 2, No. 22 (November 30, 1946), 757–763; and Edward Dunlop, "Medical Experiences in Japanese Captivity," *British Medical Journal*, 2:4474 (1946), 484.

Notes for pages 202–218

Siam Drafts. See detailed notes. Scavenging: Dunlop, *War Diaries*, 216–217, 228; Ronald Searle, *To the Kwai—and Back* (London: Collins, 1986), 102. "Any of you blokes speak English?": Harrison, *Brave Japanese*, 203. Administrative control and food: Woodhouse, Sound/IWM; Lee/SNA. Burma real estate: Teel, *Our Days Were Years*, 82–83. "What a beautiful bunch of bananas": many versions of this story are told at POW reunions.

Food along the railway: see detailed notes. Meat: A. van der Schaaf, "Veterinary Experiences as a Japanese Prisoner of War and ex-POW Along the Burma Railroad From 1941 to January 1946," *Tijdsschrift voor Diergeneeskunde*, Vol. 15, No. 104, Supplement 4 (1979), 212–228. Malnutrition rodeo: Rivett, *Behind Bamboo*, 210. "Snake!": Wright/Daws; Bramlett/UNT; Burge/UNT. The Gordon Highlanders' lasso: Blackater, *Gods Without Reason*, 102. Drought-stricken horse: Nelson, *POW*, 45; Moore/Nelson. Cooking shoe tops: Matlock/UNT.

Speedo and the Kumi Quota. Newton/AWM; A. Allbury, *Bamboo and Bushido* (London: Robert Hale, 1955), 56–57; Coombes, *Banpong Express*, 135; Coast, *Railroad*, 70; Bancroft, *Mikado's Guests*, 58; Dunlop, *War Diaries*, 192, 208, 210; Richards and McEwan, *Survival Factor*, 152ff. Japanese medical arithmetic: IMTFE, 11,415.

Sick men on the job: Gerrit Bras, "Ziekten en Hun Behandeling in Kampen Langs de Rivier de Kwai," *Nederlands Tijdschrift voor Geneeskunde*, No. 32 (August 10, 1985), 1529–1532; Ian Duncan, "Makeshift Medicine: Combating Disease in Japanese Prison Camps," *Medical Journal of Australia* (January 1983), 29–32; Dunlop, *War Diaries*, 191; Patsy Adam-Smith, *Prisoners of War* (Ringwood: Viking-Penguin,

1992), 500ff. The British doctor's moral sums: Jeffery English, *One for Every Sleeper* (London: Robert Hale, 1989), 143–144; see also Fagan/AWM. Bandy Galyean: Wallace/Daws; Pavillard, *Bamboo Doctor,* 104; Robertson, *Gap,* 226; Dunn, *Bamboo Express,* 110, 116.

The Monsoon. Wright/Daws; Weissinger/Daws; Strongg, Documents, IWM; statement of Smith, Command File, World War II, NHC; Allbury, *Bamboo and Bushido,* 57; Coombes, *Banpong Express,* 137; Peacock, *Prisoner on the Kwai,* 155–159; Adams, *No Time for Geishas,* 71.

Officers Working. Baillies MS, Documents, IWM; Robert Hardie, *The Burma-Siam Railway* (London: Quadrangle, 1984), 104–105; Ian Watt, *The Humanities on the River Kwai* (Cedar City: Southern Utah State College Press, 1982), 16; Coombes, *Banpong Express,* 112ff.; Dunlop, *War Diaries,* 208; Fisher, *Three Times a Guest,* 69. "Can't see to can't see": Fung/Daws.

Rōmusha. IMTFE, 13,654ff.; Osman/SNA; Kanahele, "Japanese Occupation of Indonesia," 304; Jan Pluvier, *Southeast Asia From Colonialism to Independence* (Kuala Lumpur: Oxford University, 1974), 237ff.; Theodore Friend, *The Blue-Eyed Enemy* (Princeton: Princeton University, 1988), 165–166; de Jong, *Koninkrijk,* Vol. 11b, Part 2, 515ff.; Brugmans, *Nederlandsch-Indië,* 505–506; van Witsen, *Krijgsgevangenen,* 66.

Cholera. In Japanese occupied territory: ATIS Research Report 92, 6ff. The epidemic on the railroad: Bras/Daws; Morris/Nelson/AWM; Pounder, Sound/ IWM; the following in Documents, IWM: Baillies, Hoops, Strongg, Vardy. See also H. de Wardener, "Cholera Epidemic Among Prisoners of War in Siam," *Lancet,* Vol. 1, No. 18 (May 1946), 637–640; Wigmore, *Japanese Thrust,* 573ff.; Walker, *Clinical Problems,* 587ff.; Coast, *Railroad,* 119ff.; Dunlop, *War Diaries,* 244ff.; Pavillard, *Bamboo Doctor,* 130ff.; Cannoo, *Bushidō,* 99ff.

The Dutch and cholera: Daws interviews with Bras, Drukker, Samethini; Beets, *Verre Oorlog,* 243; Leffelaar and van Witsen, *Werkers,* 150, 179; Frits Wolthuis, "Cholera in Thailand," *Nederlands Tijdschrift voor Geneeskunde,* No. 32 (August 10, 1985), 1538–1539; Cannoo, *Bushidō,* 104. Cholera precautions: Pavillard, *Bamboo Doctor,* 130.

Rōmusha and cholera: Escritt papers, Documents, IWM; Bancroft and Roberts, *Mikado's Guests,* 81–82; Pavillard, *Bamboo Doctor,* 130ff.: Hardie, *Burma-Siam Railway,* 105ff. "All I have is for family": Harrison, *Brave Japanese,* 199. "Use your hands": Stewart, *To the River Kwai,* 119. Burning the cholera dead: T. Douglas/ Daws; Fung/UNT; Denny, Sound/IWM; C. Lee/SNA; Coombes, *Banpong Express,* 137. Dead Tamil: Hall, *Burma-Thailand Railway,* 136. Spearing the wet beriberis: English, *One for Every Sleeper,* 153.

Escapes. This account was put together from many sources; see detailed notes.

Suicide. The figure is my educated guess. I have not been able to find more than half a dozen or so cases in railroad doctors' written notes; and no doctor I have spoken to thinks there would have been more than a dozen.

Swede Ecklund: Wright/Daws; Stone/UNT. "There is a ship!": Matlock/ UNT. Burials: Marsh, Sound/IWM.

Radios. Wigmore, *Japanese Thrust,* 557. Tom Douglas: Douglas/Daws. Donald and Max Webber: Lindy Bradley kindly supplied a copy of Donald Webber's diary. See also Daws interviews with Denham, Denholm, Readwin. The Kanchanaburi radio atrocity: Lomax/Daws; WO 235/822, PRO; *FEPOW Forum,* January–February, 1985; Lumière, *Kura!,* 151–152.

H.H. Lilley: Evans, Documents, IWM; Hoops, Documents, IWM; Rowell/ SNA; Coast, *Railroad,* 71. Philip Toosey: Toosey's papers are in Documents, IWM; see also Peter Davies, *The Man Behind the Bridge* (London: Athlone, 1991); Hamel, *Soldatendominee,* 140, 153–154; Watt, *Humanities on the River Kwai,* 14ff.

    Railroad Construction Figures. For differing compilations, see Escritt papers, Documents, IWM; "Report by Japanese Government, Burma-Thailand Railway," IMTFE, exhibit 475; Wigmore, *Japanese Thrust,* 588. Finishing the railroad and completion ceremony: see detailed notes.

Notes for pages 218–251

After the Railroad. Sabotage: Whitecross/Daws; Henderson/AWM; Escritt papers, Documents, IWM; Marsh, Sound/IWM; Stitt, Sound/IWM; James Bradley, *Towards the Setting Sun* (Chichester: Phillimore, 1982), 54; Lumière, *Kura!,* 133.

    Hopelessly sick prisoners: Boddington, Hoops, Vardy, in Documents, IWM; Fisher, *Three Times a Guest,* 72; John Durnford, *Branch Line to Burma* (London: Macdonald, 1958), 116ff. "Your 2/30th all present": Nelson, *POW,* 68; Drummond/AWM; Aspinall/AWM. See also A. Penfold et al., *Galleghan's Greyhounds* (Sydney: 2/30th Bn AIF Association, 1979).

    Japanese Figures on Deaths. IMTFE, exhibit 475. Healthy Japanese, discipline, good spirits: testimony by senior Japanese officers Banno, Hachizuka, Ishida, Nakamura, and Yanagida in WO 235/963, PRO. See also Matsuura/AWM; ATIS Research Report 83, 3ff.; van Witsen, *Krijgsgevangenen,* 261; Cannoo, *Bushidō,* 81.

    Sledgehammer to the head: Harrison, *Brave Japanese,* 168. Injecting chloroform: Wigmore, *Japanese Thrust,* 588. Rōmusha crucified: Hardie, *Burma-Siam Railway,* 133. Interpreter put in hole: Baillies, Documents, IWM; Hall, *Burma-Thailand Railway,* 203. Interpreter set on fire: Stitt, Sound/IWM. Staff not from Japan proper, and inadequate preparation: testimony in WO 235/963, PRO.

    Exact Figures for POW Dead. Wigmore, *Japanese Thrust,* 588. Japanese opinion of POWs by nationality: Spurgeon/Daws; ATIS Research Report 72, 115; ATIS Research Report 76, vi, 25; ATIS Enemy Publication 321; SEATIC Intelligence Bulletin 229, Chapter 3. "One Aussie": Thompson, "Into the Sun," Documents, IWM. See also Fisher, *Three Times a Guest,* 52; Dunlop, *War Diaries,* 275; Louis Allen, "To Be a Prisoner," *Journal of European Studies,* Vol. 16, Part 4, No. 64 (December 1986), 233–248. American deaths: Lost Battalion and *Houston* Survivors Association roster. Stensland: UNT interviews are full of stories of Stensland on the railroad. Officer survival rates: Hank Nelson, "A Bowl of Rice for Seven Camels," *Journal of the Australian War Memorial,* No. 14 (1989), 33–42.

    The spijkerploeg: Daws interviews with Bras, de Monchy, Stahlie, van Gorp, Wolterbeek; Hubert de Monchy, "Ervaringen uit Krijgsgevangenkampen in Thailand," *Nederlands Tijdschrift voor Geneeskunde,* No. 32 (August 10, 1985), 1535–1538; van Witsen, *Krijgsgevangenen,* 127; Leffelaar and van Witsen, *Werkers,* 21–31, 150.

    "Columbia, the Gem of the Ocean": Wright/Daws. Tha Muang clothing survey: Figures are in WO 235/963, PRO. Base camp businesses: Dunlop, *War Diaries,* 332, 365. Cigarette making: Smith, *And All the Trumpets,* 137ff. Charley Pryor tailoring: Pryor/UNT. Dutch laundry: Hamel, *Soldatendominee,* 159.

    Eddie Fung's birthday party: Fung/UNT. Mick the Yank: Douglas/UNT. "White Christmas": Douglas/Daws. Stage ladies: Arneil/AWM; Coast, *Railroad,*

174ff. Horse races: Hoops, Documents, IWM; Dunlop, *War Diaries,* 339, 372–373.

Japan Shipments. McInerney/Daws; Newton/AWM; Allbury, *Bamboo and Bushido,* 126; Coombes, *Banpong Express,* 148; A. Apthorp, *British Sumatra Battalion* (Lewes: Book Guild, 1988), 119–121; Whitecross, *Slaves,* 131; Cannoo, *Bushidō,* 147; Parkin, *Sword and Blossom,* 58–59; Rivett, *Behind Bamboo,* 315; Hugh Clarke, *Last Stop Nagasaki!* (Sydney: Allen and Unwin, 1984), 5. See also Peter Allen, "The Fate of the 18th Division Royal Engineers," *Royal Engineers Journal,* Vol. 106, No. 1 (April 1992), 12–19.

"I did a bum inspection": Vardy, Documents, IWM. "Chungkai, Chungkai": Smith, *And All the Trumpets,* 105.

Tropical Ulcers. Jacob Markowitz, "A Series of Over 100 Amputations of the Thigh for Tropical Ulcer," *Journal of the Royal Army Medical Corps,* Vol. 86 (April 1946), 159ff. One-legged men at Chungkai: Dunlop, *War Diaries,* 322. Tarsao amputees: Parkin, *Into the Smother,* 264–265. Artificial leg factory: Marsh, Sound/IWM. 'Arry's 'Appy Amps: Whitecross, *Slaves,* 128; Turner, Documents, IWM.

Americans and British. Wright/Daws; Michell/AWM; Apthorp, *Sumatra Battalion,* 95. Preston Stone court-martialed: Stone/UNT. "The Australians are with the Yanks": Ballinger/Daws. For a more affable view, see Fisher, *Three Times a Guest,* 77ff. The colonel's dog: Robinson/AWM. For another dog story, see Slim de Grey, *Changi: The Funny Side* (Bundall: 1991), 134ff.

Doc Hekking's radio: Hekking/Daws; Wright/Daws. The can of peaches: Wright/Daws.

V. HARD TIME
Notes for pages 253–256

Jails. For Outram Road, a basic source is the British war crimes trial WO 235/975, PRO. See also IMTFE, 12,913ff., 38,239–38,243; statement of Rogers, RG 389, B 2120, NA; Forsman/Daws; Forsman/UNT; Harrell papers; AWM interviews with S. Davis, Neilsen, Taylor, Trackson, Wells; Chew/SNA; Liau/SNA; Innes-Ker, Documents, IWM; Bradley, Sound/IWM; Bradley, *Towards the Setting Sun,* 98ff.; John McGregor, *Blood on the Rising Sun* (Sydney: Bencoolen, 1980); Bill Young, *Return to a Dark Age* (Allawah: 1991); Nelson, *POW,* 165ff.

Kempei. Nagase/AWM; SNA interviews with Choy, De Souza, Heng, Lim, Marcus, Soon; IMTFE, 12,779, 13,674ff., and PX 5732; WO 235/116, PRO; documents in RG 226, E 106, B 47, NA; statement of Reiner, RG 389, B 2177, NA; Harrell papers; SEATIC Intelligence Bulletin 229; OSS/State Department Intelligence and Research Reports, "Japan and Its Occupied Territories During World War II: The Kempei in Japanese-Occupied Territory," July 13, 1945; SCAP, "History of the Non-Military Activities of the Occupation of Japan: Trials of Class B and C War Criminals," 59ff.; Kanahele, "Japanese Occupation of Indonesia," 273; Louis Allen, "The Japanese Intelligence System," *Journal of Contemporary History,* Vol. 22 (1987), 552–554; Lord Russell, *The Knights of Bushido* (London: Corgi, 1960), 298ff.; Ronald Seth, *Encyclopedia of Espionage* (Garden City: Doubleday, 1972), 325–328; Barbara Shimer and Guy Hobbs, *The Kenpeitai in Java and Sumatra* (Ithaca: Cornell University Press, 1986); Maria Syjuco, *The Kempei Tai in the Philippines* (Quezon City, 1988); de Jong, *Koninkrijk,* Vol. 11b, Part 1, 466ff.; Cook and Cook, *Japan at War,* 151ff.; Otto Tolischus, *Tokyo Record* (New York: Reynal and

Hitchcock, 1943), 392ff.; Tan Sri Dato Mubin Sheppard, *Taman Budiman* (Singapore: Heinemann, 1979), 122ff., 141ff.; Harriet Sergeant, *Shanghai* (London: Jonathan Cape, 1991), 316; Kee Onn Chin, *Malaya Upside Down* (Singapore: Federal, 1976), 116ff.; N. Low, *When Singapore Was Syonan-to* (Singapore: Eastern Universities Press, 1973), 16–17, 74–75; Gerald Sparrow, *Not Wisely but Too Well* (London: Harrap, 1961), 134–137; Dandie, *Story of J Force,* 98–99; J. Le Bourgeois, "Prisonnier des Japonais," *Revue de Paris,* Vol. 56 (July 1949), 120–142; Johnny Funk, "The Sandakan Story," *8th Division Newsletter,* No. 7 (May–July 1985), 13, 15.

Haruku: the following in Documents, IWM: Chandler, Korteweg, Philps, Springer; Hodson, Sound/IWM; Lüning MS memoir; Leslie Audus, "Biology Behind Barbed Wire," *Discovery,* Vol. 7, No. 7 (July 1946), 211–215; Charles Roland, "Stripping Away the Veneer," *Journal of Military History,* Vol. 53 (January 1989), 79–94; Peacock, *Emperor's Guest,* 81ff.; Bulcock, *Of Death but Once,* 167ff.; Poidevin, *Samurais and Circumcisions,* 101, 159ff.; Veenstra, *Als Krijgsgevangene naar de Molukken;* Cook and Cook, *Japan at War,* 113ff.

Ambon: Chandler, Godfrey, and Stubbs in Documents, IWM; Jones, Sound/IWM; see also Carson diary, Prisoners of War, World War II, NHC; Weiss, *Below the Horizon,* 137ff.; NEFIS interrogatory report in AS/ARA I, xxvi, 11, 2; Beaumont, *Gull Force;* Courtney Harrison, *Ambon* (North Geelong: 1988); Nelson, *POW,* 84ff.

New Britain: I thank Hank Nelson for details of the British prisoners; see also IMTFE, 14, 139. Rabaul Americans and Australian coast-watcher: Murphy/AWM; Kepchia/Daws; McMurria/Daws; statements by Holguin, McMurria, and Quinones, Prisoners of War, World War II, NHC; IMTFE 14,121ff.; James McMurria, "Trial and Triumph," MS memoir; Holguin/Daws; J. Holguin, "The Experiences of Capt. Jose Holguin, USAFR, as a Prisoner of War," MS memoir; John Kepchia, *Missing in Action Over Rabaul* (privately published, 1986); Joseph Nason and Robert Holt, *Horio You Next Die!* (Carlsbad: Pacific Rim, 1987); Nelson, *POW,* 157ff.

Notes for pages 256–271

Medical Experiments. The semistarvation experiment: Ancel Keys et al., *The Biology of Human Starvation,* 2 vols. (Minneapolis: University of Minnesota Press, 1950).

Lifting weights: Murphy, Documents, IWM. American Indians at Cabanatuan: Hutchison/Daws; see also Samuel Newman, *How to Survive as a Prisoner of War* (Philadelphia: Franklin, n.d.), 24–27. Saigon: Cotton, Documents, IWM. Army Medical College, Tokyo: IMTFE, 27,809ff. Measuring penises: Duizend/Daws. Nichols Field: Vining, *Guest,* 231. Blood tests: Lewis Bush, *The Road to Inamura* (Rutland: Tuttle, 1972), 170. See also Charles Roland and H. Shannon, "Patterns of Disease Among World War II Prisoners of the Japanese," *Journal of the History of Medicine and Allied Sciences,* Vol. 46, No. 1 (January 1991), 65–85; also ATIS Research Report 117, 4ff.

"The New York clinic": Holguin/Daws; McMurria/Daws—in Nason, *Nason You Next Die,* 221, it is the Mayo clinic. Shinagawa: statement of Davis, RG 389, B 2130, NA; *Reports of General MacArthur. MacArthur in Japan—The Occupation: Military Phase, I. Supplement,* 108; SCAP, "History of the Non-Military Activities of the Occupation of Japan: Trials of Class B and C War Criminals," 199–201; *New*

York Times, September 2, 1945; Weinstein, *Barbed-Wire Surgeon,* 209–211. Ambon injections: IMTFE 13, 961–13,962, 14,001–14,006, 14,050–14,051; Harrison, *Ambon,* 127–128; Nelson, *POW,* 95. Fleet surgeon: "Final Report of Navy War Crimes Commission," 5 vols., December 1949, case 39, 21; Piccigallo, *The Japanese on Trial,* 79. Khandok: IMTFE, 14,138–14,139. "For the first time": ATIS Research Report 72, 37; ATIS Research Report 117, 4ff.; IMTFE, 14,139–14,140. Kyushu: *Japan Times,* July 1, 1978. China: Cook and Cook, *Japan at War,* 145ff. See also Besley/ Daws; Herbst/Daws; WO 235/869, 235/951, WO 235/1101, PRO; Charles Roland, "The Use of Medical Evidence in British Trials of Suspected Japanese War Criminals," unpublished paper; Whitney, *Guest of the Fallen Sun,* 47–48.

Unit 731. John Powell, "Japan's Germ Warfare," *Bulletin of Concerned Asian Scholars,* Vol. 12, No. 4 (October–December, 1980), 2–17; John Powell, "Japan's Biological Weapons: A Hidden Chapter in History," *Bulletin of the Atomic Scientists,* Vol. 37, No. 8 (October 1981) 44–52; John Powell, "Japan's Biological Weapons," *Bulletin of the Atomic Scientists,* Vol. 38, No. 8 (October 1982), 52; Peter Williams and David Wallace, *Unit 731* (New York: Free Press, 1989). Williams and Wallace kindly gave me access to the script of their TV documentary "Unit 731." In the 1980s, S. Morimura published in Tokyo a three-volume account of Unit 731 under the general title *Akuma no Hoshoku* [Gluttony of the Devil]. For Unit 644, the central China counterpart of 731: C. Hosoya et al., *The Tokyo War Crimes Trial* (New York: Kodansha, 1981), 85–86; see also Cook and Cook, *Japan at War,* 146ff. Yuki Tanaka, *Shirarezaru Sensō Hanzai [Unknown War Crimes]* (Tokyo: Ohtsuki Shoken, 1993) sets out the case for believing that Unit 731 biological war operations were planned for many parts of the Pacific war theater, and that sizable numbers of POW deaths can be connected with Unit 731 procedures.

Cabanatuan fingernails: Weinstein, *Barbed-Wire Surgeon,* 129. See also M. Clarke, "Starvation," *Simpalili: The Spectral Tarsier,* Vol. 1, No. 1 (1947), 48–50.

Lagi: every POW has lagi stories. A sampling: Morris/AWM; UNT interviews with Hard, Slate, Whitehead; La Galle diary; Honywill, Documents, IWM; Dunn, *Bamboo Express,* 49; Bush, *Clutch of Circumstance,* 156–157; Peacock, *Emperor's Guest,* 100; T. Lewis, *Changi* (Kuala Lumpur: Malaysian Historical Society, 1984), 101.

"What in the world is the matter?": Offerle/Marcello; Dunn, *Bamboo Express,* 124. Blind and legless Americans: Glusman, "Heroes and Sons," 710–711.

Yardbird Cunning. This is a very large subject. For a sampling: Daws interviews with G. Adams, Delich, Duizend, Goodman, Luitsz, Medlin; UNT interviews with Bramlett, Burge, Halbrook, Pryor; Newton/AWM; Wallace/Knox; Lüning MS memoir; La Galle diary; Peart journal, NHC; Jackson memoir, MCHC; Hoops, Documents, IWM; Pringle, Documents, IWM; Hodson, Sound/IWM; Beecher diary; K. Todd, "European Into Coolie," *Journal of the Royal Army Medical Corps,* Vol. 86 (April 1946), 182; Stephen Marek, *Laughter in Hell* (Caldwell: Caxton, 1954), generally. For more, see detailed notes.

"This is for the doctor": Jackson memoir, MCHC. Doctors playing the Japanese: Daws interviews with Bras, Hekking, Hewlett; Moss/AWM; Tisdelle diary; Bilibid death register, RG 153, 40–792, Vol. 1, NHC; statement of Kostecki, RG 389, B 2123, NA; Philps, Documents, IWM. For more, see detailed notes. Rob All My Comrades: James Bertram, *Beneath the Shadow* (New York: John Day, 1947), 114.

Warning signals: de Vos/Daws; Steltenpool/Daws; Swanton, Sound/IWM; McCracken, *Very Soon Now,* 79; Bulcock, *Of Death but Once,* 213. Sabotage: Nye/

Daws; statement of Cobb, Command File, World War II, NHC; Julien Goodman, *M.D.P.O.W.* (New York: Exposition, 1972), 107. Fakes: Burton, *Road to Three Pagodas,* 165–166; Russell-Roberts, *Spotlight on Singapore,* 254. Lice in guards' clothes: Many POWs did this. Spit in soup: Duizend/Daws. Crap in applesauce: van Heekeren/Daws; Weinstein, *Barbed-Wire Surgeon,* 285; Bancroft/AWM. Peeled bamboo: Wright/Daws; Slate/UNT; see also Donald Wills, *The Sea Was My Last Chance* (Jefferson: McFarland, 1992), 47. Whores with VD: Levenberg/Daws; Weinstein, *Barbed-Wire Surgeon,* 161; Harrison, *Brave Japanese,* 203.

Harold Johnson and money at Cabanatuan: Johnson papers, MHI; Beecher diary. See also Lyle Eads, *Triumph Amidst the Ashes* (Winona: 1985), 114–119; Weinstein, *Barbed-Wire Surgeon,* 165; Coates and Rosenthal, *Albert Coates Story,* 132; Davies, *Man Behind the Bridge,* 127.

Killing snake: Harrison, *Brave Japanese,* 140–141. Hat story, various versions: Schwarz/Daws; Fillmore/UNT; AWM interviews with Aspinall, Bancroft, Wells; Coast, *Railroad,* 152; Coombes, *Banpong Express,* 149; Nelson, *POW,* 29. Australians and the gold spike: Durnford, *Branch Line,* 139. Simon Legree: Panaotie/AWM. See also Bange/Daws; Bolt/Daws; S. Davis/AWM.

"I'll have a Hershey bar factory": Samuel Moody and Maury Allen, *Reprieve From Hell* (New York: Pageant, 1961), 161. Anything except food: Edwards, *Banzai,* 178. Towel: Clarke, *Last Stop Nagasaki,* 34.

British officer's tattoo: Fisher, *Three Times a Guest,* 85. Book of Revelation: Gordon, *Valley of the Kwai,* 59. Christmas turkey in Albuquerque and yearly variations: Every POW can recite these. Navy bell at Cabanatuan: Knox/Daws; Evans, *Kora,* 69. Officer with beard at Davao: Knox, *Death March,* 262. "Thank the Lord!": Leffelaar, *Through a Harsh Dawn,* 137. Phases of the moon: Newman, *How to Survive,* 112.

Keeping the mind sharp: Poidevin/Daws; Adair/UNT; Daman/UNT. Kraft cheese: Crandall diary, microfilm 88, NA. Betting on the benjo run: Atkinson/Daws. Poke the hog: Knox, *Death March,* 401. Popping bedbugs: Bugbee/UNT. Igniting fart gas: Scheidecker/Daws. Counting bare feet: van Heekeren/Daws.

Fading memory: Hodson, Sound/IWM; Boddington, Documents, IWM; John Fletcher-Cooke, *The Emperor's Guest* (London: Corgi, 1982), 141. "My little Jan": Harrison, *Brave Japanese,* 252.

Goldfish parade: Burton, *Road to Three Pagodas,* 161. Caged beasts: White, Documents, IWM; Lindsay, *At the Going Down,* 62. No privacy: Hall, *Burma-Thailand Railway of Death,* 114; McCracken, *Very Soon Now,* 98; Bush, *Clutch of Circumstance,* 191; Poole, *Of Love and War,* 178; Burton, *Road to Three Pagodas,* 167.

Fujita's artist's eye: Fujita/Daws. Nature: Dunlop, *War Diaries,* 119; Blackater, *Gods Without Reason,* 81. Changi wildlife: Nelson, *Story of Changi,* 179.

Survival. Another huge subject, in fact *the* subject. A sampling: Daws interviews with Davis, Drukker, Herbst, Heyne, Hoogvelt, Knox, Maple, Mroz, Murphy, L. Nelson, Obourn, Smetts, van Heekeren; UNT interviews with Burge, Chambers, Fung, Gee, Kempff, Kenner, McCall, Minshew, Rea, L. Reed, Reichle, R. Robinson, Slate, Stone; Marsh, Sound/IWM; Stitt, Sound/IWM; Philps, Sound/IWM; Kessler memoir; Beets, *Een Verre Oorlog,* 210ff.; Pavillard, *Bamboo Doctor,* 127; Nelson, *POW,* 55; Fillmore, *P.O.W.,* 76; Grashio and Norling, *Return to Freedom,* 41, 56, 70, 72; Haney, *Caged Dragons,* 114–115; Winslow, *Ghost,* 158; Stewart, *To the River Kwai,* 155ff.; Emerson, *Guest,* 90ff. John Nardini, "Survival Factors in American Prisoners of War of the Japanese," *American Journal of Psychiatry,* Vol. 109,

No. 4 (October 1952), 241–248; John Nardini, "Psychiatric Concepts of Prisoner of War Confinement," *Military Medicine,* Vol. 127, No. 4 (April 1962), 299–307; R. Bergman, "Who Is Old? Death Rate in a Japanese Concentration Camp as a Criterion of Age," *Journal of Gerontology,* Vol. 3, No. 1 (January 1948), 14–17; Stewart Wolf and Herbert Ripley, "Reactions Among Allied Prisoners of War Subjected to Three Years of Imprisonment and Torture by the Japanese," *American Journal of Psychiatry,* Vol. 104, No. 3 (September 1947), 180–193; M. Bloom and J. Halsema, "Survival in Extreme Conditions," *Suicide and Life-Threatening Behavior,* Vol. 13, No. 3 (Fall 1983), 195–206; Ian Watt, "The Liberty of the Prison," in Guthrie Moir, ed., *Beyond Hatred* (London: Lutterworth, 1969), 139–156; Beaumont, *Gull Force,* 207ff. Shorthand: Adams, *No Time for Geishas,* 123. Sketching: Collins/Daws. Sharpening the knife for Tōjō's visit: Sellers/Daws. "Faith and digging in garbage cans": Bugbee/UNT. Curly Madison: Knox/Daws. Rats in the bucket: Jeffries/Daws; Atkinson/Daws.

VI. GYOKUSAI AND CHŌMANSAI
Notes for pages 273–279

Red Cross Reports. Much documentation is in RG 200, NA; and in File 313.120, MBZ. See also *Report of the International Committee of the Red Cross on Its Activities During the Second World War,* 3 vols. (Geneva: Red Cross, 1948); *Inter Arma Caritas* (Geneva: Red Cross, 1947), 103ff.; Arthur Robinson, *The History of the American Red Cross,* Vol. 22, *Relief to Prisoners of War in World War II* (Washington, D.C: Red Cross, 1950), 247ff., 353ff.; Junod, *Warrior Without Weapons,* 252ff. Killing Red Cross workers: IMTFE, 13,512–13,513; see also Dunlop, *War Diaries,* 6–7; Lindsay, *At the Going Down,* 86–87. An example of a managed Red Cross inspection: statement of Sayan, RG 331, B 1557, WNRC. Incomplete lists of names: Adachi, "Unprepared Regrettable Events," 320. Seventy pounds of piglet: Sterling/Daws; Henning/Daws.

Allied Protests. IMTFE 49,738ff.; SCAP, "History of the Non-Military Activities of the Occupation of Japan: Trials of Class B and C War Criminals," 28ff.; Utsumi, *Horyo Toriatsukai ni kansuru Shogaikoku no Kōgishu* [Collection of Protests from Various Foreign Countries on the Treatment of POWs]; Hoyt, *Japan's War,* 256; Falk, *Bataan,* 204ff.; Dower, *War Without Mercy,* 50ff.

Japanese shipping: Mark Parillo, *The Japanese Merchant Marine in World War II* (Annapolis: United States Naval Institute, 1993), generally.

Spirit Was Crucial. Nagase/AWM; ATIS Research Report 76, iii, 9–12, vi, 9; Tasaki Hanama, *Long the Imperial Way* (Westport: Greenwood, 1970), 226–227; Agawa Hiroyuki, *Citadel in Spring* (New York: Kodansha, 1990), 85; Ienaga, *Japan's Last War,* 50; Otis Cary, *War-Wasted Asia* (New York: Kodansha, 1975), 268; Peter Suzuki, "Suicide Prevention in the Pacific War (WWII)," *Suicide and Life-Threatening Behavior,* Vol. 21, No. 3 (Fall 1991), 291–298. Bomber in Hibiya: Katō Masuo, *The Lost War* (New York: Knopf, 1946), 139; Leocadio De Asis, *From Bataan to Tokyo* (Lawrence: University of Kansas Press, 1979), 215. Tons against pounds of equipment: Harries and Harries, *Soldiers of the Sun,* 296, 313; see also Alan Millett and Williamson Murray, eds., *Military Effectiveness,* Vol. 3, *The Second World War* (Boston: Allen and Unwin, 1988), 29, 62. "If your arms are broken": ATIS Research Report 76, iii, 8; see also Friend, *Blue-Eyed Enemy,* 205.

Atrocity Stories. Generally: Fussell, *Wartime,* 116ff. See also Hoyt, *Japan's War,* 357ff. Japanese prisoners: Foreign Morale Analysis Division, OWI, Report 31, "The Attitudes of Japanese POWs: An Overall View," December 29, 1945; Ienaga, *Japan's Last War,* 49–50; Kennett, *G.I.,* 164ff. In China: Roderick Macdonald, *Dawn Like Thunder* (London: Hodder and Stoughton, 1944), 108. Sittang River: John Ellis, *The Sharp End* (New York: Scribner's, 1980), 319. Machine-gun survivors in the water: Dower, *War Without Mercy,* 66–67. Australians kill Japanese like snakes: H. Nelson/Daws. See also Close, *Documents,* IWM; McCormack and Nelson, *Burma-Thailand Railway,* 19; Barrett, *We Were There,* 439–440; Wigmore, *Japanese Thrust,* 664ff.; Denis Warner and Peggy Warner, *The Sacred Warriors* (New York: Van Nostrand, 1982), 36; J. McCarthy, *Patrol Into Yesterday* (Melbourne: Cheshire, 1963), 208ff.; Joseph Harrington, *Yankee Samurai* (Detroit: Pettigrew, 1979), 113, 156, 201, 206; Tad Ichinokuchi, ed., *John Aiso and the M.I.S.* (Los Angeles: MIS Club, 1988), 69, 72; McCormack and Nelson, *Burma-Thailand Railway,* 19; Richard Holmes, *Acts of War* (New York: Free Press, 1985), 385–386; Lamont Lindstrom and Geoffrey White, *Island Encounters* (Washington, D.C.: Smithsonian, 1990), 142. "We had one": Harrington, *Yankee Samurai,* 107. Throw prisoners from planes: H. Nelson/Daws. See also Halbrook/Marcello/UNT; Charles Lindbergh, *The Wartime Journals of Charles A. Lindbergh* (New York: Harcourt Brace, 1970), 818, 853–854, 856, 859, 875, 879–882, 902–903; Cary, *War-Wasted Asia,* 37–38, 173; Stouffer, *American Soldier,* Vol. 2, 68, 89.

Doolittle Raid. Carroll Glines, *The Doolittle Raid* (New York: Jove, 1990); Ted Lawson, *Thirty Seconds Over Tokyo* (New York: Random House, 1943).

Gyokusai. Hoyt, *Japan's War,* 357ff. Attu: ATIS Report 76, i, 3, 12ff; *The Capture of Attu* (Washington, D.C.: 1944); Howard Handleman, *Bridge to Victory* (New York: Random House, 1943), 219–222; Harrington, *Yankee Samurai,* 101. "Japanese drink blood like wine!": Morison, *Aleutians, Gilberts and Marshalls,* 50; Dower, *War Without Mercy,* 231–232; Harries and Harries, *Soldiers of the Sun,* 363ff. Tarawa: IMTFE, 14,141; Crowl and Love, *Seizure of the Gilberts and Marshalls,* 156. Japanese deaths can be followed island by island in Shaw et al., *Central Pacific Drive;* and Garand and Strobridge, *Western Pacific Operations.*

Saipan. Crowl, *Campaign in the Marianas,* 264–266; Spector, *Eagle Against the Sun,* 303ff.; Toland, *Rising Sun,* 552ff. Skulls like shish kebabs: This story came to me from Bob Richards. Korean laborers burned on Tinian: I thank Evangeline Funk for information, including photographs of the ovens. Other suicide attacks: Friend, *Blue-Eyed Enemy,* 203.

Tarawa Beheadings. IMTFE, 14,141. Nauru: *New York Times,* September 28, 1945. Ballale: IMTFE, 14,139. Wake: IMTFE, 14,972–14,976, 14,980ff.; E. Junghans, "Wake's POWs," *U.S. Naval Institute Proceedings,* Vol. 109, No. 2 (1983), 43–50.

Notes for pages 279–283

The Davao Radio. Principal interview: Hutchison/Daws. See also Cave, *Beyond Courage,* 270ff. Conditions at Davao: Calvin Jackson, *Diary of Col. Calvin G. Jackson* (Ada: Ohio Northern University, 1992), 83ff.; Betty Jones, *The December Ship* (Jefferson: McFarland, 1992); Manny Lawton, *Some Survived* (Chapel Hill: Algonquin, 1984), 101ff.; McCoy and Mellnik, *Ten Escape from Tojo* (New York: Farrar and

Rinehart, 1944), 69ff.; Grashio and Norling, *Return to Freedom*, 82ff.; McGee, *Rice and Salt*, 71ff. "If the Japanese come in": Hutchison/Daws.

Notes for pages 283–300

Prisoner Sea Transports. Much documentation, including hundreds of statements by survivors, is scattered through RG 331, WNRC, especially from B 983 on. More survivors' statements are in POW Camp files, NHC. See also IMTFE, 13,227ff., 14,454ff., 40,482ff.; WO 208/971, 209/971, 222/179, PRO; ATIS Enemy Publication 321; Knox, *Death March*, 337ff.; van Witsen, *Krijgsgevangenen*, 164ff., 172–181, 220ff.; Adachi, "Unprepared Regrettable Events," 269ff.; Comité International de la Croix-Rouge, *Protection des Prisonniers de Guerre Transportés par Voie de Mer* (Geneva: Red Cross, 1944); Joan Beaumont, "Victims of War: The Allies and the Transport of Prisoners-of-War by Sea, 1939–1945," *Journal of the Australian War Memorial*, No. 2 (April 1983), 1–7.

Tsuji training troops for shipping: Tsuji, *Singapore*, 11, 69. Banana transports: IMTFE, PX 475, 41–42. Broiler chickens: Cook and Cook, *Japan at War*, 282; see also Moriya Tadashi, *No Requiem* (Tokyo: Hokuseidō, 1968), 20–21.

Chōmansai. Much documentation in RG 331, B 983–985, WNRC; see especially statements by Arao, Baba, Fukuda, Hoda, Iio, Inukata, Kambayashi, Katō, Kawasaki, Kaneko, Mononobe, Nishiyama, Yoshitaki. See also Matsuura MS memoir, courtesy of John McBride. To compare conditions with eighteenth-century slave ships, see: Roger Anstey, *The Atlantic Slave Trade and British Abolition, 1760–1810* (London: Macmillan, 1975), 26ff.; Herbert Klein, *The Middle Passage* (Princeton: Princeton University Press, 1978), 228ff.; James Rawley, *The Transatlantic Slave Trade* (New York: Norton, 1981), 283ff.

Japanese merchant marine: Parillo, *Japanese Merchant Marine in World War II*, generally.

For documentation on the *Argentina Maru, Nitta Maru, Mate Mate Maru, Tottori Maru, Dai Nichi Maru, Montevideo Maru, Lisbon Maru, Shin'yō Maru, Rakuyō Maru, Kachidoki Maru, Jun'yō Maru, Maros Maru*, and *Toyofuku Maru*, see detailed notes. "Come over to that island": Joan Blair and Clay Blair, *Return From the River Kwai* (London: Futura, 1980), 196.

Las Piñas: Knox/Daws; Stewart/Daws; Adrian Martin, *Brothers from Bataan* (Manhattan: Sunflower University, 1992), 115ff.; Evans, *Kora!*, 79ff.

Harō Maru: Knox/Daws; and dozens of statements in RG 331, B 957, 985, 986, WNRC. See also Martin, *Brothers From Bataan*, 178–181; Evans, *Kora!*, 107ff.; Cave, *Beyond Courage*, 284ff.; Goodman, *M.D.P.O.W.*, 114ff.; Poweleit, *USAFFE*, 120ff.

Arisan Maru: statement of Binder, Command File, World War II, NHC; Calvin Graef, "We Prayed to Die," *Cosmopolitan*, Vol. 118, No. 4 (April 1945), 53ff.; Ashton, *Bataan Diary*, 295ff.; Haney, *Caged Dragons*, 173; Cave, *Beyond Courage*, 293ff.; Lawton, *Some Survived*, 113ff.

Walking skeletons: *Quan*, March 1984, 5. Smart penguins: Knox/Daws; see also Bugbee/UNT.

Oryokkō Maru: A basic source is the war crimes trial U.S. v. Toshino et al., RG 331, TR 20, Vol. 5, WNRC; see also IMTFE, 12,677ff., 13,242ff. Also Daws interviews with Anloff, Hutchison, Manning; statement of Lewin, RG 331, B 989, WNRC, and many other statements in B 989 and B 920. Command File, World

War II, NHC has many statements. See also Sharp MS, CMH, based on the diary of Nash. Also Beecher diary; Bodine diary; the papers of Gamble, Gard, and Johnson in MHI; Charles Brown, *The Oryoku Maru Story* (Magalia: 1982); Loren Stamp, *Journey Through Hell* (Jefferson: McFarland, 1993), 80ff.; Chunn, *Of Rice and Men,* 111ff.; Jacobs, *Blood Brothers,* 81ff.; Ashton, *Bataan Diary,* 280ff.; Ashton, *And Somebody Gives a Damn!* 221ff. The *St. Louis Post-Dispatch* published a fourteen-article series on the *Oryokkō Maru* by George Weller, beginning November 11, 1945.

Policy on marking POW transports: Beaumont, "Victims of War," 1–7.

United States Task Forces. I thank Edward Boone of the General Douglas MacArthur Memorial Archives for locating evidence in the Whitney papers and the Willoughby papers showing a continuing flow of intelligence concerning ship movements, especially documentary appendixes to Vol. 2 of Willoughby's reports. See also Bolitho/UNT; *New York Times,* October 22, 1944; John Morrett, *Soldier Priest* (Roswell: Old Rugged Cross, 1993), 126; Robert Brown, *I Solemnly Swear* (New York: Vantage, 1957), 140–141.

Japanese Figures on POW Deaths at Sea. Adachi, "Unprepared Regrettable Events," 269ff. "Britannia Rules the Waves": Allbury, *Bamboo and Bushido,* 168–169; Blair and Blair, *Return From the Kwai,* 165–166, 183; see also Wellard/Daws. "It took us all the afternoon": Allbury, *Bamboo and Bushido,* 180–181. Australians taking turns: Nelson, *POW,* 140ff.; see also Don Wall, *Heroes at Sea* (privately published, 1991). *Byōki Maru:* Moss/AWM; Harrison, *Brave Japanese,* 208ff.; Adam-Smith, *Prisoners of War,* 436–438, 444–446; Hall, *Burma-Thailand Railway,* 213; Parkin, *Sword and Blossom,* 75ff.

Deaths on the *Oryokkō Maru:* Chunn, *Of Rice and Men,* i; Peart journal, NHC. Company A deaths on the *Arisan Maru:* Knox/Daws; Dopkins, *Janesville 99,* 41.

VII. THE LAST STRETCH
Notes for pages 301–314

Japan. Moji and the cold winter: see detailed notes. Huddled in the snow, and heads like chilled melons: Dandie, *Story of J Force,* 201. "Frisco live": Knox, *Death March,* 417.

Japanese on Short Rations. L. Nelson/Daws; Radner/Daws; Thomas Havens, *Valley of Darkness* (Lanham: University Press of America, 1986); B. Johnston, *Japanese Food Management in World War II* (Stanford: Stanford University Press, 1953); Ibuse Masuji, *Black Rain* (New York: Kodansha, 1983), 64ff.; Edward Seidensticker, *Tokyo Rising* (New York: Knopf, 1990), 135; Jim Yoshida, *The Two Worlds of Jim Yoshida* (New York: Morrow, 1972), 35; Harries and Harries, *Soldiers of the Sun,* 219; Bertram, *Beneath the Shadow,* 162.

Bottom feeding: See detailed notes. "Snotty gobbles": Clarke, *Last Stop Nagasaki,* 76. "Elephant semen": Bush, *Clutch of Circumstance,* 150. Stalactites: Dandie, *Story of J Force,* 192.

Maimed guards: Burns/UNT; Kirkwood, Sound/IWM; Shiomi, Documents, IWM; Dandie, *Story of J Force,* 16–17; statement of Lewis, RG 389, B 2123, NA; the following statements in RG 331, WNRC: Henfling, B 930; Koury, B 962; Hepworth, B 294. WNRC has a false fist of leather and metal used by a maimed guard named Clubfist.

Kawasaki. Jeffries/Daws; Atkinson/Daws; Davidson/Daws; statement of Covalesk, RG 389, B 2133; White, *United States Marines in North China,* 143ff. Cowalski's hiding place: L. Nelson/Daws. "No food tonight": Atkinson/Daws. Shinagawa: SCAP, "History of the Non-Military Activities of the Occupation of Japan: Trial of Class B and C War Criminals," 194ff.; Lindsay, *At the Going Down,* 193–195. "Get your ass outside": Atkinson/Daws.

Hard Trading. Daws interviews with G. Adams, J. Carter, Goodman, Hubbard, Kasner, Kent, McInerney, L. Nelson, Olson, Sosvielle, Tant, Woodall; Bunch/ UNT; Evans/UNT; McDavitt/Knox; Allen, *Lost Battalion,* 87; Hubbard, *Apocalypse Undone,* 190ff.; Jack Symon, *Hell in Five* (London: Excalibur, 1992), 79–80; R. Armstrong, *San Hyaku Go* (Eugene: 1992). On the jawbone: Goodman/Daws. "Nicotine for protein": Every American prisoner knows this phrase; see also Chunn, *Of Rice and Men,* 146–147.

Only Americans traded to the death: I put the question of hard trading to POWs of all nationalities in great numbers, and this was the answer they gave, uniformly. Note, though, that the Americans of the 131st FA did *not* trade to the death; it was repugnant to their Texas brother-in-law-unit-tribal customs. See also Nelson, *POW,* 184. "This we do not tolerate": J. Carter/Daws.

Oryokkō Maru **Survivors.** The Czech: Hamel, *Soldatendominee,* 195. Lewin: Jacobs, *Blood Brothers,* 92; Chunn, *Of Rice and Men,* 118. Ninety-five skeletons, and "Okay, keep your morphine": Hewlett/Daws.

Bad health at Fukuoka 17: Daws interviews with Bras, Bronk, Duncan, Hewlett; Hugh Clarke, *Twilight Liberation* (Sydney: Allen and Unwin, 1985), 49–50.

Bankruptcy. Daws interviews with G.P. Adams, Bras, Bronk, Duncan, Feiner, Frances, Goodman, Hewlett, Horton, Humphries, Kent, McInerney, Okonski, Olson, Sosvielle, Whitecross, Wallace, Woodall; McDavitt/Knox; Bunch/UNT; Evans/UNT; Whitecross, *Slaves,* 208; Hamel, *Soldatendominee,* 189ff.; Millard Hileman and Paul Fridlund, *1051* (Walla Walla: Words Worth, 1992), 249; McCracken, *Very Soon Now,* 33. Extensive testimony on trading and bankruptcy is in U.S. v. Little, Navy, Judge Advocate General files. Hamel and Duffy: Hamel, *Soldatendominee,* 196–197. "I will be your ears": Bras/Daws.

Deficiency diseases: Bras/Daws; Thomas Hewlett, "Nightmare Revisited," unpublished paper; Thomas Hewlett, "Aftermath," unpublished paper.

Self-mutilation. Daws interviews with G.P. Adams, Bange, Becraft, Dandie, Davidson, P. Davis, Delich, Durner, Knox, Kuslak, Liskowsky, McGrew, Mroz, Obourn, Roland, Schwarz, Walk, H. White. UNT interviews with Garrison, McCall, Pryor, Reese; Robinson/AWM; the following statements in NA: Bandini, RG 200, B 1021; Rogge, RG 389, B 2124; Morris, RG 389, B 2177. Much documentation is in war crimes trial testimony, U.S. v. Iwataka, RG 331, B 9526, WNRC. For more, see detailed notes.

Self-mutilation at Fukuoka 17: Daws interviews with Bras, Bronk, P. Davis, Duncan, O'Leary, S. Schwarz, Stacy, Wallace; Scott, *90 Days,* 180–181. "Will I ever dance again?": Hewlett/Daws.

The Dog Man: Hewlett/Daws. Homosexual counseling: Daws interviews with Bras, Duncan, Hewlett. "Good riddance": Hewlett/Daws; Wallace/Daws. Rafalovich: Rafalovich/Daws.

Notes for pages 314–322

Frank Fujita. Principal interviews: Fujita/Daws; Fujita/UNT. I thank Frank Fujita for access to his unpublished diary. All direct quotes in this section are from the diary, which is excerpted in his published memoir, *Foo,* already cited. See also statement of Fujita, RG 389, B 2177, NA.

For background on Bunka Gakuin, see Ishii/AWM; statement of Frankcom, RG 389, B 2132, NA; Masayo Duus, *Tokyo Rose* (New York: Kodansha, 1983); Russell Howe, *The Hunt for "Tokyo Rose"* (Lanham: Madison, 1990). See also Bertram, *Beneath the Shadow,* 135ff.; Bush, *Clutch of Circumstance,* 180–181; Nelson, *POW,* 180.

B-29 Bombing of Japan. For background, see Ronald Schaffer, *Wings of Judgment* (New York: Oxford University Press, 1985); Martin Sherry, *The Rise of American Air Power* (New Haven: Yale University, 1987); E. Bartlett Kerr, *Flames Over Tokyo* (New York: Donald Fine, 1991); Howard Hansell, *Strategic Air War Against Japan* (Maxwell Air Force Base: 1980); Thomas Coffey, *Iron Eagle* (New York: Crown, 1986); Havens, *Valley of Darkness,* 176ff. "Scorched and boiled": Schaffer, *Wings of Judgment,* 152. See also La Galle diary; Fosco Maraini, *Meeting with Japan* (New York: Viking, 1960), 408ff.; Chester Marshall, *Sky Giants Over Japan* (privately published, 1984).

Downed Airmen. IMTFE, 13,499–13,500, 13,846–13,865, 15,033–15,040, 28,887, 28,890–26,900, 30,239–30,246, 38,026–38,027, 38,030, 38,032, 38,050–38,052, 38,056, 38,633, 40,771; ATIS Research Report 72, Supplement 1; ATIS Research Report 134, 3–4; Richard Hill, *My War With Imperial Japan* (New York: Vantage, 1989), 360–368; Cook and Cook, *Japan at War,* 110–111. Bicycle Camp: Hodson, Sound/IWM. Japanese home islands: Adachi, "Unprepared Regrettable Events," 285–286; SCAP, "History of the Non-Military Activities of the Occupation of Japan: Trials of Class B and C Criminals," 58ff., 127ff.; *Reports of General MacArthur. MacArthur in Japan—The Occupation: Military Phase, I. Supplement,* 108; Martin Caidin, *A Torch to the Enemy* (New York: Ballantine, 1960), 79–80. Kyushu: Ienaga, *Japan's Last War,* 189–190. Niigata: Davidson/Daws. Hakensho: Dandie, *Story of J Force,* 202–203. Beaten to death by fishermen: R. Manoff, "American Victims of Hiroshima," *New York Times Magazine,* December 2, 1984, 116.

Notes for pages 322–327

Retaking Corregidor and Manila. Edward Flanagan, *Corregidor* (Novato: Presidio, 1988); Edward Flanagan, *The Angels* (Novato: Presidio, 1989), 199ff.; Toland, *Rising Sun,* 667ff.; Manchester, *American Caesar,* 467ff. "If we run out of bullets": Friend, *Blue-Eyed Enemy,* 205. "When killing Filipinos": Anthony Arthur, *Deliverance at Los Baños* (New York: St. Martin's, 1985), 183. See also Gladys Savary, *Outside the Walls* (New York: Vantage, 1954), 178ff. Iwo Jima: Figures on deaths vary; see Dower, *War Without Mercy,* 45. Okinawa: Harries and Harries, *Soldiers of the Sun,* 376–377.

"One hundred million die": Sherry, *Rise of American Air Power,* 240. See also Meirion Harries and Susie Harries, *Sheathing the Sword* (London: Hamish Hamilton, 1987), 36; Dandie, *Story of J Force,* 204.

"Prevent prisoners of war." IMTFE 14,533, 14,725; see also ATIS Research Report 72, Supplement 1, 15ff. Palawan: CINCPAC-CINCPOA Escape and Evasion Report 23, and statements of Bogue, Barta, McDole, NHC; ATIS Research Report 133; Bergamini, *Japan's Imperial Conspiracy,* 1094.

"Oru men die": Edwards, *Banzai,* 172. Japanese digging and building pillboxes: IMTFE 11,487; Luitsz/Daws; Leffelaar and van Witsen, *Werkers,* 281–282; Arthur

Marder et al., *Old Friends, New Enemies,* Vol. 2 (Oxford: Oxford University Press, 1990), 575; Stewart, *To the River Kwai,* 173.

"Extreme measures": IMTFE, 12,782–12,783, PX 1465, 14,724–14,728; see also Military Intelligence Division, "Captured Japanese Instructions Regarding the Killing of POW," February 26, 1945, RG 389, B 2223, NA; Edwards, *Banzai,* 259ff.

Miyata: Fletcher-Cooke, *Emperor's Guest,* 315. Fukuoka 17: Hewlett/Daws. Kanchanaburi: Hard/UNT. Prisoners take action: Knight/UNT; Kessler memoir; Knox, *Death March,* 433; Haney, *Caged Dragons,* 135, 140. "Frontally towards a machinegun post": Dunlop, *War Diaries,* 378. Molotov cocktails: Jackson memoir, MCHC. Fujita's plan: Fujita/Daws; Fujita, *Foo,* 252. See also Frank and Shaw, *Victory and Occupation,* 774–775; Bilyeu, *Lost in Action,* 214; Joseph Petak, *Never Plan Tomorrow* (Valencia: Delta, 1991), 379; Rivett, *Behind Bamboo,* 329.

Pakenbaroe railroad: For background and detail, see Henk Neumann and E. van Witsen, *De Sumatra Spoorweg* (Middelie: Pieter Mulier, 1985), generally; van Witsen, *Krijgsgevangenen,* 69ff.; IMTFE, 13,569; statement of Gorski, RG 389, B 2120, NA; Thompson, "Into the Sun," Documents, IWM. "Long walk": Hodson, Sound/IWM; see also Duff/Daws; Murphy/Daws.

Sandakan-Ranau: IMTFE 13,344–13,404, 13,420–13,435; Athol Moffitt, *Operation Kingfisher* (Sydney: Angus and Robertson, 1989); Don Wall, *Sandakan Under Nippon* (Sydney: 1988); Don Wall, *Abandoned?* (Sydney: 1990); Adam-Smith, *Prisoners of War,* 375ff.; *Sydney Morning Herald,* November 1, 1989. Australians escape: AWM interviews with Botterill, Braithwaite, Campbell, Short. Formosan guard: IMTFE, 13,378.

Notes for pages 327–332

Harry Jeffries and Oklahoma Atkinson at Odate. Principal interviews: Jeffries/Daws; Atkinson/Daws. All direct quotes are from Atkinson/Daws. For the Sendai camps generally, see Gilles diary, RG 331, B 957, WNRC; statement of Groneck, RG 331, B 957, WNRC; statement of Covalesk, RG 389, B 2133, NA; statement of Covalesk, RG 331, B 962, WNRC.

VIII. OVER AND OUT
Notes for pages 333-349

A-bombs. "Prompt and utter destruction": Peter Wyden, *Day One* (New York: Warner, 1985), 227. See generally Committee for the Compilation of Materials on Damage Caused by the Atomic Bombs in Hiroshima and Nagasaki, *Hiroshima and Nagasaki* (New York: Basic Books, 1981). Hiroshima POWs: *New York Times,* July 12, 1970; Barton Bernstein, "Unraveling a Mystery: American POWs Killed at Hiroshima," *Foreign Service Journal,* Vol. 56, No. 10 (October 1979), 17ff.; Barton Bernstein, "Hiroshima's Hidden Victims," *Inquiry,* August 6 and 20, 1979. "A rain of ruin": Wyden, *Day One,* 288. "Look there": Manoff, "American Victims of Hiroshima," 124. Nagasaki POWs: Rene Schäfer, *Terug Naar Fukuoka 14* (Amsterdam: Jan Mets, 985); J. Stellingwerf, *Fat Man in Nagasaki* (Franeker: Wever, 1980); Clarke, *Twilight Liberation,* 96ff.; Barton Bernstein, "Doomsday II," *New York Times Magazine,* July 27, 1975, 7ff. One bomb: Wyden, *Day One,* 280. Two other airmen:

Bernstein, "Unraveling a Mystery," 17ff.; *Quan,* August 1978, 6.

"Americano joto nai": Dandie, *Story of J Force,* 205. "Automatic bomb": Ray-burn/UNT. Grapefruit: Mallonee papers, MHI. "Genshi bakudan": John Hersey, *Hiroshima* (New York: Knopf, 1985), 82. "Adam bomb": Jacobs, *Blood Brothers,* 107. The emperor's broadcast: Toland, *Rising Sun,* 944ff.

Osaka: SCAP, "Trials of B and C Class Japanese War Criminals," 140ff.; Fukuoka: 156–157. Celebes: David Sissons, "War Crimes Trials," *Australian Encyclopedia* (Terrey Hills: 1988), Vol. 8, 2,980–2,983. Unit 731: Williams and Wallace, *Unit 731,* 84–86. See also WO 235/1021, PRO.

Reprisals and Nonreprisals. A sampling: Nelson/Daws; Stecklein/Knox; Louis Allen, "Not So Piacular," *Proceedings of the British Association for Japanese Studies,* Vol. 5, Part 1 (1980), 113–120; Berry, *Prisoner of the Rising Sun,* 218; Clarke, *Twilight Liberation,* 91, 130–131; Hamel, *Soldatendominee,* 217; Roy Parkin, *The Sword and the Blossom* (London: Hogarth, 1968), 232; Bush, *Clutch of Circumstance,* 242; Symon, *Hell in Five,* 89–90. "Get up and fight": Clarke, *Twilight Liberation,* 121.

Food Drops. This is a subject very vivid in POWs' memories. A sampling: Daws interviews with Atkinson, Bange, Davidson, Henning, Jeffries, McQuinn, L. Nelson, Pitcher, Sellers, Spurgeon, Wallace; UNT interviews with Adair, Bunch, Detre, Evans, Halbrook, Kenner, Knight, Koury, Minshew. For more, see detailed notes. "Glad to meet you": Sparkman/UNT.

Arithmetic of Food Drops. Twentieth Air Force Tactical Mission Report, August 27–September 20, U.S. Air Force Historical Research Center; Craven and Cate, *The Pacific to Matterhorn,* 734ff.; *Reports of General MacArthur. MacArthur in Japan—The Occupation: Military Phase, I. Supplement,* 97–99. Deaths on the ground: This is my estimate, arrived at simply by noting every on-the-spot report.

Overeating: Jeffries/Daws. "Stay in camp": Gordon/UNT. Sport: Daws interviews with Duncan, Hewlett, Okonski; Allen, *Lost Battalion,* 132. Taking swords: Emerson, *Guest of the Emperor,* 86ff. Commandeering trucks and trains: Harrison, *Brave Japanese,* 259ff. Robbing bank: Nelson, *POW,* 201; Clarke, *Twilight Liberation,* 6; Harrison, *Brave Japanese,* 268; Dandie, *Story of J Force,* 154–155, 209–210. The second-best geisha house: Luitsz/Daws. Sprinkling salt: Evans/UNT.

Liberation in Manchuria. Gibson/AWM; Herbst/Daws; Tisdelle diary; Curtis, Oral History, MCHC; the following papers in MHI: Beebe, Lawrence, Mallonee, Mitchell, Peck; Nelson, *POW,* 194–195; Petak, *Never Plan Tomorrow,* 393ff., 421ff.; Allen, *Lost Battalion,* 155ff.; Quinn, *Love Letters to Mike,* 317; Clarke, *Twilight Liberation,* 145ff.; Lindsay, *At the Going Down,* 208ff.; Tsuji Masanobu, *Underground Escape* (Tokyo: Booth and Fukuda, 1952), 222.

Fujita swims out: Fujita/Daws. Recovering POWs: Action reports of the navy task forces evacuating POWs are in NHC; for an overview, see "Report of Surrender and Occupation of Japan," February 11, 1946. Reports of the army recovery teams are in RG 389, B 2244, NA. Forrest Knox: Knox/Daws. The scene at the ports and on board ship: see detailed notes. Everything was new: Bange/Daws; Boyce/Daws; Upton/Knox. Shirley Temple was engaged: Sellers/Daws.

Deaths on the Way Home. Maple/Daws; Sellers/Daws; Gibson/AWM; Curtis, Oral History, MCHC; *Benjo News,* August, 1991, 5; John Lane, *Summer Will Come Again* (Fremantle: Fremantle Arts Centre, n.d.), 206; Petak, *Never Plan Tomorrow,* 431; Fletcher-Cooke, *Emperor's Guest,* 328; Clarke, *Twilight Liberation,* 85; Dandie, *Story of J Force,* 120; Weinstein, *Barbed-Wire Surgeon,* 301.

"Baka": Stewart, *To the River Kwai,* 35. The boy interpreter: Shiomi, Documents, IWM. "Now we are friends": Many POWs have a version of this. Yokohama Earthquake Fund: Parkin, *Sword and Blossom*, 216. See also Newton/AWM; IMTFE 49,690.

Singapore guard: Botterill/AWM. Uncle John: Liam Nolan, *Small Man of Nanataki* (New York: Dutton, 1966). Charlie Chaplin: *Benjo News*, December 1991, 2. Tateyama: Douglas/UNT. Smiley: Pryor/UNT. Kanemura: Offerle/UNT. Niihama: De Vos/Daws. Widow: Detre/UNT. For more, see detailed notes. Many POWs report that kindly Japanese were Christians—statistically a very small minority in the Japanese population and armed forces. "You can't hate them all": Nelson, *POW*, 156.

Cowalski on Guam: Jeffries/Daws. Ice cream: Pitcher/Daws.

Notes for pages 349–358

RAPWI. The basic document is Earl Mountbatten, *Report to the Combined Chiefs of Staff by the Supreme Allied Commander, South-East Asia, 1943–1945* (London: 1951). See also Kirby, *The Surrender of Japan*, 243–249; Charles Cruickshank, *SOE in the Far East* (New York: Oxford University Press 1983), 239ff.; Gideon Jacobs, *Prelude to the Monsoon* (Philadelphia: University of Pennsylvania, 1982), xi–xxxiv; Louis Allen, *The End of the War in Asia* (London: Hart-Davis, 1976), generally; Wigmore, *Japanese Thrust*, 632ff.; *The Netherlands Red Cross Feeding Team Report on Nutritional Survey in the Netherlands East Indies* (1946); van Velden, *Japanse Burgerkampen*, 457ff.

POWs off the Burma-Siam railroad: Blackater, *Gods Without Reason*, 206; Coast, *Railroad*, 240–241. Children: Daws interviews with Muijser, Powning, ten Brummelaar, van Iterson. Airdrop: George Colley, *Manila, Kuching and Return 1941–1945* (San Francisco: privately published, 1946), 44. Peeling bread: Derwent Kell, *A Doctor's Borneo* (Brisbane: Boolarong, 1984), 160.

Reprisals. Irrawaddy River: Yuji Aida, *Prisoner of the British* (London: Cresset, 1966), 51. Bougainville: H. Nelson/Daws. Balikpapan: Poidevin, *Samurais and Circumcisions*, 129. Labuan: Duff/Daws. Borneo story: I thank Hank Nelson for clarification. See also Russell Braddon, *Japan Against the World* (New York: Stein and Day, 1983), 146; Tom Harrisson, *World Within* (London: Cresset, 1959), 313ff. Nakom Pathon: Nagase Takashi and Watase Masaru, *Tigers and Crosses* (Bangkok: Allied Printers, 1990), 22. See also Richard Adams, *The Day Gone By* (New York: Knopf, 1991), 367–369; Allen, "Not So Piacular," 113–126. Kempeitai: Shimer and Hobbs, *Kenpeitai in Java and Sumatra*, 61ff.; Cook and Cook, *Japan at War*, 119–120.

The Indonesian Situation. Daws interviews with Banens, Schepel, Voll, Wollraven; Anthony Reid and Akira Oki, *The Japanese Experience in Indonesia* (Athens: Ohio University Press 1986), 334ff.; N. Hofstede, *De Slaven van Roku Ban* (Franeker: Wever, 1979), 207; Leffelaar and van Witsen, *Werkers*, 341ff., 380ff., 403ff. I thank David Marr for information on Japanese who stayed in French Indochina after the war.

"Have you got a roster?": Wright/Daws. "Do you have malaria? Do you still like girls?": Wright/Daws. The barefoot army captain: Fillmore, *Prisoner of War*, 132. Blucher Tharp: statement of Thompson, RG 200, B 1023, NA. "You tell my friend Slug": Wright/Daws, Hekking/Daws. "My god": Wright/Daws. "Are you kidding?": Wright/Daws. "Be our guest": Wright/Daws.

John Harrell: I thank Roger White and Otto Schwarz for access to copies of the Harrell papers. Schwarz and the Australians: Schwarz/Daws; Schwarz/UNT. *Houston* men on Borneo: Colley, *Manila, Kuching and Return*, 39. On Sumatra: Schwarz/Daws. In Thailand: Schwarz/Daws; Nicol Smith and Blake Clark, *Into Siam* (Indianapolis: Bobbs-Merrill, 1946), 249.

"Matlock, you want a ride?" and "Son, is that you?": Matlock/UNT. Abilene reunion: Fujita/Daws; Fujita, *Foo,* 344. Slug Wright and Doc Hekking: Wright/Daws; Hekking/Daws.

Notes for pages 358-359

"Put it behind you": Every POW has a version of this. "They looked down my throat": Minshew/UNT. Two out of three dead in Asia: Dopkins, *Janesville 99,* 41–44. "I don't remember": Knox/Daws. "Is that right": Knox/Daws.

Notes for pages 359–361

Deaths. Forrest Knox's outfit: Doherty, "Too Little, Too Late," 275–283. 131st and *Houston:* Lost Battalion and *Houston* Survivors Association roster. Wake Island: Urwin, "Defenders of Wake," 440ff.; Frank and Shaw, *Victory and Occupation,* 750. For the Pacific-Asian theater context of these deaths, see Dower, *War Without Mercy,* 294ff. Comparisons with Europe: Kennett, *G.I.,* 185–186. Comparisons with the eastern front: McCormack and Nelson, *Burma-Thailand Railway,* 162ff. See also IMTFE, 40,537, 49,594; Urwin, "Defenders of Wake," 446ff.; Roland and Shannon, "Patterns of Disease," 67ff.; Richard Severo and Lewis Milford, *The Wages of War* (New York: Simon and Schuster, 1989), 293.

Black Plague: The Black Plague lasted between three and four years and killed about one in three. What happened POW camp by POW camp approximated in duration and severity what happened village by village in Europe.

IX. EVER AFTER
Notes for pages 363-376

War Crimes Trials. For the Tokyo trial, the basic source is the 27-volume edition of IMTFE by Pritchard and Zaide; for context, see the introductory essay and the judgment. For B and C Class crimes, see copious trial documents and reports in various archives: American, NA, WNRC, NHC; Australian, AWM and AA; British, PRO; Dutch, MBZ. See also Chaen, *Nihon B-C-Kyū Sempan Saiban Shiryō* [Materials Relating to Japanese B and C Class War Crimes Trials]. In the 1980s, Chaen published several other collections of documents relating to trials of B and C Class war criminals. See also Piccigallo, *The Japanese on Trial.* Russell, *Knights of Bushido,* summarizes atrocities. Also Adachi, "Unprepared Regrettable Events," 322; Louis Allen, "Japanese Literature of the Second World War," *Proceedings of the British Association for Japanese Studies,* Vol. 2, No. 1 (1977), 129ff.; Charles Roland, "The Use of Medical Evidence in British Trials of Suspected Japanese War Criminals," unpublished paper.

Tōjō's suicide attempt: William Craig, *The Fall of Japan* (New York: Dial, 1967), 315ff.; Courtney Browne, *Tojo* (New York: Holt, Rinehart and Winston, 1967),

5–6, 211ff.; "Snafu Suicide," *Life,* September 24, 1945, 36–37. "Tell this yellow bastard": Toland, *Rising Sun,* 986.

Yamashita: Frank Reel, *The Case of General Yamashita* (Chicago: University of Chicago Press, 1949); Richard Lael, *The Yamashita Precedent* (Wilmington: Scholarly Resources, 1982); Ichinokuchi, *John Aiso and the M.I.S.,* 142–143. Homma: U.S. v. Homma, RG 331, B 1671, WNRC; Swinson, *Four Samurai,* 242–243; *New York Times,* April 3, 1946.

Sugamo. Much documentation in RG 331 and RG 338, WNRC. See also John Ginn, *Sugamo Prison* (Jefferson: McFarland, 1992); Kodama Yoshio, *Sugamo Diary* (Tokyo: Radiopress, 1960); Hanayama Shinshō, *The Way of Deliverance* (New York: Scribner's, 1950); Shiroyama Saburō, *War Criminal* (Tokyo: Kodansha, 1977); Dan Kurzman, *Kishi and Japan* (New York: Obolensky, 1960), 225ff.; Arnold Brackman, *The Other Nuremberg* (New York: Morrow, 1987), 227ff.; Oliver Statler, "The Barber and the Brass: Recollections of the 1946 Tokyo Trials," *EastWest* (Spring 1985), 12–17. Shanghai hangman: Roper, Documents, IWM. "I'm going to rip your bloody head off": An eyewitness told this story at a dinner party forty-five years later; I thank Norah Forster for recording it. United States Navy: "Final Report of the Navy War Crimes Commission," 5 vols., December 1949, NHC. "If you need me to find them": statement of Laporte, RG 389, B 2126, NA. "I am at complete liberty": statement of Covalesk, RG 331, B 962, WNRC. Hangman from Yokohama: Ginn, *Sugamo,* 234. Springing the trap: Private letter of the hood and lever man.

"Remember Pearl Harbor": "The Bridge of General Hideki Tojo," *United States Navy Dental Corps Update* (August 1991), 12–13. Hanging A Class criminals: *New York Times,* December 24, 1948; William Sebald, *With MacArthur in Japan* (New York: Norton, 1965), 171ff.; Browne, *Tojo,* 235–236; Shiroyama, *War Criminal,* 291ff.; Hanayama, *The Way of Deliverance,* 254ff.; C. Boyd, "Exaltation and Hindsight," *Montclair Journal of Social Science and Humanities,* Vol. 3, No. 2 (1974), 79–96.

Sentences on B and C Class Criminals. These are collated nation by nation in Piccigallo, *Japanese on Trial.* See also L. de Groot, *Berechting Japanse Oorlogsmisdadigers in Nederlands-Indië* (den Bosch, Art & Research, 1990). The Shinagawa doctor: Craig, *Fall of Japan,* 285ff.; *New York Times,* September 2, 1945; Bergamini, *Japan's Imperial Conspiracy,* 140–141, 1197. The Australian Ambon trial: CRS, A471, item 81, 709, AA. Sone Ken'ichi: The trial of Sone is in file 322.191, Japan Vonnissen, 1–50, MBZ. For more on Sone, see detailed notes. Sone's brain: Bras/Daws.

Opinions on the War Crimes Trials. Hosoya, *Tokyo War Crimes Trial;* Richard Minear, *Victor's Justice* (Princeton: Princeton University Press, 1971); Tsurumi Kazuko, *Social Change and the Individual* (Princeton: Princeton University Press, 1970), 138–179; Iritani Toshio, *Group Psychology of the Japanese in Wartime* (New York: Kegan Paul, 1991), 201ff.; Harries and Harries, *Soldiers of the Sun,* 392ff.; Ienaga, *Japan's Last War,* 237–238; Bergamini, *Japan's Imperial Conspiracy,* 1108–1109; Peregrine Hodson, *A Circle Around the Sun* (New York: Knopf, 1992), 71–74, 139, 150–154, 210–213, 264–267; K. Steiner, "War Crimes and Command Responsibility," *Pacific Affairs,* Vol. 58, No. 2 (Summer 1985), 293–298; R. John Pritchard, "The Nature and Significance of British Post-War Trials of Japanese War Criminals, 1945–1948," *Proceedings of the British Association for Japanese Studies,* Vol. 2, Part 1 (1977), 189–219; R. John Pritchard, "The Historical Experience of British War Crimes Courts in the Far East, 1946–1948," *International Relations,* Vol. 6, No. 1 (May 1978), 311–326; R. John Pritchard, "Lessons from British Proceedings

Against Japanese War Criminals," *Human Rights Review*, Vol. 3, No. 2 (Summer 1978), 104–121; G. Dickinson, "Manus Island Trials: Japanese War Criminals Arraigned," *Journal and Proceedings, Royal Australian Historical Society*, Vol. 38, No. 2 (July 1952), 67–77; Richard Glenister, "B and C Class War Crimes Trials Held by Australia: Fair Trial and the Geneva Convention" (unpublished paper); Ian Buruma, *The Wages of Guilt* (New York: Farrar Straus Giroux, 1994); Adachi Sumio, *Gendai Sensō Hōki Ron* [A Discussion of Modern War Legislation] (Tokyo: 1979), 174–178; Fujiwara Iwaichi, *F Kikan* (Hong Kong: Heinemann, 1983), 194, 289ff.; F. Hart, "Yamashita, Nuremberg and Vietnam: Command Responsibility Reappraised," *Naval War College Review*, Vol. 25, No. 1 (September–October 1972), 19–36; Andrew Gilchrist, *Bangkok Top Secret* (London: Hutchinson, 1970), 222–231; Mark Gayn, *Japan Diary* (New York: Sloane, 1948), 338–340. See also the Kodansha documentary film "The Tokyo Trial."

"Five years a slap": The Sugamo Committee, "A Factual and Statistical Survey of the Inmates in Sugamo," File 322.191, Japan, Algemeen, Part II, 1952–1953, BMZ; see also Friend, *Blue-Eyed Enemy*, 189.

Australian executions: Sissons, "War Crimes Trials," 2,980–2,983; McCormack and Nelson, *Burma-Thailand Railway*, 78, 83ff., 127ff. For a perspective on Australian views of wartime Japan, see Humphrey McQueen, *Japan to the Rescue* (Port Melbourne: Heinemann, 1991), 295ff.

MacArthur's Deal with Unit 731. Powell, "Japan's Germ Warfare," 2–17; Powell, "Japan's Biological Weapons," 44–52; Williams and Wallace, *Unit 731*, 133, 195, 207, 210, 215; Edward Behr, *Hirohito* (New York: Villard, 1989), 163ff. Soviet trial of Unit 731 men: *Materials on the Trial of Former Servicemen of the Japanese Army Charged with Manufacturing and Employing Bacteriological Weapons* (Moscow: Foreign Languages Publishing House, 1950).

Clemency. Robert Wolfe, ed., *Americans as Proconsuls* (Carbondale: Southern Illinois University, 1984), 226–259. Sasakawa Ryō'ichi: David Kaplan and Alec Dubro, *Yakuza* (New York: 1987), 79–81; J. Roberts, "Ryoichi Sasakawa: Nippon's Right-Wing Muscleman," *Insight* (April 1978), 8–15. Kodama Yoshio: Kaplan and Dubro, *Yakuza*, 64ff.; David Boulton, *The Lockheed Papers* (London: Jonathan Cape, 1978), 45ff., 270. Naitō Ryō'ichi and Kitano Masaji: Williams and Wallace, *Unit 731*, 240–241. Tsuji Masanobu: Tsuji, *Underground Escape;* Murakami Hyoe, *Japan: The Years of Trial* (Tokyo: Japan Culture Institute, 1982), 110–112; Ward, *Killer They Called a God*, 248ff., 274, 280, 288, 295ff., 305ff.; Harries and Harries, *Soldiers of the Sun*, 291–292; Bergamini, *Japan's Imperial Conspiracy*, 915, 943, 956ff., 1107, 1173; Toland, *Rising Sun*, 325, 336–337; Swinson, *Four Samurai*, 77, 161ff., 170–171; 246. Kishi Nobusuke: Kurzman, *Kishi and Japan*, 302.

Kempeitai: Shimer and Hobbs, *Kempeitai*, 14. Refined Spirit Association: Cook and Cook, *Japan at War*, 167. Shrines: *New York Times*, December 23, 1948; *Nippon Times*, May 7, 1956; Shiroyama, *War Criminal*, 1–2; Browne, *Tojo*, 235–236, 242–243; Harries and Harries, *Sheathing the Sword*, 174.

Yasukuni: Cook and Cook, *Japan at War*, 448ff.; John Potter, *A Soldier Must Die* (London: Frederick Muller, 1963), 1–3; Russell Brines, *Until They Eat Stones* (Philadelphia: Lippincott, 1944), 289; Funasaka Hiroshi, *Falling Blossoms* (Singapore: Times, 1986), 41, 114; ATIS Research Report 76, iii, 19; ATIS Enemy Publications 72, 2; Escritt, *Beyond Three Pagodas Pass*, 56; W. Newell, "The Nature of the *Kami* in the Yasukuni Shrine at Its Foundation and at the Present Time," unpublished paper.

Notes for pages 376–396

POWs Postwar. "The second thing": Nelson, *POW,* 210. "If I don't do it every day": Erickson/Daws. Robert Taylor: Billy Keith, *Days of Anguish, Days of Hope* (Garden City: Doubleday, 1972). Boy holding the stick: Nardini/Daws. The Texas family funeral: Self/Daws. "Didn't you get bored . . . ?": Every POW has a version of this; see also Philip Brain, *Soldier of Bataan* (Minneapolis: Rotary Club, 1990), 67. The Australian cobbler: Wallace/Daws; see also Clarke, *Twilight Liberation,* 157. The boy from D Battery: Bramlett/UNT; Chambers/UNT. Eight Americans from the Philippines: *New York Times,* August 15, 1947.

    Working Imitation of Normality. Every POW has his own private version. A sampling: Daws interviews with Crow, Mroz, L. Nelson; UNT interviews with Brain, Minshew, Thompson. On this subject it is instructive to listen to POWs' wives. Monroe Woodall: Woodall/Daws. Kelly Bramlett: Bramlett/UNT. Frank Fujita: Fujita/Daws.

    "I believe I'll quit these big casinos": Atkinson/Daws. Atkinson at reunions: Davidson/Daws; L. Nelson/Daws. "Goddamn": Atkinson/Daws.

    Reparations. Robert Ward and Frank Schulman, *The Allied Occupation of Japan* (Chicago: American Library Association, 1974), 1117ff.; T. Ohno, "United States Policy on Japanese War Reparations, 1945–1951," *Asian Studies,* Vol. 13, No. 3 (December 1975), 23–45; Adachi, "Unprepared Regrettable Events," 323.

    Compensation. Canada: Carl Vincent, *No Reason Why* (Stittsville: Canada's Wings, 1981), 237ff. Dutch colonials: I thank Nick Vos of Stichting ICODO and Sjoerd Lapré of Stichting Japanse Ereschulden for information. See *Guide for the Victims of Persecution During the 1940–1945 War Who Are Resident Outside the Netherlands* (Rijswick: 1975); J. Ellemers and R. Vaillant, *Indische Nederlanders en Gerepatrieerden* (Muiderberg: 1985). "The Hague is the widow of the Indies": Daws interviews with Bras, Hekking, van Iterson.

    Physical Suffering. A sampling of postwar medical studies from different times and places: Bernard Cohen and Maurice Cooper, *A Follow-Up Study of World War II Prisoners of War* (Washington, D.C.: Veterans Administration, 1954). H. Richardson, *Report of a Study of Disabilities and Problems of Hong Kong Veterans, 1964–1965* (Canadian Pension Commission, 1965); *P.O.W.* (Washington, D.C.: Veterans Administration, 1980); D. Patrick and P. Heaf, *Long-Term Effects of War-Related Deprivation on Health* (London: 1981); Ian Duncan et al., *Morbidity of Prisoners of War* (Sydney: POW Association, 1985); P. Watson, *A Study of the Post-Captivity Health of Ex-Prisoners of War of the Japanese* (Blackpool: 1985); Gustav Gingras and Carol Chapman, *The Sequelae of Inhuman Conditions and Slave Labour Experienced by Members of the Canadian Components of the Hong Kong Forces, 1941–1945, While Prisoners of the Japanese Government,* 2 vols. (War Amputations of Canada and Hong Kong Veterans Association of Canada, 1987); Charles Guest and Alison Venn, *Studies of Morbidity and Mortality of Former Prisoners of War and Other Australian Veterans* (Melbourne: Dunlop Foundation, 1990). Some of these major studies include psychiatric material in their bibliographies. The Dutch have done most to investigate "camp syndrome"; I thank Nick Vos of Stichting ICODO for guidance on this subject. VA doctors: I have heard this any number of times from POWs talking among themselves at reunions; see also Stan Sommers, ed., *The Japanese Story* (Marshfield: AMEXPOW, 1980), 65ff. (one of many compilations done for American Ex-Prisoners of War, Inc.). "Dear Charles": private letter from one POW to another.

Forrest Knox: Knox/Daws; Knox, *Death March,* 478ff. The deaths of Oklahoma Atkinson and Harry Jeffries: personal knowledge.

POWs and the United Nations. Gingras and Chapman, *Sequelae of Inhuman Conditions;* Queensland Ex-POW Reparations Committee, *Nippon Very Sorry— Many Men Must Die* (Bowen Hills: Boolarong, 1990); McCormack and Nelson, *Burma-Thailand Railway,* 7–9, 57, 120ff., 140ff. Other compensation suits: From the beginning of the 1990s there has been a steady stream of media reports on various suits.

Japanese Internees in the U.S. United States Department of the Interior, War Relocation Authority, *The Evacuated People* (Washington, D.C.: 1946); *Impounded People* (Washington, D.C.: 1946); and Commission on Wartime Relocation and Internment of Civilians, *Personal Justice Denied* (Washington, D.C.: 1982). Internment camps as concentration camps: Allan Bosworth, *America's Concentration Camps* (New York: Norton, 1967). Roger Daniels et al., eds., *Japanese Americans* (Seattle: University of Washington Press, 1991); Michi Weglyn, *Years of Infamy* (New York: Morrow, 1976); Martin Grodzins, *Americans Betrayed* (Chicago: University of Chicago Press, 1949); John Tateishi, ed., *And Justice for All* (New York: Random House, 1984); Daisuke Kitagawa, *Issei and Nisei* (New York: Seabury, 1967); Dillon Myer, *Uprooted Americans* (Tucson: University of Arizona Press, 1972); Daniel Davis, *Behind Barbed Wire* (New York: Dutton, 1982); *Honolulu Sunday Star-Bulletin and Advertiser,* February 25, 1990; *Hawaii Herald,* March 16, 1990. Pissing on the plaque: another judgment call where I am withholding a name.

Stanbrough and Reed at Bicycle Camp: Stanbrough/Daws. Slug Wright and Doc Hekking touring: Wright/Daws; Hekking/Daws. See also Bange/Daws; Delich/Daws.

The Thai with bad dreams: *U.S. News and World Report,* December 3, 1990, 14. Nightmares: Every POW has bad dream stories—a topic on which POWs' wives can speak in detail. See also J. Kluznik et al., "Forty-Year Follow-up of United States Prisoners of War," *American Journal of Psychiatry,* Vol. 143, No. 11 (November 1986), 1443–1446. POW in the trailer camp: another case where I have thought it best to withhold a name.

Arisan Maru reunion: This took place in September 1983. Rabaul reunion: Daws interviews with Holguin, Kepchia, McMurria; Murphy/AWM; *New York Times,* August 6, 1986; *Los Angeles Times,* April 8, 1990.

Amarillo sukiyaki: *Chit Chat,* February 1968. The khaki undershirt: Scheidecker/Daws. Wake-up call: Hekking/Daws. Man from the *Houston:* Wilkinson/ Daws. Otto Schwarz's newsletter is called *The Blue Bonnet.*

The yearly Lost Battalion and *Houston* Survivors reunions are chronicled in their roster and newsletters. The plaque was finally dedicated on May 4, 1994.

INDEX